fresh

TO MY BILLY BOBO

*Always,
your flower girl*

First published in 2017 by

Glitterati Incorporated
New York | London

New York Office:
630 Ninth Avenue, Suite 603
New York, New York 10036
Telephone: 212 362 9119

London Office:
1 Rona Road
London NW3 2HY
Tel/Fax: +44 (0) 207 267 8339

www.GlitteratiIncorporated.com | media@GlitteratiIncorporated.com
for inquiries

First edition, 2017

Library of Congress Cataloging-in-Publication data is available from the publisher.

Hardcover edition ISBN: 978-1-943876-44-0
Printed and bound in China
10 9 8 7 6 5 4 3 2 1

fresh

FRESH FLOWERS... FRESH ARRANGEMENTS... FRESH IDEAS

Sybil Brooke Sylvester

Foreword | Charlotte Moss   Preface | Charles McNair

Glitterati
INCORPORATED
New York | London

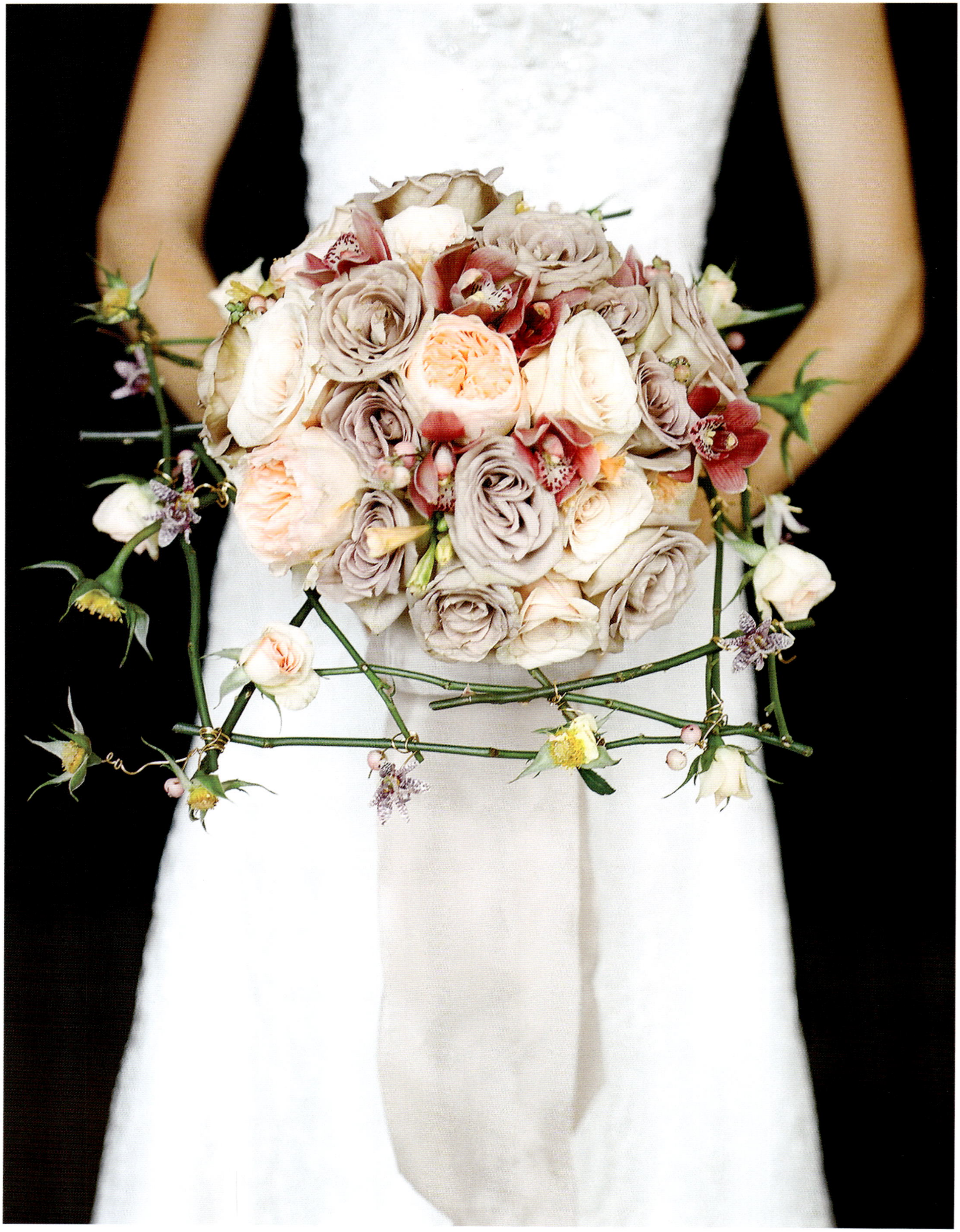

CONTENTS

a breath of fresh air

by Charlotte Moss

A breath of fresh air is exactly how I would describe Sybil Sylvester. Scroll back several years ago in Atlanta when I first met Sybil at a dinner hosted by Margot Shaw, owner of *flower* magazine. The next day I was to be on a panel at Atlanta Decorative Arts Center and Sybil was to give a demonstration on floral design. I was very short on time and should have gone to see a couple of antique dealers. Because I had spent time with Sybil the night before and was so charmed by her down-to-earth approach, her sincerity, and her downright determination to make sure that her audience left her presentation empowered and fearless with flowers, I just had to bear witness to whatever this little redheaded fireball had to share. Share she did.

In true southern style Sybil held no cards back. She shared tips, tricks, trial-and-error, all the while had us in hysterics. Her natural, matter-of-fact manner is translated to her *au naturale* style of arranging.

fresh is her approach to her arrangements and to her business. What will delight you in this book first and foremost is that this approach lacks rules. Sybil begs you to experiment and to play. She encourages you to personalize with containers foraged for or temporarily forgotten in the back of closets and with things not designed as containers at all, they just look like a good idea waiting to happen. She believes that a walk in the woods can be like a treasure hunt, producing curly branches, roots, pinecones, nuts and bark that looks like sculpture. Found objects can add measurably to your raw materials making your flower arranging possibilities infinite! Sybil would not want you to feel limited in any way, and *fresh* is evidence of that.

We have all had those moments when the arrangement that looked great before we went to bed, well, it just had a bad night and nothing will revive it. So maybe you should start with Sybil's First Rule: where she shares, once again, six easy steps to prep your flowers so they are just as happy in the morning as they were before bedtime. Think of Sybil's First Rule as insurance; take solid advice from a pro, and listen up. And don't forget to look at her list of supplies, which will make you look like a pro. Then, fix a cup of tea, settle in to your favorite place to read *fresh* and let Sybil tell you the rest.

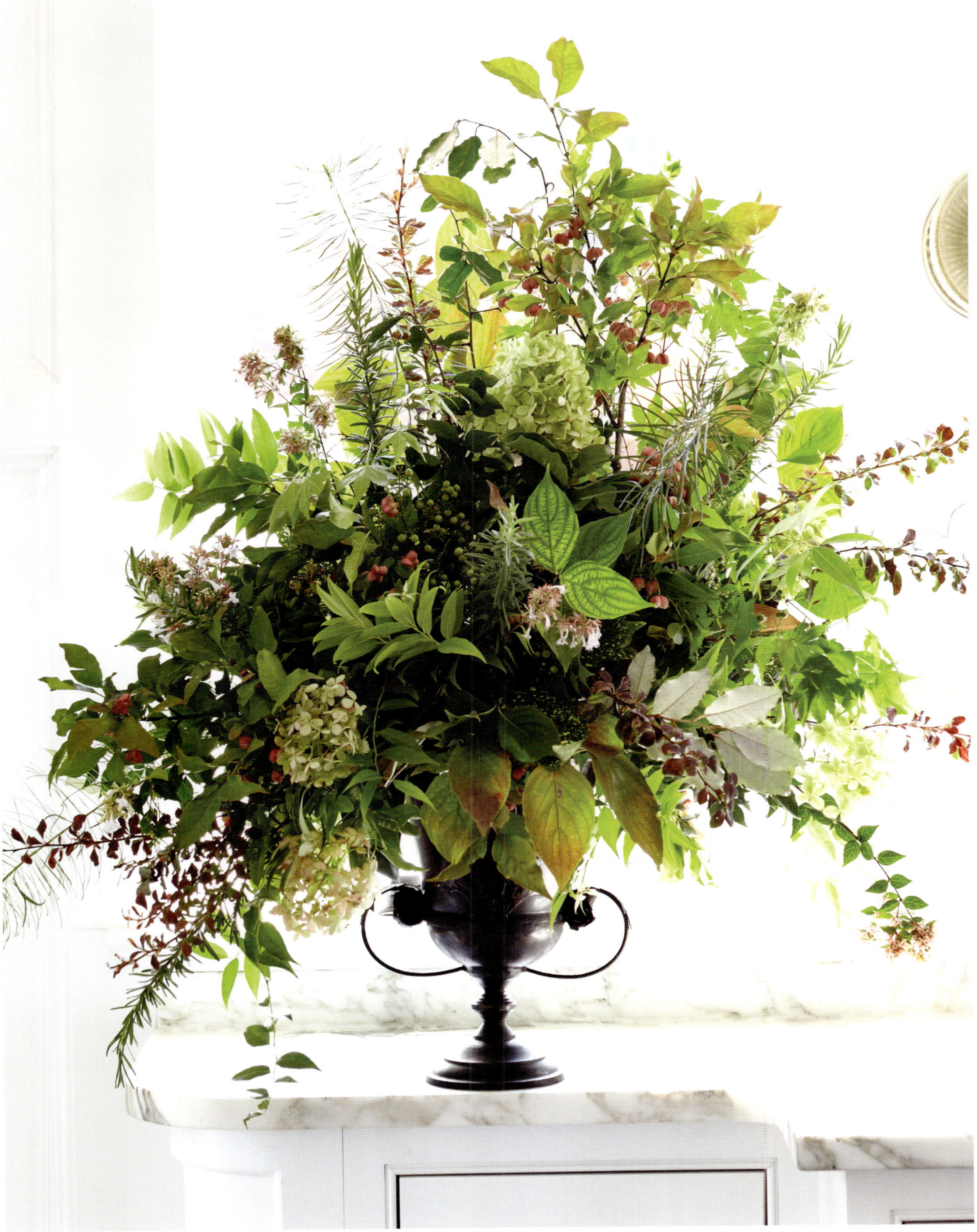

I grew up in Dothan, Alabama, on a dirt street. Fifty yards behind my house rose a 100-acre forest, a jungle of shadows and smilax, tulip poplar and tangle, privet and poison ivy.

My mother heroically raised six kids, four born in the first six years of her marriage. Mama fed us, clothed us, bathed us, doctored us, disinfected us. She tamed us. We all lived to adulthood somehow, no matter how many times we ate bad things growing on the sides of trees or played with matches in forts built of pine straw.

Even more, Mama attempted with all her might to tame the forest around our little 1960s home.

She started planting flowers.

Her azaleas grew big and bushy. They crawled the perimeter of the house like a giant green caterpillar, flowering every Easter with pink and white blooms that went off in the retina—bang! Her little seed gardens brought the very first signs of cultivation to the fringes of the forest primeval. (Nights, we heard wildcats mate and foxes bark just beyond the illumination of the back porch bug light.)

Mama set out roses, including rambling wild ones. Here and there, the yard raised sentinel flags of crimson and peach and yellow from May to the end of July. She put out camellias that flowered in peppermint and alabaster. The native sasanquas blossomed about the time college football kicked off. Japonicas got into action a little later, those blooms sometimes hanging around long enough to see Santa Claus.

Mama's relaxed gardening style paralleled her parenting. So what if a bed had a few so-called weeds? Those goldenrods and Indian pinks and coreopsis looked pretty too.

Little by little, thanks to my mother, the shady edge of an Alabama forest took on color and charm. Civilization arrived.

Mama didn't get a lot of credit for her green thumb. Daddy didn't much care for flowers. He gave Mama little encouragement for her beautification efforts.

Once, her African violets, a back porch collection of clay pots and fat purple blooms, got smashed in some disagreement. I remember Mama sweeping up black potting soil and red shards, tears running down her face.

More than once, a careless McNair with a lawn mower ran over a rose. We raised a calf for a while, and of course it escaped and ate Mama's flowers. The woods sent stinkbugs, rusts, thrips, worms, aphids, you-name-it after anything bright and pretty she tried to grow.

> "Sybil's wonderfully creative book presents a paradox. She has civilized the wild flower, turned the bloom by the side of the stream ... mainstream."

Mama kept at it. If the neighborhood beautification society never showed up with a plaque, so what? Mama just kept planting and pulling. Flowers sprang from her footsteps.

It seemed to be enough. Mama understood that one rose in a forest made a difference.

She had one moment, though, that let us all see her in a new light.

Each year, the Garden Club held an annual flower show, and members of the club submitted decorations to be judged in different categories—roses, camellias, lilies, etc. As with many events in small towns, it got competitive. Bragging rights matter among people with not a lot to brag about.

Honestly, none of us in the family even knew my mother entered the competition.

So when the telephone rang one evening, and the McNair kids suddenly got a summons to put on our shoes and load up in the station wagon, it seemed a bother. I remember complaining as Daddy drove. We made our way across town to the public library, where the flower show occupied a spacious room.

Mama never said a word. She herded McNairs up the library steps. Inside, we passed giant bouquets of red roses and displays of hyacinth with blooms like red bugles.

Then we stopped.

A booth bore my mother's name—Nora Joyce McNair. Behind the card stood a ... well, what?

A piece of art.

A rust-crusted metal cross stood in a base of black soil from our own yard. A snarl of rusted barbed wire entwined the cross. The display looked dug up from a battlefield.

A single blood-red wild rose glowed in all that twisted metal.

Below it, my mother's handwriting:

Midst the war's great curse
Stands the Red Cross nurse
She's the rose of no-man's land

It was beautiful. Powerful. Utterly unlike anything else in the room.

A blue ribbon—first place—hung on the front of the booth with the red, red rose.

My Mama found that rose.

My mama is that rose.

No single flower has meant so much in my life.

beginnings

When I look back on what made me fall in love with flowers, I can't help but conclude that I thought of them as my friends. As a child, I spent countless hours picking flowers and playing with them. I loved them from the very beginning. I continue to have the childlike fascination I had growing up with flowers, fairies, mushrooms, and mosses. I spent many a day creating and making everything from clover and daisy chains to fairy houses to little violet or pansy bouquets to picking armloads of daffodils to arrange in jelly jars.

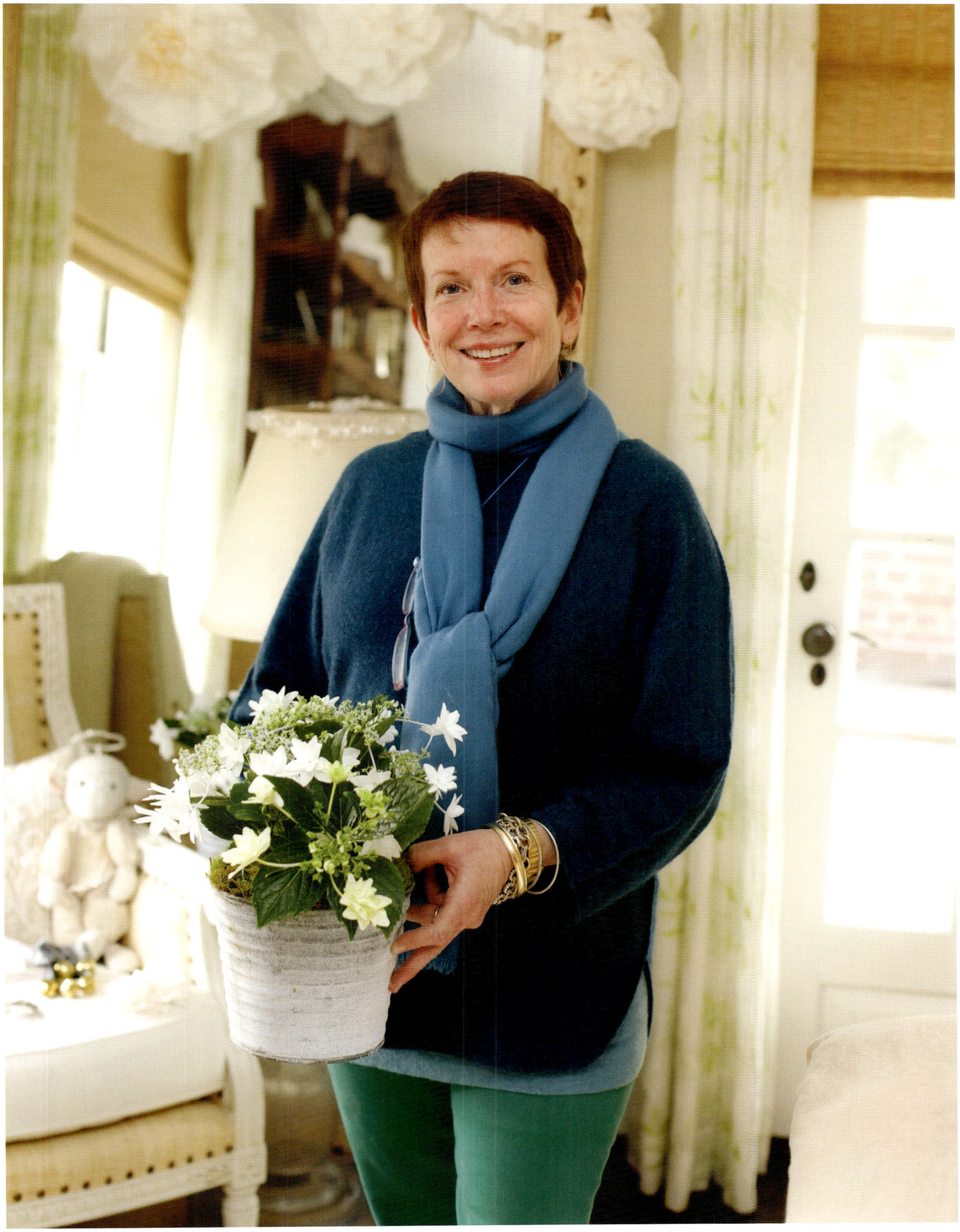

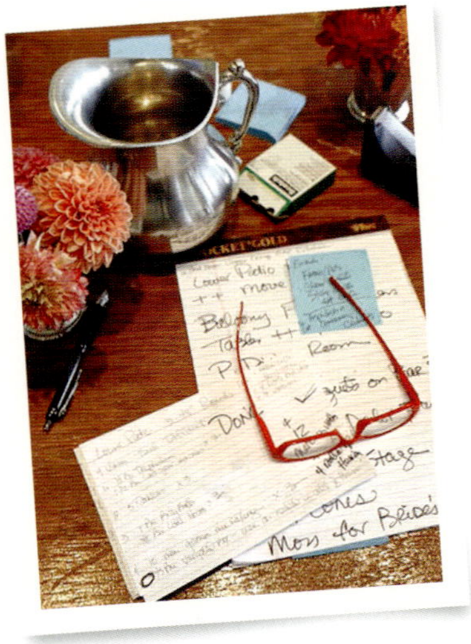

In all the years of working on this book, the Rodgers and Hammerstein song, "Happy Talk," ran through my head …

"You've gotta have a dream. If you don't have a dream, how you gonna have a dream come true?"

I was born in Baton Rouge, Louisiana, into a traditional family. I had what seems to me to have been a typical 1950s/1960s upbringing as number four in a family with five children. I spent my earliest years playing under magnolia trees and then piling into our Woodie station wagon with the whole brood for adventures with Mama and Daddy. I remember going to see the sugar cane fields and chewing on a fresh cut stick of sugar cane and my Mama showing me a buttercup and making sure she rubbed the pollen on my chin. I also remember returning home to the beauty of the giant bougainvillea vine that cascaded over our front door and the wonderful heady scent when all the magnolias and gardenias were in bloom. We moved to Birmingham, Alabama, when I was 5—so early flower memories are hard to pull up. I do remember that my maternal Granddaddy always, always made sure the band played "The Yellow Rose of Texas" for me every time I entered a room or restaurant or party—even though I never lived in Texas! I did have very blonde hair, and I loved being associated with a rose.

An artistic streak along with athletic ability runs through our family as well as exceptional minds. I fall in there somewhere—we won't say exactly where—but in my early years I would describe myself as an outgoing Tom Boy/Girlie Girl who could hold her own in school and on the playground and the diving board along with the golf course! Not one family member influenced me through great floral design or the gift of gardening to help me choose my path. My mother's life long best friend, Lula Rose Blackwell—"Aunt Lula Rose" to me—would be who I would point to and bestow responsibility for influencing my path toward floral design. Lula Rose was the go-to, haute couture floral designer in Old Mountain Brook, and Mama and Aunt Lula Rose got together and thought that I might like to help with her flower business. I started helping at the age of 12. My work assignments were to tote flower buckets and strip roses, among other things. As I learned, my duties expanded into container preparation, and I learned all the must-do basics that are invaluable steps to proper floral design. I then advanced to joining the team to install wedding arrangements in the churches and reception flowers at the Country Clubs. I was still a bucket toter and occasionally the "Hander" of flowers to the arranger. I certainly received loads of instruction and How-To techniques along with the dreaded No-Nos. Once I got my drivers license, I was sent out on gathering expeditions to collect roadside flowers such as Queen Anne's Lace, Blackeyed Susans, and Butterfly weed that enhanced the arrangements. They also instructed me as to how to prune branches from bushes in the garden so I didn't go through and clear cut someone's hedge. These foraging trips led to my fascination with everything in the wild and how it only enhances a flower arrangement. All in all, my experience working for Aunt Lula Rose and Mrs. McReynolds and the other ladies on the Flower Basket team were invaluable. The first time they allowed me to twirl a little piece of smilax, having been collected by my hands in the woods, onto a sconce at the Country Club I thought I had died and gone to heaven …. I was hooked. I never actually "did" flowers for them—but years later the first time I went out and gathered my materials, prepared my own container, and created an actual greenery arrangement I shocked myself because it worked and it was beautiful. I took it forward from there. Birmingham has a very strong, deep respect and tradition in the

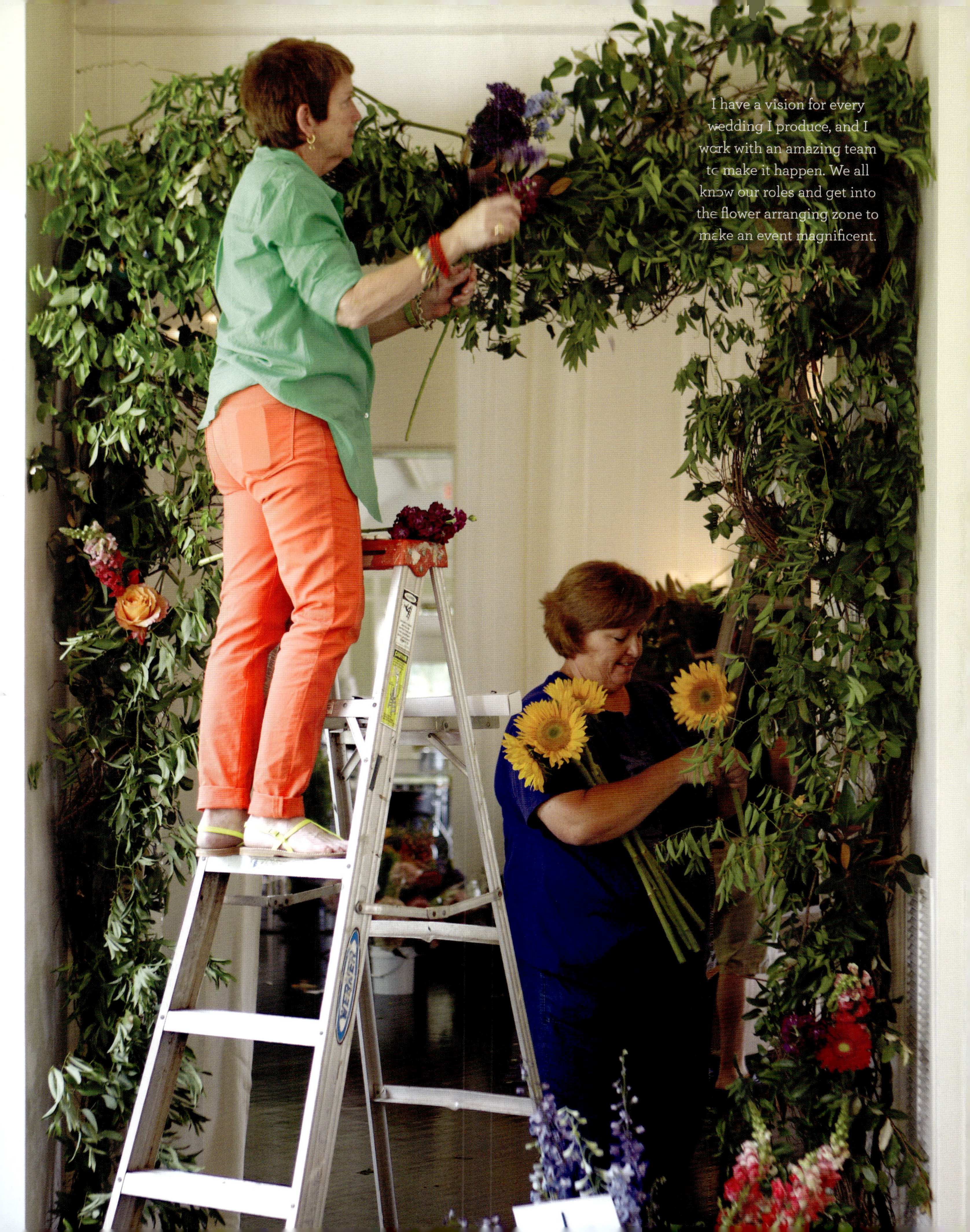

I have a vision for every wedding I produce, and I work with an amazing team to make it happen. We all know our roles and get into the flower arranging zone to make an event magnificent.

field of floral design and I am very fortunate to have learned from true masters.

I headed off to school and then was married and started having babies, and friends were always asking me to help do flowers for little things. It was fun to swoop in and collaborate. Finding flowers for parties was a huge challenge—I certainly couldn't purchase at the wholesale floral business because I wasn't an actual "business." I became friendly with a few ladies who would sell me flowers from their gardens. I had my family's yards to collect from, and I had my foraging, or I'd stop my car and send my children scurrying to grab something on the roadside that I just "had to have."

I think it was these times when I was only able to gather a little of this and a little of that—as the days that carved out the Wildflower "look" which is very natural, locally gathered, and seasonal with an element of surprise. When you have to make something pretty out of what you have on hand, you rely on your innate creativity, and it works.

My next flower shop job was when my oldest, Robert, was a baby. I worked at Village Florist in Mountain Brook Village for Virginia Williams. I almost lost my job working there because I hated to use the stiff wholesale greenery such as leather leaf ferns. Mrs. Williams not only had fresh flowers, but throughout her little shop she also had blooming potted plants and greenery in hanging baskets. I would snip a little here and a little there to create (in my eye) a more natural, woodland-like arrangement. She told me I had to stop because she wasn't going to be able to sell the plants—even though I was being careful like Aunt Lula Rose had taught me! I couldn't bring myself to stop—I just had to have the softer greenery. My days were numbered. I was saved by an order from a gentleman from Tuscaloosa. He called long distance and said he wanted me to make his wife an arrangement. He was making the 60 mile trip to Birmingham to pick it up because the first one I made for him a few weeks before, that he had taken home to his wife, was a huge success. She had said that it was the "most beautiful arrangement she had ever seen." My foraging continued.

Like so many of us, I divorced and was faced with earning a proper living to support my family. Hence, my banking days began along with side gigs to help fund birthday presents and Santa. I helped Peggy Conway, a sweet lady who had also helped Aunt Lula Rose and Mrs. McReynolds. She worked from her home like Lula Rose had, and things felt familiar being back in the floral end of the wedding/party business. Once again, I never really "did" flowers to any scale but I did prep work, flower conditioning, cutting yard greenery, making the hand-wired corsages and boutonnieres and flower girl circlets. All the really hard, tedious jobs that they rooked me into doing by telling me I was so good at the task. Nothing like the power of praise! Again, I was working with flowers and learning on the job. I also began creating dried flower wreaths and garlands. It was the craze then, and I rode that wave. I worked making silk flower arrangements on Saturdays at a local gift shop and that led to me doing window displays as well. Then I was asked to help a few ladies dress their houses up for Christmas... remember I am still working at the bank fulltime and raising my children! My life was busy and breathless, hard and so rewarding ... and I needed more.

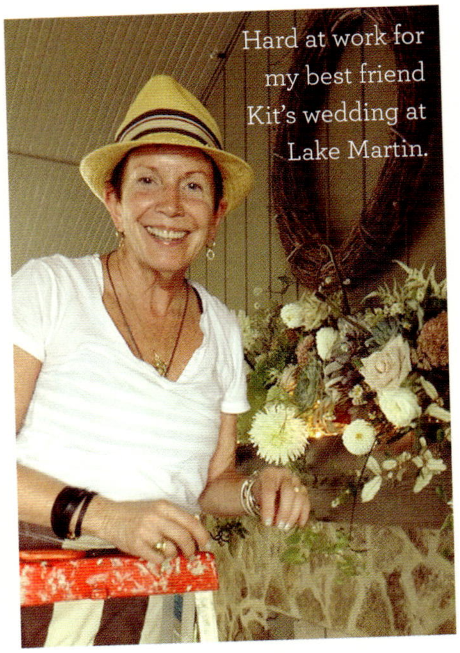

Hard at work for my best friend Kit's wedding at Lake Martin.

Mrs. Conway knew of a new flower shop opening in downtown Birmingham. They were looking for a manager. She recommended me—I was so flattered. But, I couldn't see how I could leave my solid bank job—insurance, security. I was wooed away by a good salary to cover my now out-of-pocket expenses and the thrill of working with flowers. I began at Le Marché aux Fleurs. The store was ahead of the times in Birmingham and a lovely shop. It was an oasis in the heart of the city, with all the office buildings towering overhead. We offered the bucket shop concept for a flower shop; each flower could be purchased by the stem. Customers could come in and buy whatever mix they chose, or we'd be set free to create what we chose for a specific budget. It was very fast paced and extremely rewarding work, and I learned TONS about the flower shop inner workings.

I loved working for Judith at Le Marché and all that I experienced in those years, but the best part is that it was at the shop where I met my husband Bill. He was an attorney downtown, and he was on the dating scene. So he would come in and purchase flowers for other girls, and we became friends. I guess he was flirting, but it didn't occur to me at the time until he asked me on a date one Friday afternoon. I was busy for the weekend and that began a series of missed opportunities that went on for quite awhile. Eventually, we grabbed a quick lunch one day and the rest is history...sort of.

Bill was my biggest fan, and he is responsible for me getting up the courage to open my business and make it official. I started in our garage and then expanded to my first shop, called Wildflower Designs, in 1996. Bill was so thrilled because he could finally park in the garage again, and I got the flowers out of the washing machine (I used it as a deep bucket to hold fresh flowers)! He had his house back...but then I was at the shop for all hours working to get things off the ground. Two sides to every coin!!!

My concept for my shop was that I wouldn't send anything out on delivery that I wouldn't want to receive myself. I was tired of all those ugly pressed glass floral vases that Mama had shelves and shelves of, and I wanted the container to be one everyone would want to keep and enjoy. I spent every free second scouring antiques markets and flea markets for unusual vintage pieces. Many of my first arrangements were made in old sap buckets that I sourced from up East, older mixing bowls or teacups or handmade pottery pieces and vintage lunchboxes.

For many years, by necessity, I had foraged and gathered flowers and materials for my arrangements, and I still insisted on unusual cut greenery for the arrangements—still no leather leaf! Cute little Galax leaves were available through the wholesale florist so I did embrace them and used them frequently in our mixes. There was an empty garden space outside the door to my shop so we planted a crazy quilt type of garden to be a spot where we could cut herbs and unusual things to add to our arrangements. This practice was a choice that set me apart.

The magazines were extremely supportive of me from the beginning. I had done photo styling and flowers for photo shoots for several years, but as I was opening the doors to my shop I was also commissioned by *Southern Accents* to create a series of Wedding bouquets that were shot in color and ran as full page pictures. I was ahead of my time evidently because people were amazed at the colorful "Wedding" bouquets. I also had two weddings featured in the inaugural issue of *Southern Living Weddings* and later I was asked to write and create supporting arrangements for an ongoing article in *Southern Accents* named "Flower School." The column ran for three years in the magazine, and then I was fortunate enough to be linked with *flower* magazine, and I hold the position as Contributing Editor for that glorious publication. I am very proud of the work I have done for these magazines and others and of their support. As a result of the printed press, I have been able to build my business through word of mouth and concentrate on pretty things and keep the quality to my standards.

With the help of my staff, we were able to keep the Wildflower concept alive and my business continued to grow. The resolutions I'd tucked close to my heart were and are the guidelines that give clients insight into my style and employees the information they need to get every arrangement right and

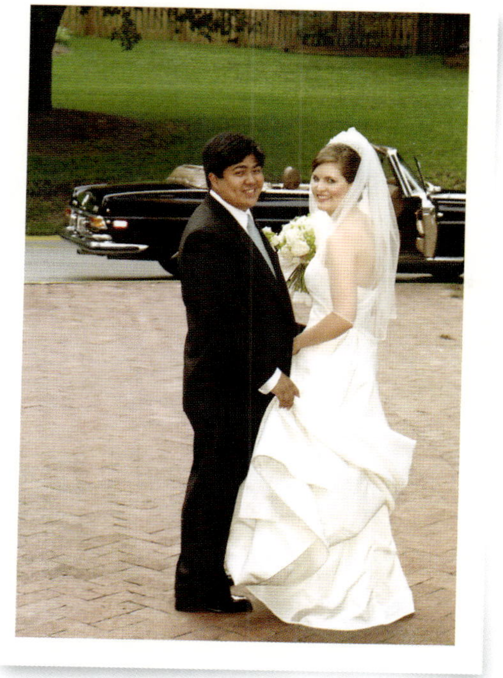

All those years of hard work helped me be prepared for planning my own daughter Brooke's wedding. What a glorious day!

ready to go into the delivery van.

As I have researched and prepared for this book, I am awestruck by the number of wonderful clients that I have had over the years and by the sheer number of events from small luncheons, brunches, wedding showers, baby showers, dinner parties (large and small), weddings and anniversary celebrations, to list a few, that I have been a part of. Then we could discuss the 55+ flower demonstrations and lectures that I have taught over the last 15 years...all the students I have instructed ...or the many fundraising events that I have been involved in ...on and on and on. I reflect on all of these wonderful people who have trusted their life celebrations to me, and I am very touched and grateful. I remember each event individually as if it were one of my children. What an amazing path that I have found myself on and how very proud I am of what I have accomplished. And, there is more to come!!!

When I stop and reflect, the one theme that seems to dance through my flowers is always the addition of soft garden greenery or gathered unusual blooms or berries or vines or pods. Anything that takes the magnificent, the elegant, the precious flower arrangement and humbles it a bit. I am pleased with the end result with a few grasses, vines, or alley-found treasures tucked in to soften things and make the finished arrangement seem more natural and "down to earth."

I have come full circle. My shop is closed, and I work from my studio behind my home, sometimes by myself, sometimes with a whole collection of long time local helpers along with helpers who will travel in from nearby states to join the Wildflower gang. We are a tightknit team who I liken often to a quilting bee. We work amiably together to reach a finished goal...we share knowledge of our craft, we laugh together and cry together and support each other, and we share a huge pride in our finished product.

Luckily I've made time for travel, time for my children and grandchildren and my patient husband Bill, who is still my greatest supporter. I have entered a new level of floral designing—I get to travel around the world giving lectures and floral demonstrations and making new friends who I cherish along the way. It is just the way it has all turned out—nothing was planned in any certain way. The driving force has been my creativity that loves to come rushing out when I least expect it. I will have an idea... the next thing you know I am covered with goose bumps and I know I'm onto something great... I follow that idea to where it takes me. My life and lessons have brought me to this moment, and I am still learning.

spring

My favorite season officially arrives for me when tiny wild violets pop up everywhere begging me to pick them. The violets are followed by tiny lavender muscari, pink hyacinths, and yellow narcissus emerging among all the pansies. The cycle continues, and the earth wakes up. Then one day I realize that everything is glowing chartreuse green, the color of new growth.

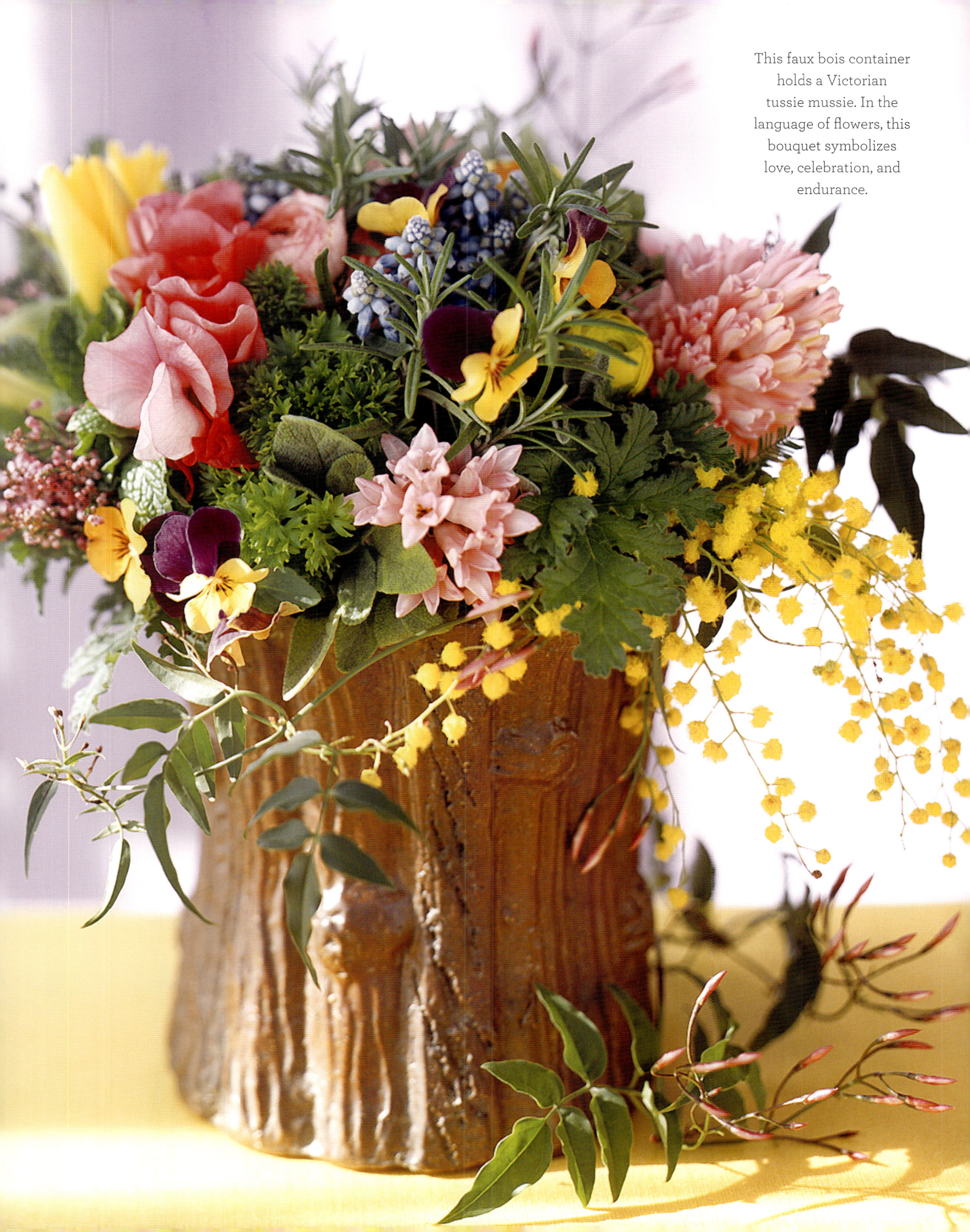

This faux bois container holds a Victorian tussie mussie. In the language of flowers, this bouquet symbolizes love, celebration, and endurance.

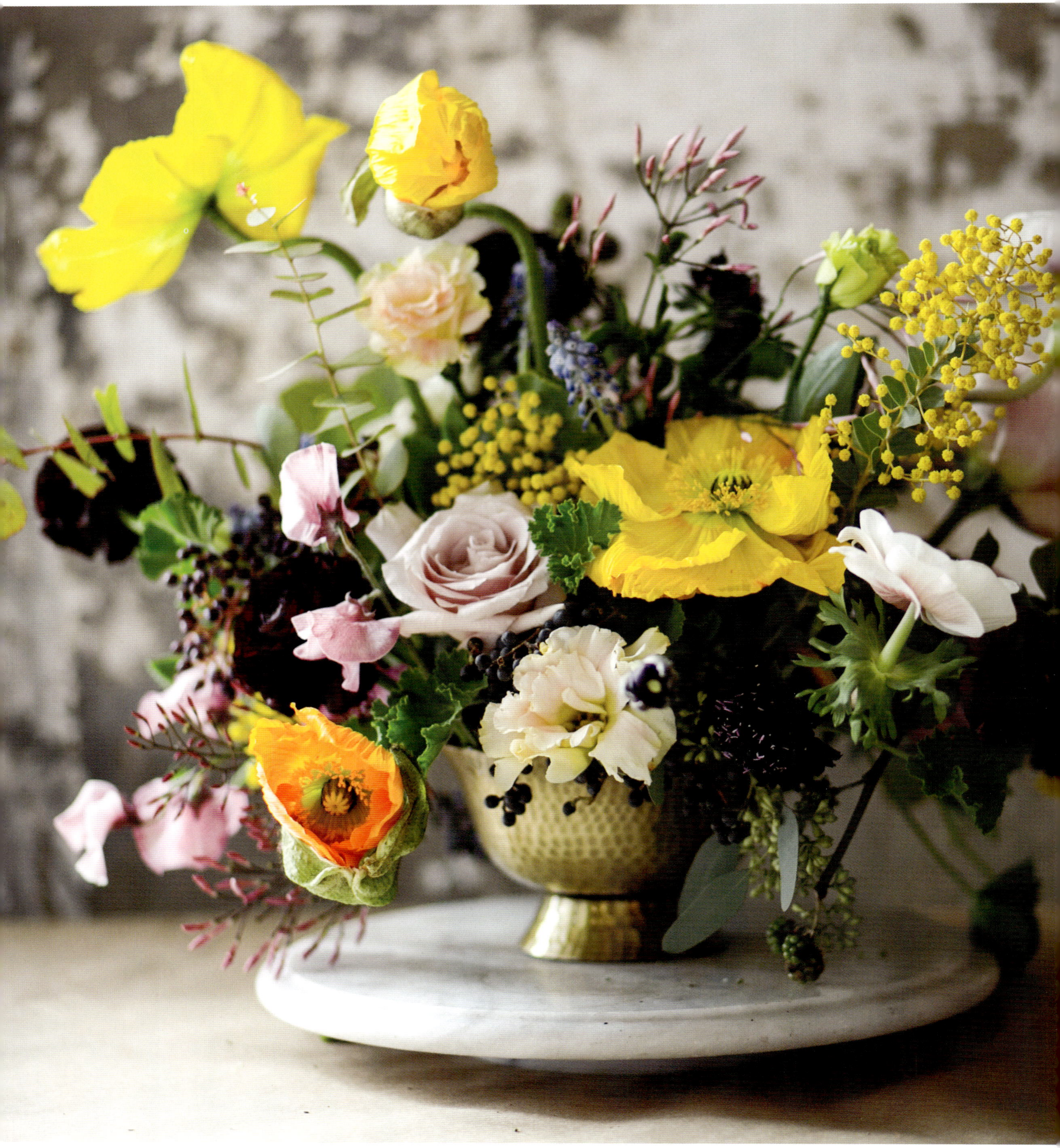

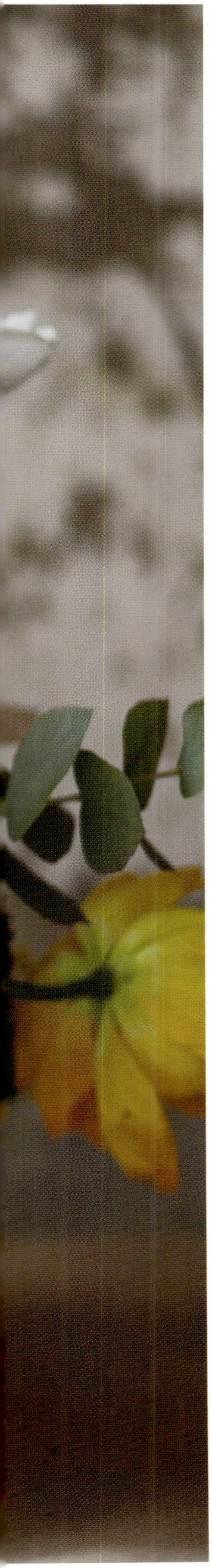

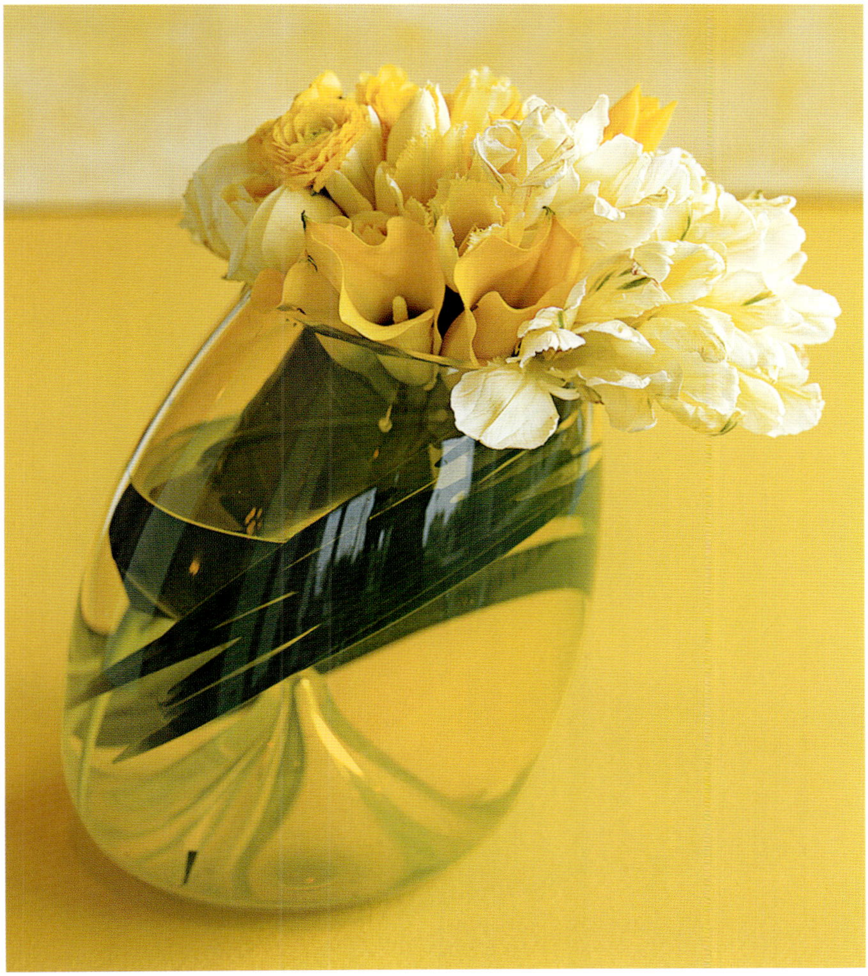

above: By clustering several different types of yellow flowers, a simple arrangement become more complex and interesting. I used a yellow glass vase.
The swirl of submerged lily grass covers all the different stems and gives the container more interest *left*: The floral collection of natural ingredients established as de rigueur by Constance Sprye is back in fashion. My modern twist is the unusual color combination. Deep eggplant-colored scabiosa and ranunculous play off the black eye of the anemone, softened with dusty shades of mauve and getting a jolt from bright pops of yellow. Even the textures, with wispy vines and dancing greenery, lighten the overall effect. Bees and butterflies can certainly fly through this one.

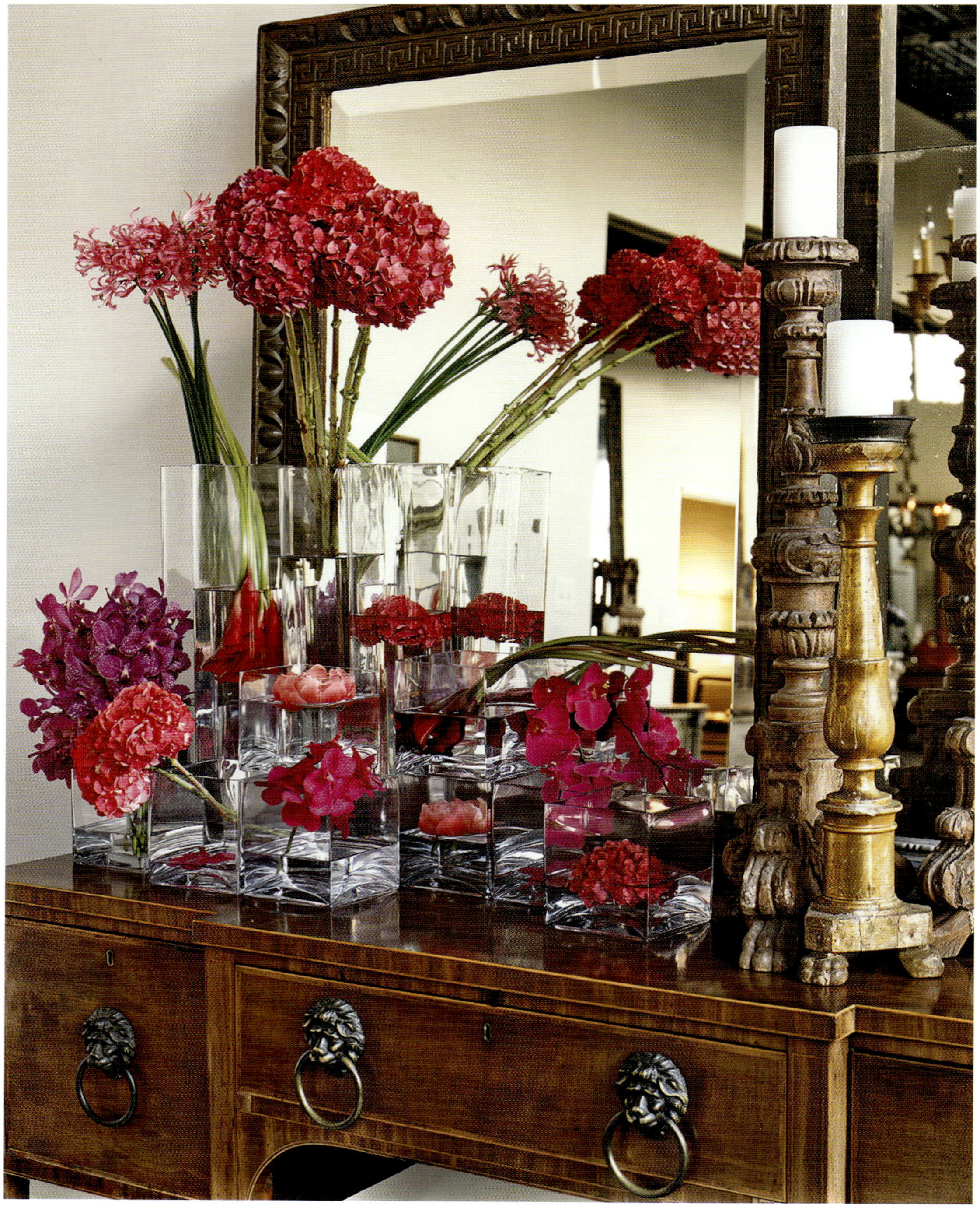

above: This floral display evokes a graphic skyline. I wanted the drama of a modern installation in a traditional setting: flowers leaning on the lips of clear glass vases, floating or submerged under the water line; massed single colors that complement each other to create a nontraditional arrangement. Each element could stand alone, but together they create a real show.

right: A rustic basket on a mahogany sideboard! That's the kind of contrast I think we all need. Take down the fine and make it less imposing; mix herbs and roses and showcase the beauty of each. I normally avoid using scented flowers around a table with food, but these herbs are so food friendly that I think my exception is warranted.

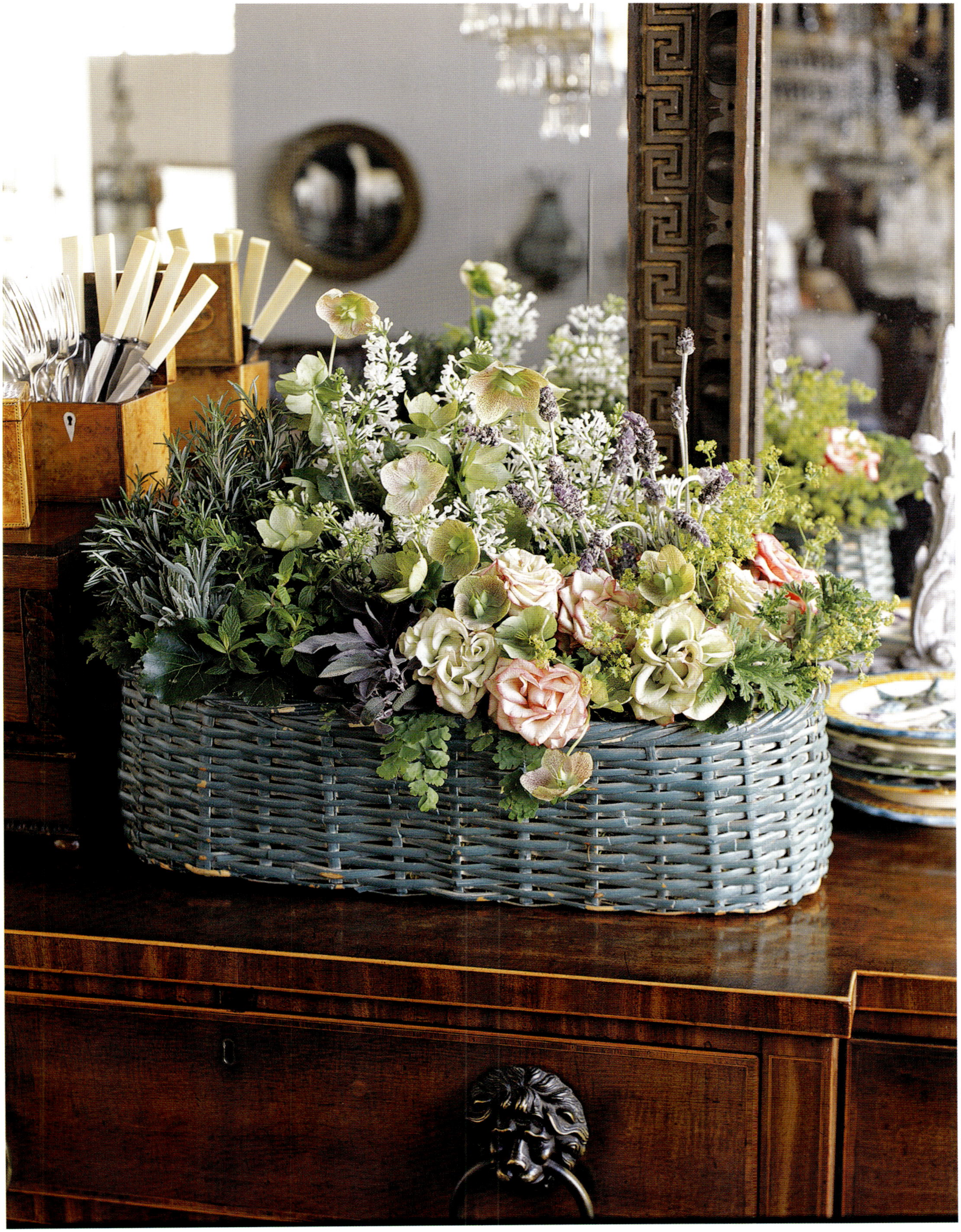

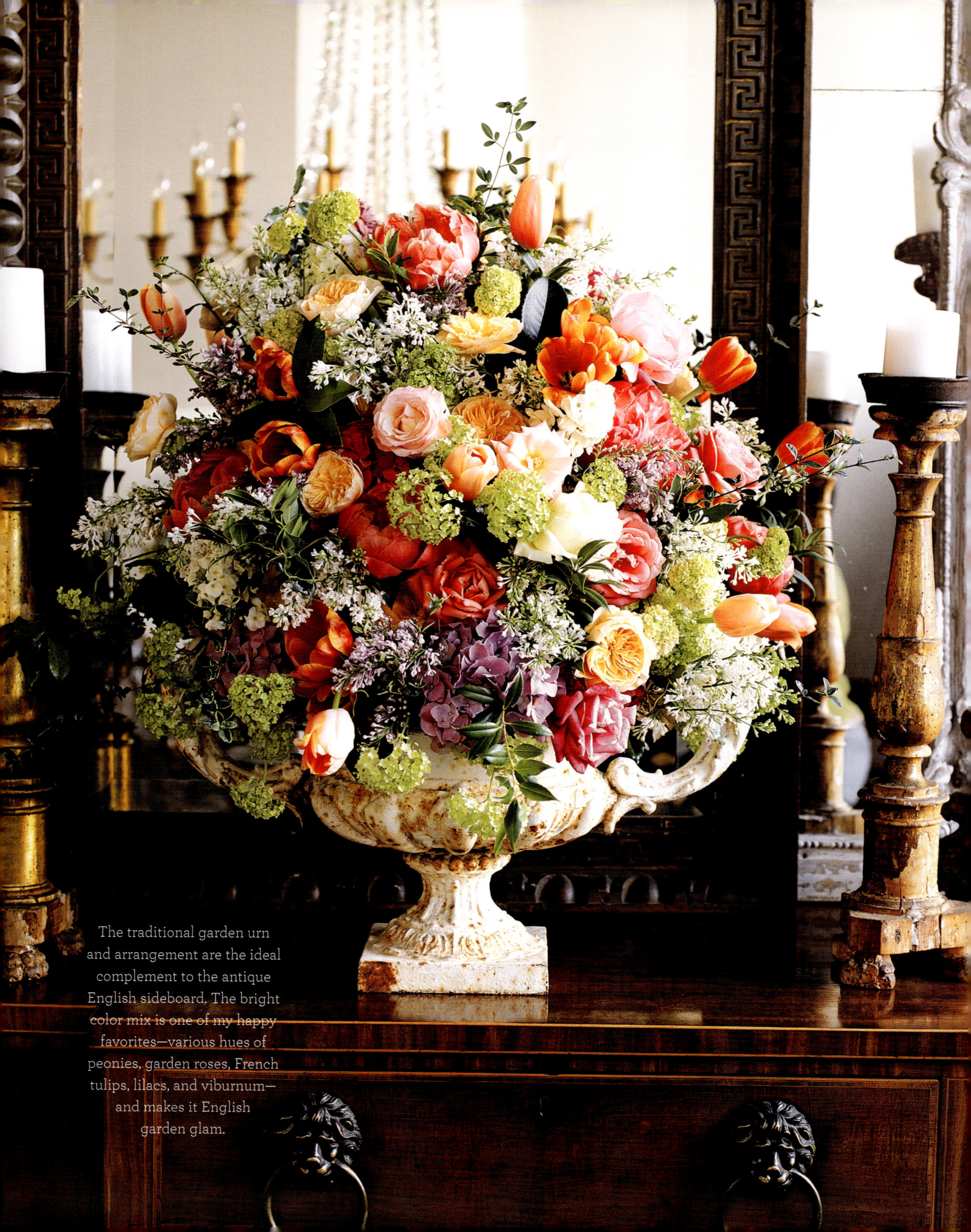

The traditional garden urn and arrangement are the ideal complement to the antique English sideboard. The bright color mix is one of my happy favorites—various hues of peonies, garden roses, French tulips, lilacs, and viburnum—and makes it English garden glam.

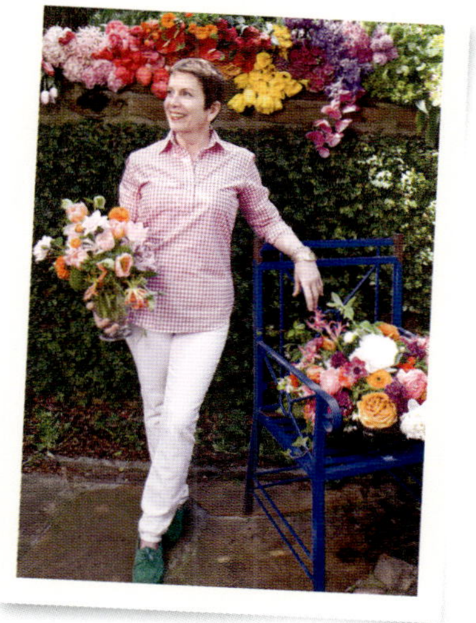

This English-inspired garden arrangement started with a visit to my garden where I cut enough branches to green in the arrangement before I even added any flowers. It's this sense of natural lushness that has become my signature: English style Sybilized.

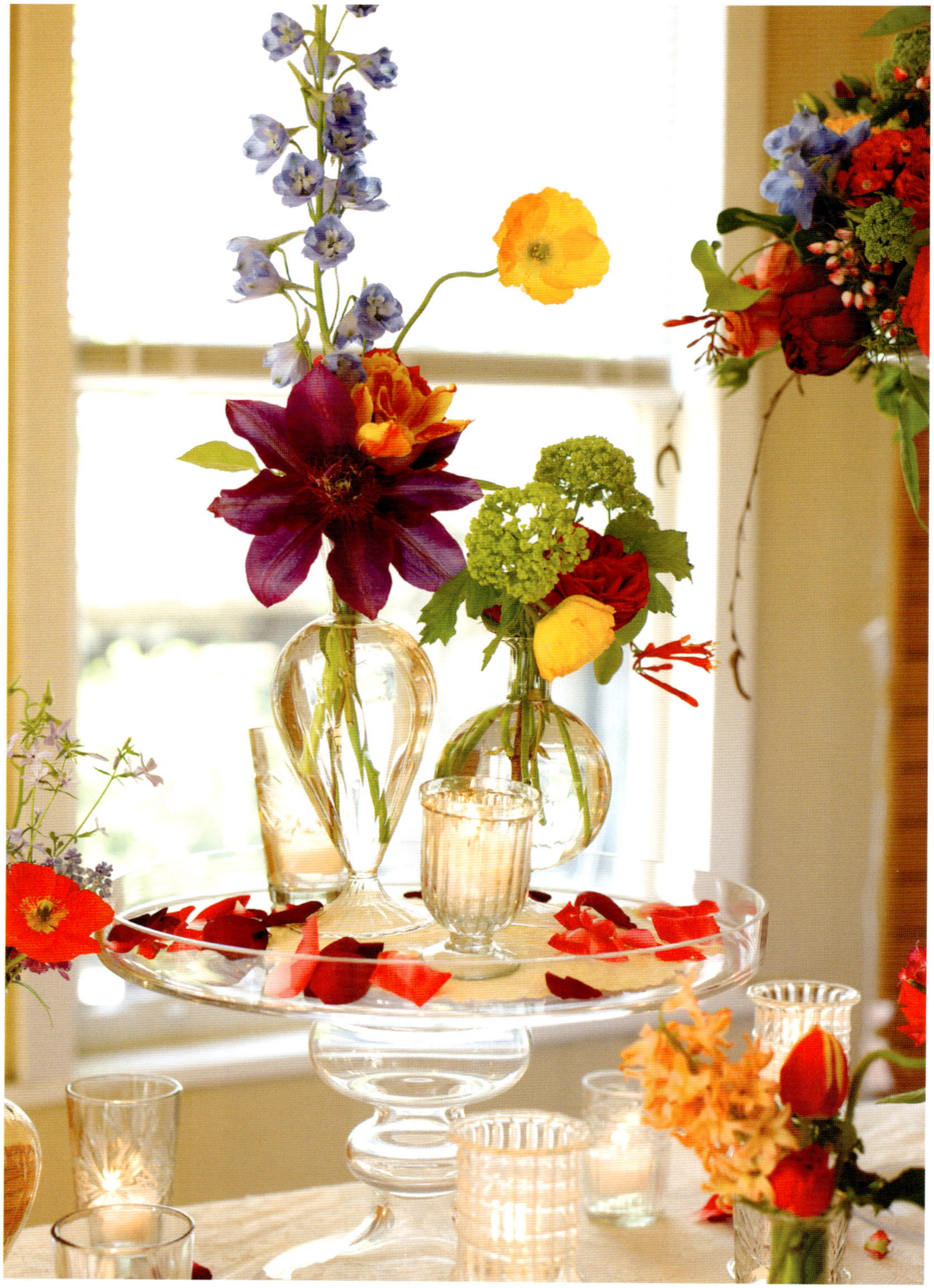

above: Ninety percent of the flowers in this composition were gathered straight from my garden, conditioned, and arranged to delight. I anxiously await my clematis blooms each season ... the star of this grouping. *right:* Lately I lean more and more toward tone on tone floral arrangements. Here is a mix of peach to coral to orange flowers, interspersed with my go-to chartreuse green for a pop. My garden treasures were added at the end: dancing columbine.

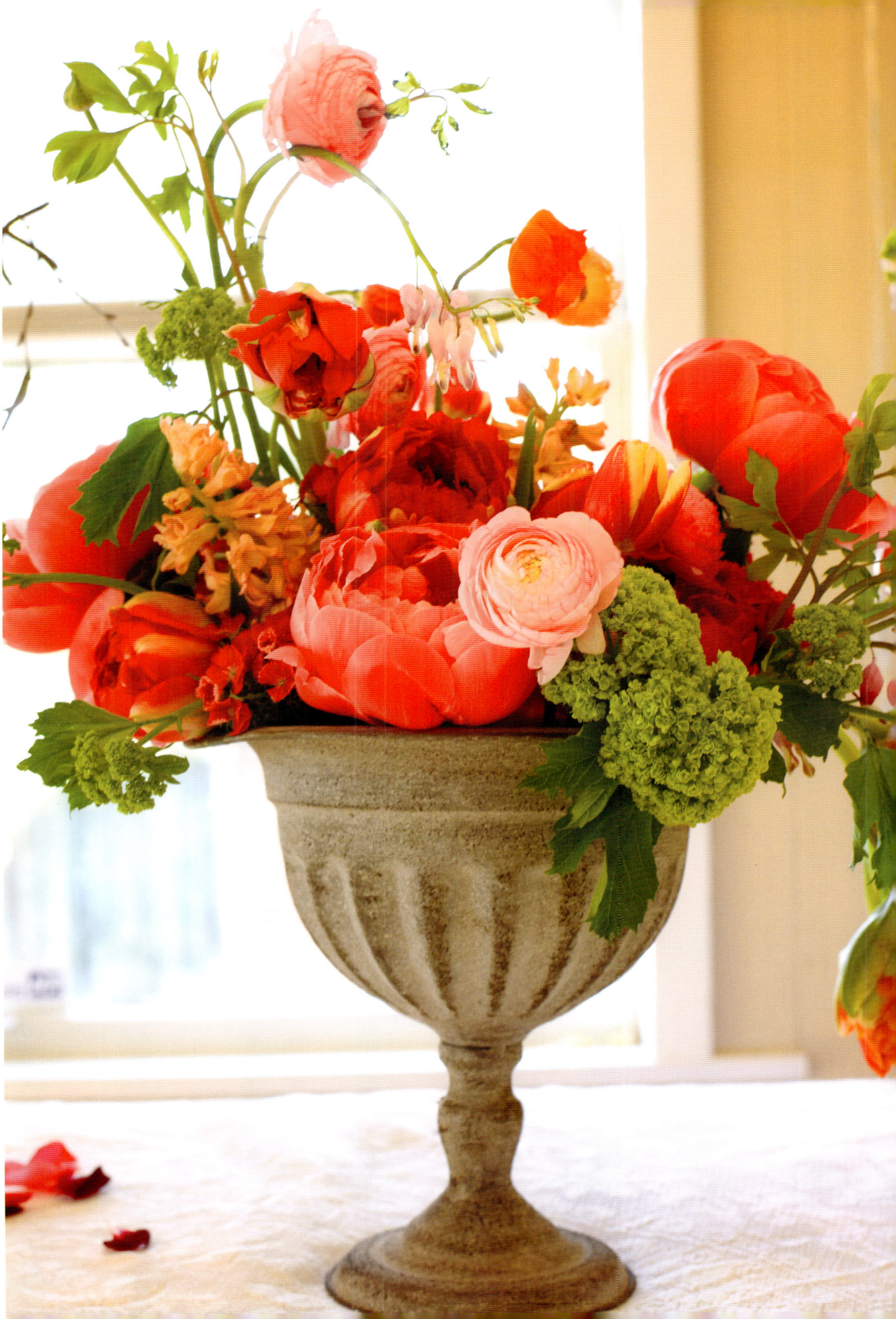

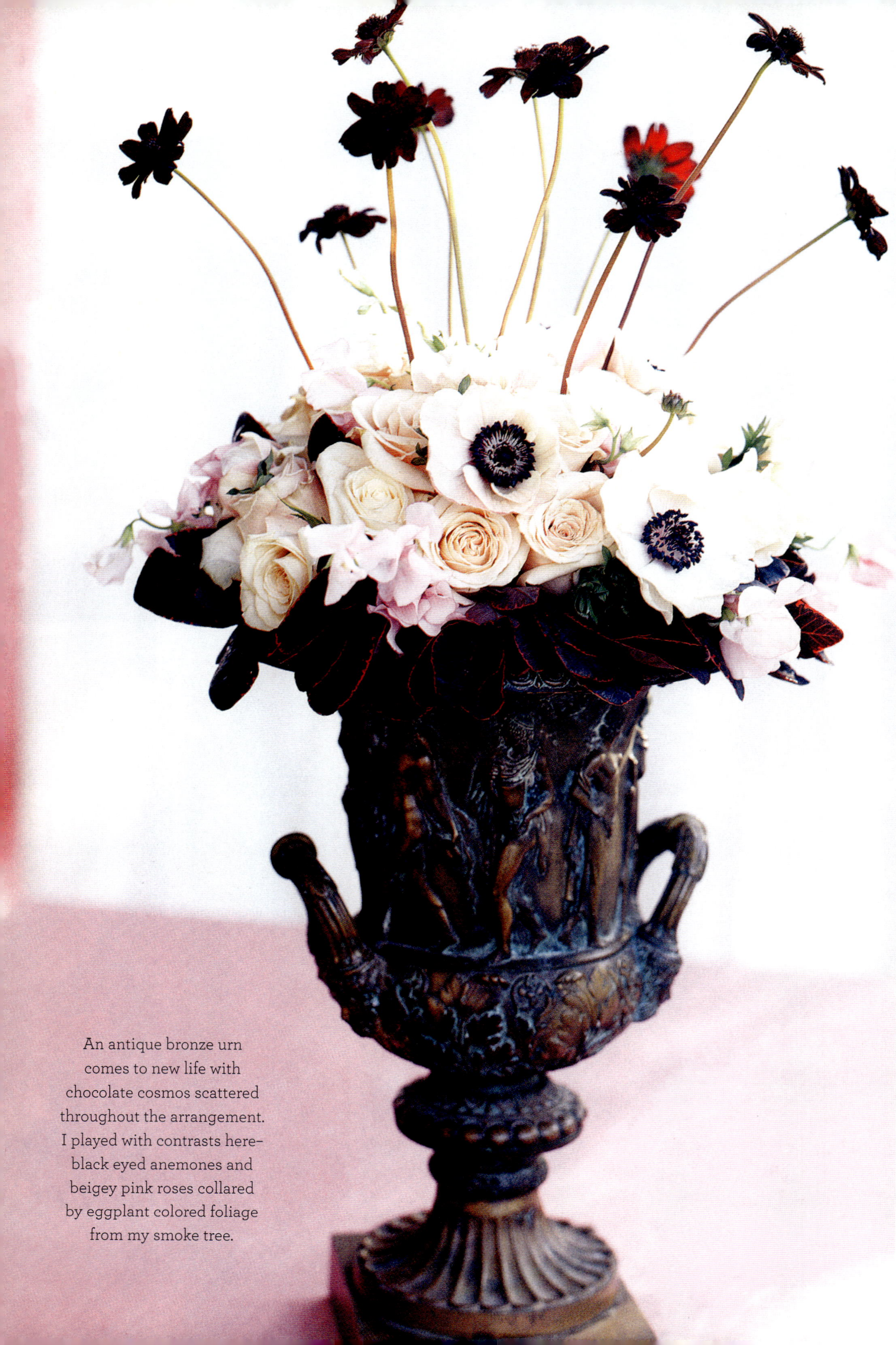

An antique bronze urn comes to new life with chocolate cosmos scattered throughout the arrangement. I played with contrasts here–black eyed anemones and beigey pink roses collared by eggplant colored foliage from my smoke tree.

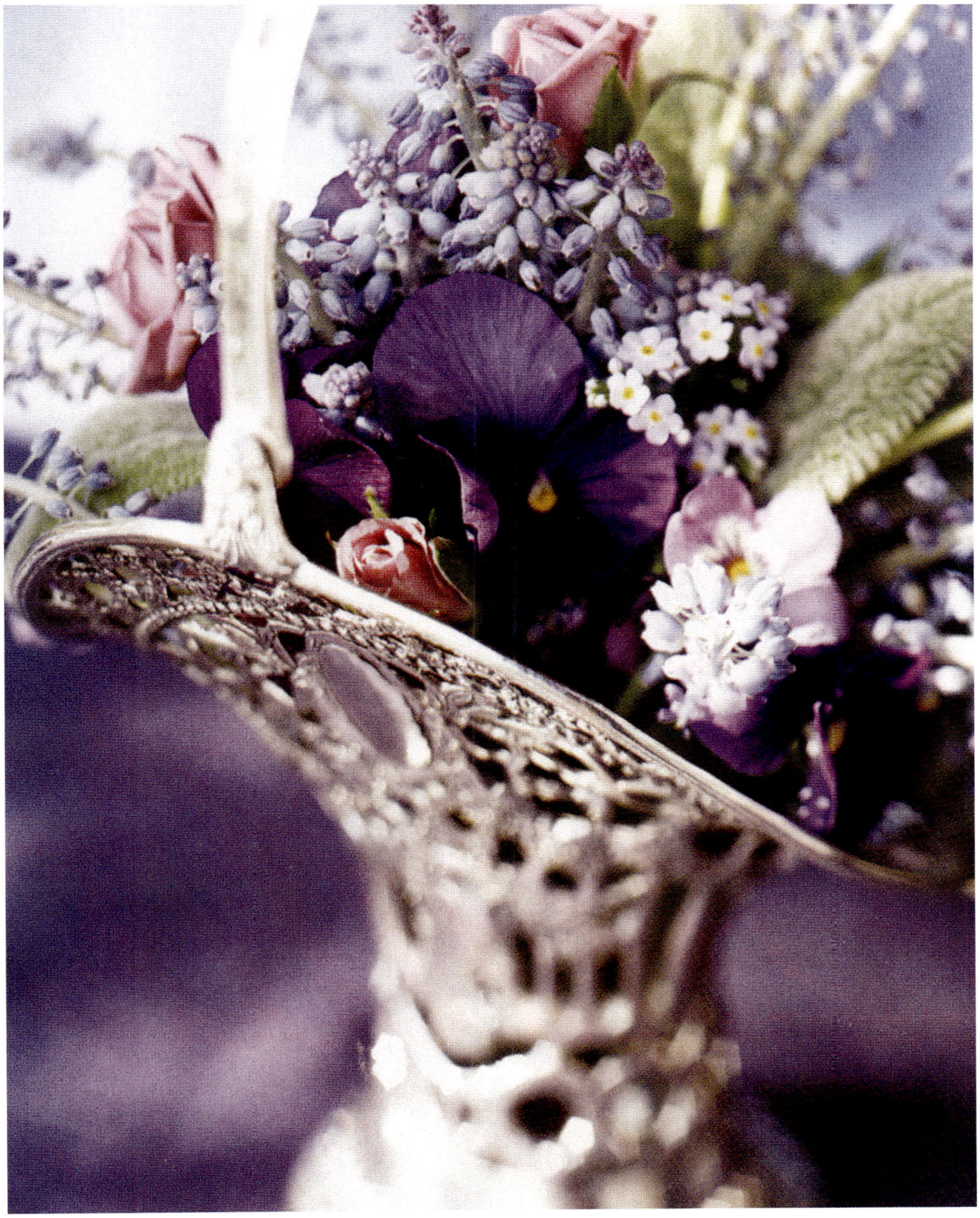

WHERE THERE'S A WILL THERE'S A WAY. THIS RETICULATED SILVER BASKET REQUIRED INGENUITY. I PLACED A GLASS VOTIVE CUP INSIDE TO HOLD WATER.

This 5-inch-tall antique sterling silver flower basket is a favorite of mine, but it's difficult to arrange flowers in because it doesn't hold water. It begs: "put flowers here." The only "florist" flower is a lavender spray rose that I trimmed and split into three. The precious forget-me-nots, pansies, and furry lamb's ear leaf came from my garden.

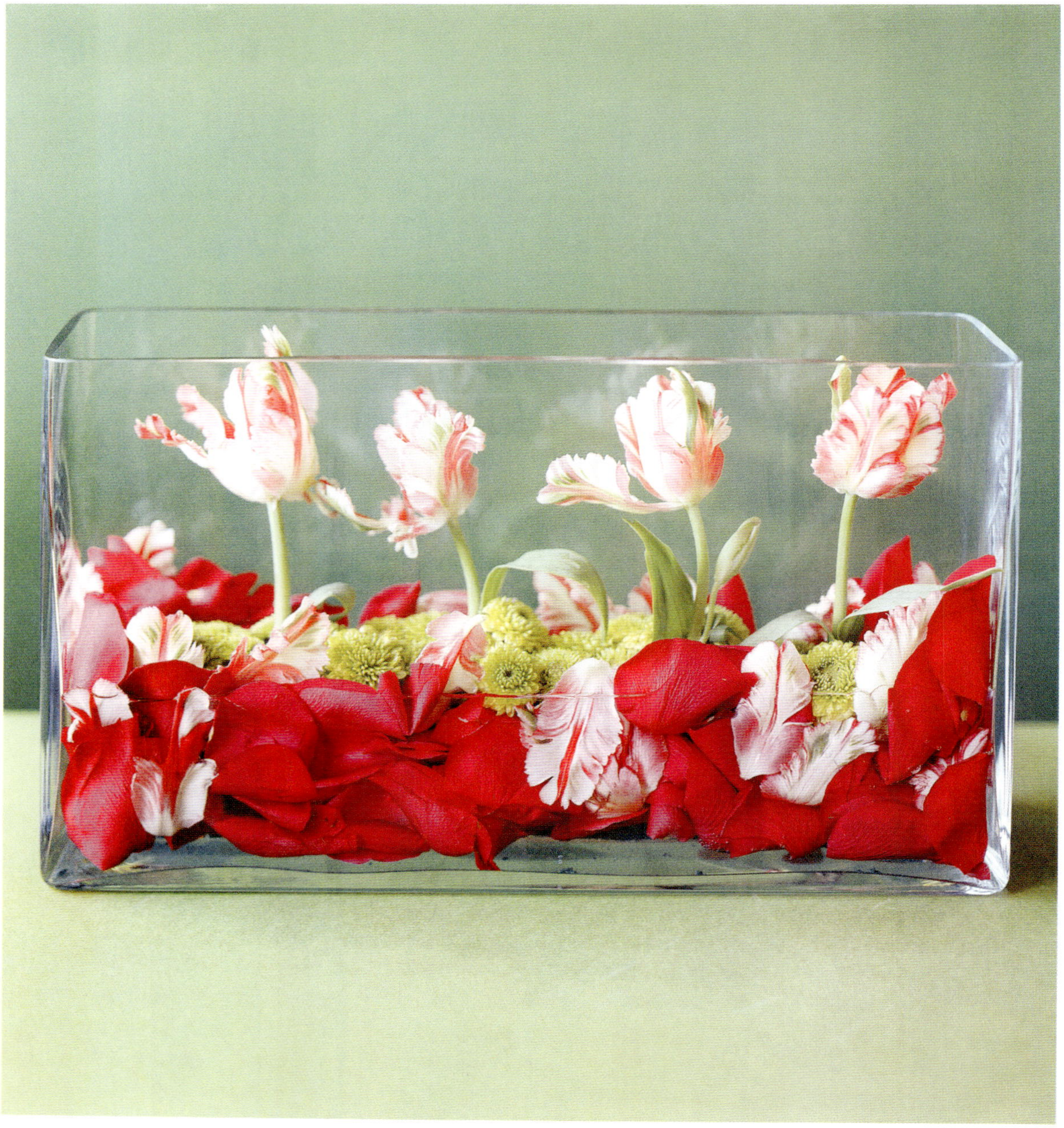

above: By massing the rose heads below the lip of the glass container, the arrangement becomes a modern twist on the Japanese art of ikebana. The Irish moss evokes a bed of grass, and the roses emerge lush and colorful, almost as in a fantasy. *right:* This arrangement reflects my mindset when pairing a container with flowers. The elegant cachepot has gilt feathering. The gold centers of the coral peonies duplicate this feathery feel. Though the arrangement is not complicated, it has an exceptional presence.

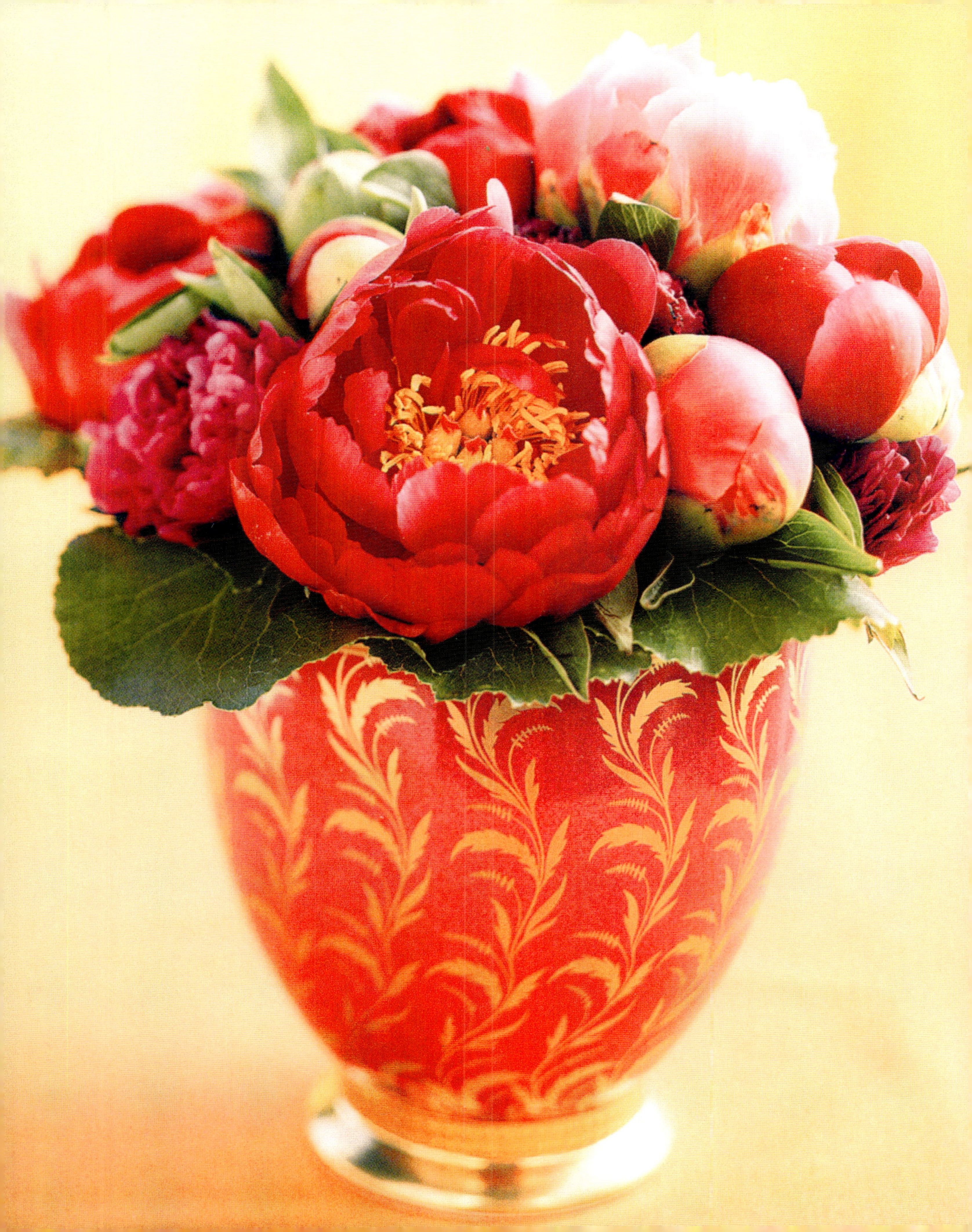

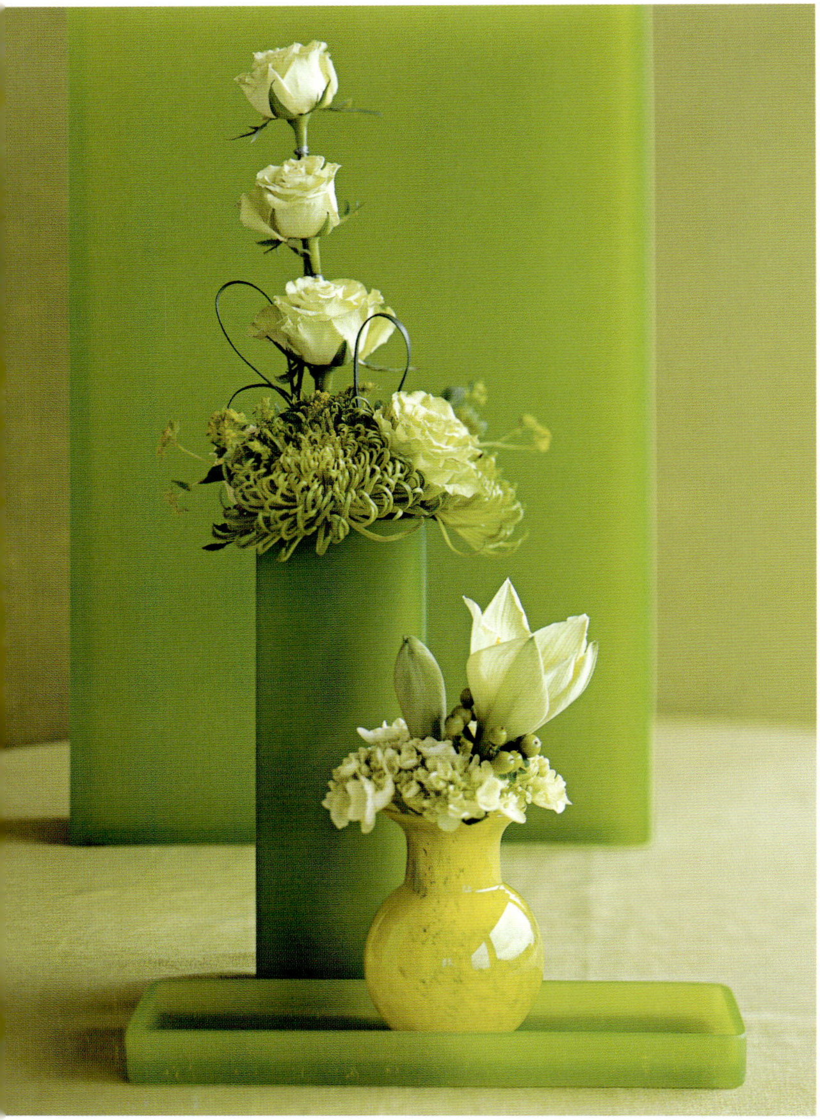

Green flowers mixed into green Martha Sturdy containers (I want to live in her world)—it's all part of this dream coming true. I broke my own rules by wiring three roses in a line with loops of lily grass to mimic leaves.

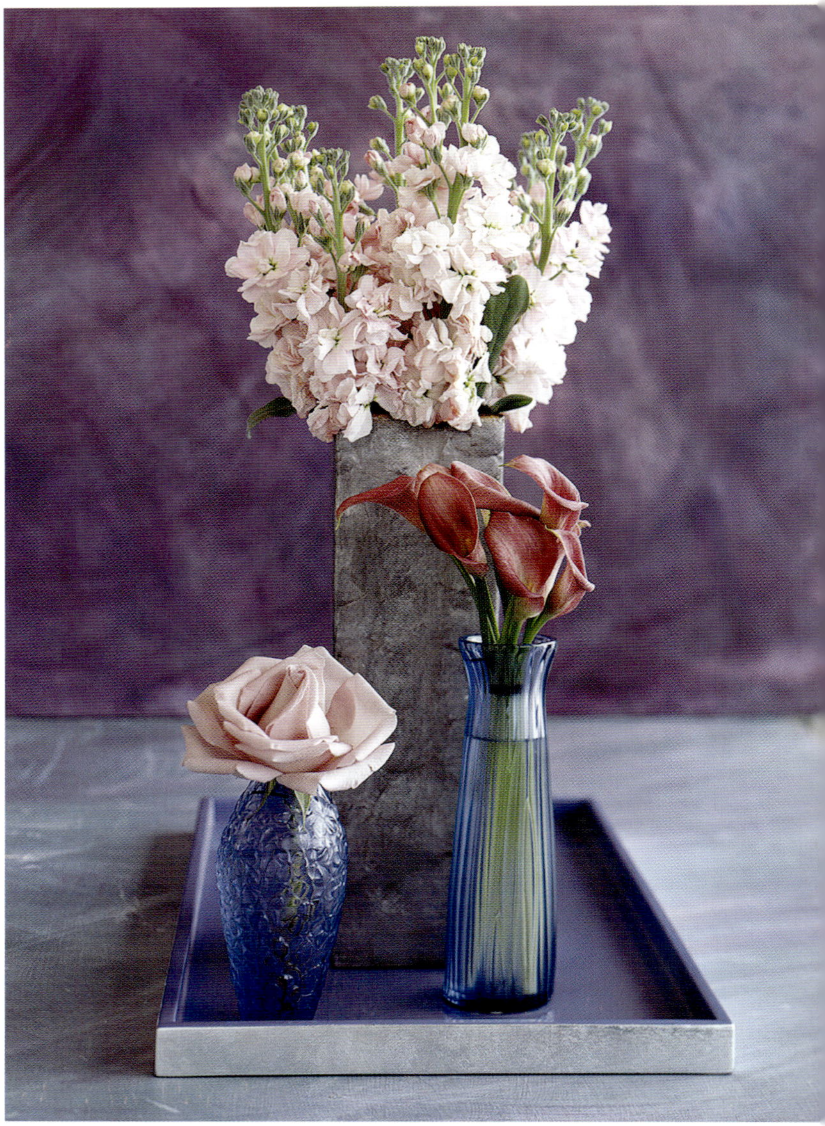

I like to call the color of the palest flowers "ice lavender." The plum-toned mini calla lilies bind the grouping together, giving weight with their deeper tones. I love lavender because as you see the final result is always so soothing and easy to enjoy.

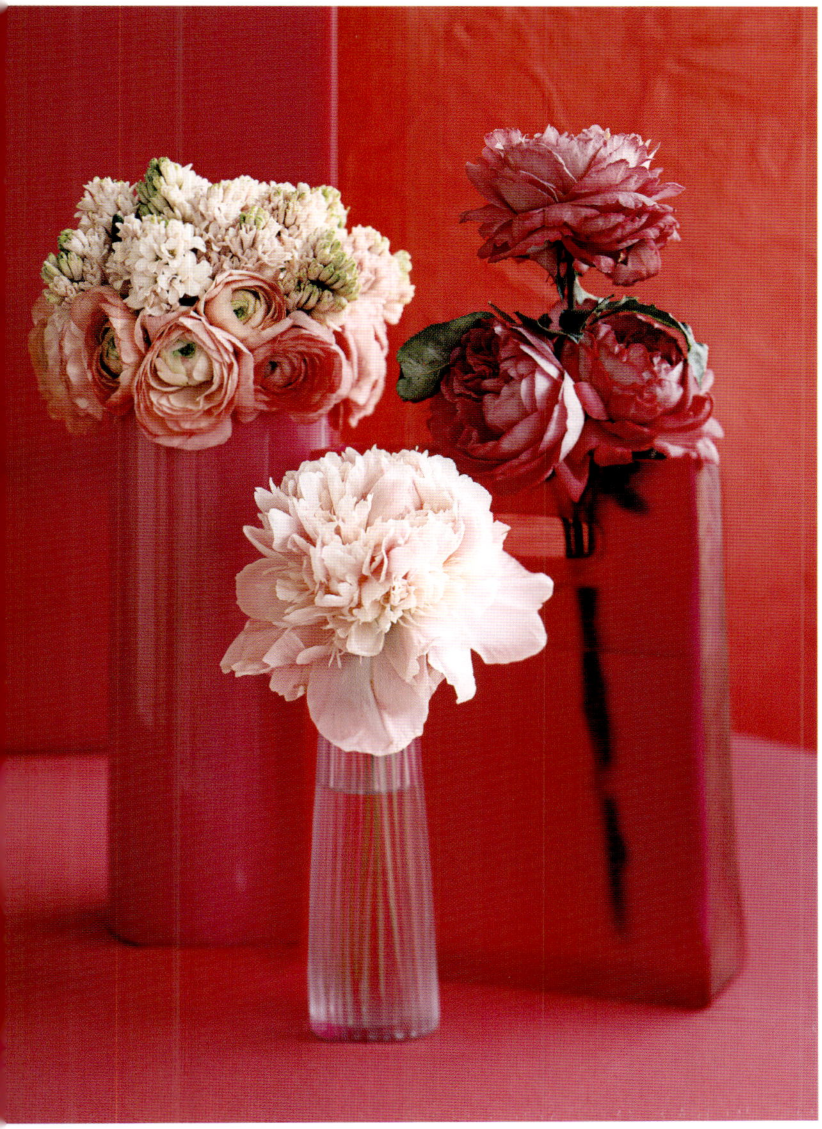

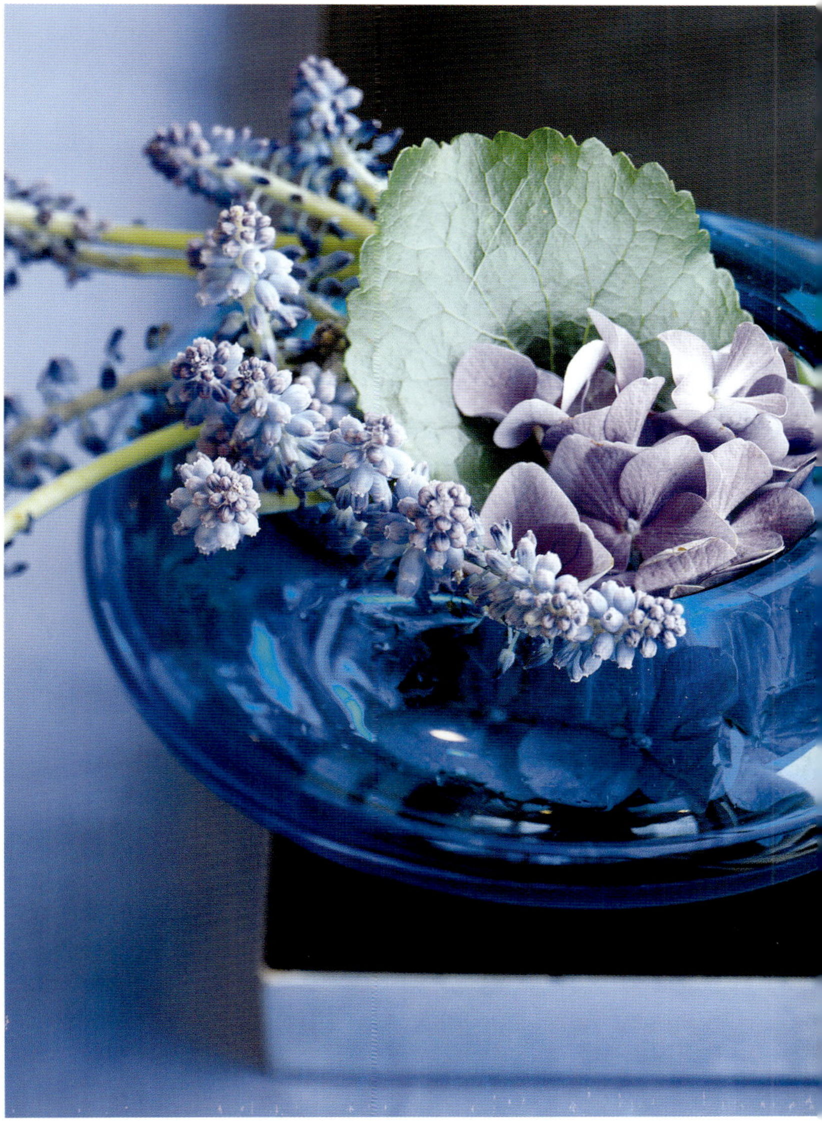

Textural vases hold lush and fluffy flowers—peonies, garden roses, hyacinths, and ranunculus. Don't be afraid to use a combination of pinks from your garden. They will always work together. Grouping flowers by color—you'll never go wrong.

This blue glass bowl is so beautiful it could stand on its own, but this understated arrangement makes it even more special. The image packs a huge punch, but the tiny bowl fits in the palm of my hand.

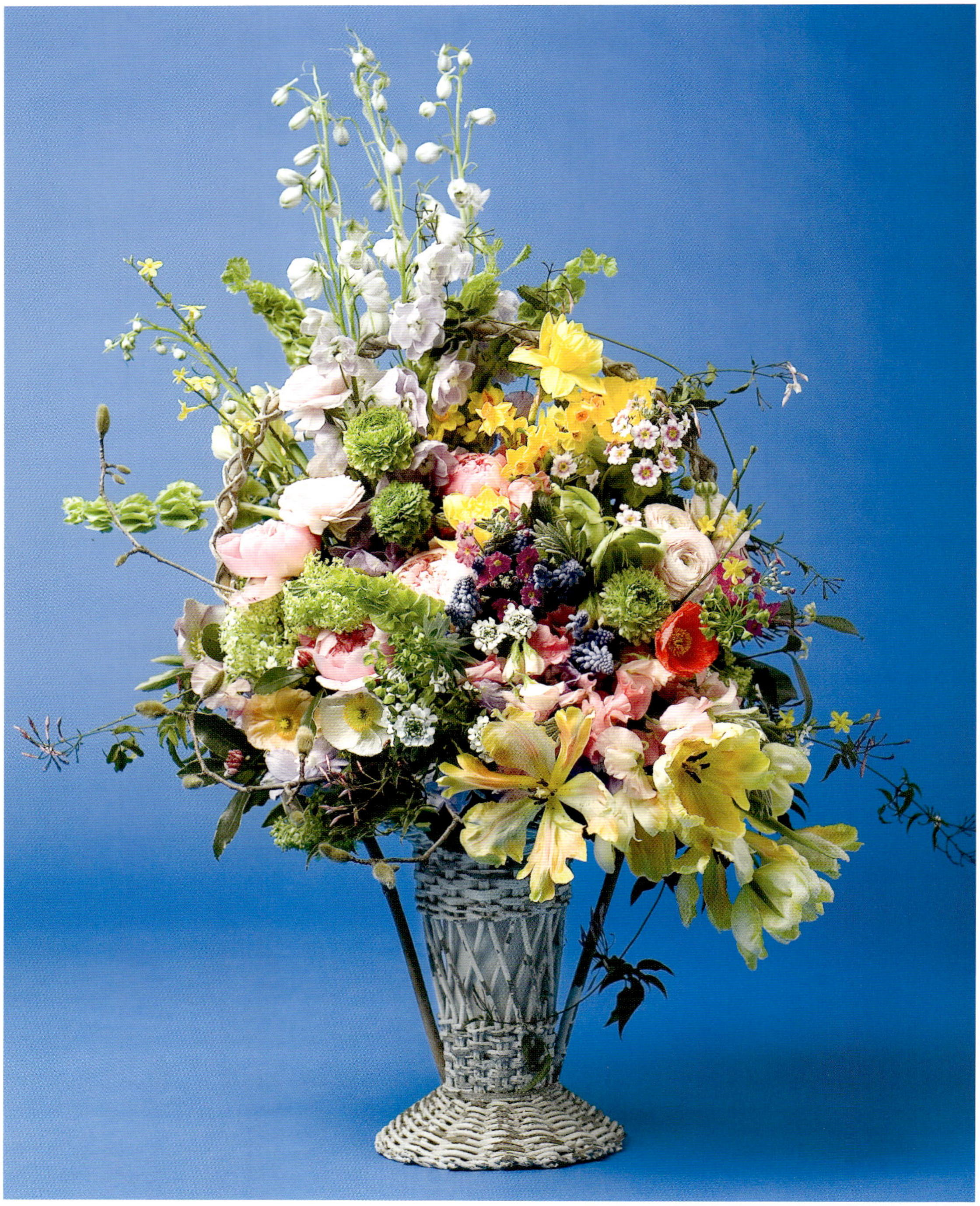

AS A TRIBUTE TO THE EXERCISE OF DEPICTING PAINTINGS THROUGH FLOWERS AS PRACTICED IN ART IN BLOOM EXHIBITIONS AT MUSEUMS ACROSS THE COUNTRY, I CREATED MY OWN VERSION. ALL WITH SPRING FLOWERS.

The closeup on my Dutch-master inspired arrangement shows the diversity of the materials I used. I see lavender, primula, euphorbia, candy tuft, hellebores from my garden and a huge array of other beautiful flowers in a wicker container with great patina.

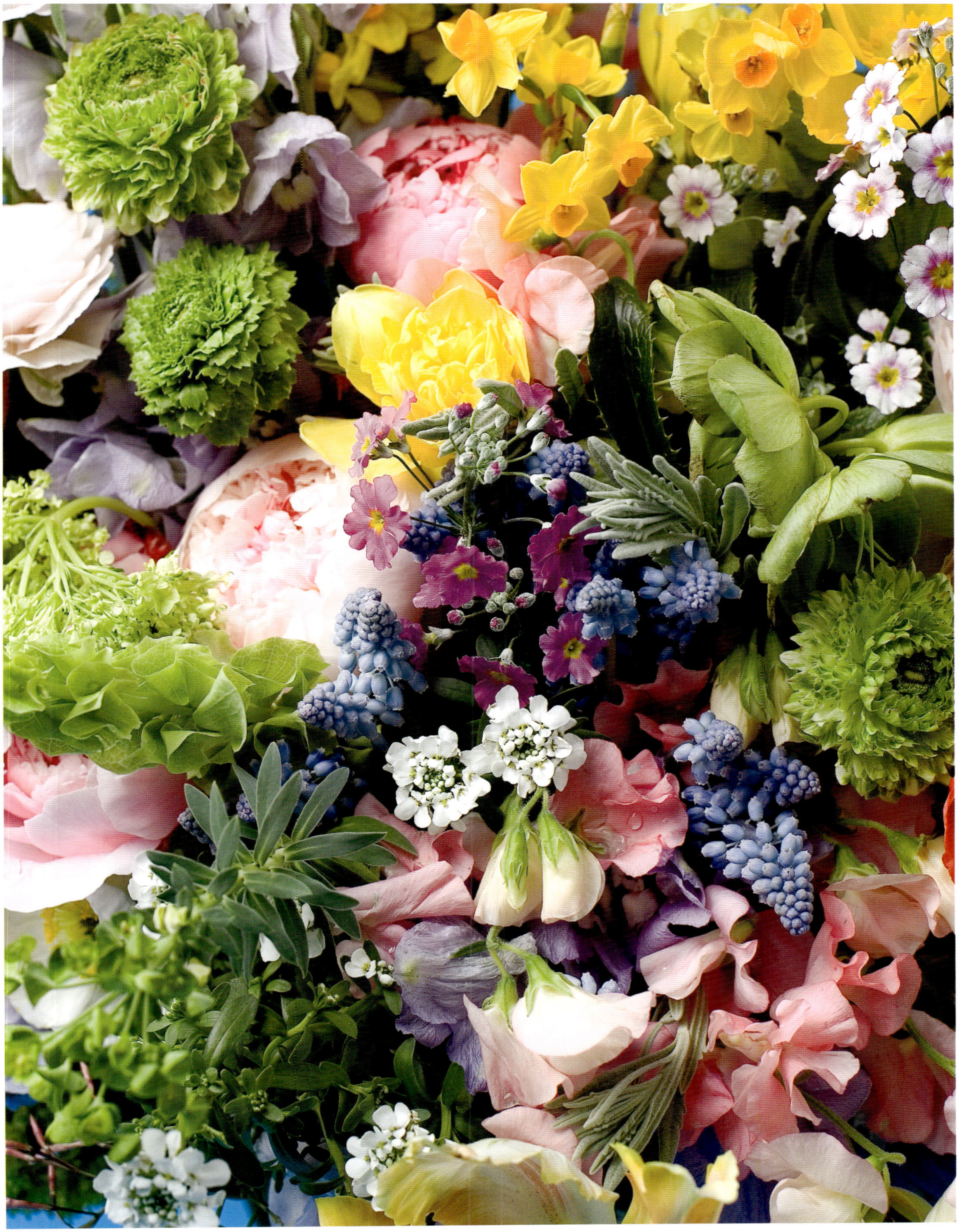

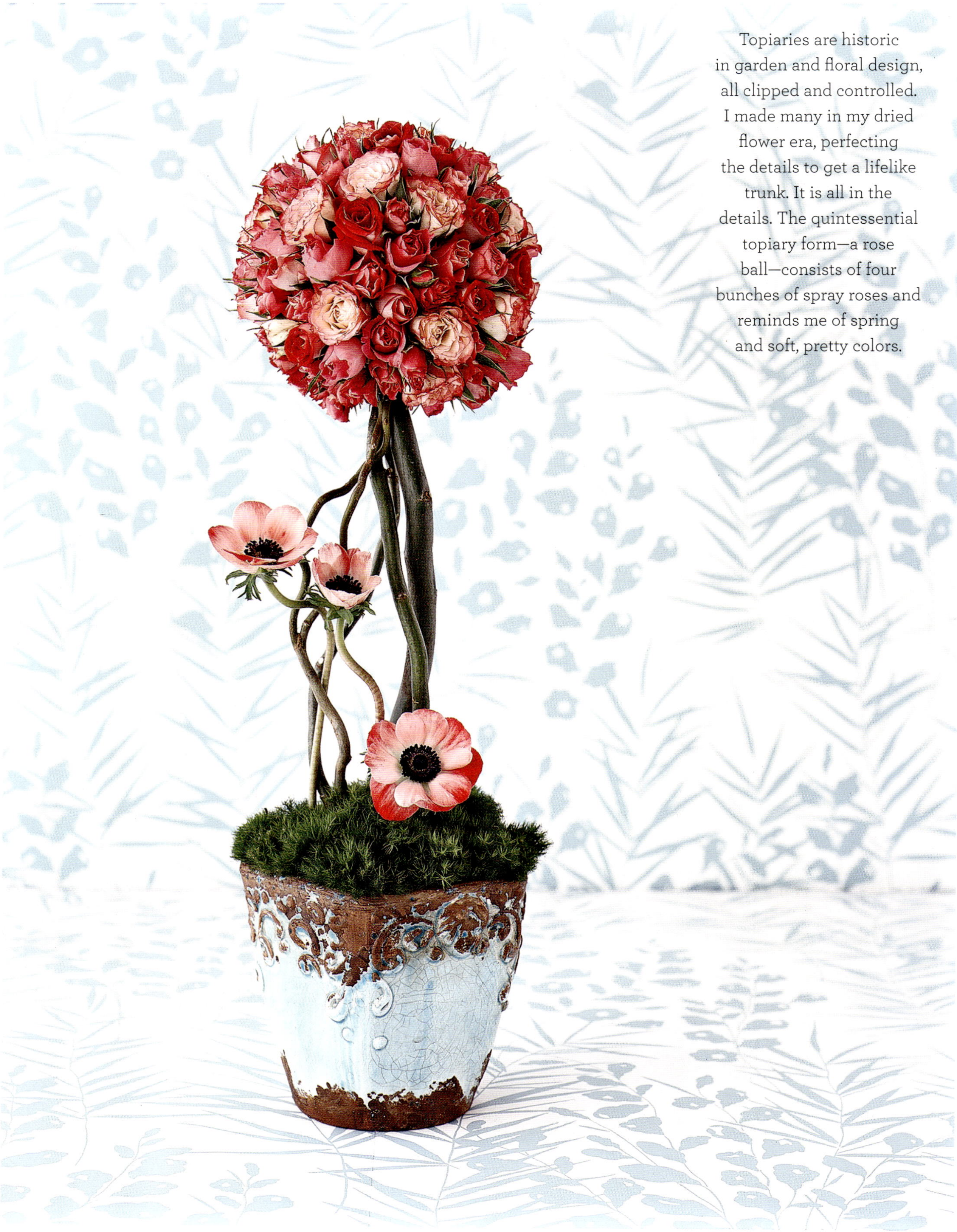

Topiaries are historic in garden and floral design, all clipped and controlled. I made many in my dried flower era, perfecting the details to get a lifelike trunk. It is all in the details. The quintessential topiary form—a rose ball—consists of four bunches of spray roses and reminds me of spring and soft, pretty colors.

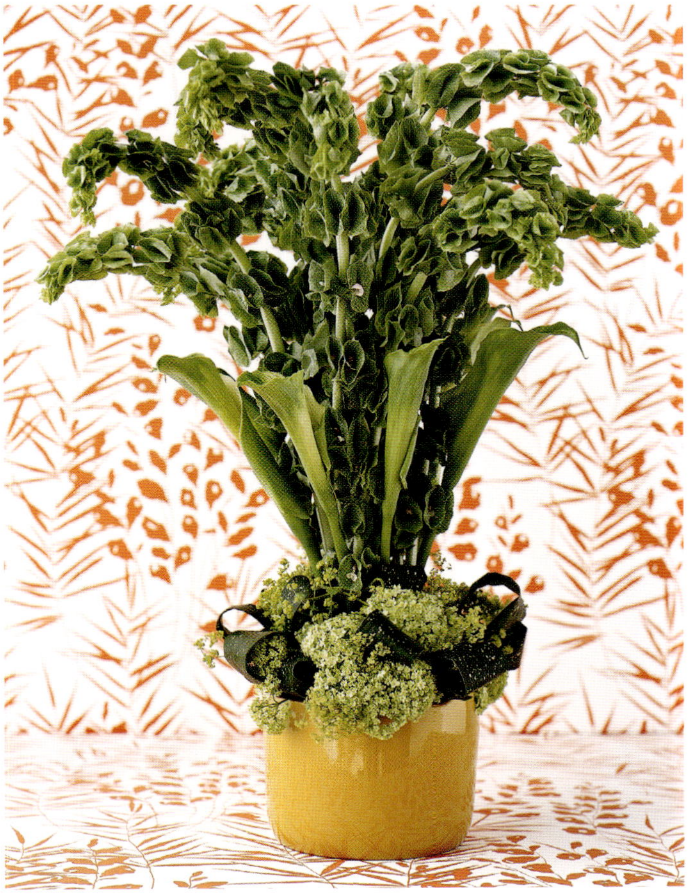

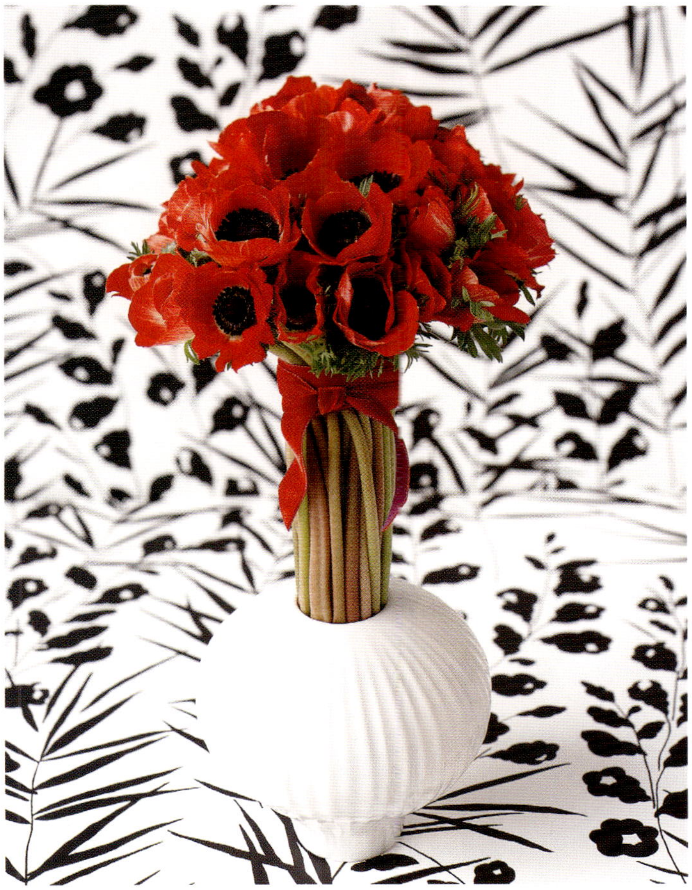

left: Once again, my go-to color: green. I was inspired by new foliage on the trees that emerge this time of year. I created a topiary-ish look starting first with a cluster of belles of Ireland surrounded by 'Green Desire' calla lilies, finished off with green snowball viburnum, lady's-mantle, and loops of tropical leaves. *right*: The cluster of black-eyed red anemones with their wide faces makes a bold impact standing tall inside the short white vase. Many times keeping it simple makes the strongest statement.

HERE ARE SOME OF MY EXAMPLES OF SHOWING OFF FORCED BULBS WITHOUT ALWAYS HIDING THEIR ROOTS:

top left

For this antique wooden case, I imagined a gurgling stream with clusters of bulbs popping up along the shore. Twisted kiwi branches, sunny daffodils, lilies of the valley, and ranunculus surround a rambling row of pink hyacinths and the stream of baby's tears down the center of the box.

top right

As I mentioned before, keeping it simple makes a huge impact. I've forced muscari bulbs, removed them from their pot, washed the bulbs and roots, and "planted" them into a bed of sea glass within a clear glass vase.

bottom left

I bought pots of forced hyacinth bulbs and washed their roots—a time consuming but rewarding job—and put them in a clear, low rectangular vase (the stems are strong enough to stand on their own). I cut the newest stalks and added them and then let a few blossoms float, representing the hyacinth in almost all its stages of growth.

bottom right

I see this arrangement as an updated daffodil garden with a Japanese influence. Simply bound bamboo create an arbor to support the weak daffodil stems as they grow taller. Notice the Martha Study vase and tufts of wheat grass forming tassels on top of the bamboo supports.

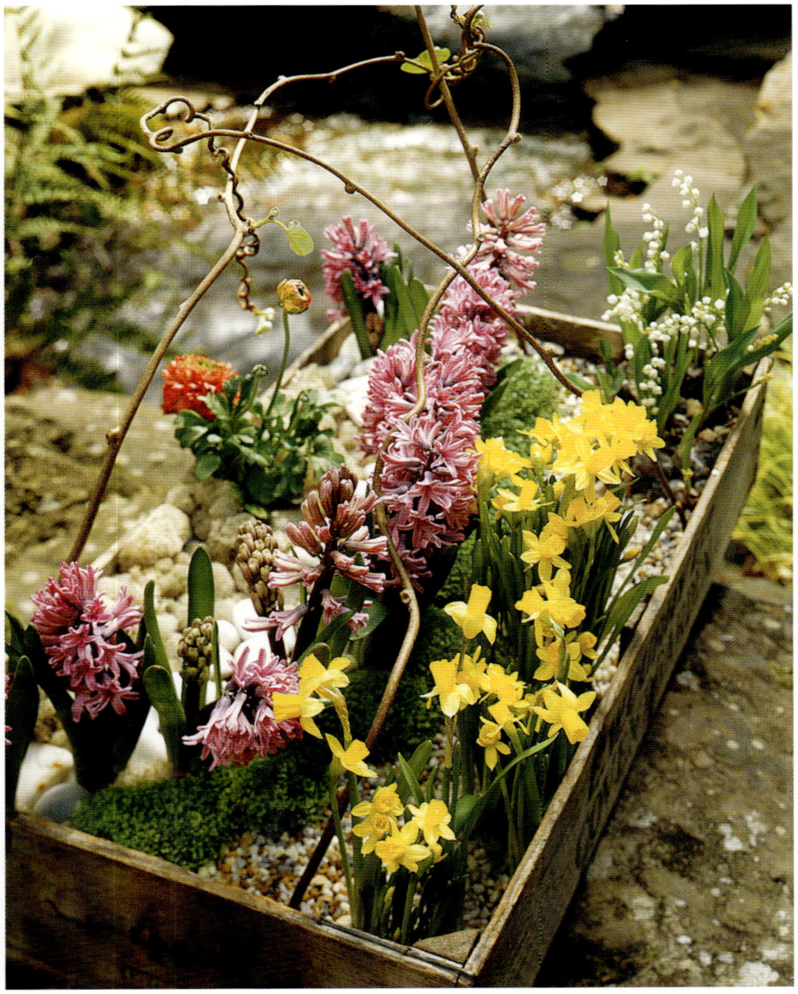
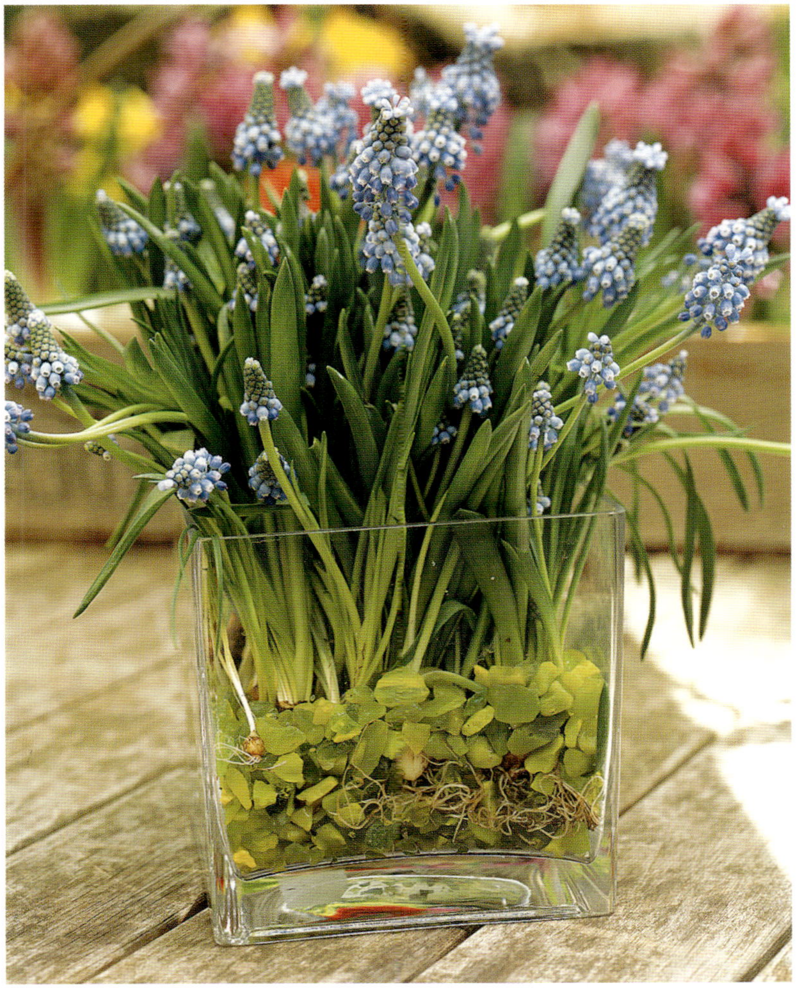
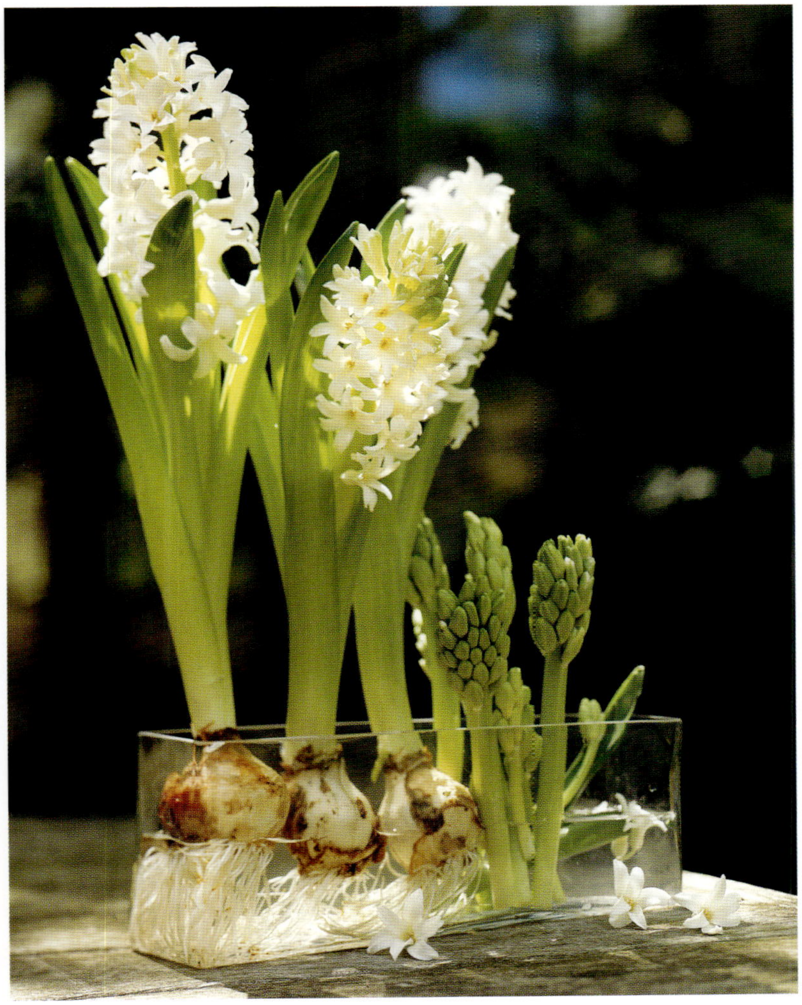
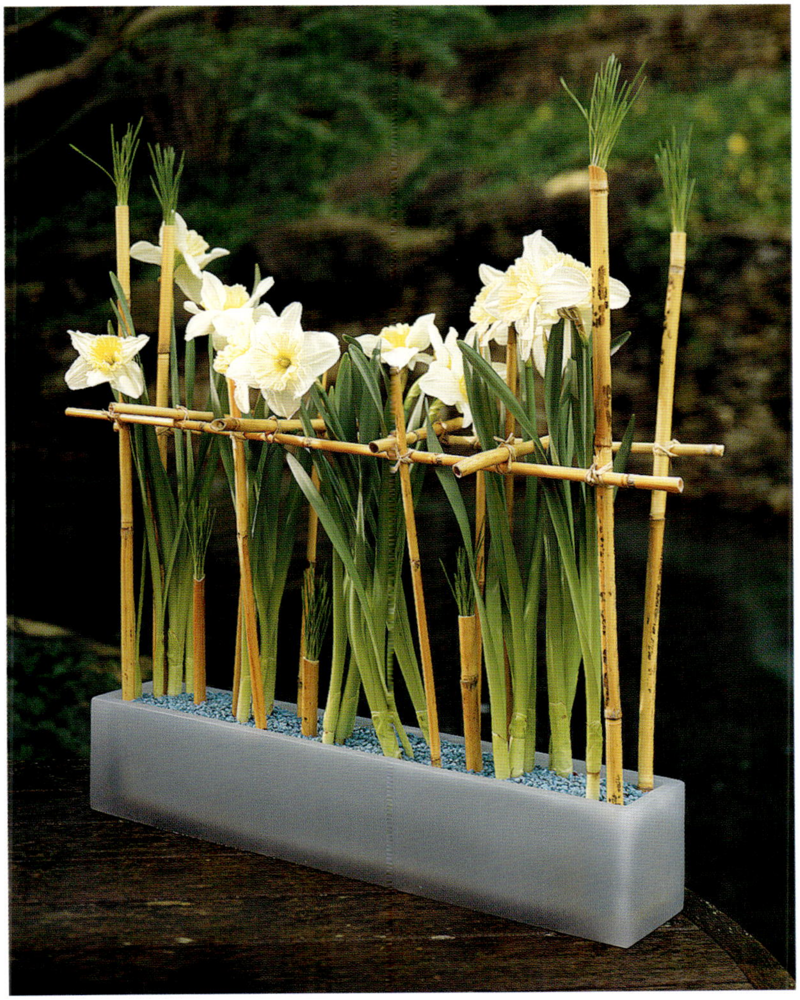

summer

My summer begins when really great tomatoes start being available. I know, tomatoes are not flowers, but I just don't believe summer is here until I have my first perfect tomato. Flower-wise, I'd say French blue hydrangeas and roses along with gardenias and magnolia blossoms are the first real sign the seasons are changing. Followed by all the summer favorites: Queen Anne's Lace, Hostas, and Zinnias being the Queen Bee for me. Their colors are so beautiful, and their simplicity is a comforting memory from my childhood.

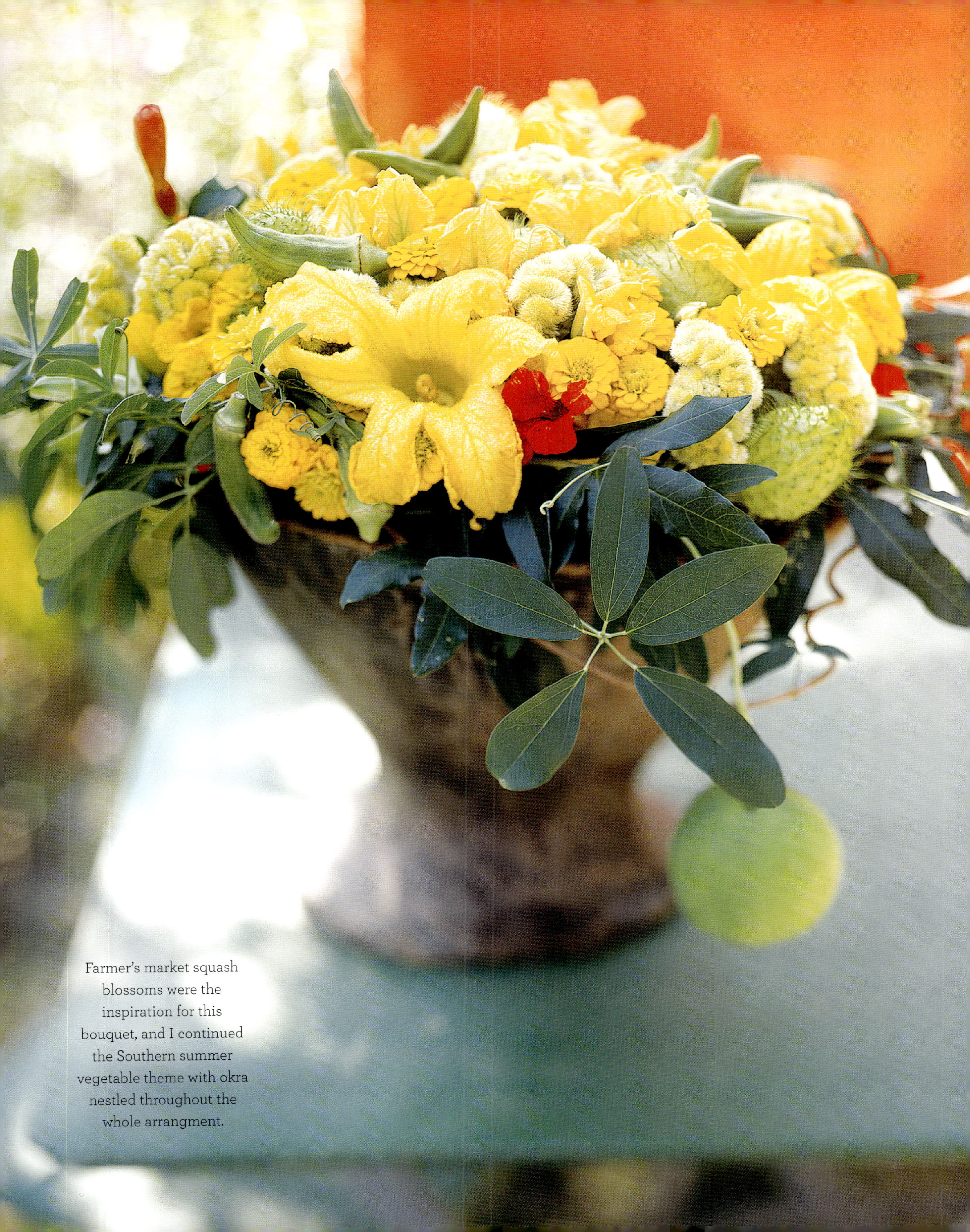

Farmer's market squash blossoms were the inspiration for this bouquet, and I continued the Southern summer vegetable theme with okra nestled throughout the whole arrangment.

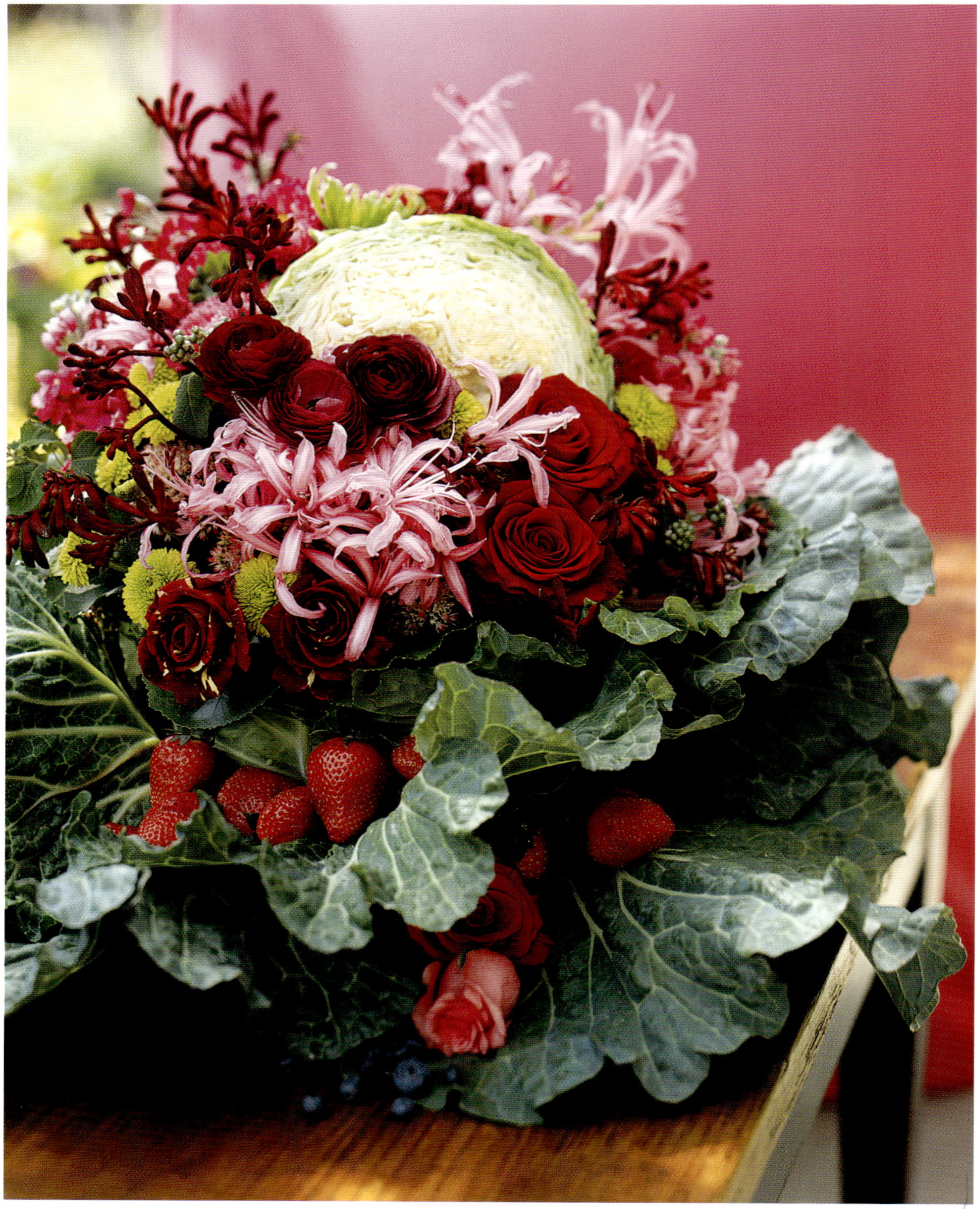

above: What bigger, better blossom than a cabbage with its robust leaves and its multi-colored center? On its own, it can work as a centerpiece, but with the addition of tiers of flowers, it becomes art. An arrangement like this is especially great on an entrance hall credenza with a wall behind it. *right*: I see this arrangement as a full-blown testimony to flower varieties that are available in the red hot summer months. With fruit—figs, blueberries, and green apples—mingling with a profusion of dahlias, zinnias, and angelwing begonia, the effect is lush and bold, dramatic and sultry.

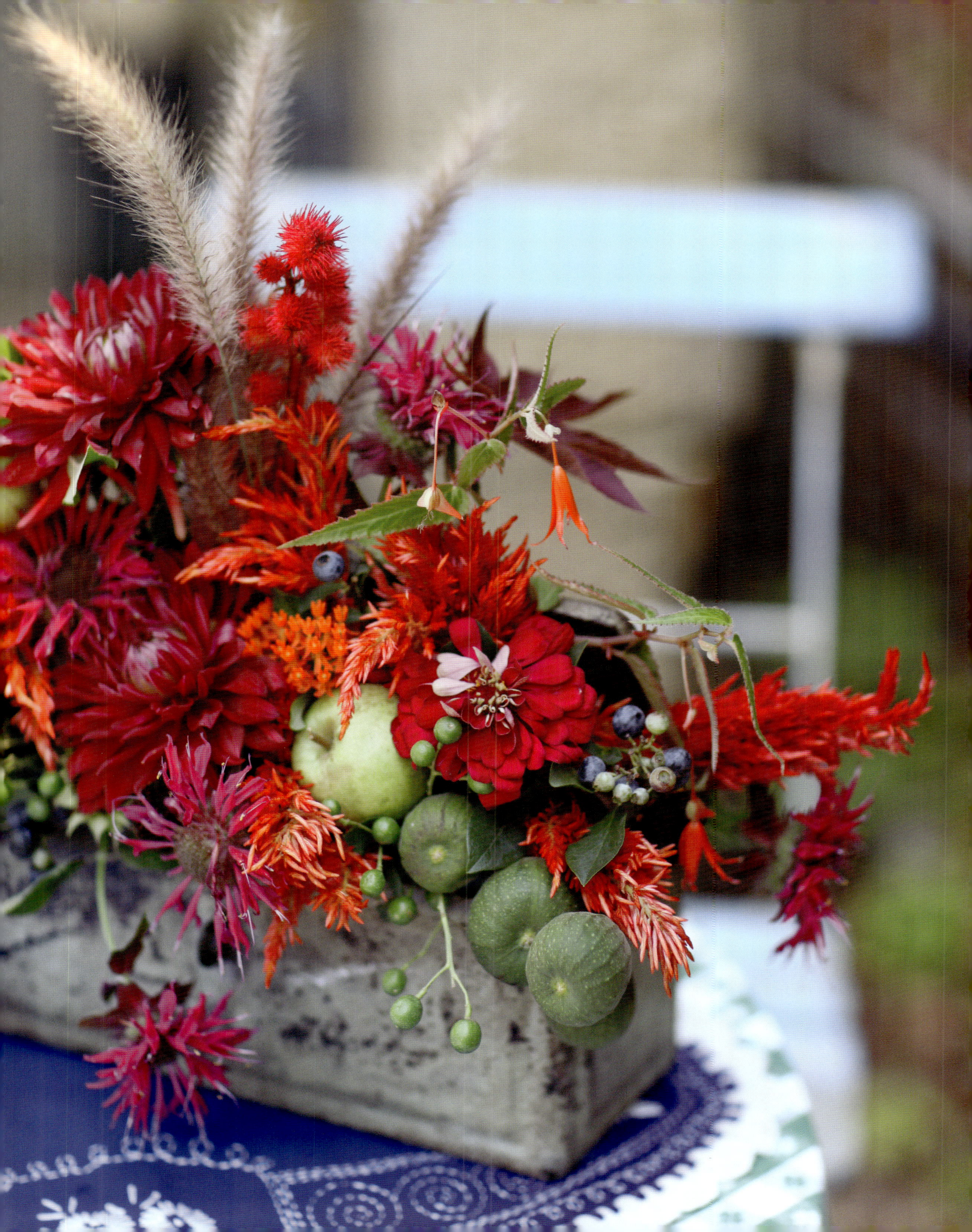

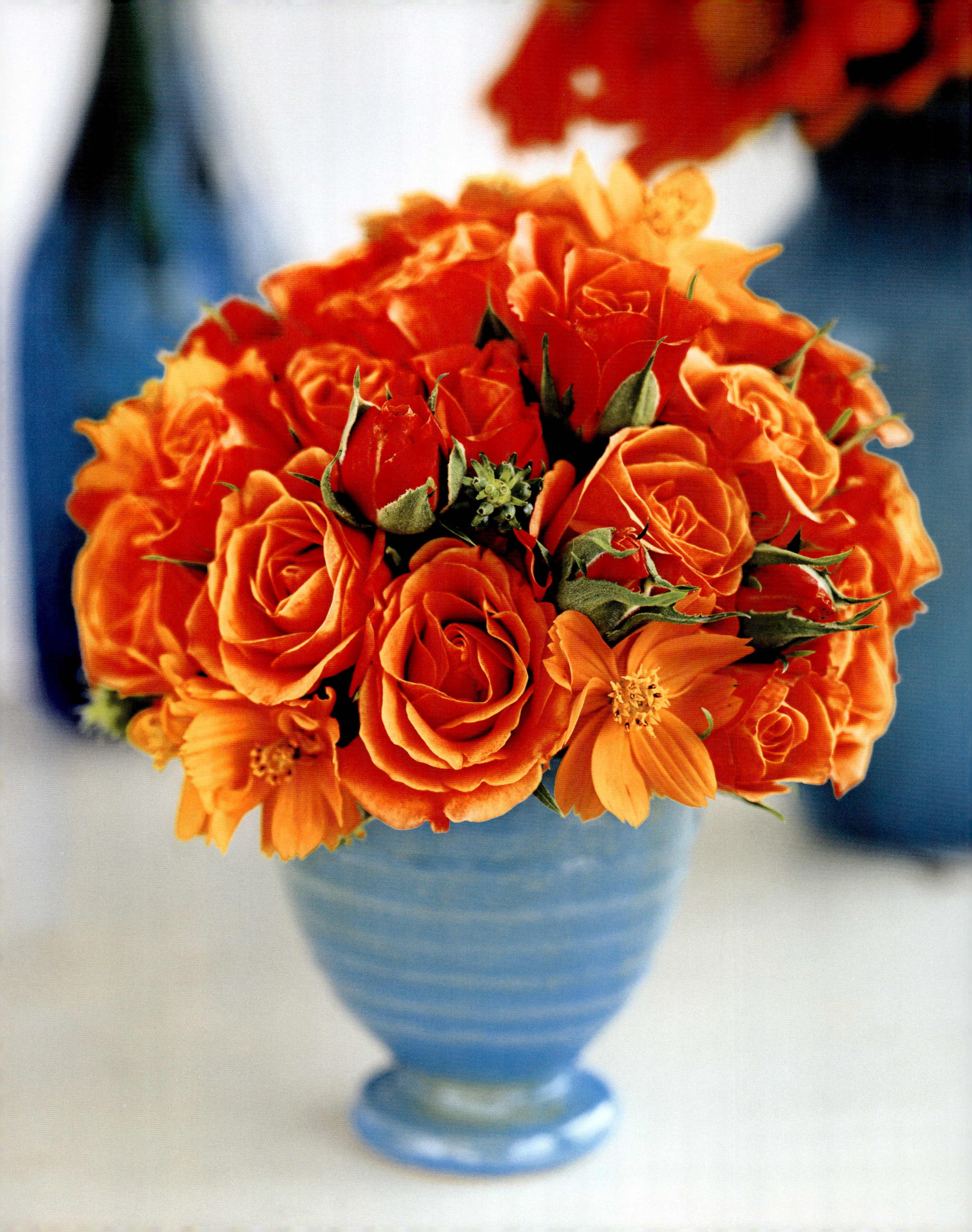

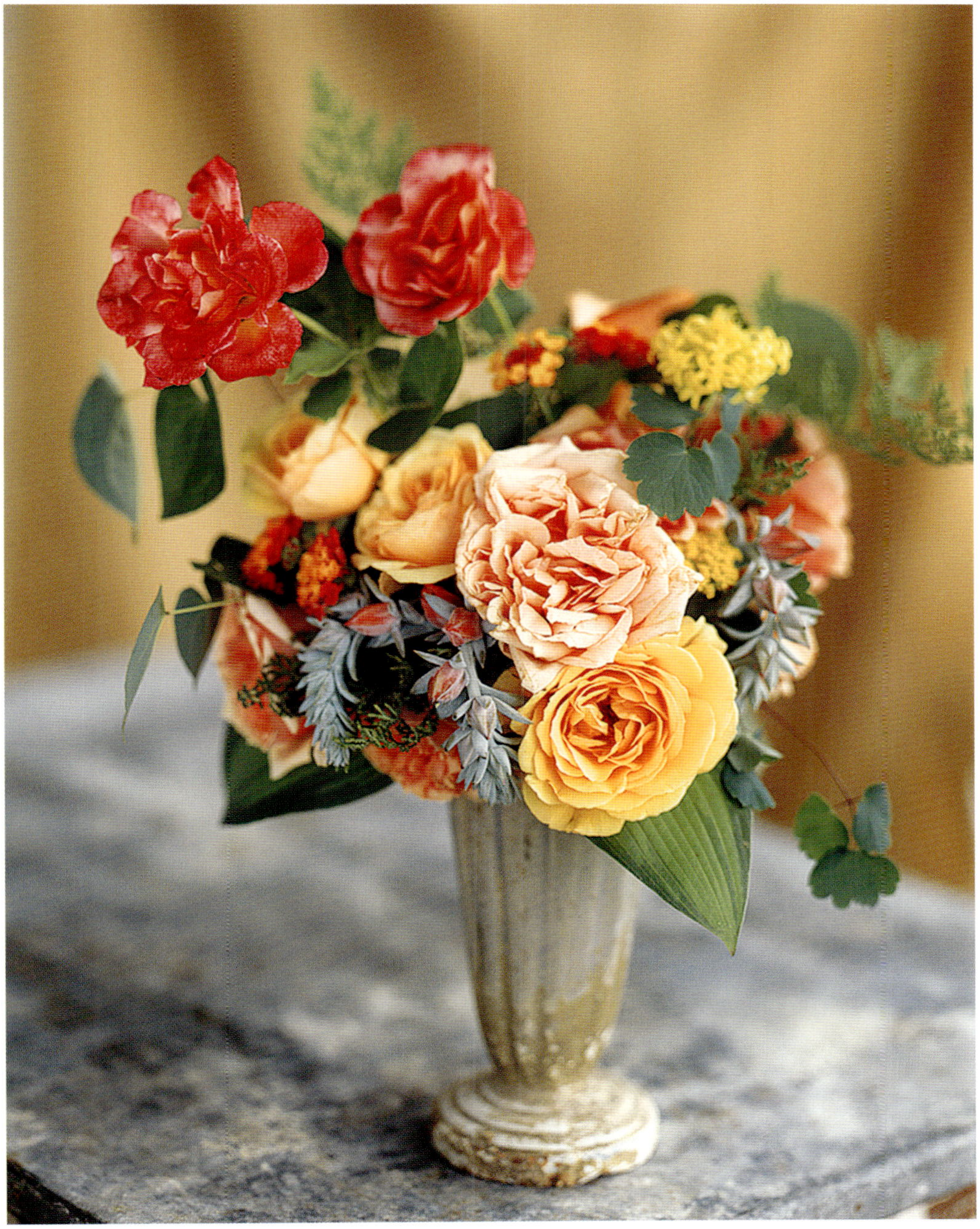

above: This vessel is actually an antique Hungarian funeral vase that I found on a shopping expedition. Little by little—that's how I started arranging this, pulling from what I could get my hands on in the garden. *opposite*: Instead of putting a plant into this tiny turquoise pot, I used it as a vase and hand-tied these garden flowers, creating a bouquet to go inside. Unlike many arrangements, I left the greenery around the roses in tact and even added a little to give the arrangement a more fresh-from-the-garden feel.

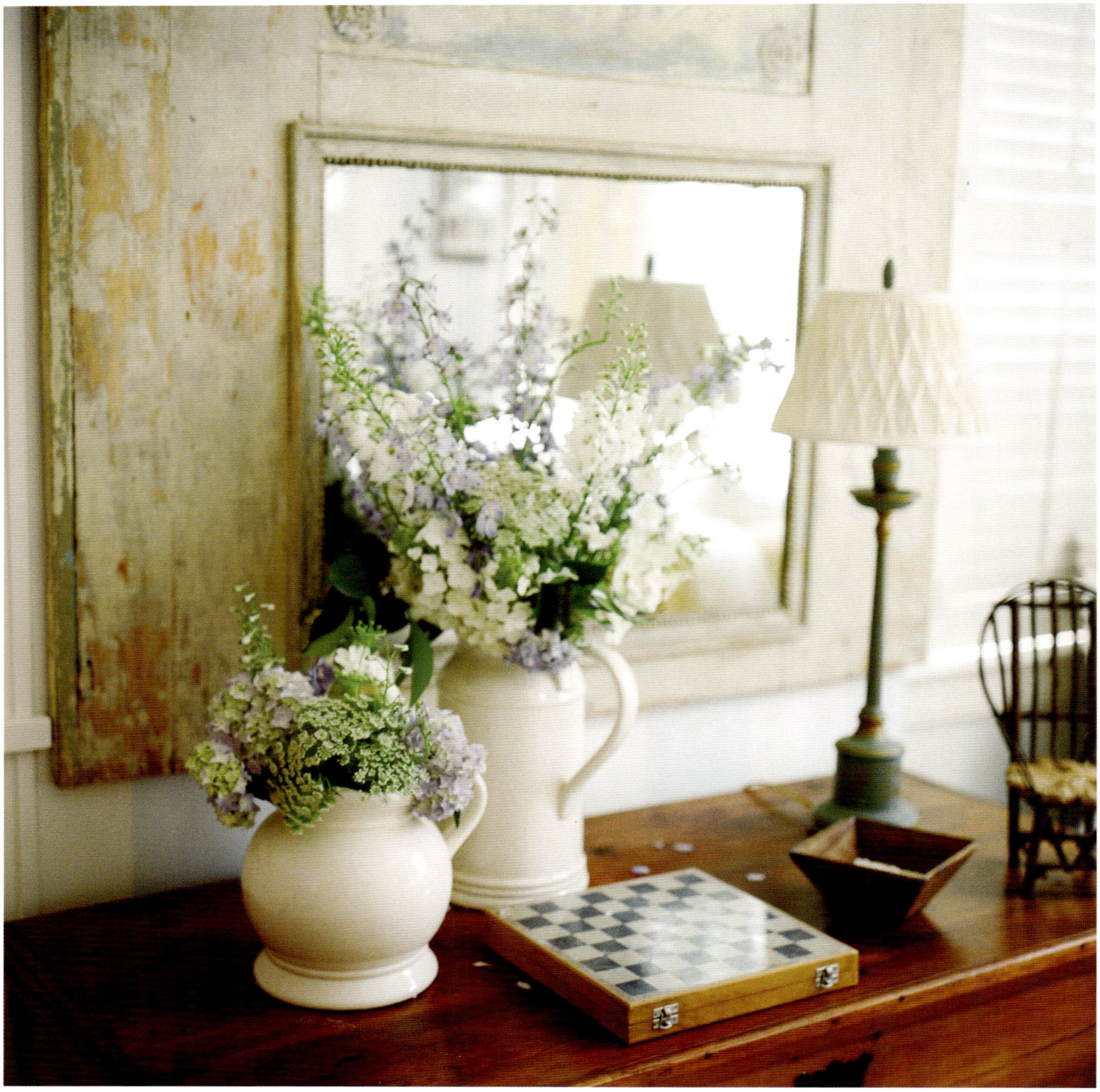

WHENEVER I DO A PARTY OR AN EVENT, I ALWAYS CHECK OUT THE LOCATION FIRST, TO GET A FEEL FOR THE SPACE AND ITS POTENTIAL!

My best loved look when I arrange flowers is for them to appear as if they are actually growing in the garden. Here I filled two white ironstone pitchers (I love white ironstone's humble simplicity) with French hydrangeas, hybrid delphiums, and snowflake hydrangeas. It's a perfect summer arrangement: fresh and loose, with cool tones of white, blue, and lavender.

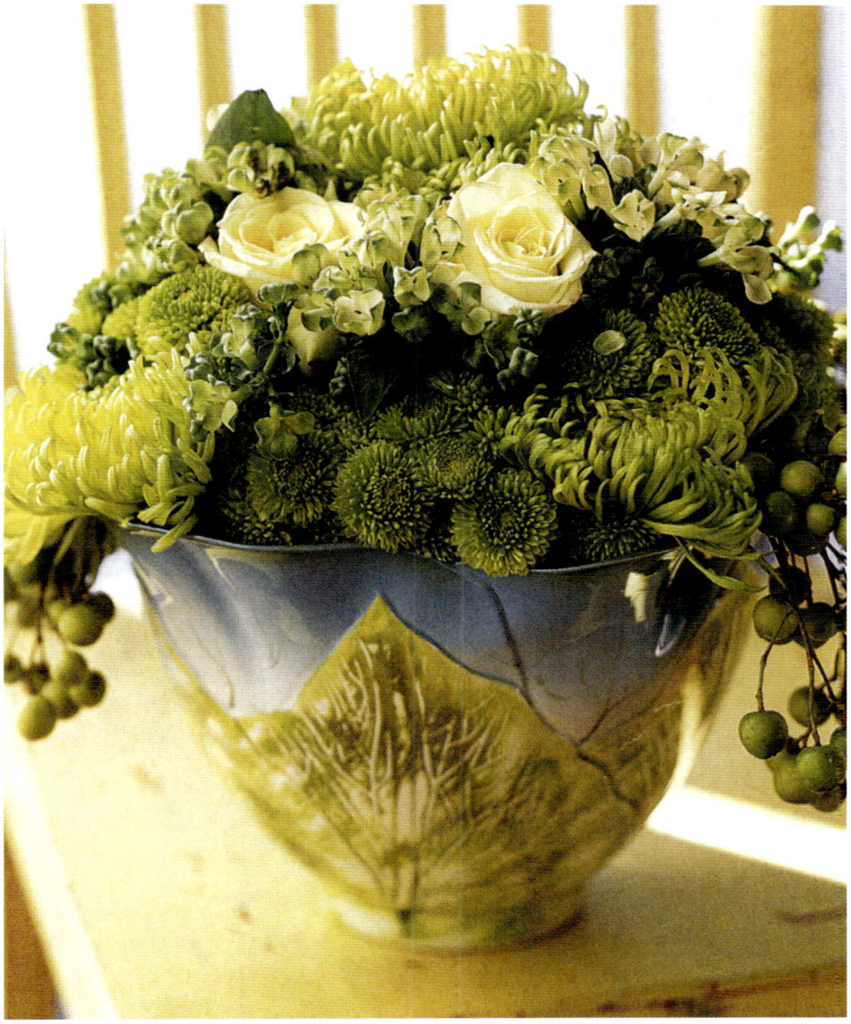

The container dictated this arrangement because of its pretty blue and green. I remember my Mama telling me, "No mums, no baby's breath, no leather leaf ferns." She pretty much put a nail in the coffin for me using those flowers. But Kermit mums are different. And so is its Fuji mum cousin—the Shamrock.

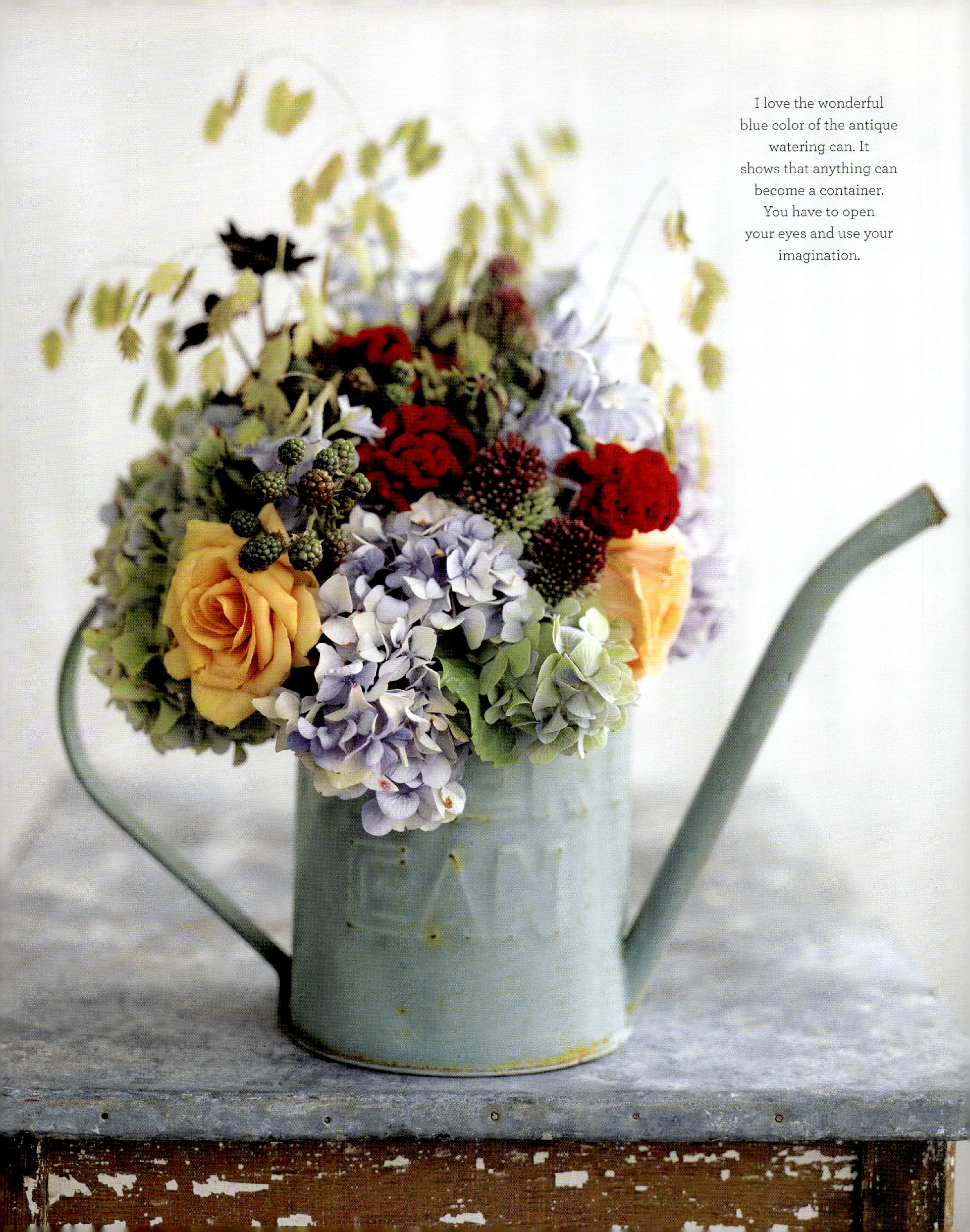

I love the wonderful blue color of the antique watering can. It shows that anything can become a container. You have to open your eyes and use your imagination.

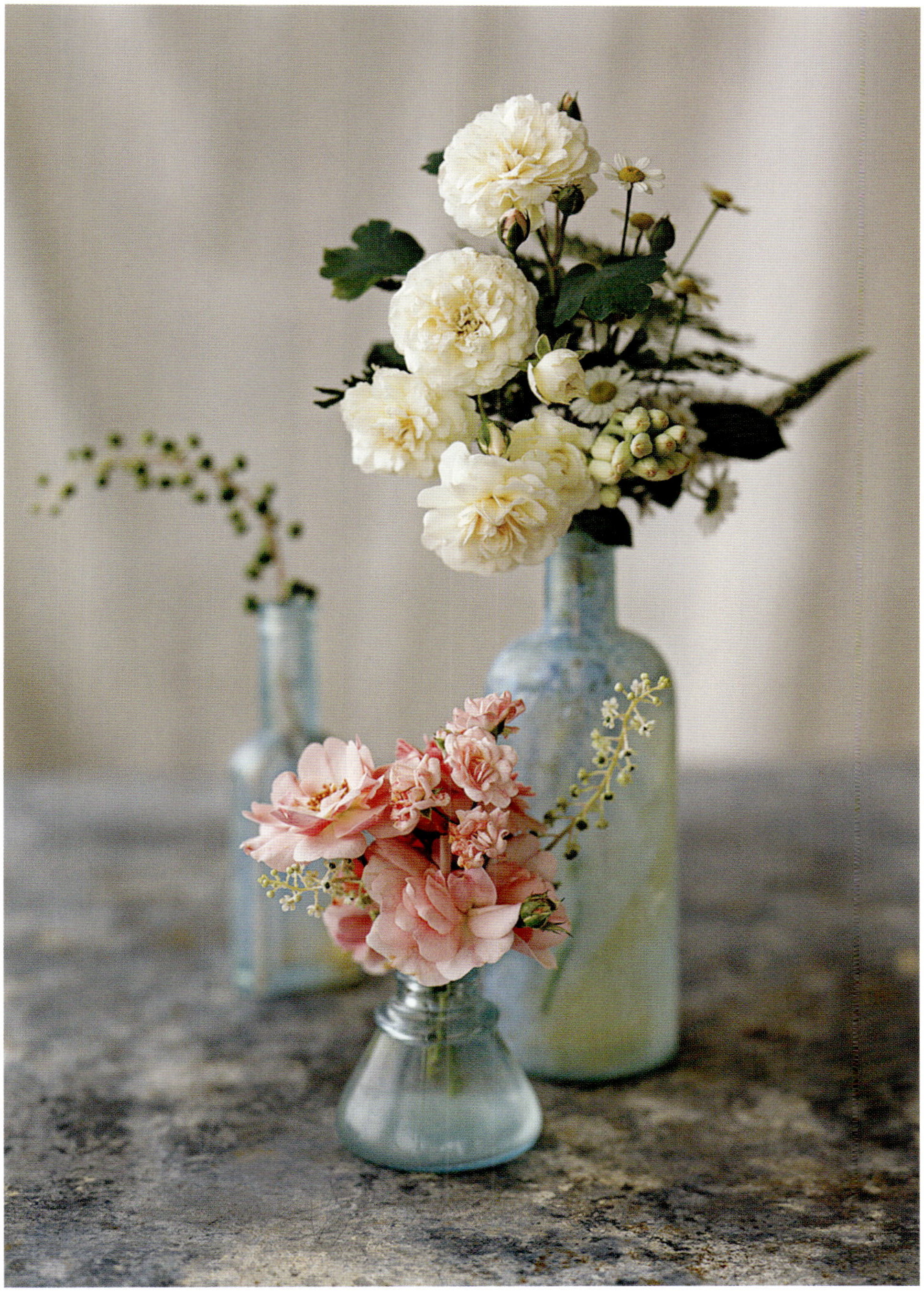

ONE THING TO REMEMBER WHEN YOU'RE DOING AN ARRANGEMENT: KEEP TURNING THE CONTAINER SO THAT IT'S PRETTY FROM ALL SIDES.

Bottles that have been in fires take on an iridescent pink tone that makes complementary shade blossoms even more beautiful. These glass vases, with their different shapes, are as much a part of the arrangement as the flowers themselves.

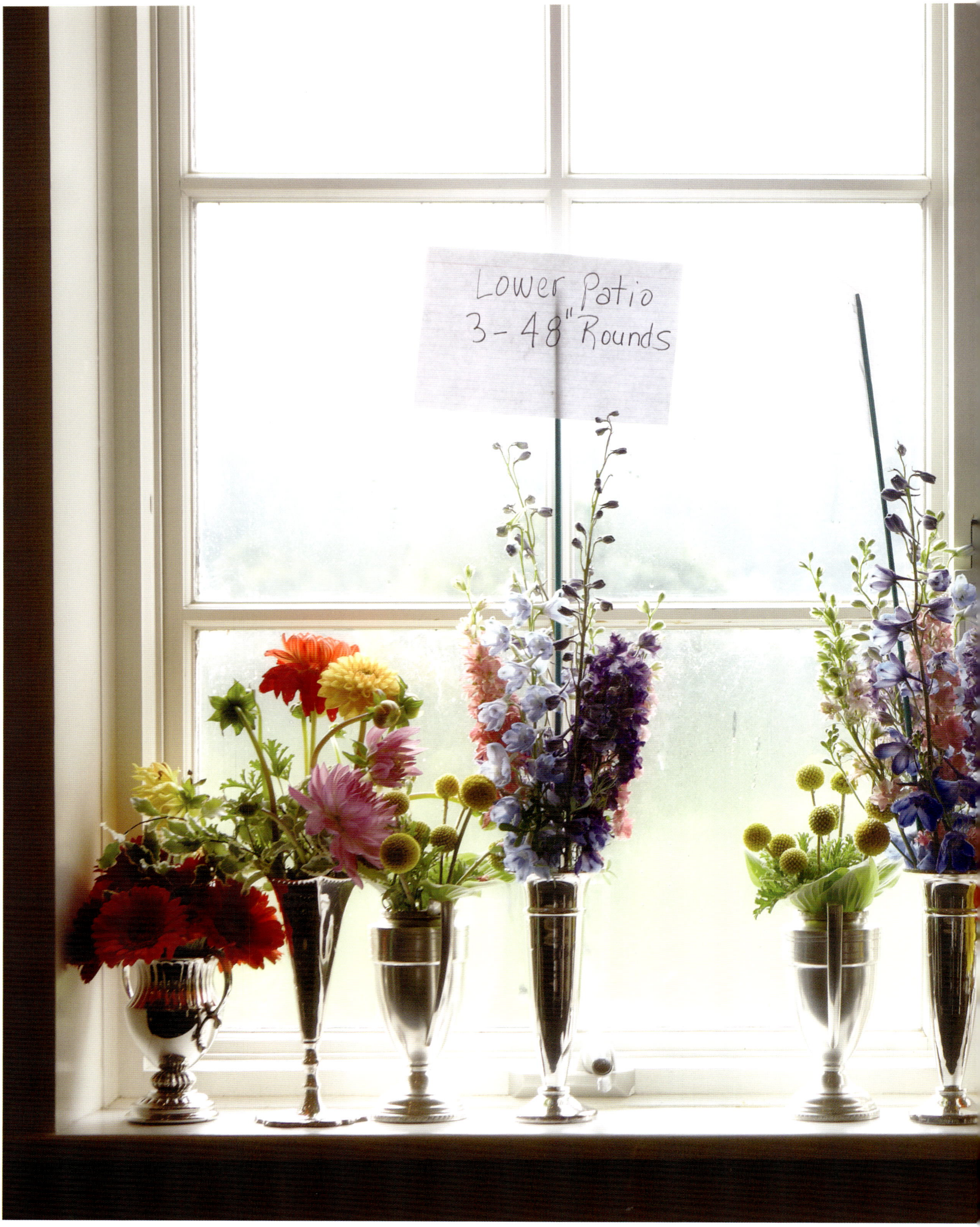
Lower Patio
3-48" Rounds

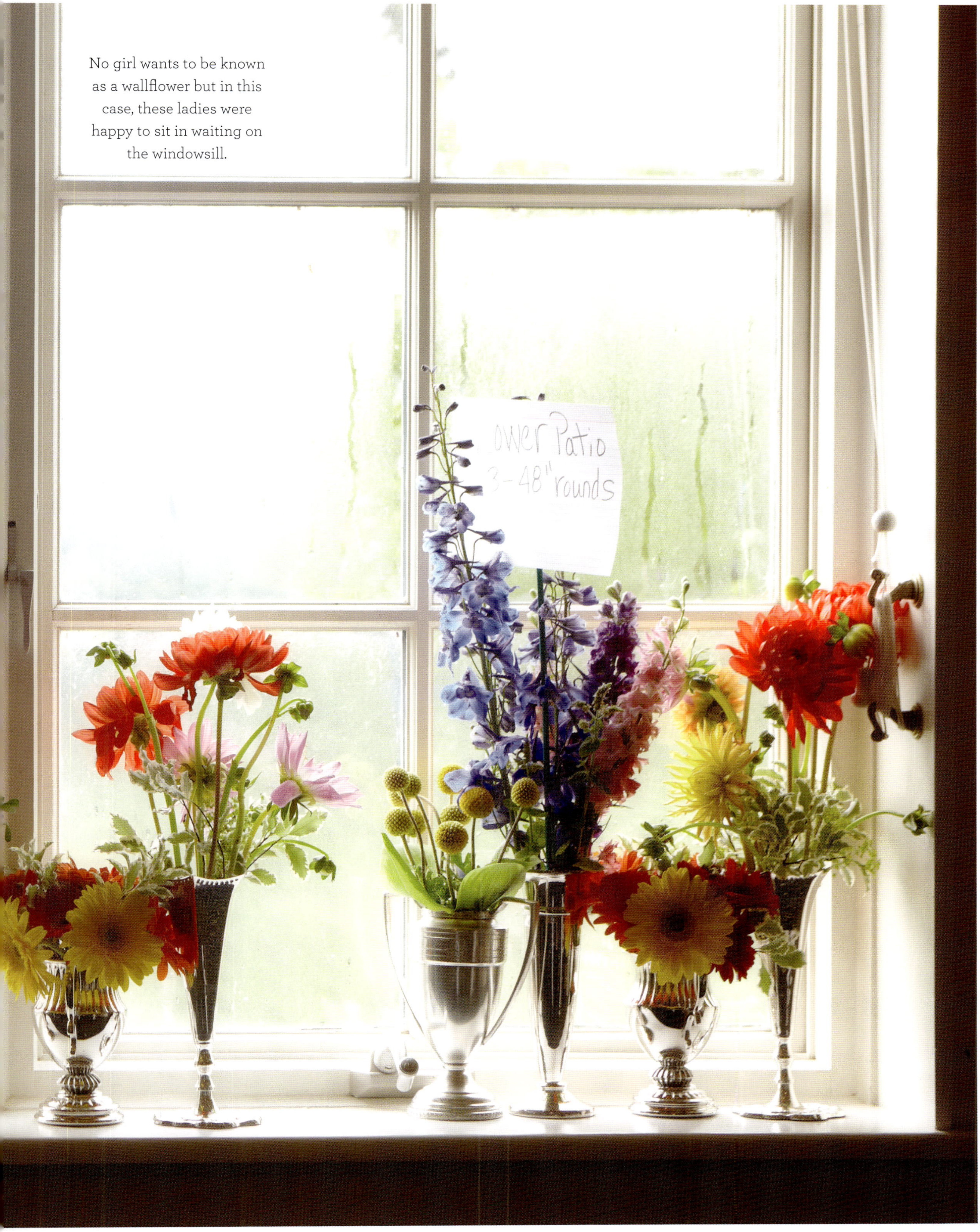

No girl wants to be known as a wallflower but in this case, these ladies were happy to sit in waiting on the windowsill.

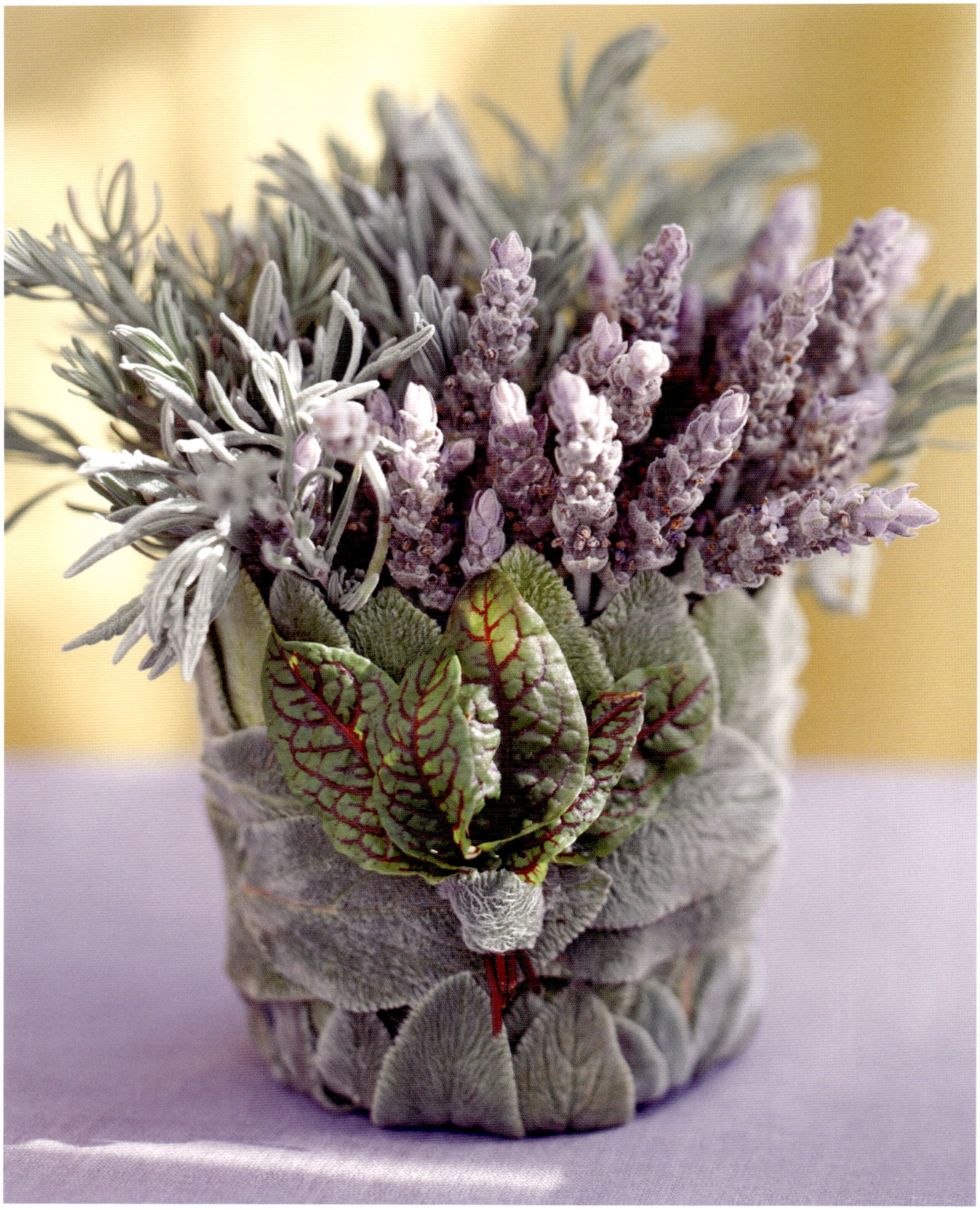

above: To create this container, I covered it with double-sided carpet tape and layered lamb's ear to cover the base. I tried hot glue first, but that turned the leaves brown. I filled the container with lavender blossoms and its silver foliage. Then I added the little spray of sorrel leaves on the front. *right*: I purchased this rustic pot at a grocery store in Highlands, North Carolina, a reminder that you can find treasures anywhere. I was inspired by the colors of the porcelain vine (which trails out of the pot), a treasured gift from my daughter that thrives in my garden.

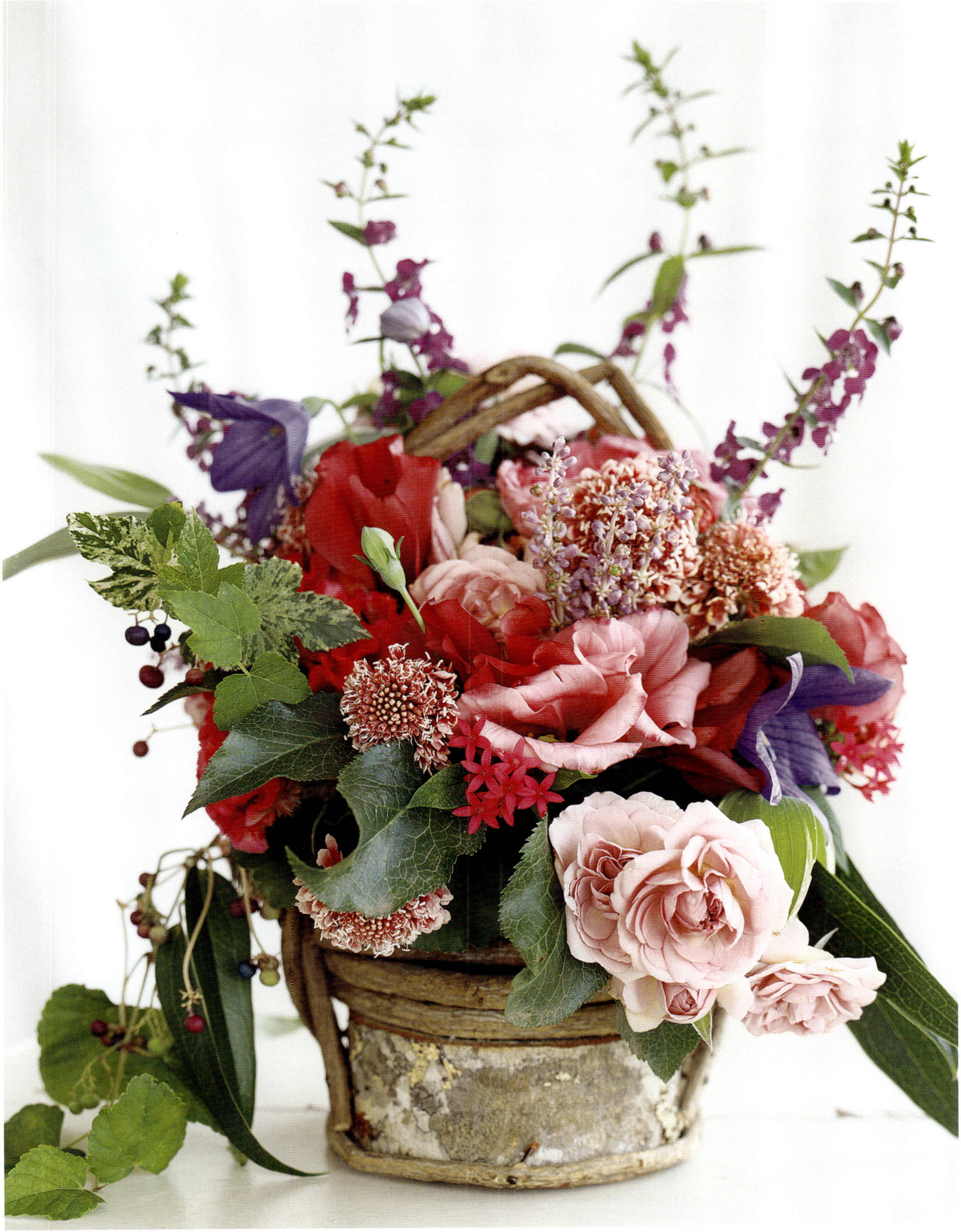

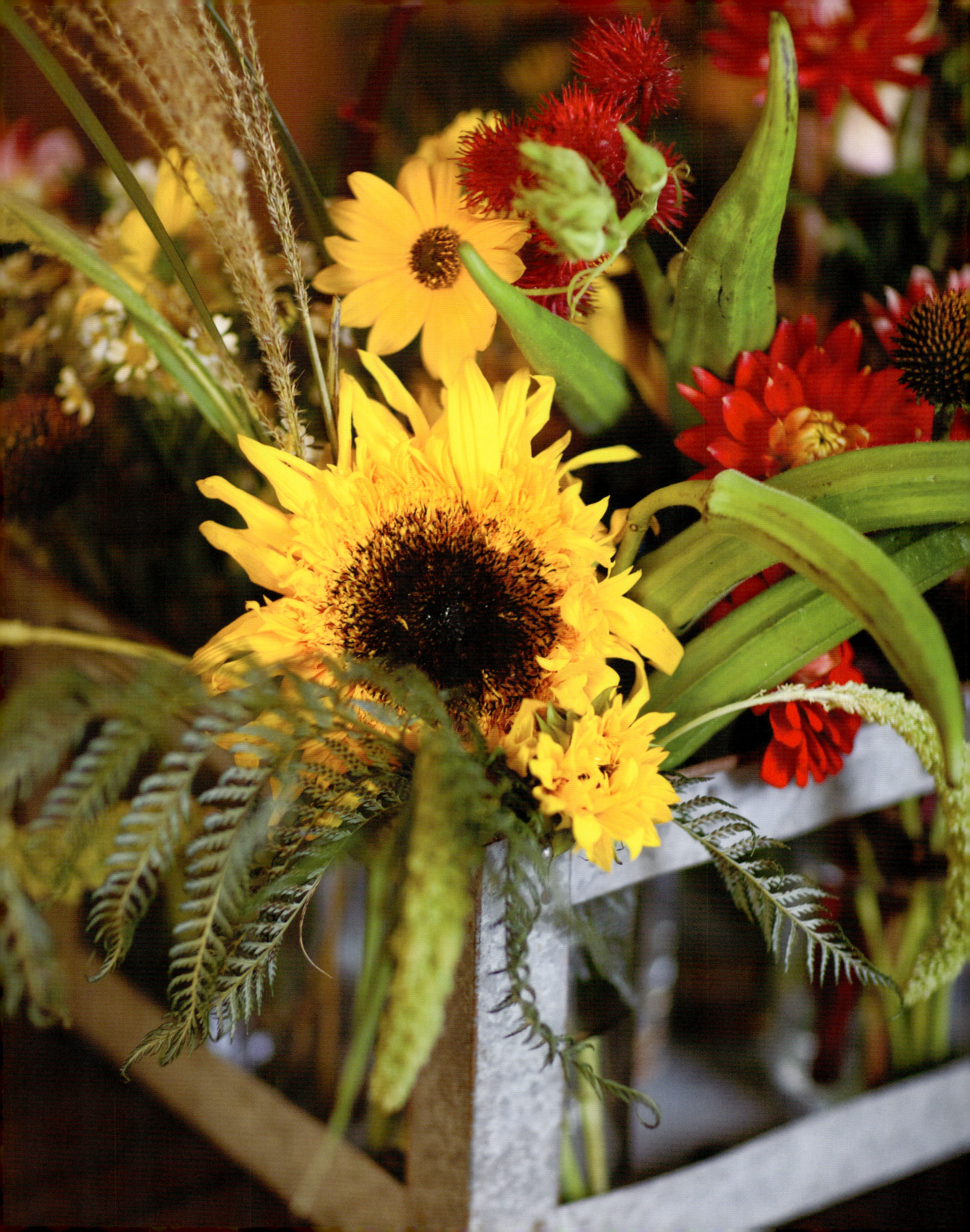

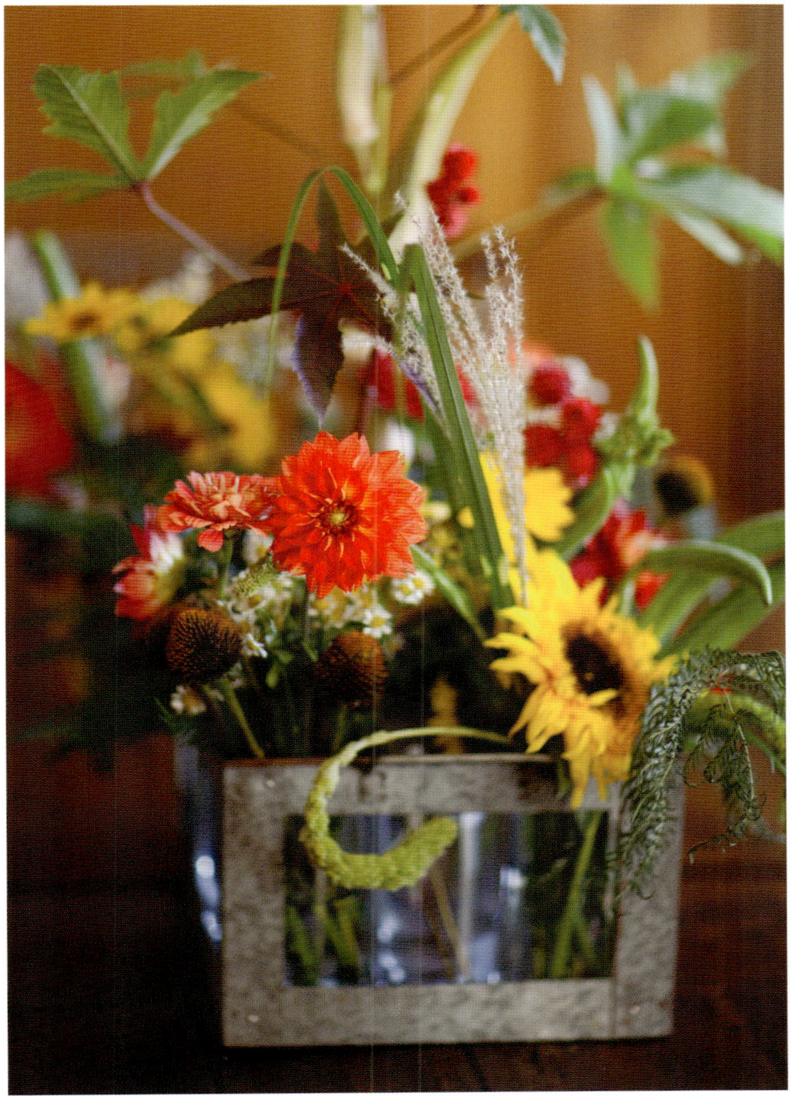

above and opposite: There is nothing like a crate of mason jars overflowing with fresh gathered garden flowers and the unexpected addition of okra on its branch to say summer. I clustered four mason jars in a rustic carrier and loaded them up with vegetables and flower garden blossoms and greenery. The basket can be transported and work as a single large arrangement or separated with individual bouquets in the jars.

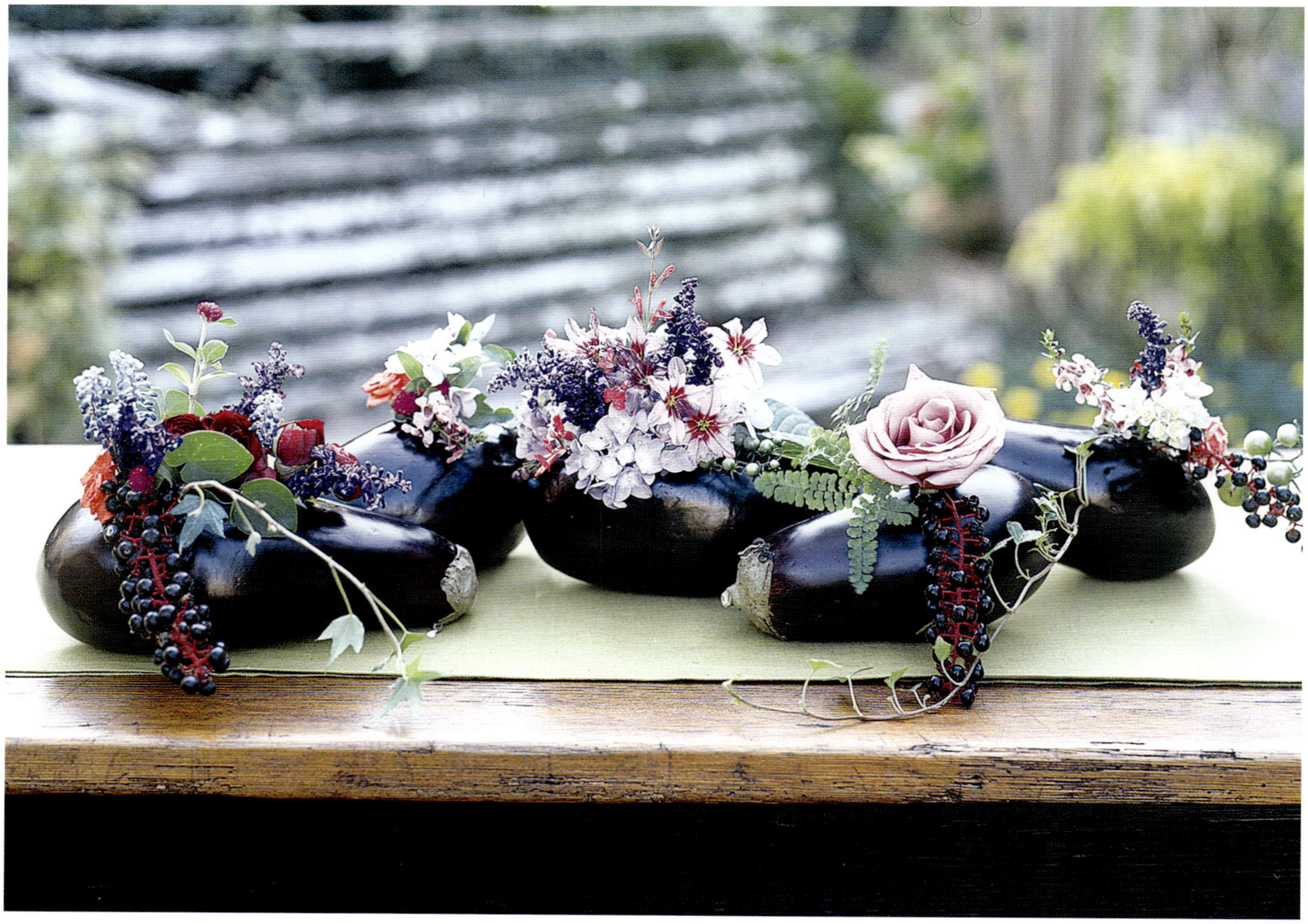

VEGETABLES HAVE MANY BENEFITS! THEY CAN EVEN SERVE AS A TEMPORARY WATER SOURCE FOR YOUR FLOWERS.

I scooped out a plug from the eggplants and wedged a piece of wet oasis into the hole. Then I tucked in a combination of things from my garden—muscari, hydrangeas, maidenhair fern. But my favorite touch is the baby green cherry tomatoes.

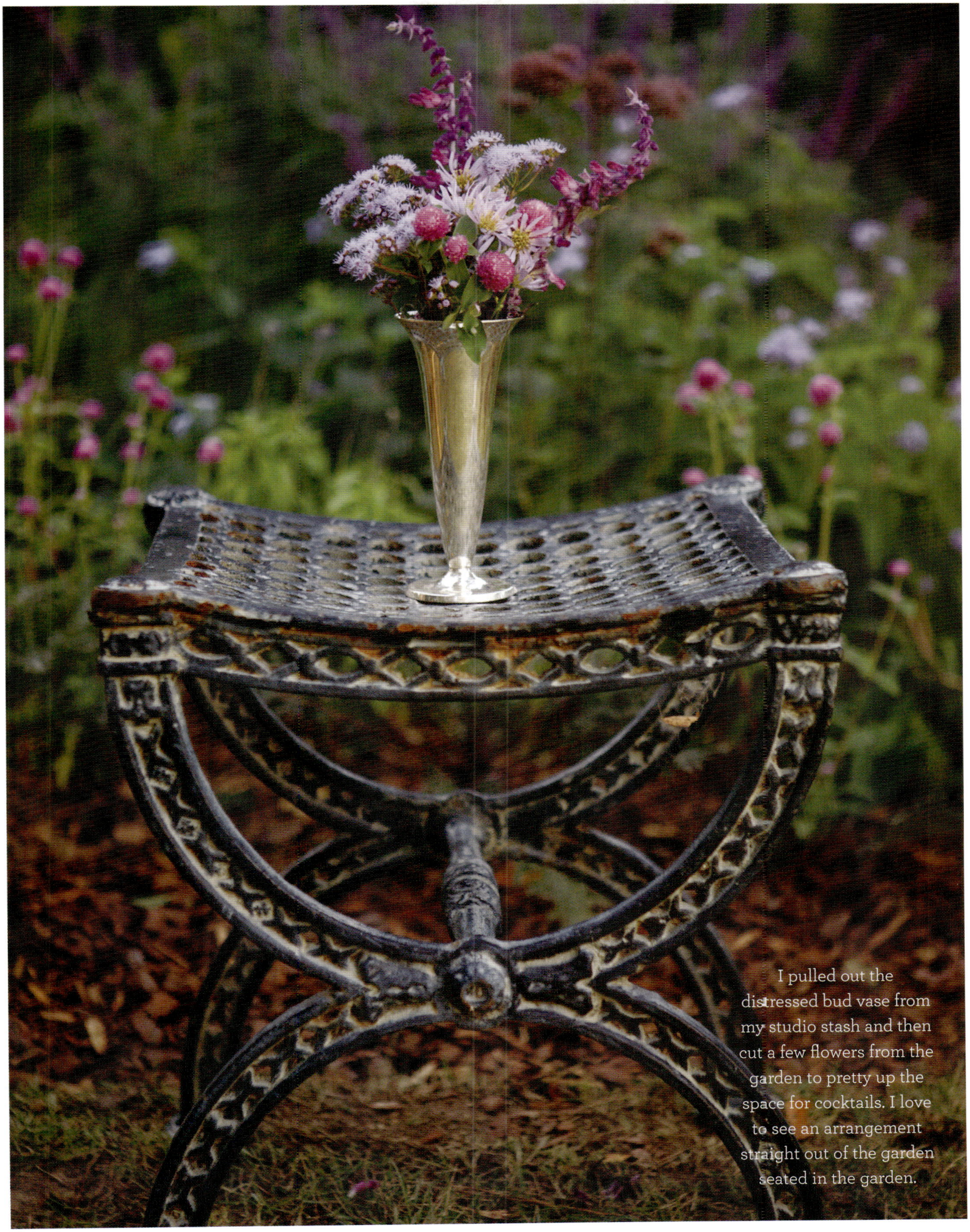

I pulled out the distressed bud vase from my studio stash and then cut a few flowers from the garden to pretty up the space for cocktails. I love to see an arrangement straight out of the garden seated in the garden.

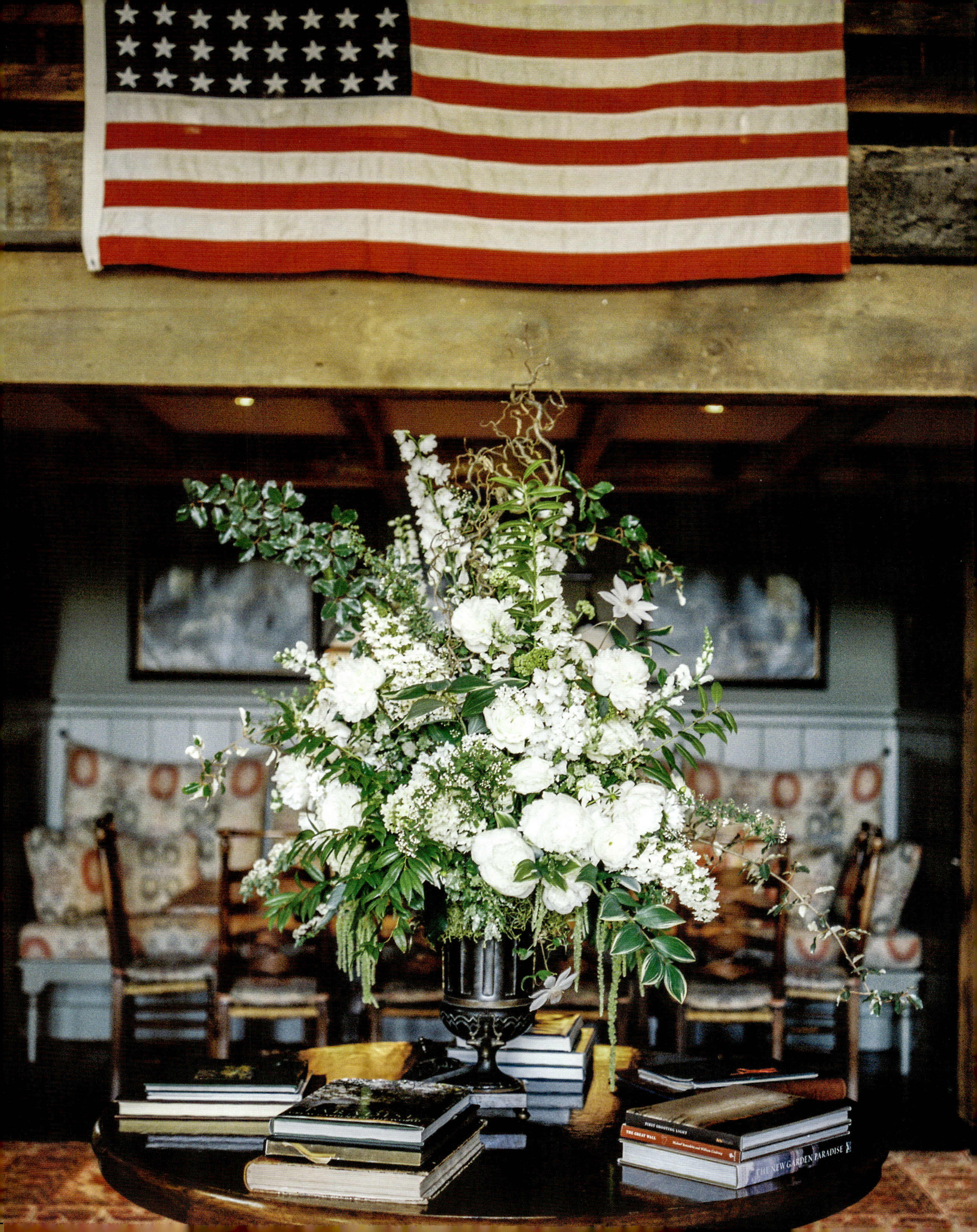
FIRST SHOOTING LIGHT
THE GREAT WALL
THE NEW GARDEN PARADISE

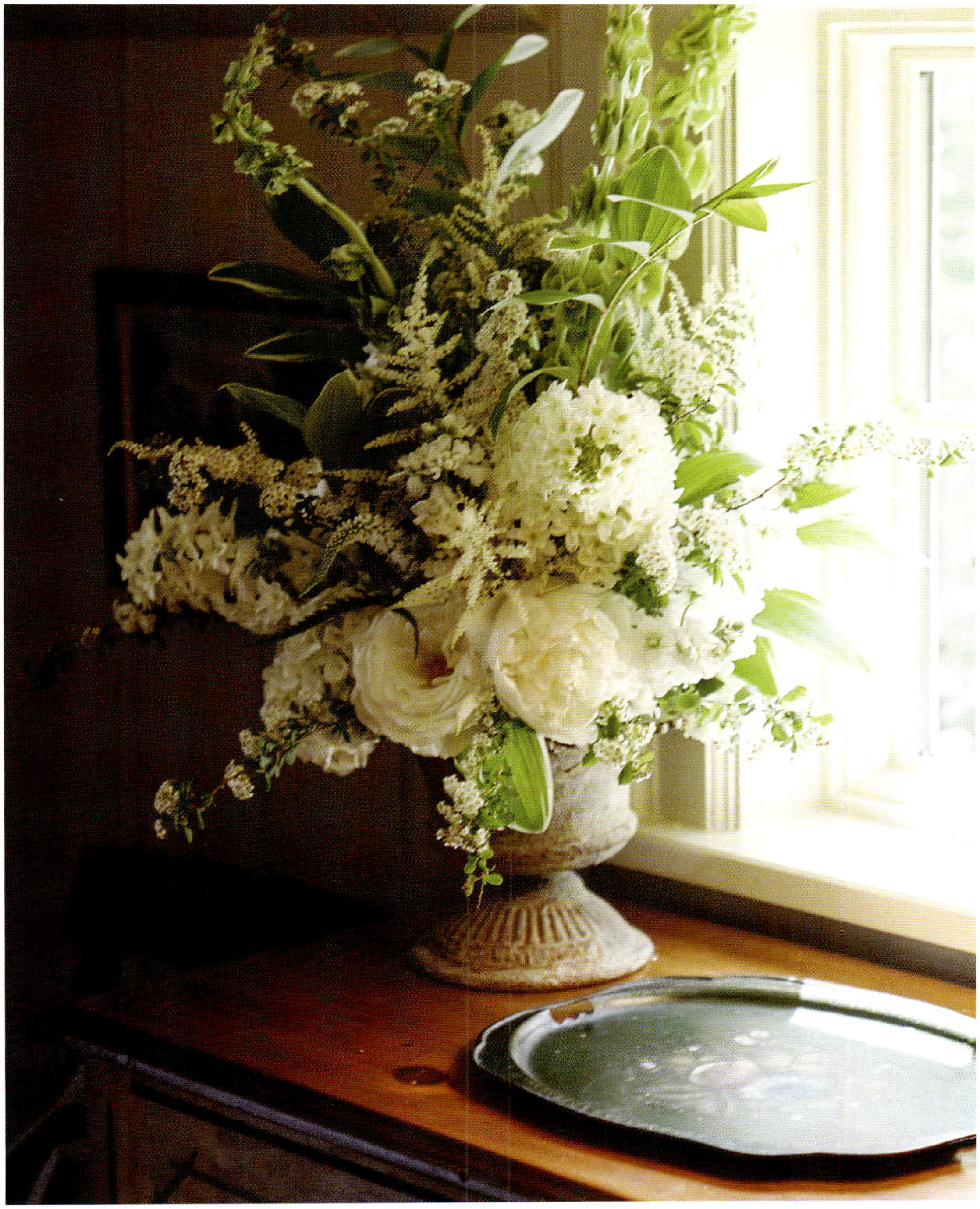

above: Highlands, North Carolina, is a treasure trove of summer gardens with endless sources of flowers and greenery that makes putting arrangements on every tabletop easy and fun. *opposite*: I love an entry hall center table arrangement that greets guests and comes together from what is growing in the garden. Branches and vines, hydrangeas and roses celebrate summer and the relaxed spirit of the North Carolina mountain getaway.

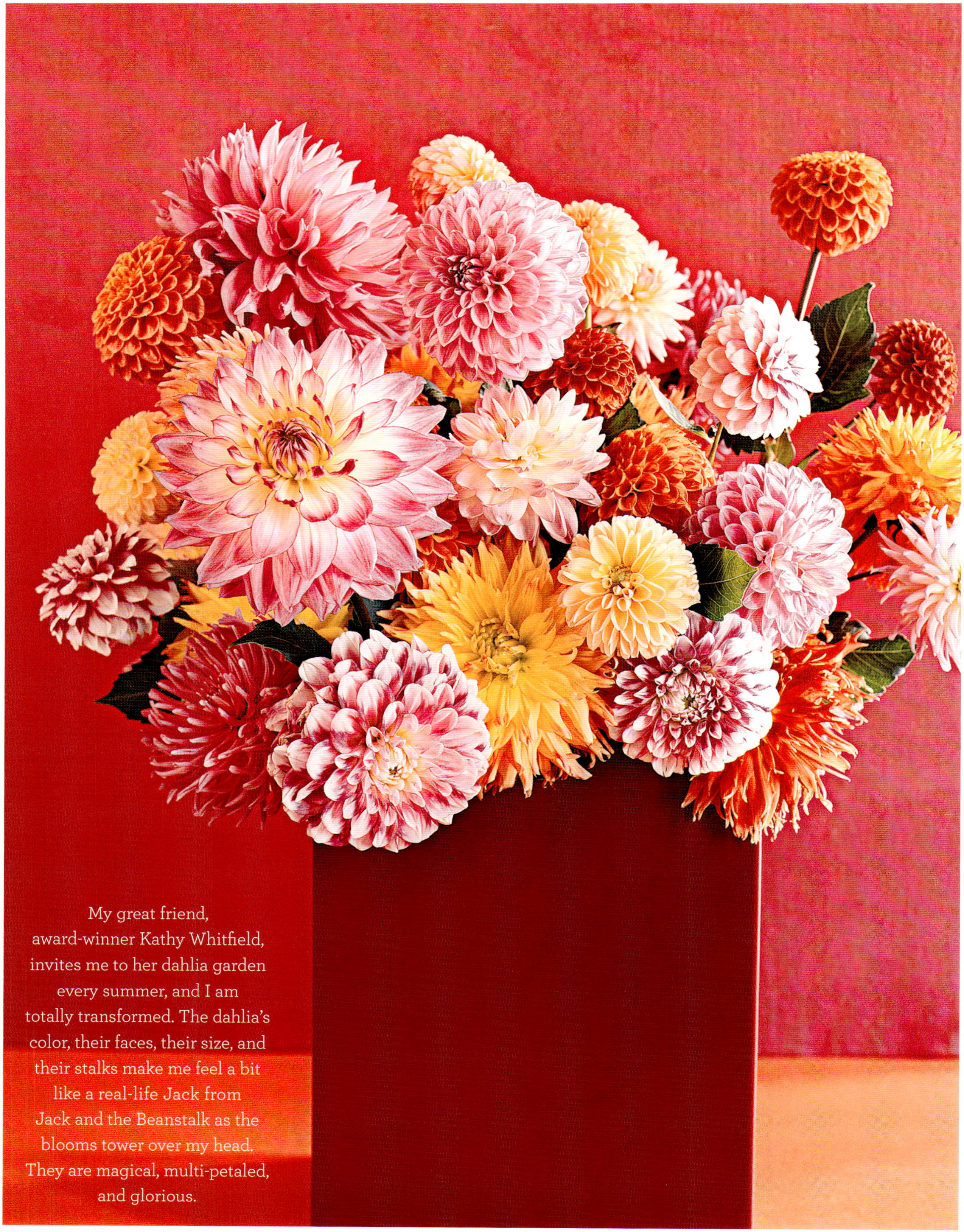

My great friend, award-winner Kathy Whitfield, invites me to her dahlia garden every summer, and I am totally transformed. The dahlia's color, their faces, their size, and their stalks make me feel a bit like a real-life Jack from Jack and the Beanstalk as the blooms tower over my head. They are magical, multi-petaled, and glorious.

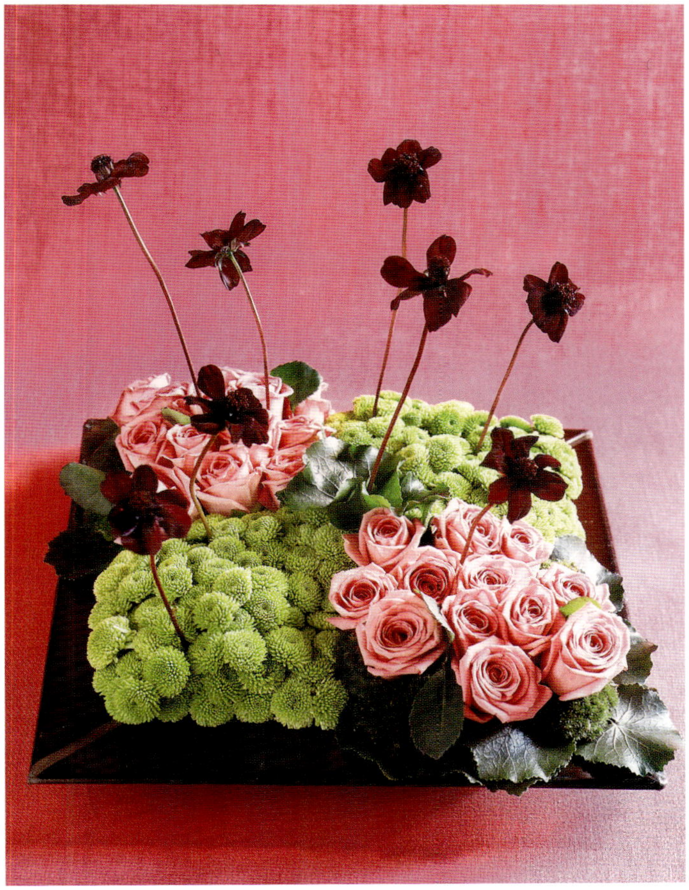

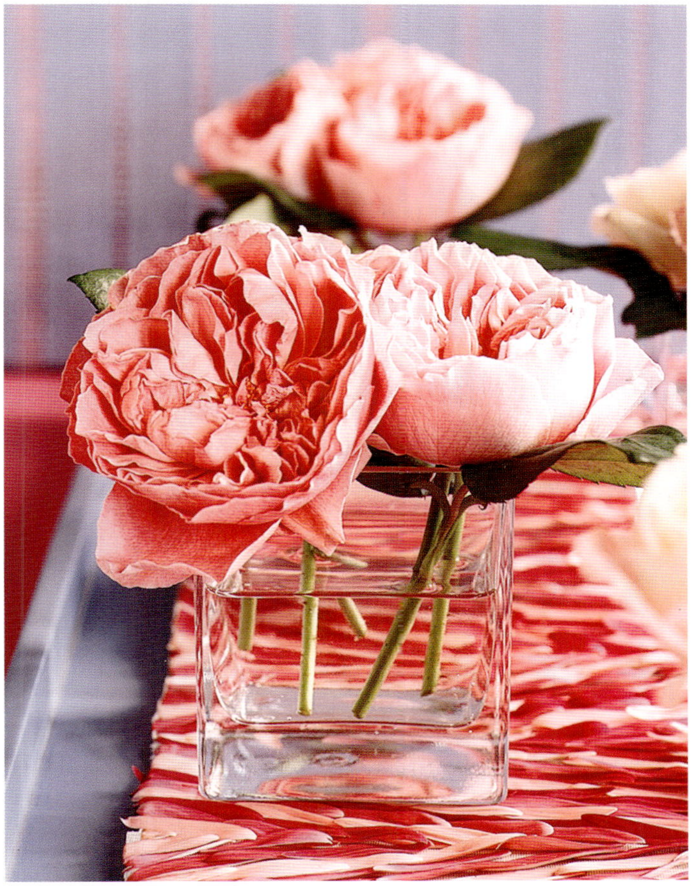

above: This is one of those arrangements that can happen with so many different kinds of flowers. I love the pattern of pink and green at the base, like a layer of moss, with sprightly cosmos dancing amid it all. Pink and green is such a preppy classic combination that you can never go wrong. *right*: I was inspired by Bargello needlework and wanted to reproduce the look with flower petals (Gerbera daisies in this case). I kept the arrangement in the refrigerator overnight, and it was beautiful all day the following day. But beware: this carpet is a one-day arrangement.

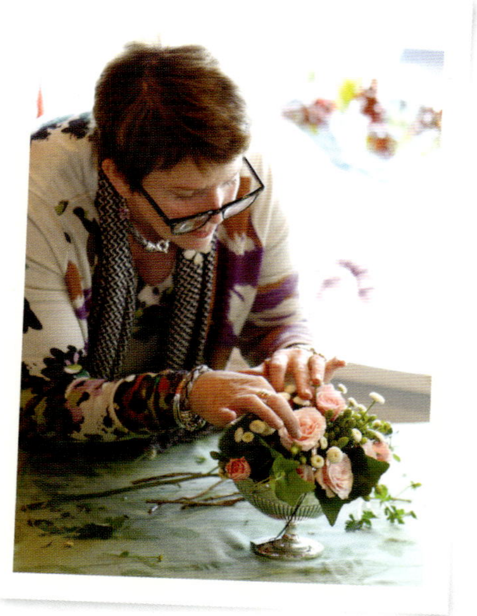

I LOVE TO GROUP SMALL CONTAINERS, SILVER ESPECIALLY. I UNEARTH THE HAND-ME- DOWNS, PUT-AWAY-NEVER-TO-BE-USED PIECES, AND THEN POLISH THEM UP WITH A LOT OF DETERMINATION AND ELBOW GREASE.

They are easy to arrange—put two or three or five on a table, all different heights. Clustered together they make a strong statement, but they are also pretty and delicate. These petite arrangements came together easily, but they required trimming flowers and working out a balance that still looked organic. Often the containers, like the floral painted pitcher, dictate the flowers. The ultimate container is a mint julep cup. The silver cruet is so beautiful on its own that it doesn't need much—just a little hyacinth—to dress it up.

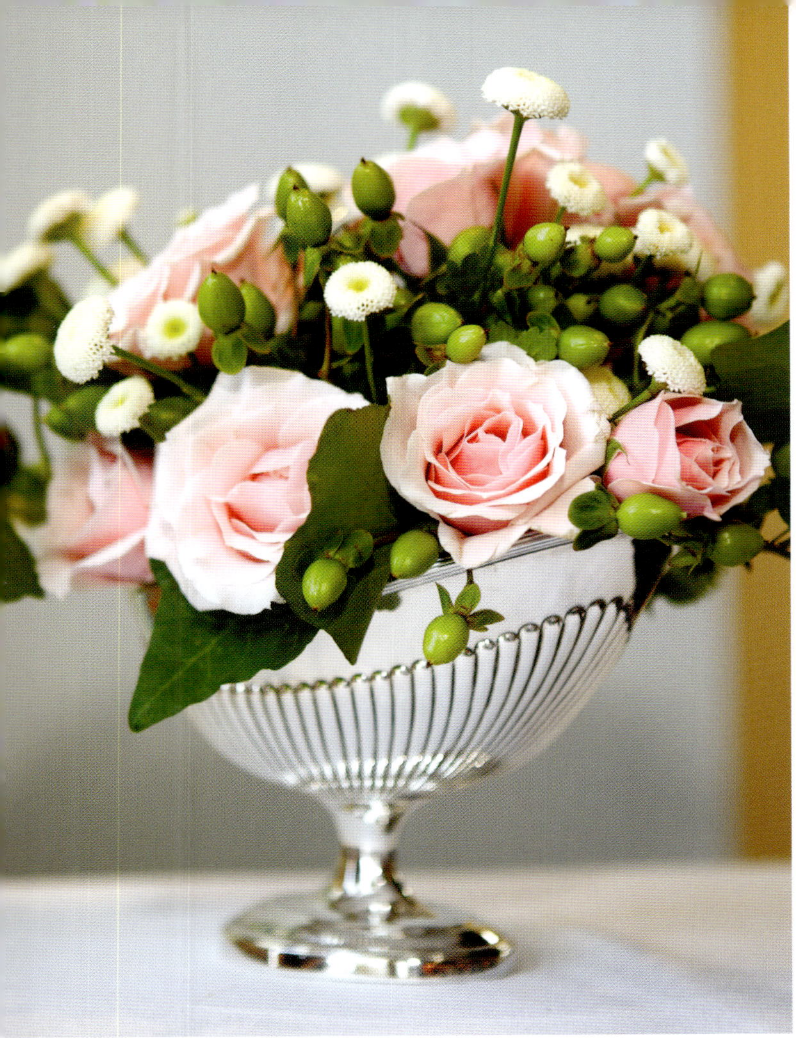
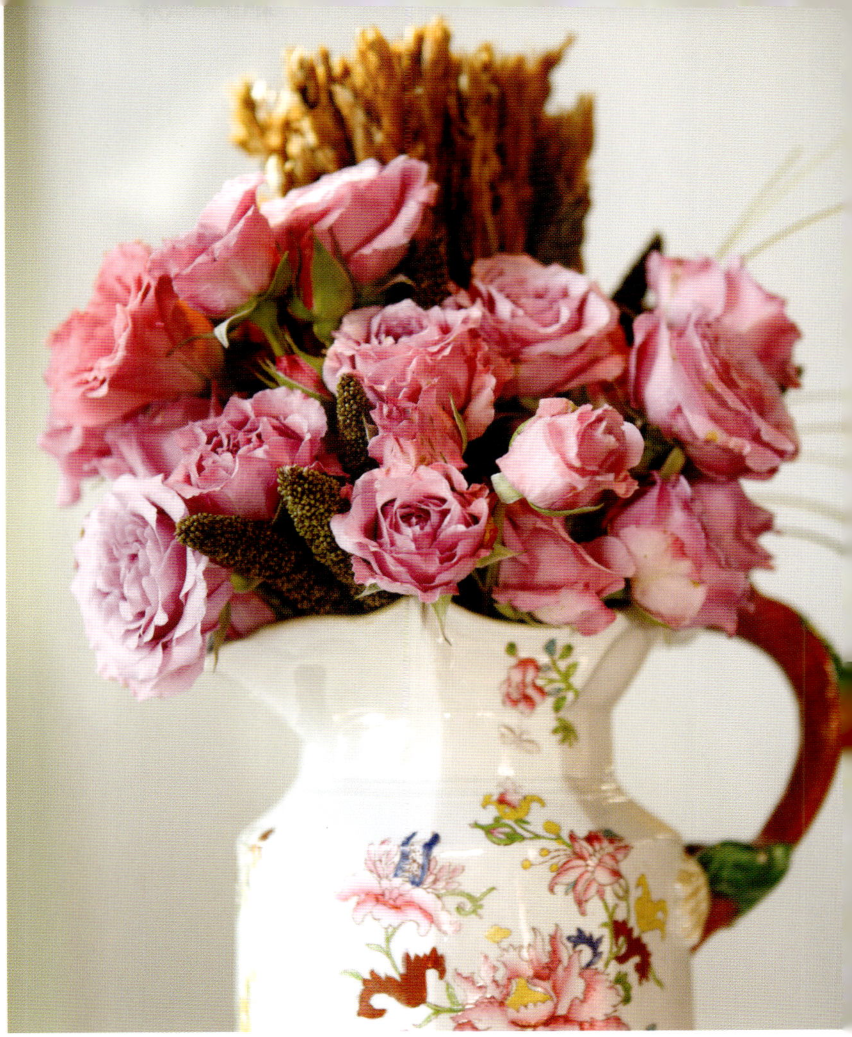
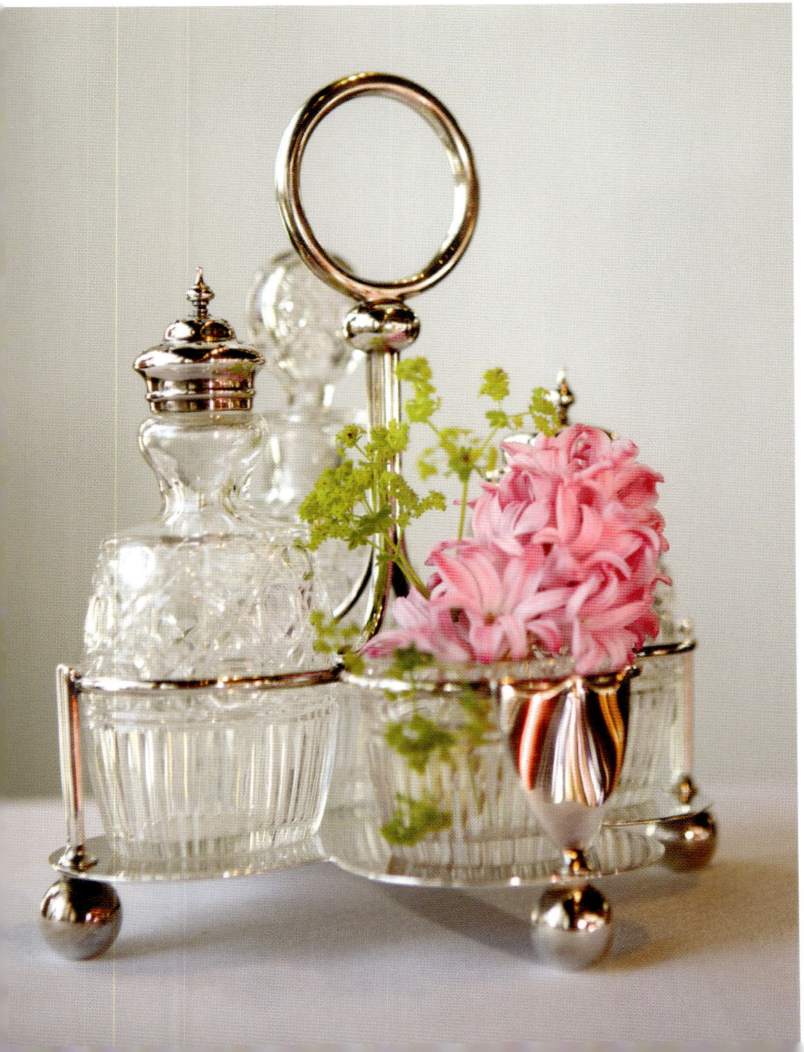
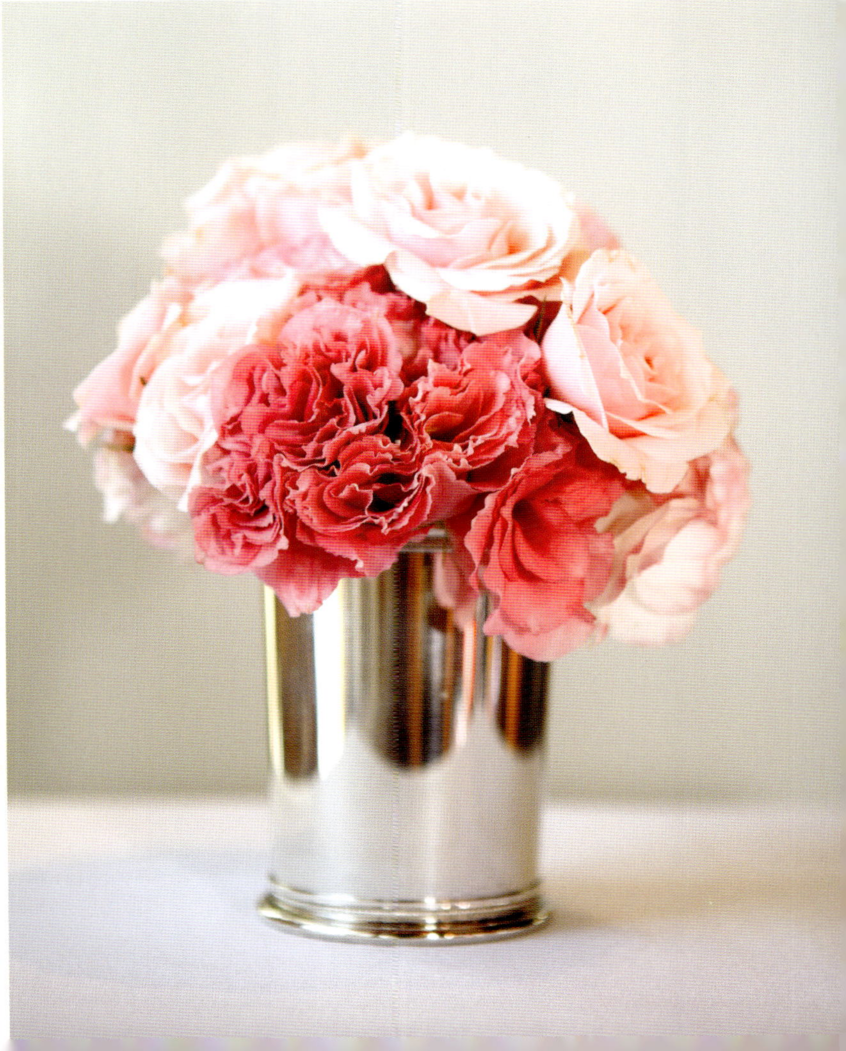

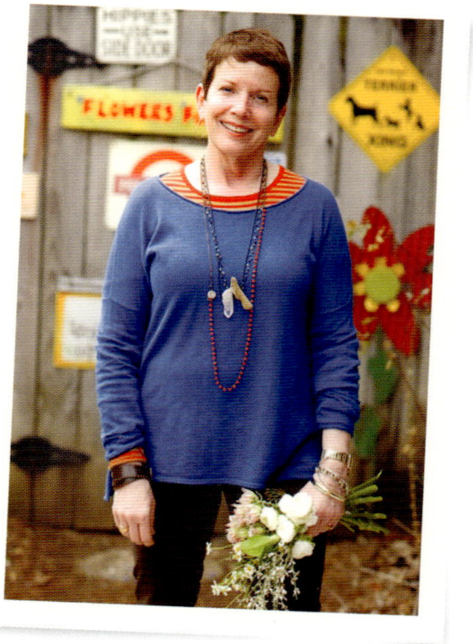

One of my favorite quotes is from Erma Bombeck: "When I stand before God at the end of my life, I would hope that I would not have a single bit of talent left, and could say, 'I used everything that you gave me.'"

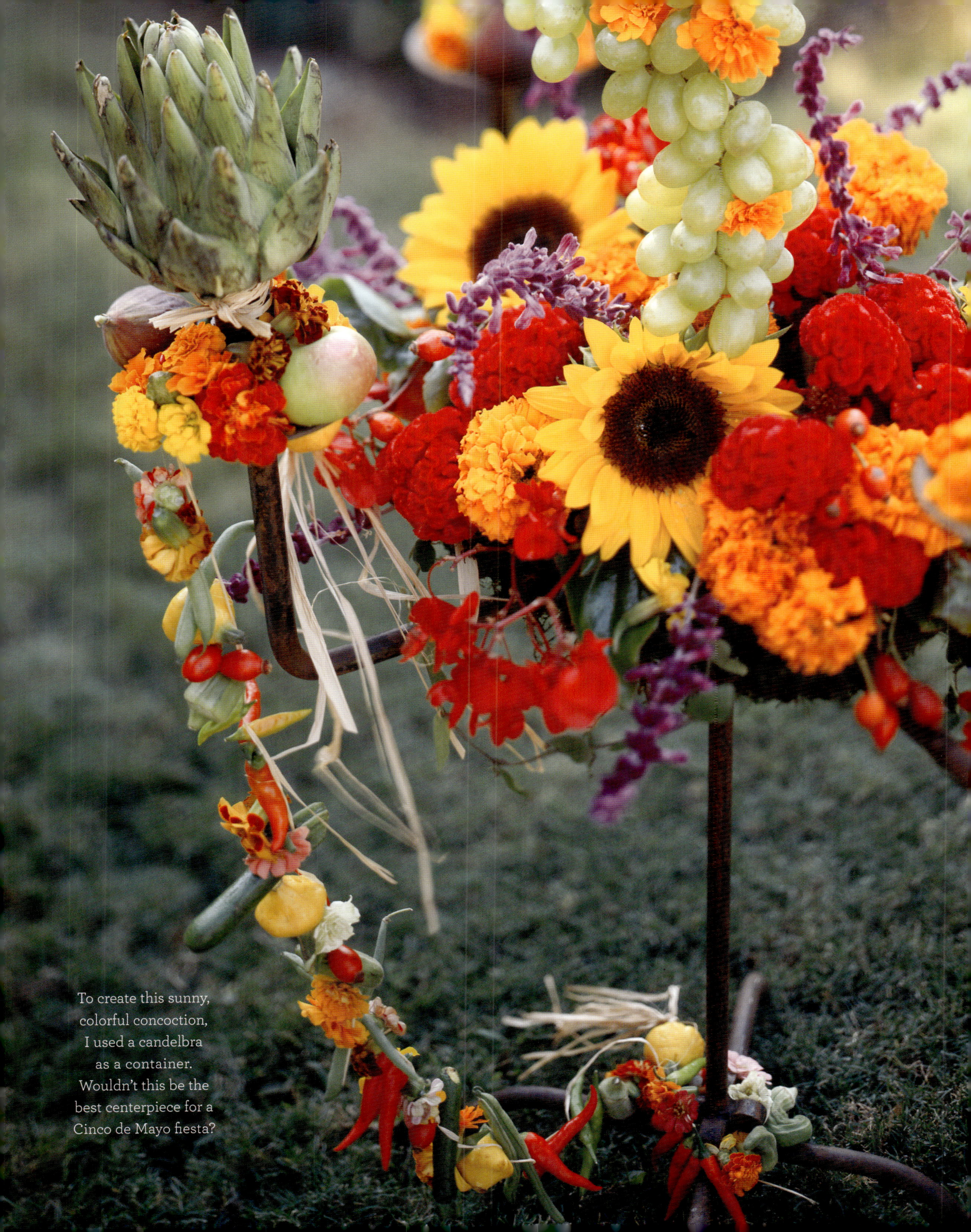

To create this sunny, colorful concoction, I used a candelbra as a container. Wouldn't this be the best centerpiece for a Cinco de Mayo fiesta?

autumn

When I think of Fall, I think of flowers and plants that are available for those last few months of the year, that fall out of favor after Thanksgiving. Autumn definitely suggests a warm color palette, but as you'll see in some of my designs, you can shake it up a bit. Fall offers a touch of coolness in the air, the promise that the sweltering Alabama heat will not last forever. As the days get shorter and football madness sets in, I find myself puttering more and more in my garden. I reflect on how grateful I am to live in a place where we truly have four seasons of the year and how those four seasons are the clock that makes me tick.

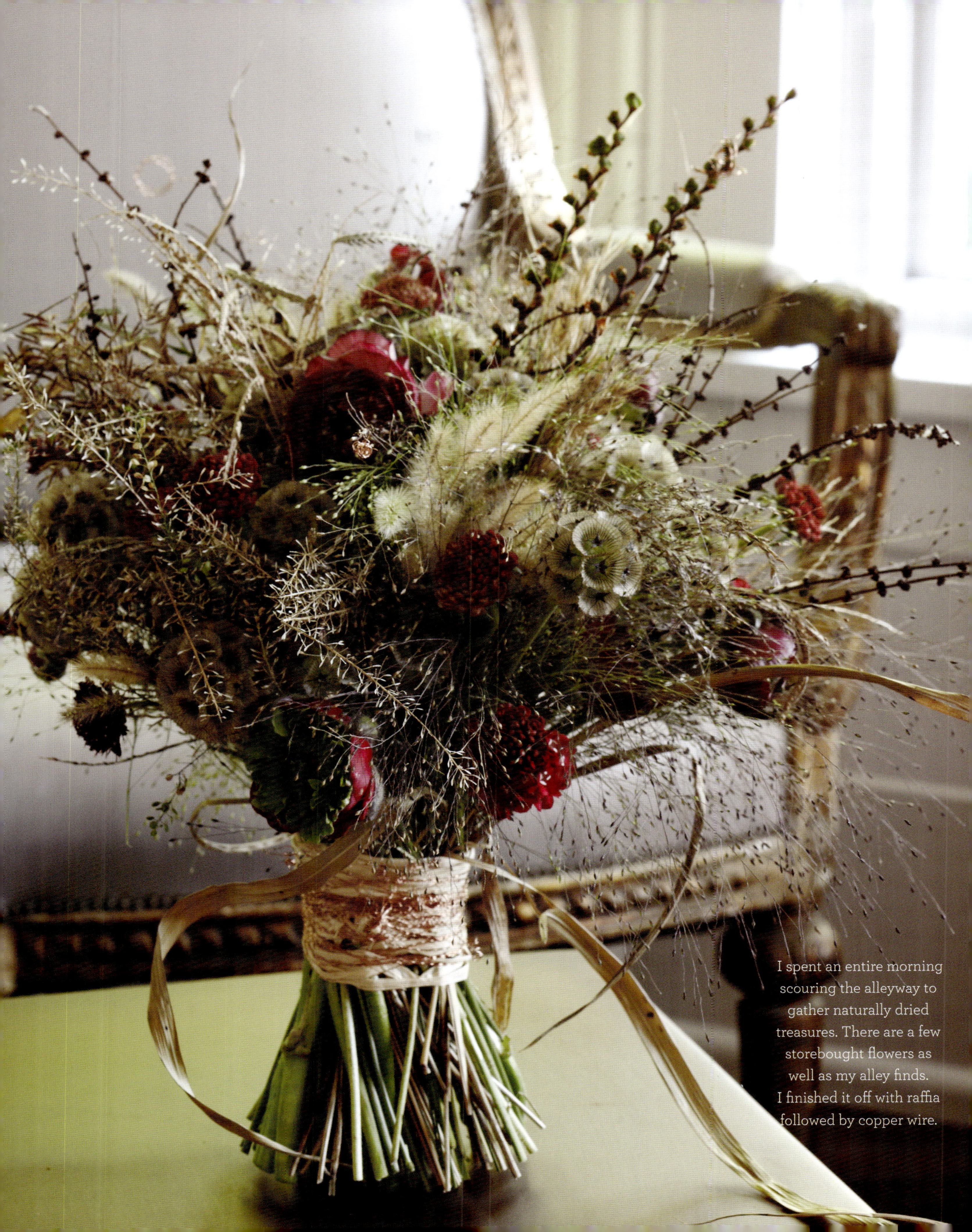

I spent an entire morning scouring the alleyway to gather naturally dried treasures. There are a few storebought flowers as well as my alley finds. I finished it off with raffia followed by copper wire.

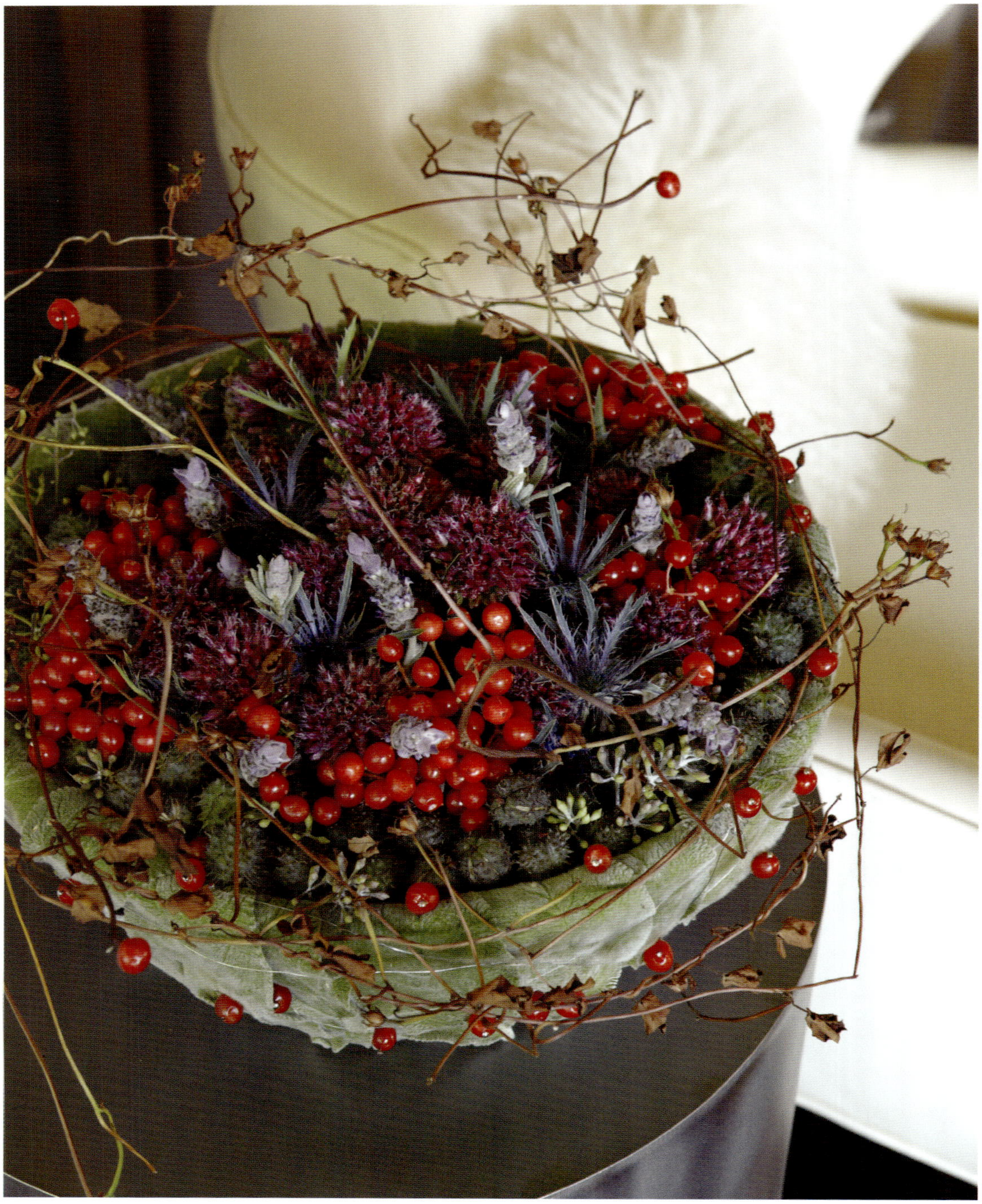

above: I handmade this container by gluing lamb's ear leaves over each other like scales on a fish. I actually used a wire mesh colander as the base for my leaves and worked from the bottom up and around. I then placed a water tight container with wet oasis inside my bowl. *right:* Soft autumn tones that evoke the colors of fall seemed the correct response to an antique hunt-themed container. I can see it on an old Southern huntboard with silver pitchers and julep cups surrounding it as riders quench their thirst and head off for the day. I used hypericum berries here; they're in just about every arrangement we create or receive. But they have great texture and grow in so many different colors.

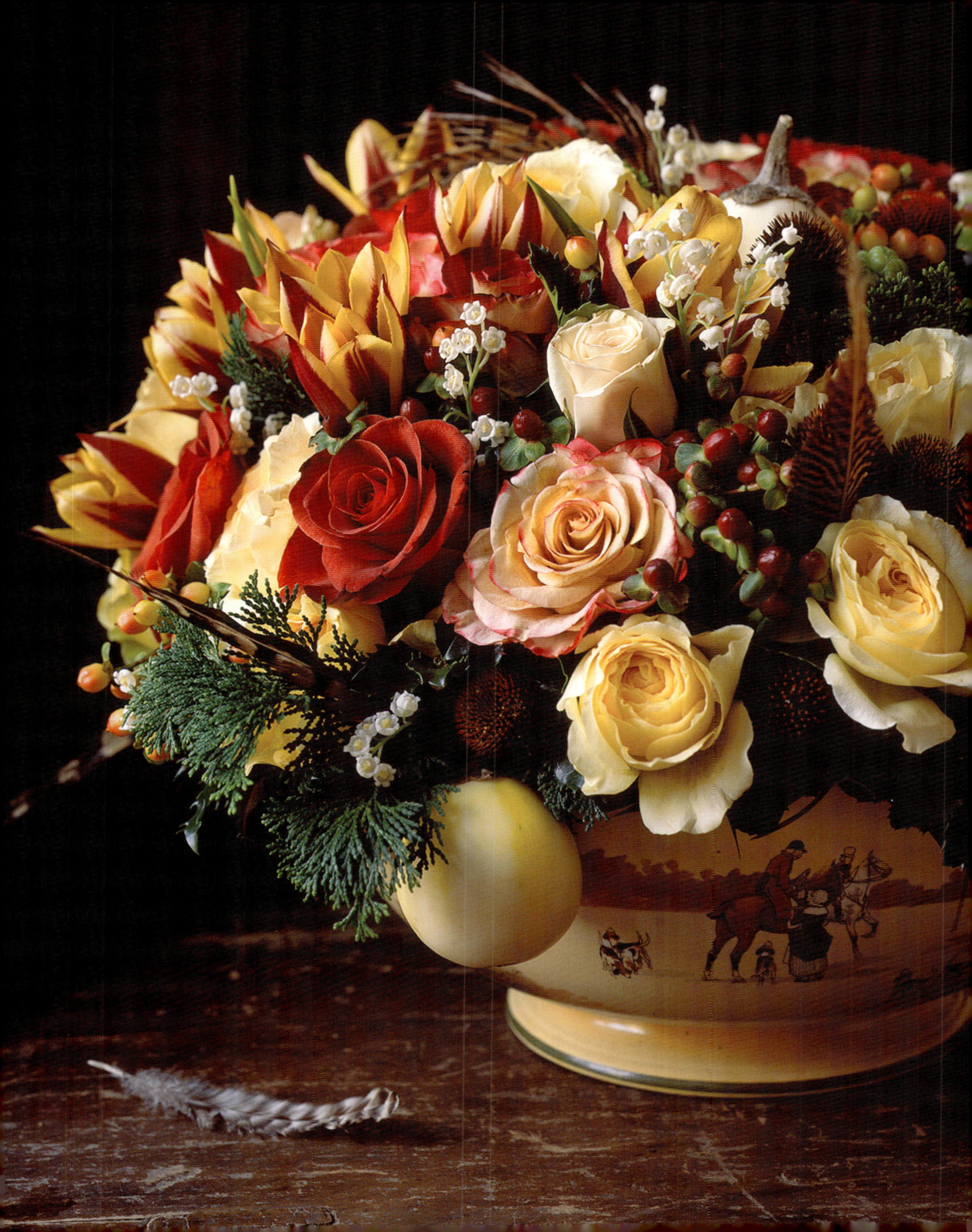

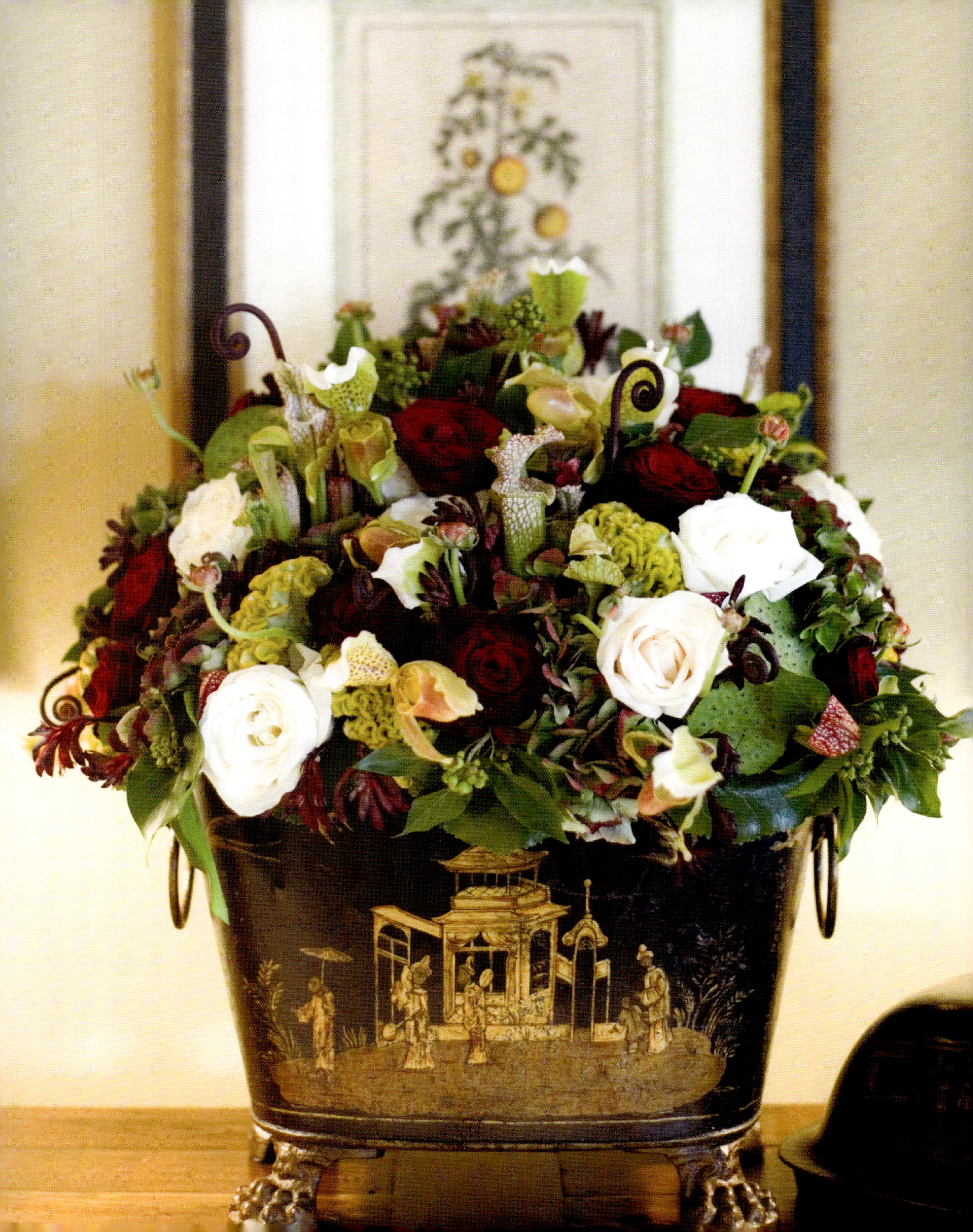

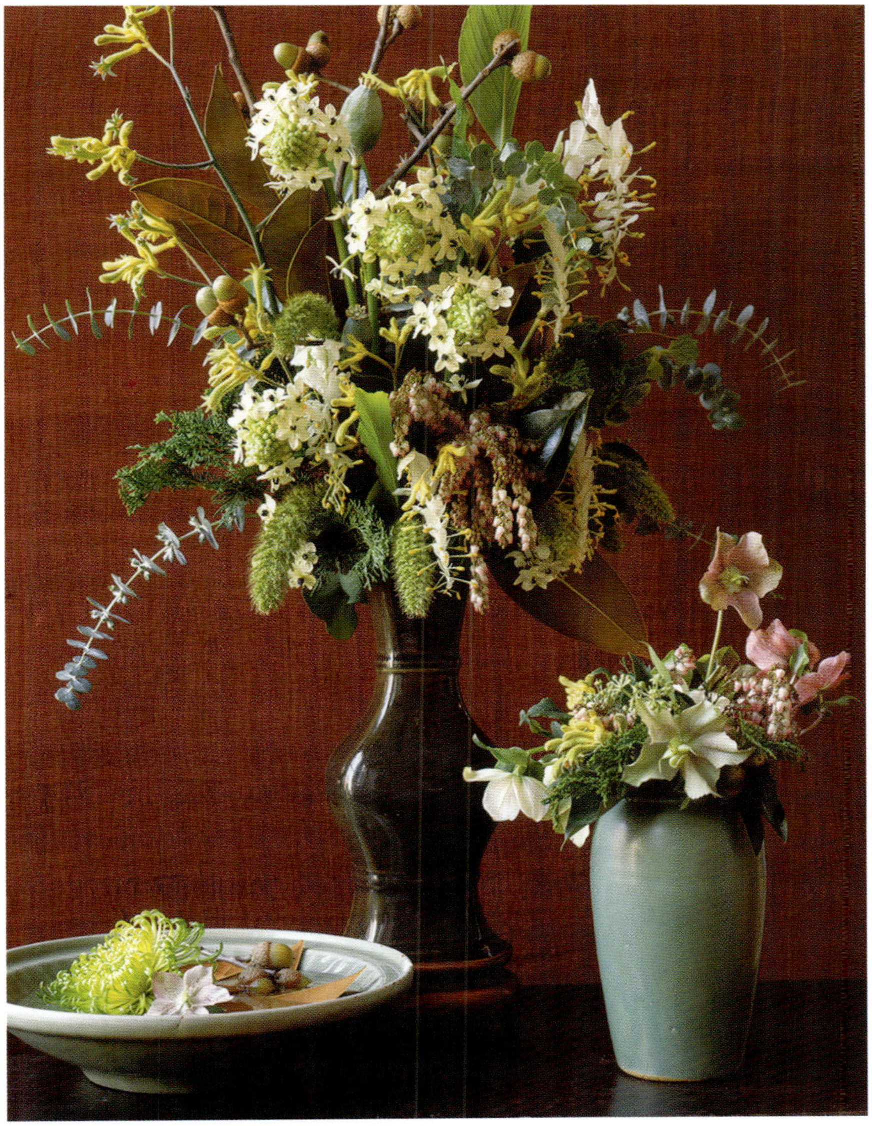

above: This grouping feels very Asian inspired to me. I guess it's a Sybilized version! I mixed cascading ginger lily blossoms with pierus that reminds me of blossoms adorning a Geisha's hair. Their elegance mixed with acorns on the branch and poppy pods and millet really excited me. Like burlap and lace! *left*: The tole chinoiserie container set the tone of the floral arrangement, which includes an exotic mix of flowers—black beauty and sahara roses, red kangaroo paw, lotus pods, tree ivy. It's the ultimate contrasting composition—light and dark flowers, fine and ubiquitous foliage, an elegant and yet humble metal container.

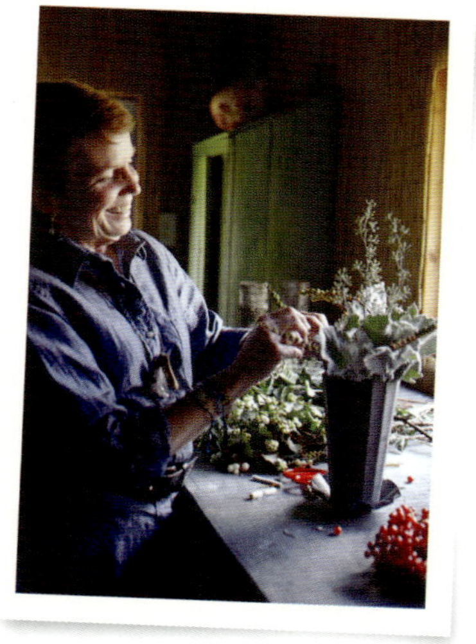

I always have to use
everything and
create an arrangement
that pleases my
eye before I'll stop.
No matter how long
my day has been,
this last arrangement
is always my
favorite of the day.

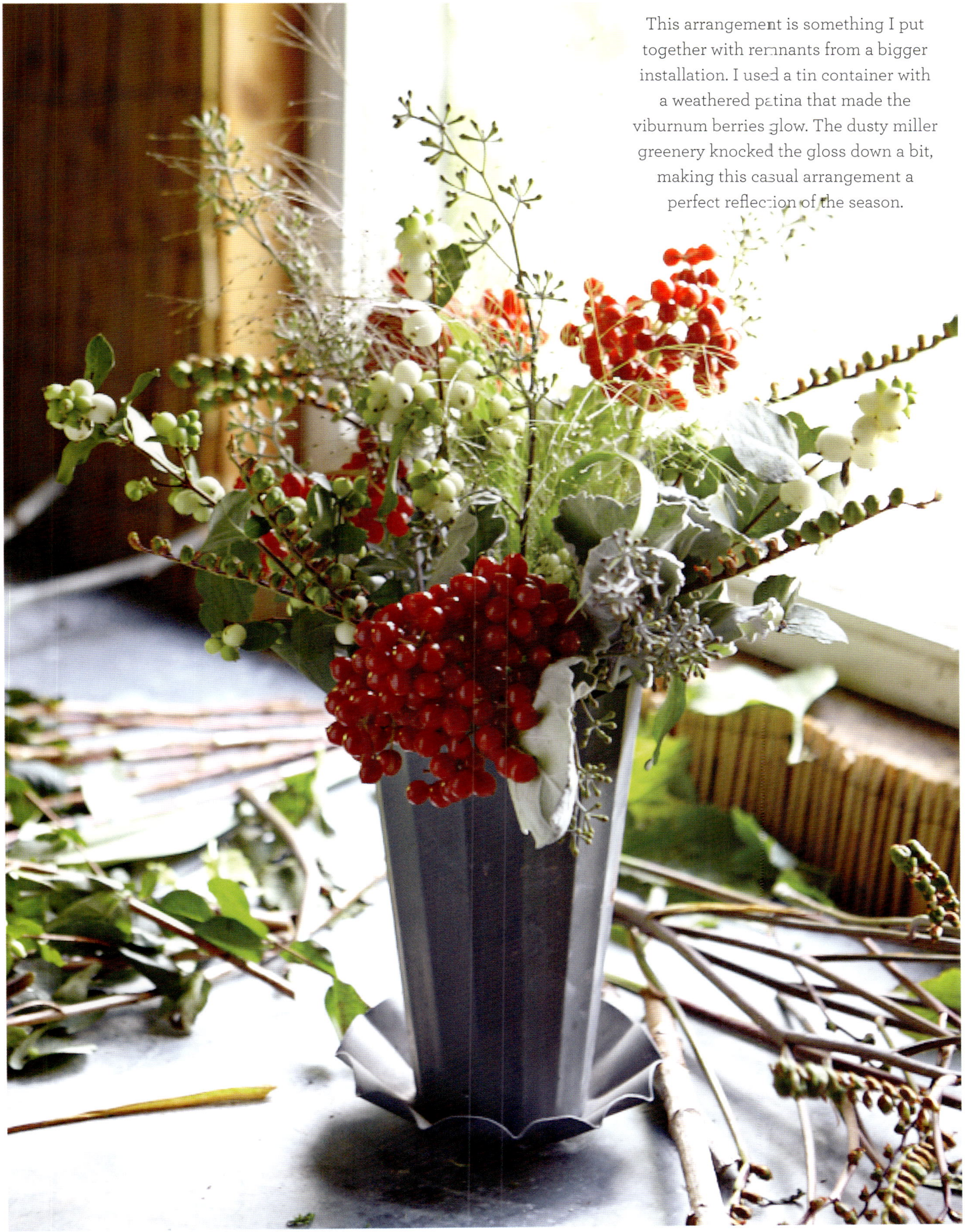

This arrangement is something I put together with remnants from a bigger installation. I used a tin container with a weathered patina that made the viburnum berries glow. The dusty miller greenery knocked the gloss down a bit, making this casual arrangement a perfect reflection of the season.

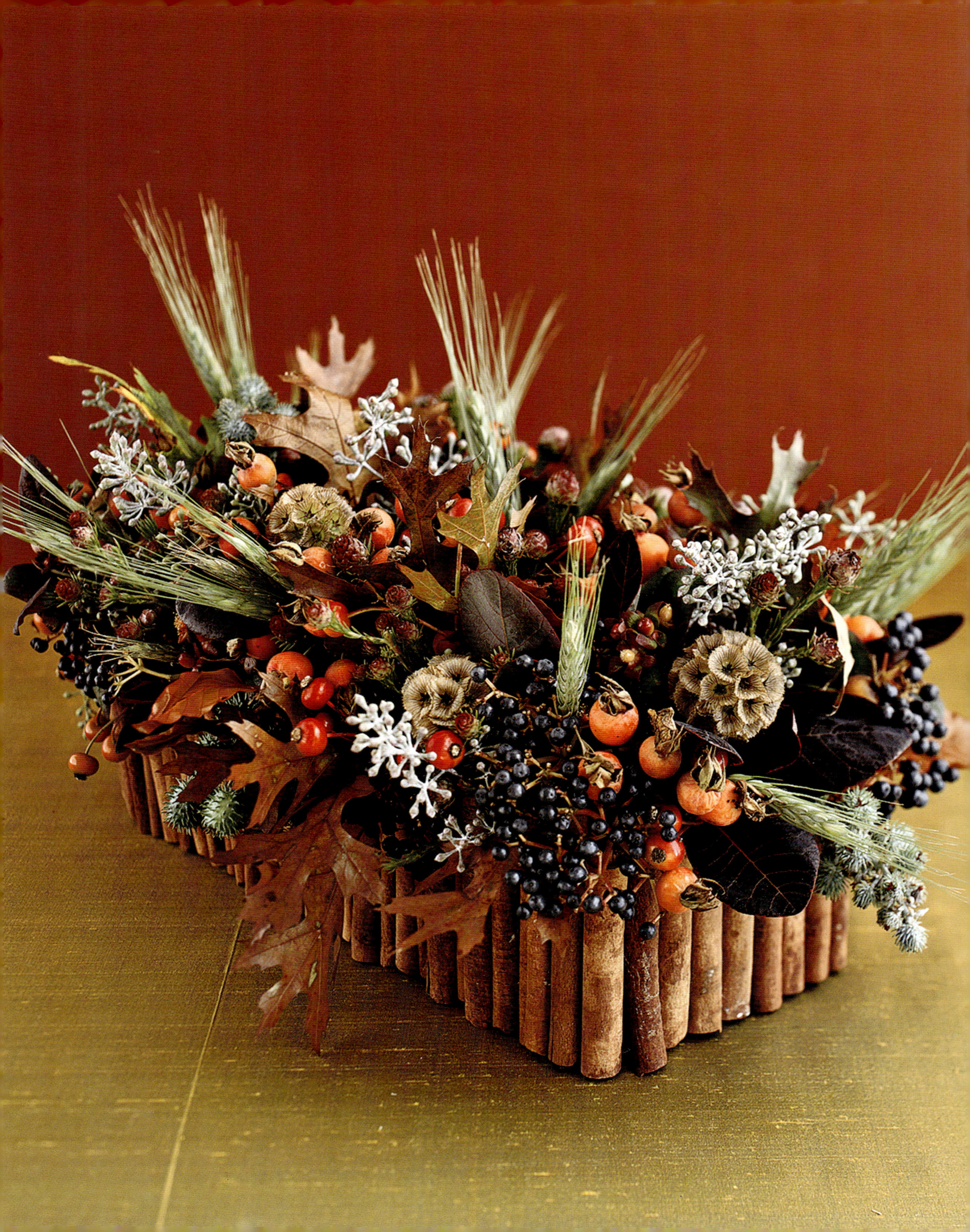

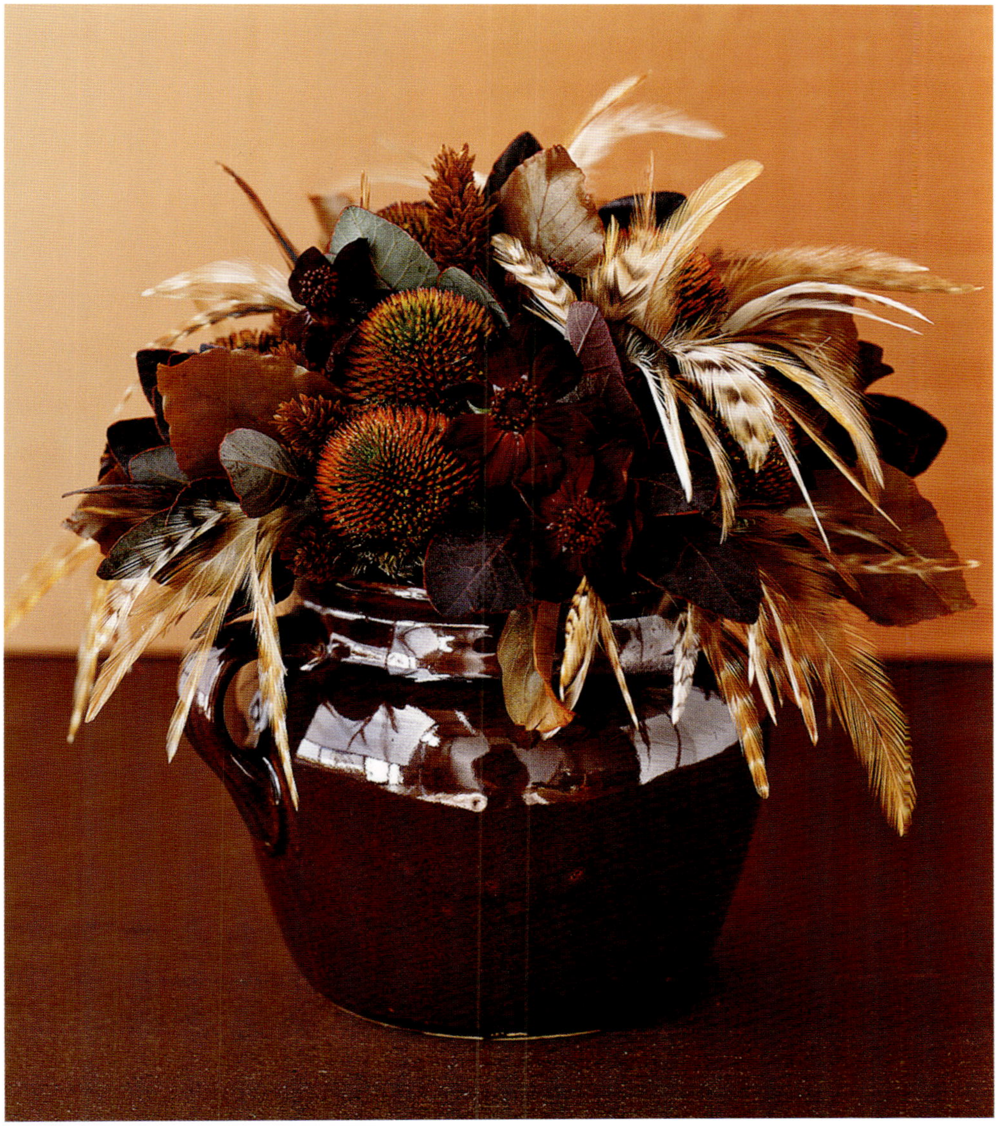

above: Lush and autumnal, this arrangement started with feathers from an arts and crafts store. I separated them into small clusters that I wired together. To complement the dark brown container, I chose the darkest foliage of the smoke tree and then grouped pods from the center of cone flowers with preserved beech foliage, dried preserved grass called phalaris, and chocolate cosmos. *left*: I ran double-sided carpet tape around a straight-sided container and covered the sides with aspidistra leaves. I then hot-glued cinnamon sticks to the outside. The result looks like a rustic fence filled with a medley of fall foliage, seed heads, pods, and berries. It is so textured, it resembles a tapestry.

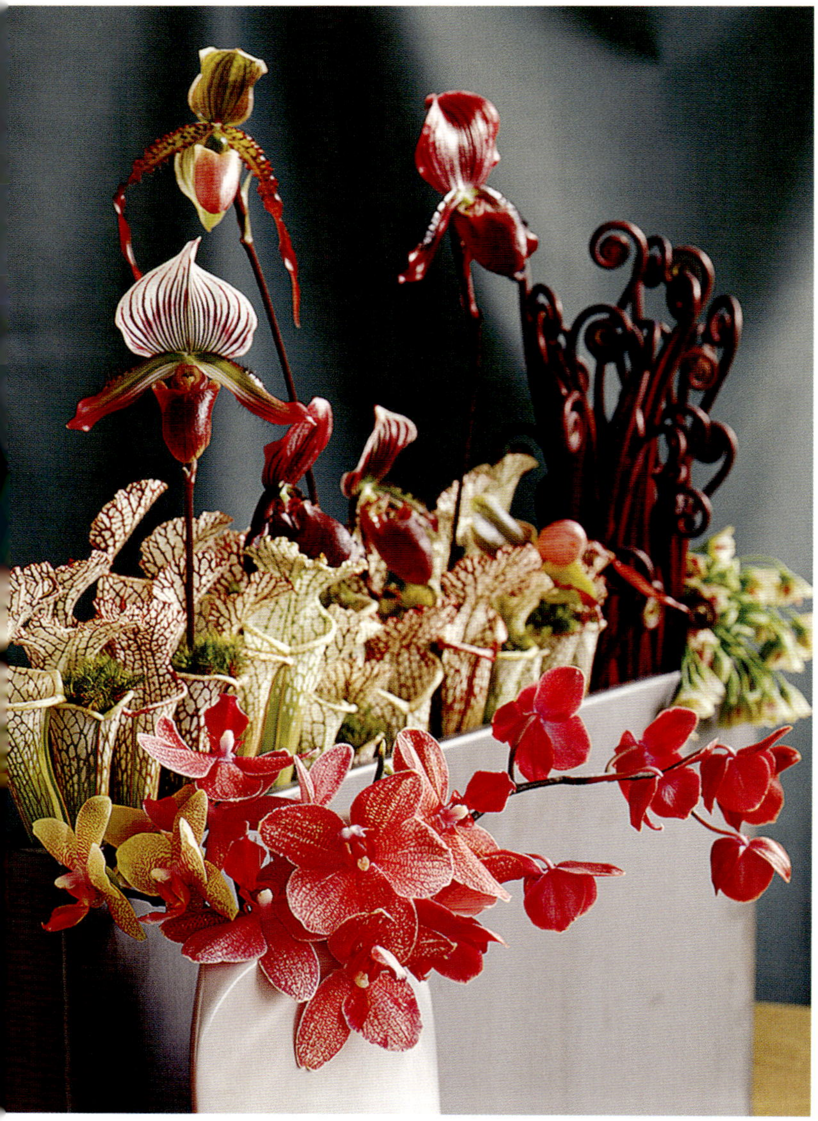

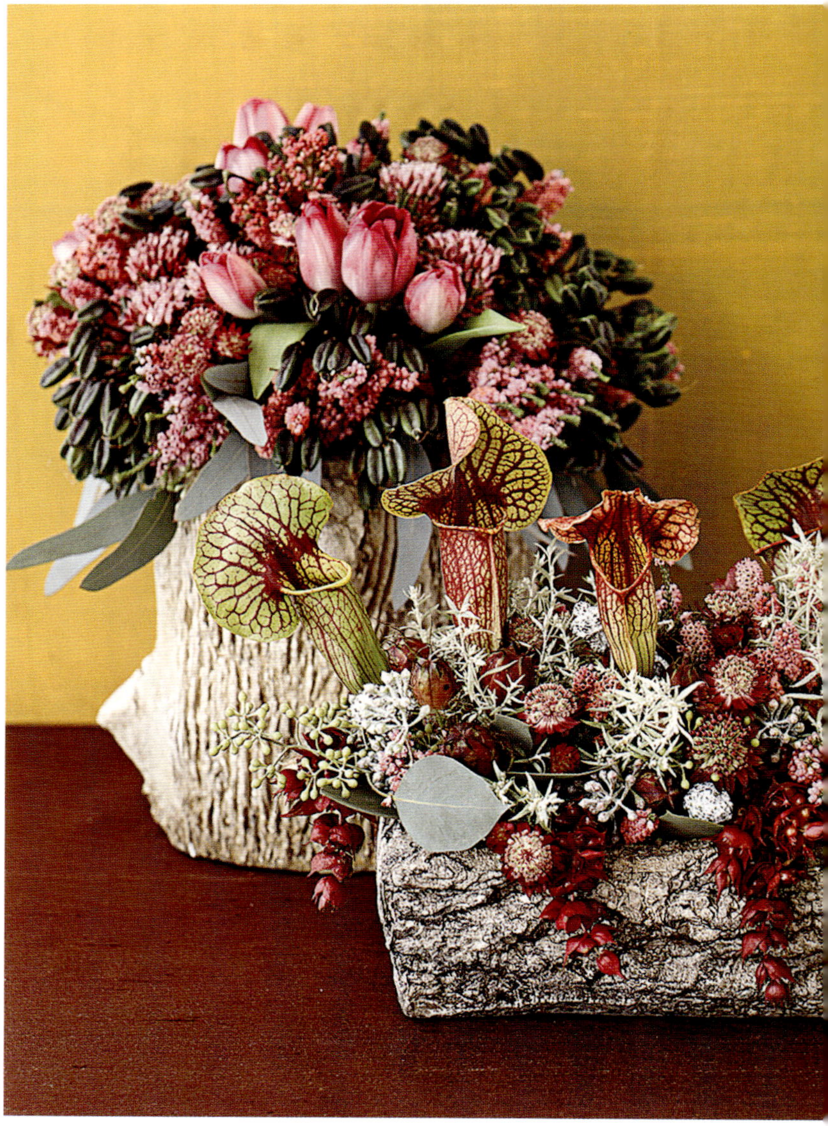

These woodland materials just fit the opening of this zinc box, where flat grays play off the plum and eggplant shade of the lady slipper orchids. I love the mix of exotic orchids with the pitcher plants and fern fronds.

Instead of rust and gold, these plum-toned arrangements explore another side of fall. The concrete faux bois d'arc containers lend themselves to the color palette. This textural mix of natural materials is very typical of my work.

some like it hot

MY ARRANGEMENTS HAVE PERSONALITIES AND A LITTLE SEX APPEAL, STRETCHING OUT THEIR ARMS AND STRIKING A POSE WITH SENSUOUS STEMS AND LUSH PETALS. AND, IN AUTUMN, MY PALETTE GETS MORE SULTRY WITH DEEP PURPLES AND NUANCED GREENS AND GOLDS.

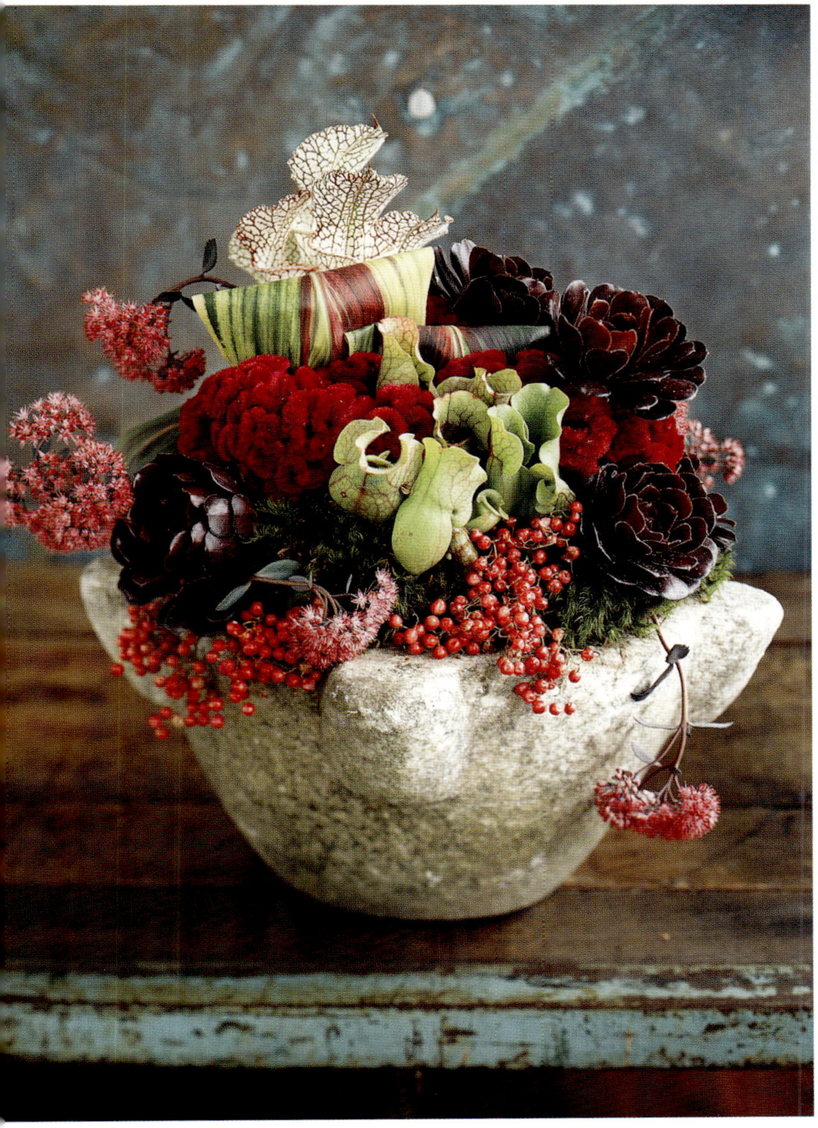

I used pitcher plants and their flower seed heads in this creation. These exotic beauties are grown especially for the flower industry—not gathered from a protected wildflower bog. I am totally dedicated to preserving our wetlands!

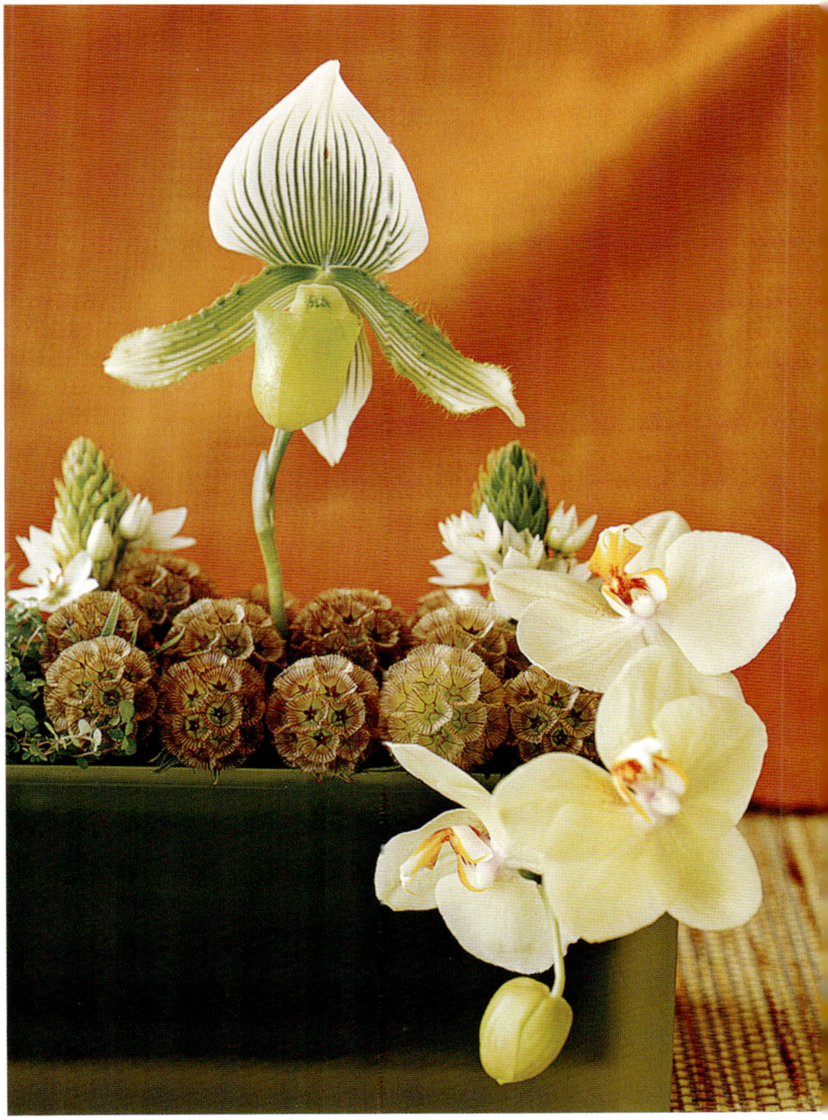

Lady Slipper Orchids give the arrangement sex appeal with their outstretched petals and curvaceous stems. Strangely beautiful, the scabiosa pods, with their rich tan color, honeycomb look, and delicate yet bold texture, are available summer through fall.

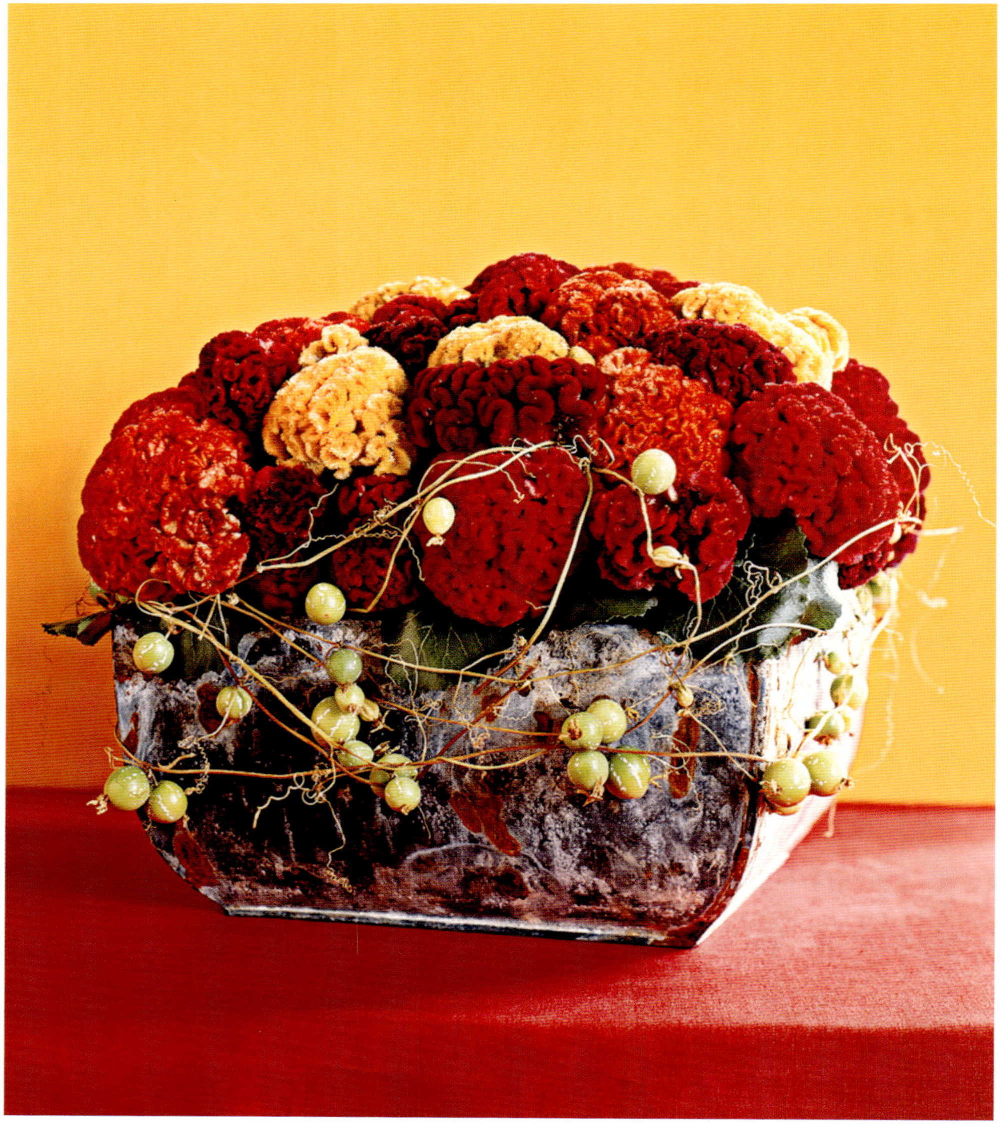

I OFTEN LOOSELY WRAP MY ARRANGEMENTS IN VINES THAT I FORAGED FROM SOME ALLEY, FIELD, OR GARDEN. THEY EXTEND THE BOUQUET BEYOND THE CONFINES OF THE CONTAINER AND LOOSEN UP THE FLOWERS.

The folds and curves of coxcomb celosia remind me of brain coral – that's been brightly painted. The flower heads also look like velvet, and it's all you can do not to pet them. Just as a chef highlights a seasonal food ingredient, I am all about coxcomb, which is always spectacular by fall.

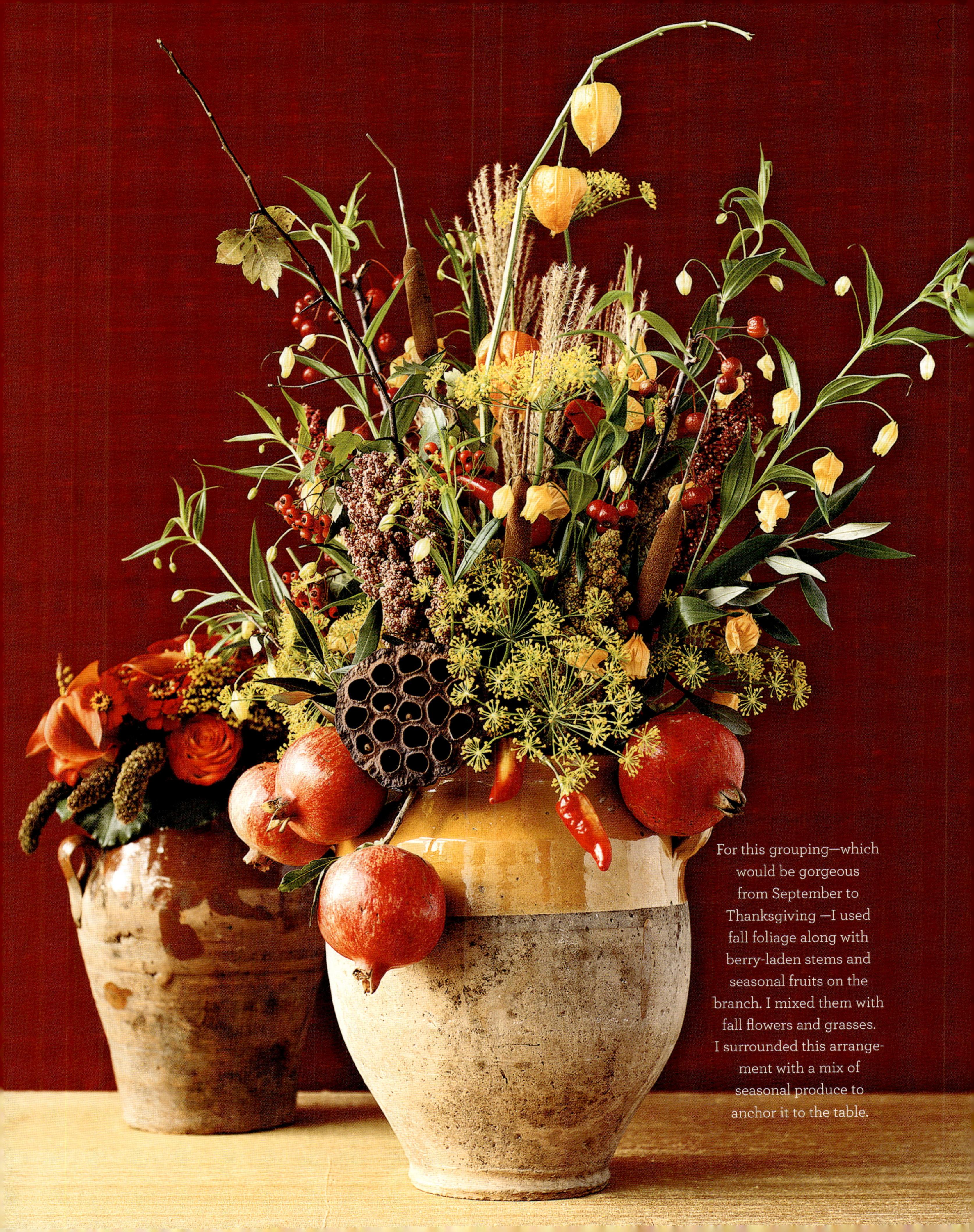

For this grouping—which would be gorgeous from September to Thanksgiving—I used fall foliage along with berry-laden stems and seasonal fruits on the branch. I mixed them with fall flowers and grasses. I surrounded this arrangement with a mix of seasonal produce to anchor it to the table.

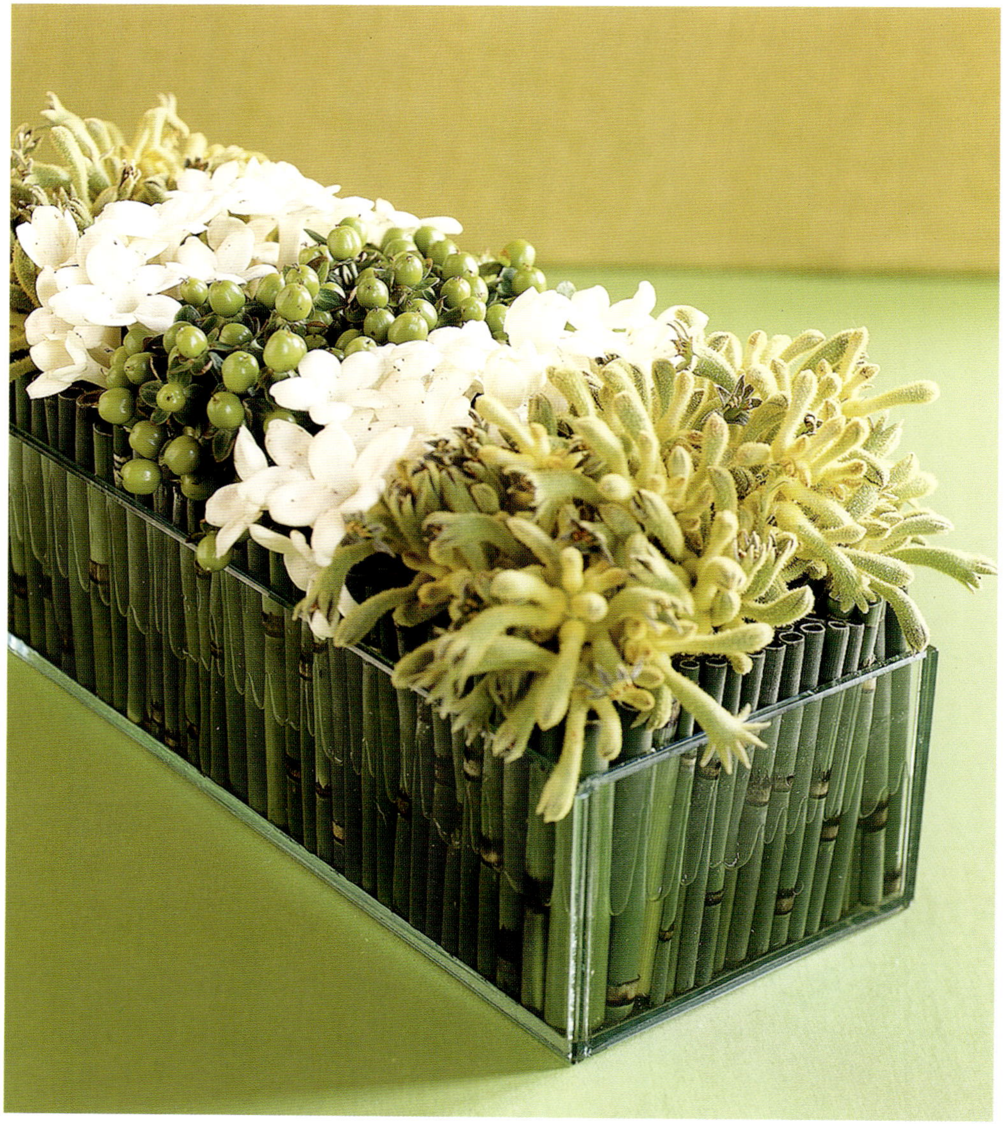

above: Stephanotis, considered the traditional wedding flower, smells magnificent. The down side is that it will get a brown face if it gets moist. As those flowers fade, take them out of the arrangement and replace them with fresh ones or switch out other flowers that are less fragile. *right*: I just can't leave an orchid plant plain in the pot! Especially if it has a plastic hair-clip holding the stem upright and attached to a wooden stick. This is my example of how an orchid should be properly dressed up. The prehistoric looking fur-encased element is a giant fern frond, available at the flower market.

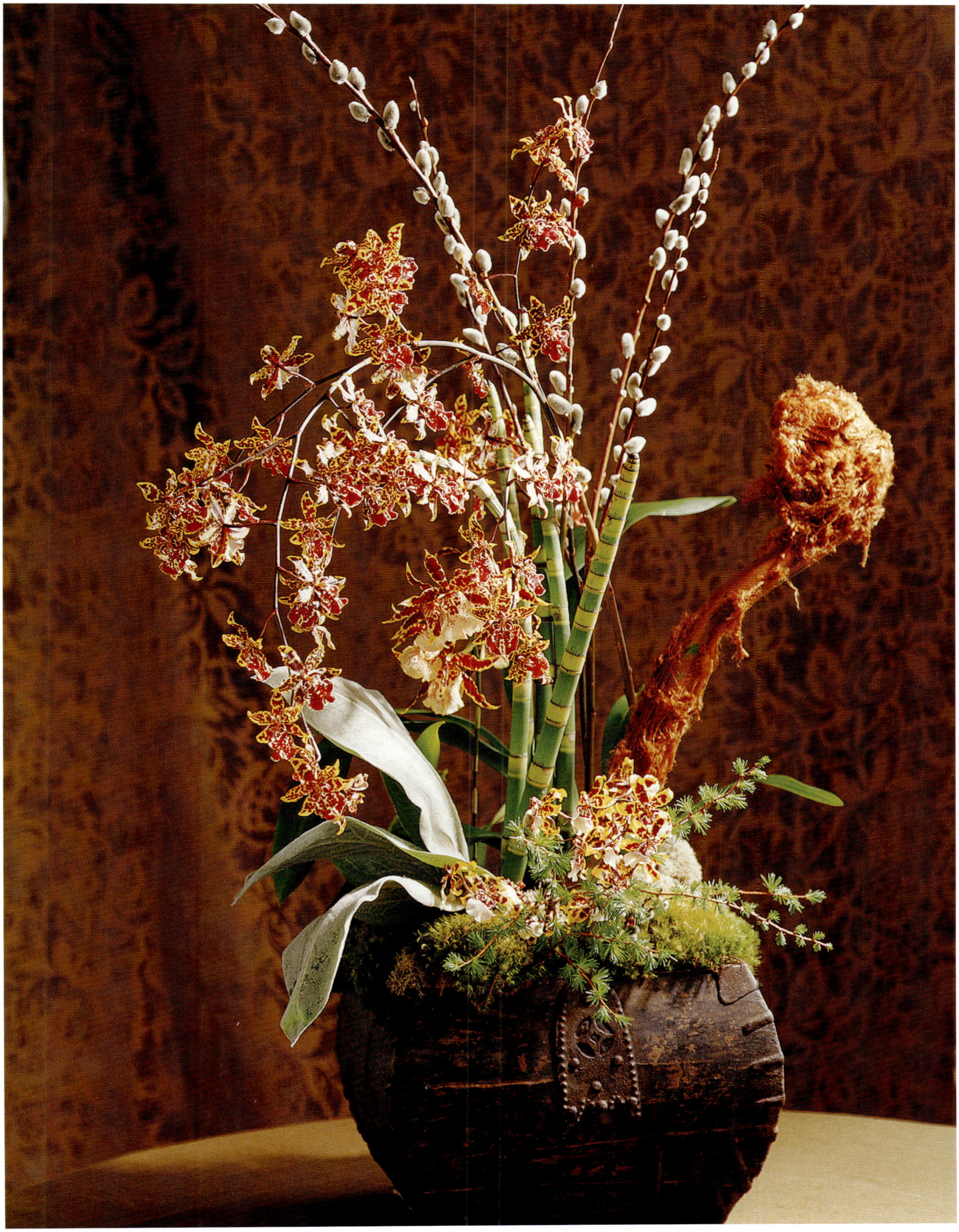

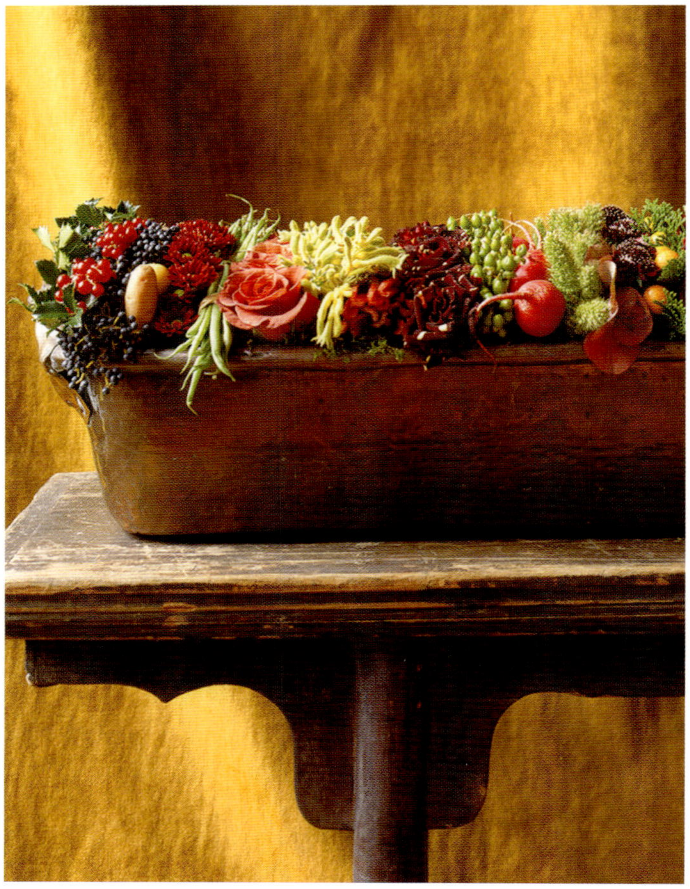

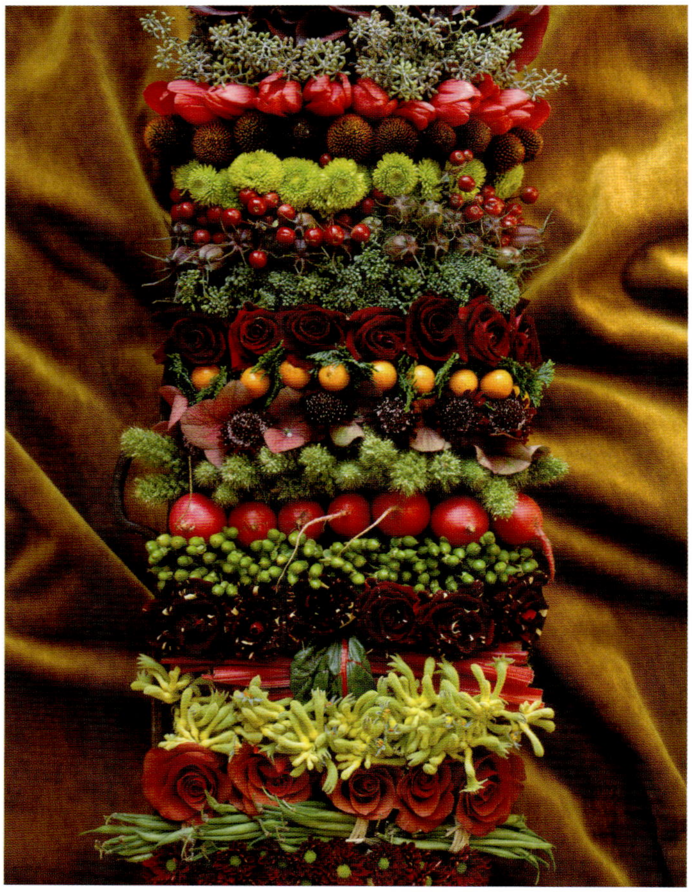

The antique copper fish poacher begged for grouped, seasonal, fresh flowers so I tried a checkerboard design first. But I ended up with stripes, which are so graphic when you look at them from above. It would be a great centerpiece for a large Thanksgiving table, when friends and distant and close family members congregate. My favorite stripe has to be the bundles of Swiss chard tied with a leaf.

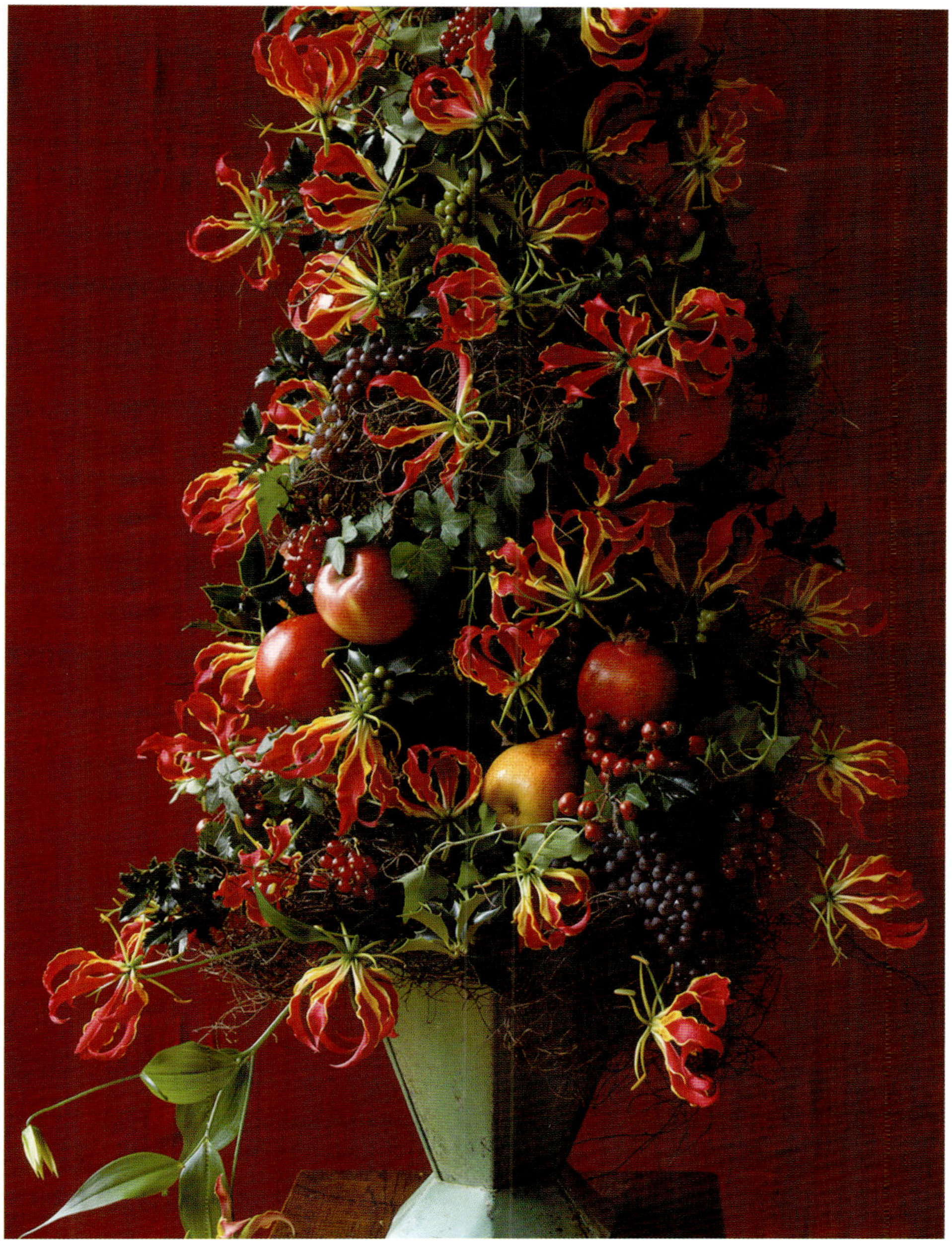

The base of the topiary is a grapevine cone that I placed in a rustic metal container. I first added greenery around the cone, using water picks/vials to keep the greans fresh and just pushing the picks into the grapevine form. I added fruit next, using wood floral picks to secure them into the cone. The finishing touch is the dancing gloriosa lily blossoms turning in every direction.

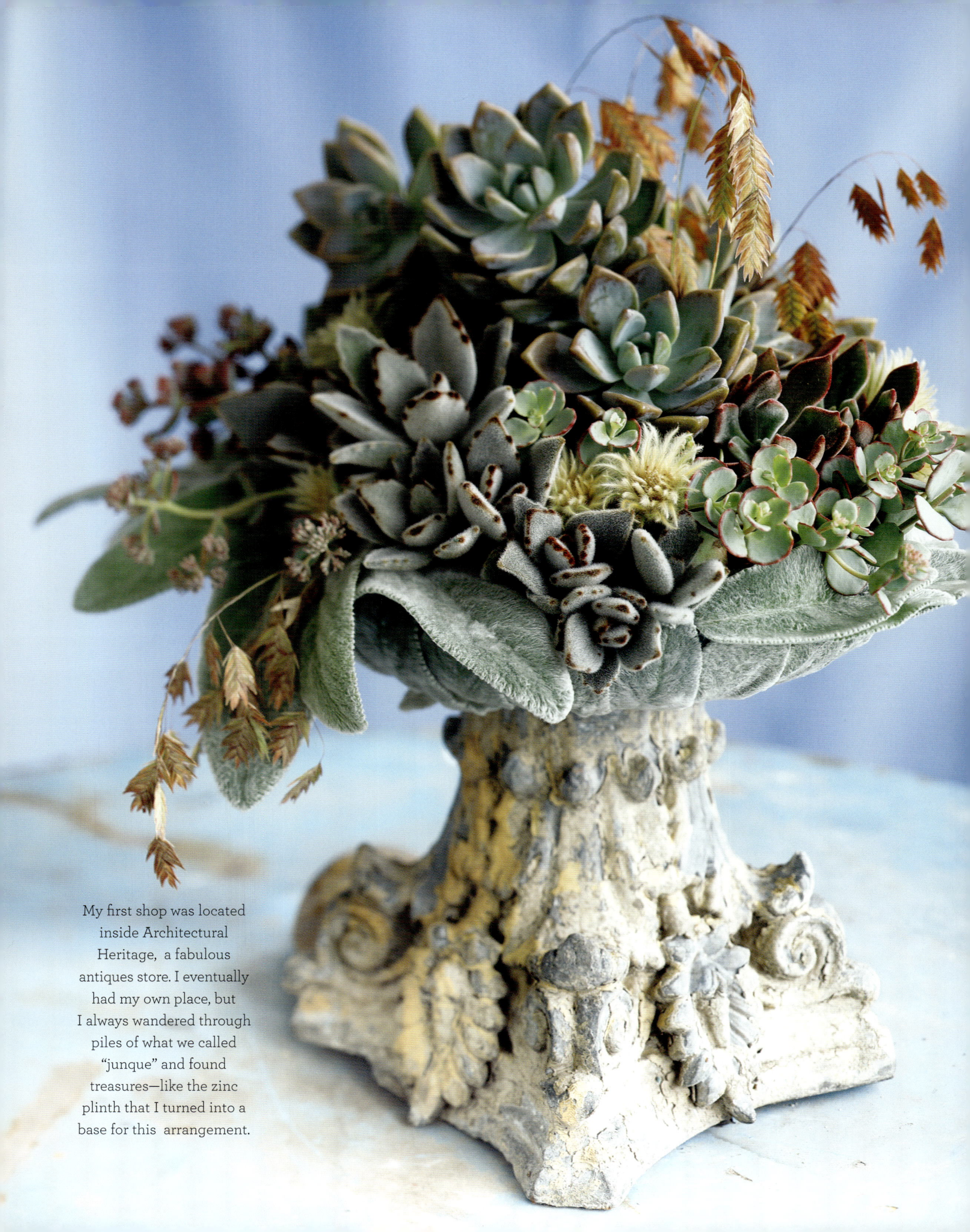

My first shop was located inside Architectural Heritage, a fabulous antiques store. I eventually had my own place, but I always wandered through piles of what we called "junque" and found treasures—like the zinc plinth that I turned into a base for this arrangement.

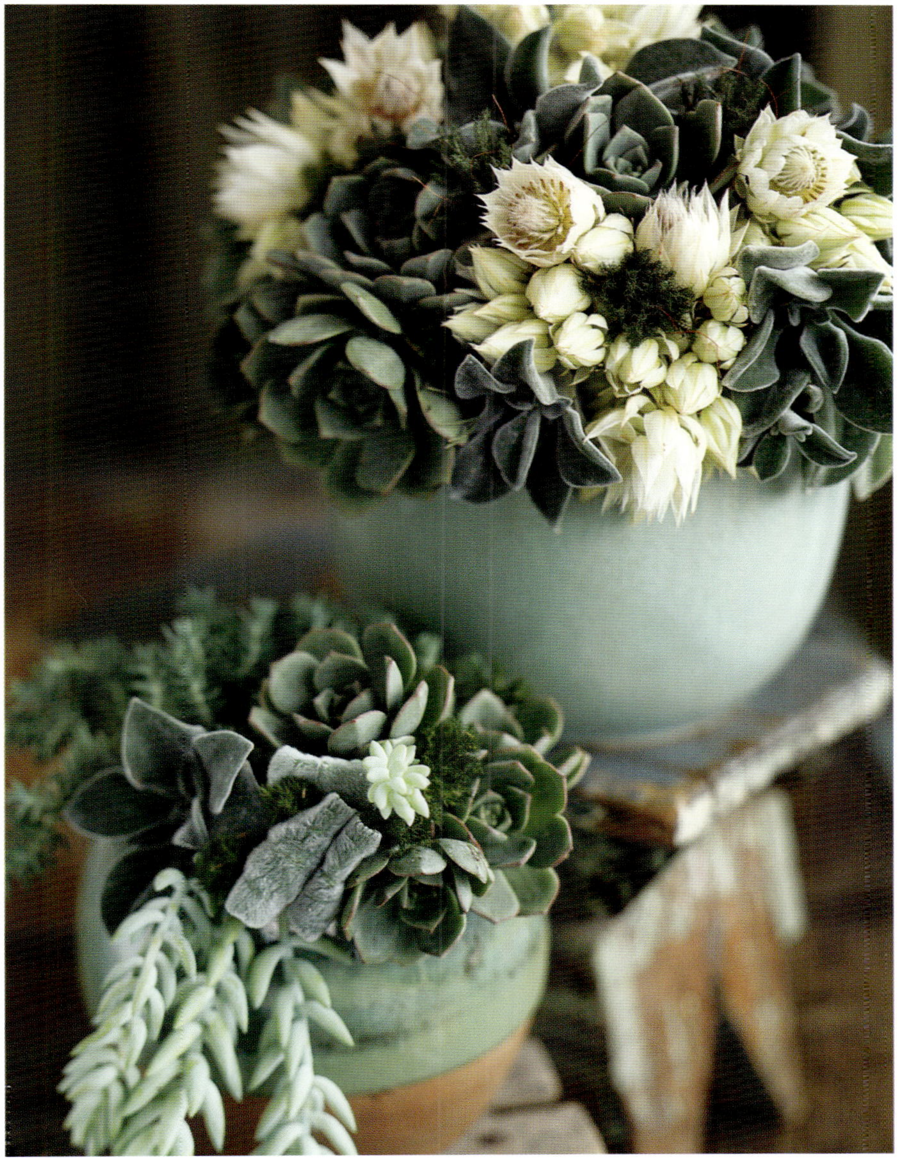

I CREATED THESE SUCCULENT ARRANGEMENTS WHEN WE WERE GOING THROUGH A PARTICULARLY LONG DROUGHT IN BIRMINGHAM.

The idea of succulents appealed because of their color and texture but also their ability to withstand heat and dryness. I used succulents with blossomlike faces combined with one of my favorite unique flowers: bridal blush protea. Then I assembled them so the arrangement looks like flowers tucked in vases.

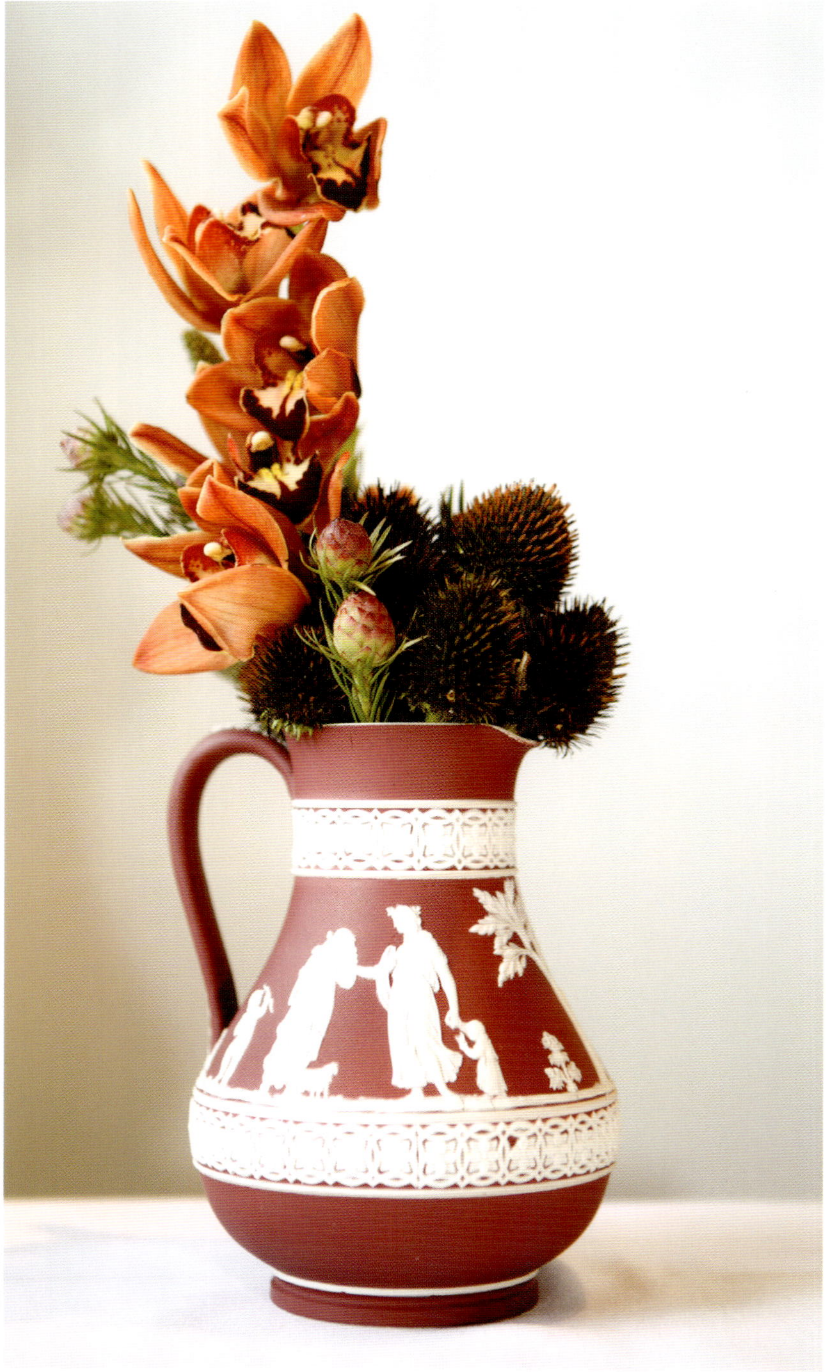

above: The red Wedgwood Jasperware pitcher is unexpected—we usually see blue—and elegant, so I brought in orchids and coneflowers to complement the texture and color. *right*: Simply dramatic—a dark calla lily with a coneflower and mums tucked loosely into a clean-lined, white vase. The contrast gets a wink with grasses folded over, emphasizing the elegant angles of the container and flower. I made a nod to Japanese ikebana, but this arrangement came to life almost all on its own.

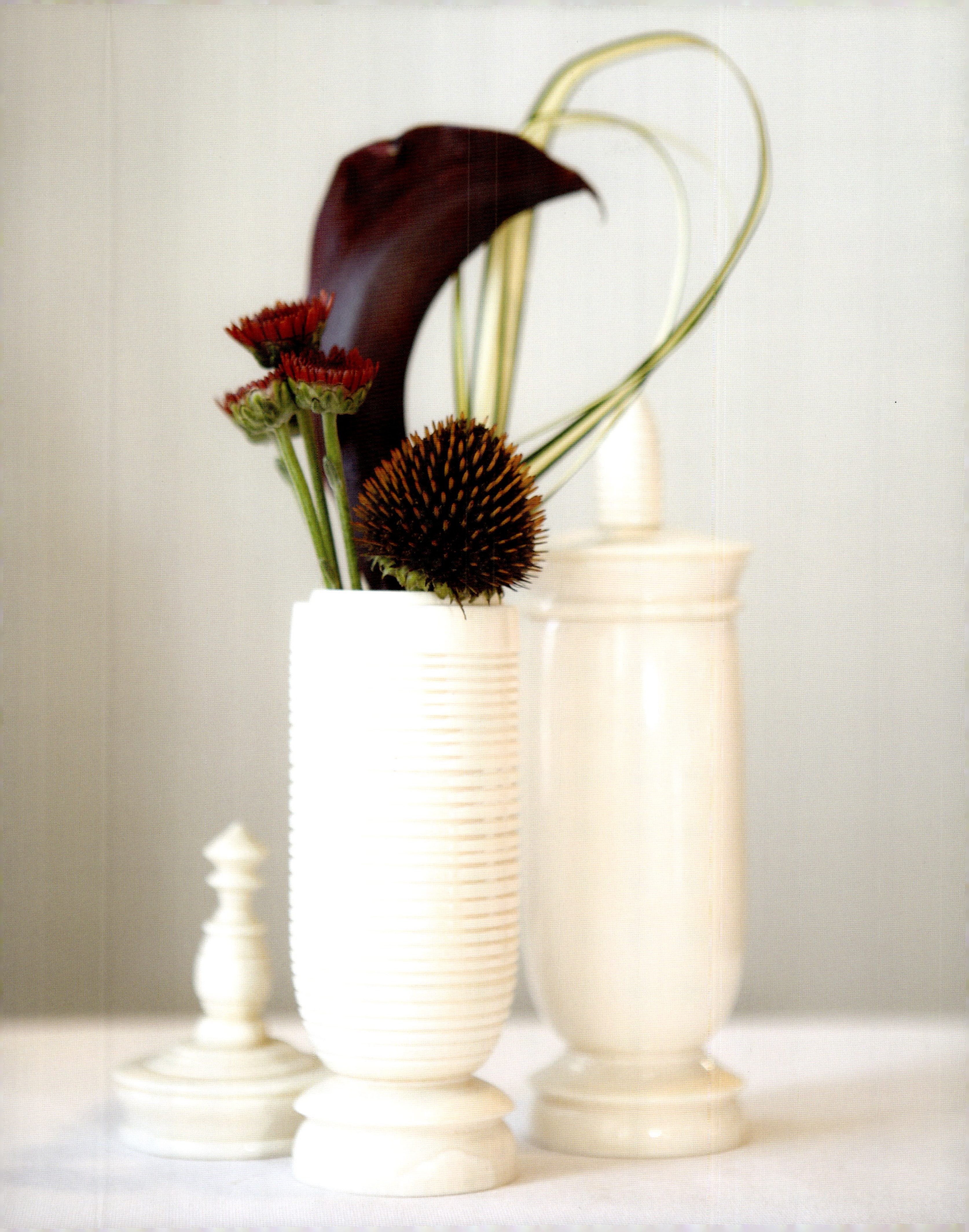

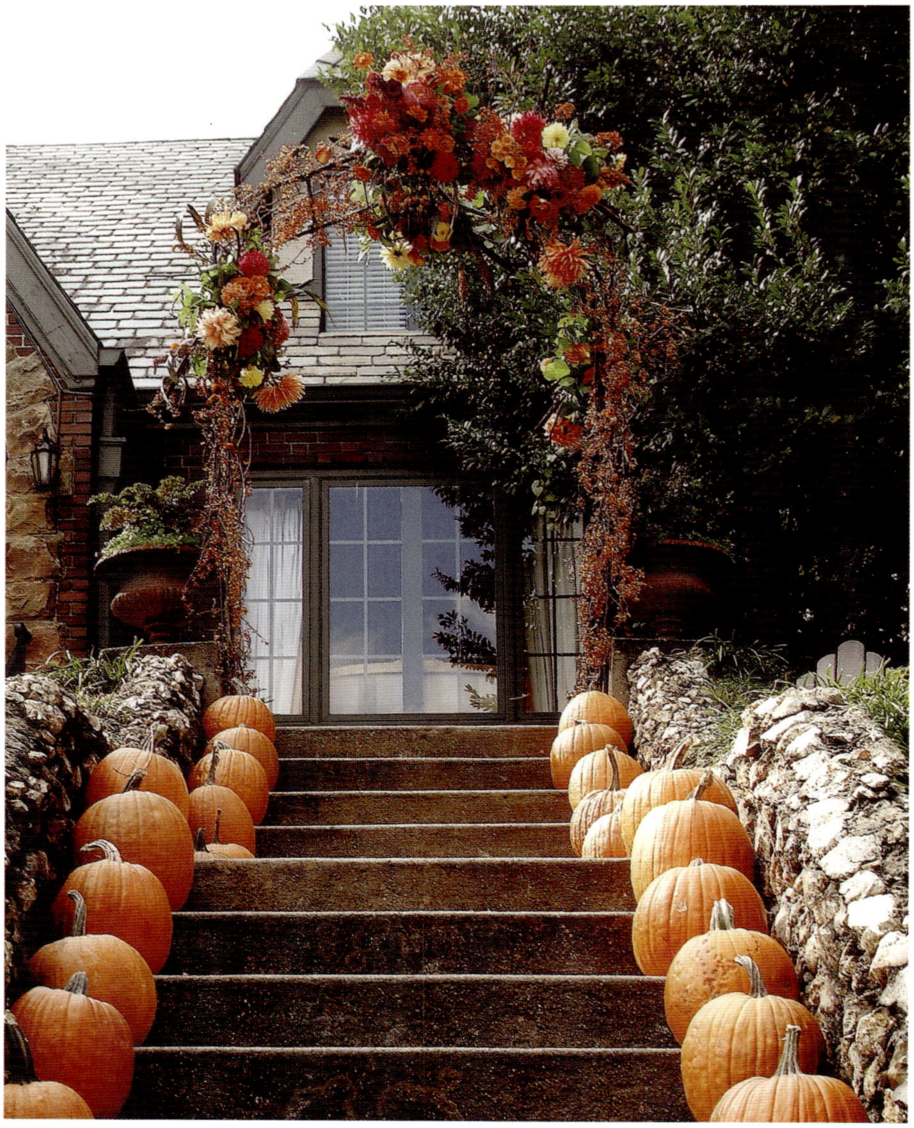

above: This fall flower arch got its spectacular start with a truckbed full of pumpkins I bought at our farmer's market. Stairstepping their way up the front walk, the pumpkins lead to a dahlia, mum, greenery, and vine arch that heralds a autumn harvest wine and cheese dinner. When we do things up in Birmingham, we do things right! *right*: When using herbs, always strip the bottom portion of each stem. They are tiny and can be flimsy, so I separate them into similar bundles that I tie off with raffia. Treating each bundle as if it were an individual flower, I combine them to form a nosegay. Although the preparation takes more time than the actual making of the bouquet, the end result is worth the effort.

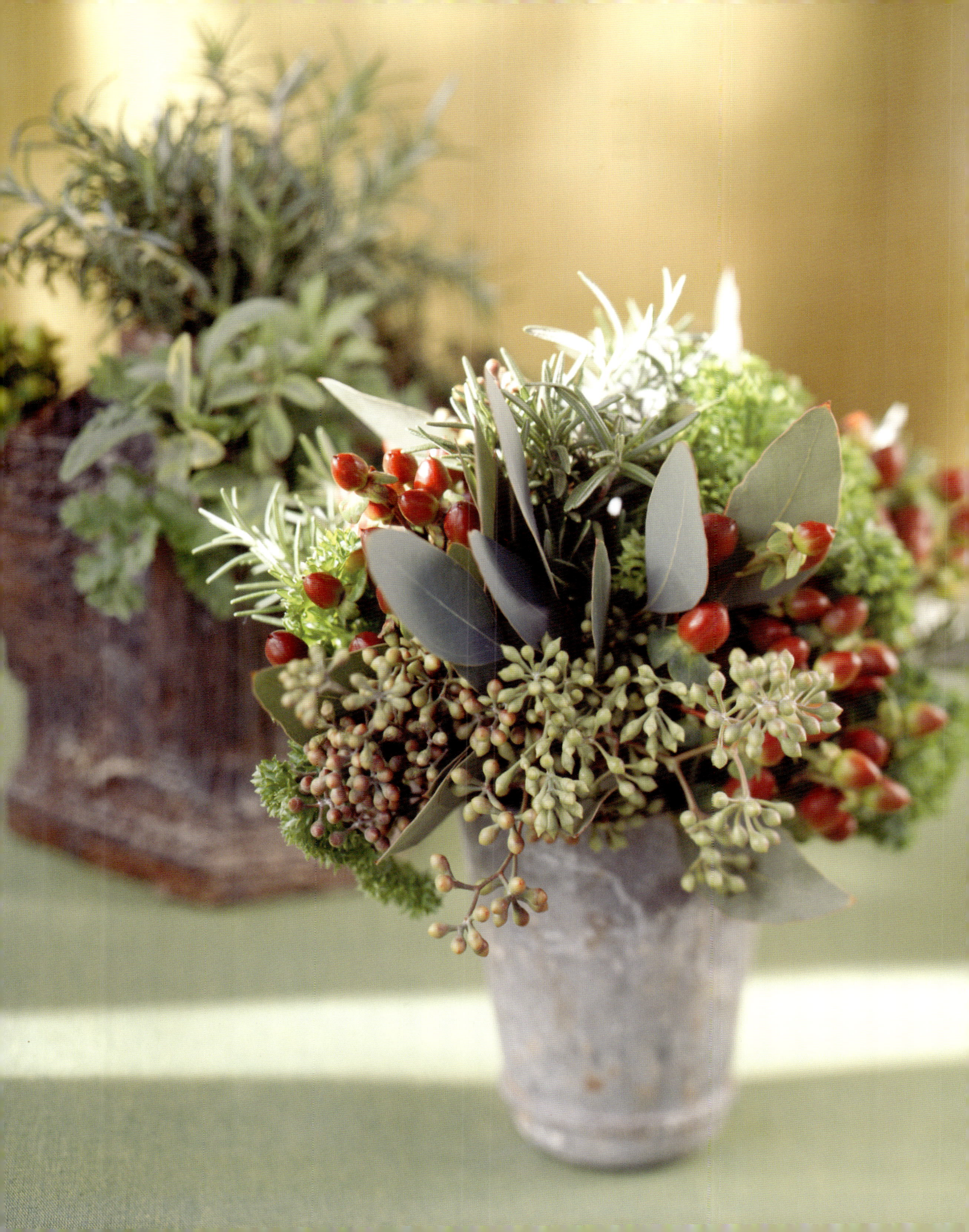

winter

Winter doesn't really take hold in Alabama until after the New Year—except for rare occasions, such as a snowy Christmas morning a few years past. During the holidays, we put bulbs in the garden and wait for the first sign of spring's approach. The last few years my prolific French blue hydrangeas have been nipped by a late frost. My fingers are crossed and double crossed that they will bloom next summer. In the mean time, sculptural branches, evergreen foliage, bold berries, and forced bulbs bring color and life to the cold winter months. They lay the ground work for spring and animate stark surfaces, reminding us that the earth provides no matter the season.

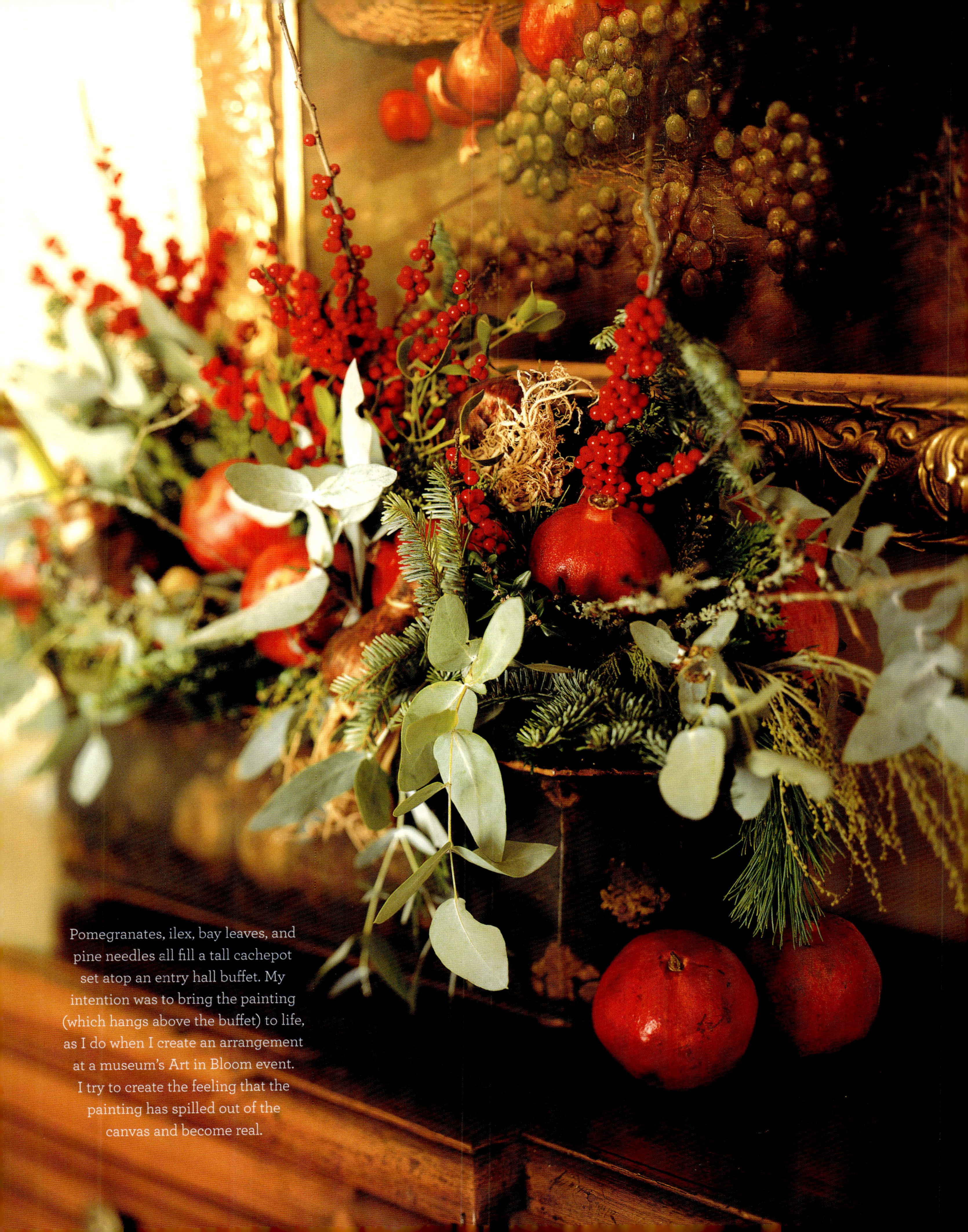

Pomegranates, ilex, bay leaves, and pine needles all fill a tall cachepot set atop an entry hall buffet. My intention was to bring the painting (which hangs above the buffet) to life, as I do when I create an arrangement at a museum's Art in Bloom event. I try to create the feeling that the painting has spilled out of the canvas and become real.

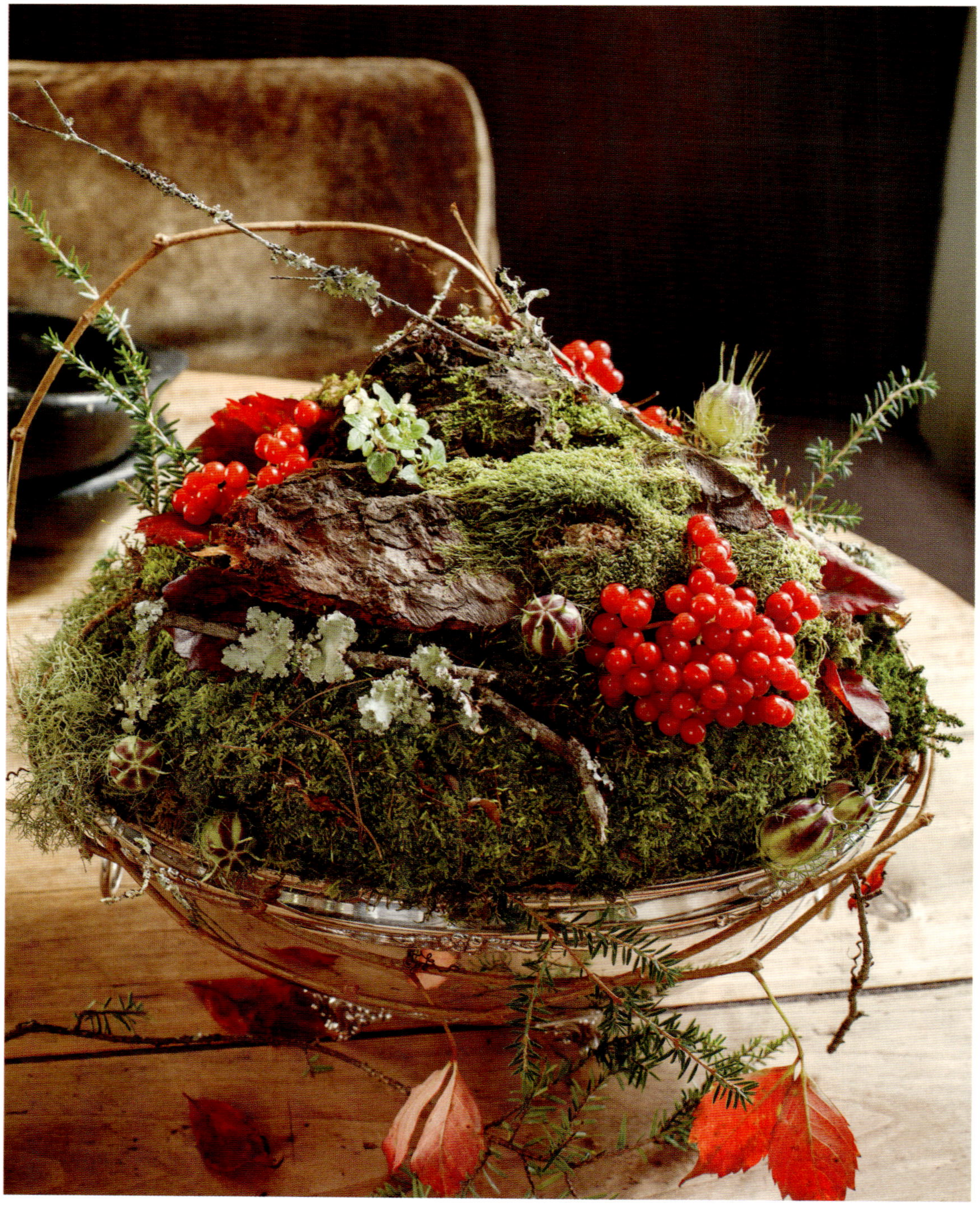

above: A moss-encrusted piece of bark that I discovered on a hike in North Carolina was the starting point for this arrangement. I foraged a few clusters of lichen-covered branches then added gloriosa lilies and more foraged materials to the silver tureen. *right:* I created this woven container from rose stems, vines, and branches. Then I added the Harry Lauder's walking stick – which are the twisted and gnarled wooden pieces. It's bound together like a four-layer tikki raft and stuffed between the layers with mosses and lichen. I used clear test tubes to hold flowers in place. The snow effect comes from cotton boles.

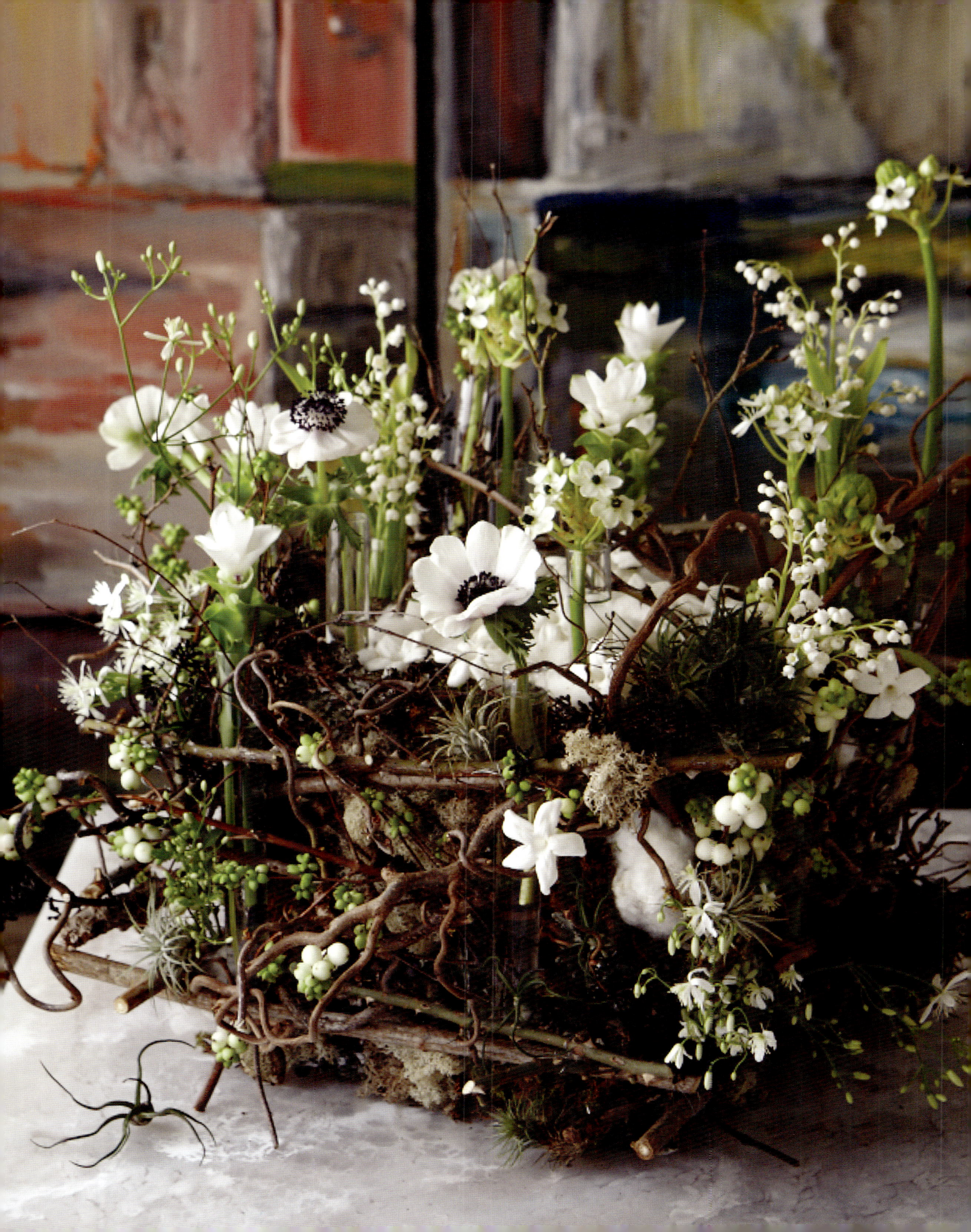

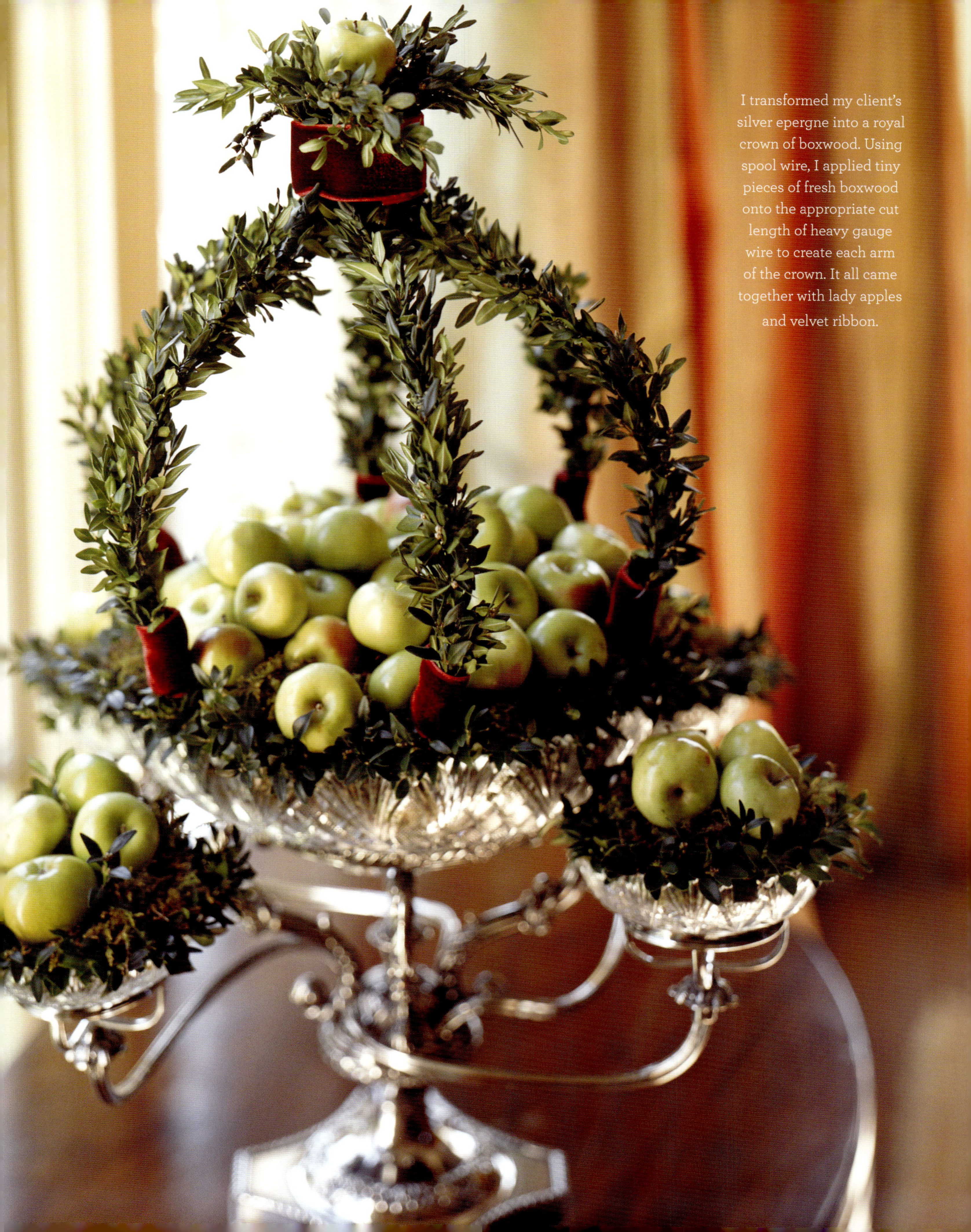

I transformed my client's silver epergne into a royal crown of boxwood. Using spool wire, I applied tiny pieces of fresh boxwood onto the appropriate cut length of heavy gauge wire to create each arm of the crown. It all came together with lady apples and velvet ribbon.

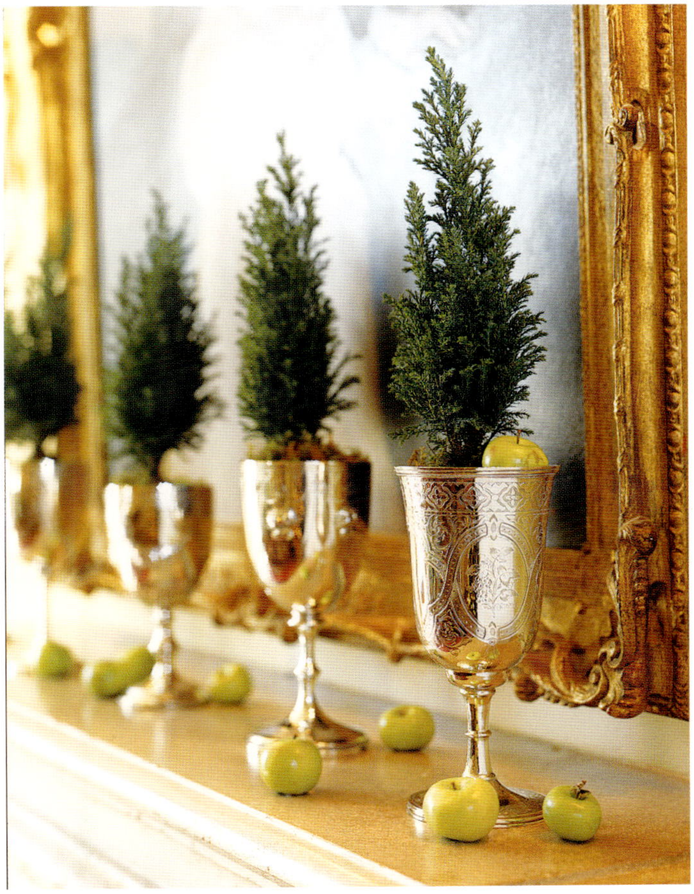

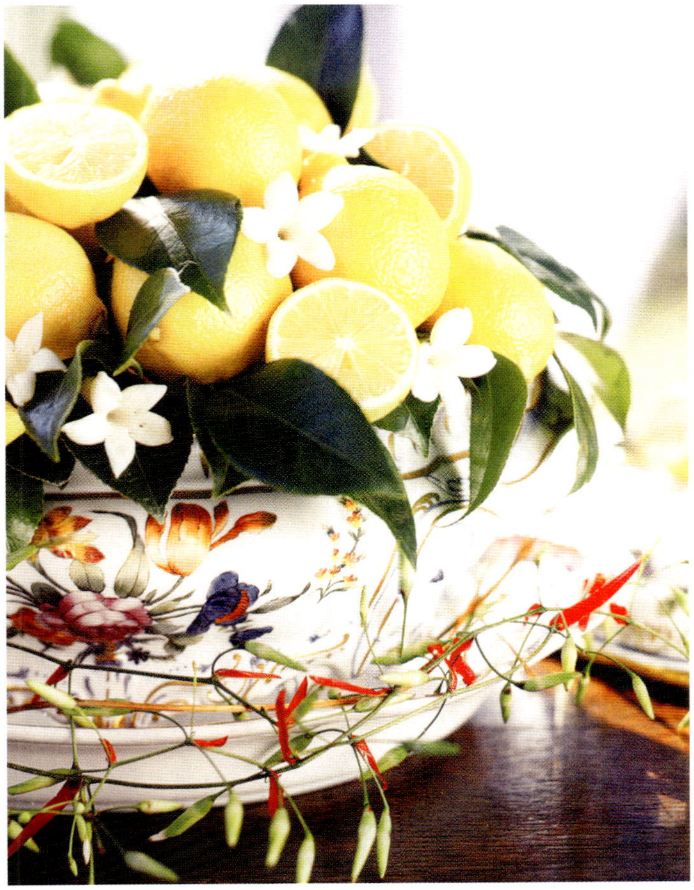

above: I planted a collection of silver goblets with miniature cedar trees to place along a dining room mantle. It lasted through the holidays because we remembered to give them a little water from time to time.
right: The Herend soup tureen has a porcelain lemon lid, which inspired the choice to use actual lemons in the arrangement, perfect for a winter seated ladies' luncheon because it is refreshing and low, promoting easy conversation. The jasmine and firecracker vines helped the tureen's decoration extend to the table.

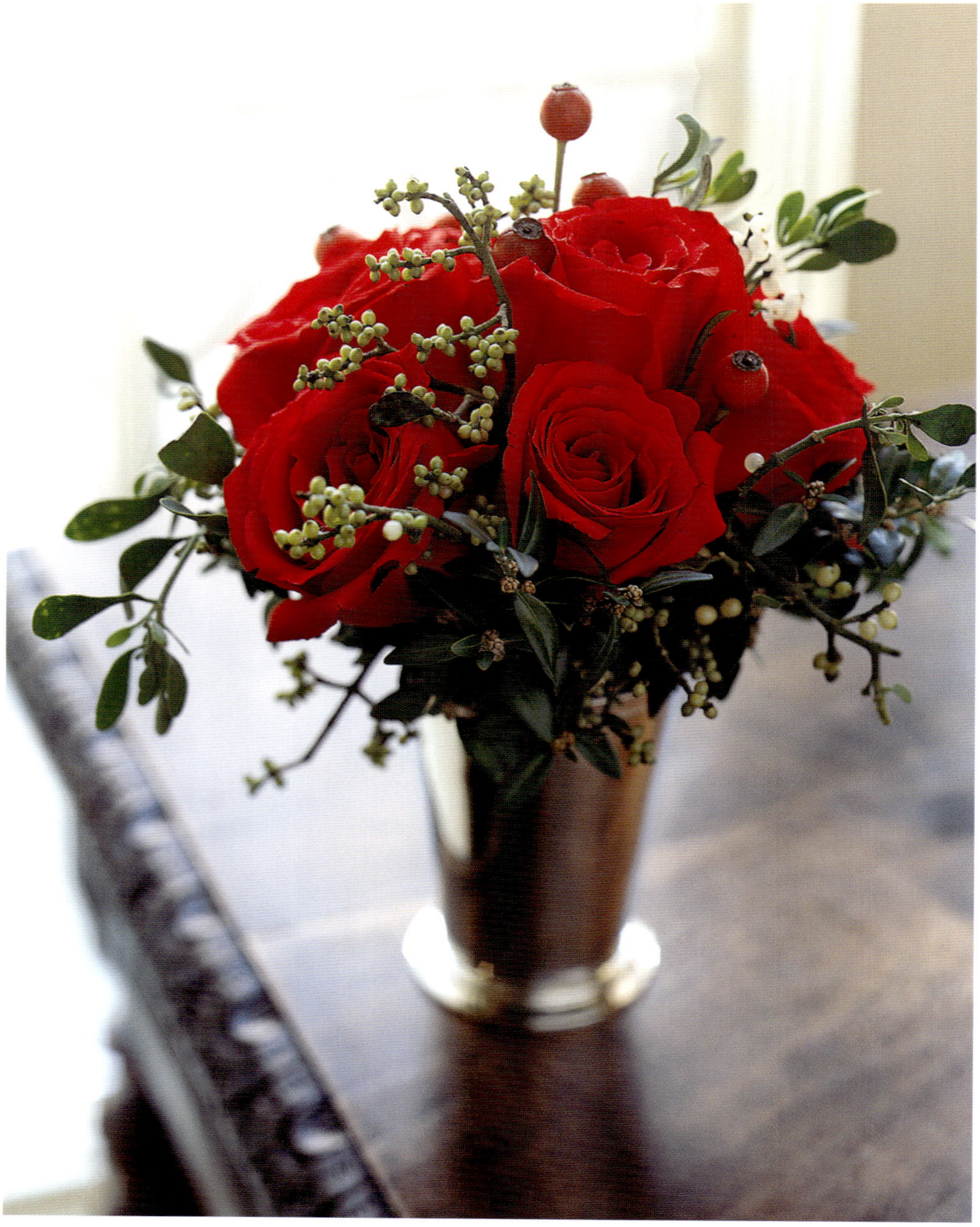

above: A sweet cluster of roses, boxwood, rosehips, and mistletoe berries in a mint julep cup does double duty. It holds the mint julep in May and flowers the rest of the year. *right*: I massed a collection of mercury glass vases atop a buffet and then pulled out all the red and green stops—with pine and nandina branches, magnolia leaves, ranunculus blossoms, and ribbons. It was not a complicated composition, but it's an effective winter arrangement that will last for several weeks.

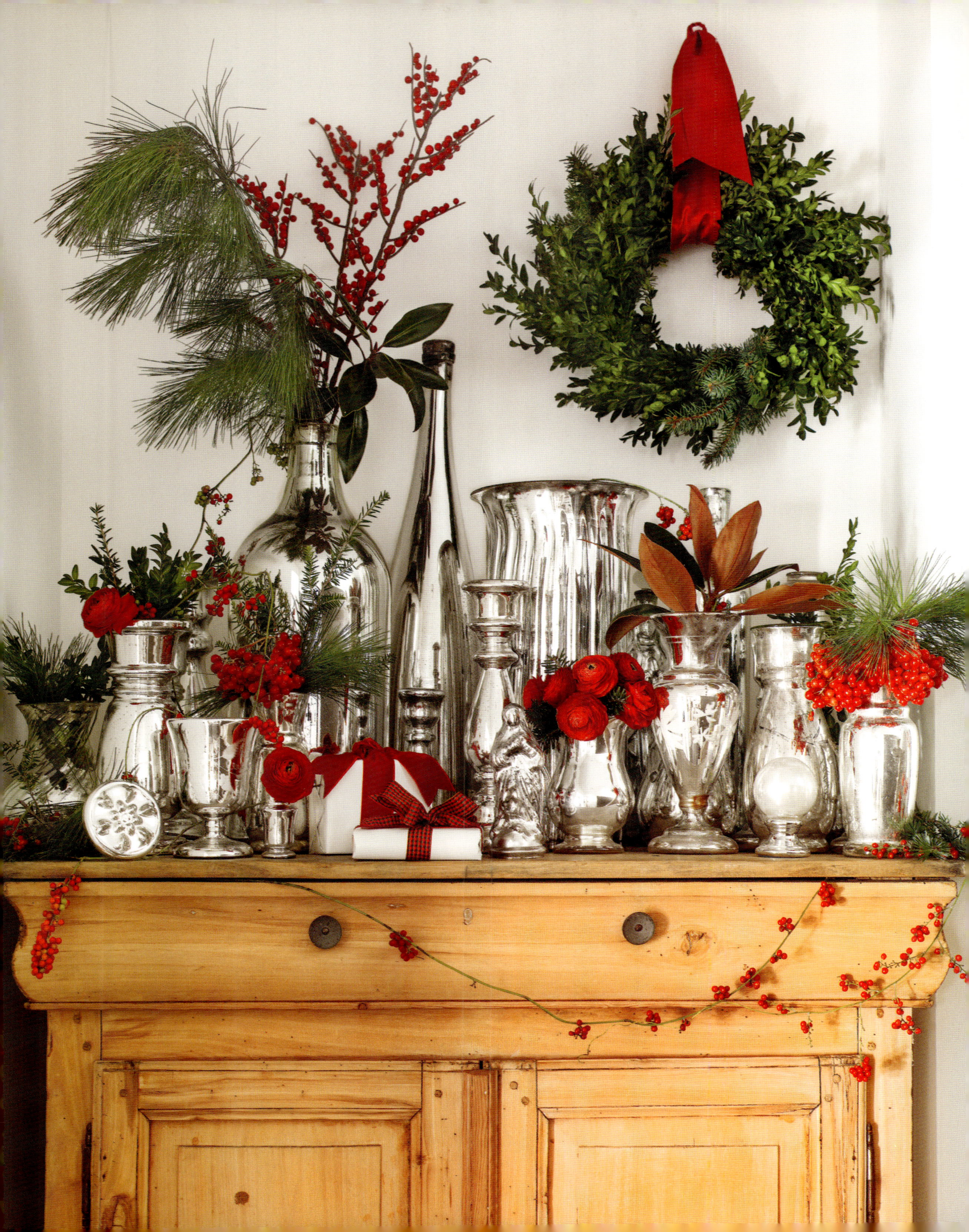

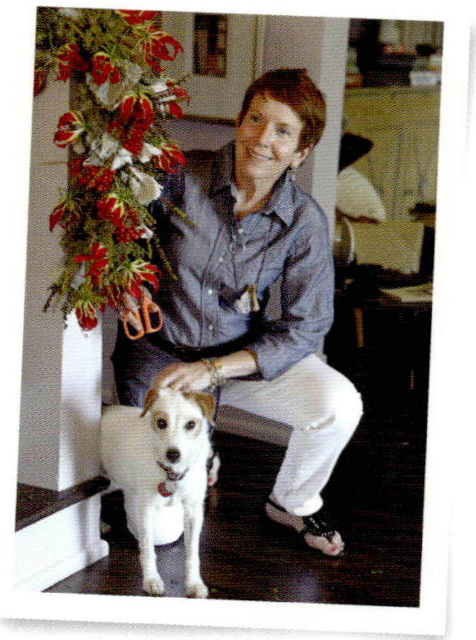

The traditional side of me comes out during the holiday season, and I love the use of reds and greens. But sometimes a room's design is more suited to alternate color combinations.

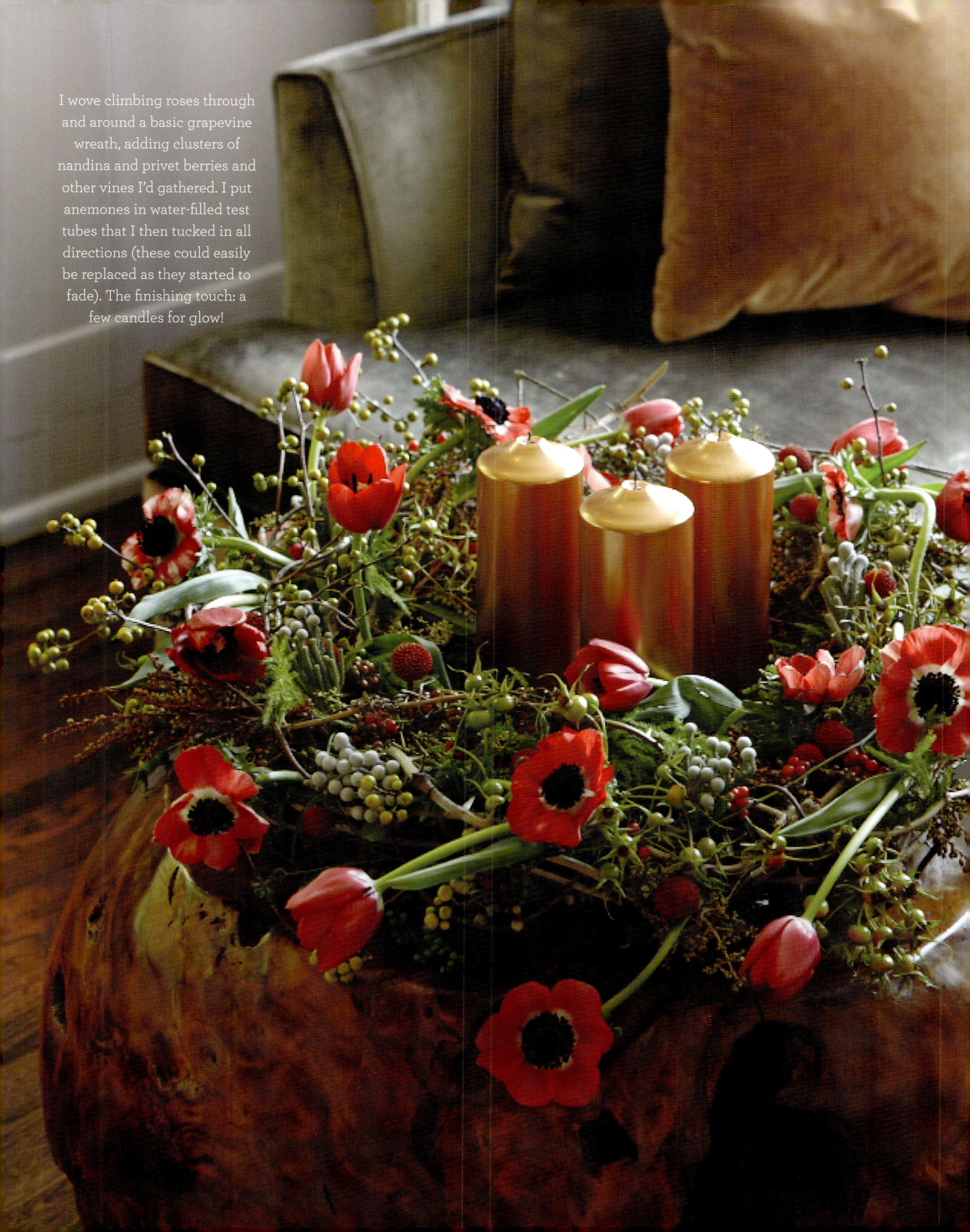

I wove climbing roses through and around a basic grapevine wreath, adding clusters of nandina and privet berries and other vines I'd gathered. I put anemones in water-filled test tubes that I then tucked in all directions (these could easily be replaced as they started to fade). The finishing touch: a few candles for glow!

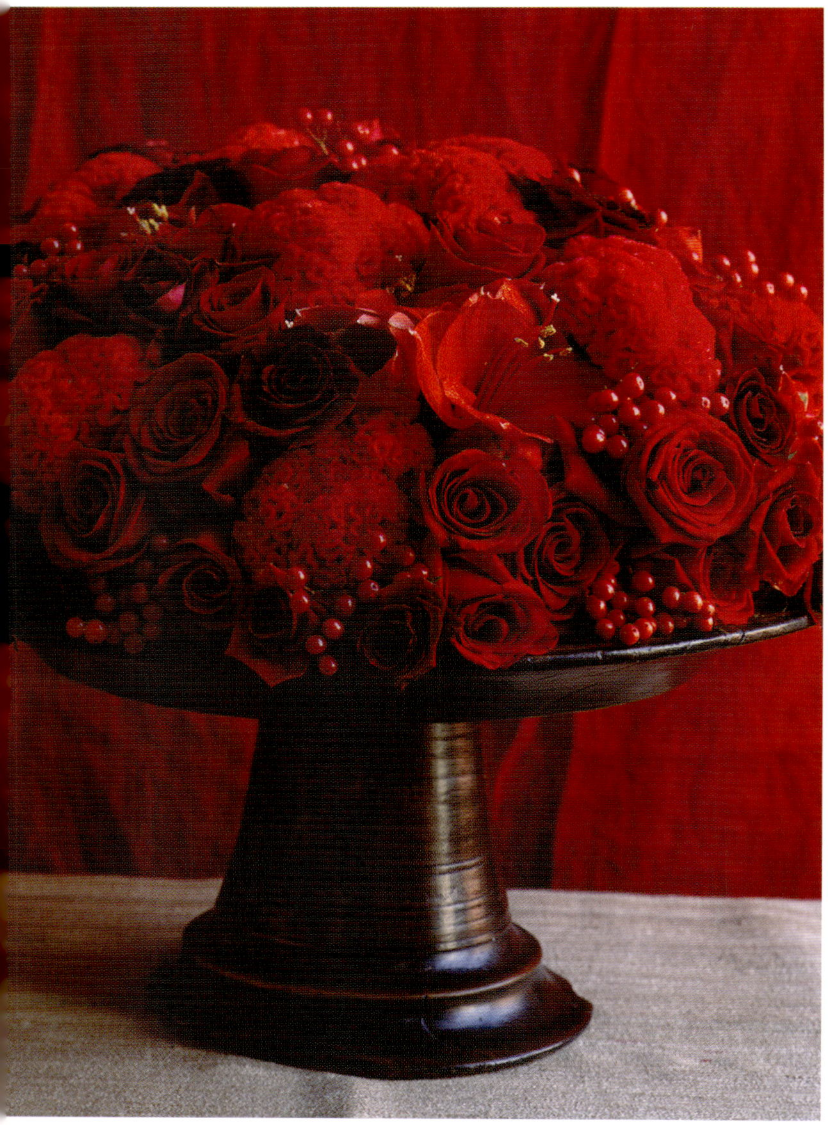

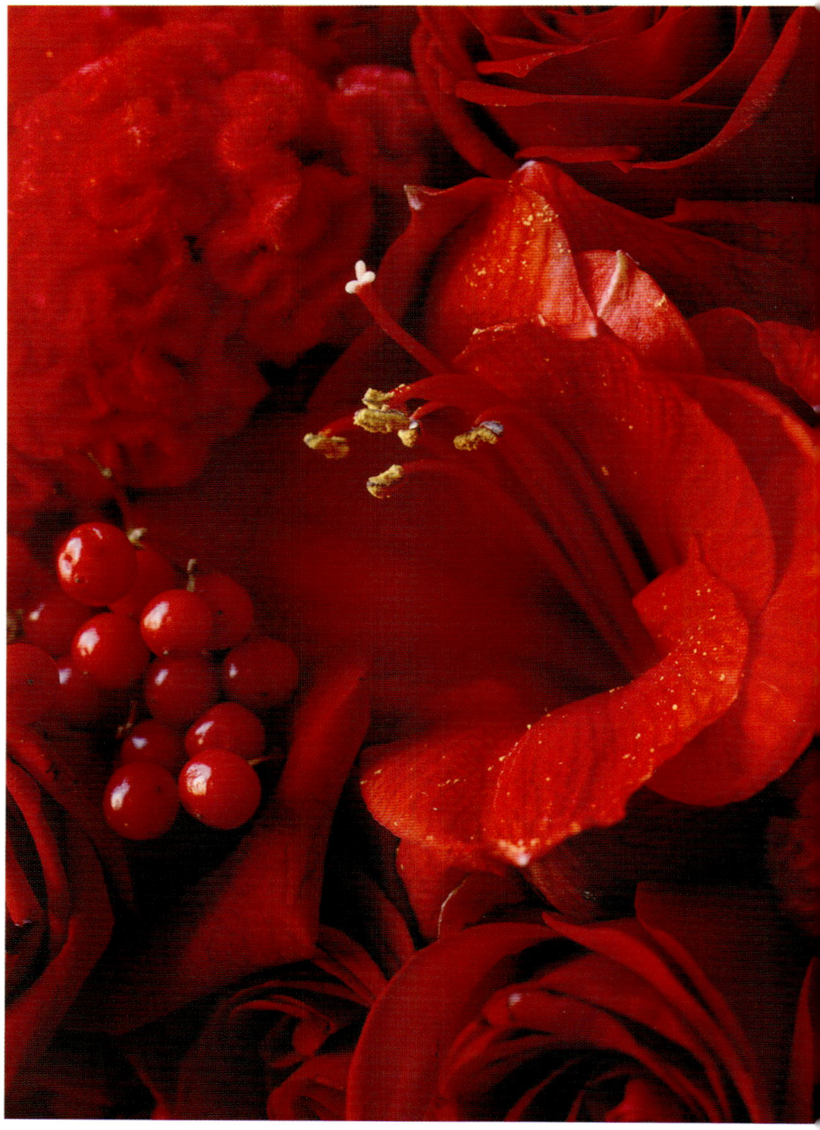

What does it say about me that I went through a 15-year stage—actually I think I may still be in it—where red is my favorite color? Put an assortment of red flowers in my hand, and look out, you'll get something like this—dramatic and strong, pungent and really beautiful. At the center of a table or on a sideboard, the red arrangement, with its decadent approach to cake, subverts the expected dessert presentation.

all about the baroque

IN THE COLDER MONTHS, WHEN WE YEARN FOR COLOR AND NEW GROWTH, IT'S ENORMOUSLY SATISFYING TO BRING TOGETHER FLOWERS AND FRUIT AND CREATE A LUSH BALANCE THAT TIPS THE DRAMATIC SCALES.

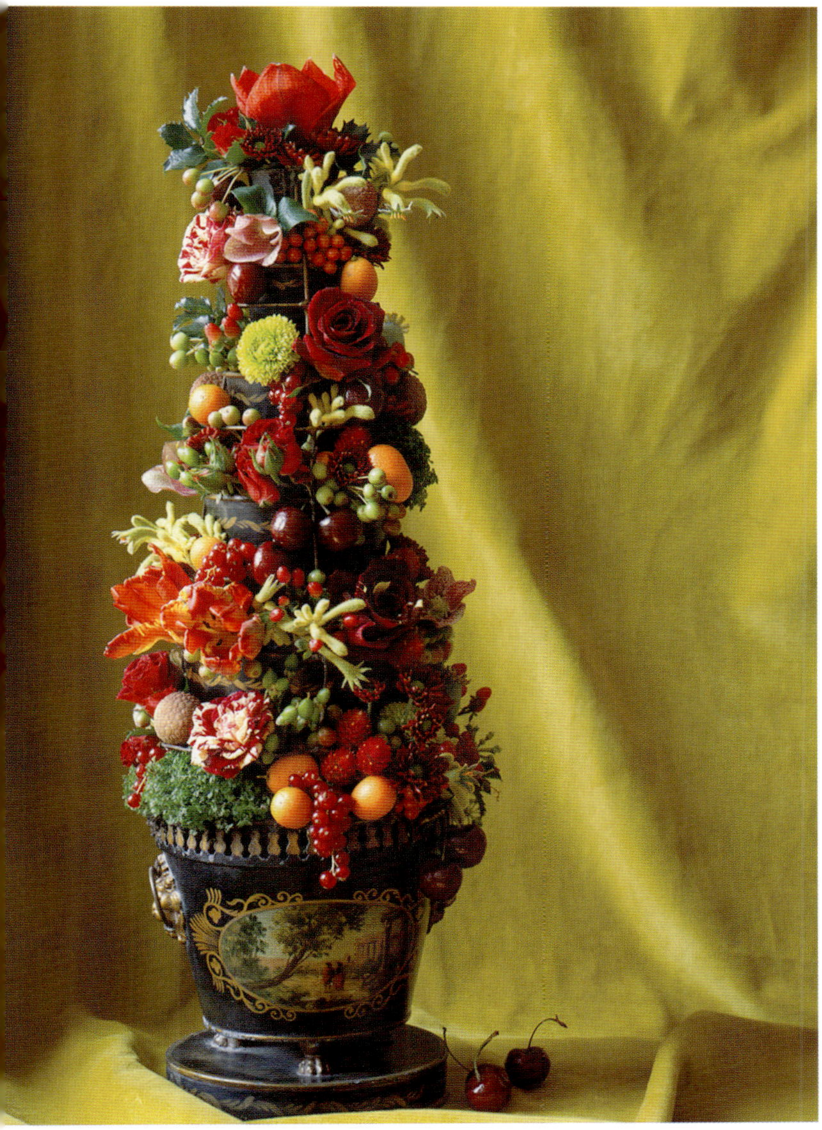

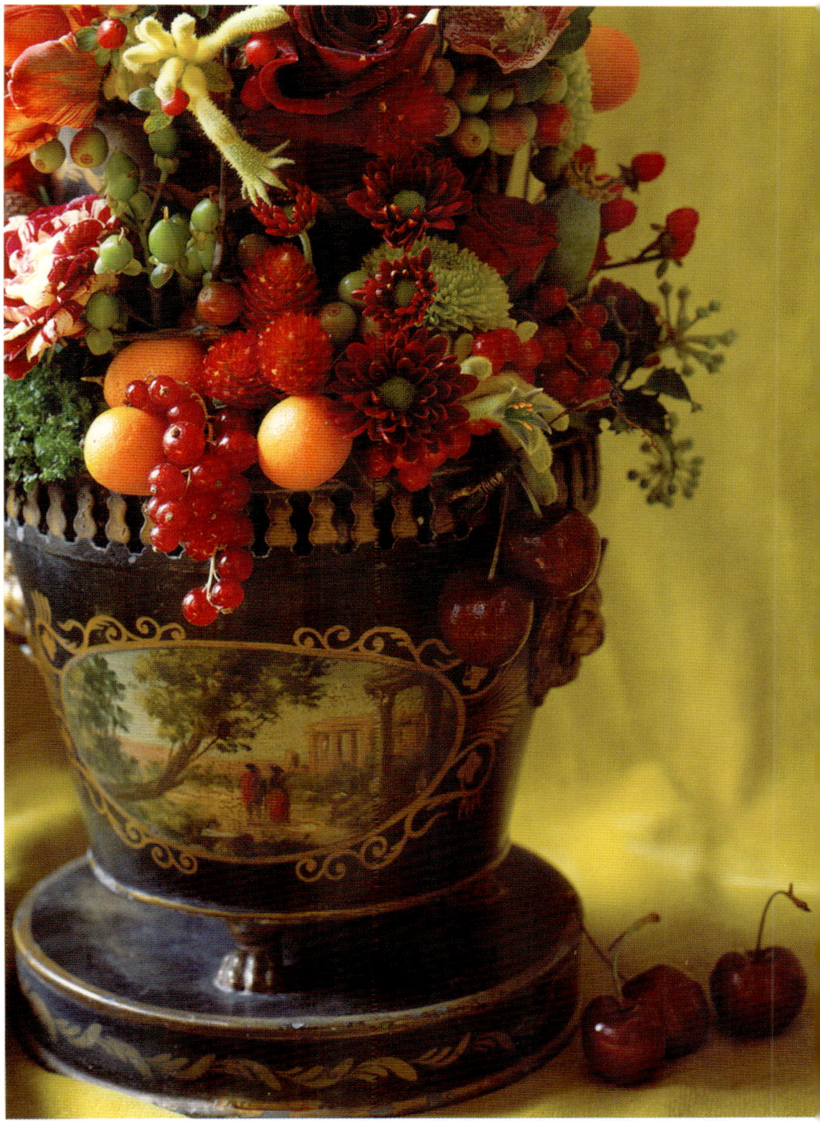

Starting with what has to be my all-time favorite container—I love the traditional scene painted on the simple pot—I assembled a whole collection of tiny fruits and small buds with various berries, all tucked into the tiers that would be elegant on a sideboard or console. I added lighter flowers and berries to the topiary at higher heights, being careful to only partially obscure the container because it's unique decoration is part of what makes the arrangement special.

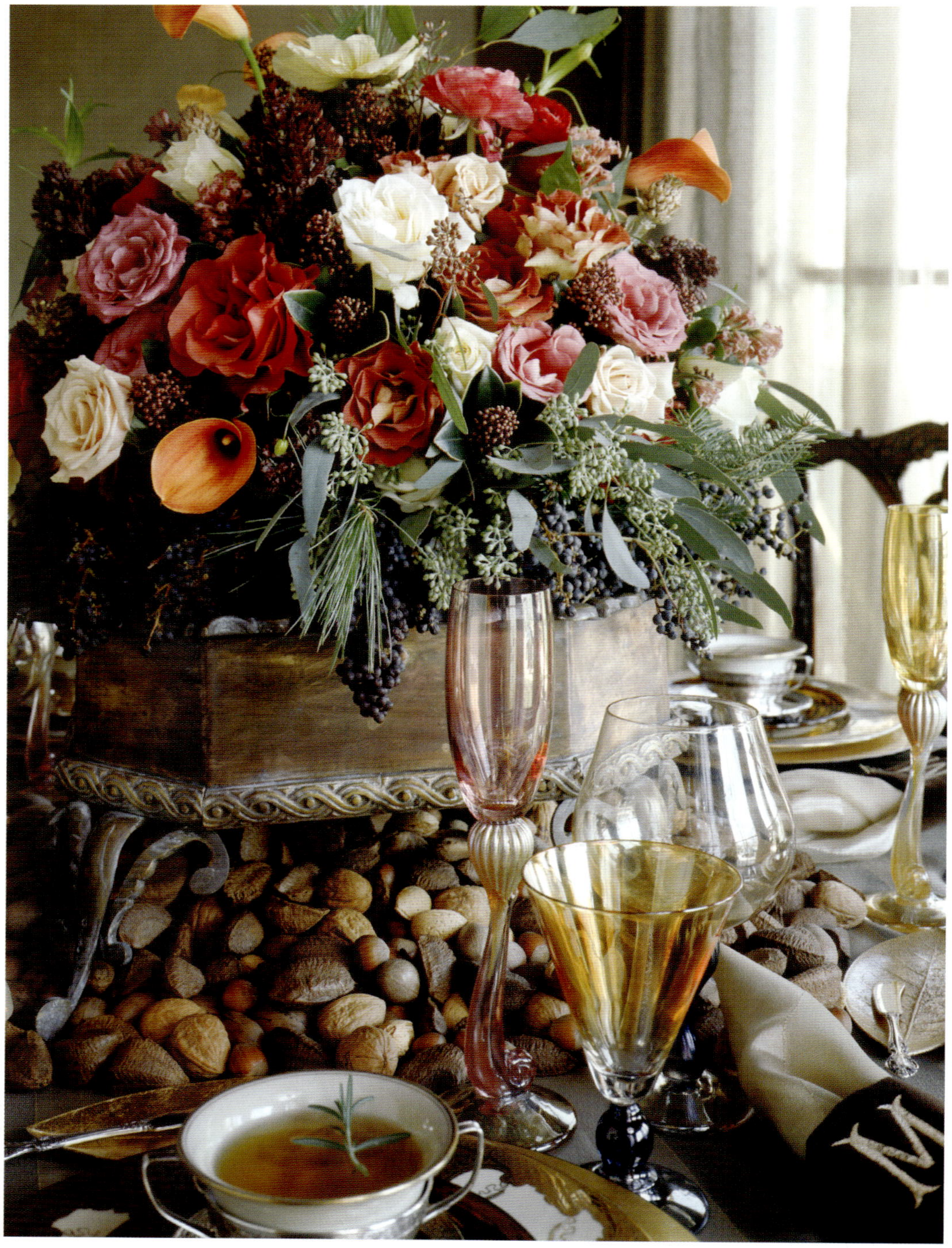

above: To fill the void between the feet of the antique copper container and the tabletop, I gathered nuts underneath. The nuts were another element of the arrangement that could work for any occasion, from pre-Thanksgiving to New Year's Eve. *right:* A testament to the fact that you can find elements for a great centerpiece right outside your front door. I placed mercury glass ornaments and a few greenery balls into the arrangement in lieu of fresh flowers. I love the back side of the Little Gem magnolia leaves that bring out the warm wood tones of the tabletop.

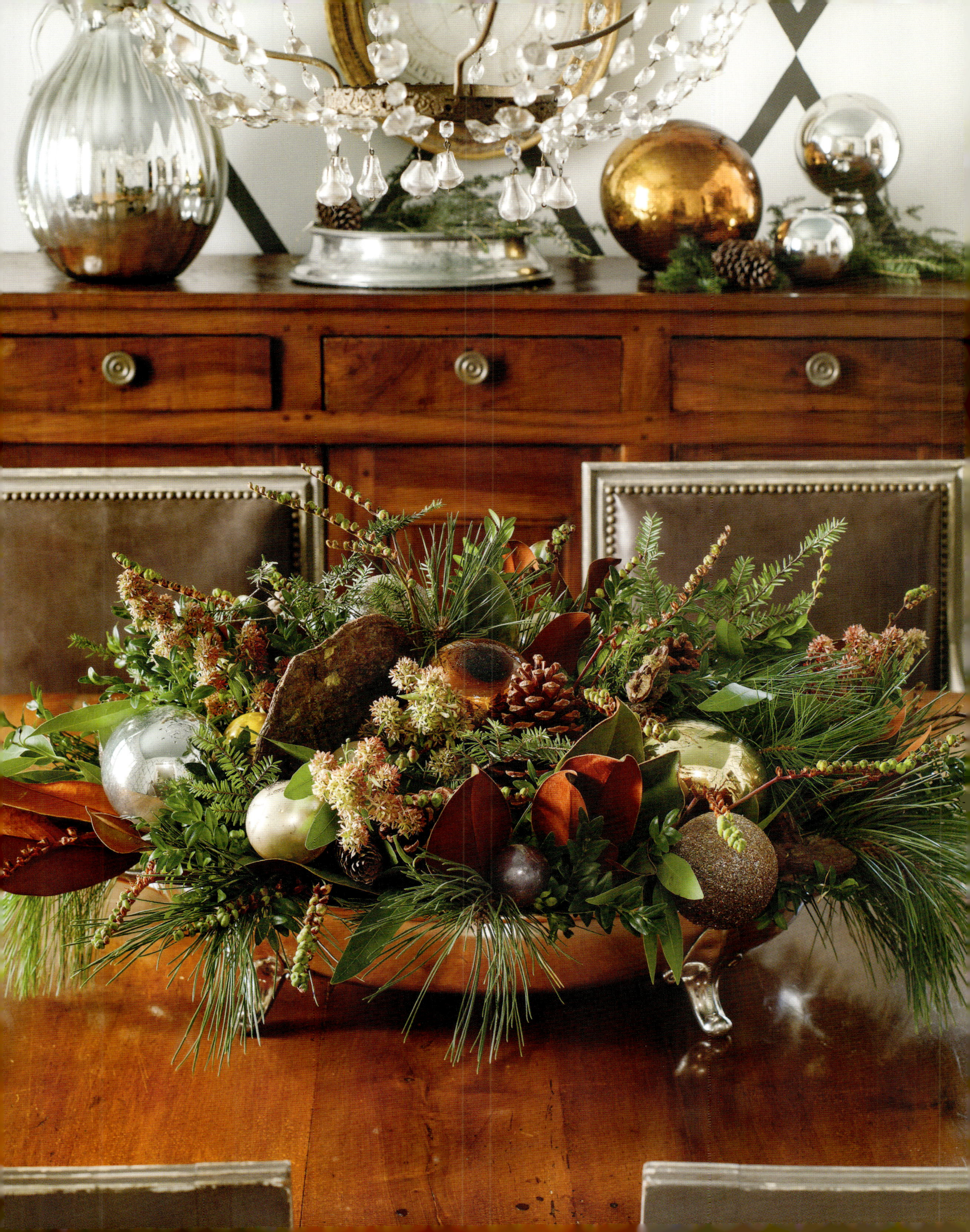

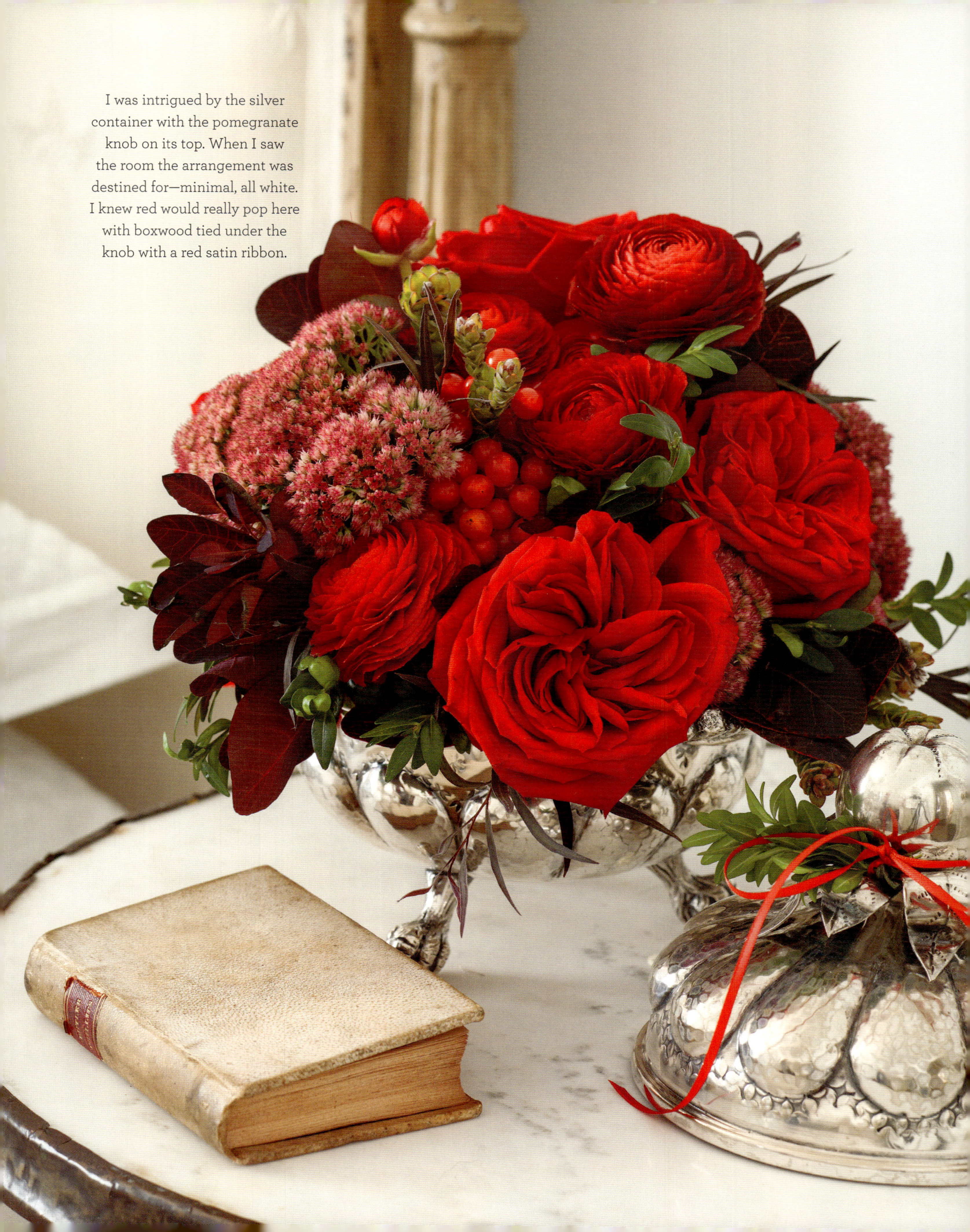

I was intrigued by the silver container with the pomegranate knob on its top. When I saw the room the arrangement was destined for—minimal, all white. I knew red would really pop here with boxwood tied under the knob with a red satin ribbon.

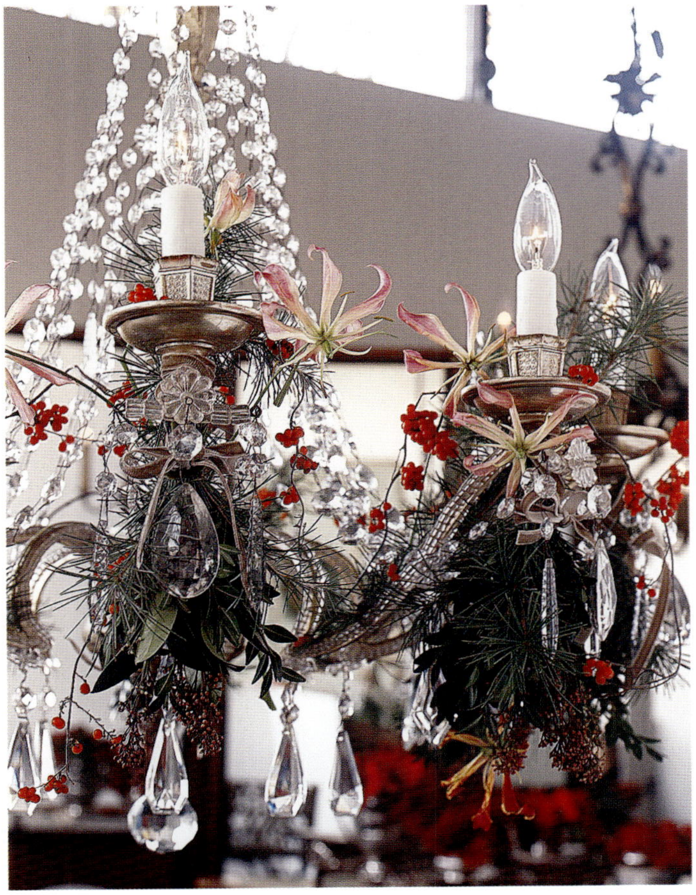

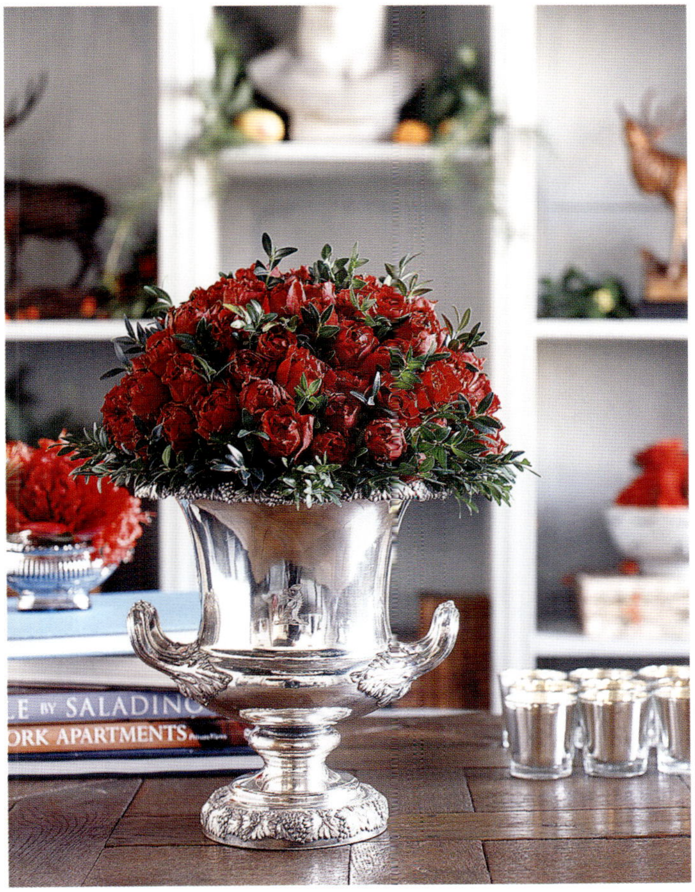

above: I created greenery tassels and tied the bundles to the chandelier arms with velvet ribbons. Then I twirled wild red berry throughout. Lastly, I tucked long-stemmed gloriosa lily in test tubes and hid the glass in the greenery. It looks so right on the chandelier arms that, once we took it down, the chandelier looked a little naked. *right:* A holiday run for the roses in this arrangement. I filled an antique silver wine cooler wth red roses and tulips, then tucked in sprigs of boxwood. This is one of those arrangements where I could use oasis, but I used chicken wire instead, and the effect is just as magical.

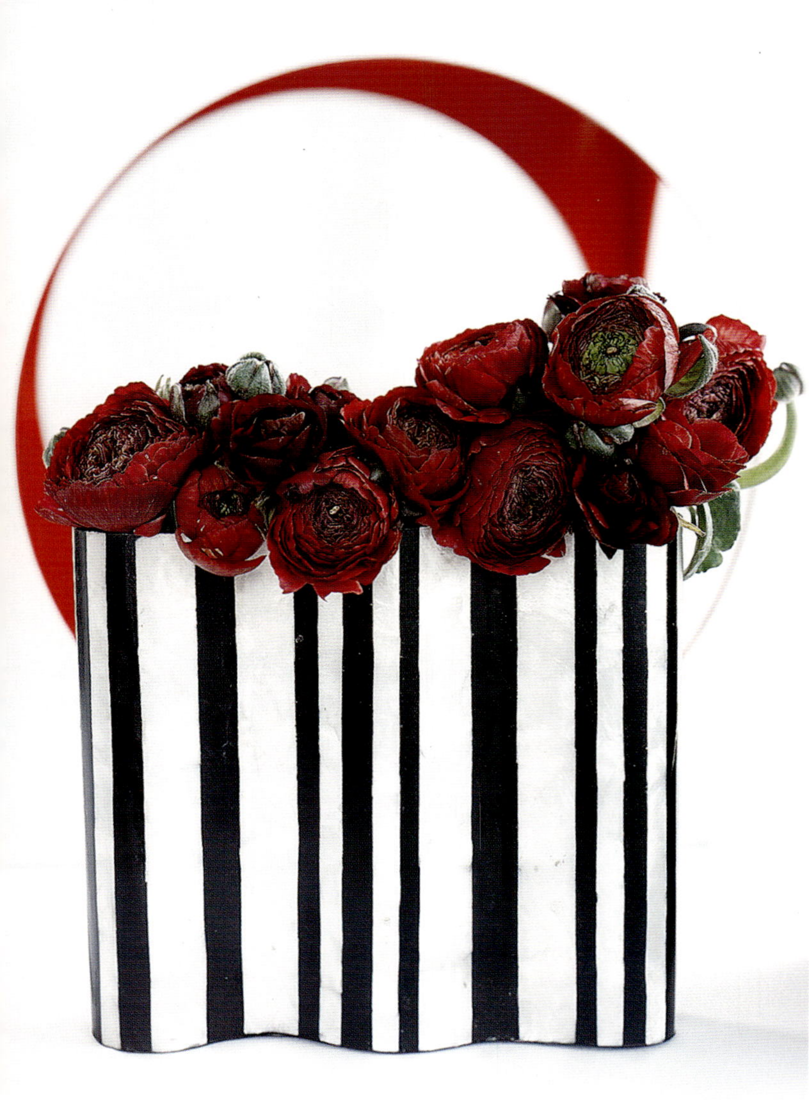

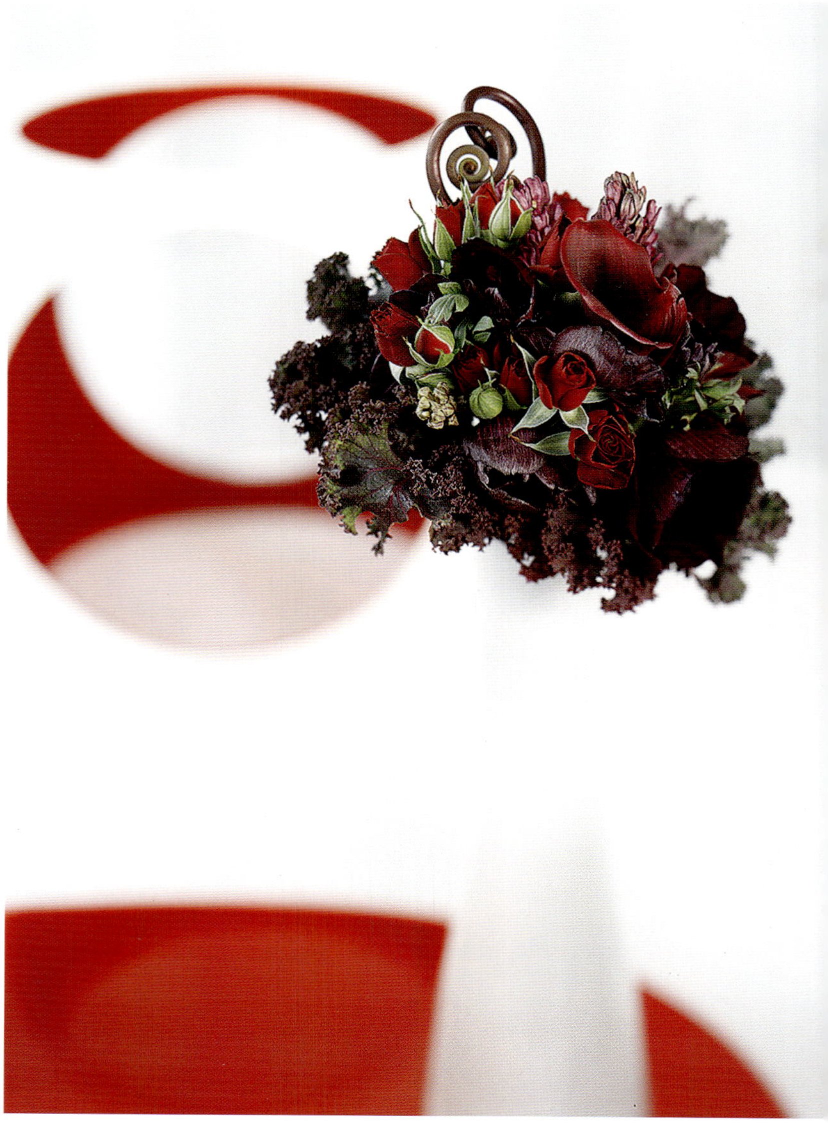

Dark flowers could become a black mass without some contrast, be they leaves or blossoms with green centers, in this case. It's a graphic package—black and white container with dark flowers, and it makes for a dramatic and original arrangement.

I created a nosegay with kale leaves at the base and then clustered the callas and roses in the center. I wired the fiddlehead ferns to face each other and make a heart—a nice Valentine's Day touch.

a flair for drama

THERE ARE VERY FEW TRULY BLACK FLOWERS; THERE SEEM TO BE MORE VARIETIES OF DEEP, DARK BURGUNDY AND WINE AND PLUM SHADES COMING ON THE MARKET. THE VERY FIRST FLOWER THAT I REMEMBER SEEING THAT WAS SO DARK IT STRUCK ME AS BLACK WAS A MINI CALLA LILY "SHWARZWALDER." THEY CONVEY SOPHISTICATION AND DEPTH.

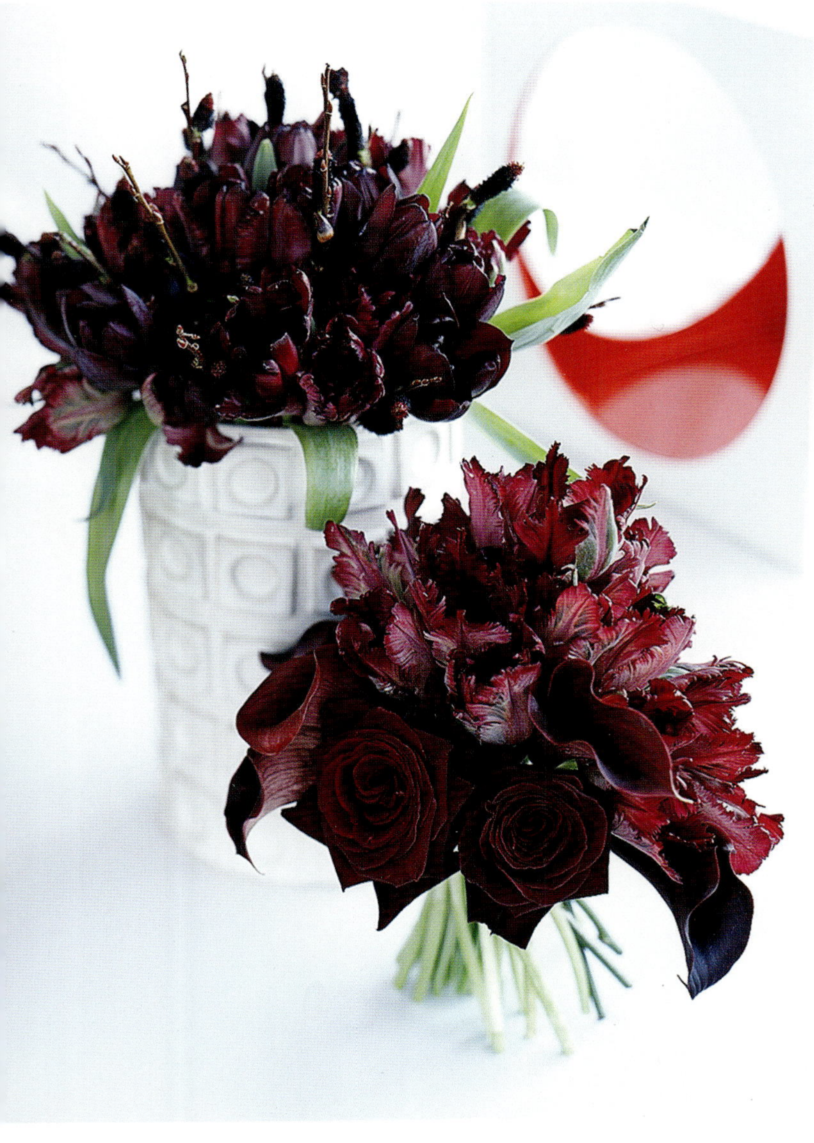

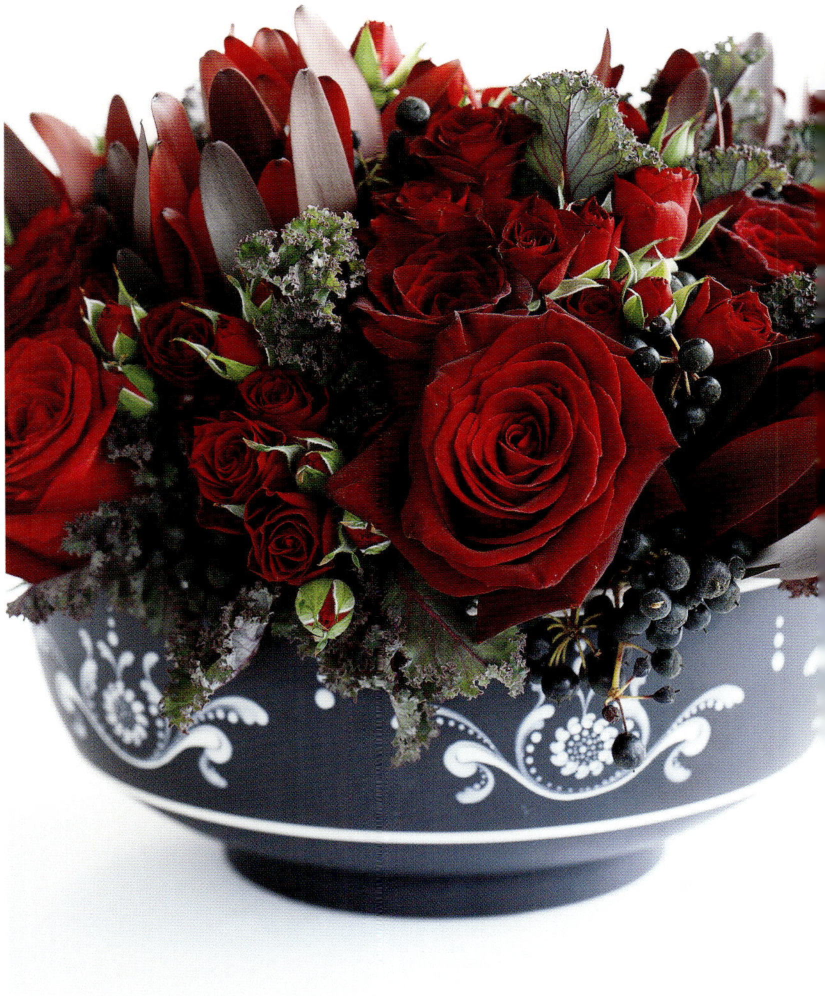

Ruffled petals and deep shades of red make me think of an intimate evening occasion. The colors seem designed to keep company with a glass of cabernet, but I think the addition of flowers with hints of green plays up the contrasts among the different blossoms.

Dark red and black berries underscore the richness of the black basalt bowl, taking a traditional palette and updating it with a fresh treatment and an unexpected combination of plants.

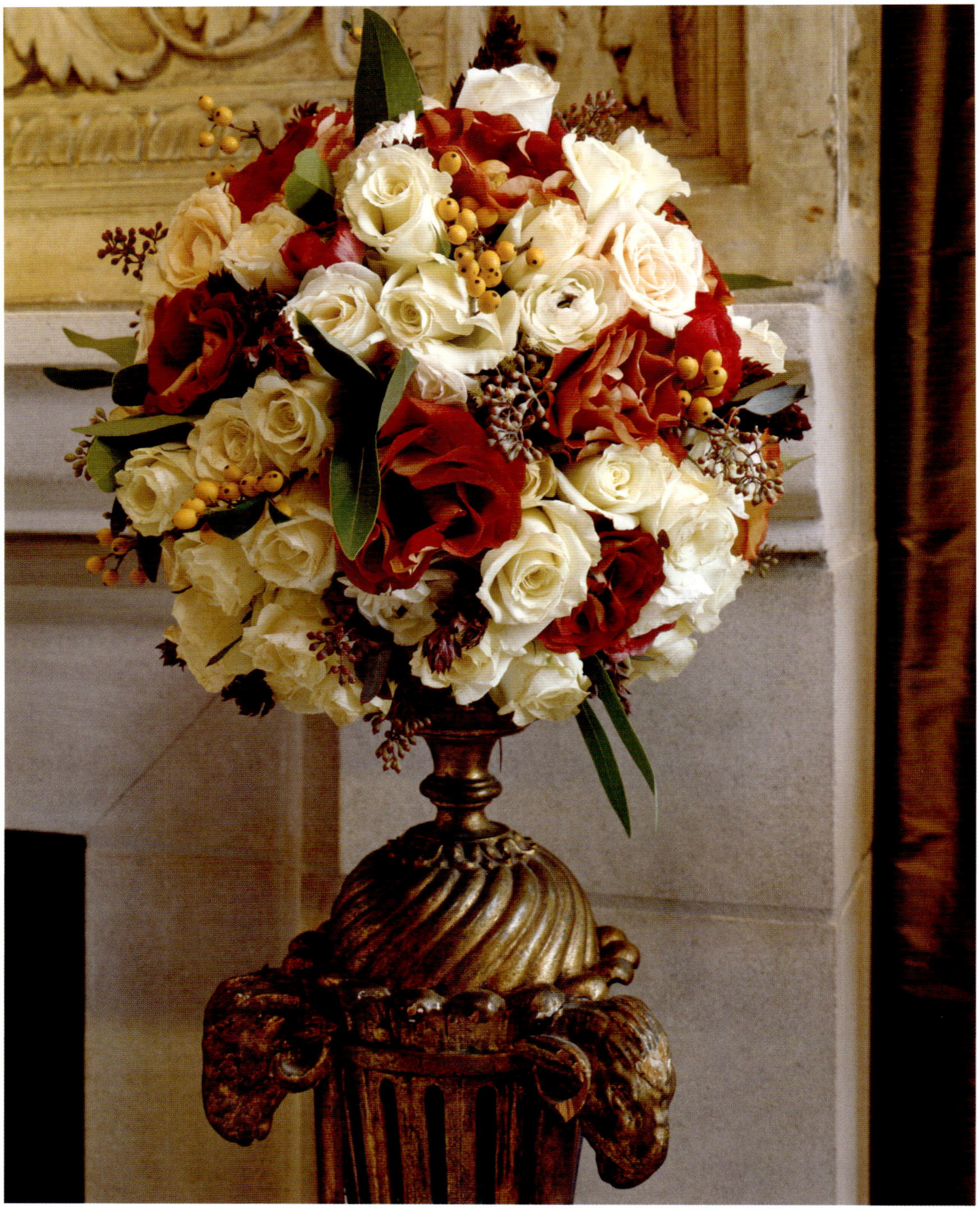

above: This is actually one of the very first flower spheres I ever made. I saw this lovely tall finial, and it begged me to add a top knob—so of course it had to be made up of fresh flowers. *right:* I chose a muted palette to complement the room's design and added greenery to the crown of the bust, a "Sybil" touch to watch overt the flowers that include terra-cotta and Sahara roses, chocolate cosmos, clematis vine turned into seedpods, and dried shelf mushrooms.

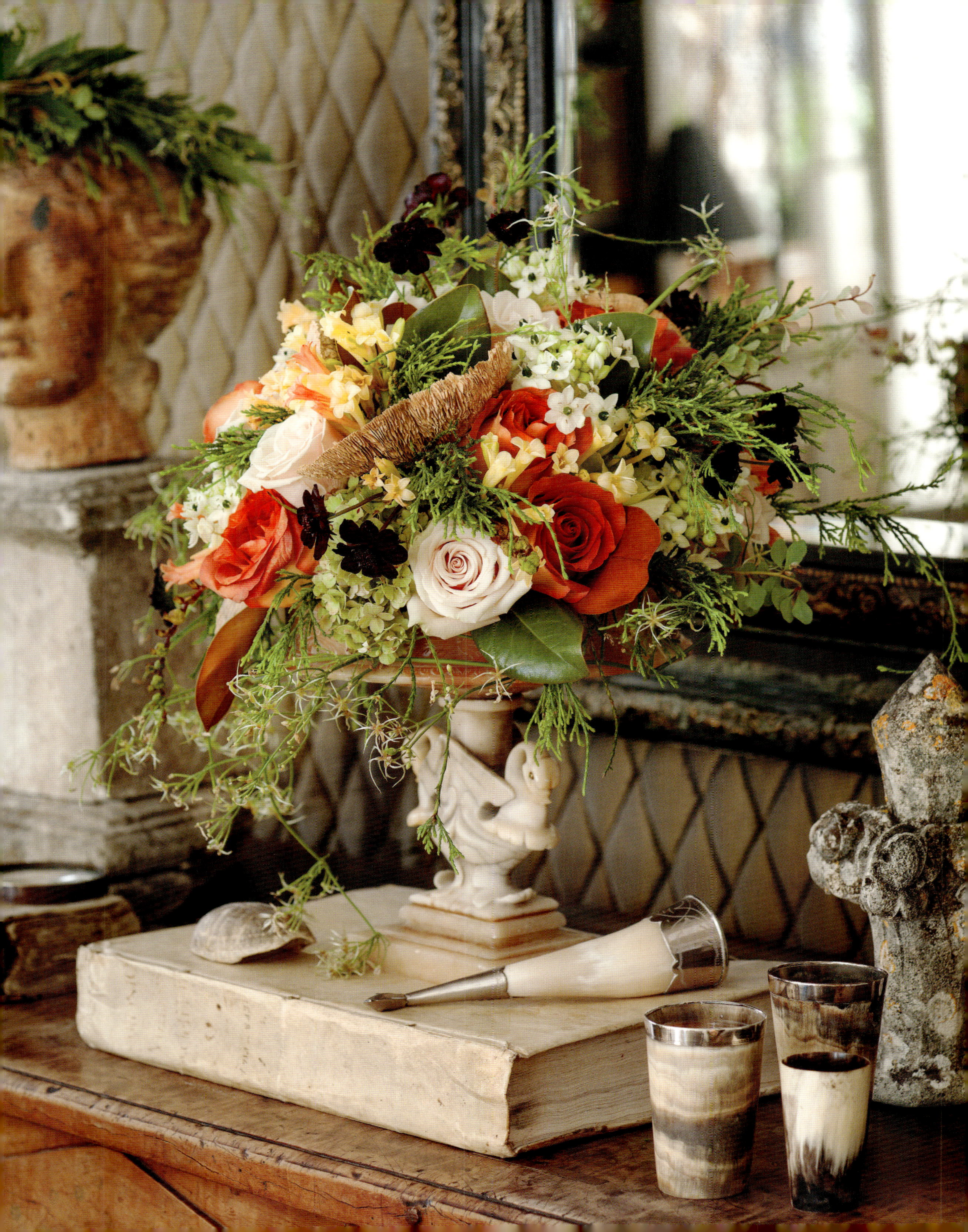

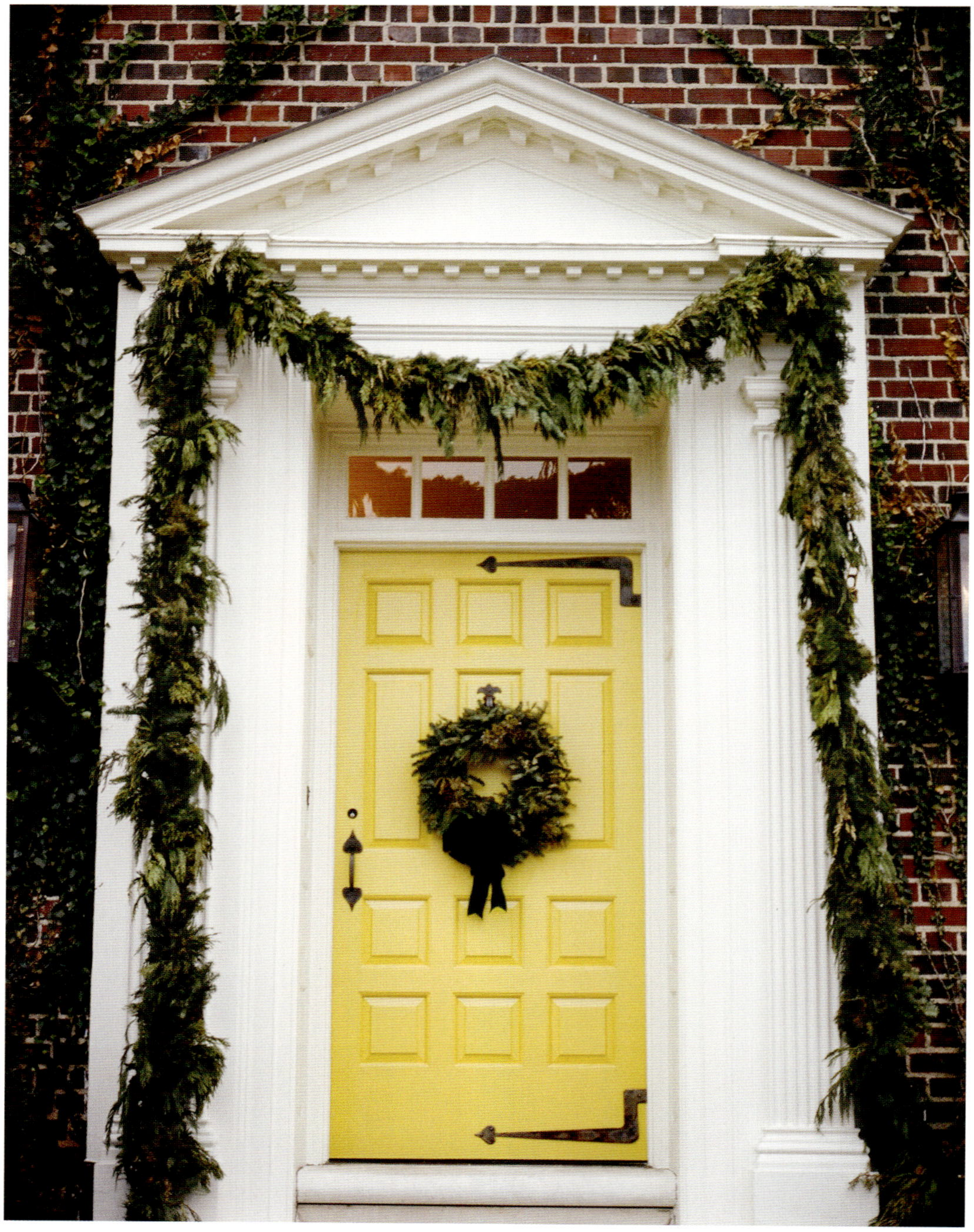

above: A traditional home calls for traditional decorations for the holidays, but things can be jazzed up a bit for a Holiday Home Tour. We kept everything all green for the exterior, and I went for the Wow factor as the guests entered the front door. *right:* The staircase garland was a mixed deluxe heavy garland that I entwined with a pine garland then added spray painted King protea blossoms and yellow oncidium orchid stems that had been water tubed to keep them fresh. The orchids complemented the Clarence House wallpaper, and the pine cones played up the warm wood tones in the space.

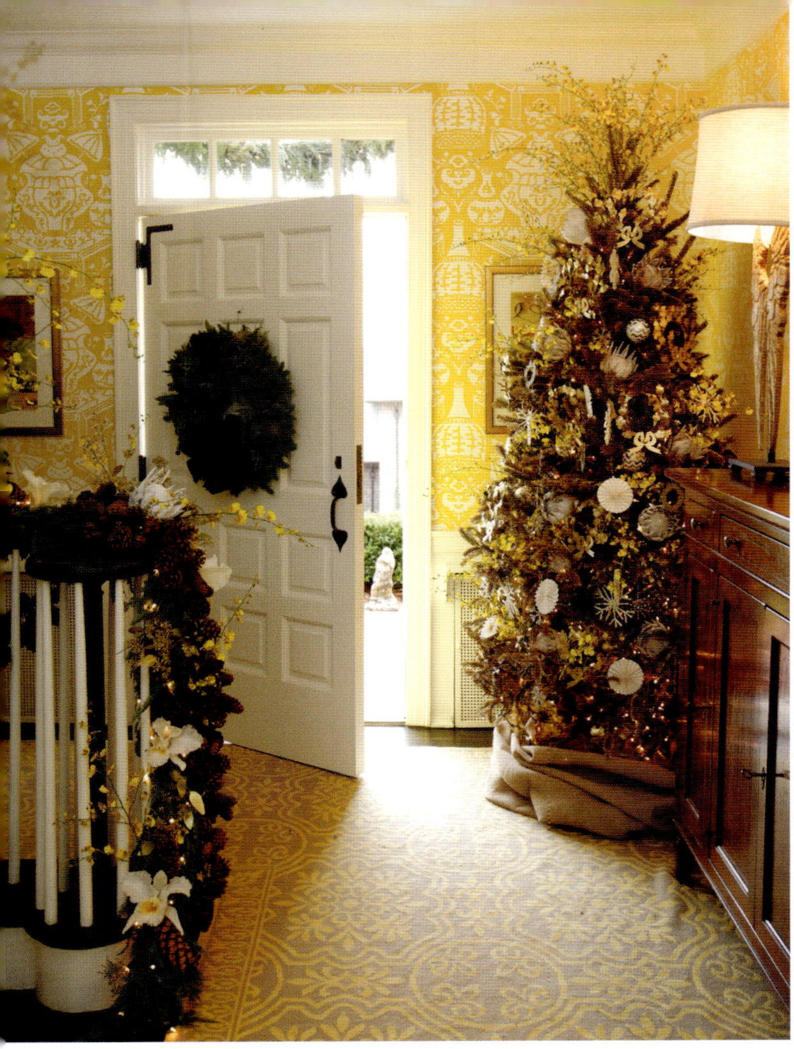

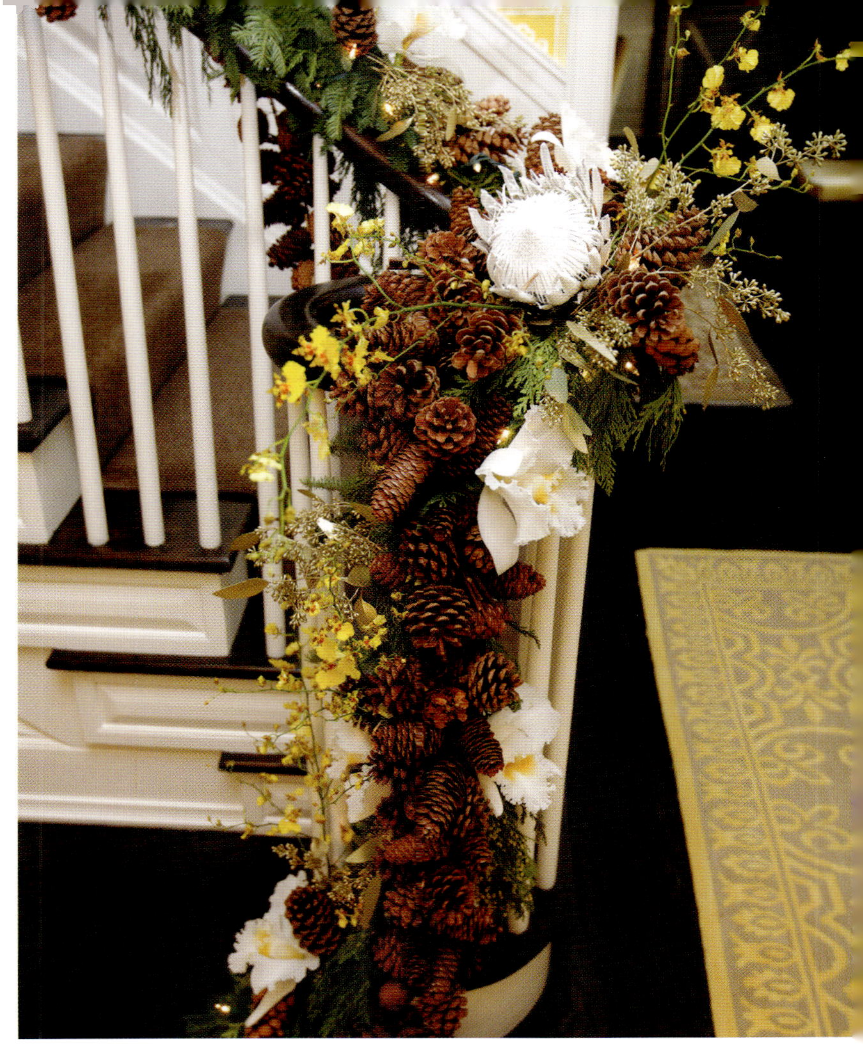

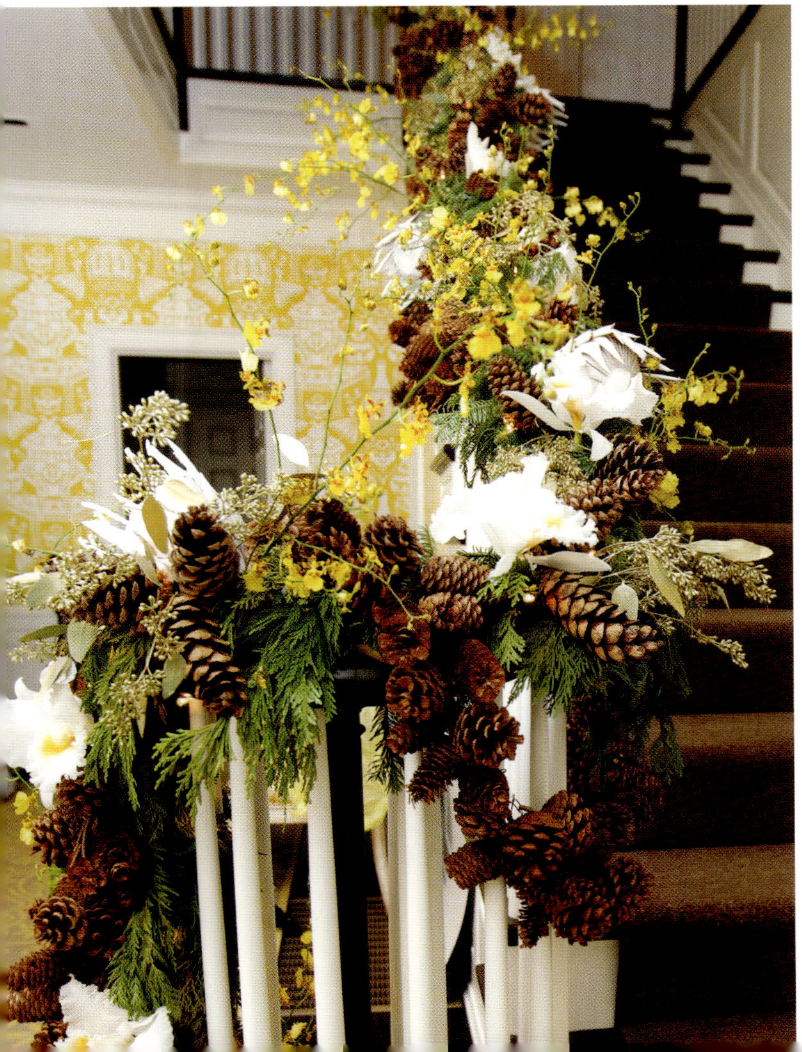

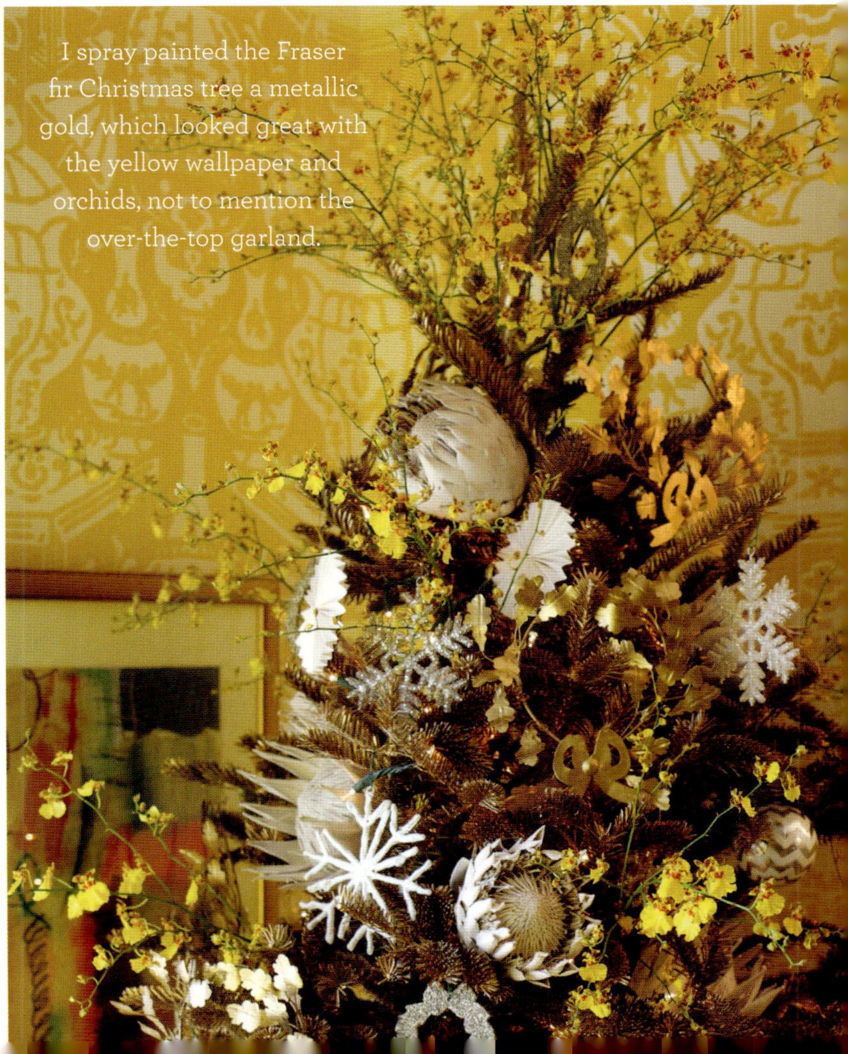

I spray painted the Fraser fir Christmas tree a metallic gold, which looked great with the yellow wallpaper and orchids, not to mention the over-the-top garland.

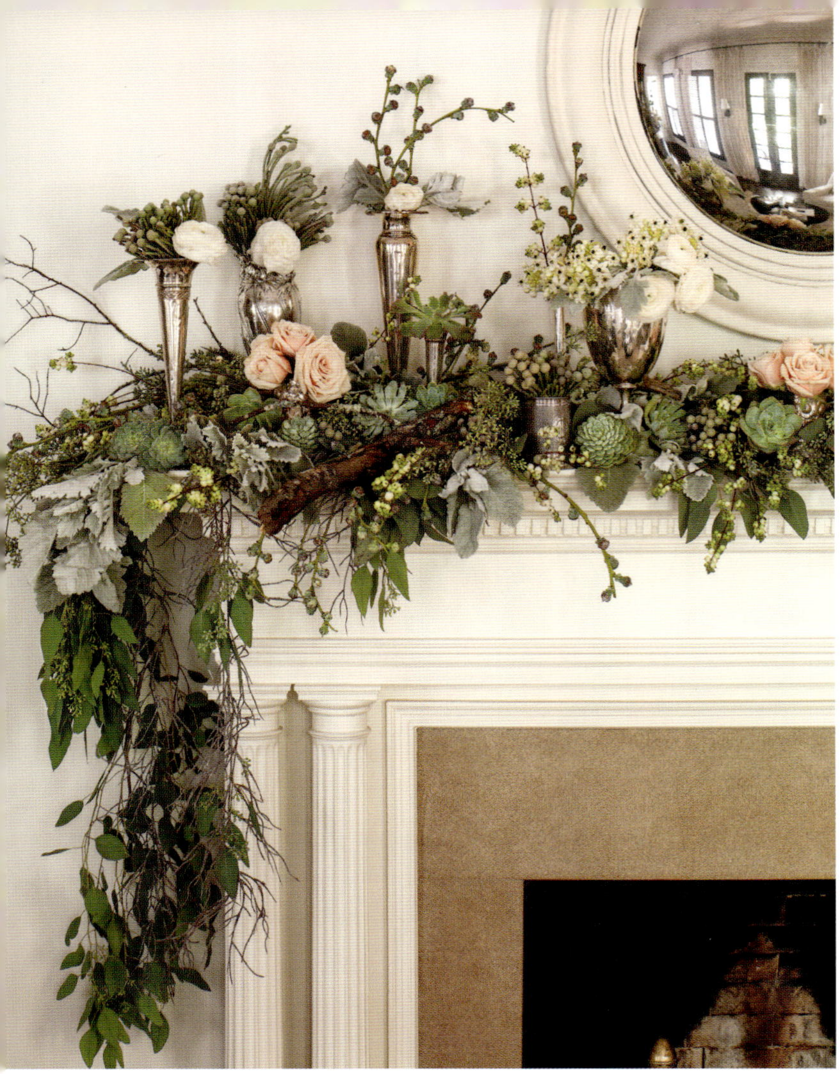
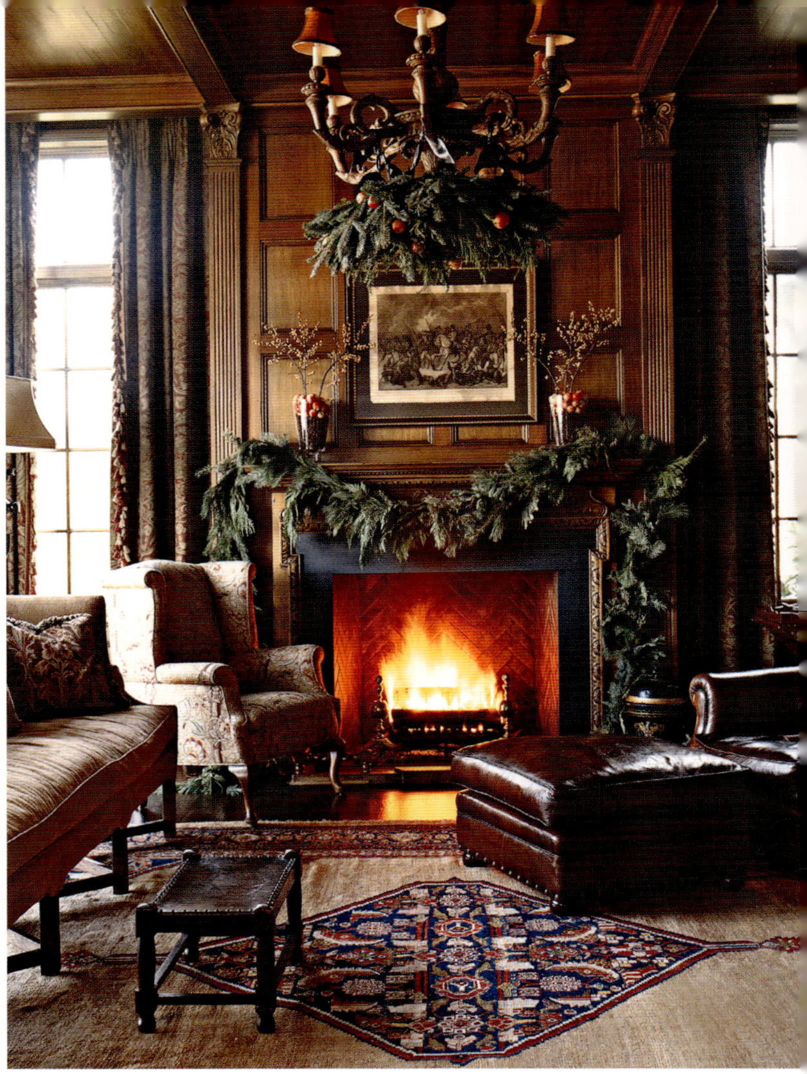
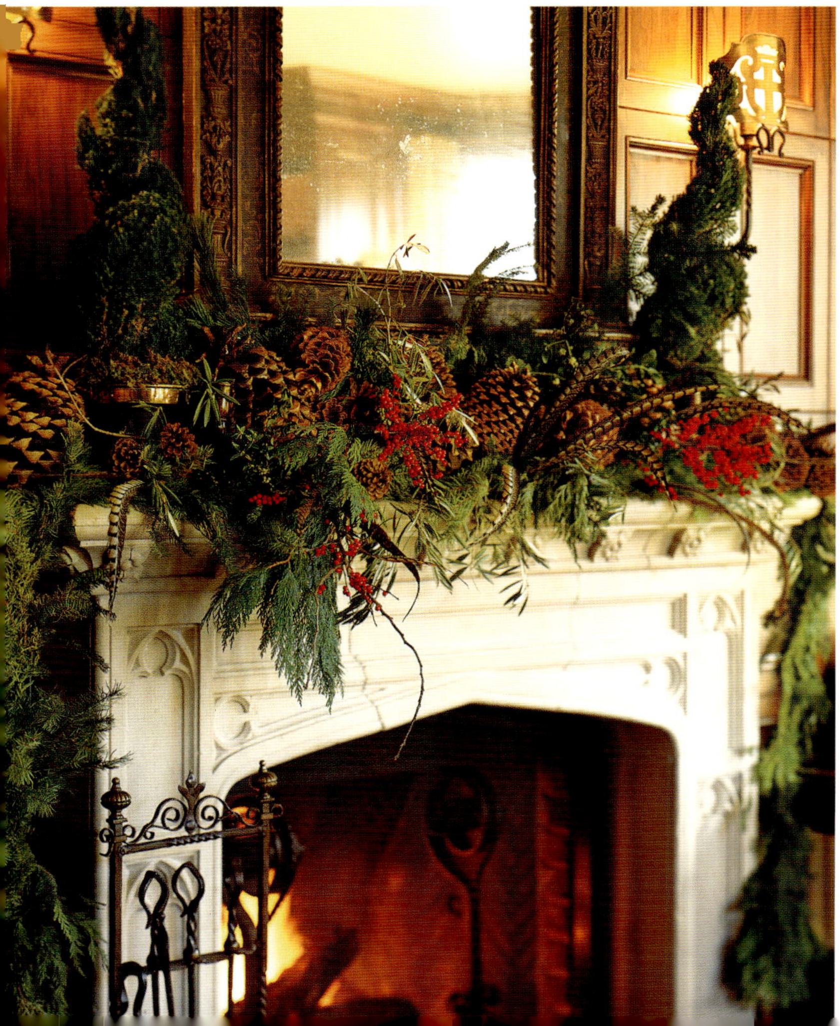
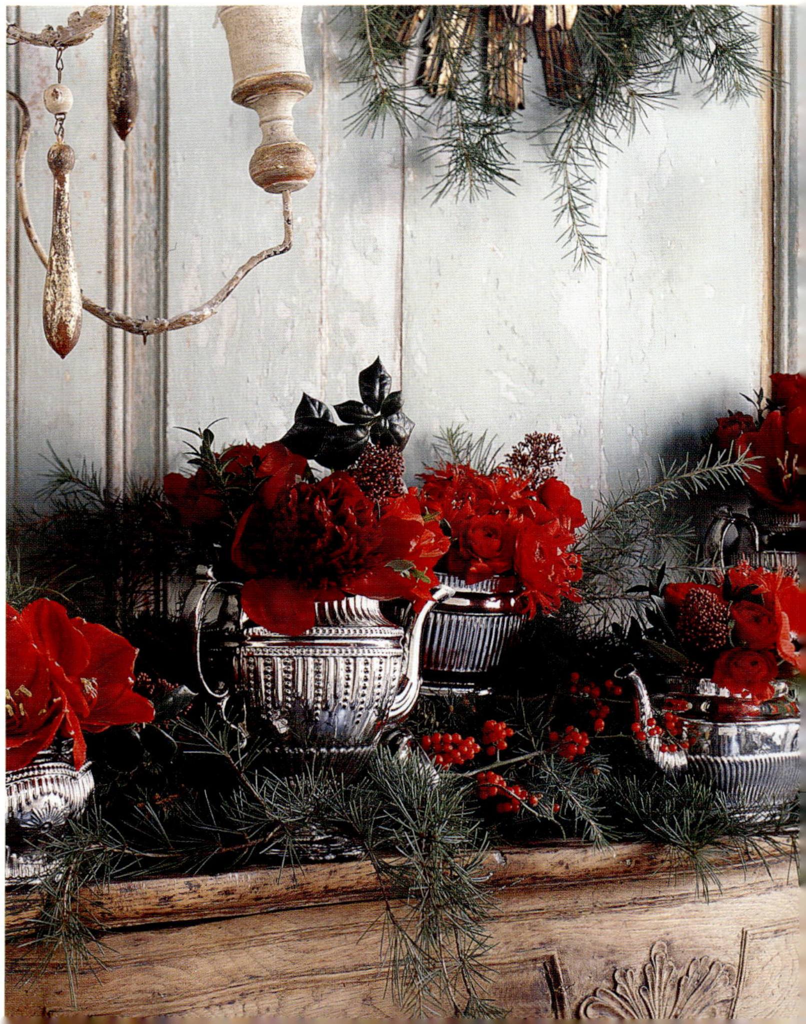

FIREPLACE MANTELS

decking the hearth for the holidays

I love decorating fireplace mantels for the holidays. It's almost like festooning a stage set for a performance. I love foraging the grounds and the forests for materials, using treasures like pine cones and berries that are almost icons of the winter months. I also think about the decorations in the rest of the house, what events the house will host during its four to six week period of holiday decoration, and practical considerations such as how can I make it last? There's rarely a prescribed plan. Sometimes I order a base garland. Others I put one together from what's on hand in Birmingham. But it's always a success—how can it not be?

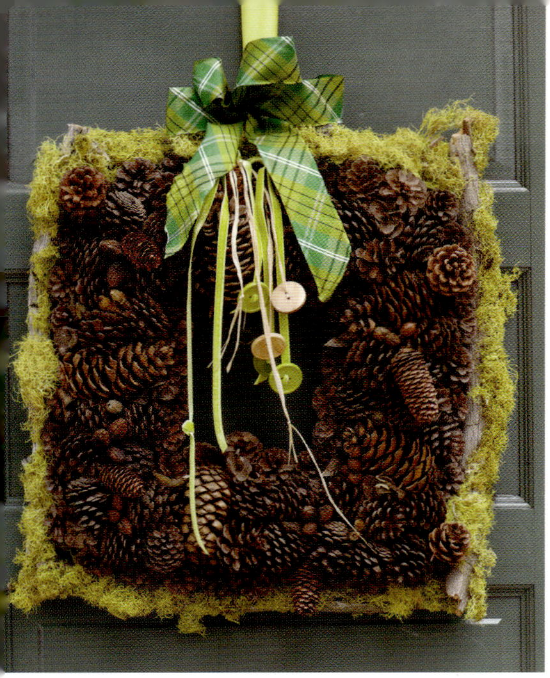
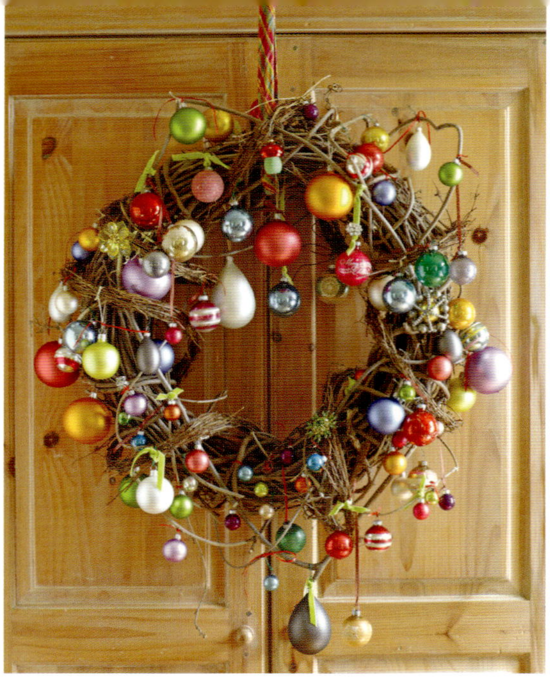
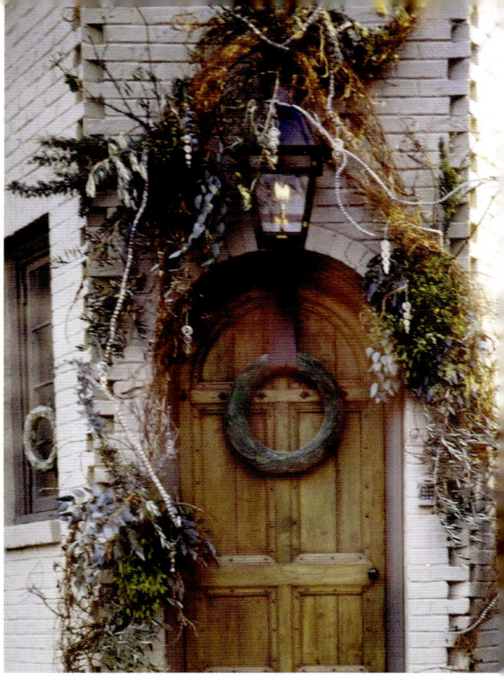
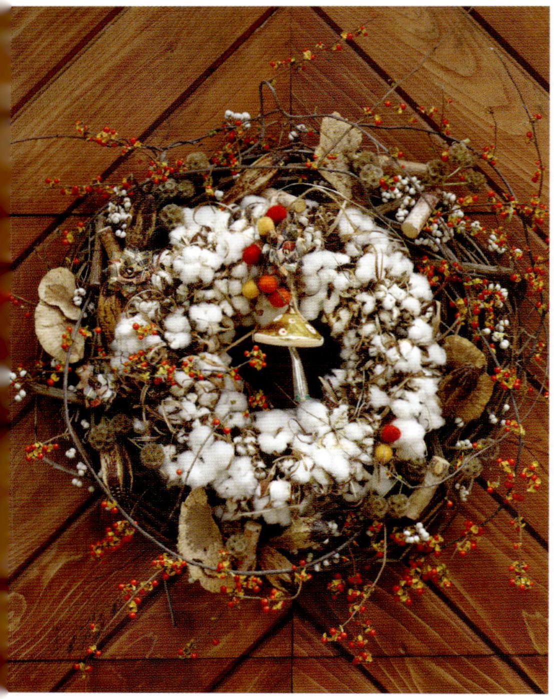
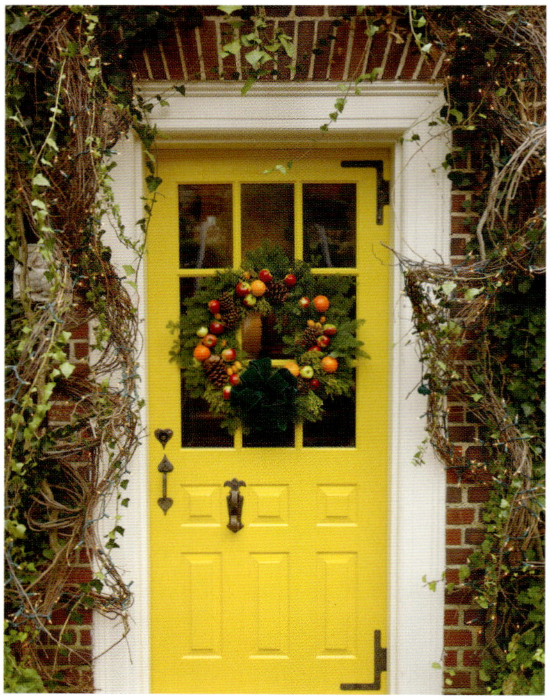
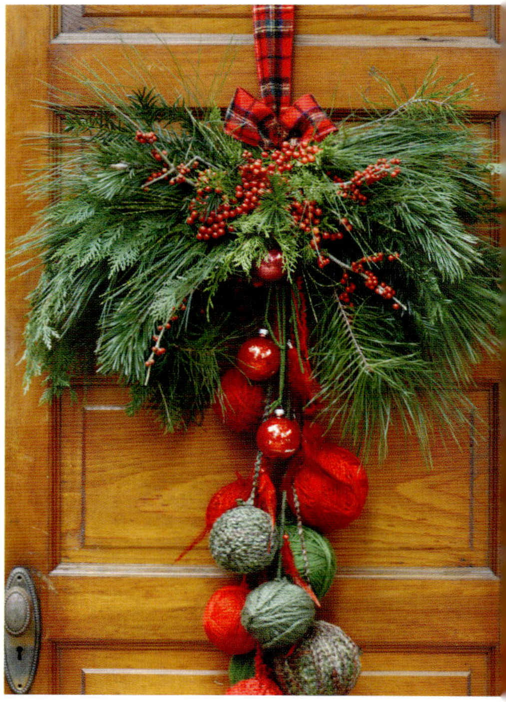
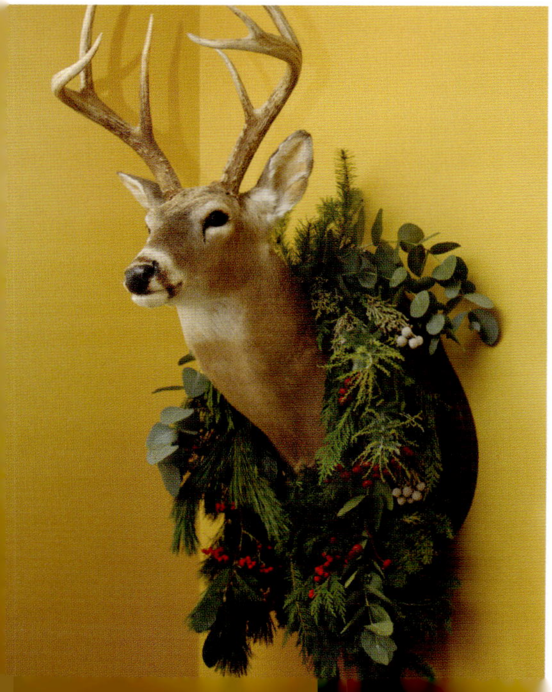
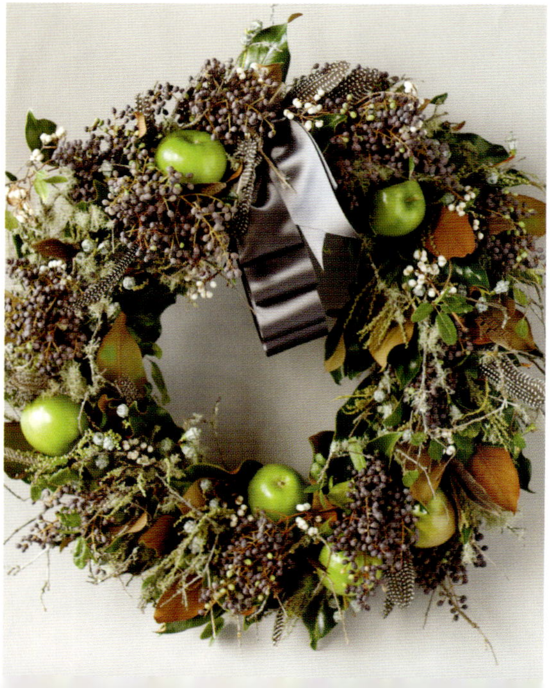
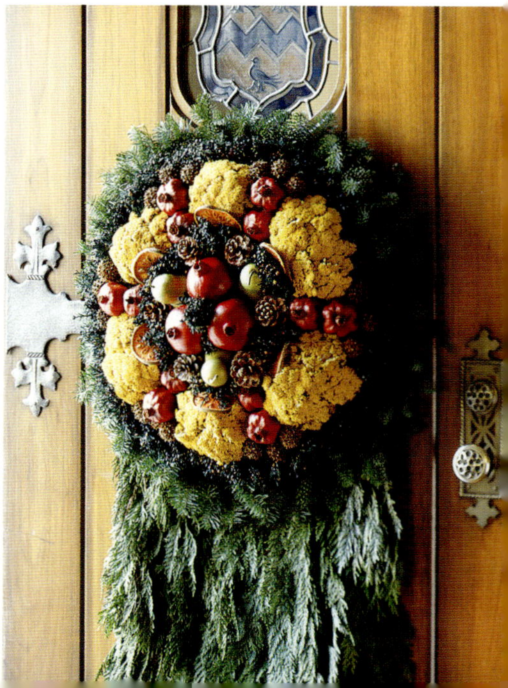

CHRISTMAS WREATHS

wishing happy holiday

The architecture of the houses I decorate at Christmas is so diverse that the design of each wreath I create is necessarily unique as well. Some doors are dark stained wood, heavy and traditional, so I create a basic, lush mixed greenery wreath, albeit festooned with "Sybilized" touches. Other doors are bright and painted or modern and a little too simple, so I ramp the decorating up a notch and bring in fruit or ornaments, cotton and twigs. I occasionally eschew the standard round wreath and create instead a square or other out-of-the box style, just to keep things FRESH.

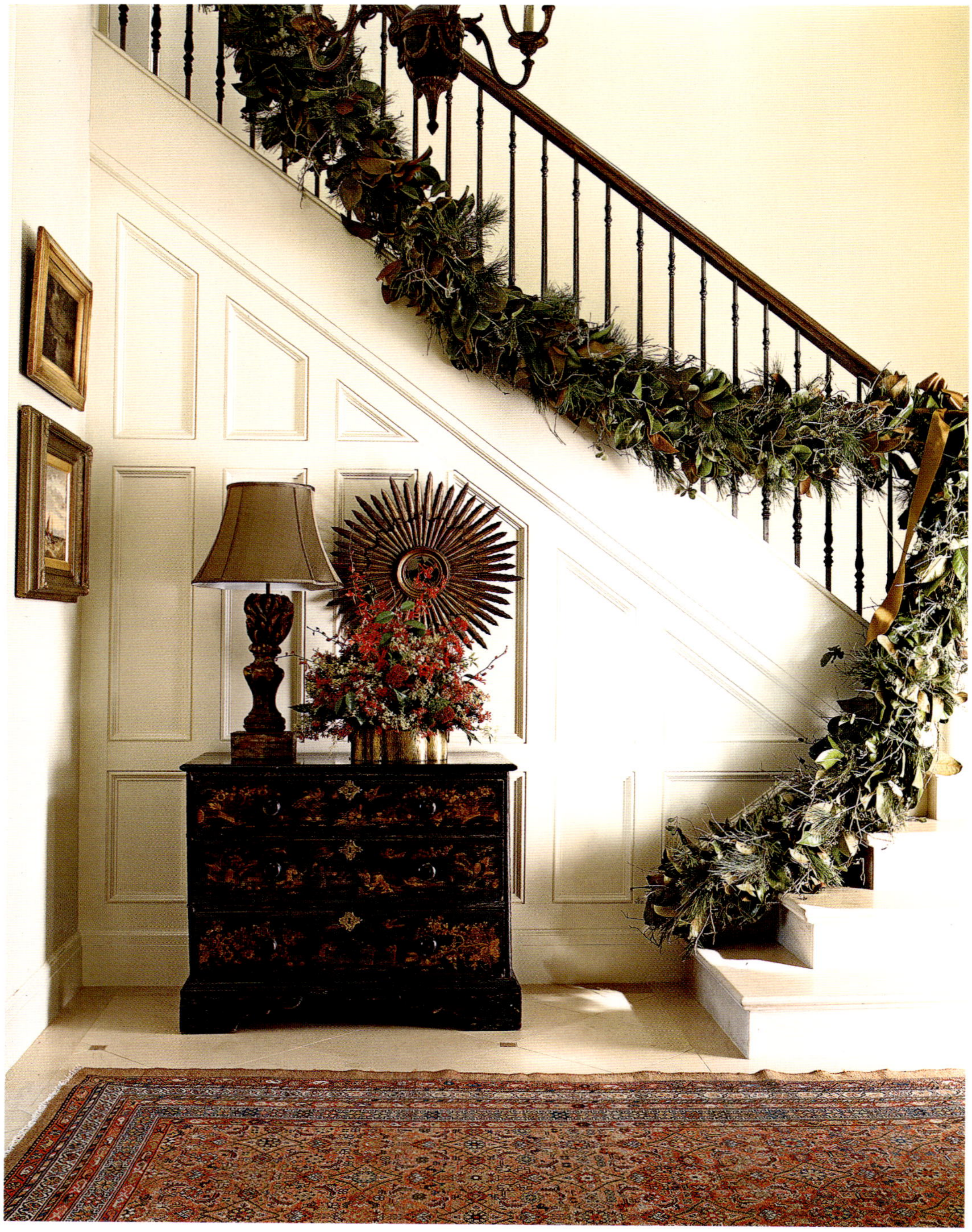

above: The entry hall and dining room are the first rooms you see in the house so I did them up and made them work for the season, with a lush, heavy garland on the banister and a pretty bouquet on the table.
right: I love this time of year—it's an opportunity to re-decorate for a few months, dress the house up in jewels and baubles, and then start fresh in January.

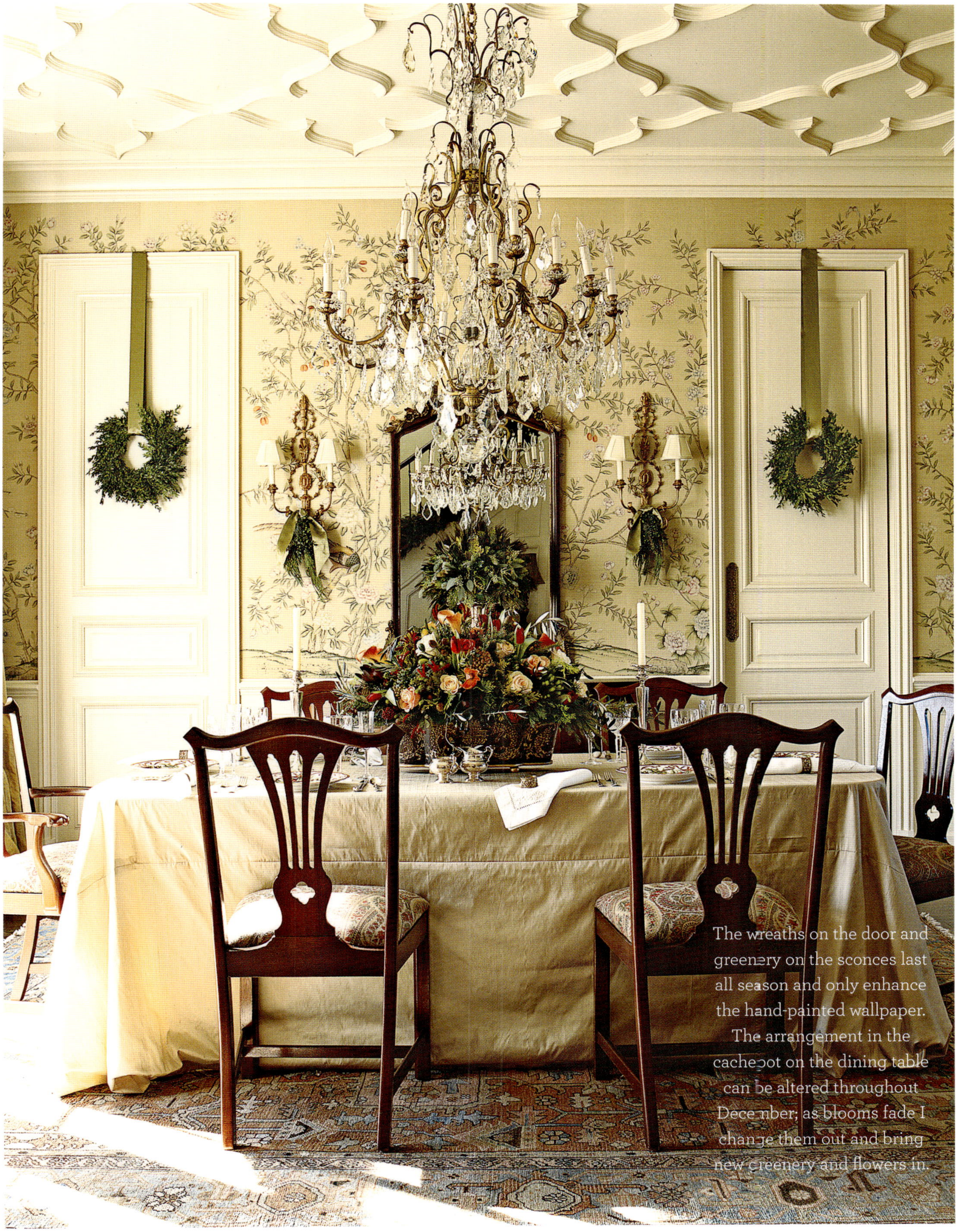

The wreaths on the door and greenery on the sconces last all season and only enhance the hand-painted wallpaper. The arrangement in the cachepot on the dining table can be altered throughout December; as blooms fade I change them out and bring new greenery and flowers in.

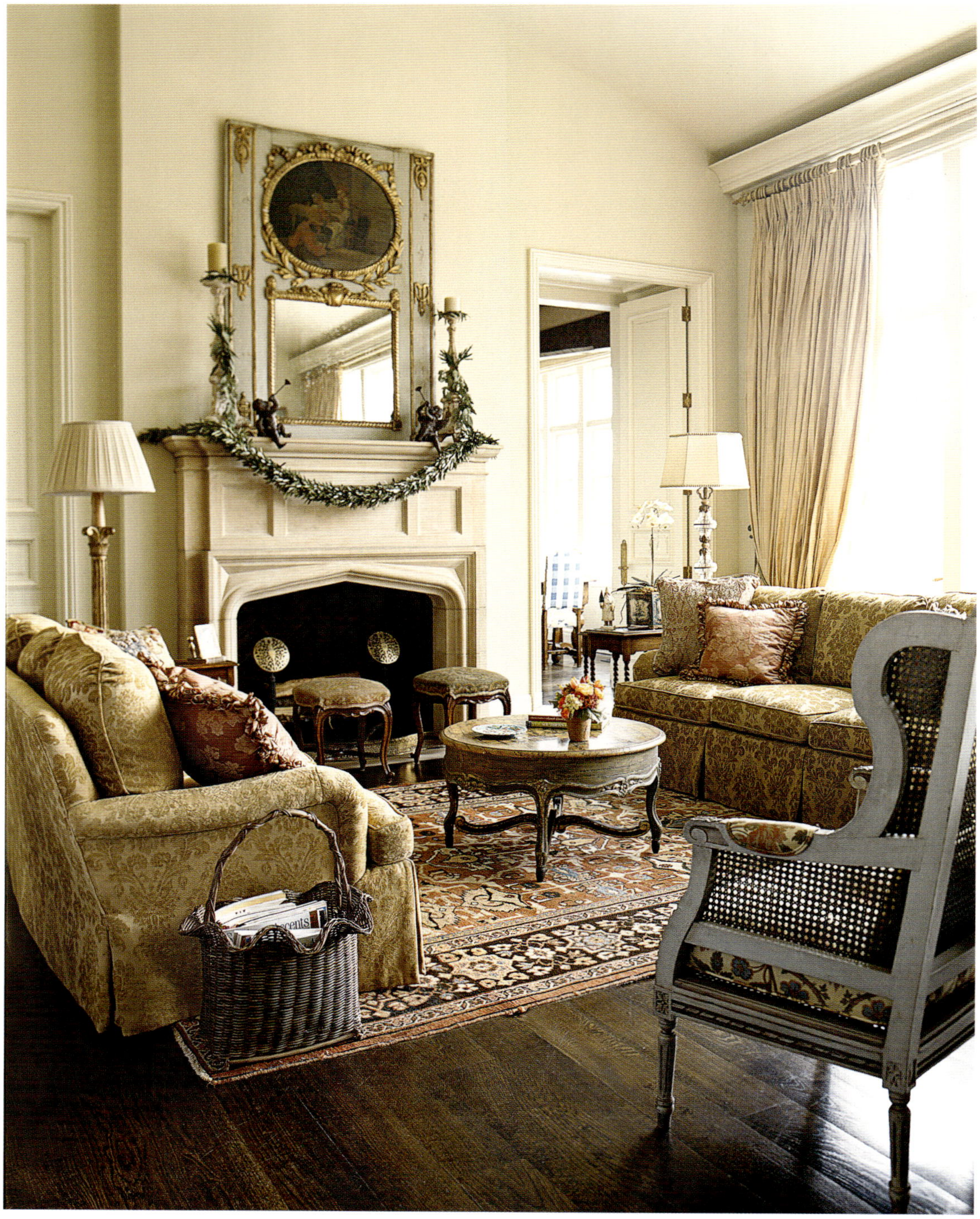

THE ONLY THING I DID ON THAT TREE WAS ADD THE BLUE RIBBONS, AND IT MADE THE WHOLE THING SPECTACULAR.

above: This is a pretty house, and the colors are subtle. I didn't want to do anything jarring so I created a tailored garland for the mantel. *right*: The only real shock of color is the blue satin ribbons, but they coordinate with the art behind the tree so the feel of the space is still refined.

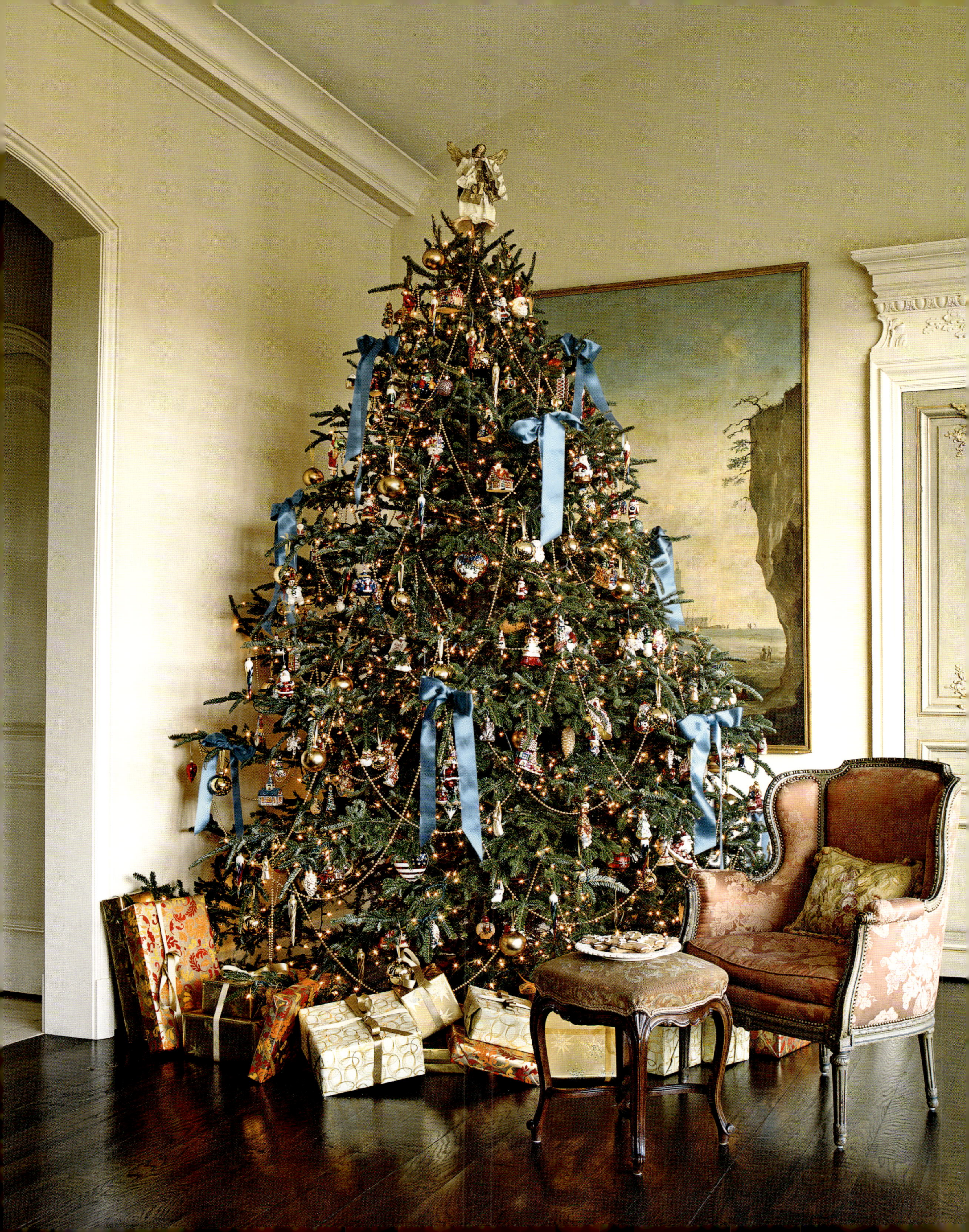

celebrations

My calendar is booked full of weddings and bouquets, arrangements for anniversaries and congratulations. But what really fills the pages are the events that I orchestrate throughout the year. There are many fundraisers and birthday parties, balls and holidays to help make beautiful as well as "Sybilized." I'm in a meeting or at the flower market or scouting a location almost every day of the week. And it's always fun. The challenges, the ideas, the people I meet make every occasion special. I just add to my family, cherishing the memory of each event almost as if it's one of my very own children.

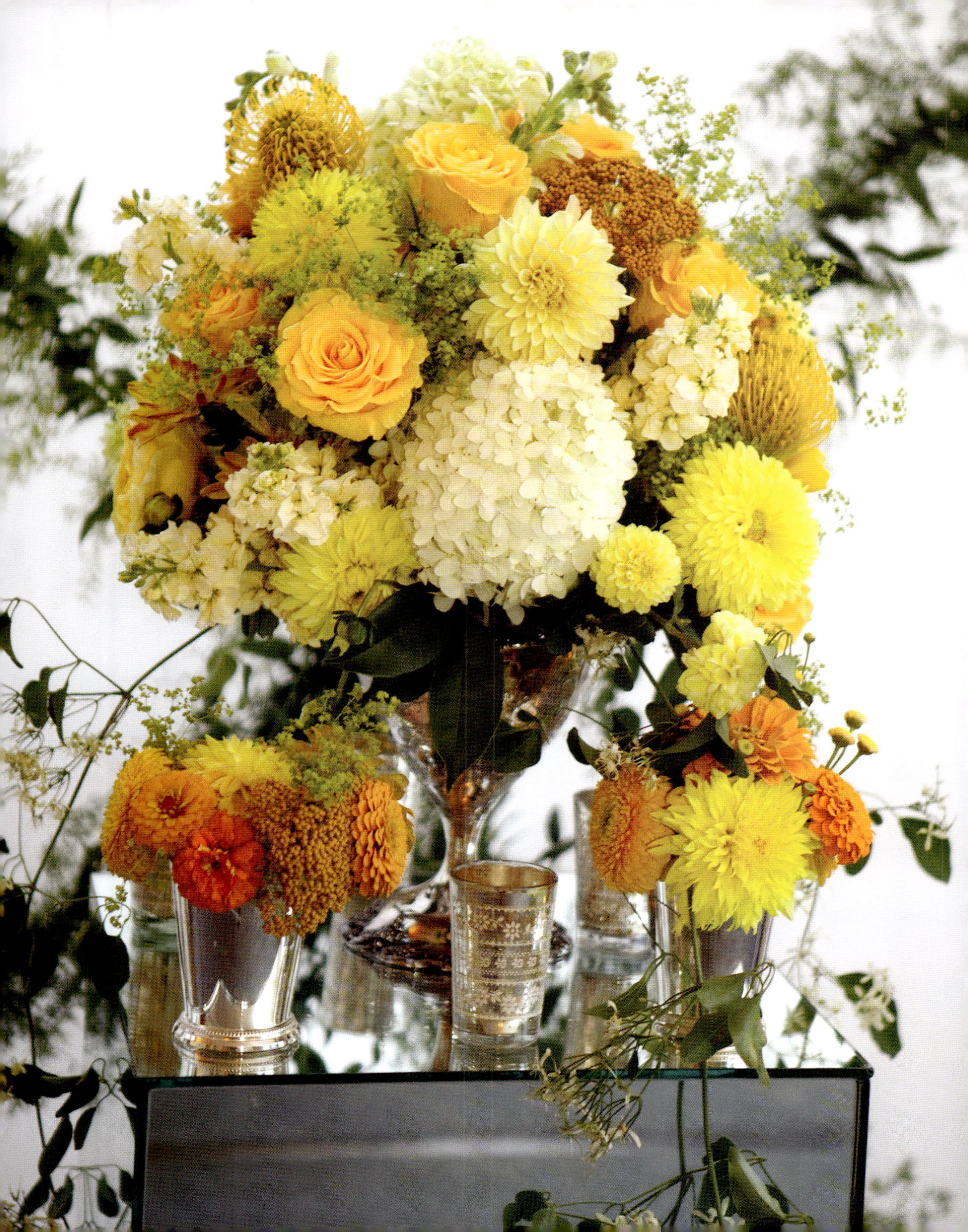

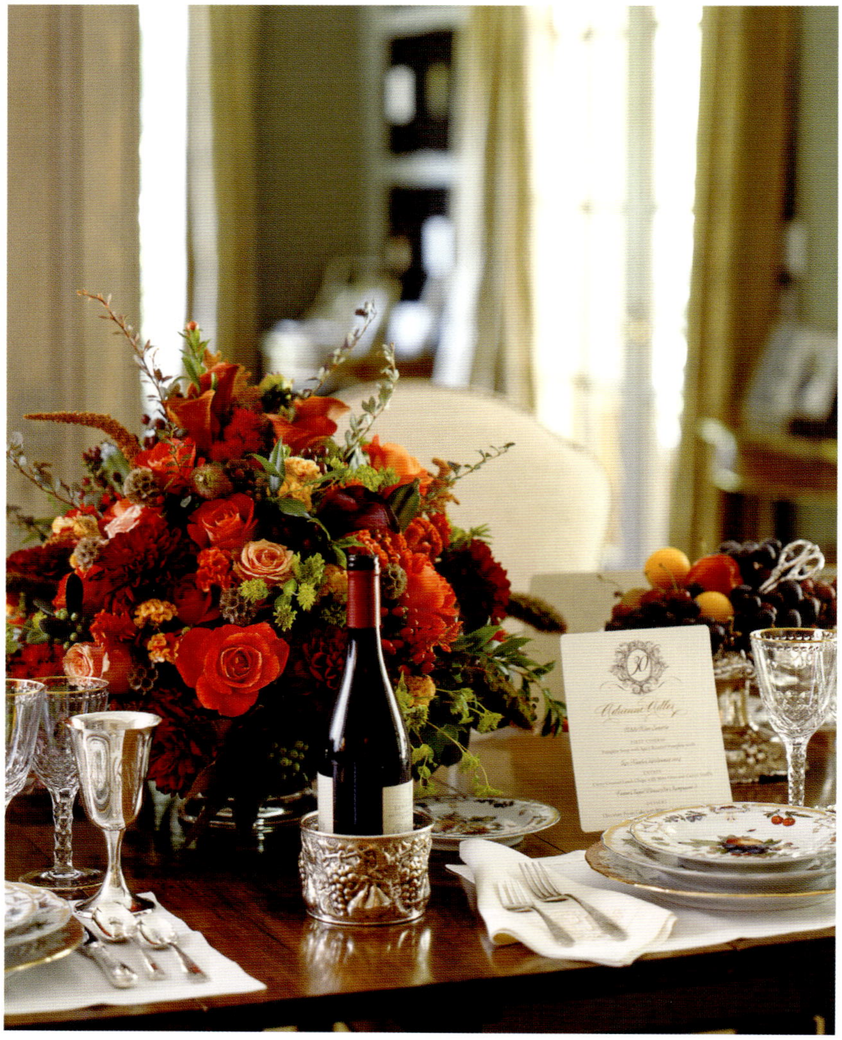

FORMAL DINNER

putting on the ritz

For this occasion, we dressed things up a bit, or as we say in Alabama, "Put on the Dog!" It's a thrill to pull out the heirloom silver pieces, your best china and crystal, and the special linens that stay tucked away waiting to be remembered. The plan this evening was for wonderful food and conversation and to linger over a glass of wine and enjoy cheese and fruit as the finish to the meal.

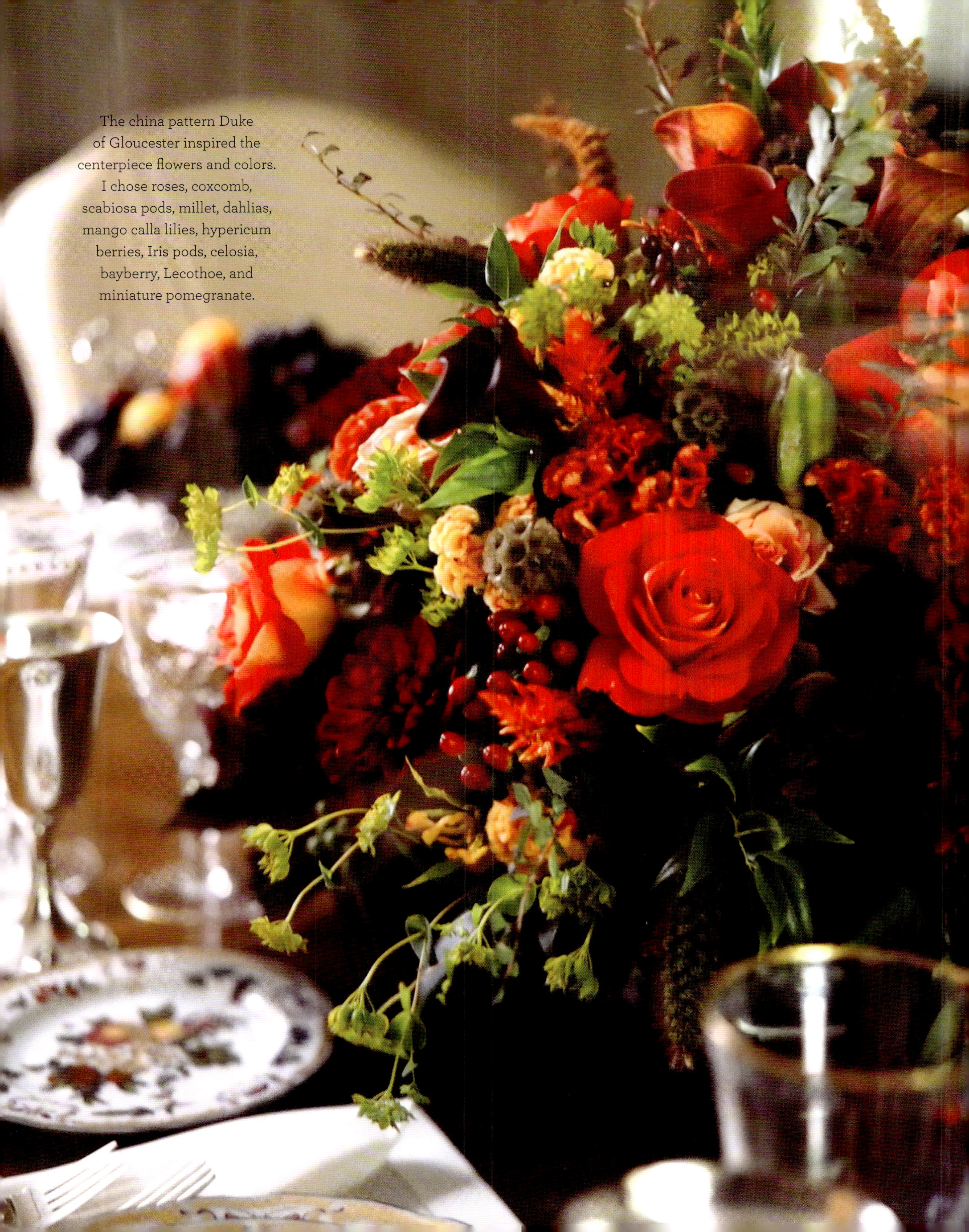

The china pattern Duke of Gloucester inspired the centerpiece flowers and colors. I chose roses, coxcomb, scabiosa pods, millet, dahlias, mango calla lilies, hypericum berries, Iris pods, celosia, bayberry, Lecothoe, and miniature pomegranate.

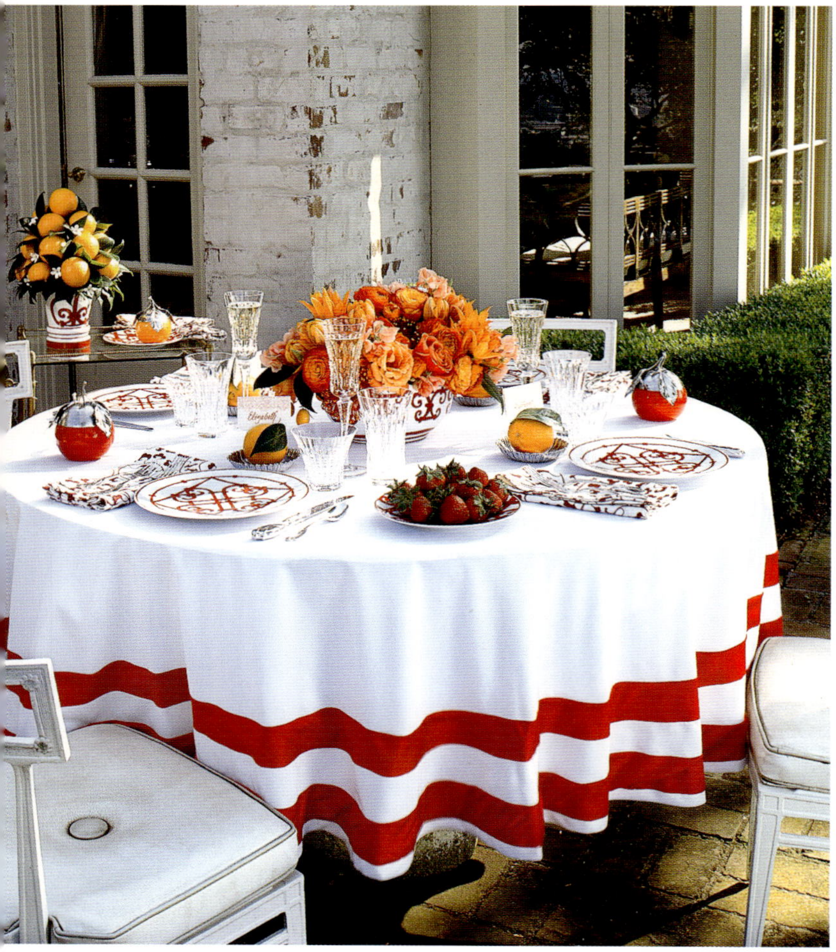

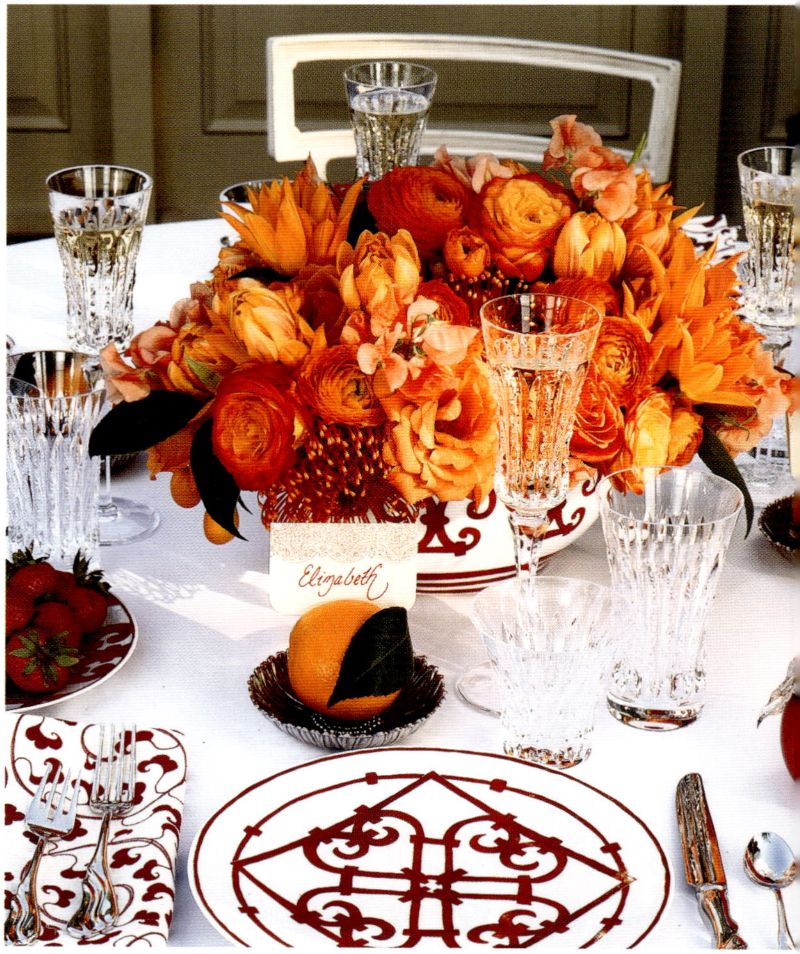

INTIMATE BRUNCH

summertime cool

What could be more fun than combining red and orange, mixed with graphic prints and fresh fruit? This brunch was early one weekend, before the heat of the day set in. Instead of working with cool blues, I chose intense colors and cooled them off with a crisp custom-made white linen tablecloth foundation.

I anchored a dome of chicken wire in place in the tureen and started adding every orange flower I could get my hands on. Clusters of kumquats on branches made me want to use oranges as place card holders. The tablecloth was custom-made to coordinate with the china, and I created the orange topiary on the tea cart to create a visual link with the centerpiece.

WORDS OF WISDOM

1.

When I get a call for a party, the first thing I always do is visit the location or house. It makes no sense to do flowers and decorations for a space that will look totally at odds with the hosts and the guests and the location!

2.

Then we talk. A lot. I want to know about the type of party, who are the guests, what is the feeling they're going for, what they will wear, what will they be serving throughout the event.

3.

Next I look around. I open closets and cabinets. I look at the style of the house to make sure the style of the house and the feel of the party can all work together.

4.

It's the cabinets I love. That's where I see containers where other people don't, vessels that can be lined to hold flowers, long overlooked silver or pots that will make the event more special and personal.

5.

Next we talk about the guests. The big secret to throwing a great party, luncheon, get-together, brunch, fete is really simple, but I cannot tell you how easy it is to miss. Never forget to plan and put your guests' needs and comforts above all else. If you take care of your guests, and they feel the attention—you can't lose. And guess what – you'll have a great time too.

6.

The Kiss of Death: Never Assume Anything. You have to make sure of everything, that you have crossed everything off your list.

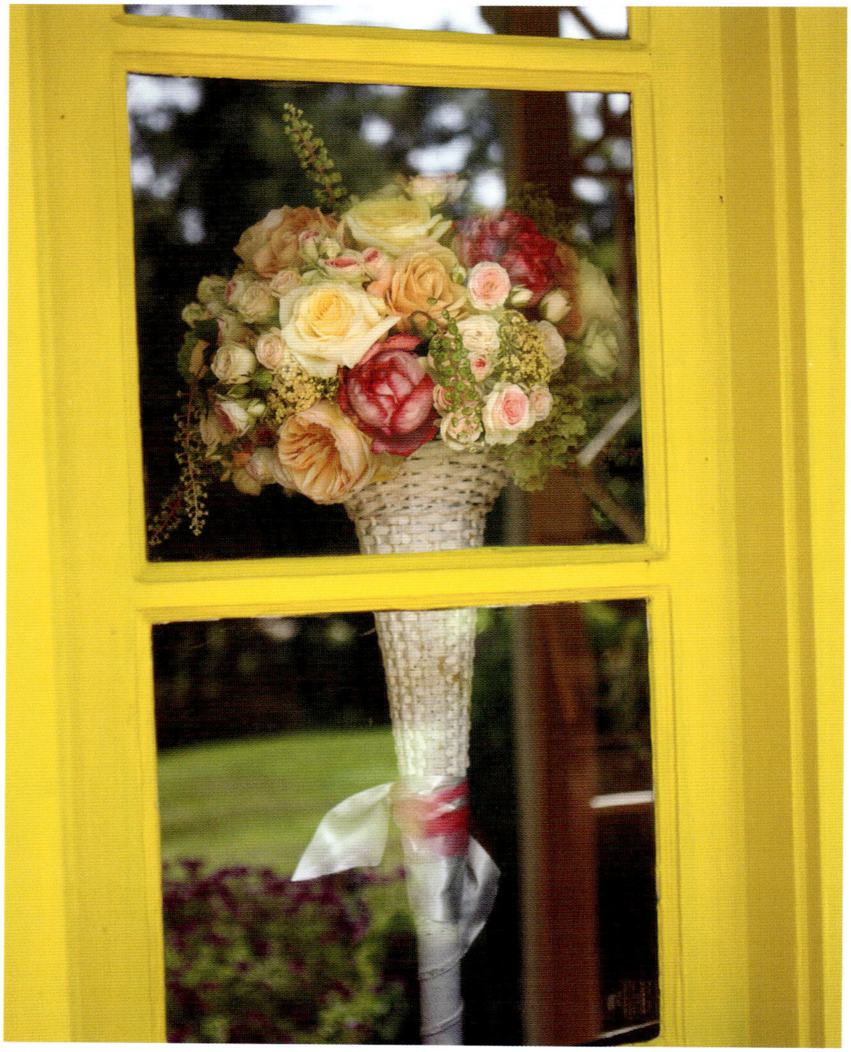

BRIDAL SHOWER

fresh as a spray rose

I have a good friend who has been with me through it all, and I have helped her through the years with parties and weddings and events large and small at her beautiful house. When she hosted a bridal shower for a special young friend, I kept the feeling young and still traditional. We used mostly antique white iron urns and an antique Victorian wicker plant stand that stood sentry by the front door.

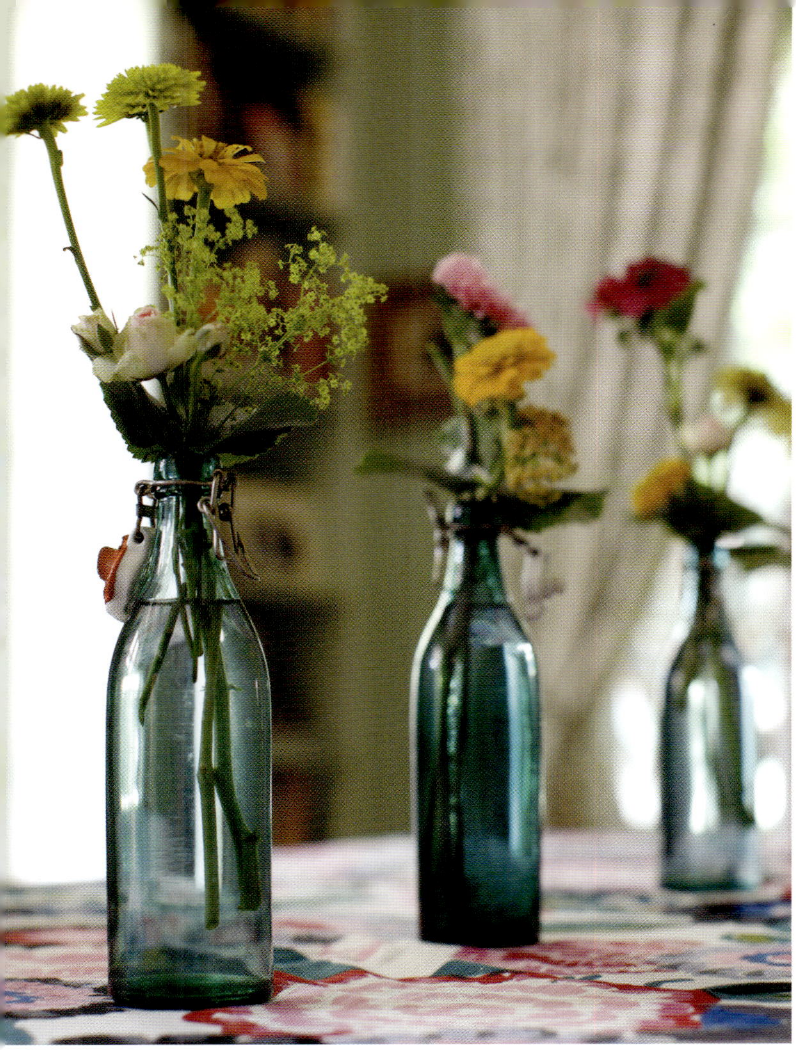

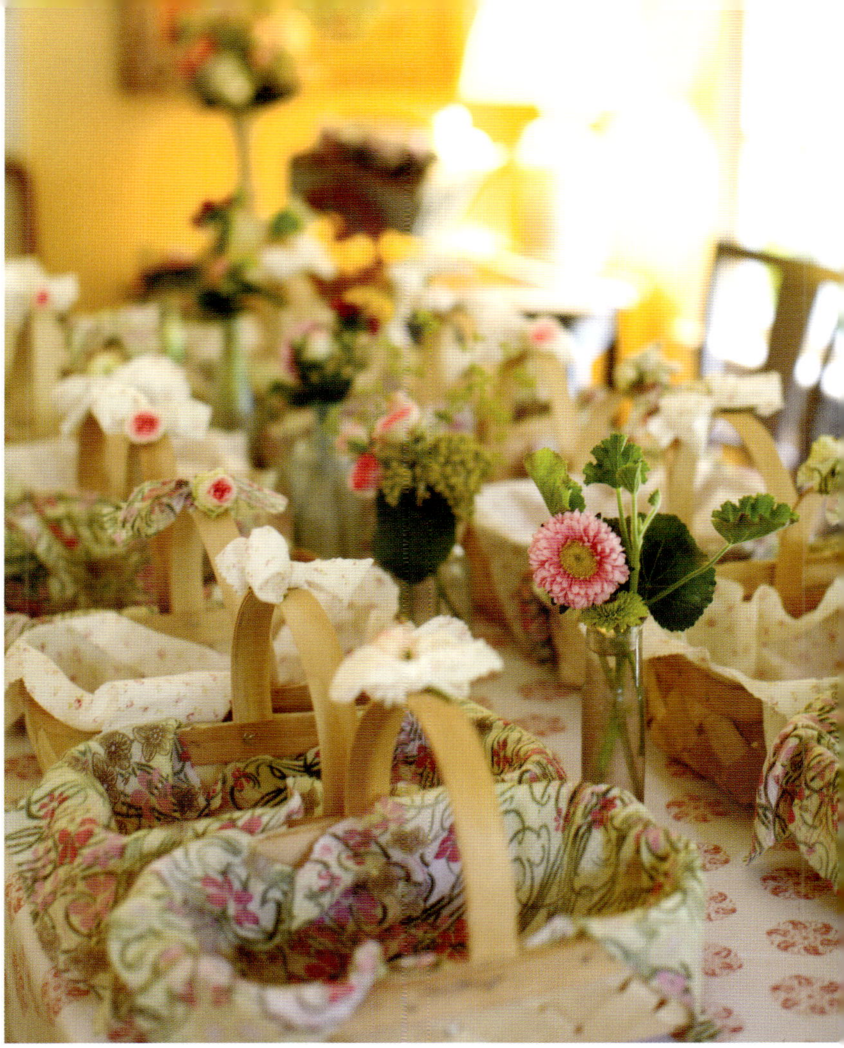

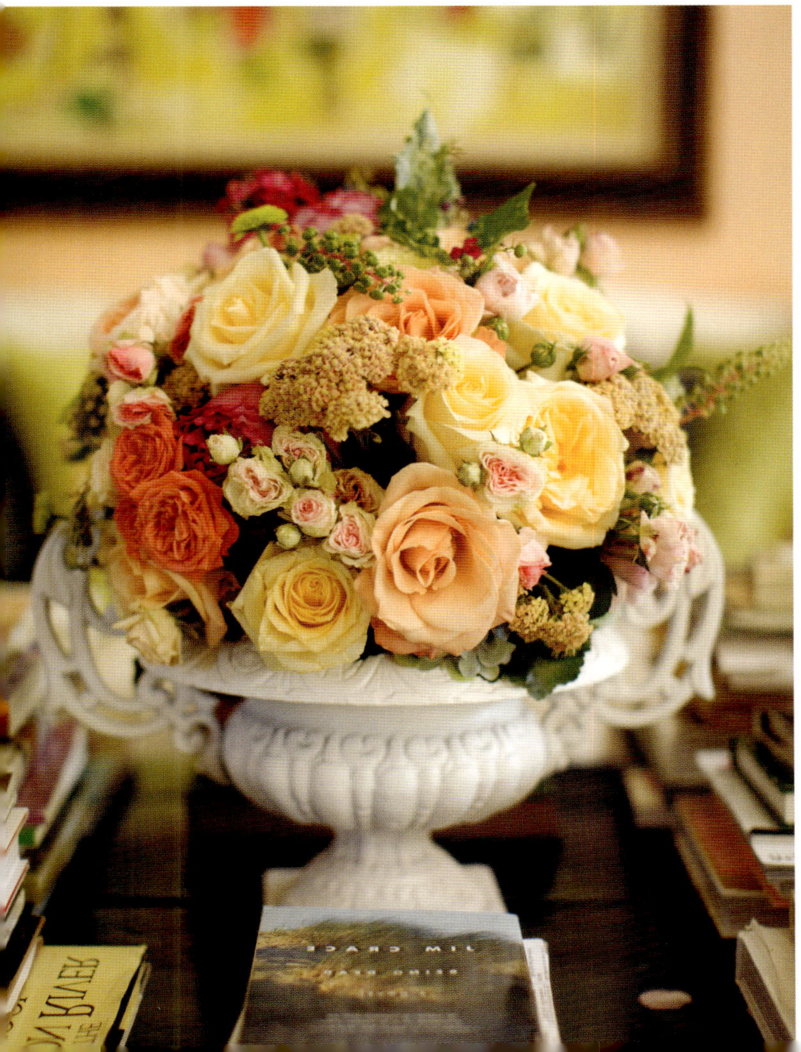

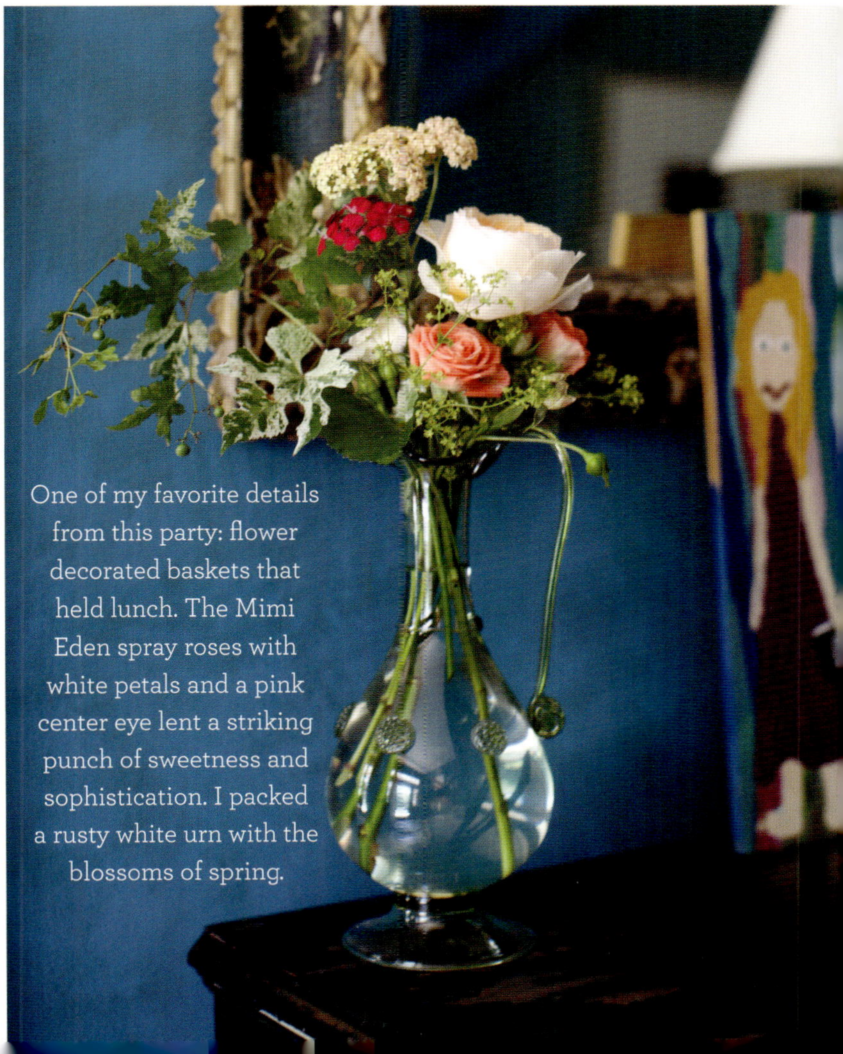

One of my favorite details from this party: flower decorated baskets that held lunch. The Mimi Eden spray roses with white petals and a pink center eye lent a striking punch of sweetness and sophistication. I packed a rusty white urn with the blossoms of spring.

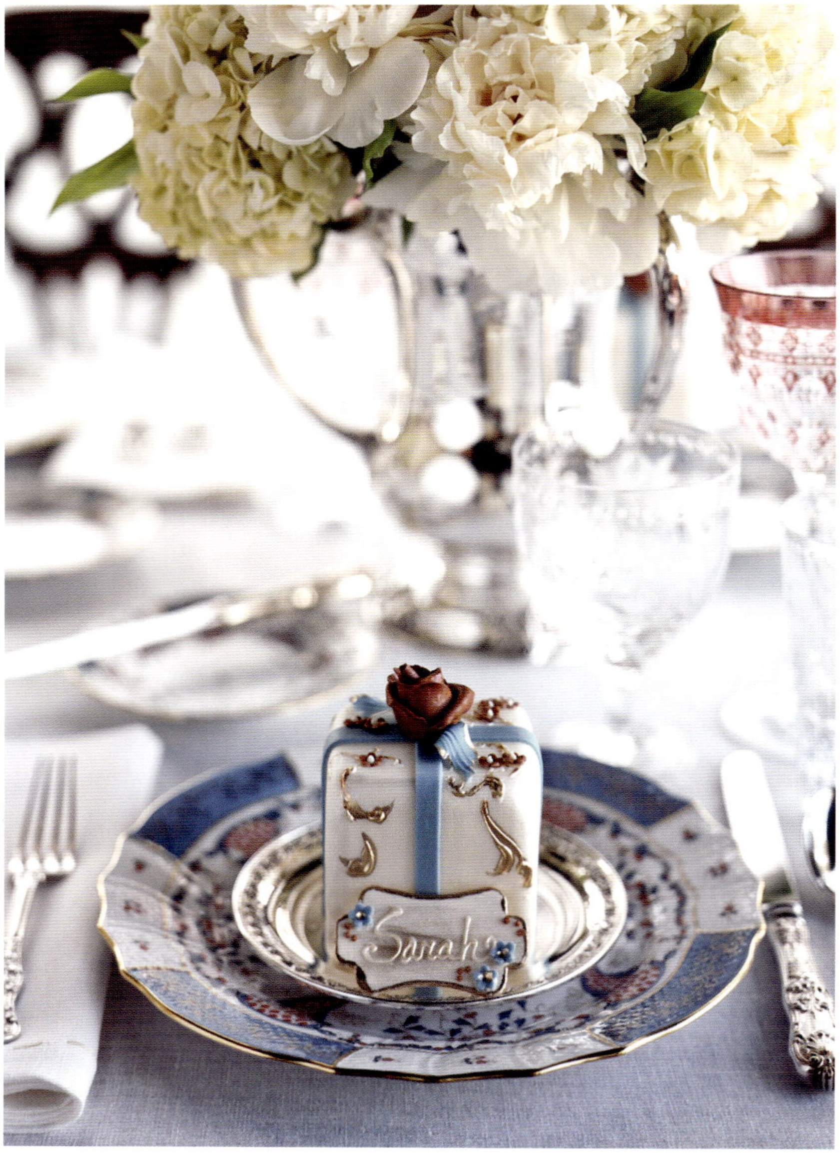

BIRTHDAY LUNCH

sparkles with elegance

My inspiration was the ultimate Southern ladies-who-lunch affair that celebrates a mother and grandmother. We brought out all the traditional heirloom finery—that is both beautiful and a foundational part of the collective memory of every guest.

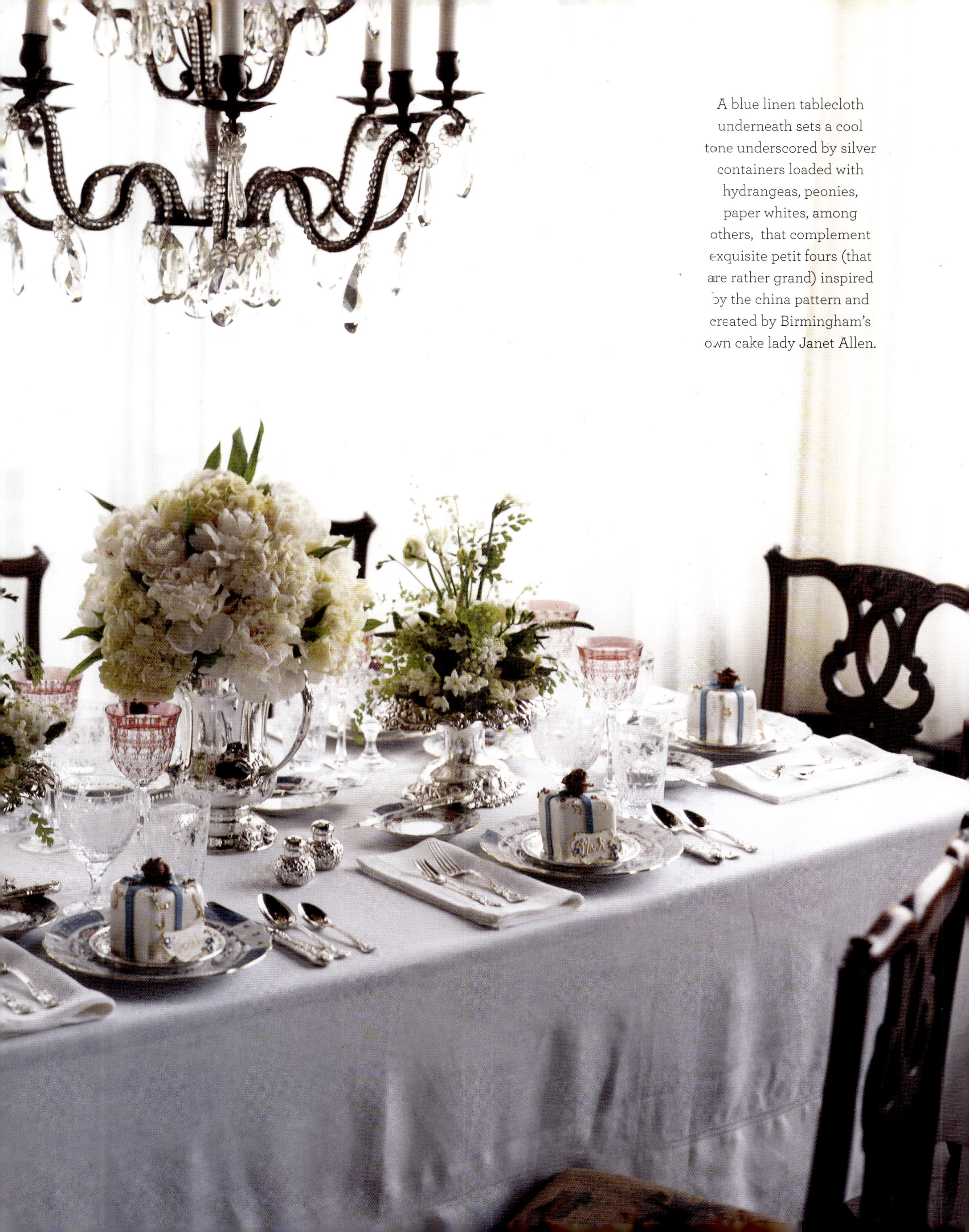

A blue linen tablecloth underneath sets a cool tone underscored by silver containers loaded with hydrangeas, peonies, paper whites, among others, that complement exquisite petit fours (that are rather grand) inspired by the china pattern and created by Birmingham's own cake lady Janet Allen.

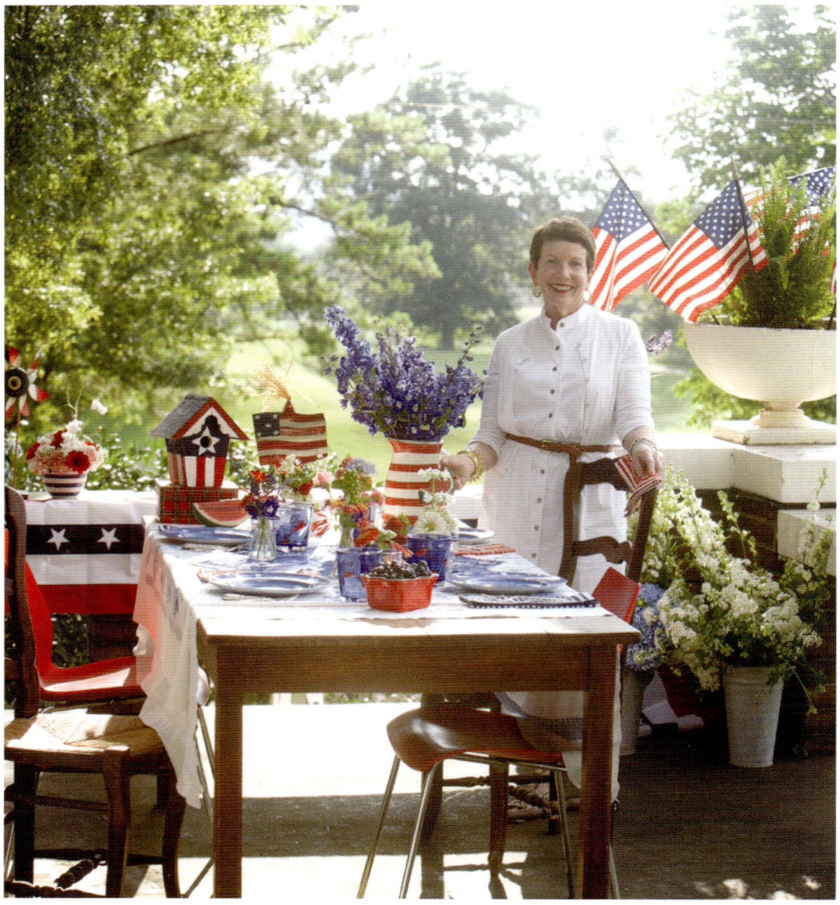

FOURTH OF JULY

until the fireworks

For years, I've collected silly patriotic flea market finds, so it was fun to pull them all out for an afternoon front porch Fourth of July cocktail supper. I went all out and junked it up a bit, but that was the point. We waved flags, cooked out, and waited for the fireworks over the golf course. Relaxation, celebration, and Uncle Sam!

Do not be afraid to mix and match anything red and white, blue and white, or all three – including linens, china, glassware, containers, and flowers. It's fun in the collecting and in the displaying. My collection comes from relatives, flea markets, garage sales, and who knows where else. It almost grows on its own now!

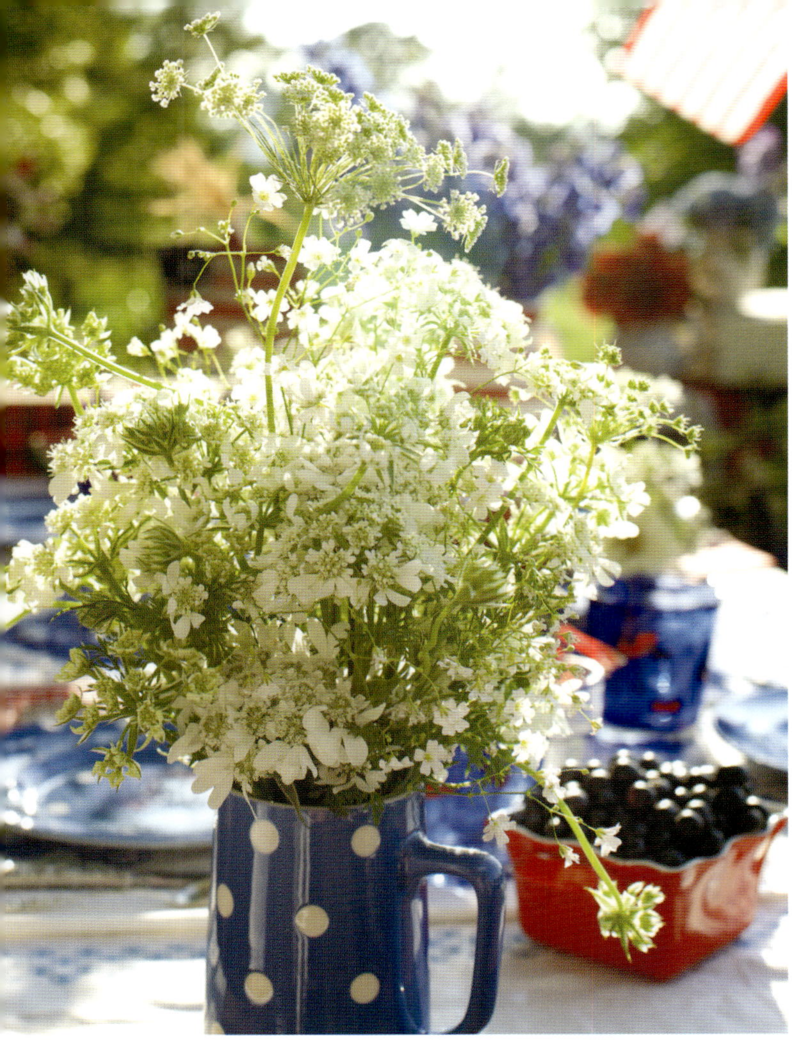
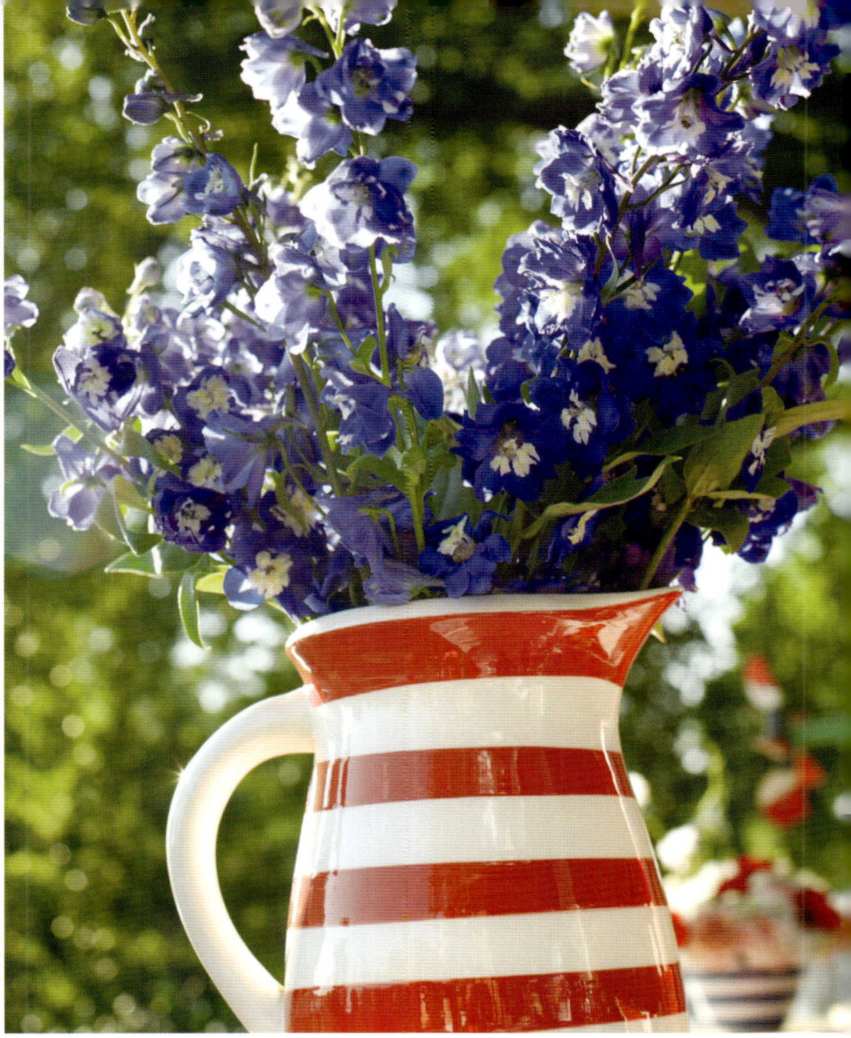
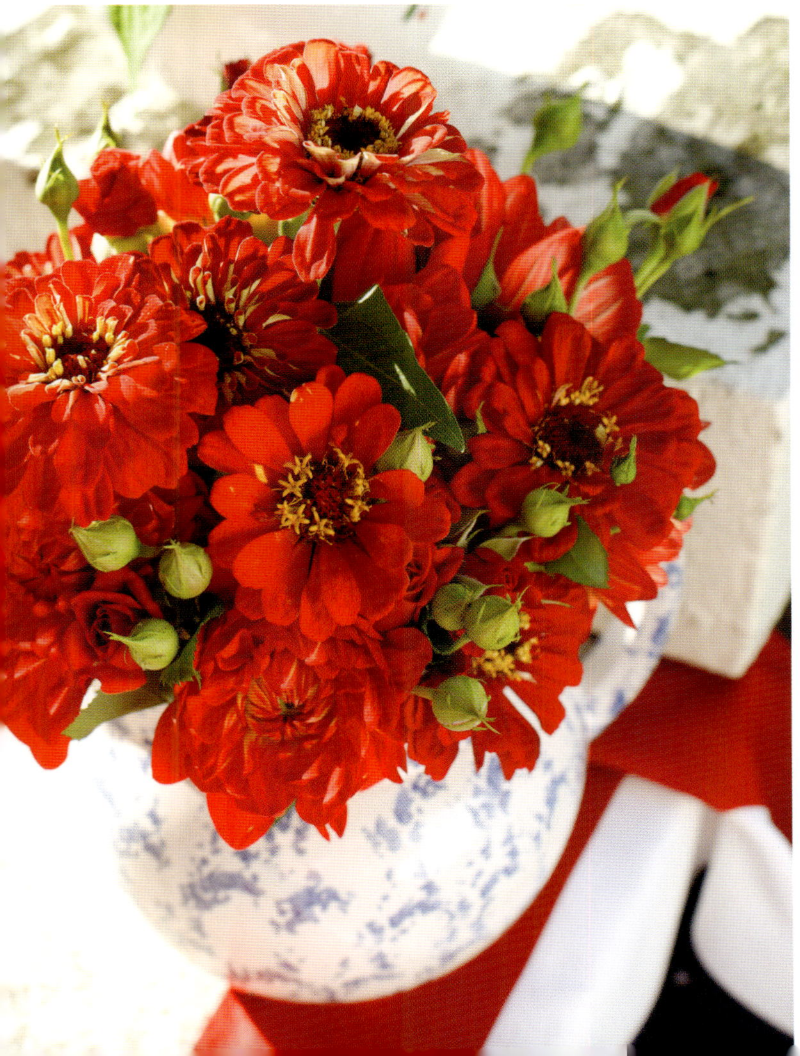
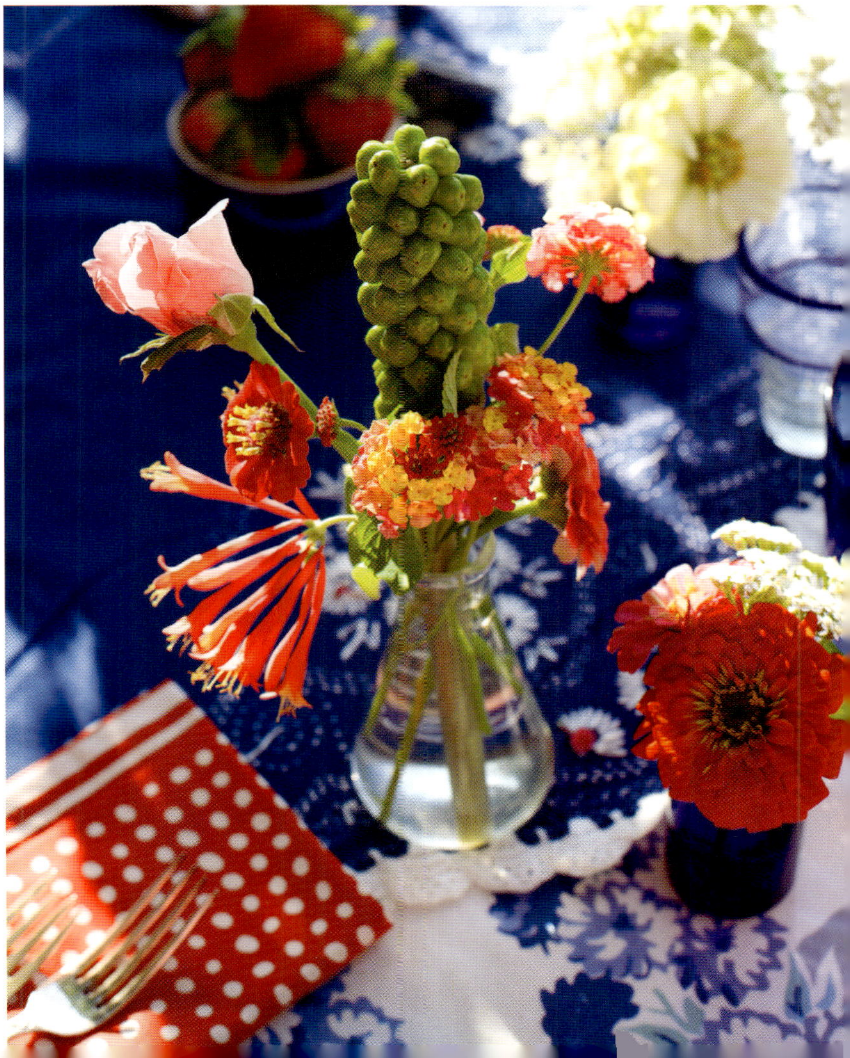

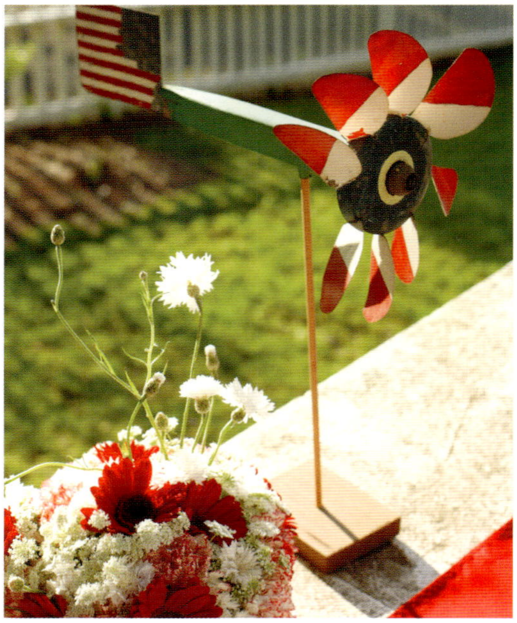

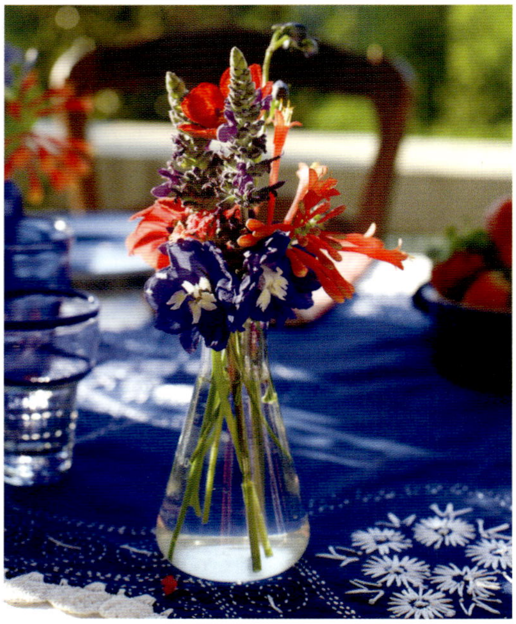

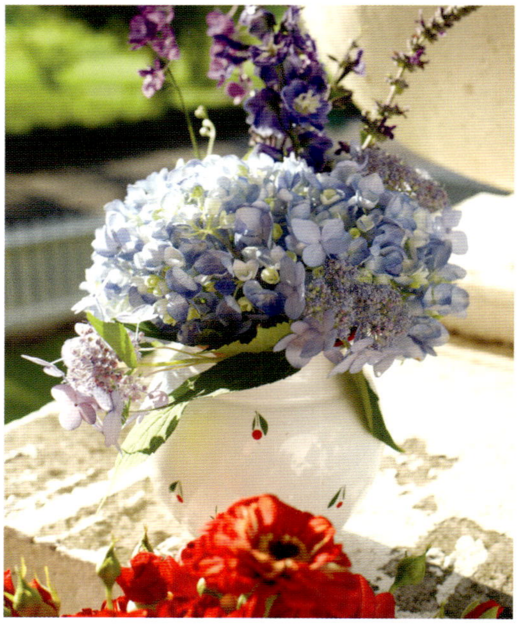

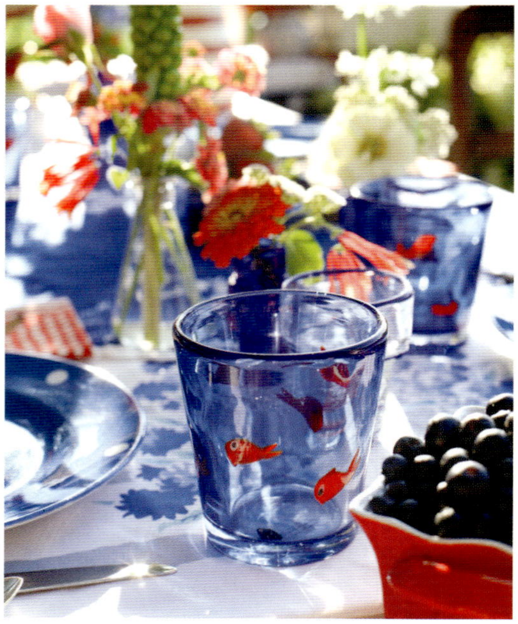

I HAVE ALWAYS BEEN A SUCKER FOR UNCLE SAM AND YANKEE DOODLE DANDY. OVER THE YEARS, I'VE TROLLED FLEA MARKETS AND AMASSED QUITE A COLLECTION OF RED, WHITE, AND BLUE PIECES—FOLK ART, POTTERY, FLAGS, LINENS, EVEN FLATWARE AND GLASS—THAT WE LOVE TO BRING OUT FOR EACH SUMMER CELEBRATION.

We always get comments on how beautiful the pre-arranged flowers are in the French sap buckets. So for this event, we massed together bunches of like flowers to make a big impact. I also picked flowers from the garden and filled little blue glasses and vases with them.

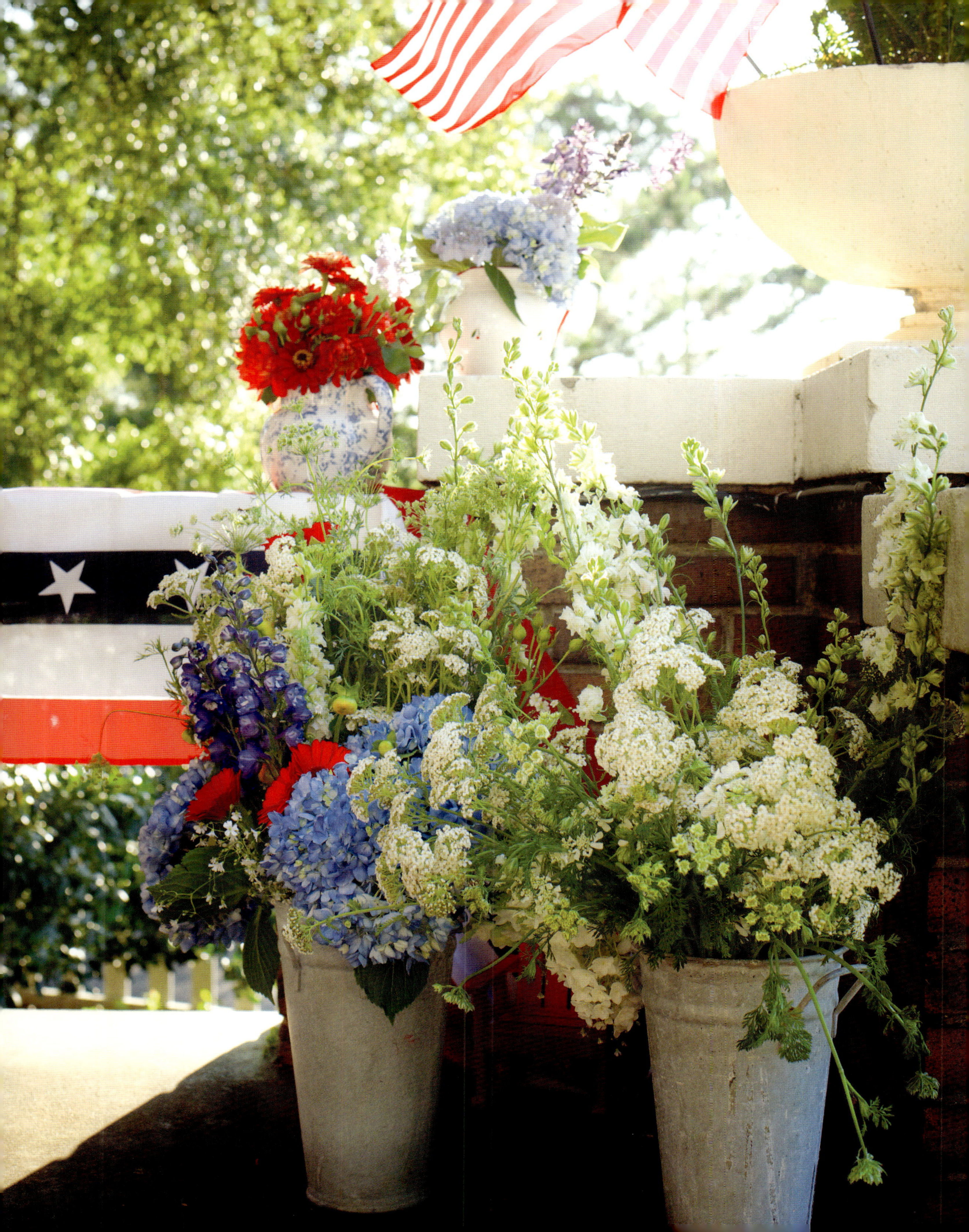

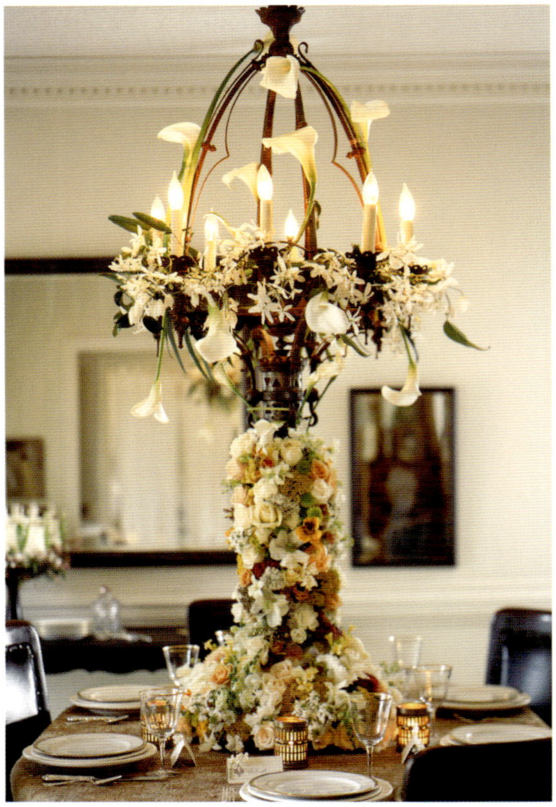

GOLDEN WEDDING ANNIVERSARY

celebrating fifty years

I set the scene for an intimate dinner party for family and close friends. The wife loves all things floral so I played off the neutral colors and soft textures in the house and went a little nuts with the flowers. The flower tower combines yellow cynthranthus flower with camel, Vendela, and Sahara roses and reaches up to touch the iron chandelier that I decked out with calla lillies and stephanotis. The tablesetting is restrained, porcelain plates and crystal wine glasses, in deference to all the action at the center of the table and the fun of the occasion.

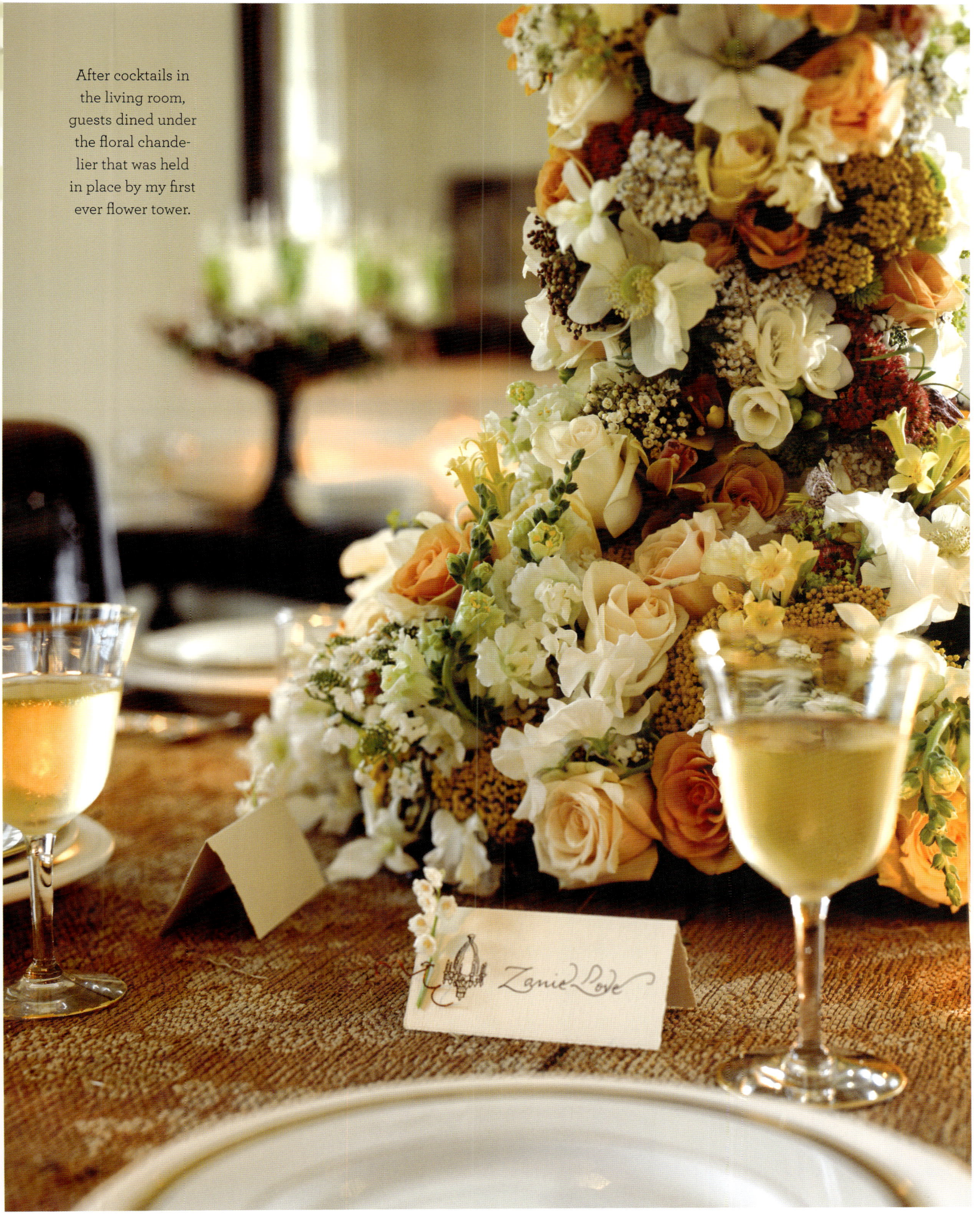

After cocktails in the living room, guests dined under the floral chandelier that was held in place by my first ever flower tower.

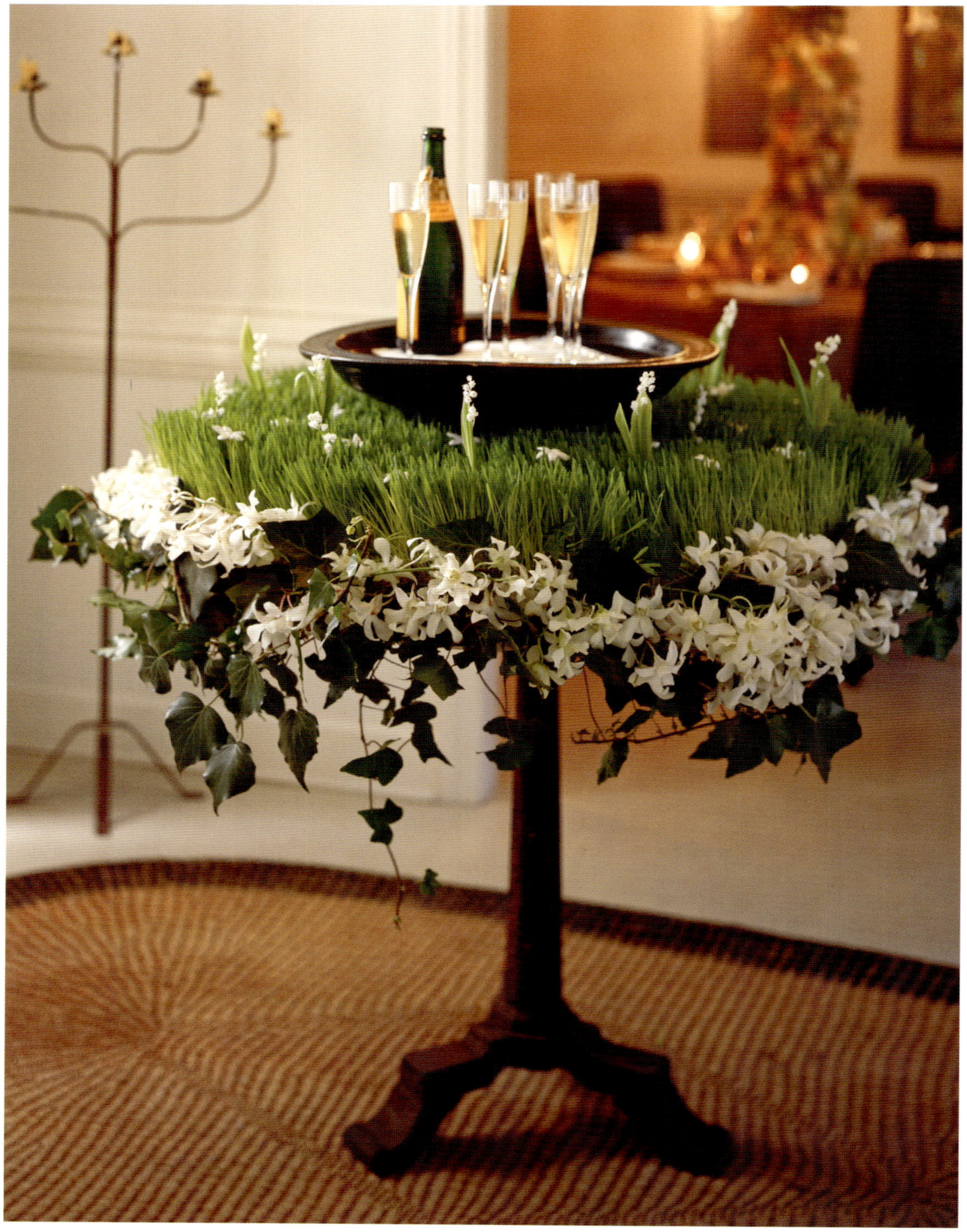

Guests entered the house to find a champagne table greeting them in the entrance hall. Homemade coconut cake was a family tradition, although it wasn't always dressed so elegantly. For this party, I used stephanotis blossoms as candle holders and surrounded the cake with lily of the valley and jasmine vine.

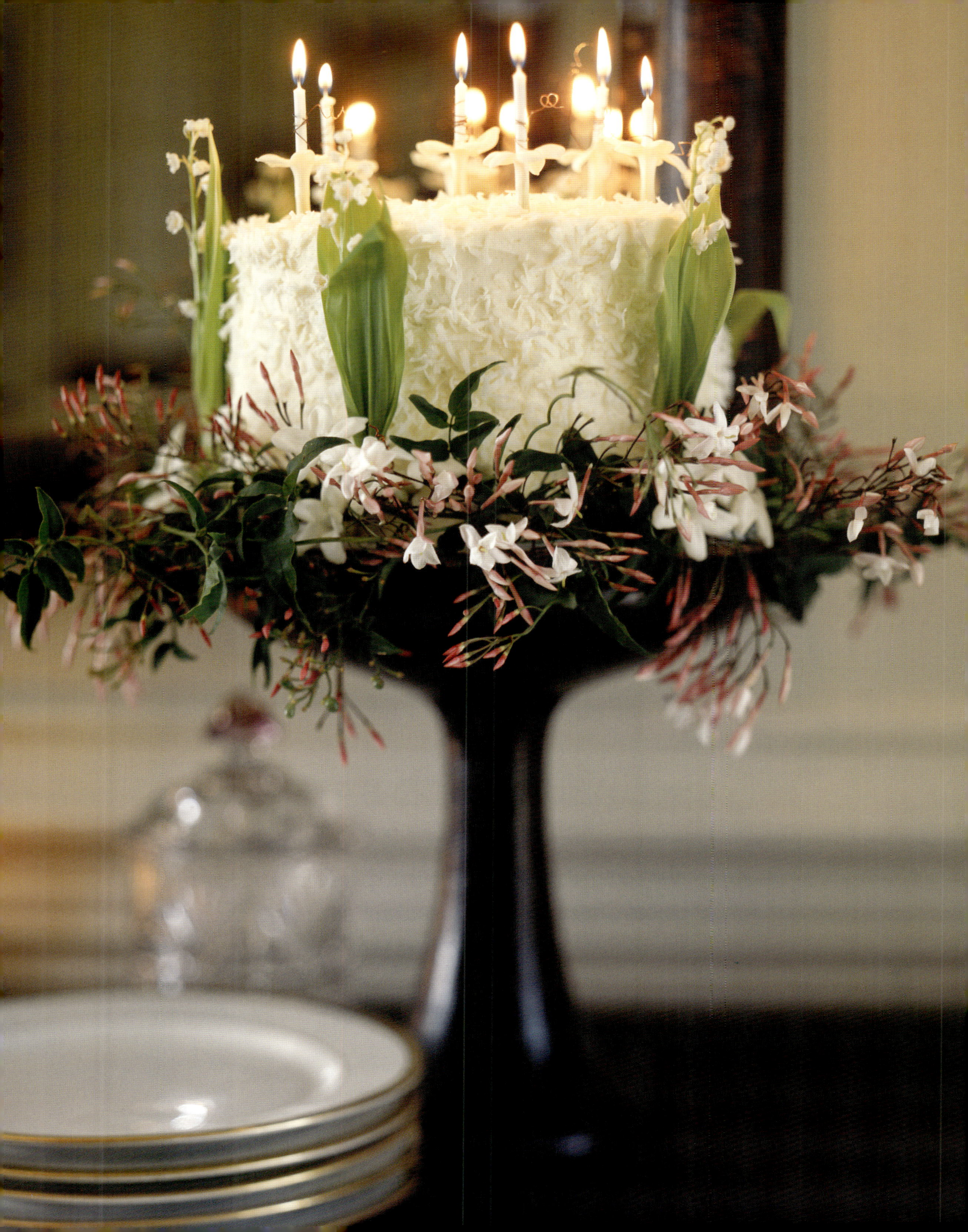

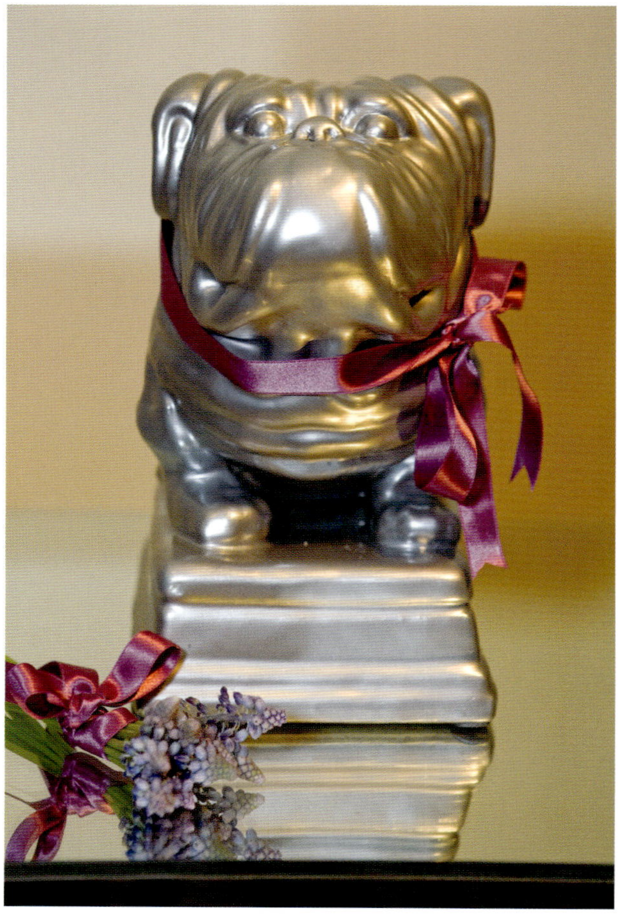

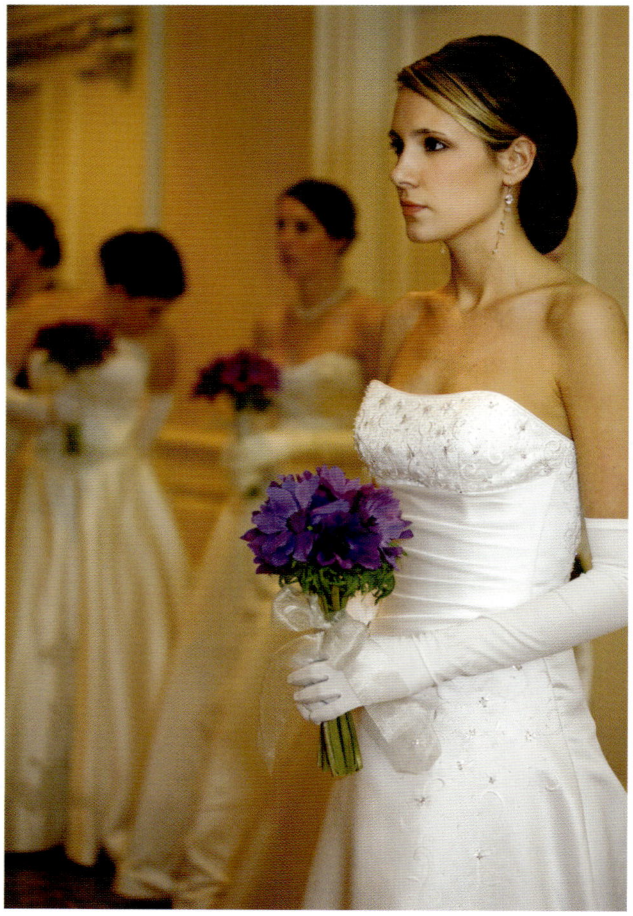

DEBUTANTE BALL

must wear a white gown

It's an annual Southern tradition, and this specific one occurs the Saturday night before Christmas. There are reams and reams of information on all the traditions that are celebrated each year at this event, and I am fortunate to be on the team to make the magic happen. The host club's colors are silver and purple, and their mascot is the bulldog. This particular year was the club's 50th anniversary so we went all out and all traditional.

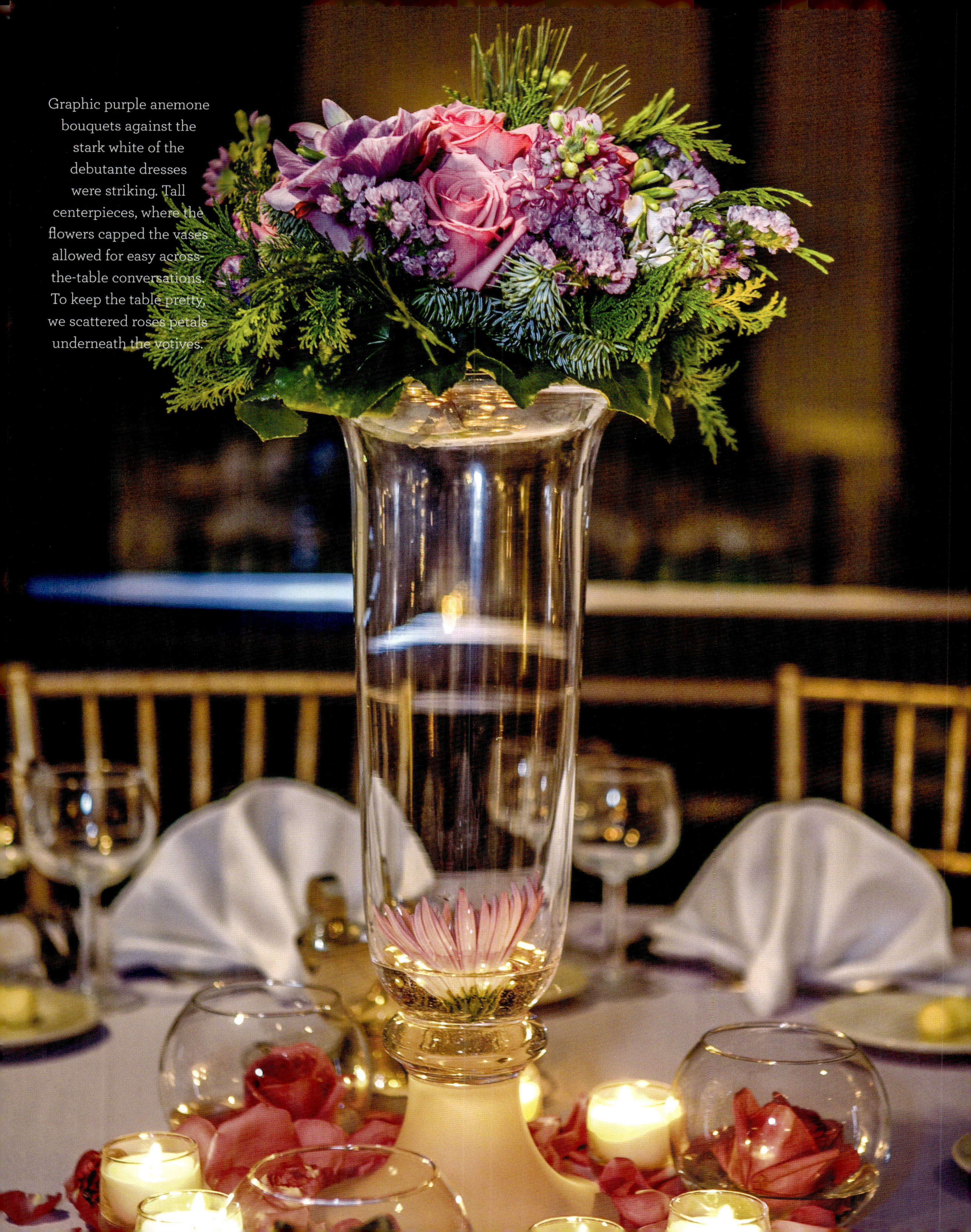

Graphic purple anemone bouquets against the stark white of the debutante dresses were striking. Tall centerpieces, where the flowers capped the vases allowed for easy across-the-table conversations. To keep the table pretty, we scattered roses petals underneath the votives.

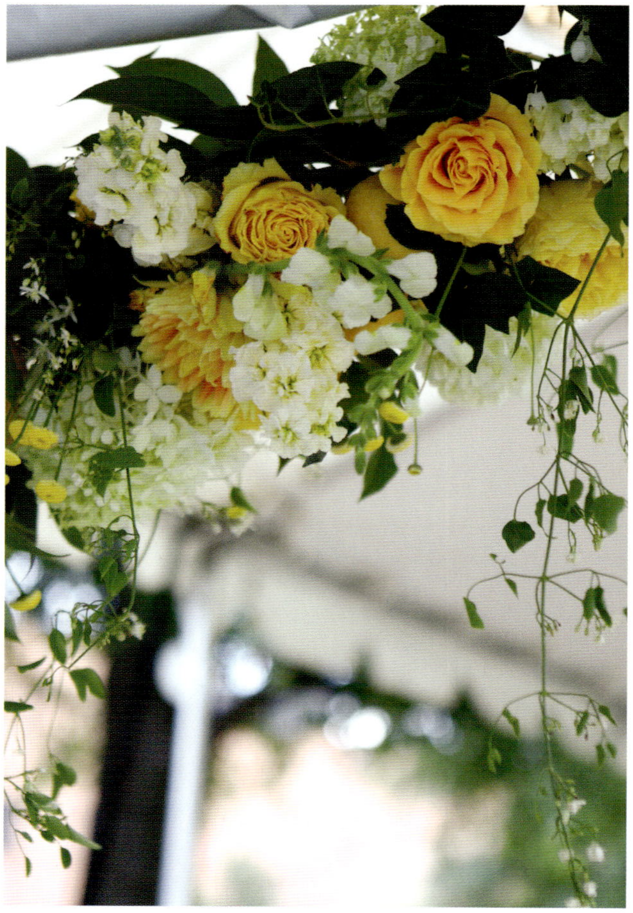

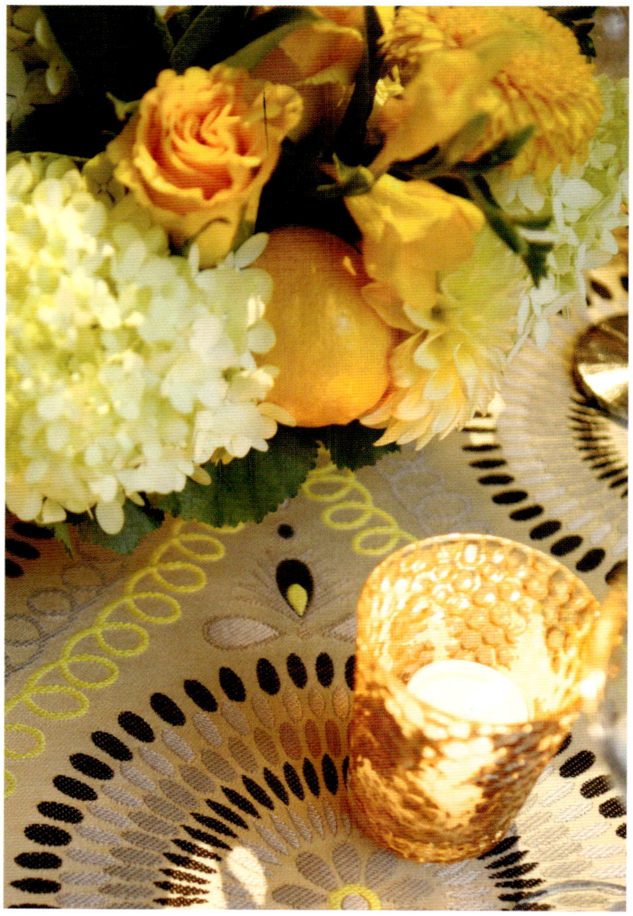

MAESTRO'S BALL

alabama symphony orchestra

The annual fundraiser is a not-to-miss black-tie event in Birmingham. Held every September, the gala follows a spine tingling concert in the concert hall. Then six to seven hundred guests make their way to a giant tent village that we create each year for a seated gourmet dinner. The theme of the party reflects the theme of the music that the guests have just heard. I have dutifully attempted to translate and incorporate into the dinner tent an atmosphere along with table decorations that do the beloved symphony justice.

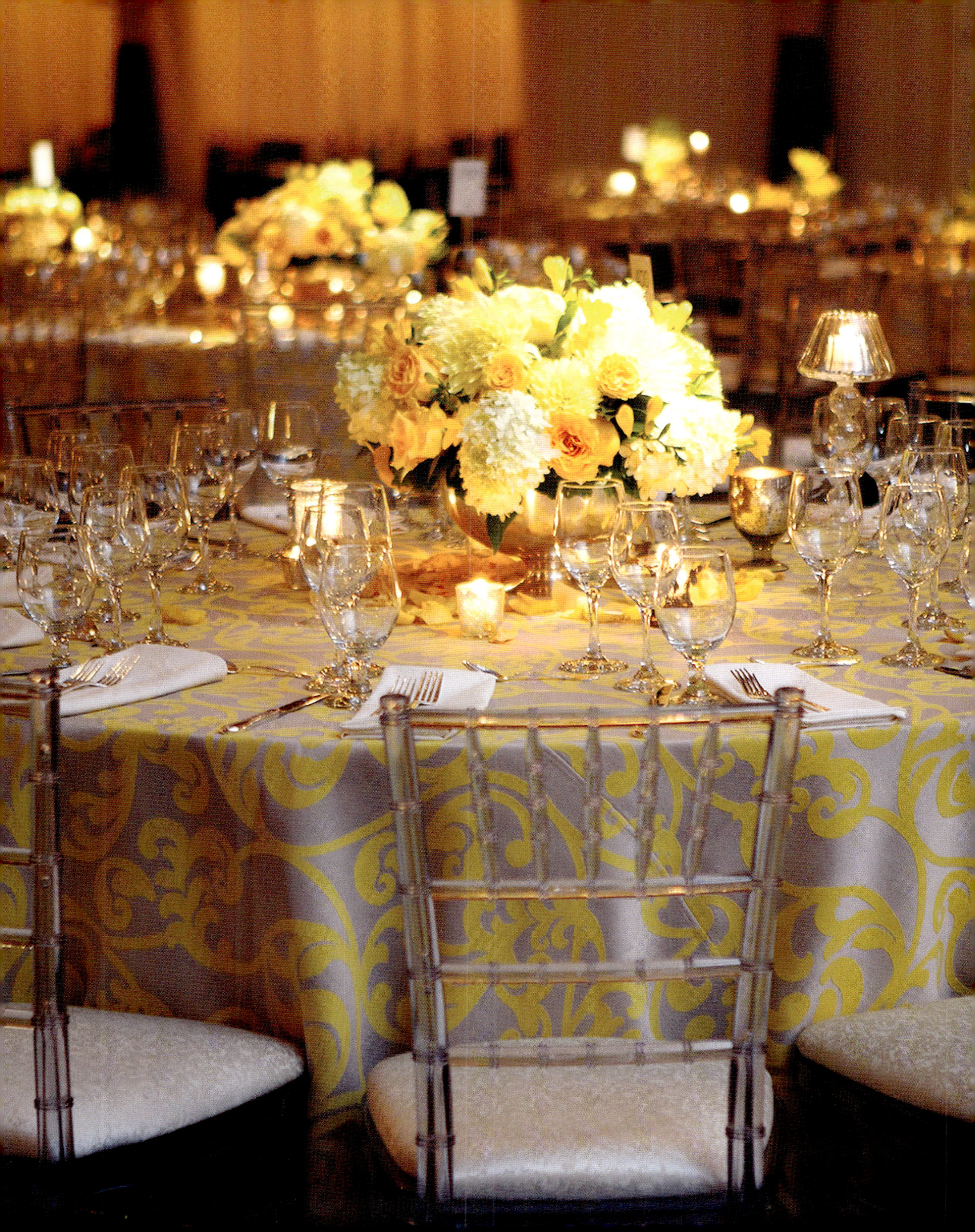

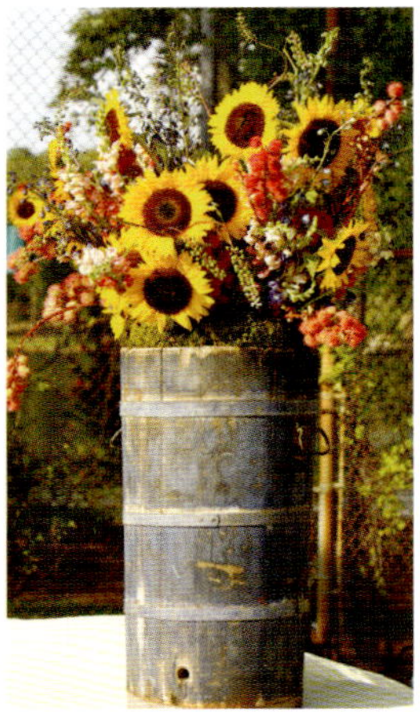

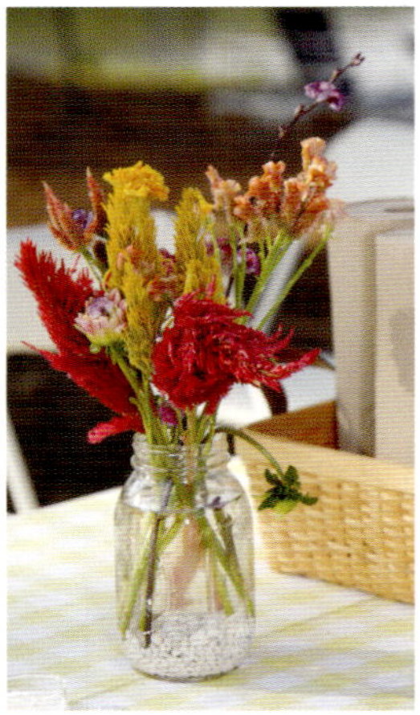

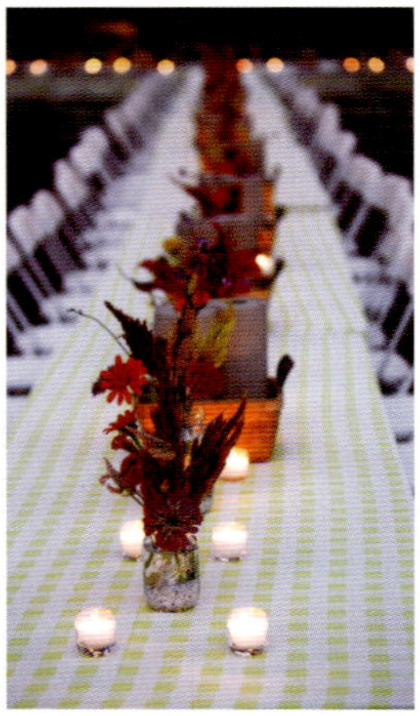

LAKE PARTY

a southern shrimp boil

A favorite Alabama pastime is the Southern Shrimp Boil, and in Birmingham, we like to do it at the lake. There was a huge field nearby for croquet and Frisbee and soccer and then a grove of pine trees closer to the water. I wanted to string bulb lights, so I used the trees as my poles. Then we set up a really long "T" shaped table and added baskets with paper towels to solve the inevitable mess of peeling shrimp shells. Interspersed mason jars full of summer flowers traded space with votive candles. It was a really fun night—I know because I was a guest!

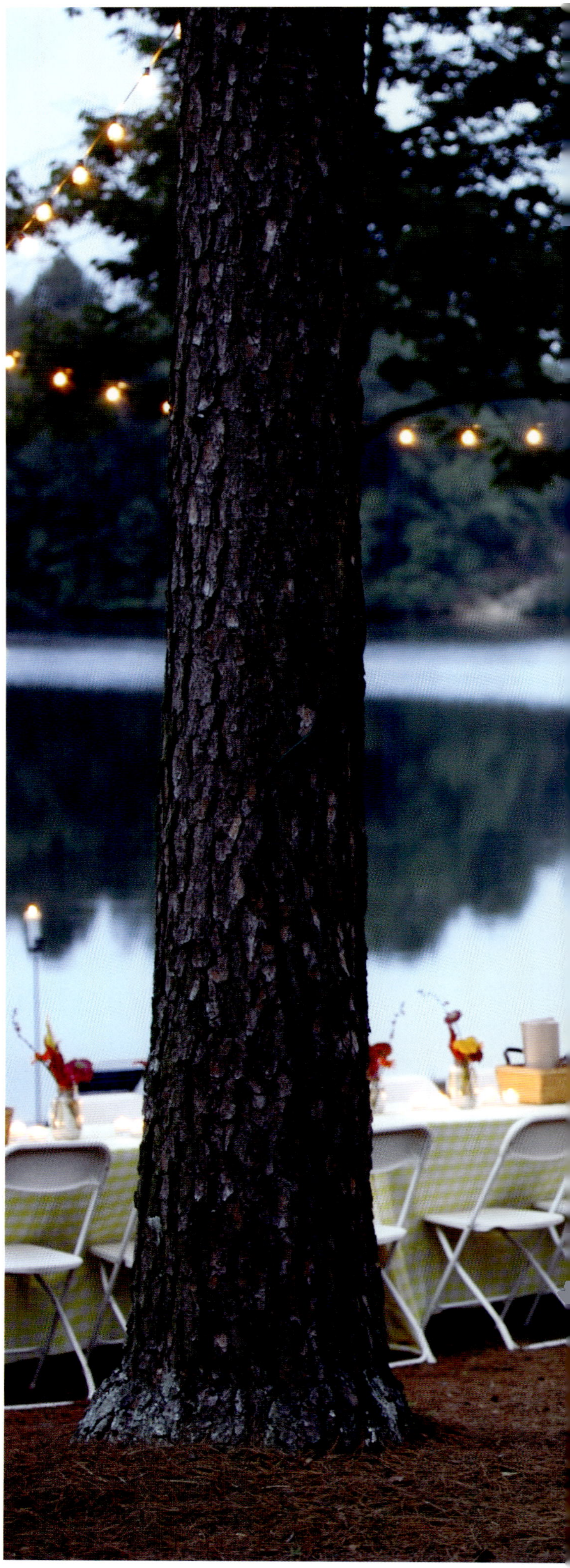

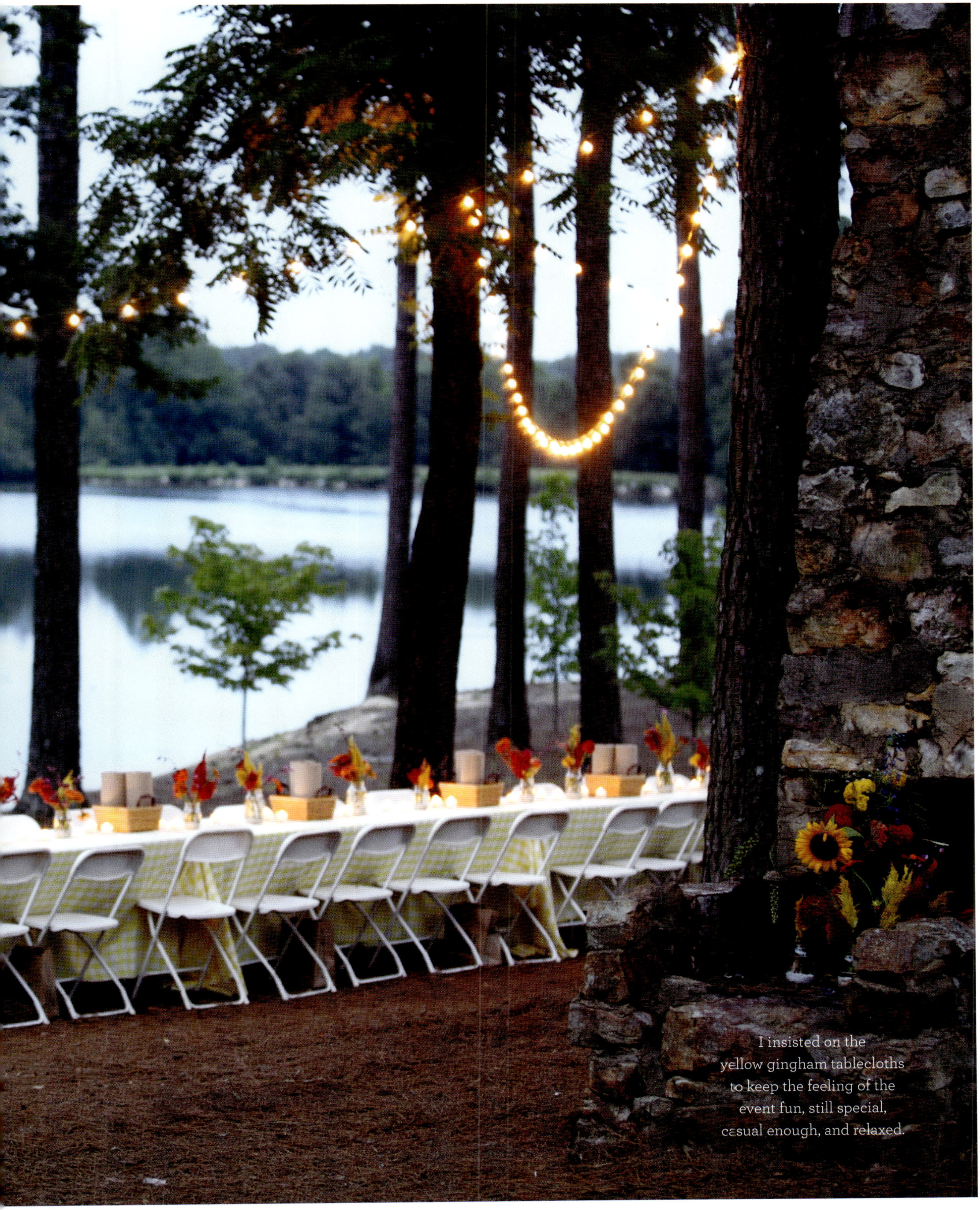

I insisted on the yellow gingham tablecloths to keep the feeling of the event fun, still special, casual enough, and relaxed.

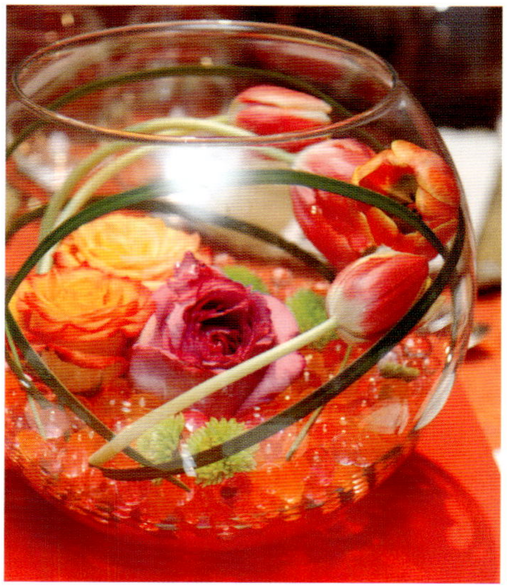

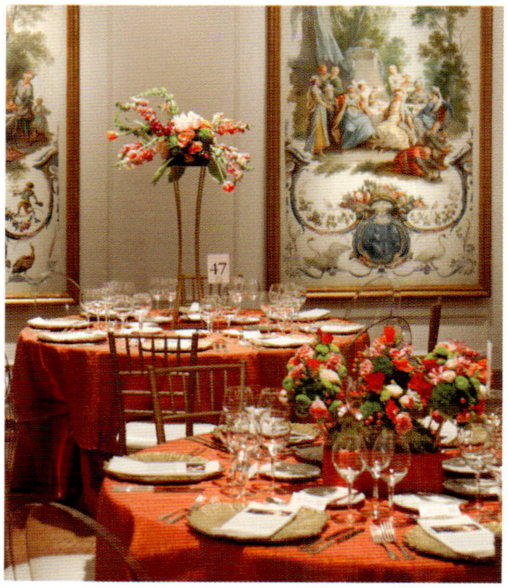

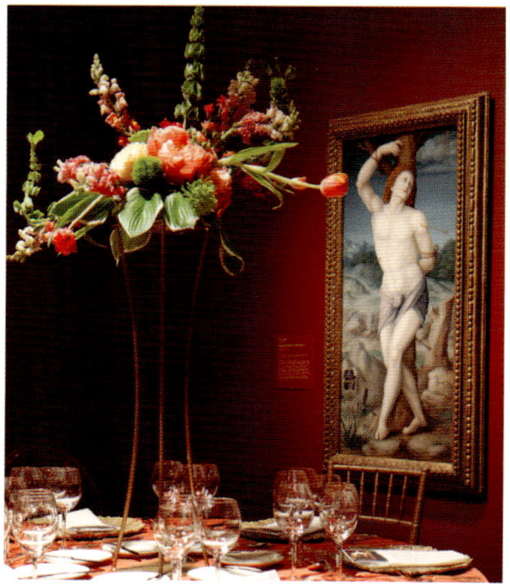

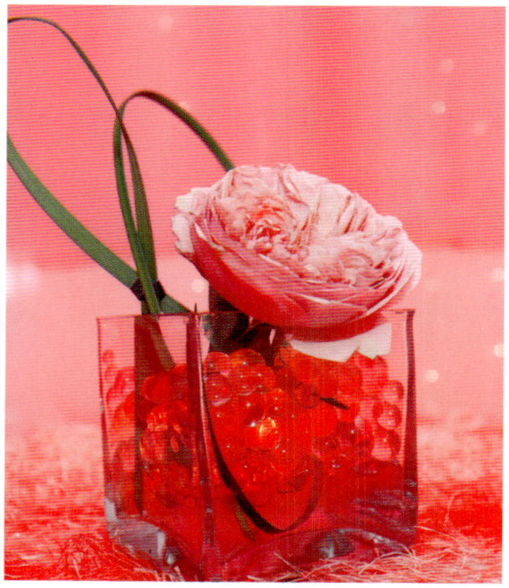

MUSEUM GALA

birmingham museum of art

Throughout the years I've been fortunate to create the setting for the crème de la crème of social and fundraising events in Birmingham—the Museum Ball. It's a black-tie event held throughout the museum, with amazing food prepared by top Birmingham chefs. Guests are wined and dined among glorious masterpieces and sculptures, and it is a very rare treat because it breaks all the rules. On any given day, you're not even allowed to have a bottle of water in your pocket book.

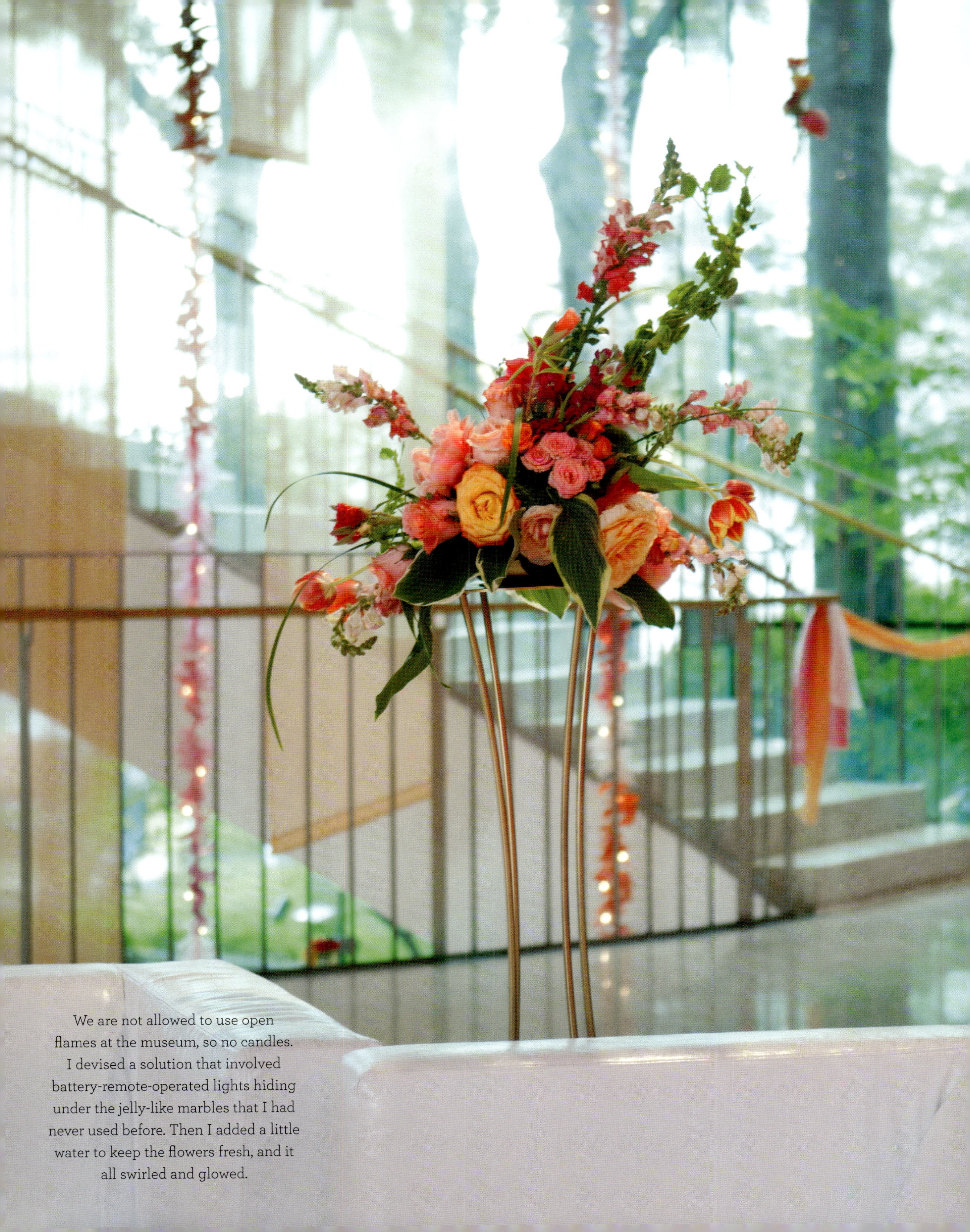

We are not allowed to use open flames at the museum, so no candles. I devised a solution that involved battery-remote-operated lights hiding under the jelly-like marbles that I had never used before. Then I added a little water to keep the flowers fresh, and it all swirled and glowed.

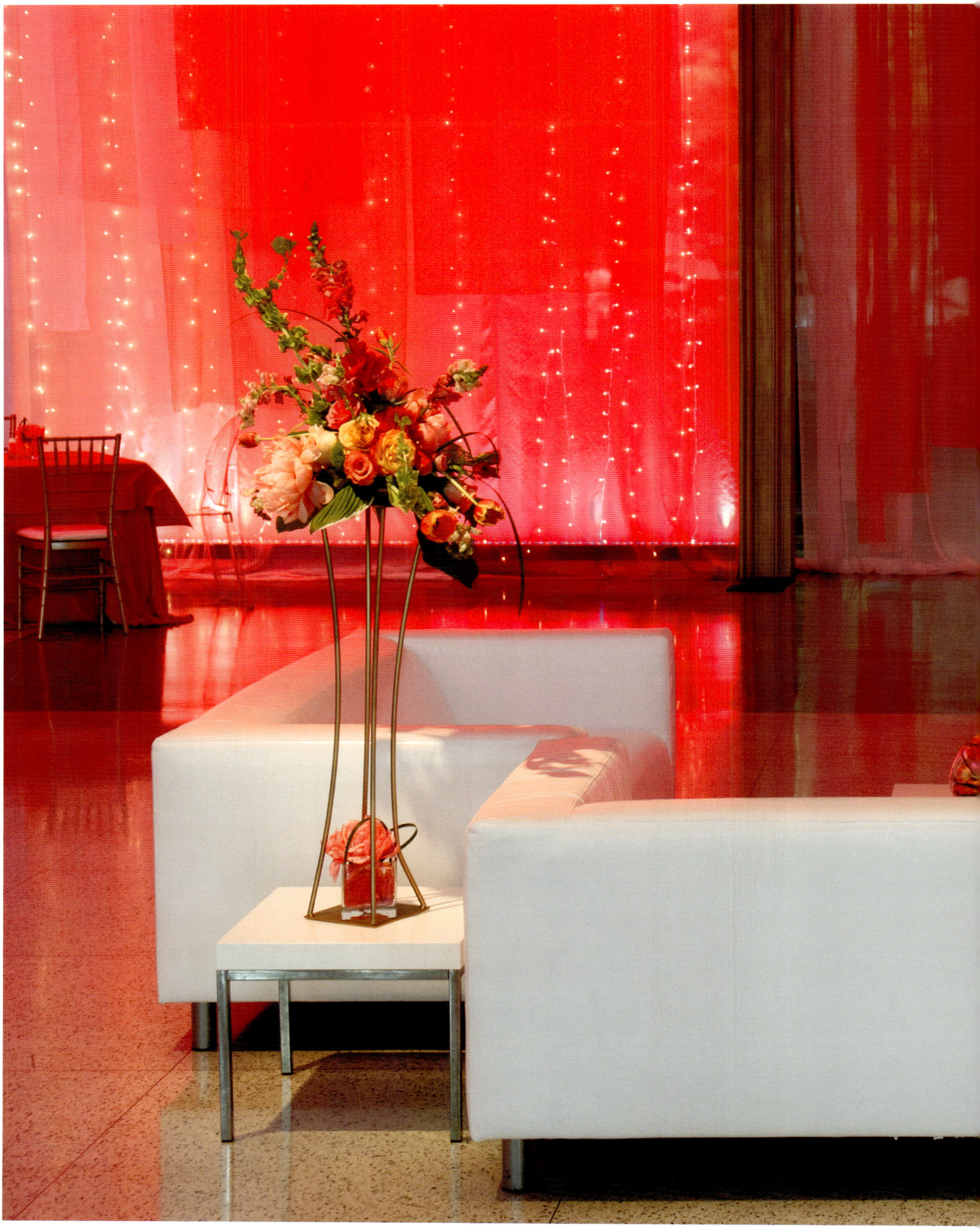

I CHOSE LOTS OF DRAPING TO HELP DEVISE AND DEFINE AREAS OF THE PARTY. I HAD THE IDEA TO MIX IN SOFT LINEN FABRICS AND HANG THEM, ALMOST AS IF THEY ARE FABRICS HANGING LIKE SHEETS ON THE LINE DRYING IN THE SUN.

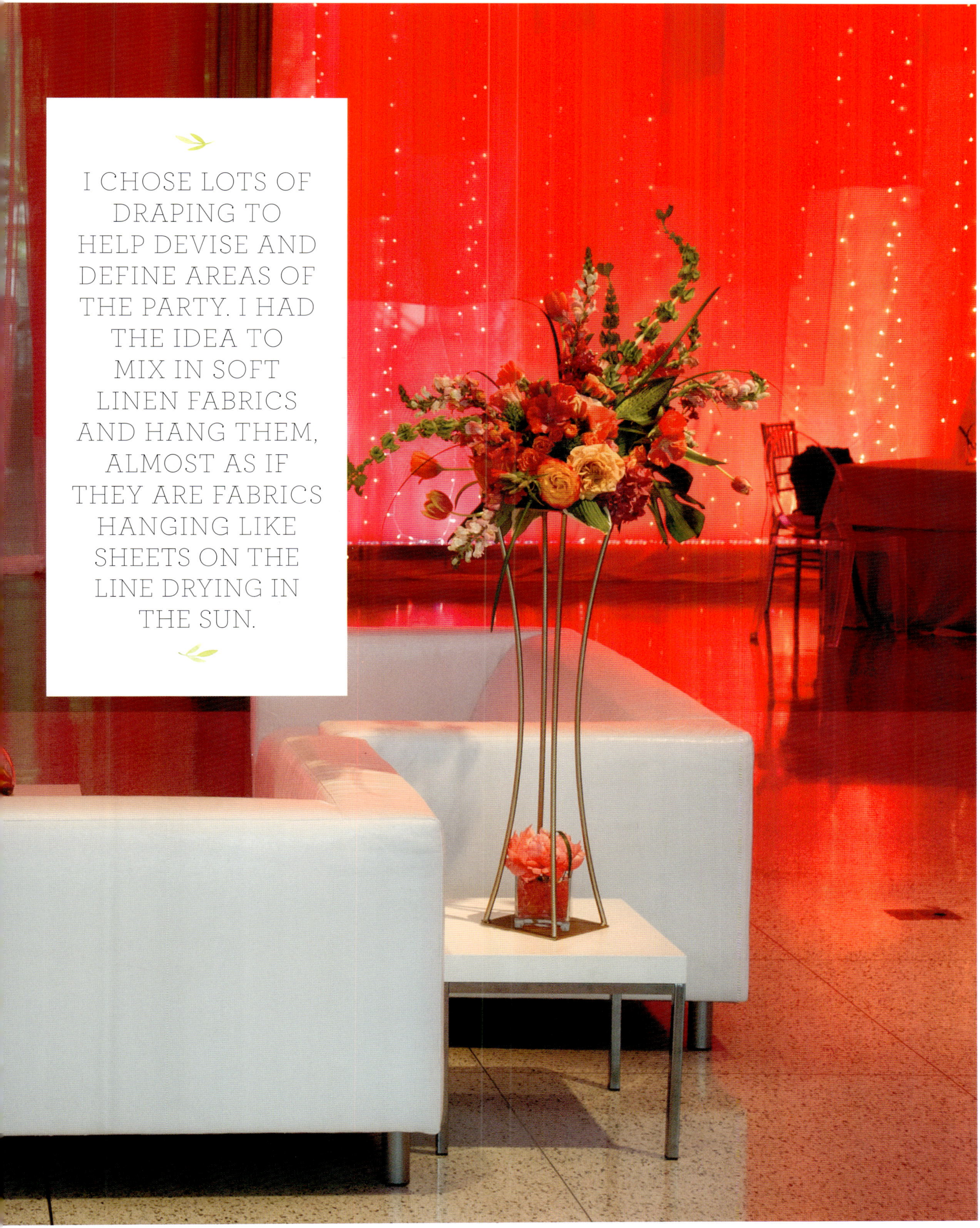

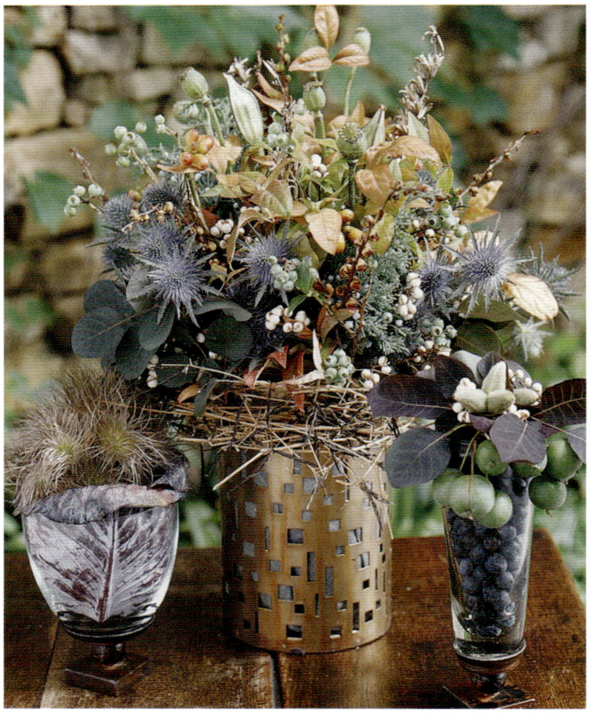

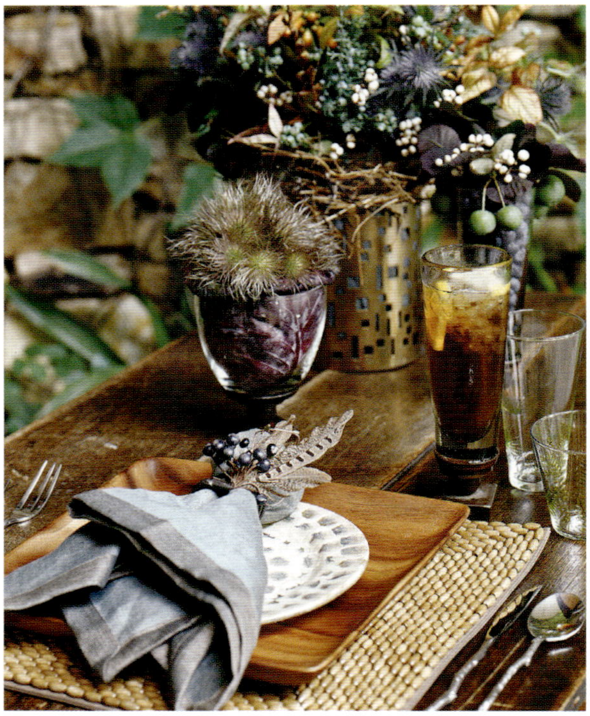

DOVE HUNT

rustic en plein air

What a totally fun day—whether you are lucky enough to attend an all-out styled and decorated fete following a morning in the fields or you have a sandwich in a brown sack and a coke while resting on a hay bale. This was one of those rare over-the-top Dove Hunt luncheons where the guests felt pampered and indulged. It was a day not to be forgotten.

I started with a brass hurricane lantern (by my favorite artist Martha Sturdy). I lined it with a linen napkin and then placed a plain glass cylinder inside to hold the flowers and water. Then I added a grapevine collar around the mouth of the vase, creating the feel of a bird's nest to cradle the arrangement. The wine goblet is lined with purple cabbage leaf. I added water to hold the seed pods—for a little Sybil signature whimsy. I filled the champagne flute with blueberries then added water and tucked a grouping of pods and leaves into the top—almost like a little hat.

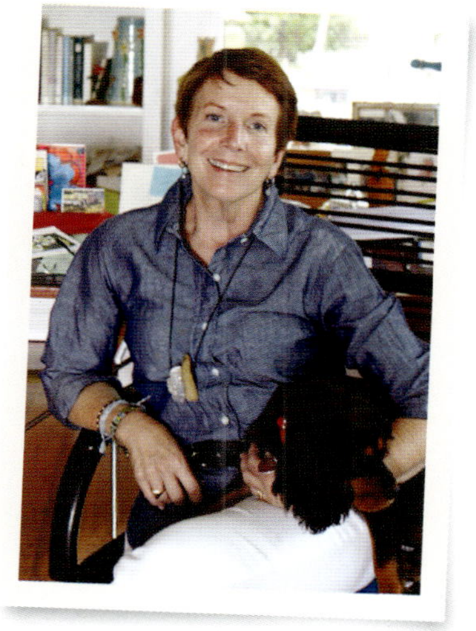

CENTERPIECES

Centerpieces can go in so many directions, so I have hit upon a current solution that we are liking. I've always mixed styles—not wanting the room to look too cookie cutter—but now we are using at least 3 designs that fall at different price points. You get a big impact at an averaged price, which brings the overall pricepoint of the event down. It is more complicated for my team but works for an overall look and budget considerations. I never like for flower arrangements to look like they came off of an assembly line.

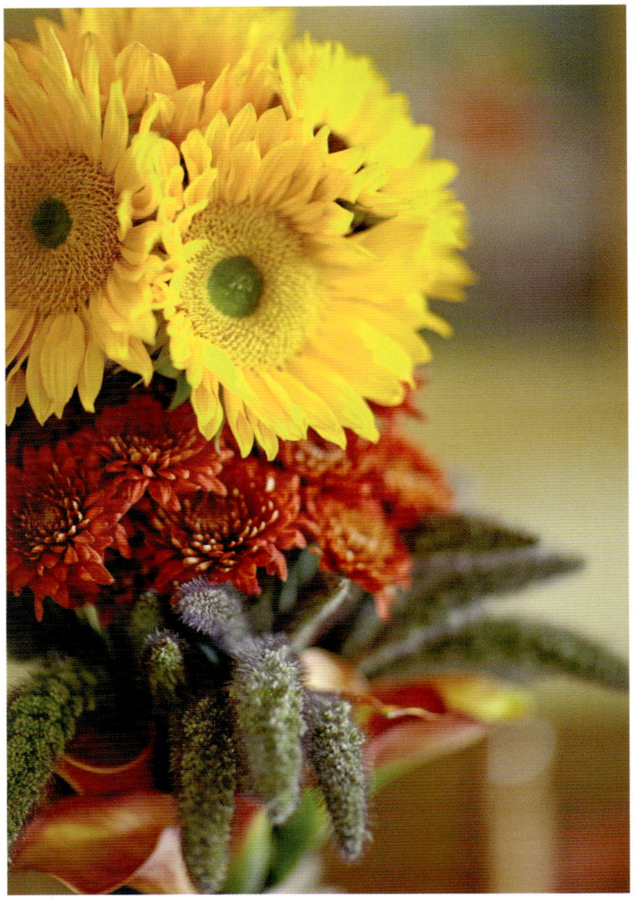

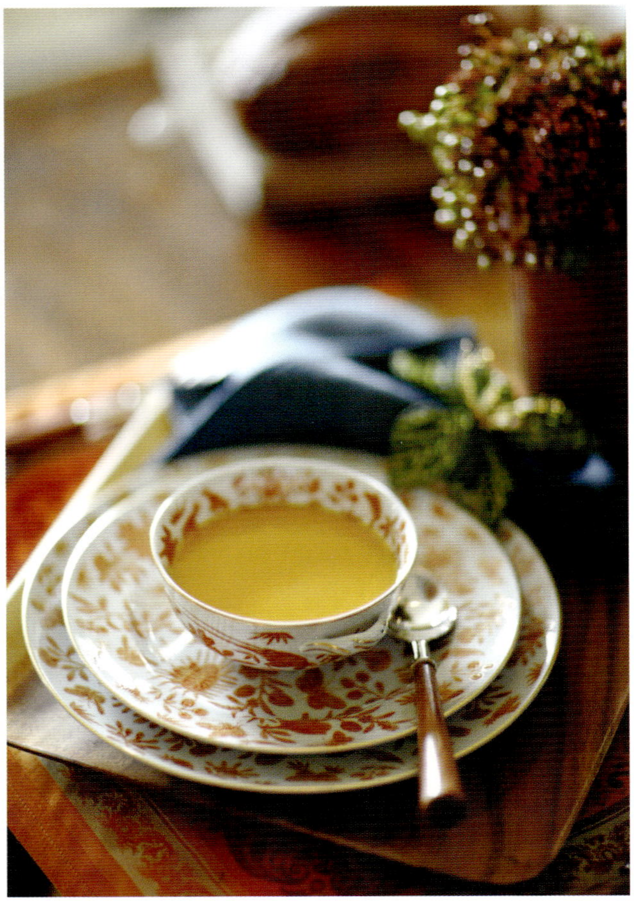

THANKSGIVING DINNER

all about the harvest

One of the things I cherish the most about my work is being trusted to come in and fix and do what I see as appropriate for my clients' family celebrations. This family is laidback with great cooks and laugh-so-hard-you-cry stories to enjoy while giving thanks for all. I kept the dinner on the casual side, but still beautiful for the holiday.

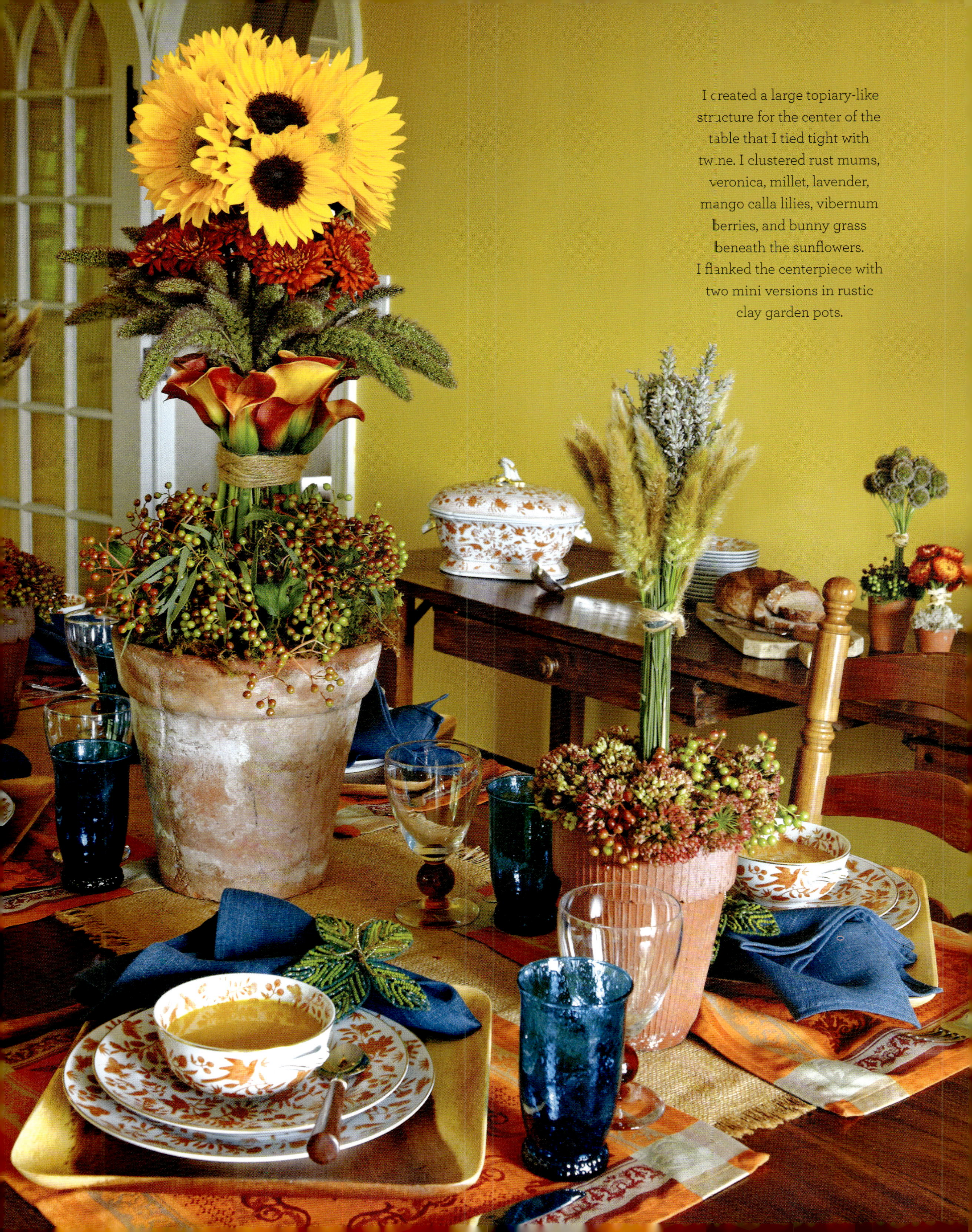

I created a large topiary-like structure for the center of the table that I tied tight with twine. I clustered rust mums, veronica, millet, lavender, mango calla lilies, vibernum berries, and bunny grass beneath the sunflowers. I flanked the centerpiece with two mini versions in rustic clay garden pots.

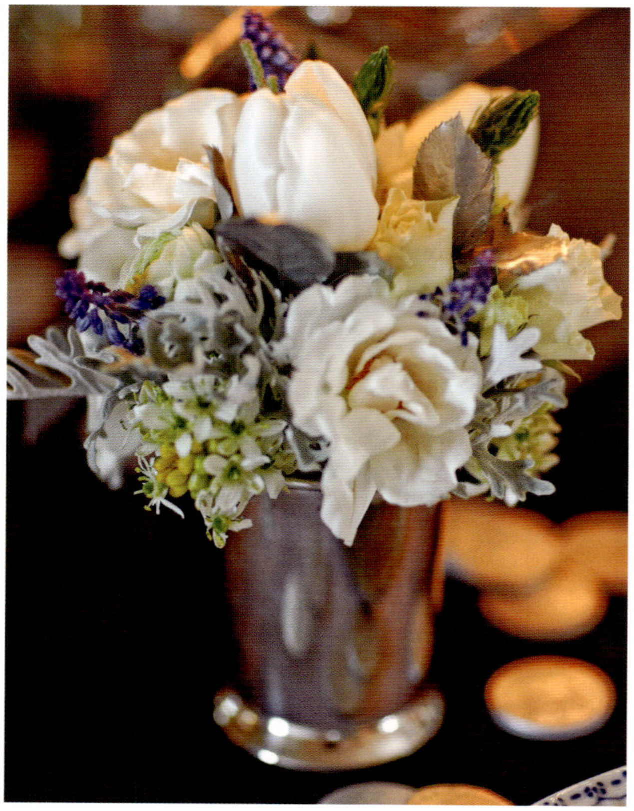

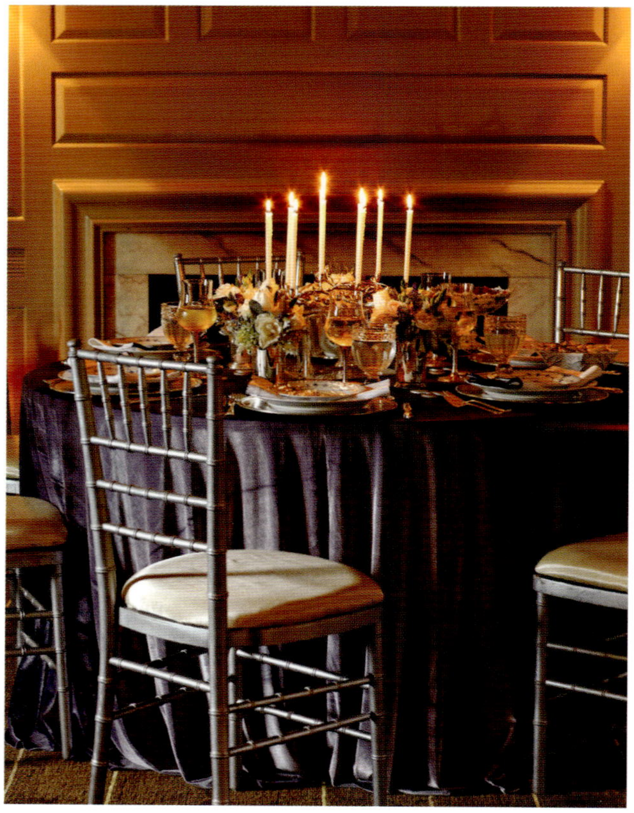

HANUKKAH

festival of eight days

It's such a special family time and deserved a pretty presentation for all who gathered. We worked with traditional silver and blue colors that made the table elegant: the Menorah and silver chairs, silver julep cups holding flowers, special lucky silver coins sprinkled on the table, blue and white patterned china, and tiny blue flowers mixed in with white flowers and dusty miller "silver" foliage.
I especially love the plum velvet cloth that helped to meld the silver and blue and add an elegant base for the entire table.

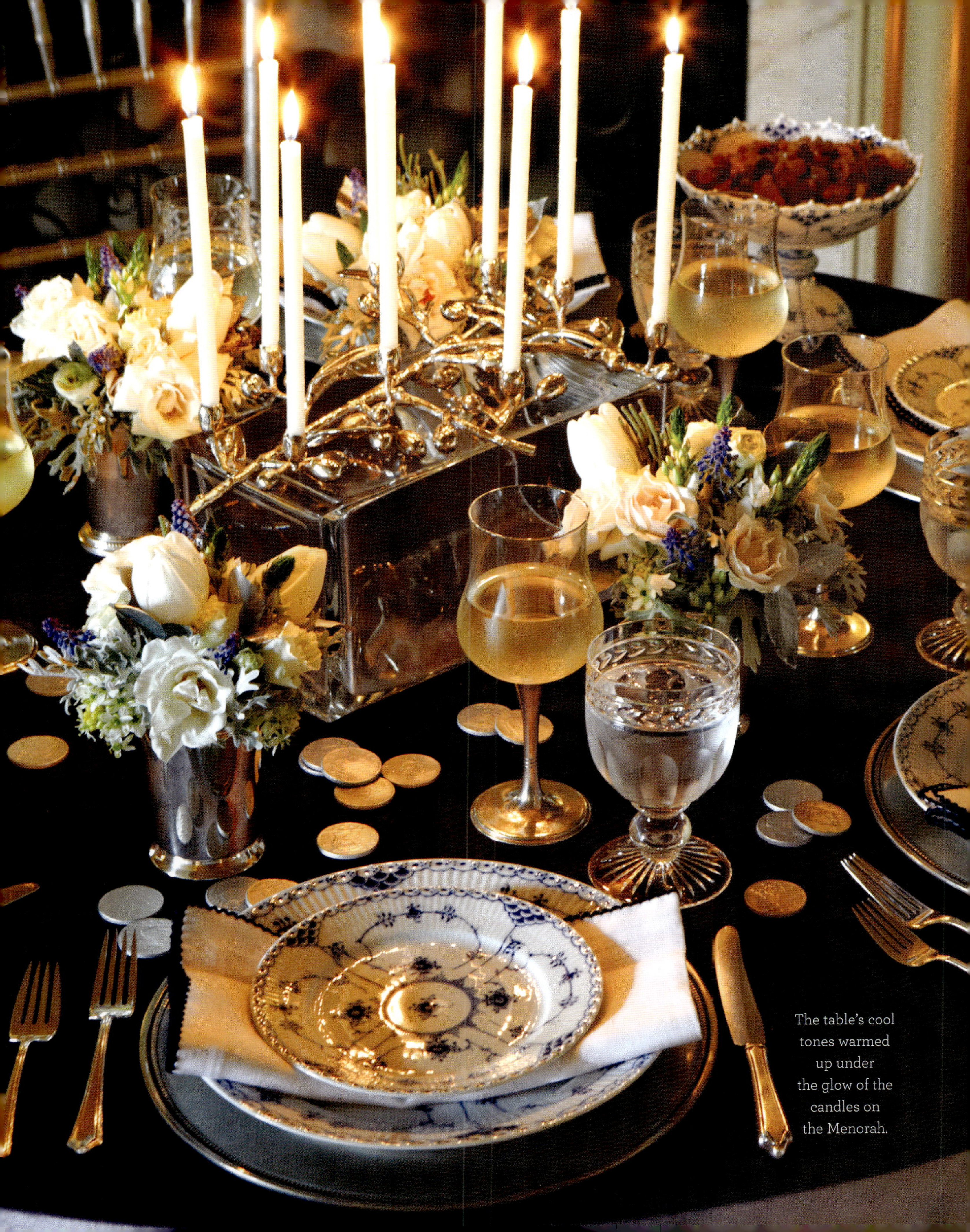

The table's cool tones warmed up under the glow of the candles on the Menorah.

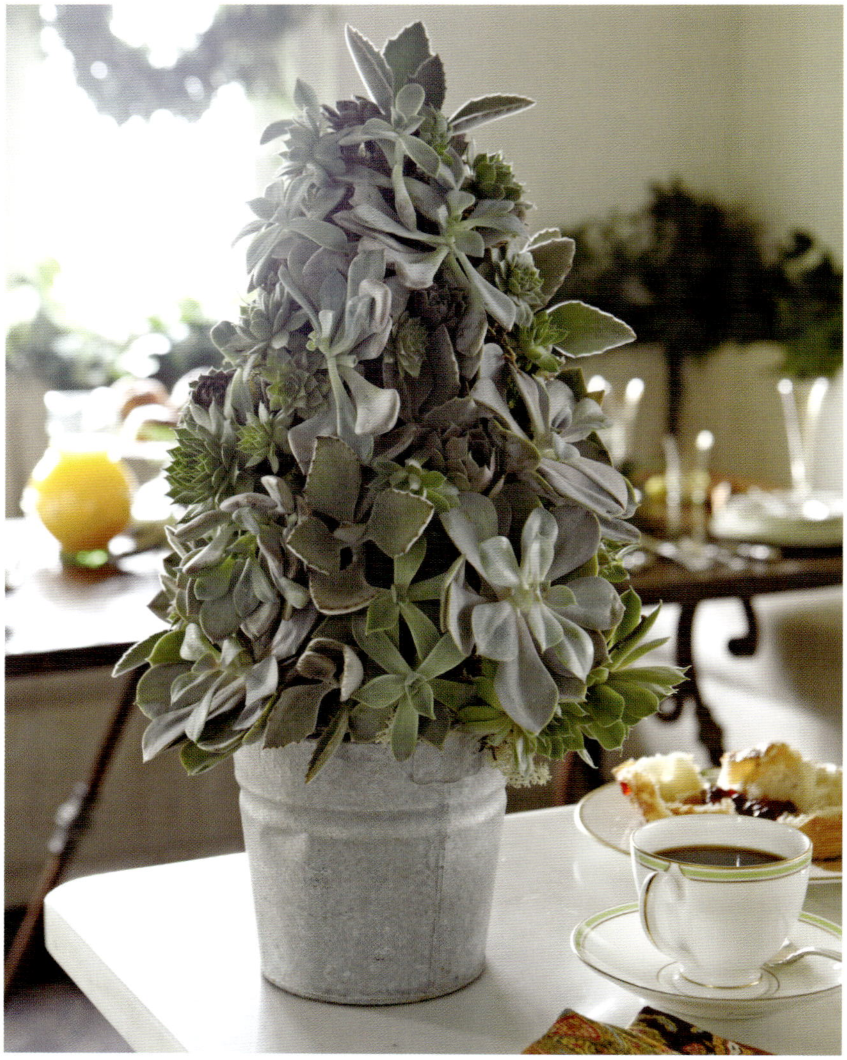

CHRISTMAS BREAKFAST

right where I want to be, slippers and all

C'est Noel says it all! I made the sign out of plumber's copper tubing, and we hung it behind the head of the table. I banked the banquet seating area with a Christmas garland composed of branches of holly and pine and eucalyptus tucked in. The centerpiece is essentially a planted garden that I created from green lichen branches stacked around a center container. Inside are purple flowers mixed with succulents and mercury balls for a little sparkle.

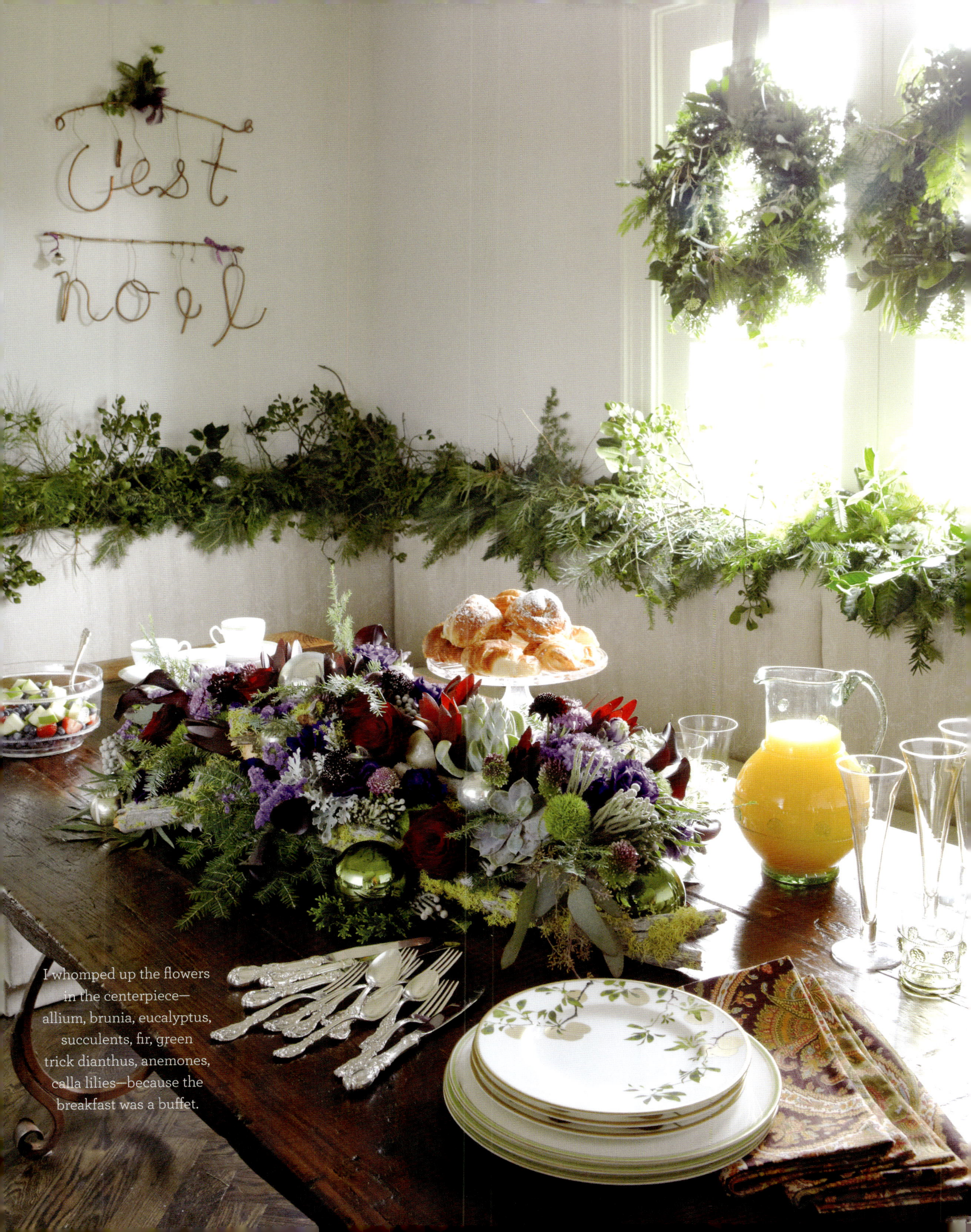

I whomped up the flowers in the centerpiece—allium, brunia, eucalyptus, succulents, fir, green trick dianthus, anemones, calla lilies—because the breakfast was a buffet.

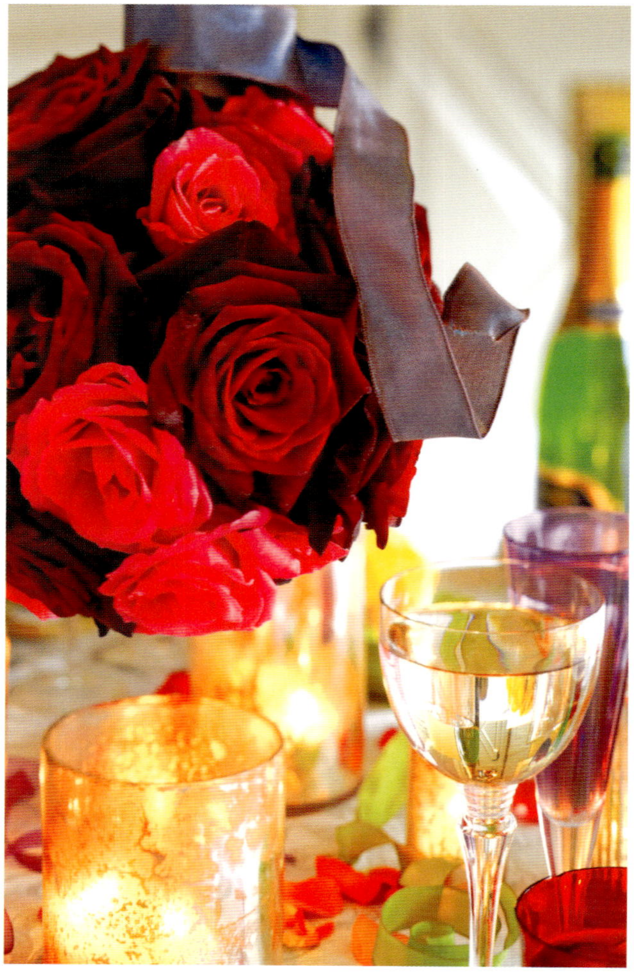

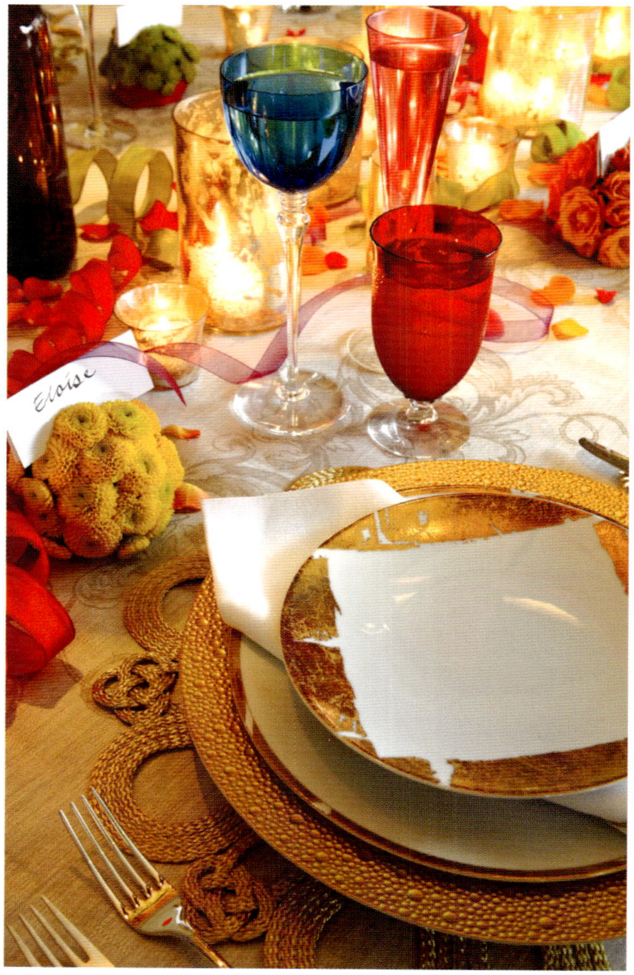

RING IN THE NEW YEAR

for "auld lang syne"

As often happens, my eyes went straight to the light fixture. I knew we could use it to create drama centered over the table. Instead of going the all white route, which often happens after Christmas when people are over the over red and green, I went a little nuts with colors! All that's missing here are the hats, shakers, and poppers that come out at midnight.

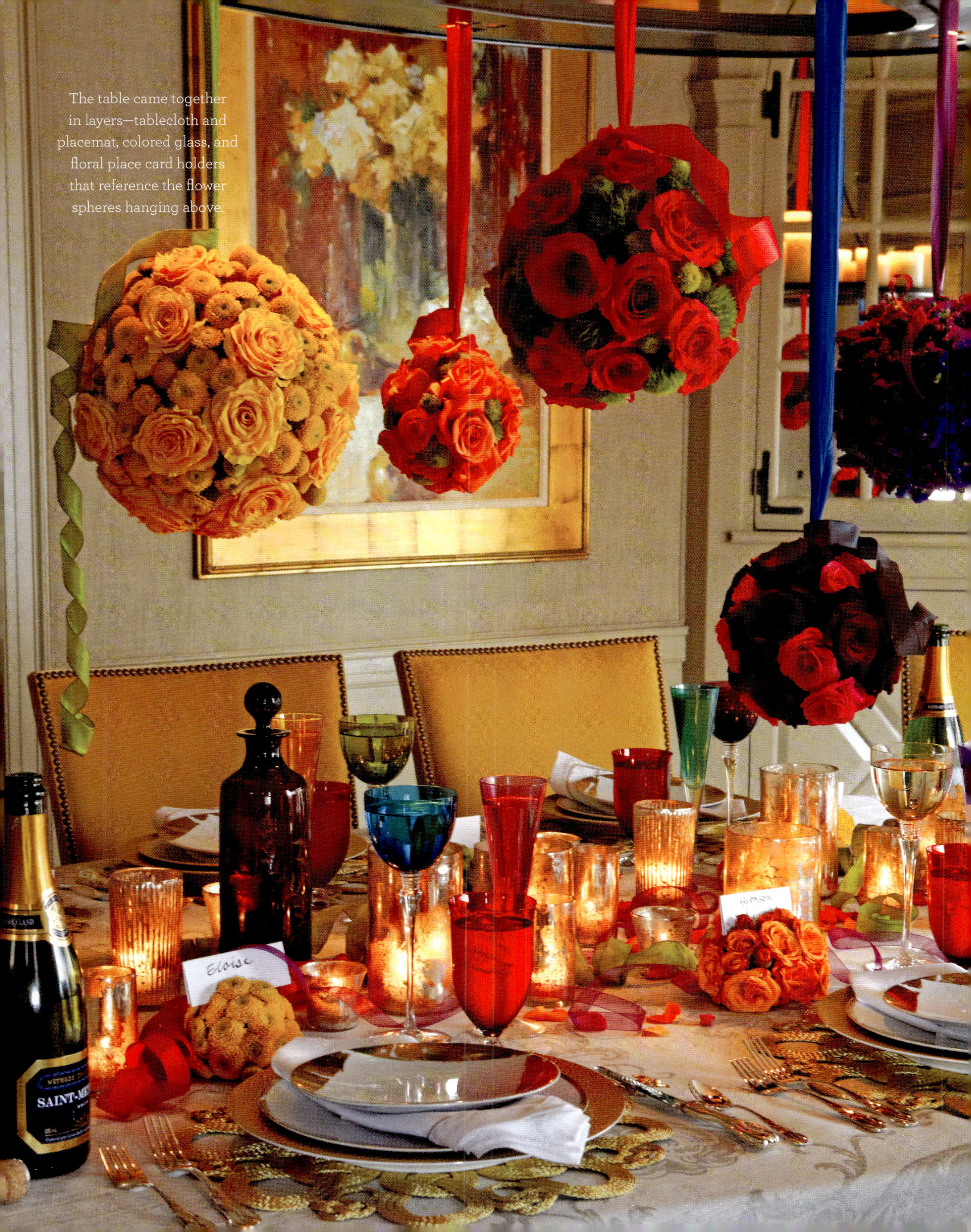

The table came together in layers—tablecloth and placemat, colored glass, and floral place card holders that reference the flower spheres hanging above.

weddings

Obviously, I am Southern, and I have always been profoundly impacted by what Southerners call a "proper wedding." We do it our way—family silver, an heirloom handkerchief in the bride's bouquet, linen and lace tablecloths, mixed with thoughtful reflections that represent the adorable couple getting hitched. Of course, gorgeous flowers, delicious food, and wonderful music are part of the day too. We include traditional touches, along with fun and whimsy. Rarely is there a seated dinner for all in attendance. Usually, it's a full on party—with cocktails flowing, massive food buffets with local favorites, and seating for a portion of the group because the band is so great, no one stays seated for long.

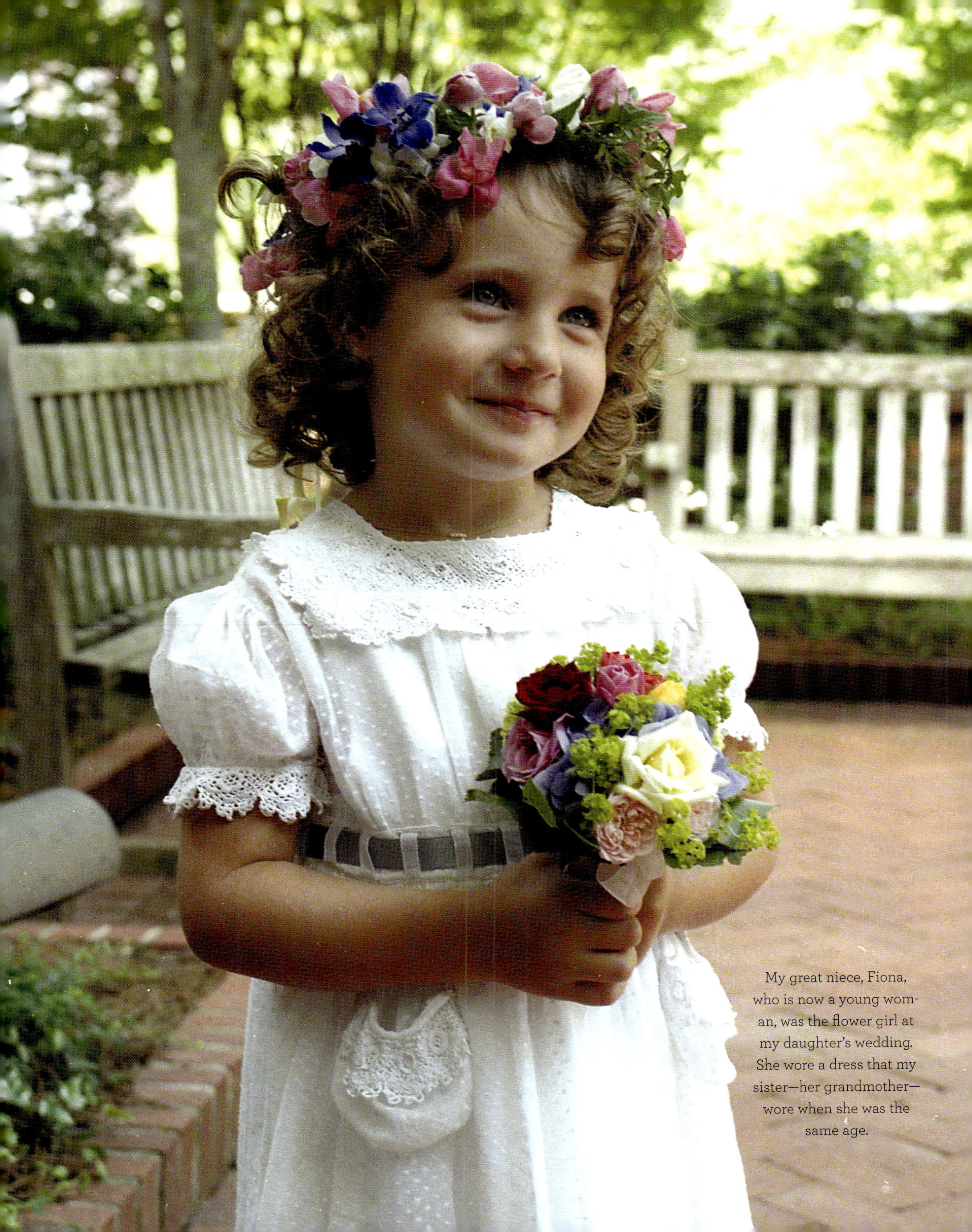

My great niece, Fiona, who is now a young woman, was the flower girl at my daughter's wedding. She wore a dress that my sister—her grandmother—wore when she was the same age.

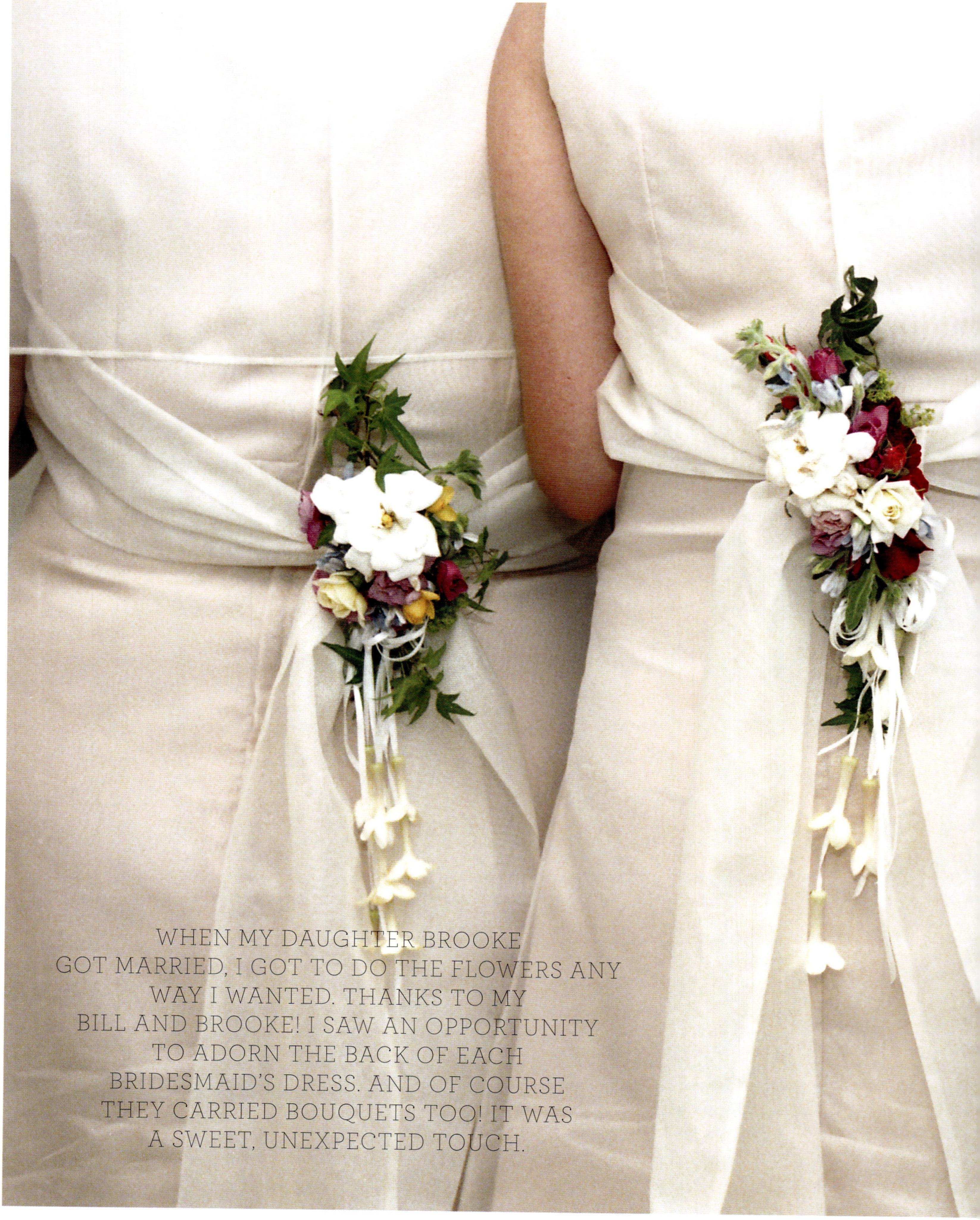

WHEN MY DAUGHTER BROOKE GOT MARRIED, I GOT TO DO THE FLOWERS ANY WAY I WANTED. THANKS TO MY BILL AND BROOKE! I SAW AN OPPORTUNITY TO ADORN THE BACK OF EACH BRIDESMAID'S DRESS. AND OF COURSE THEY CARRIED BOUQUETS TOO! IT WAS A SWEET, UNEXPECTED TOUCH.

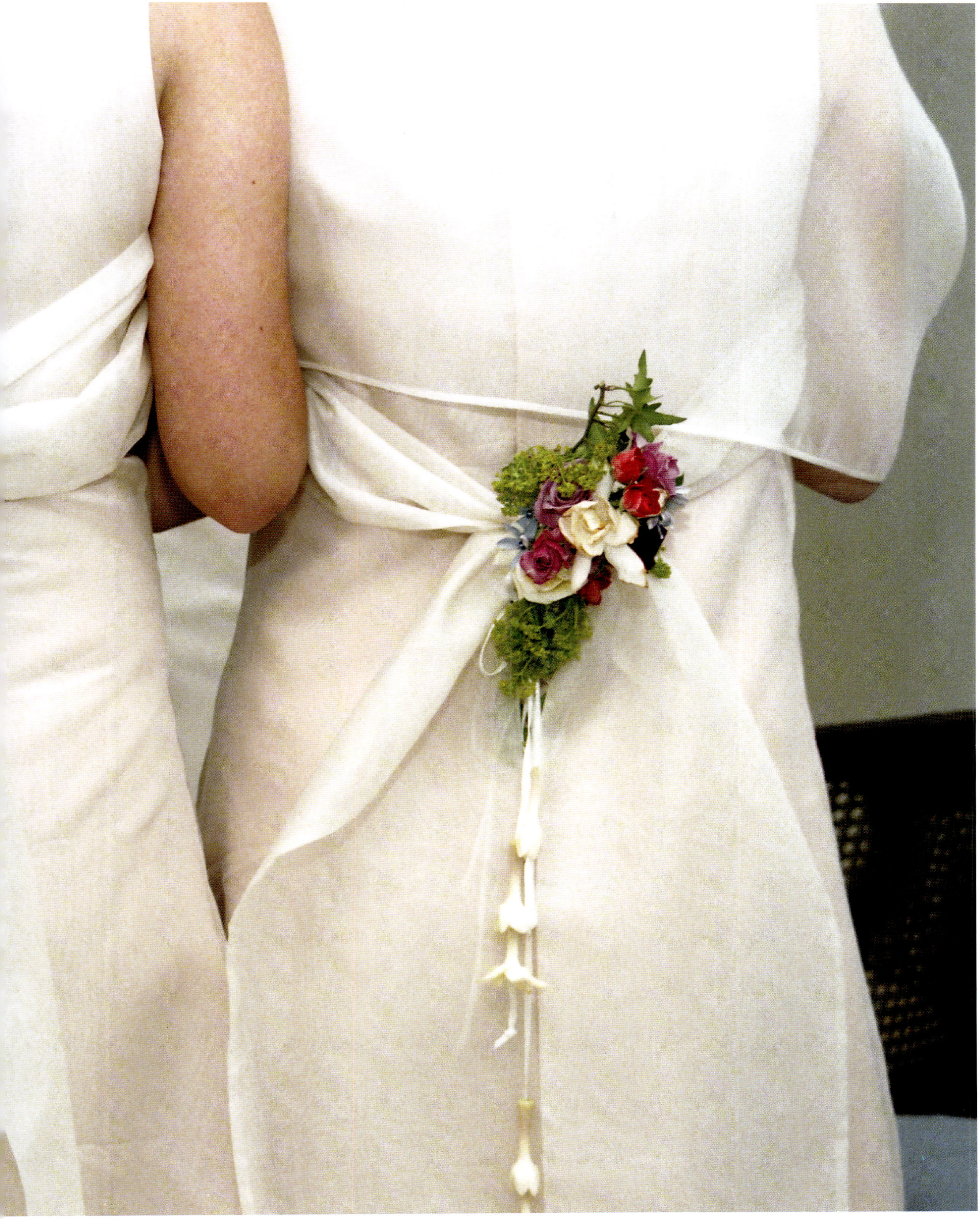

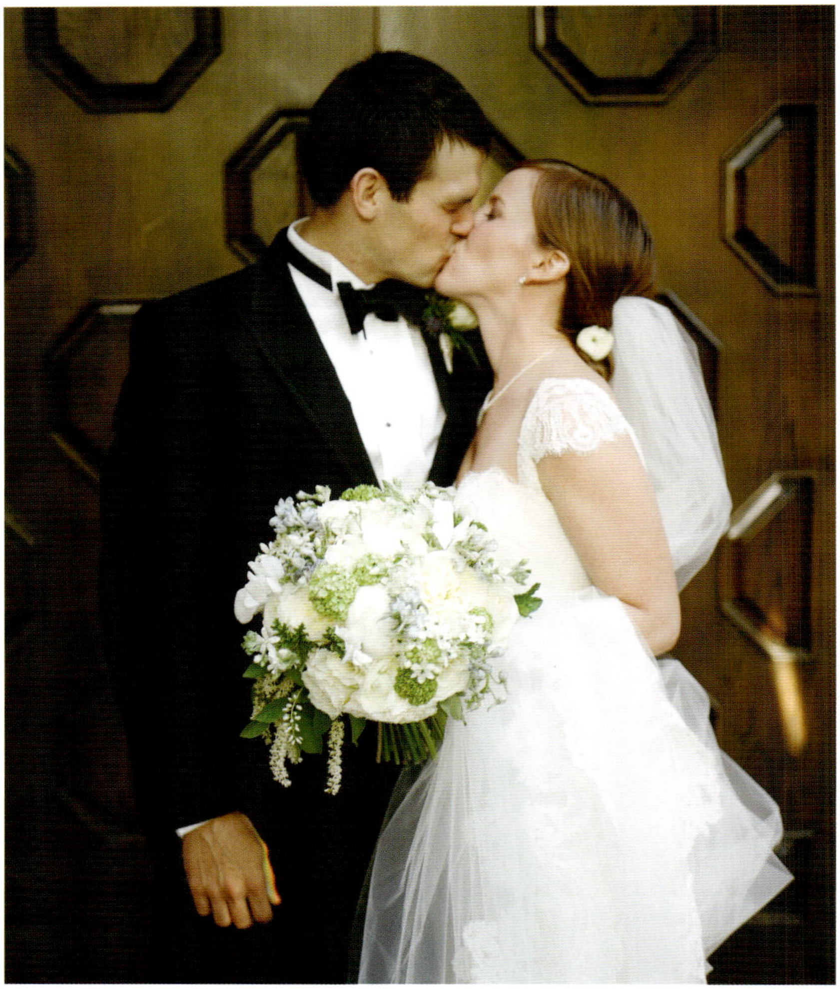

KATIE & MICHAEL

a fresh take on tradition

This wedding has all the elements of tradition with the ceremony held at a church and the reception at the country club, but then it all gets very personal. I think of the friends I made, the sweetness, kindness, and beauty of everyone involved. I met Katie and her Mama many months before the wedding. We talked about Katie's dream event, and then we planned it all: the care for the guests and transportation needs; parties beforehand; the wedding and reception; even the breakfast the morning after for the out of towners. .

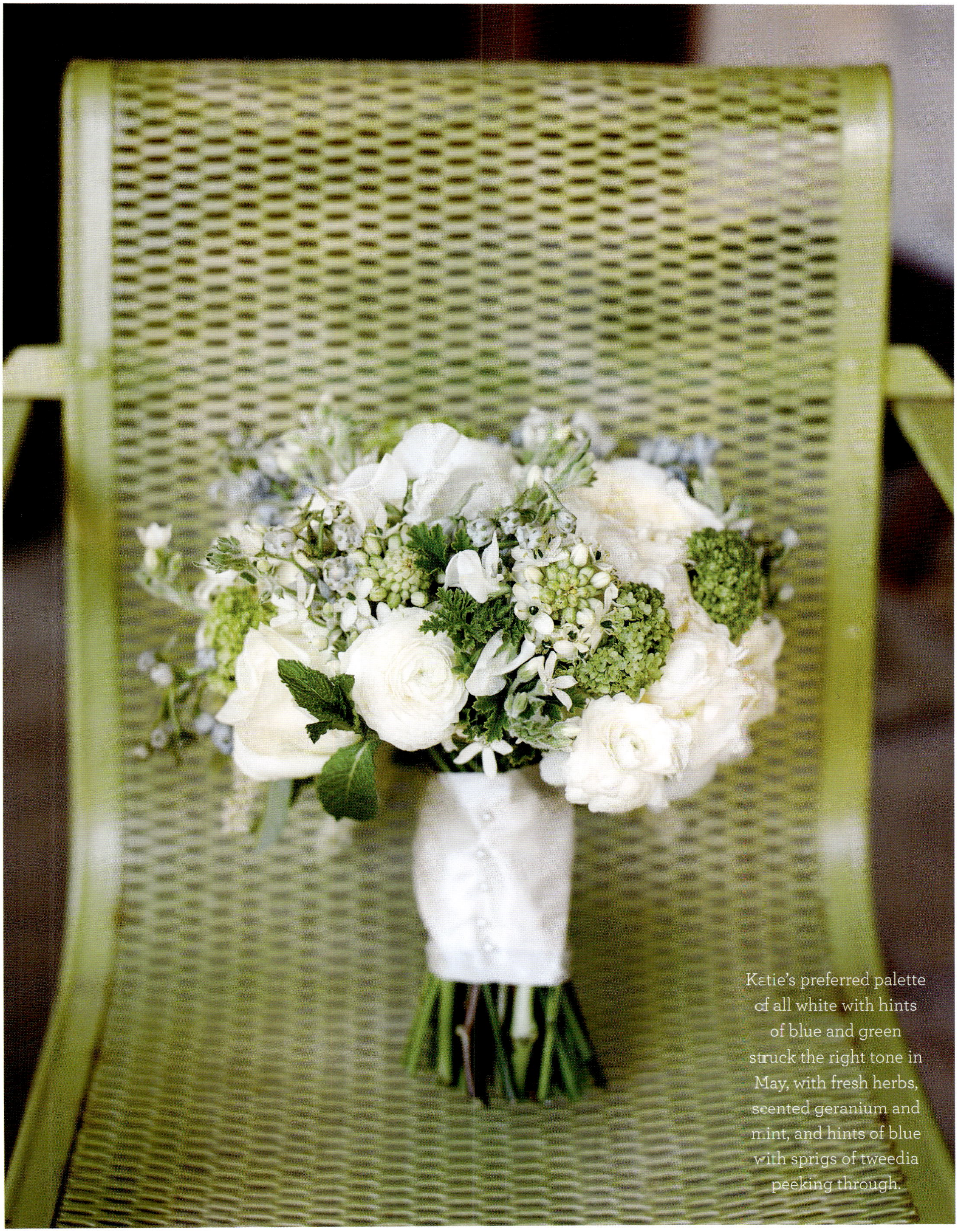

Katie's preferred palette of all white with hints of blue and green struck the right tone in May, with fresh herbs, scented geranium and mint, and hints of blue with sprigs of tweedia peeking through.

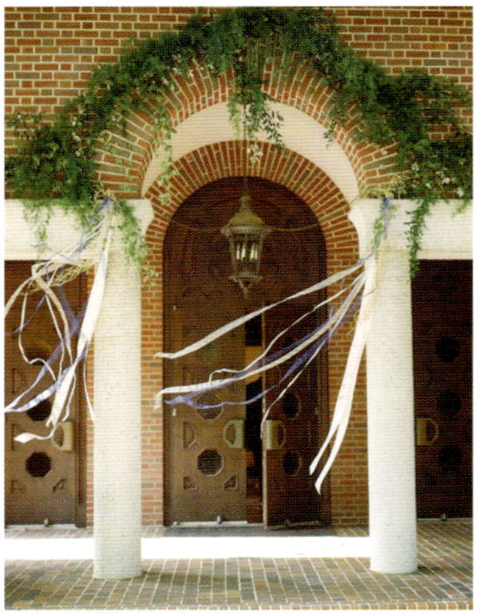
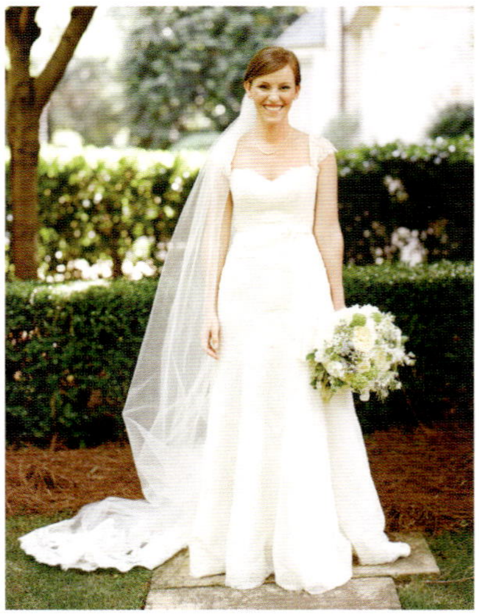
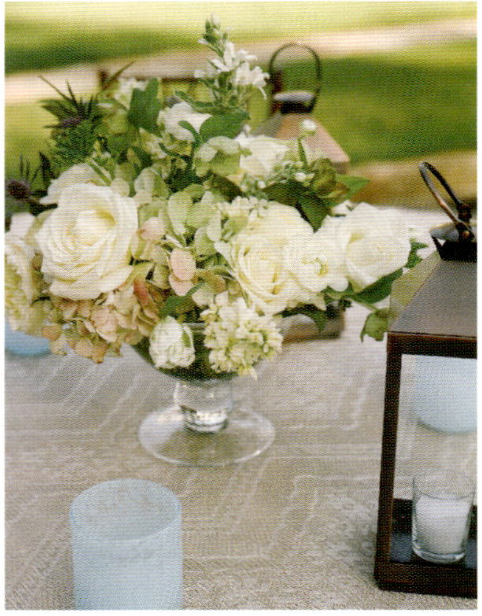
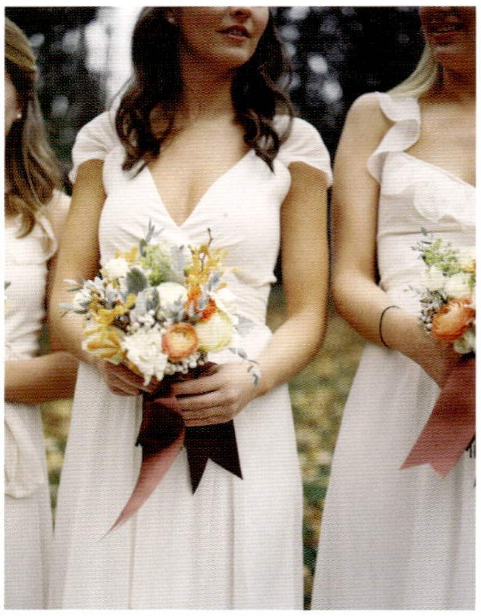
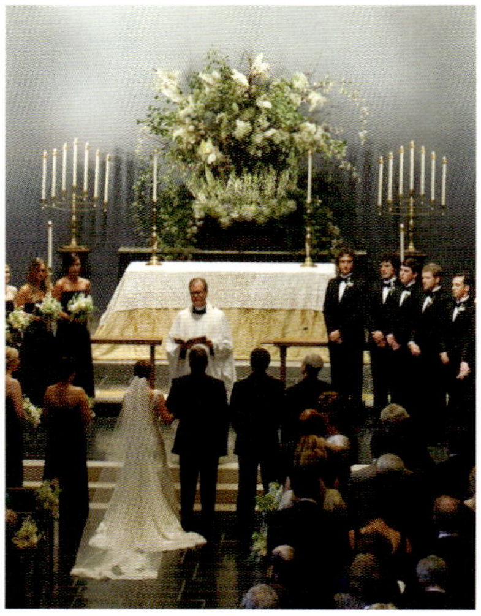
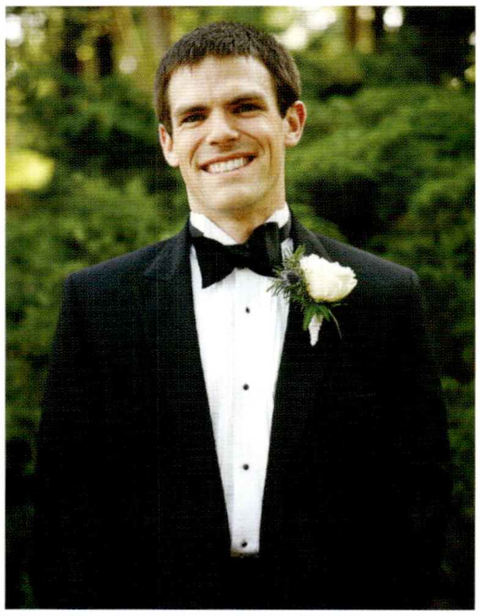
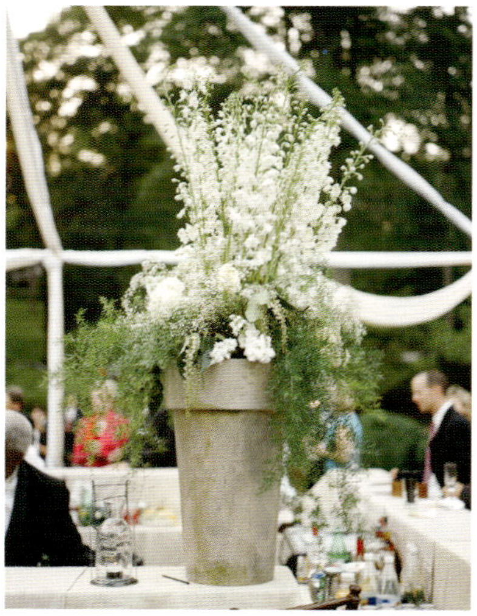
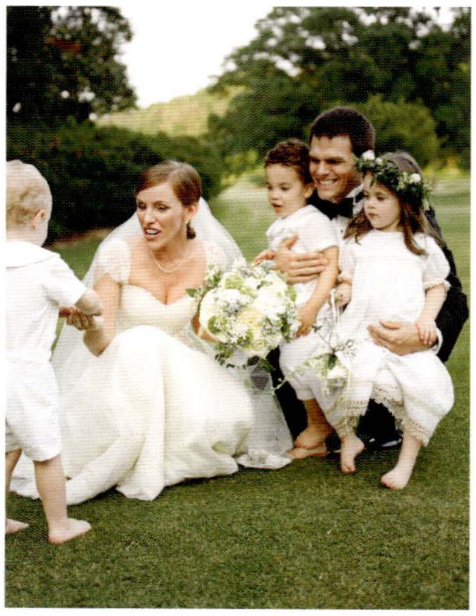
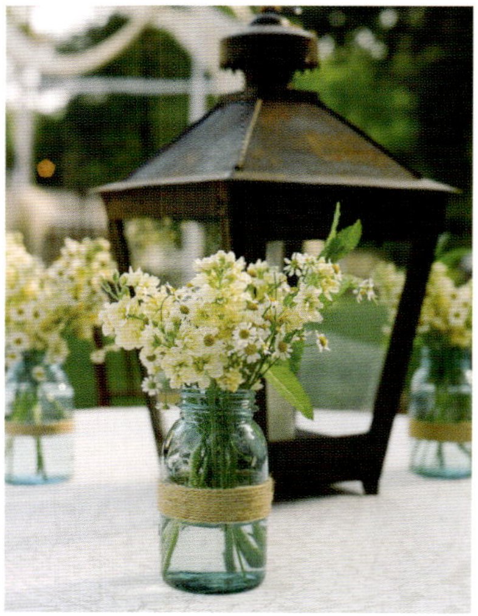

I created a decorative relationship between the church and the reception location, tying color schemes and mood together from one location to the next. We made tabletop arrangements with clear goblets and blue shaded mason jars to keep the feeling not too formal. And we invited everyone from the family pup to nieces and nephews—to throw extra unpredictability and charm into the day.

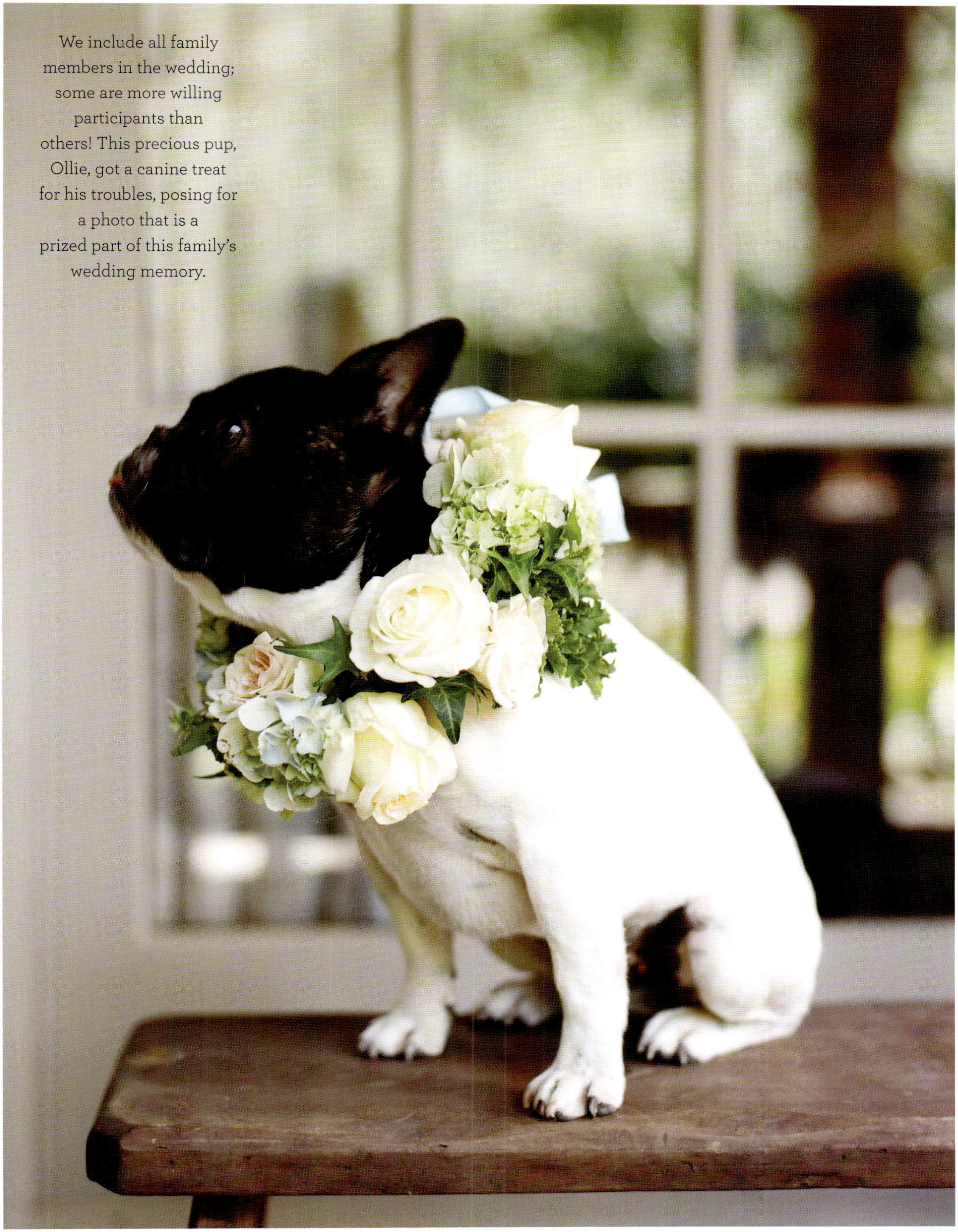

We include all family members in the wedding; some are more willing participants than others! This precious pup, Ollie, got a canine treat for his troubles, posing for a photo that is a prized part of this family's wedding memory.

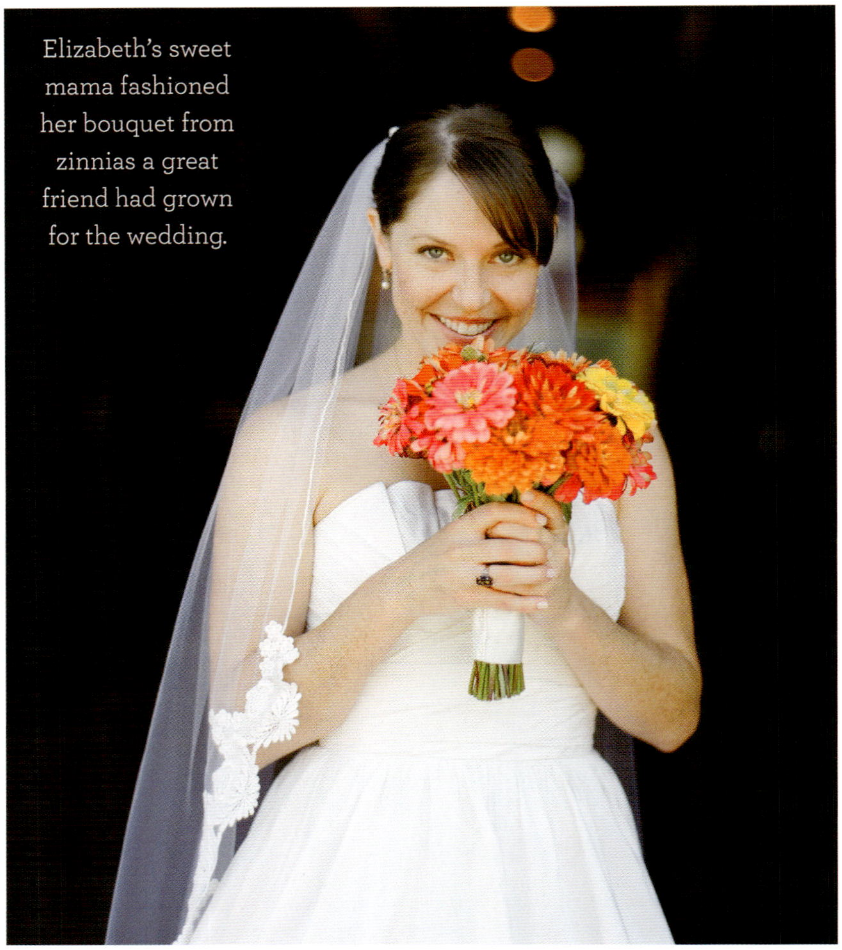

Elizabeth's sweet mama fashioned her bouquet from zinnias a great friend had grown for the wedding.

ELIZABETH & NELSON

on the banks of the black warrior river

Nelson grew up hunting and fishing and being out in the woods at the family farm that borders a bend in the Black Warrior River. He has always been our "nature" boy (he's also my nephew) so we were pleased when he became the Black Warrior Riverkeeper and then thrilled as his relationship with outdoor loving and adventurous Elizabeth developed. It was no surprise that they wanted their wedding at the place they love so much, but then the reality of what we were facing hit home! There were lots of obstacles, but one look at these photos, and you'll see we conquered them all and created a glorious event.

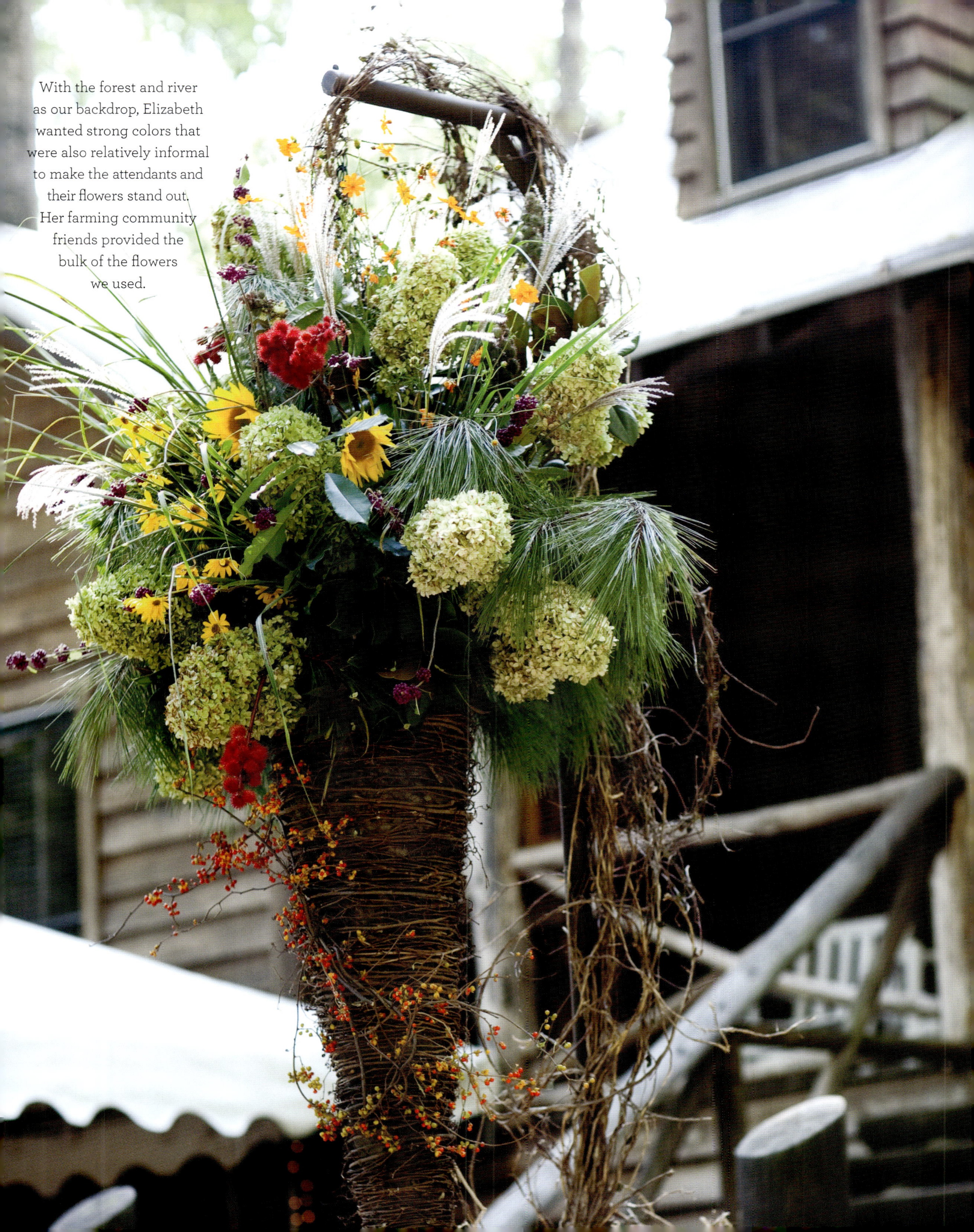

With the forest and river as our backdrop, Elizabeth wanted strong colors that were also relatively informal to make the attendants and their flowers stand out. Her farming community friends provided the bulk of the flowers we used.

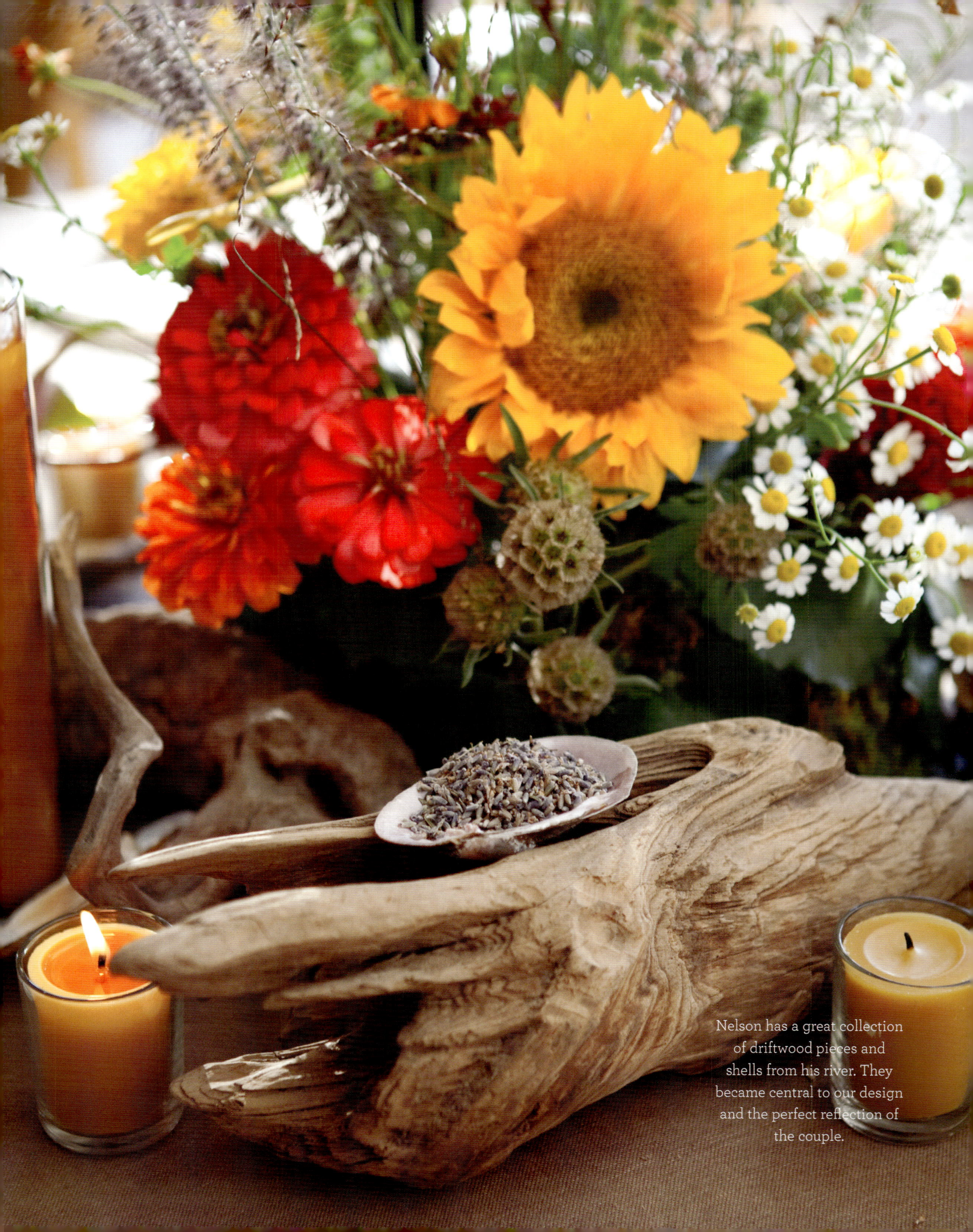

Nelson has a great collection of driftwood pieces and shells from his river. They became central to our design and the perfect reflection of the couple.

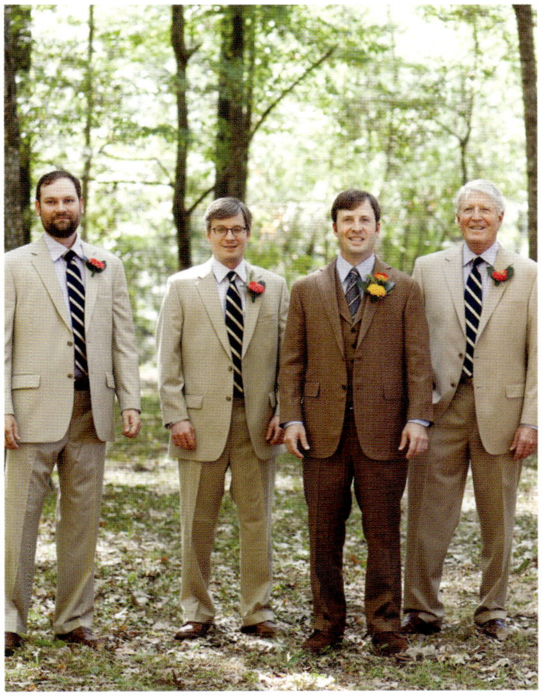

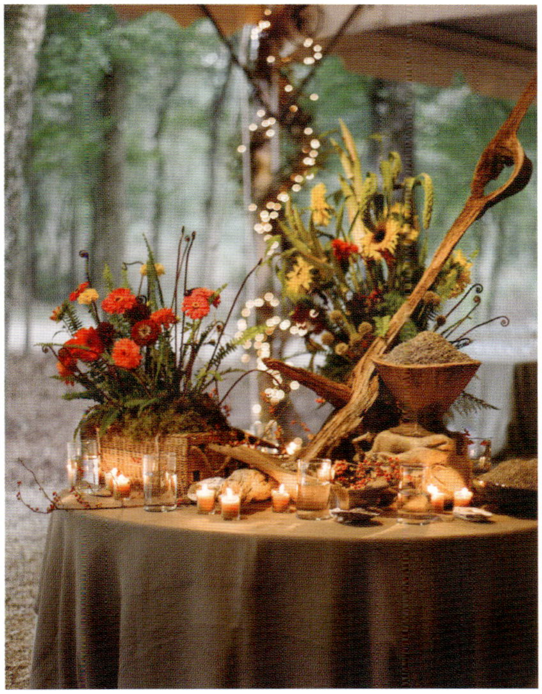

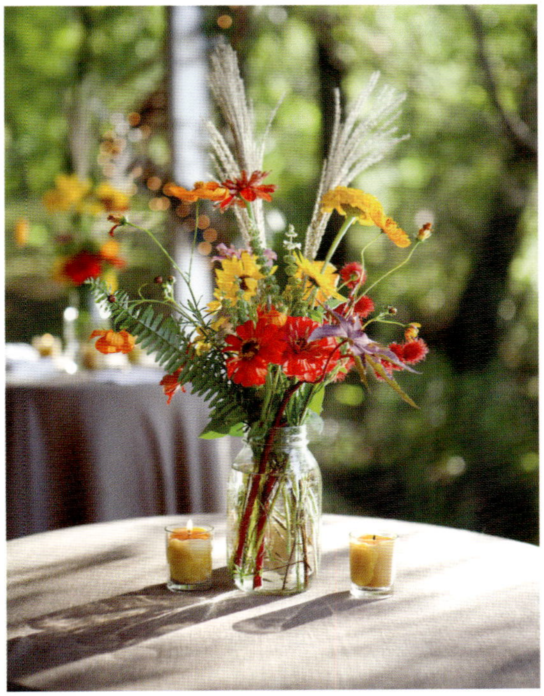

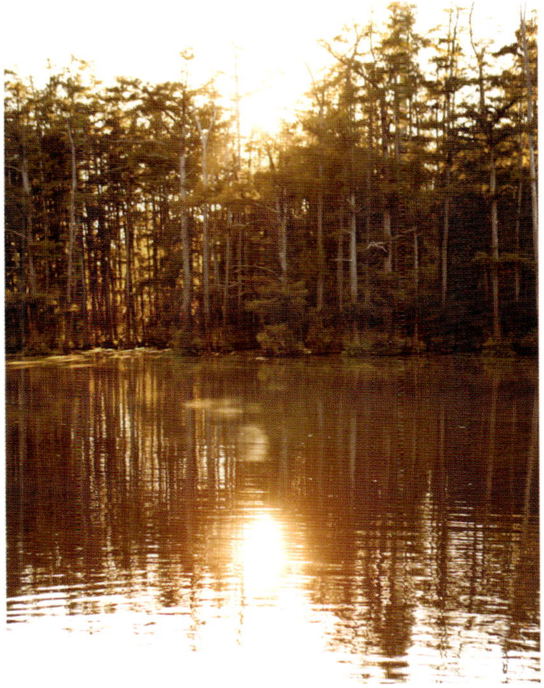

THEY LEFT THE RECEPTION IN A METAL FLAT BOTTOMED "JON BOAT" AND CAMPED OUT IN A YURT FOR THEIR WEDDING NIGHT.

They took me four-wheeling to see the wedding site by the river—a fun first for me. The orchestrating was a challenge. I have a mandate that we have to make all guests comfortable—no matter the age. It worked with a little foraging and a lot of ingenuity.

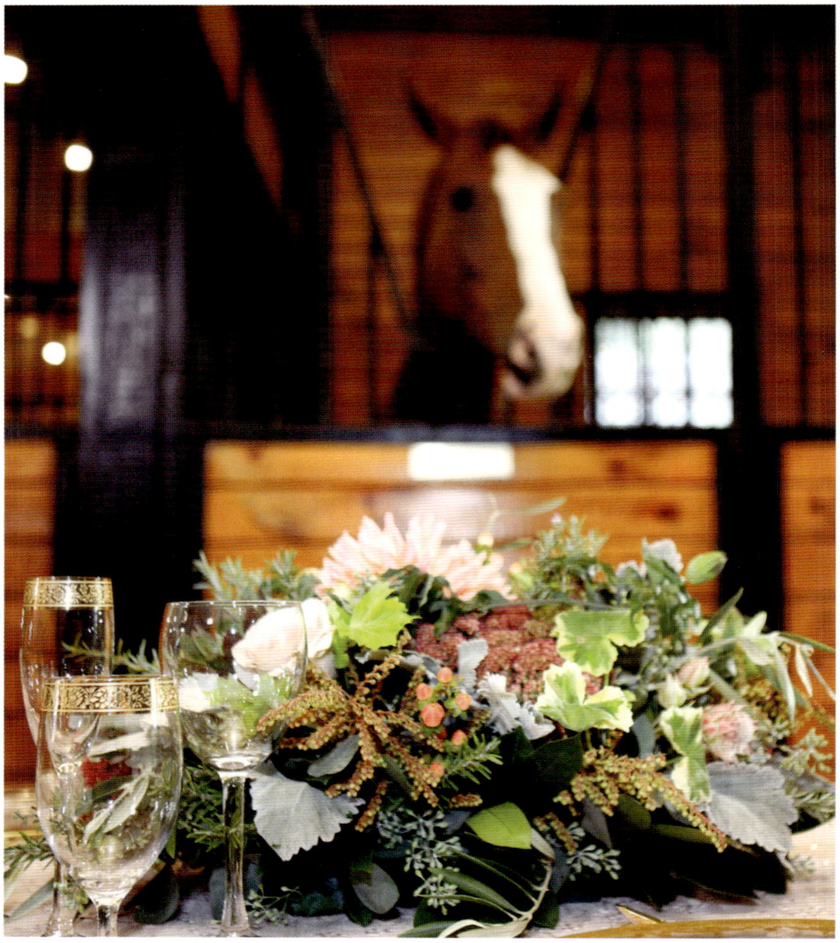

ARDEN & WILLIAM

for the love of horses

We have a world-class equestrian center right outside of Birmingham. The first time I visited, my only comparison was Blackberry Farm in Tennessee. Arden has photographed many of the weddings I've produced, so she was keen to have her own ceremony be personal and unique to her and William. They both love horses, so we chose their barn, at their equestrian center, as the site for the wedding and pre-reception dinner.

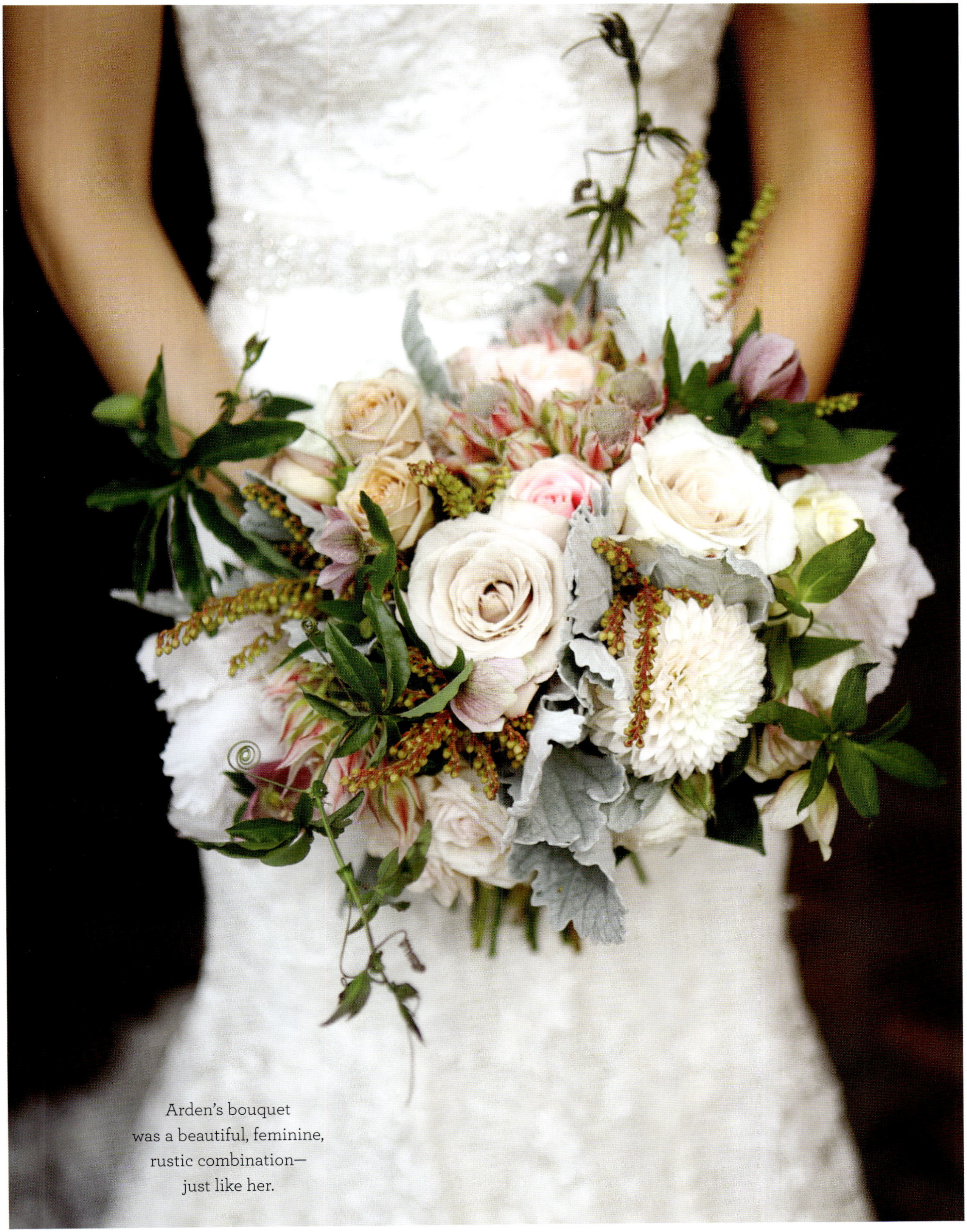

Arden's bouquet was a beautiful, feminine, rustic combination—just like her.

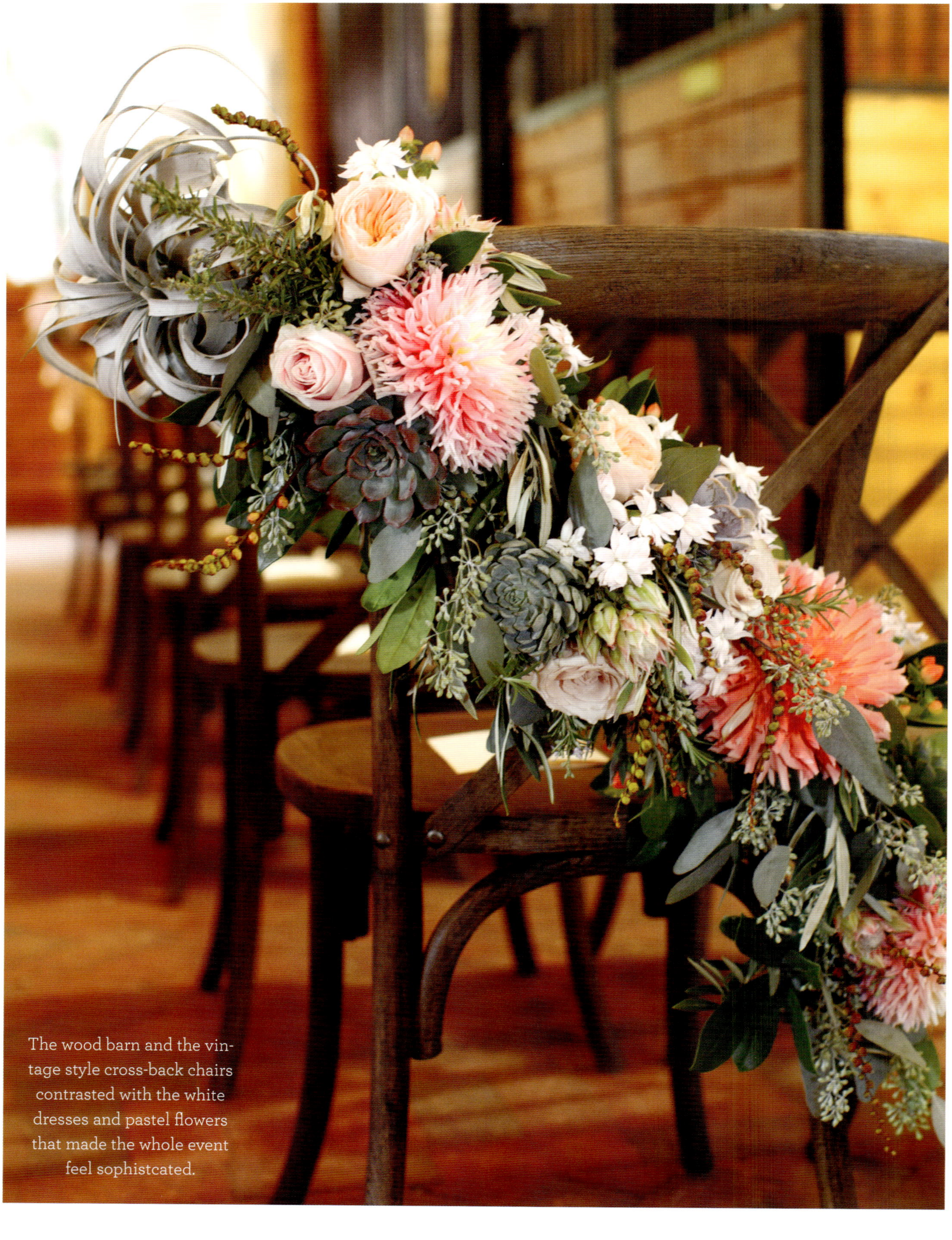

The wood barn and the vintage style cross-back chairs contrasted with the white dresses and pastel flowers that made the whole event feel sophistcated.

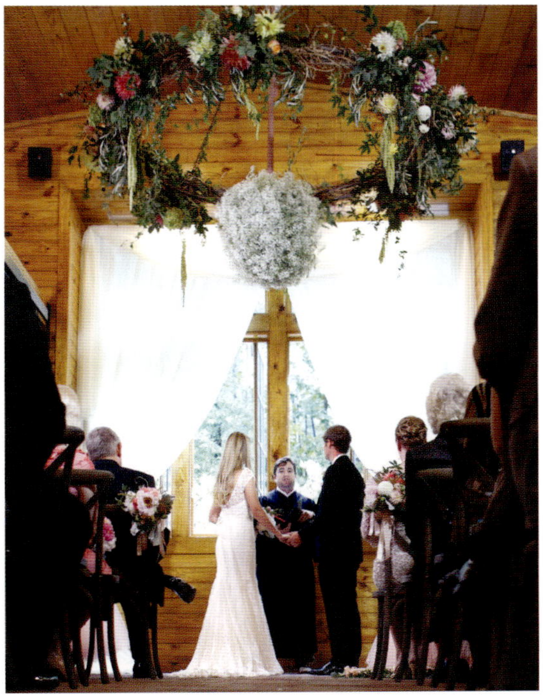

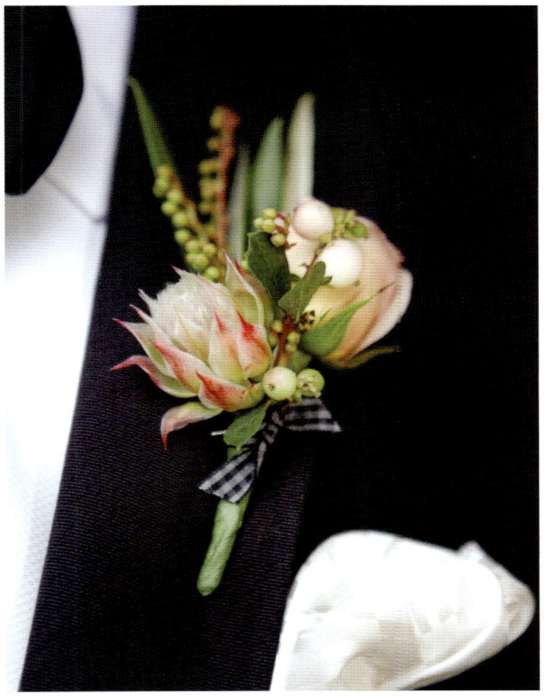

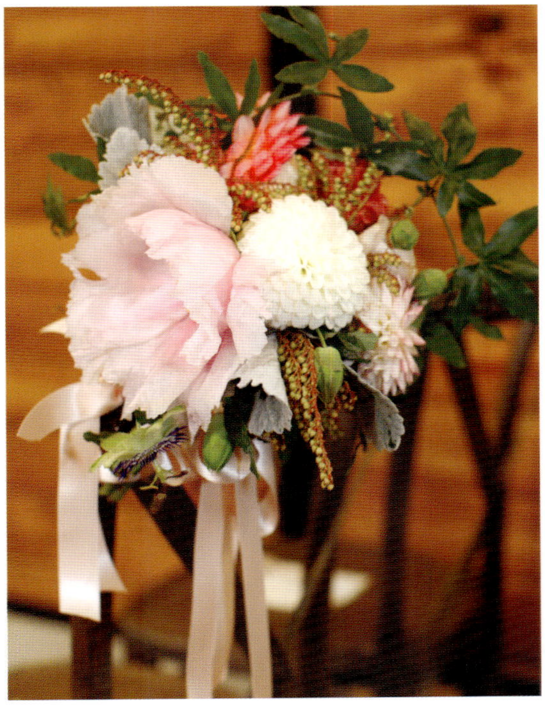

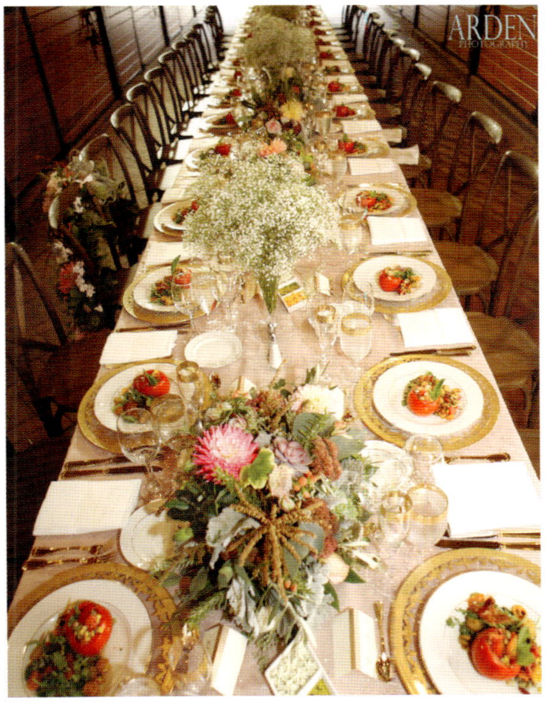

ARDEN IS SUCH A FORCE IN THE WEDDING SCENE THAT WE ALL LENT A HAND. I DID THE WEDDING AND DINNER; ANOTHER FLOWER FRIEND DID THE DANCE PARTY AFTER.

We strung a lush garland of succulents, seeded eucalyptus, dahlias, and roses as pew markers. The seated dinner that followed spanned a long table that filled the longest hallways of stalls. The horses reached out, almost joining in the conversation.

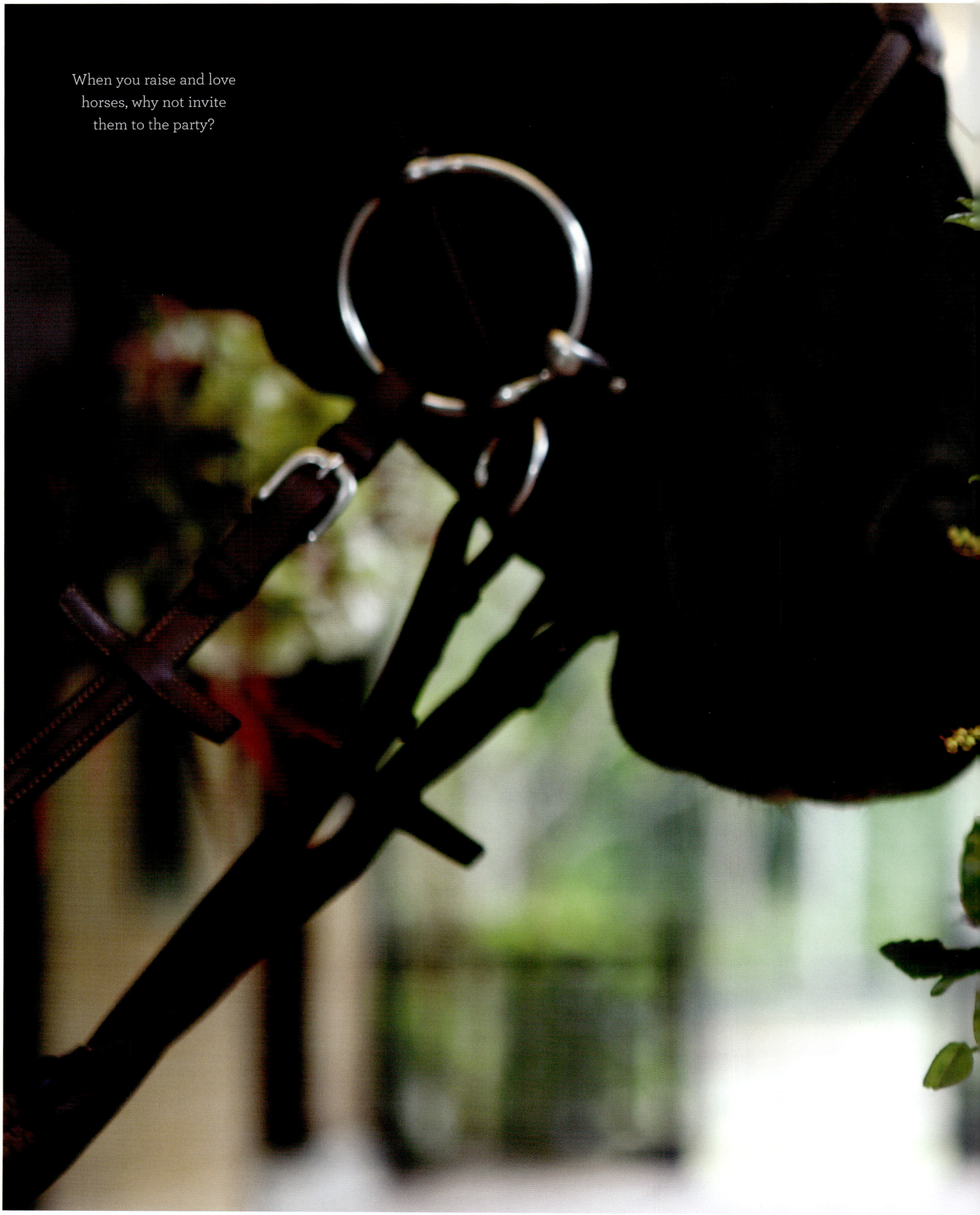

When you raise and love horses, why not invite them to the party?

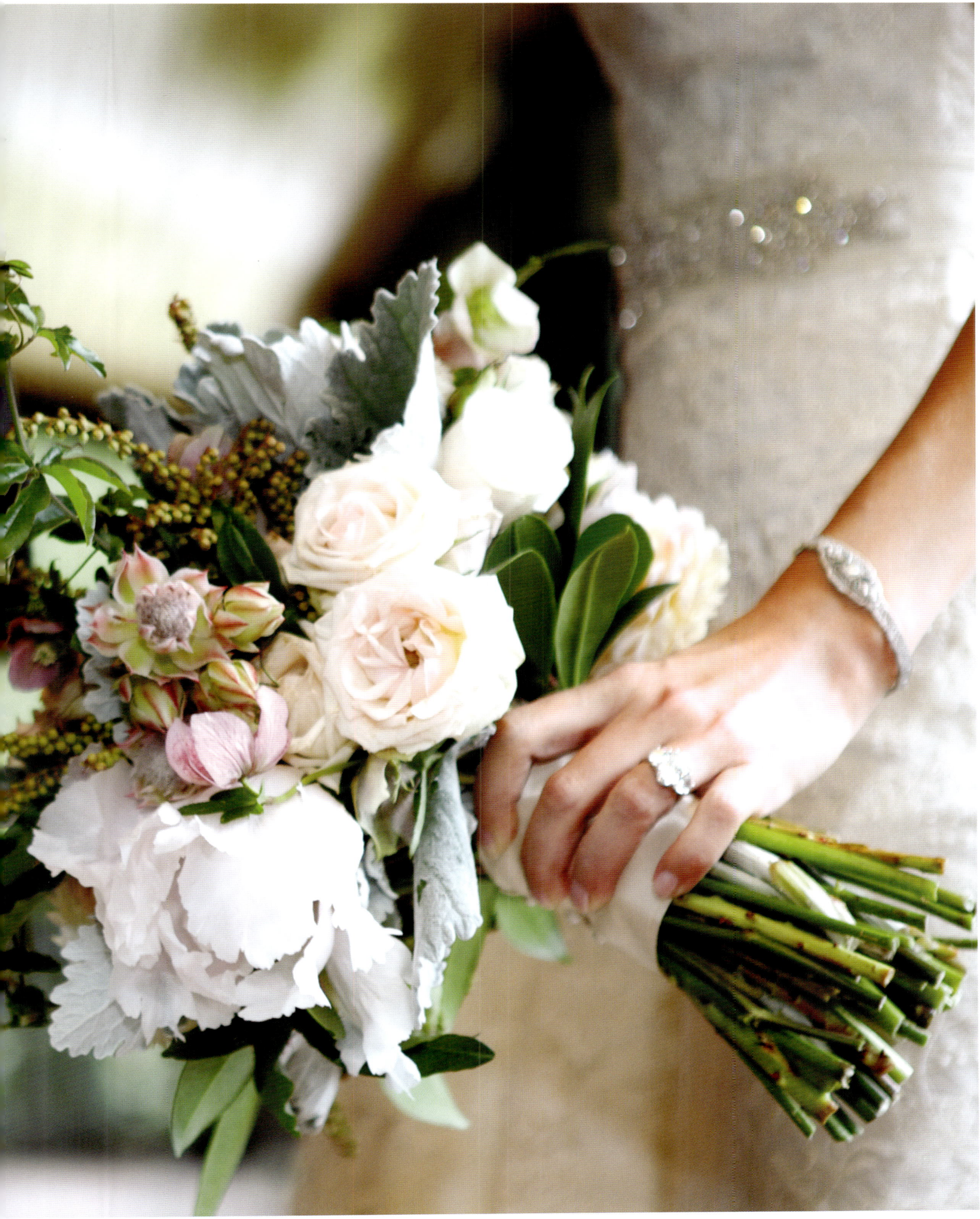

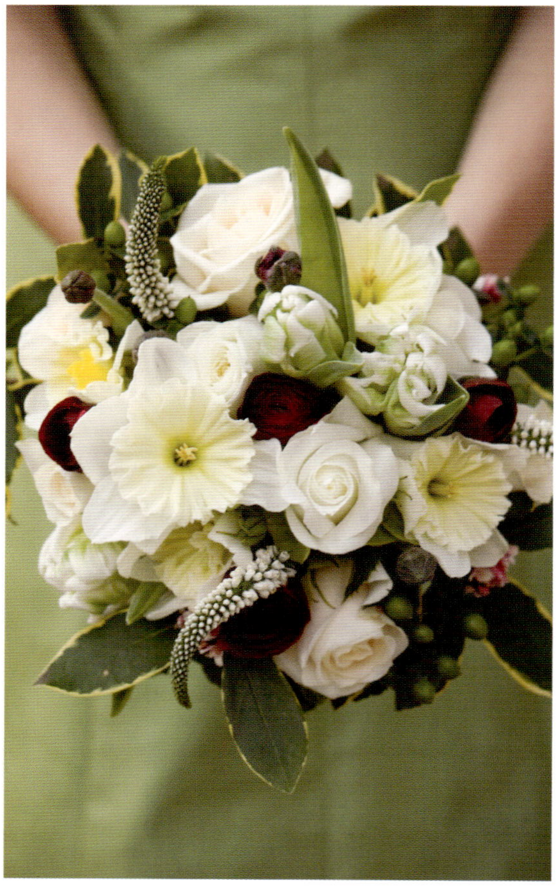

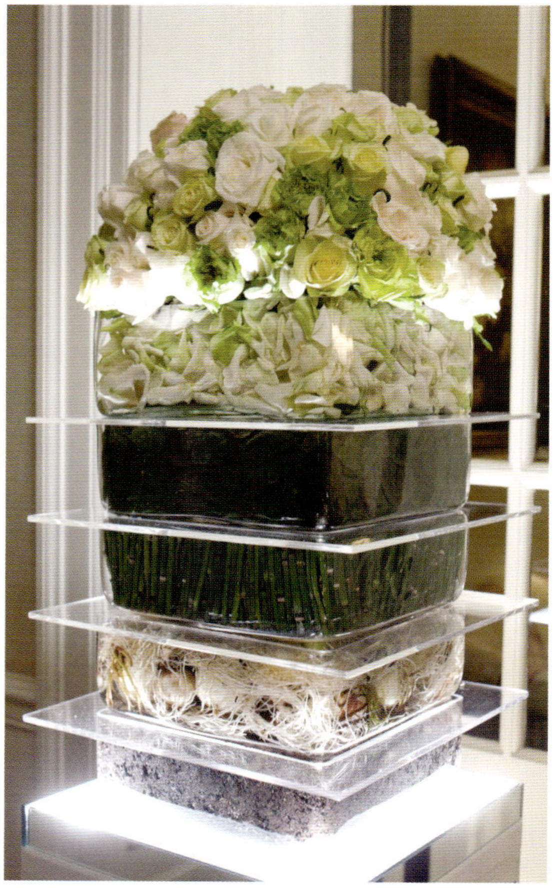

ELIZABETH & CHIP

green with the glory of spring

The promise of spring's arrival combined with Southern traditions made this wedding feel young and fresh. I enlisted the help of a gardening friend to force daffodils and other bulbs. I didn't need the bulbs to be blooming—I just needed some green on the top emerging from the bulbs and an advanced root system to show the bulb with clean roots below. I mixed them all in clear glass vases with river rocks at the base and blooming quince branches extending out.

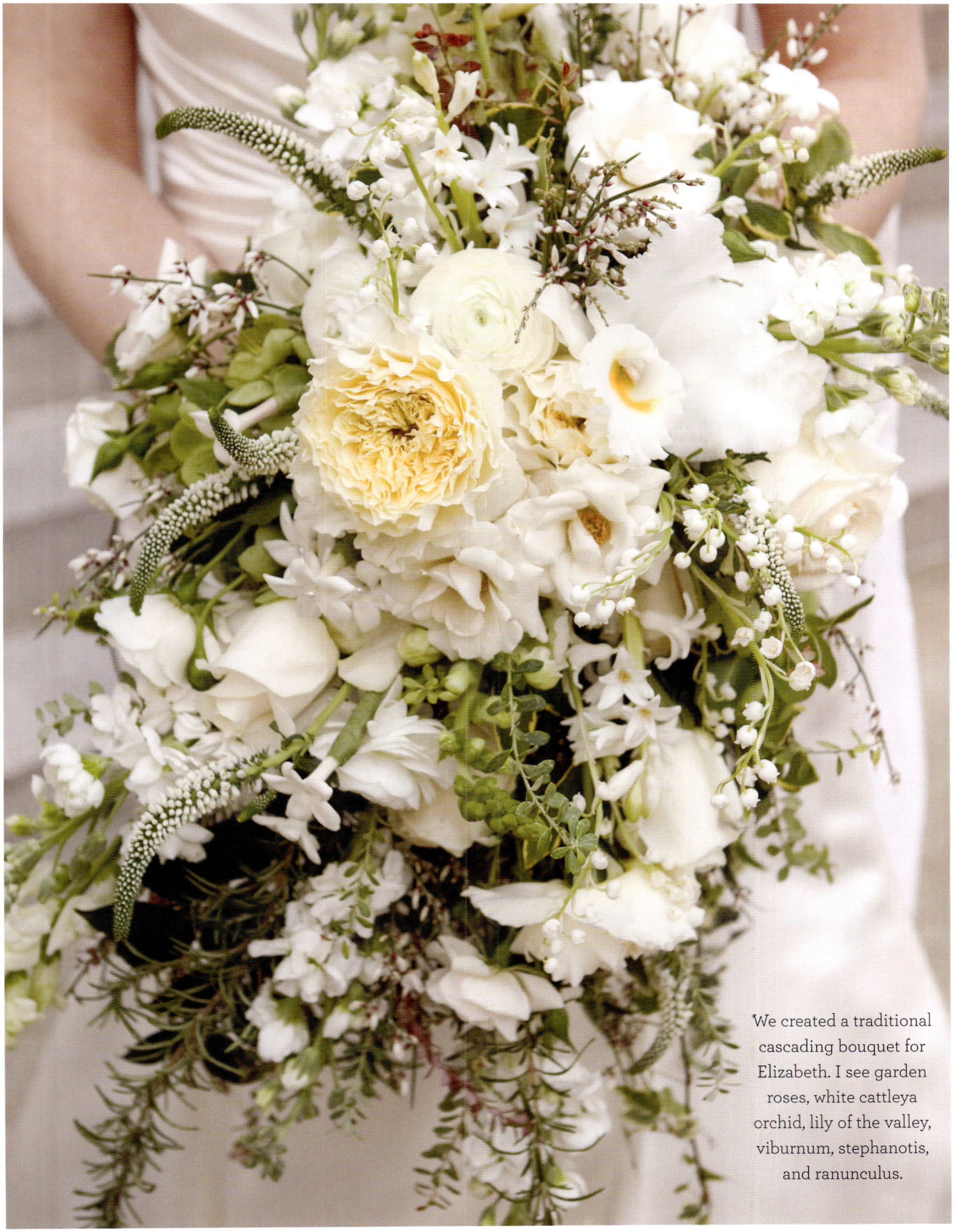

We created a traditional cascading bouquet for Elizabeth. I see garden roses, white cattleya orchid, lily of the valley, viburnum, stephanotis, and ranunculus.

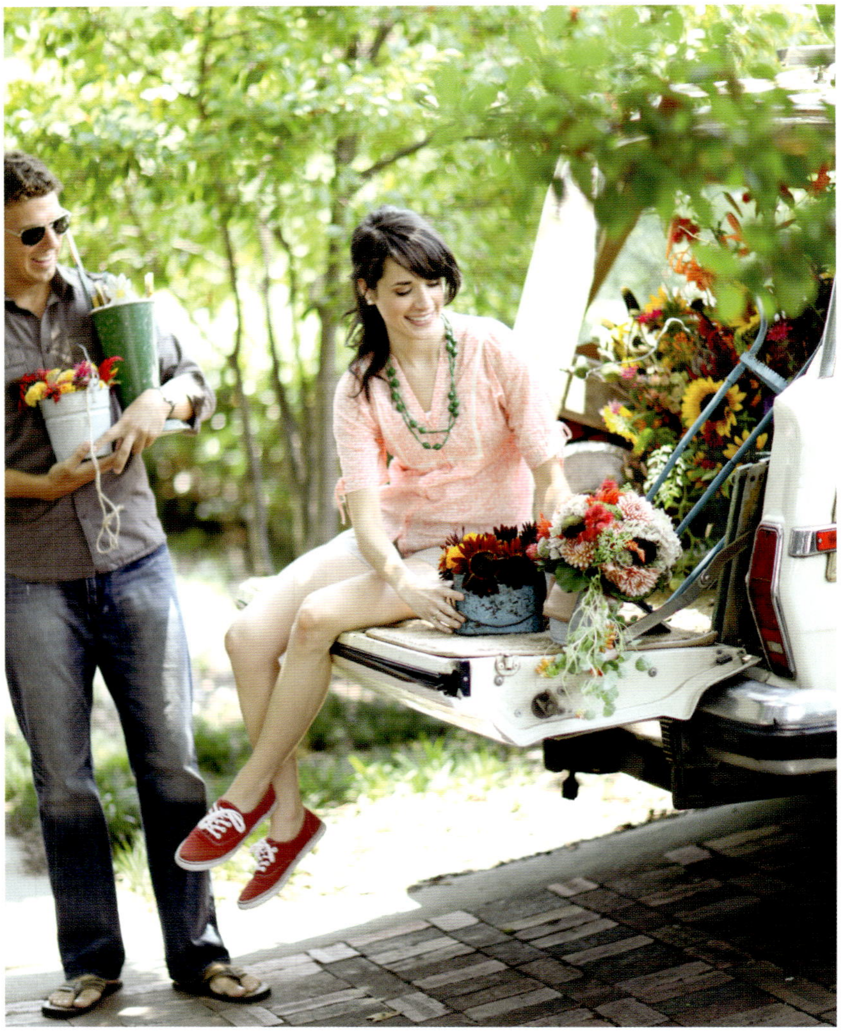

PAMELA & JOHN

a community celebration

This was my first all gathered and locally sourced "green" wedding. Everything was perfect: flower contributions from some of our favorite gardens, red keds, casual vibe, bicycle getaway, and a natural feel that kept the mood relaxed and festive and intimate. All the guests had a hand in the event!

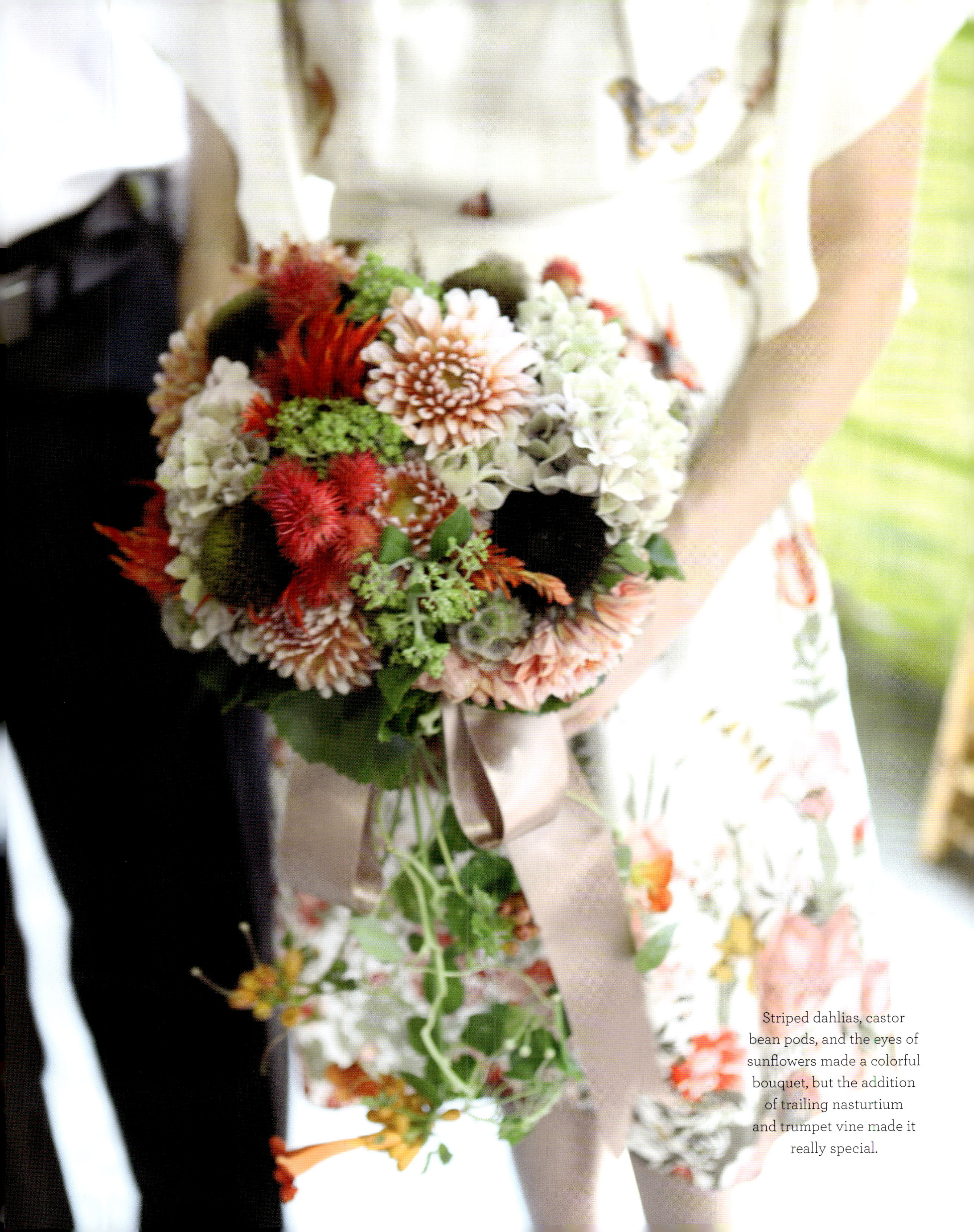

Striped dahlias, castor bean pods, and the eyes of sunflowers made a colorful bouquet, but the addition of trailing nasturtium and trumpet vine made it really special.

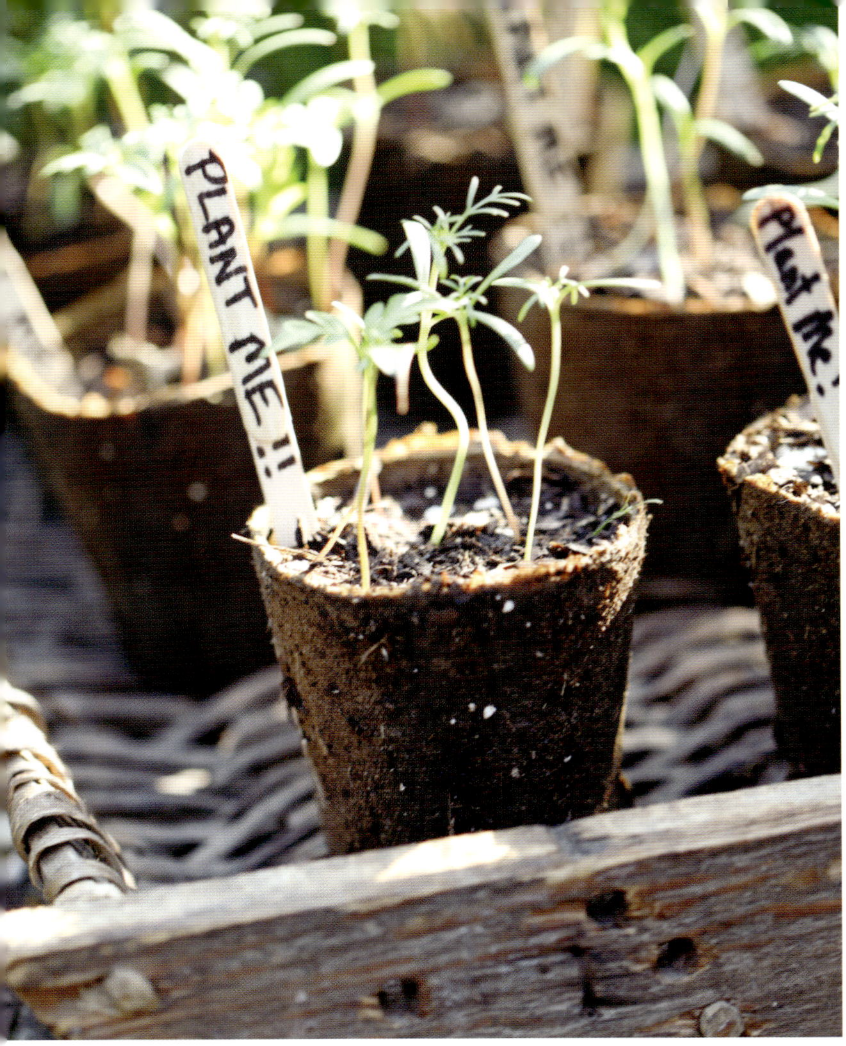
PLANT ME!!
Plant Me!
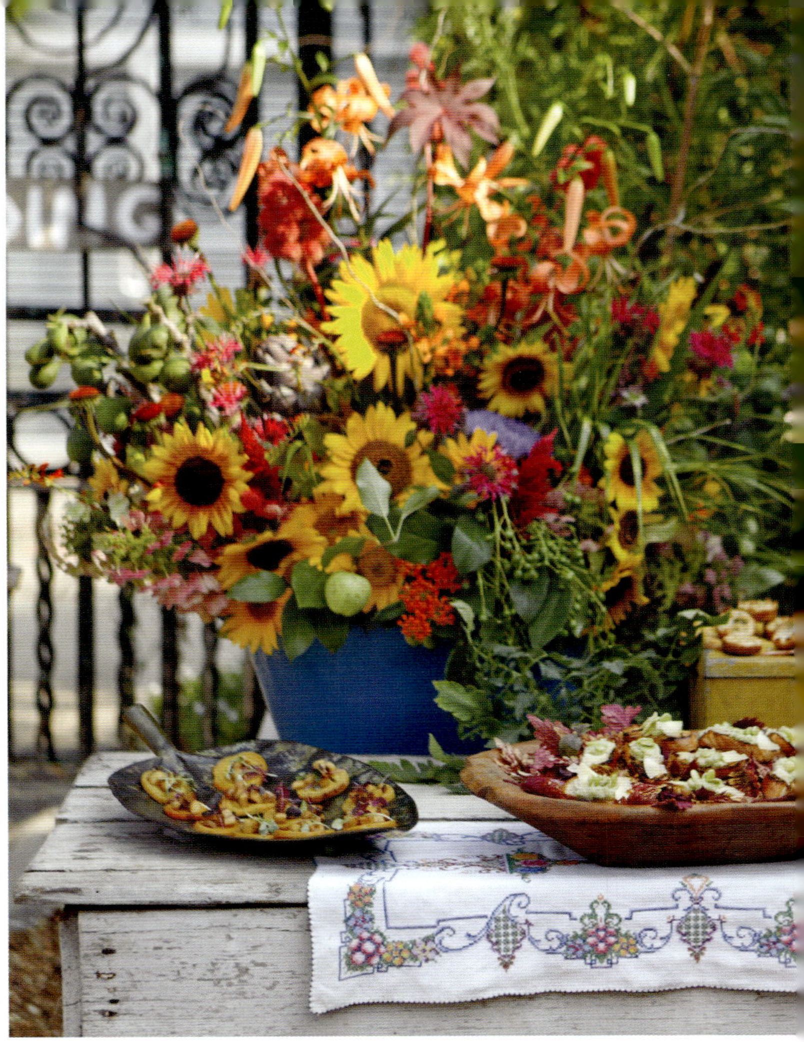
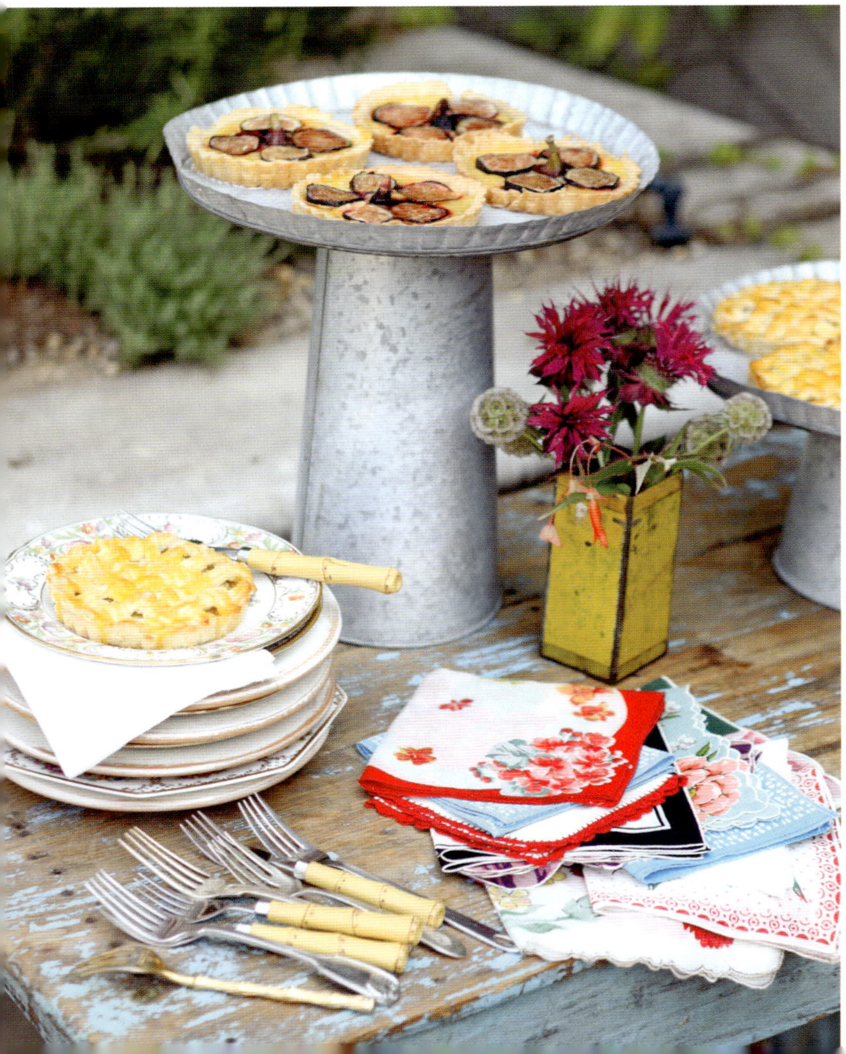
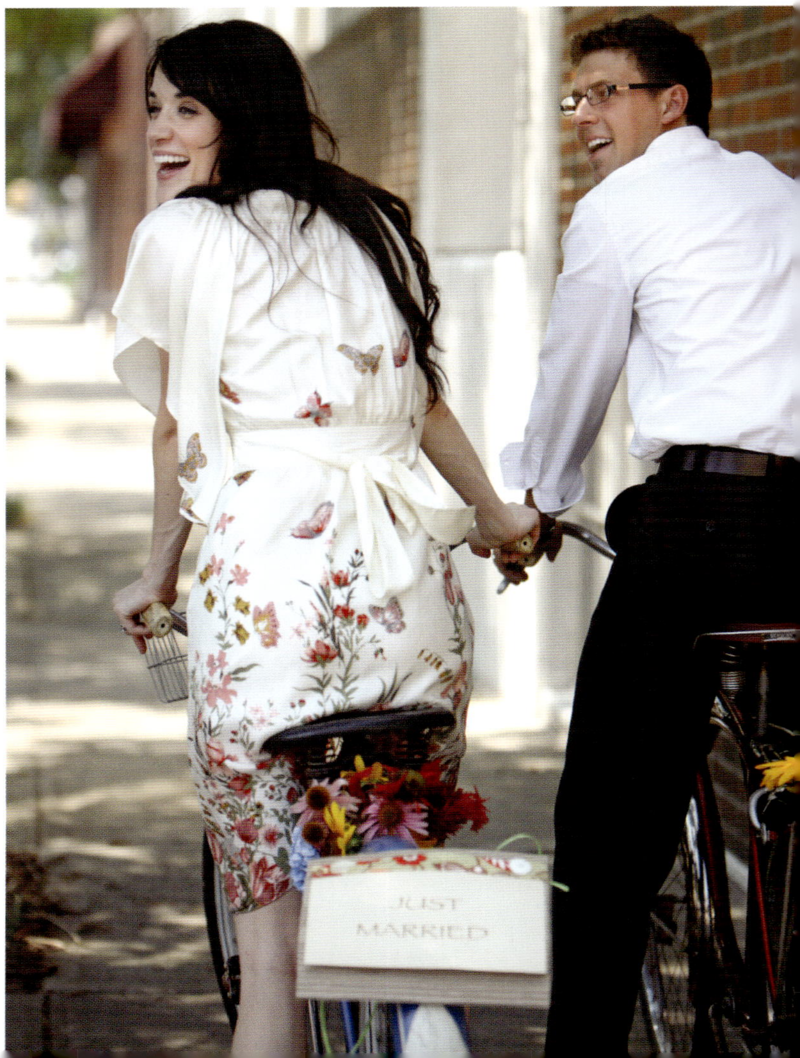
JUST
MARRIED

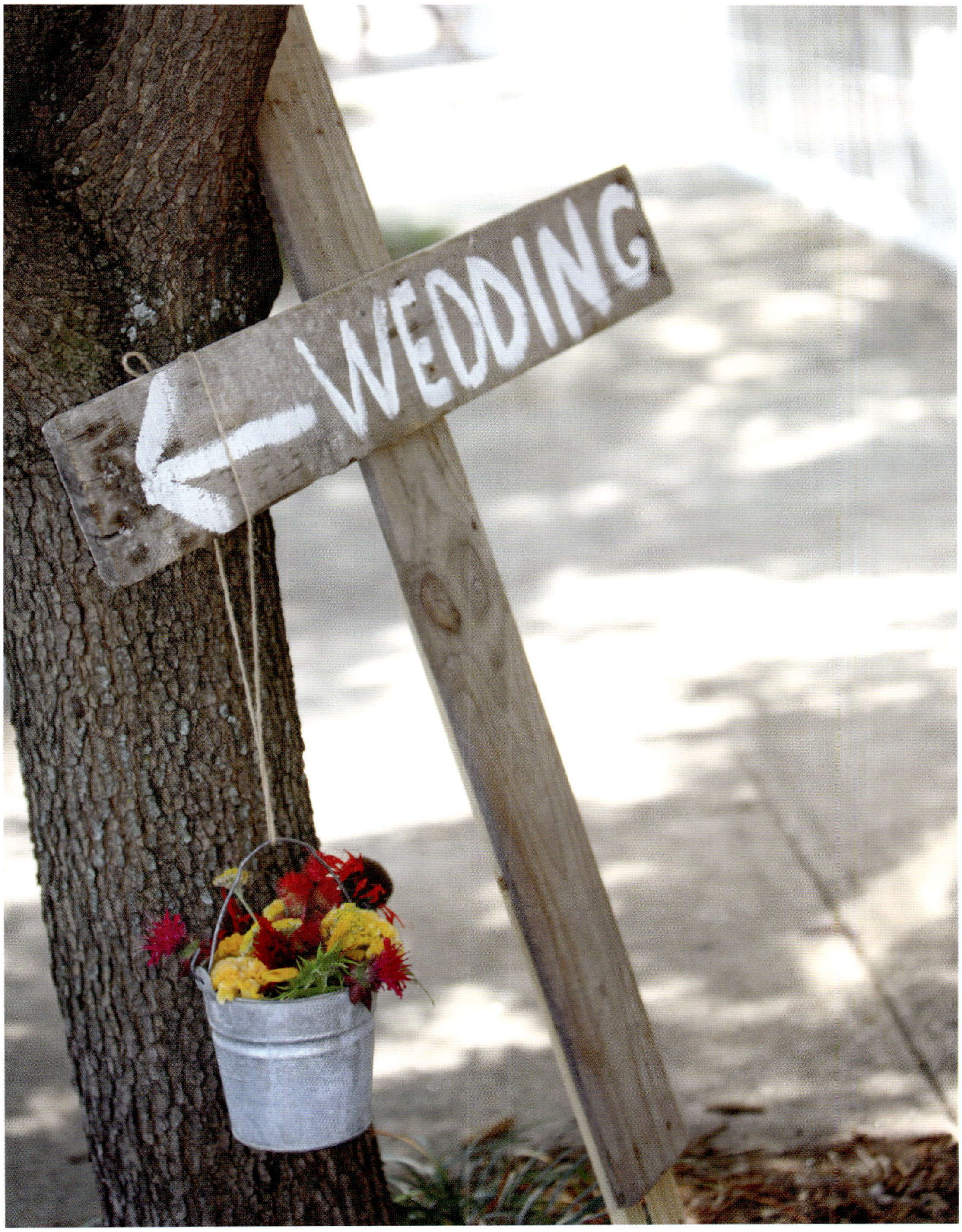

THE WEDDING AND RECEPTION WERE AT PEPPER PLACE, THE SITE OF BIRMINGHAM'S FABULOUS SUMMER FARMER'S MARKET AND MY SHOP.

Not only did we gather blooms from neighborhood gardens, we collected flatware and containers from friends. The whole event felt like a community celebration with vintage French market baskets, distressed tables, vintage lace, and delicious food prepared by one of our favorite chefs, Chris DuPont.

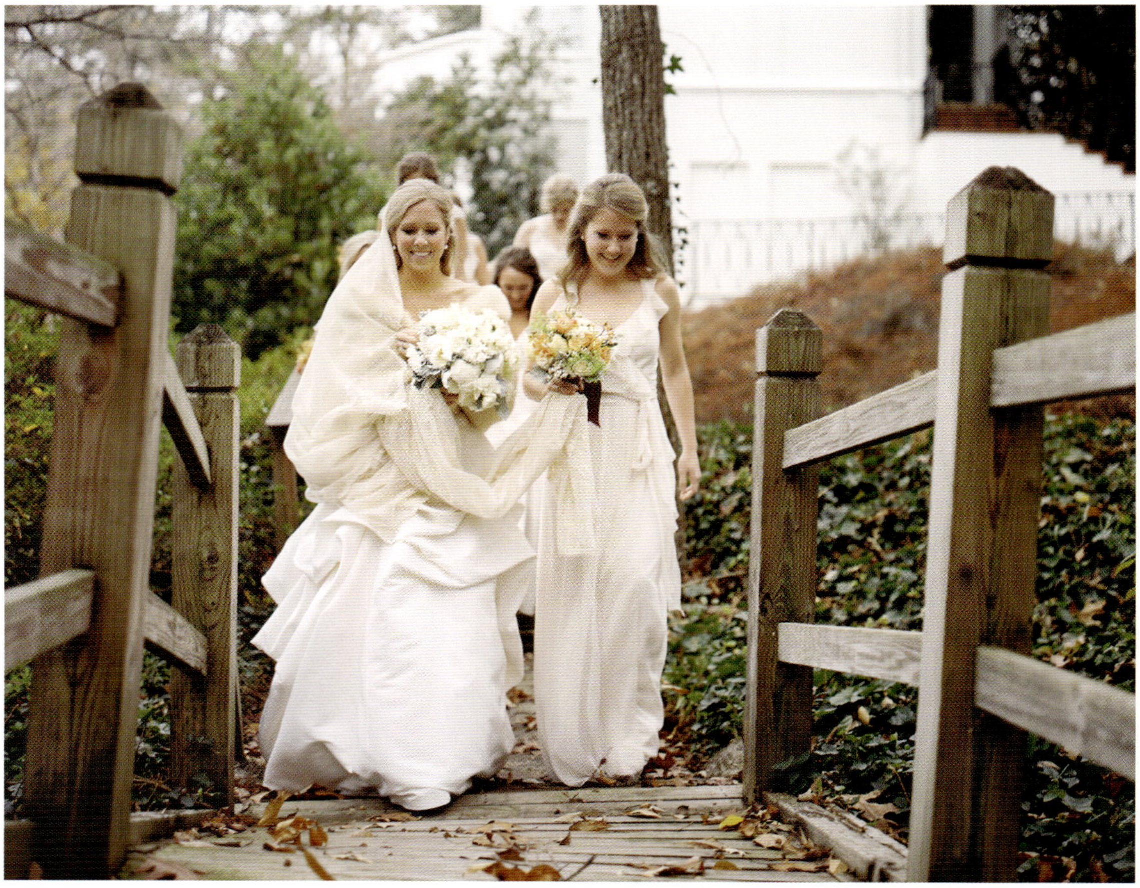

VIRGINIA & ANDREW

youthful ode to traditional autumn

I have been so privileged in my work to get to know my clients really well over the years and create bonds. Virginia's mama falls in this category. We just click! I have enjoyed our collaboration over the years, and I was thrilled to work with Virginia, who is a designer and has fabulous ideas. She wanted to enhance the antebellum club house, which was the site of the reception, without taking away from its character. We used fall colors mixed with magnolia and fall leaves and other graphic elements to give it a current feel.

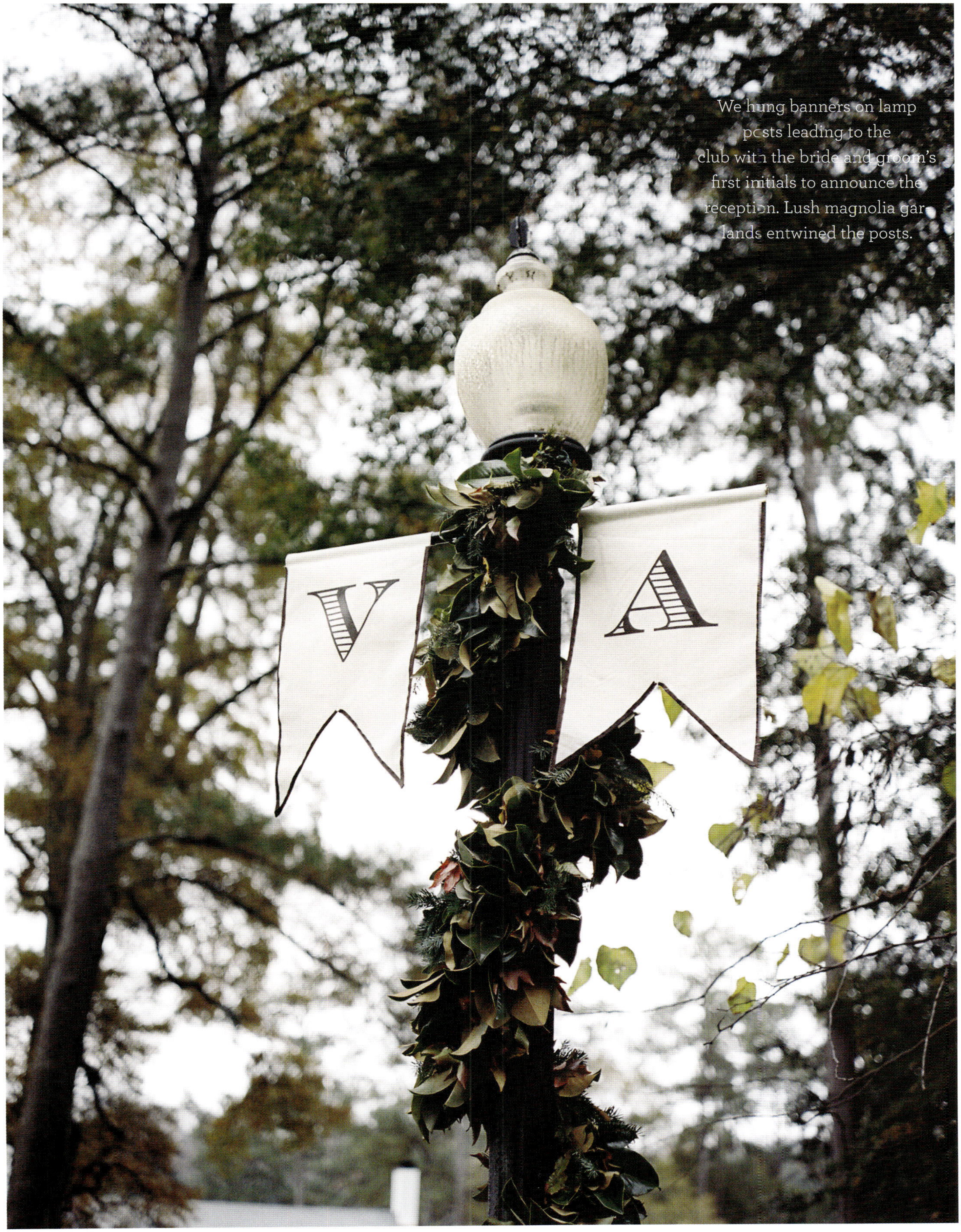

We hung banners on lamp posts leading to the club with the bride and groom's first initials to announce the reception. Lush magnolia garlands entwined the posts.

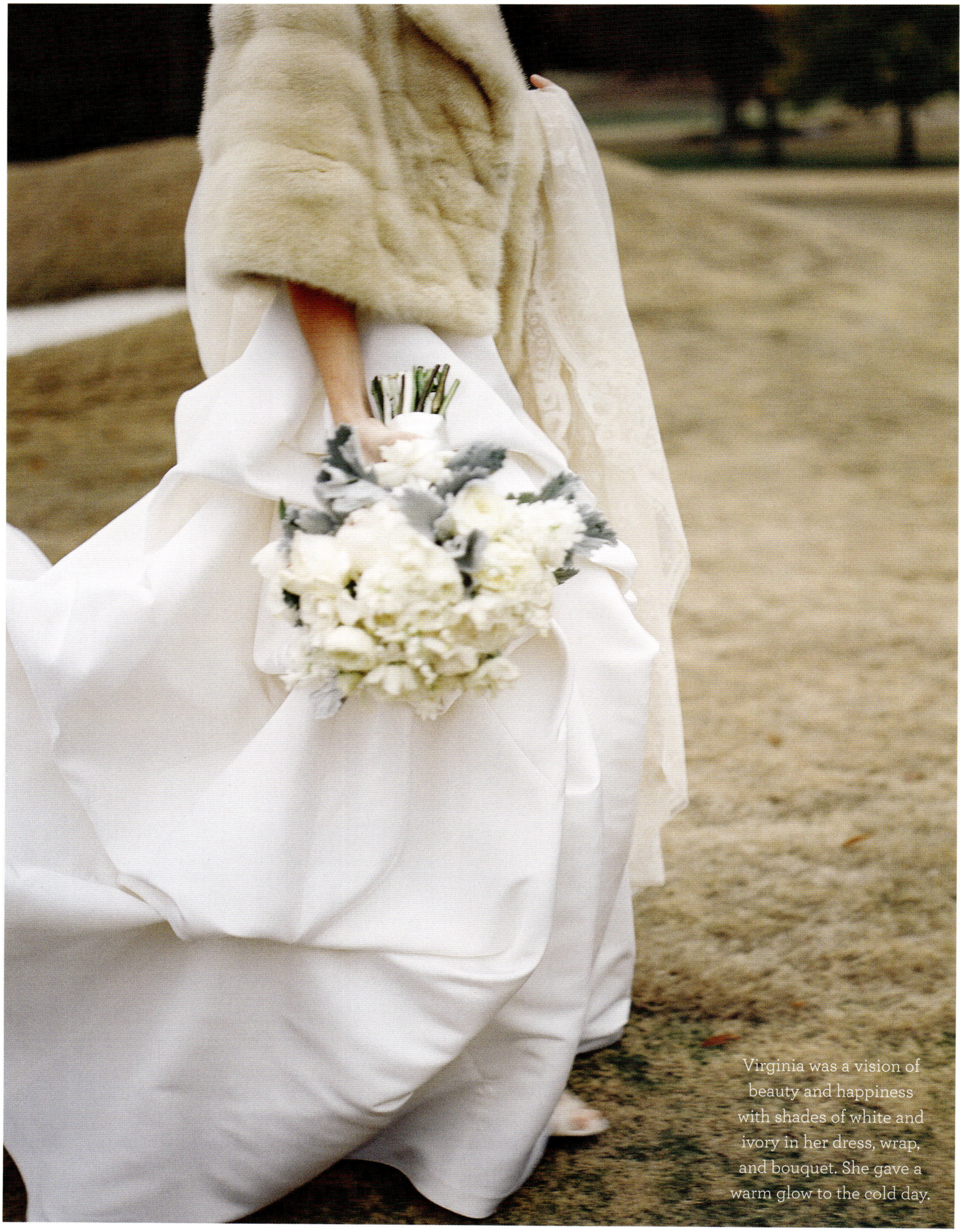

Virginia was a vision of beauty and happiness with shades of white and ivory in her dress, wrap, and bouquet. She gave a warm glow to the cold day.

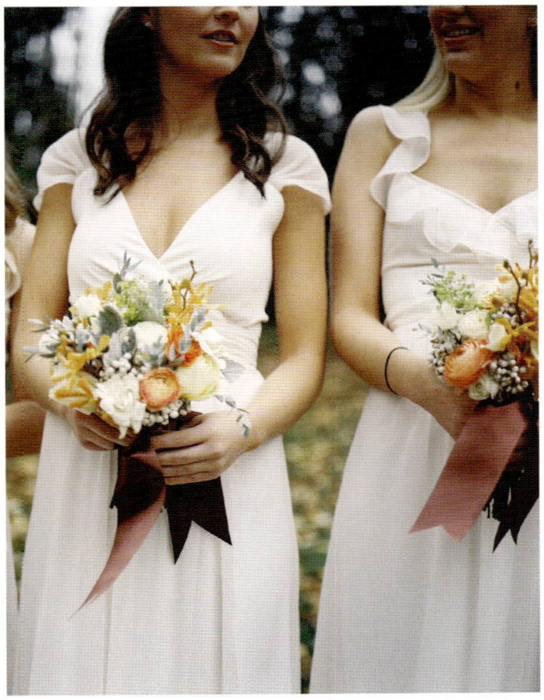

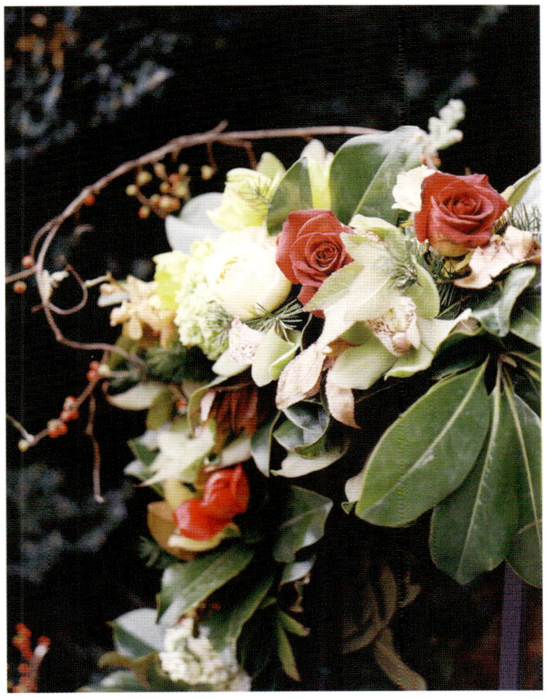

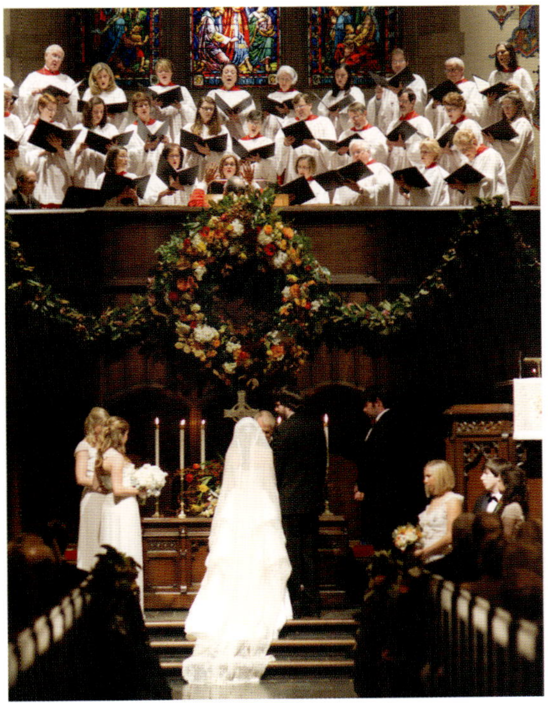

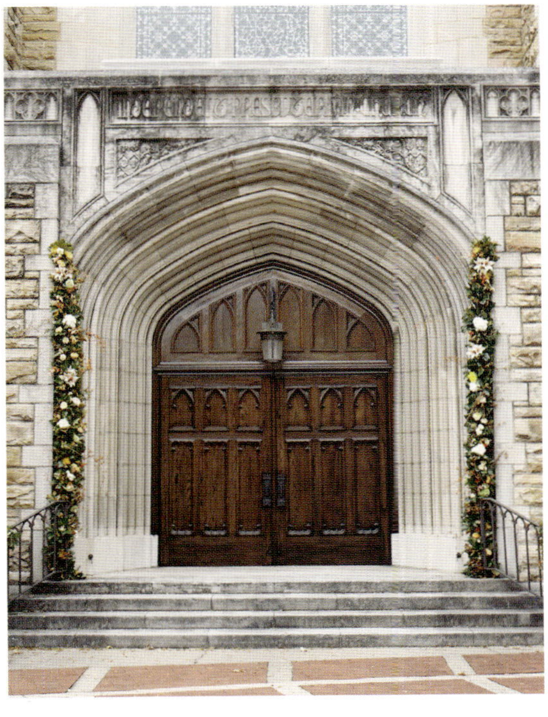

Rust and apricot hued flowers, like ranunculus, orchids, and garden roses, wrapped in brown satin ribbon contrasted elegantly against the backdrop of the bridesmaids's cream dresses and the traditional setting. Longtime members of their church, the family prevailed on the choir to be a part of the service. To stay warm on an unseasonably frigid day, Virginia wore her grandmother's fur wrap—adding to the elegance and tradition of the occasion.

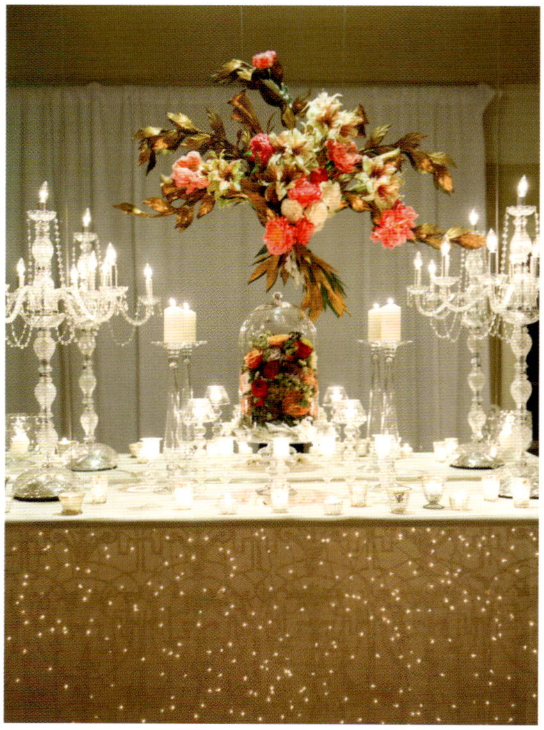

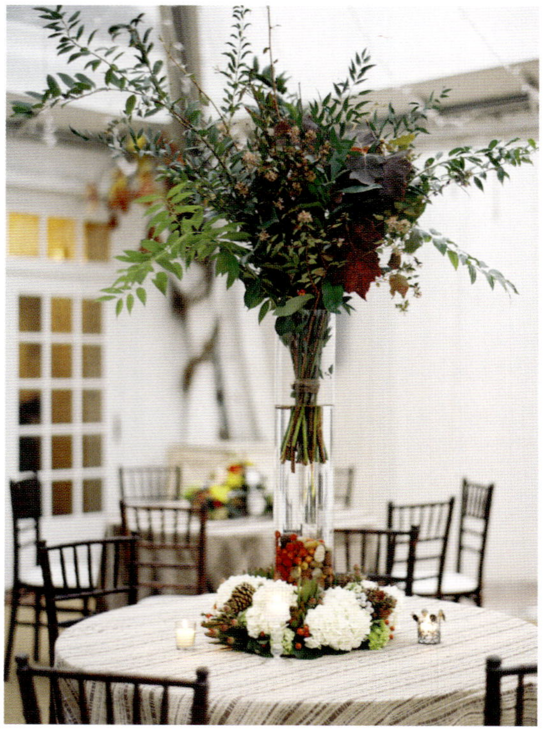

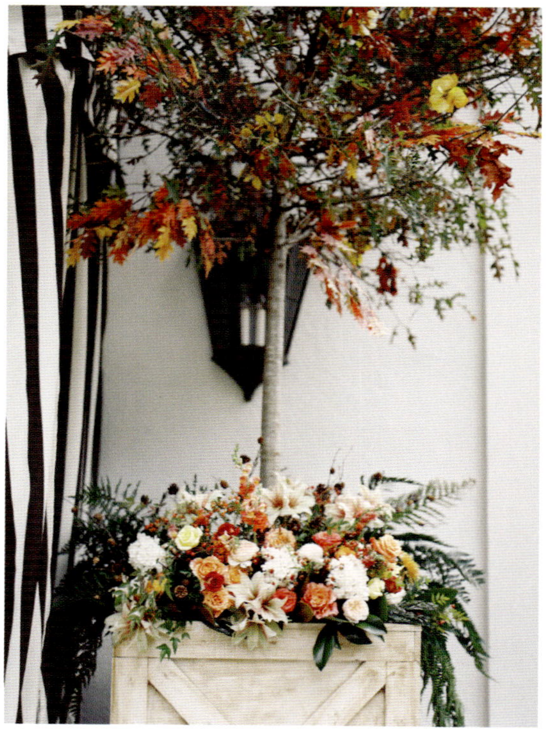

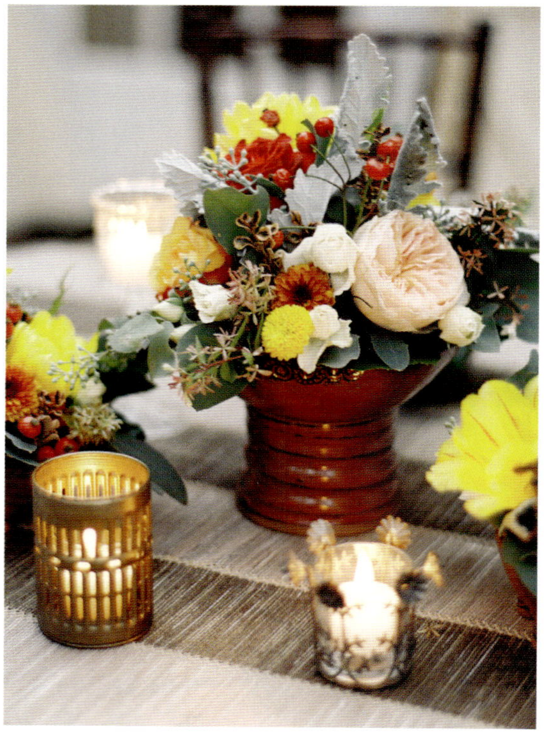

We collaorated with a great rental company in South Georgia, and they were able to produce the striped entry awning we had dreamed up. We then used fall colors mixed with magnolia leaves and also created fall trees that brought the outdoors inside for the party.

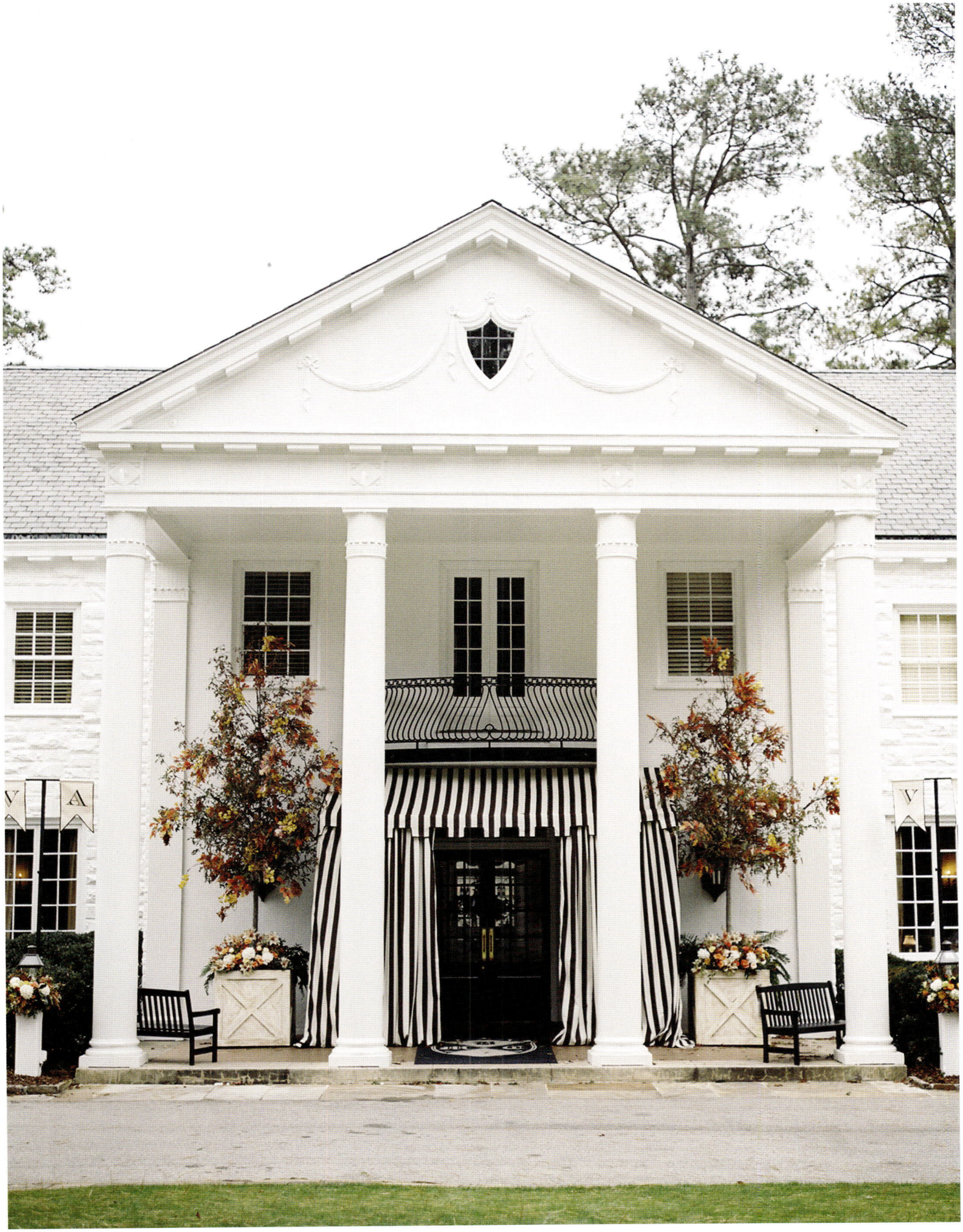
V
A
V

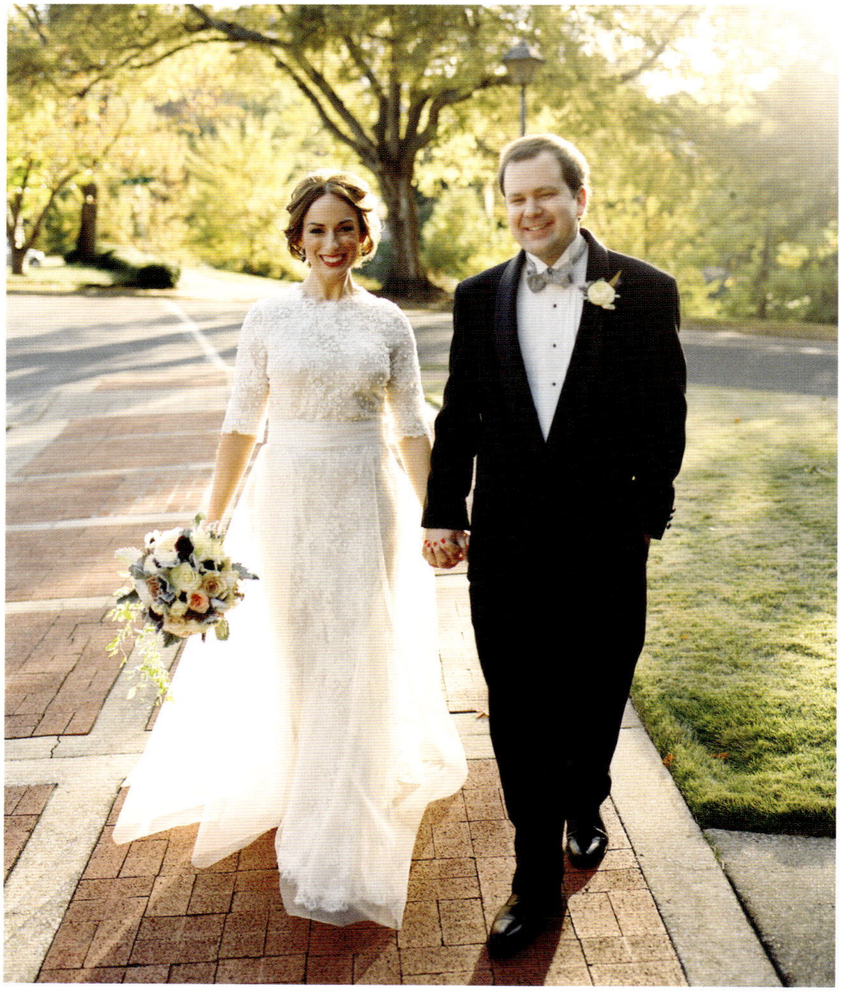

MEGAN & BARNETT

fashion forward and channeling chanel

Megan is a fashion stylist, and our inspiration came from a recent Chanel fashion show in Paris. The models walked around a long center buffet that was overladen (Marie Antoinettish) with tiered platters of fruit and sweets, intermingled with loads of crystal—candelabra, chandeliers, and containers. Her lace dress was timeless, a flattering silhouette the great designer would have loved.

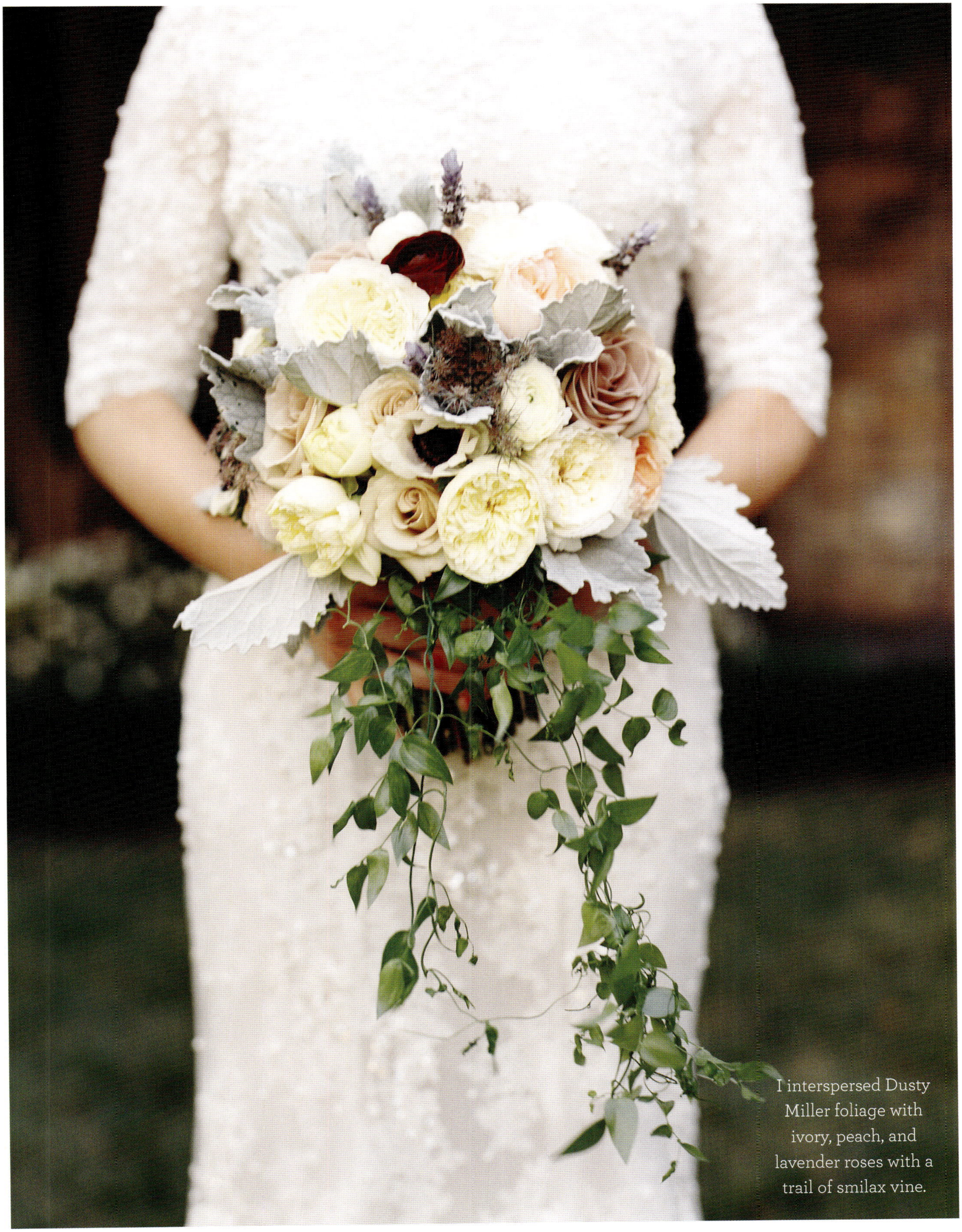

I interspersed Dusty Miller foliage with ivory, peach, and lavender roses with a trail of smilax vine.

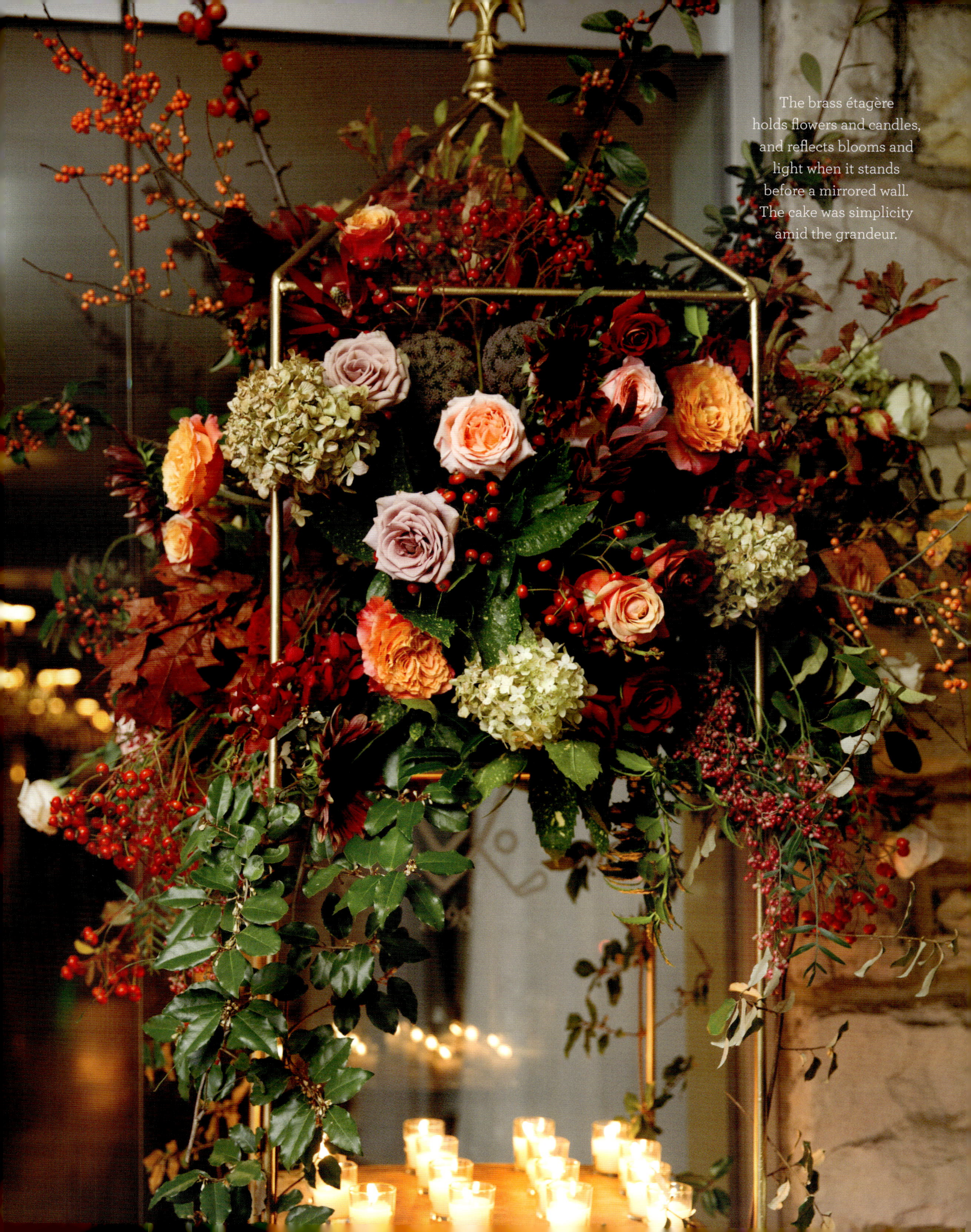

The brass étagère holds flowers and candles, and reflects blooms and light when it stands before a mirrored wall. The cake was simplicity amid the grandeur.

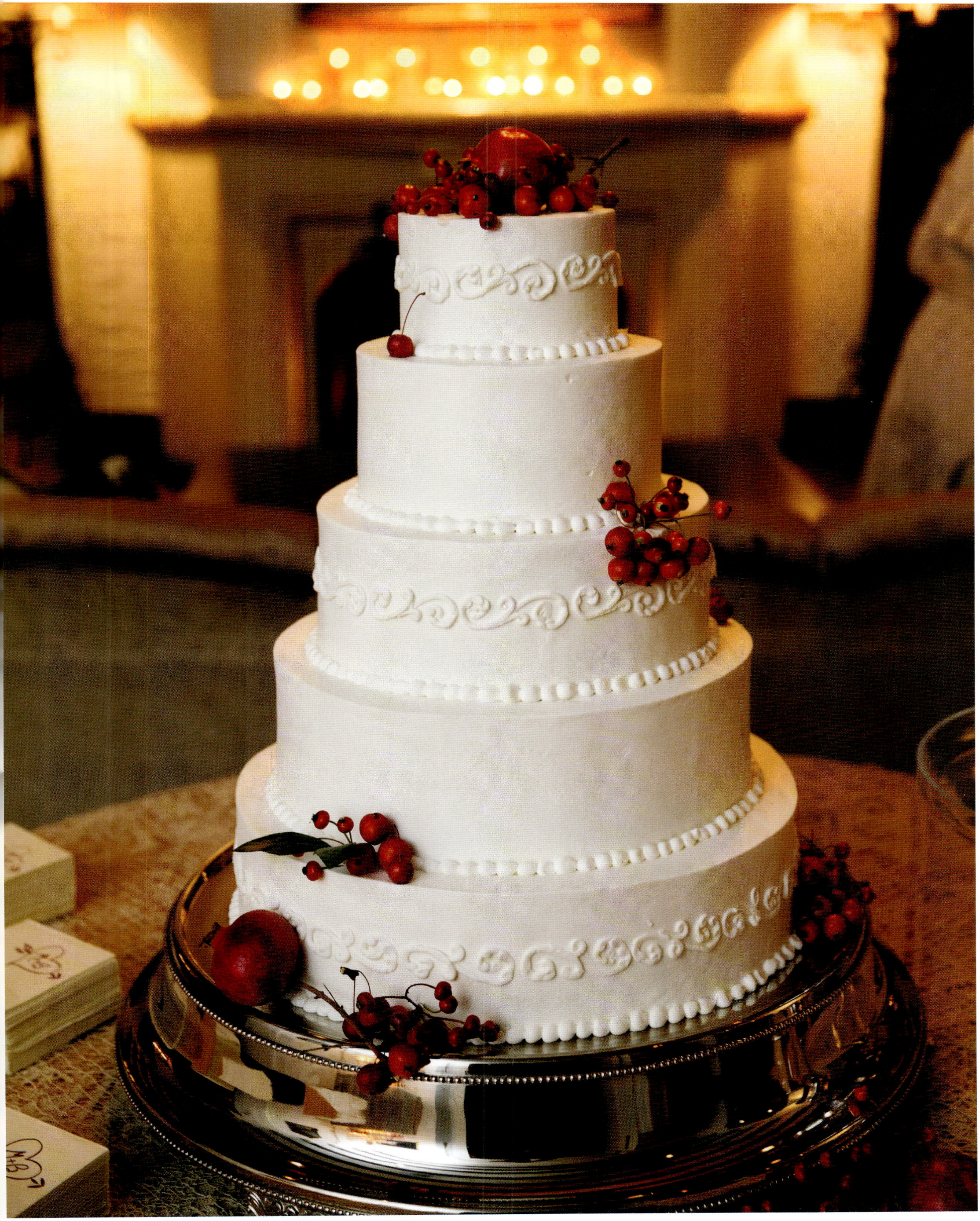

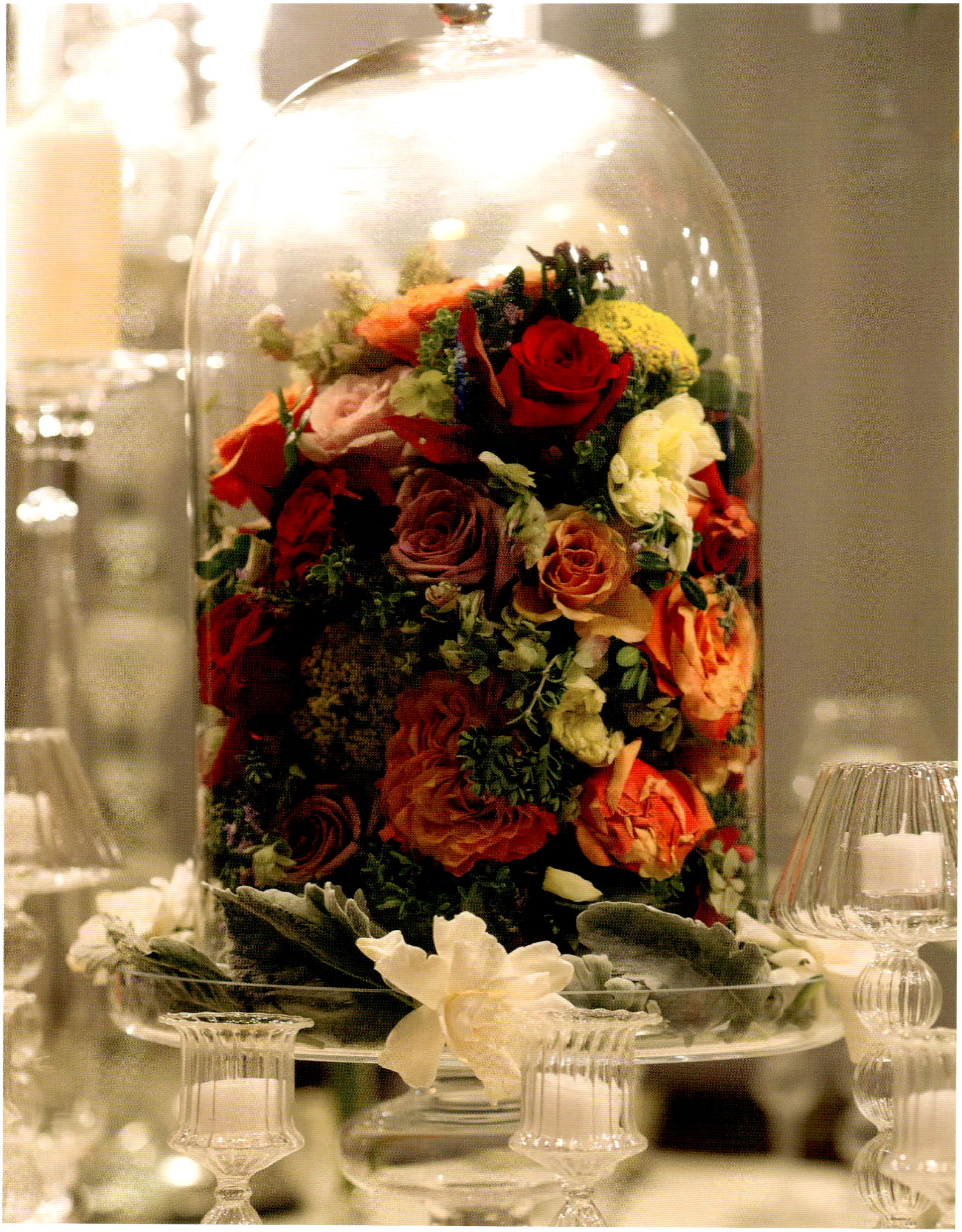

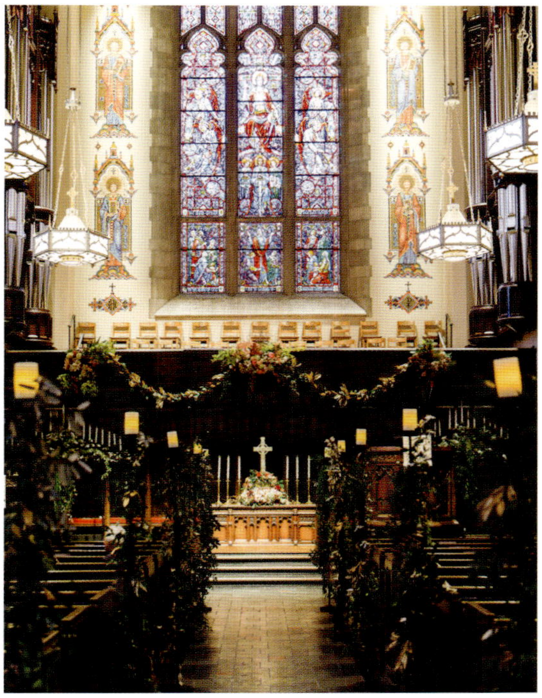
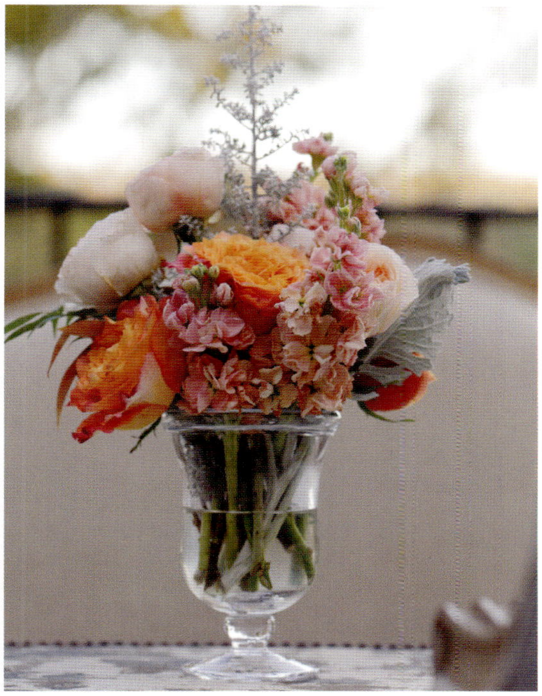
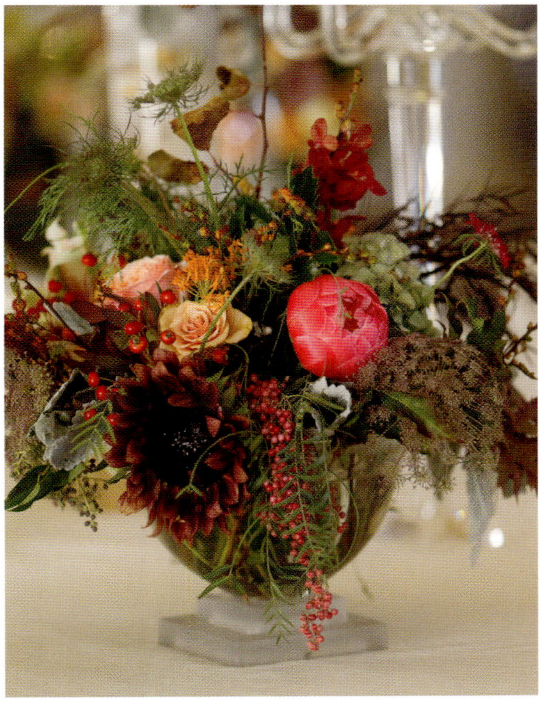
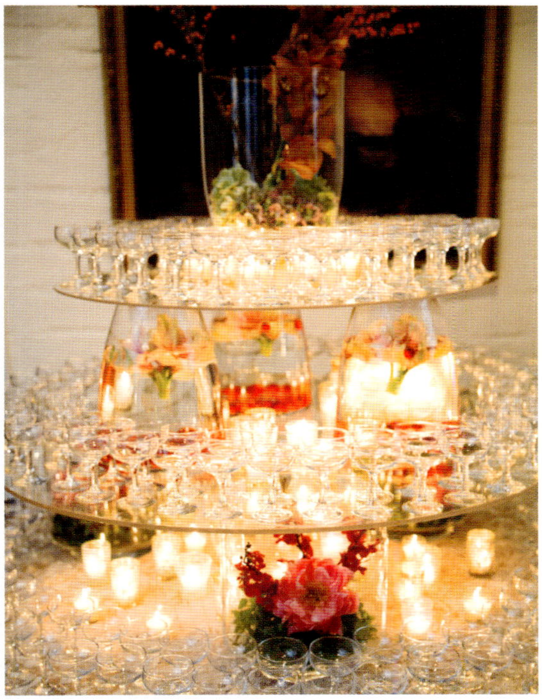

A feeling of sophisticated opulence and elegance tied the church and reception together. With masses of flowers and crystal, a champagne tower that comes to life with candles and floating blooms, and a cloche-covered tower of roses, the effect was glittering and magical, unlike anything I've done before.

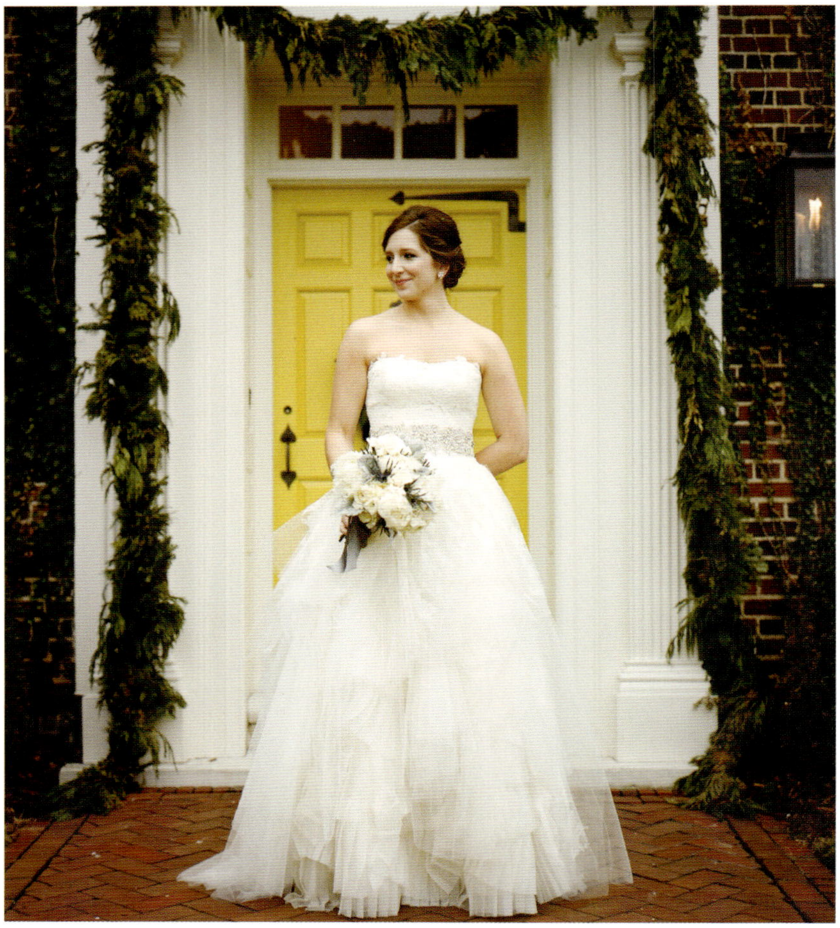

SALLY & STEVEN

completely inspired by downton abbey and love

This was a family wedding, so we pulled out all the stops, and I had a blast putting it together. It was during the holidays, and the reception was at the Country Club of Birmingham, with wood beams and fireplaces, all old English Manor in inspiration. I had the best time hanging clusters of mistletoe with golden laurel circlets at various heights across the ceiling. Each table was unique. Bud vases and votives mixed with golden wooden compotes holding flowing arrangements. Candles and more candles kept pace with Christmas garlands, little lights, shimmering pine cones, and jingle bell shakers that sent the couple off on the great adventure of life.

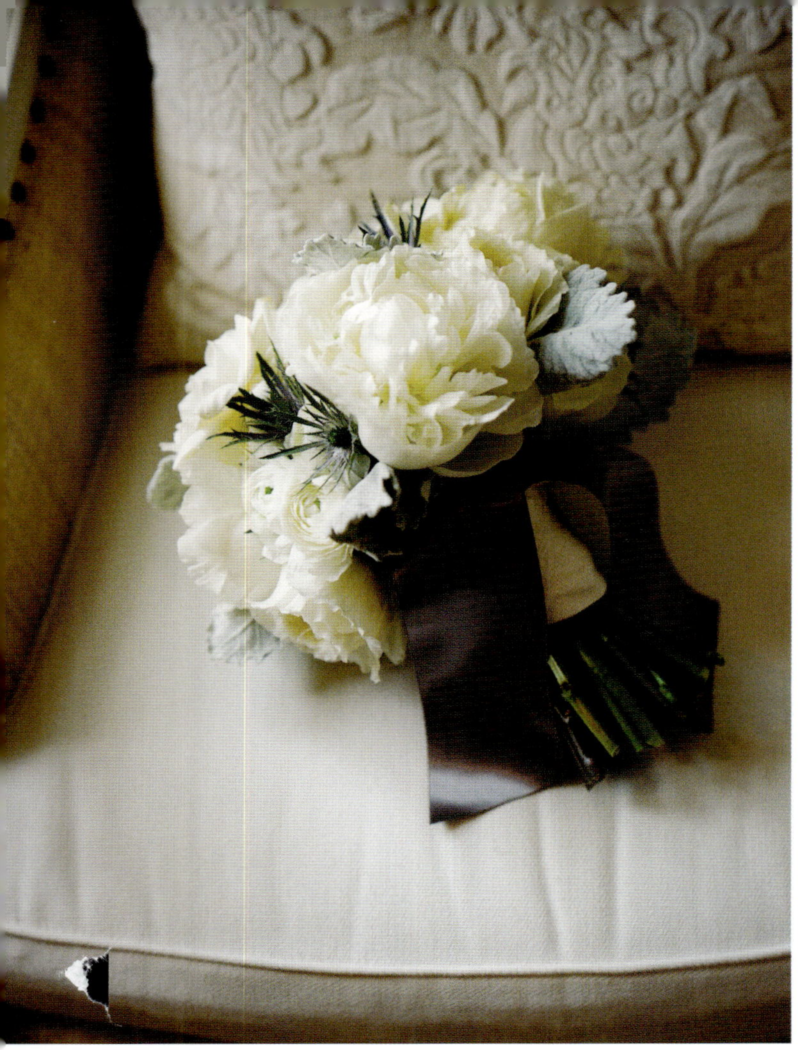
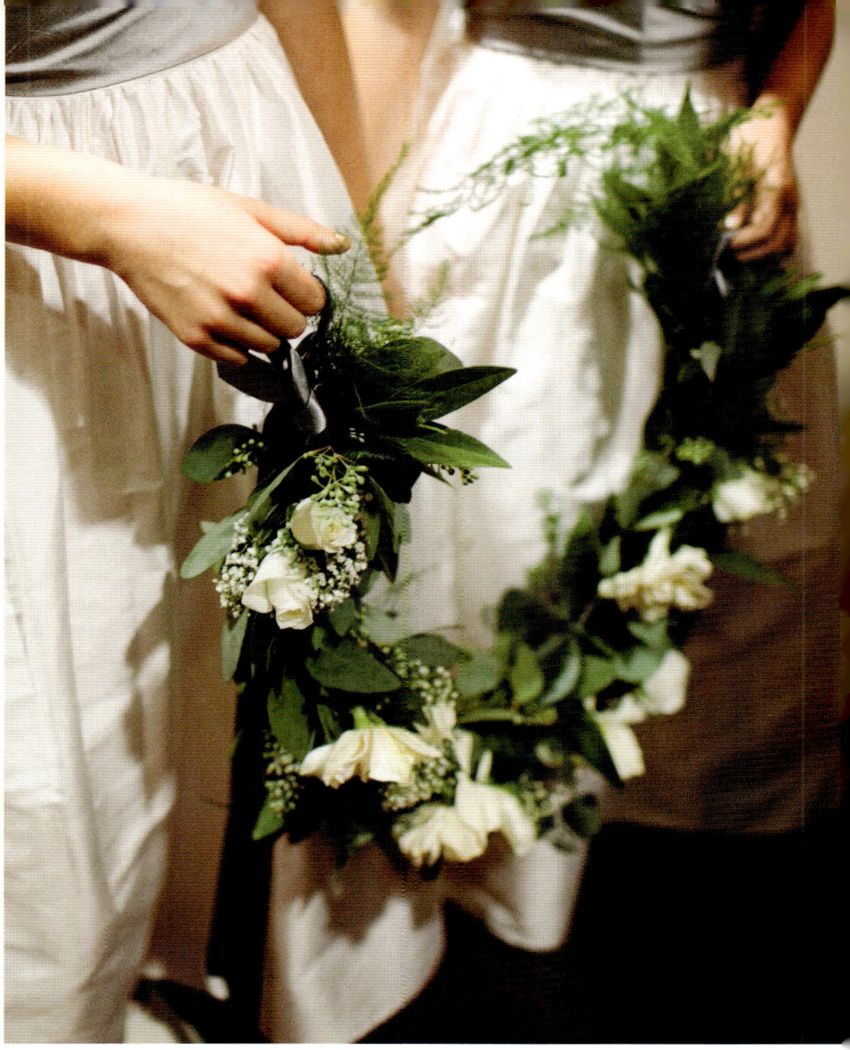
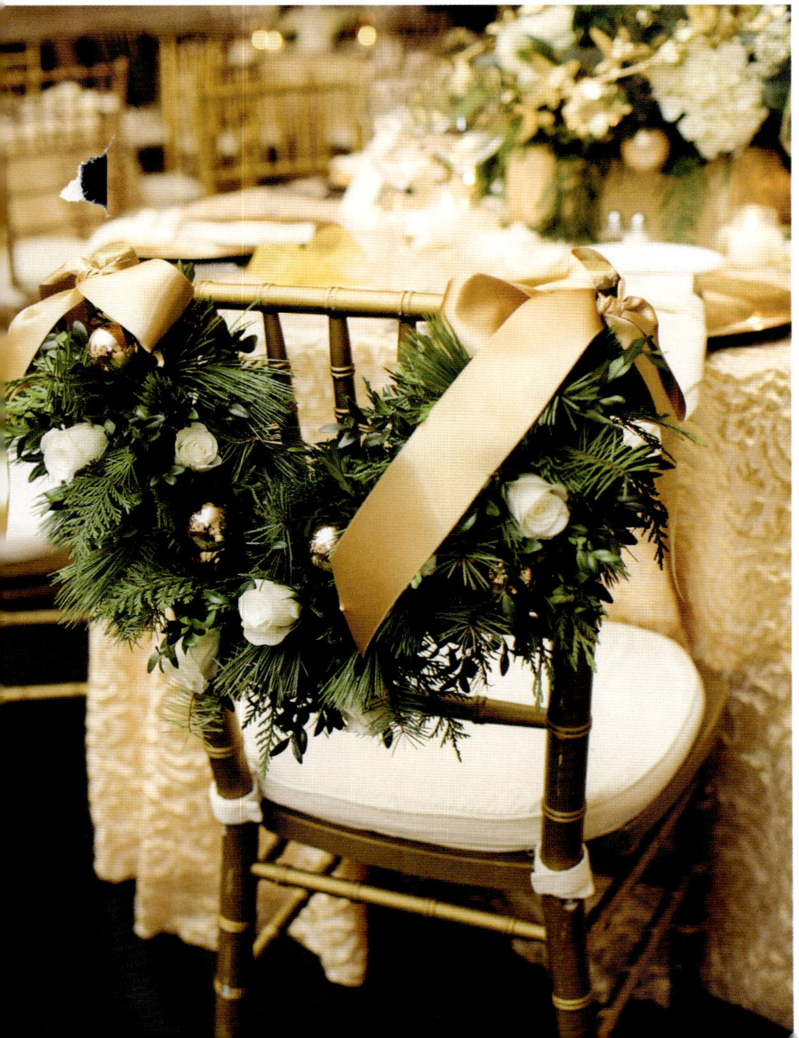
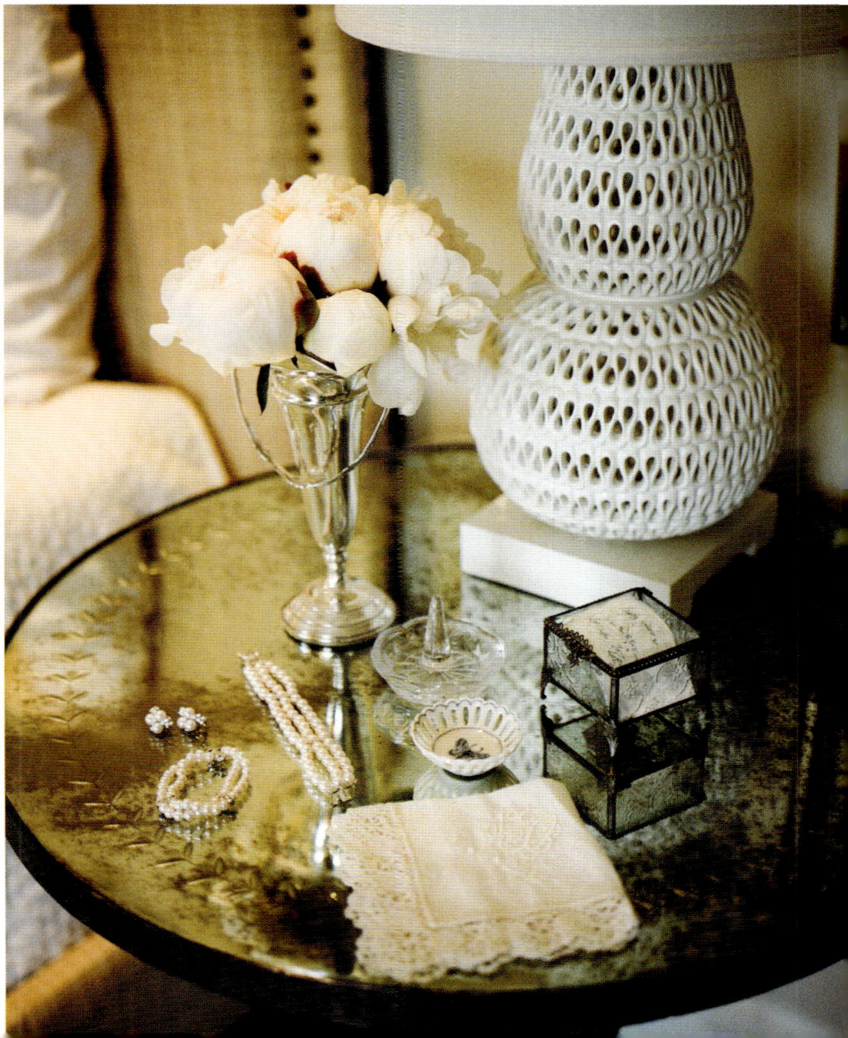

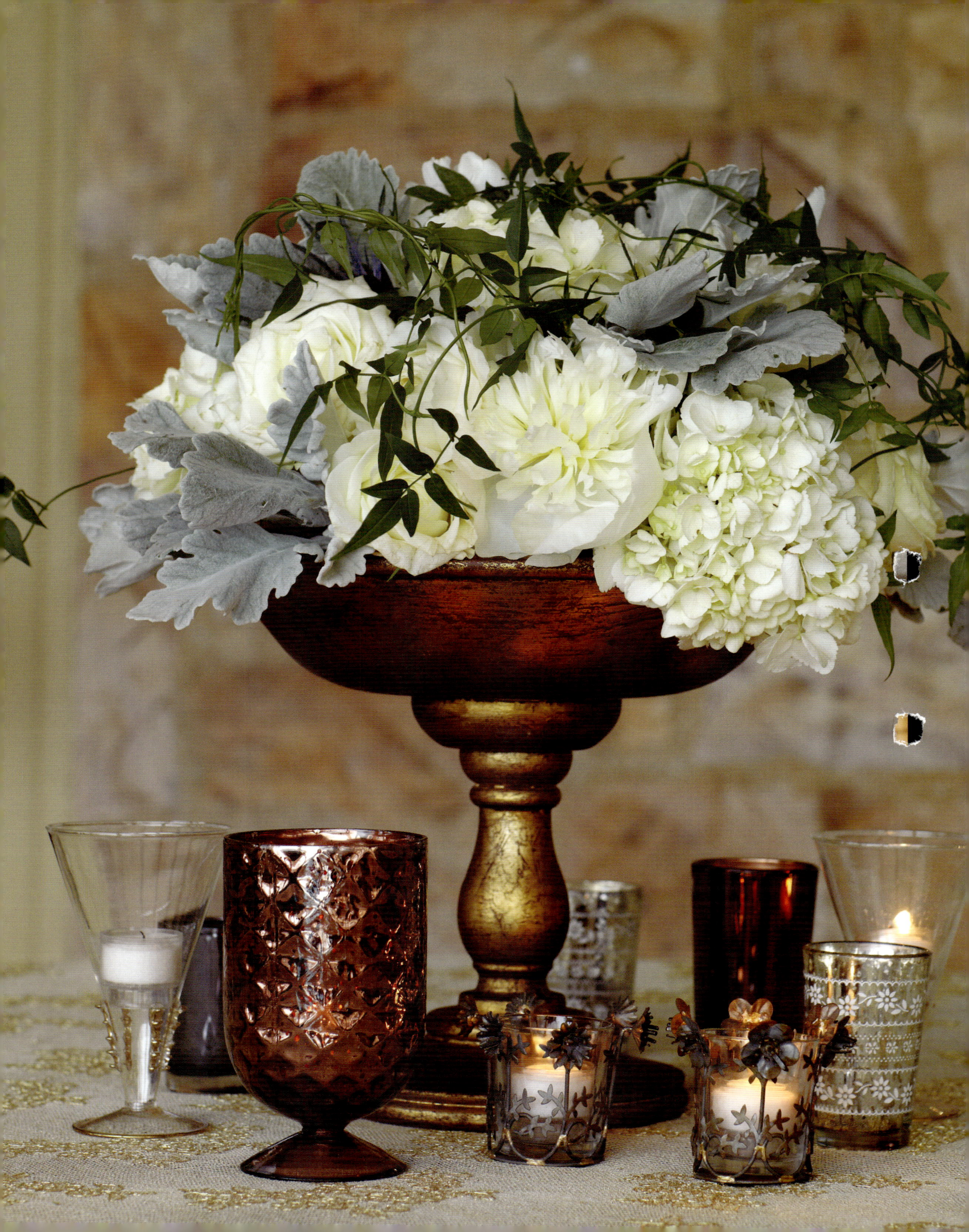

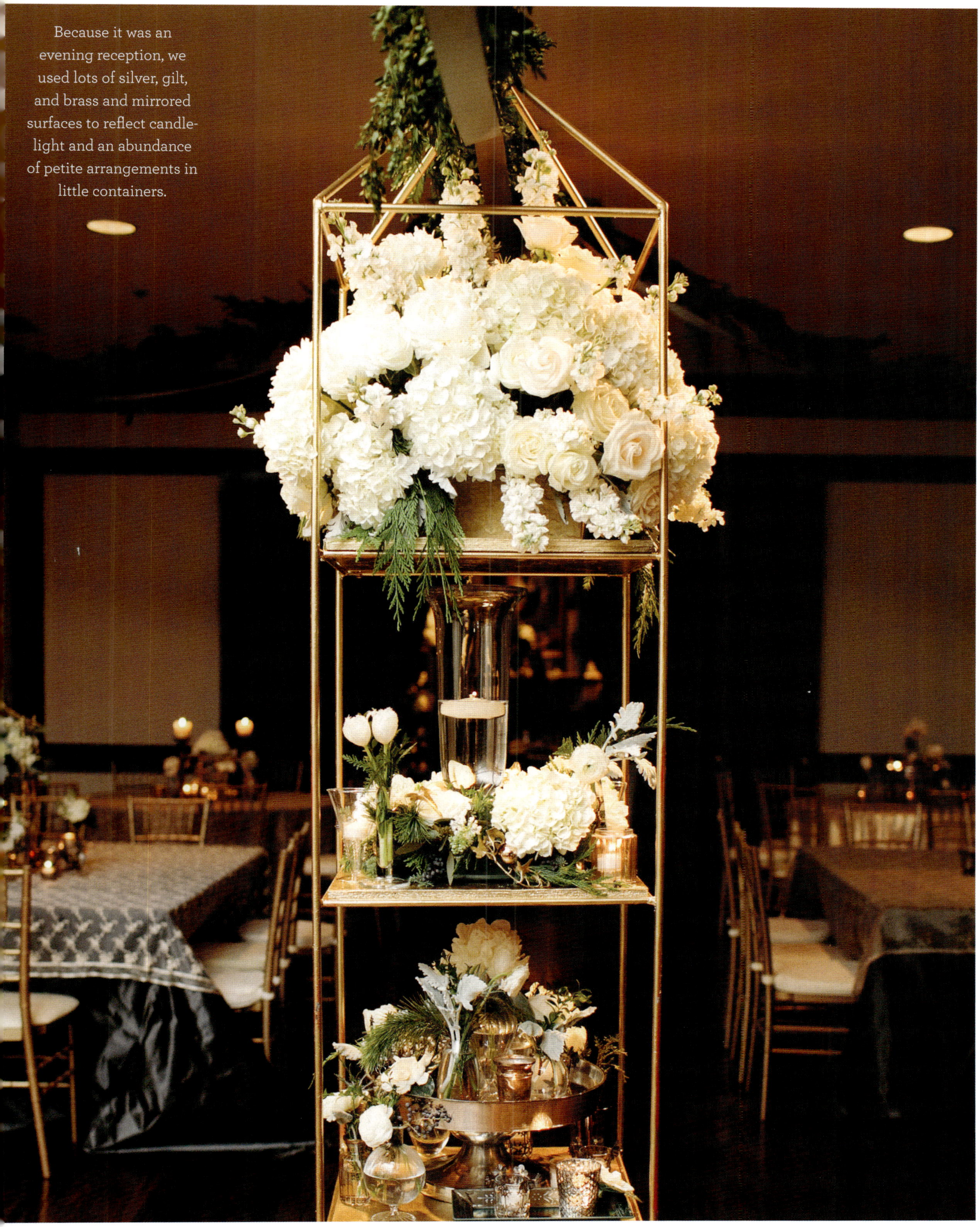

Because it was an evening reception, we used lots of silver, gilt, and brass and mirrored surfaces to reflect candlelight and an abundance of petite arrangements in little containers.

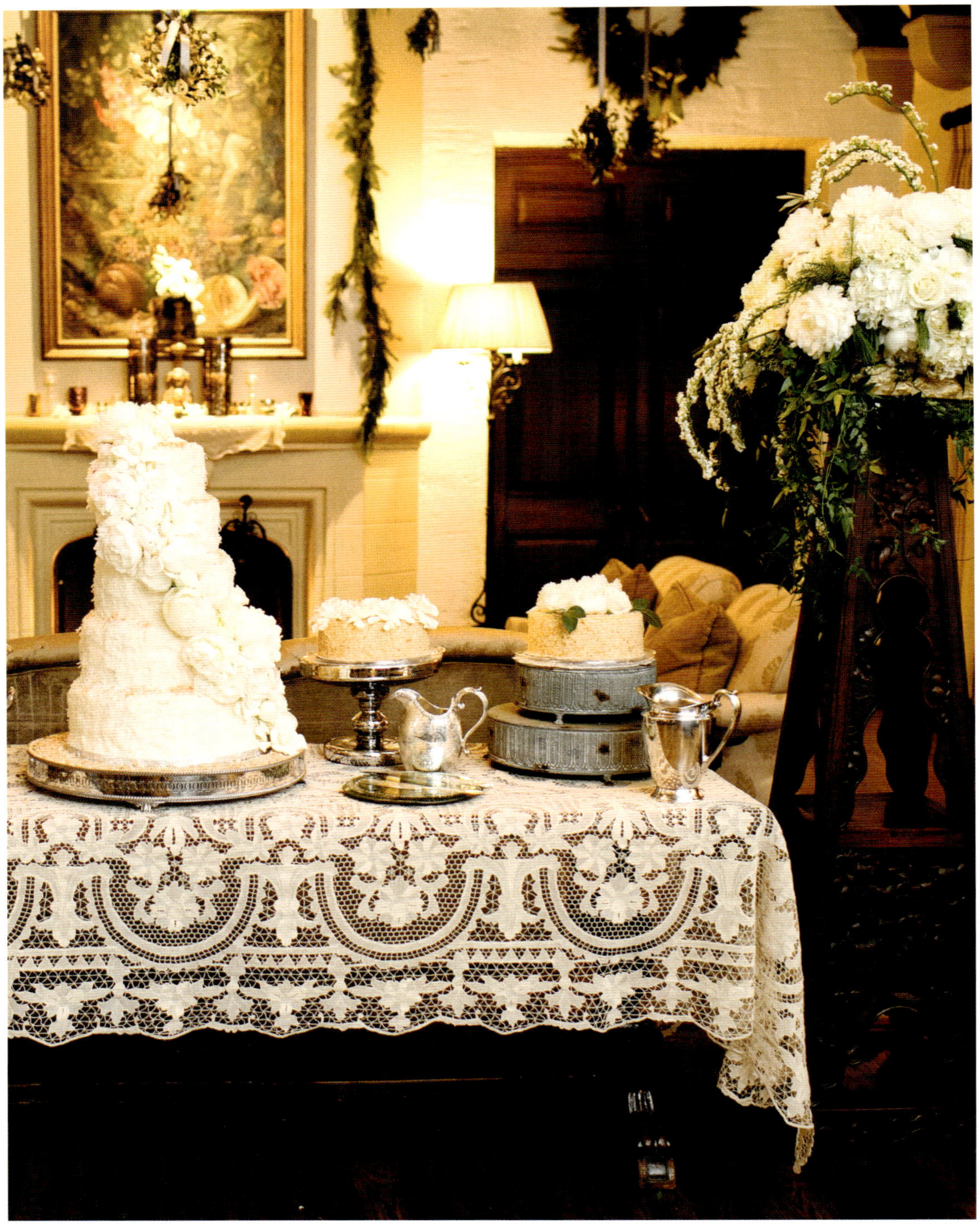

SALLY HAS ALWAYS CALLED ME "GAGA." I DON'T KNOW WHY, BUT BY THE END OF THIS WEEKEND, I WAS "LADY GAGA." I WONDER IF I'LL EVER LIVE IT DOWN!

The cakes and mistletoe made us rename the living room "The Kissing Room." Sally's bridesmaids wore charcoal gray dresses so we decided to hang charcoal gray doorway treatments to give the rooms more intimacy. We removed paintings throughout the dinner spaces and replaced them with various golden mirrors decorated with tiny wreaths adorned with golden laurel wreaths. They made everything glow and twinkle.

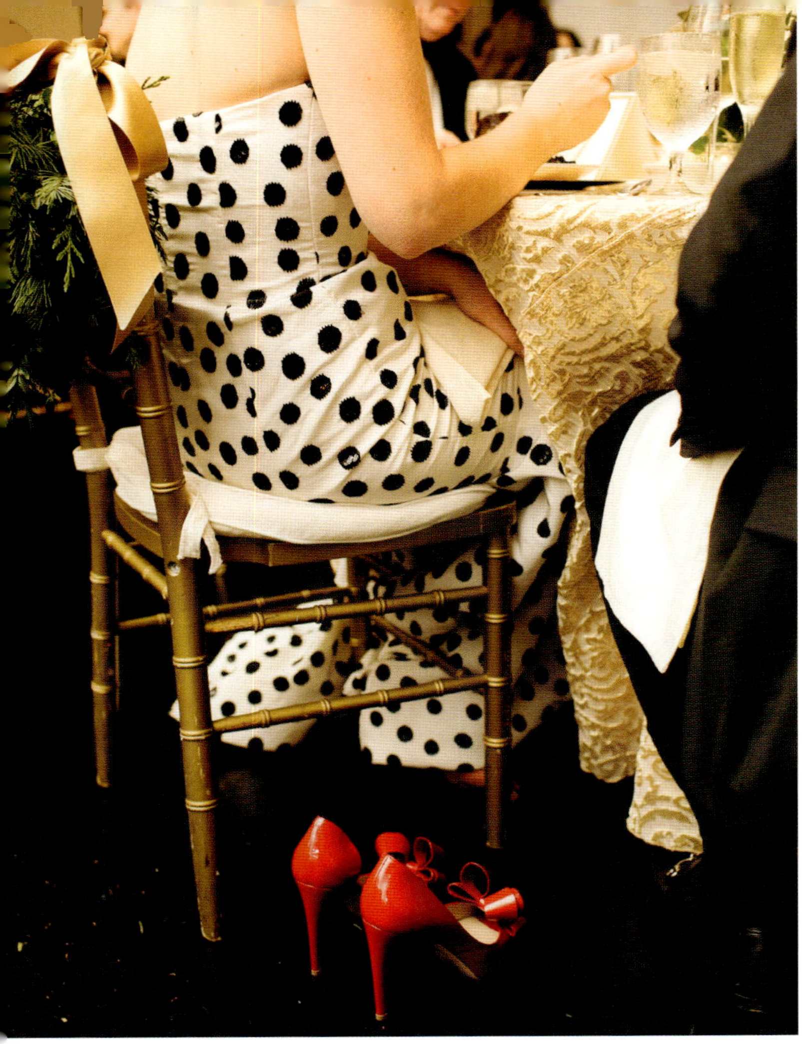
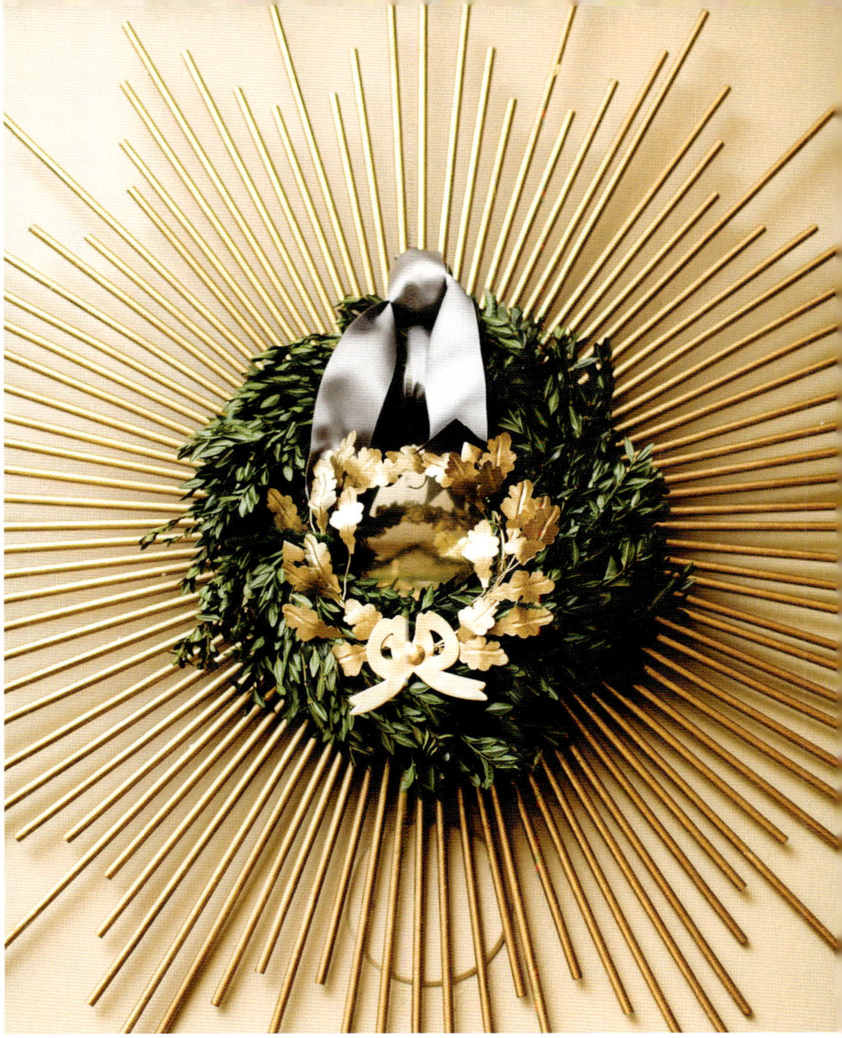
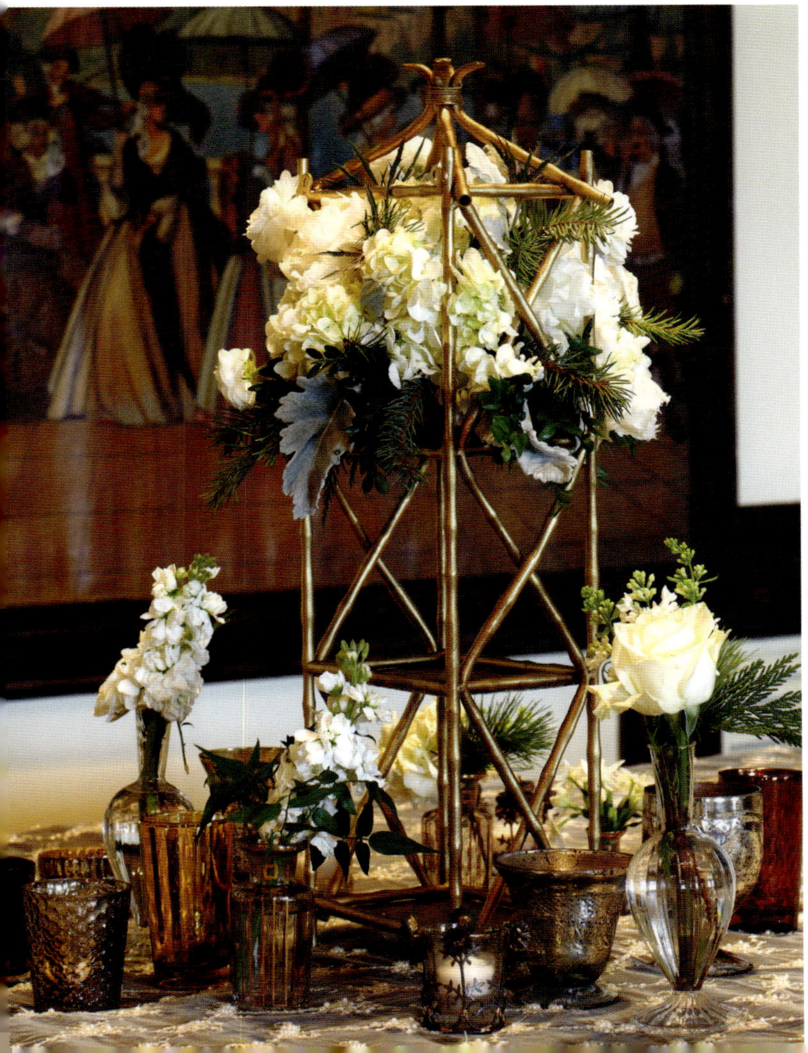
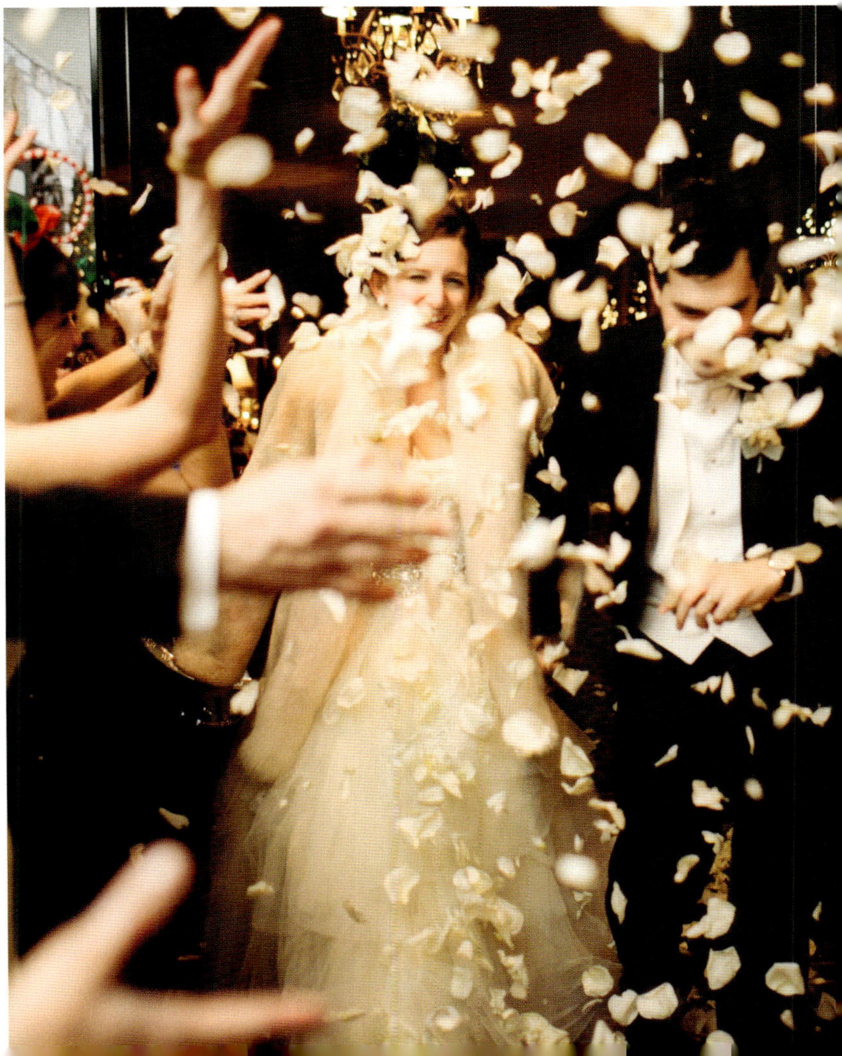

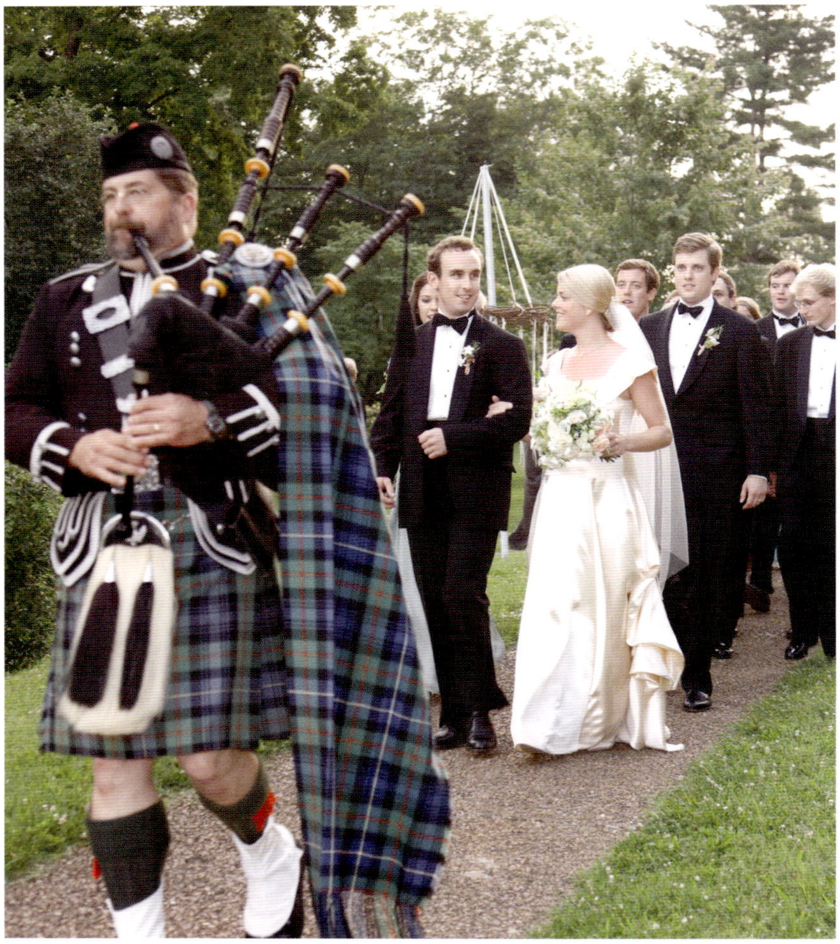

KATHERINE & SAM

all saints' chapel in sewanee, tennessee

I met with Katherine's mama to coordinate her destination wedding and do the flowers. That meant I would be traveling back and forth, from Birmingham to Sewanee, to iron out the logistics. I fell in love with the entire family and Sewanne and the Chapel, one of the most beautiful churches in this country, in my opinion. I kept the decoration pretty simple, to not compete with the beauty of the setting and the tradition of the church. The bagpipes alone stole the show!

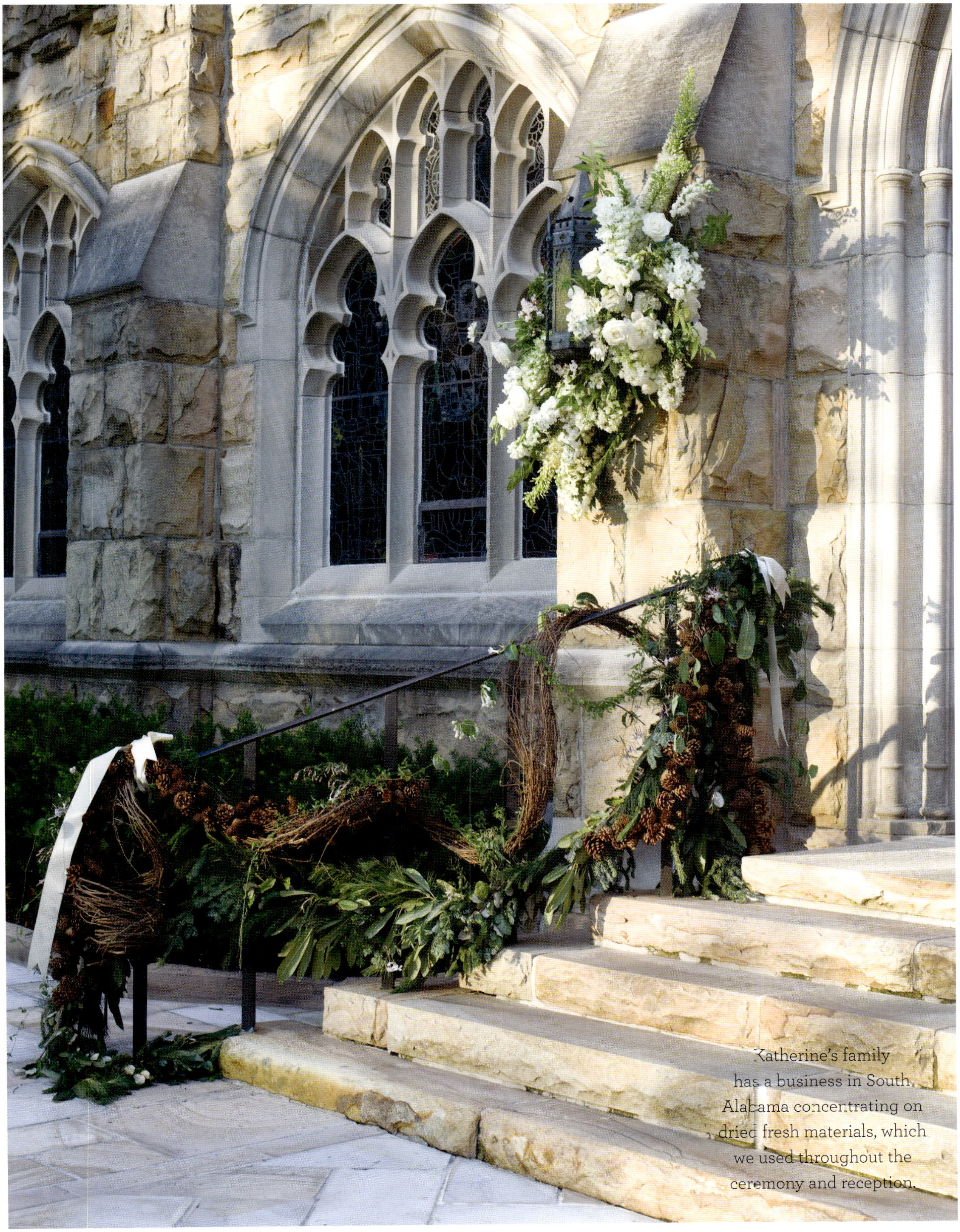

Katherine's family has a business in South Alabama concentrating on dried fresh materials, which we used throughout the ceremony and reception.

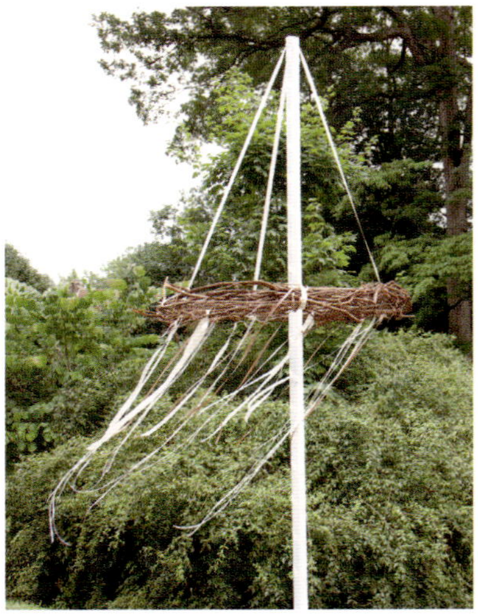
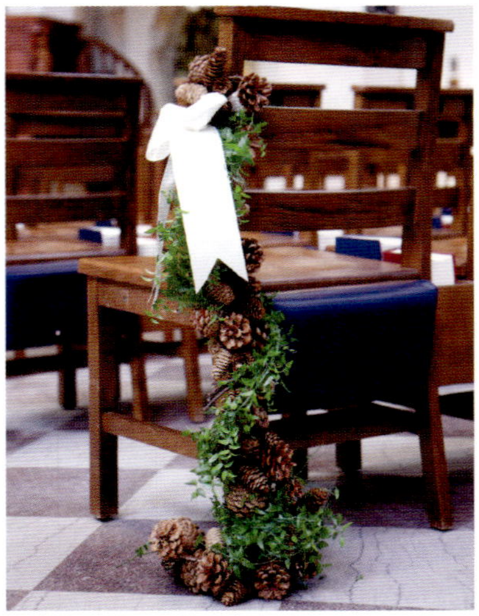
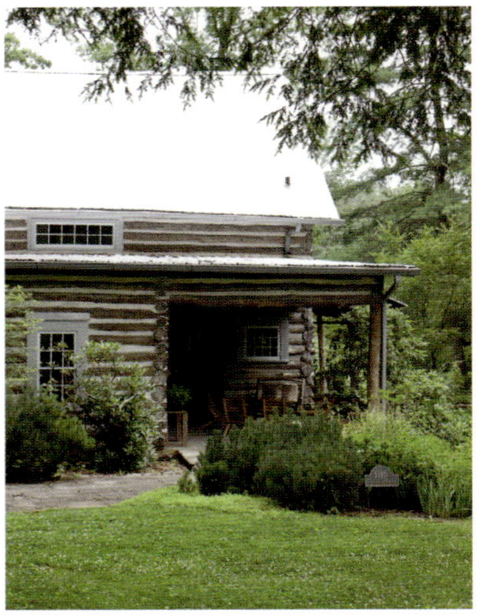
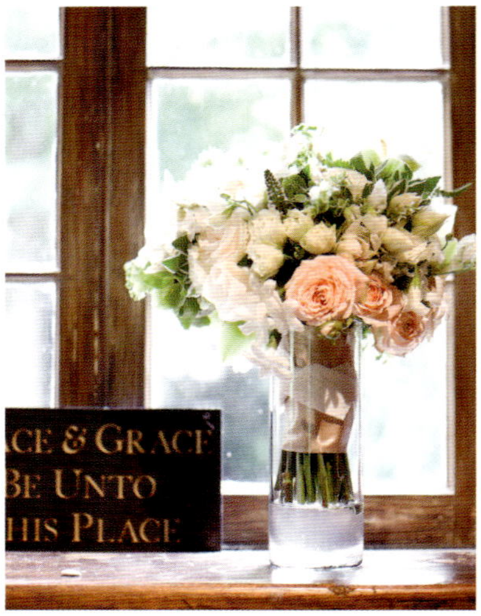

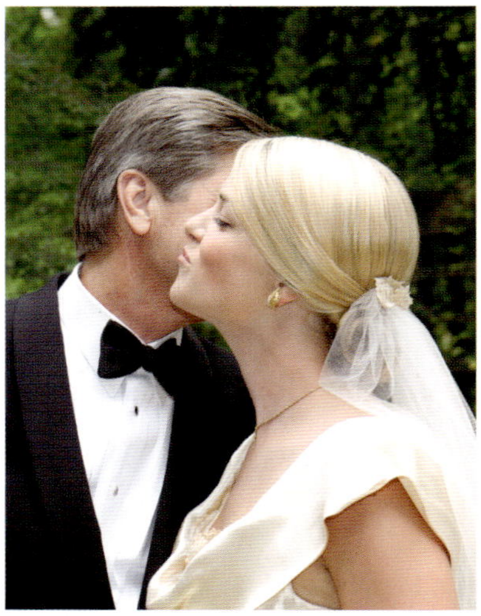
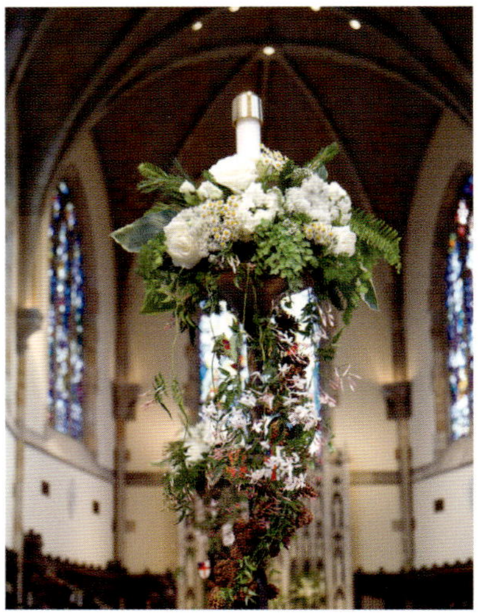
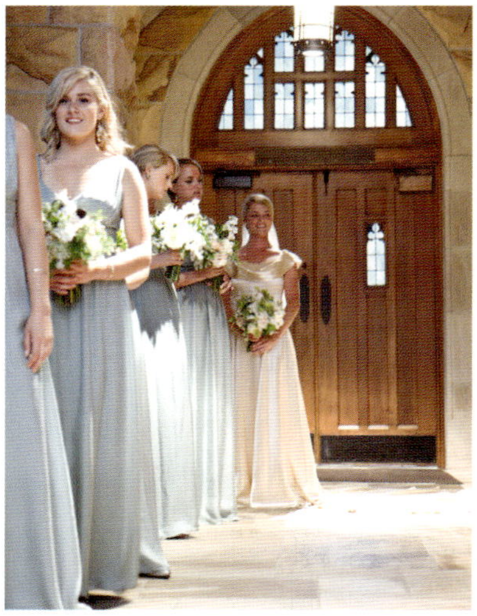
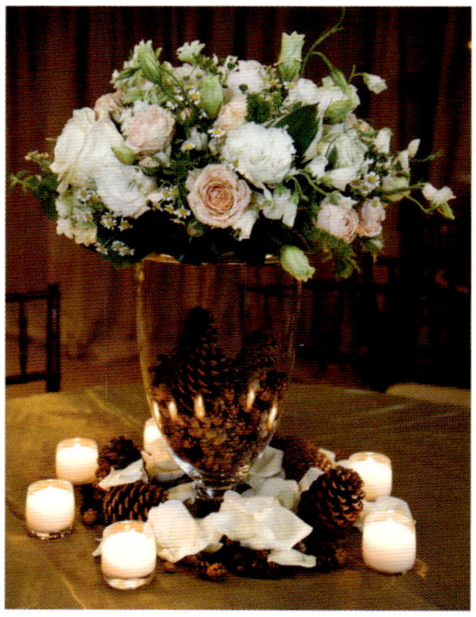
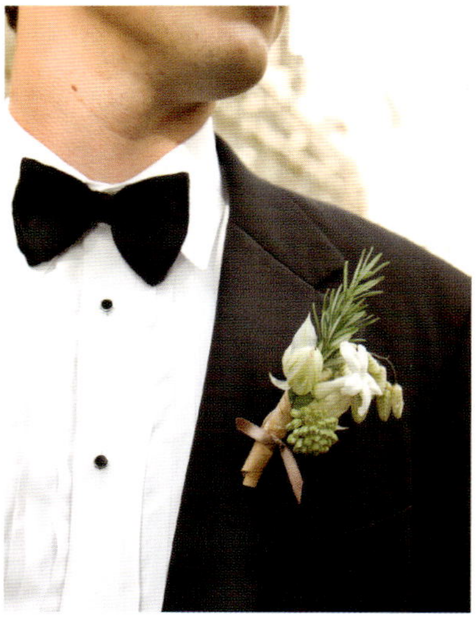

I made a maypole to mark the location and add to the merriment. For the flowers, my team and I pulled in loads of hosta and seasonal Southern greenery mixed with magnolia and lamb's ear, mushrooms, grasses, and birch bark vine, not to mention lots of herbs. The whole event was serene and peaceful, with light streaming through the stained glass in the church and the acoustics of age and tradition echoing throughout the space.

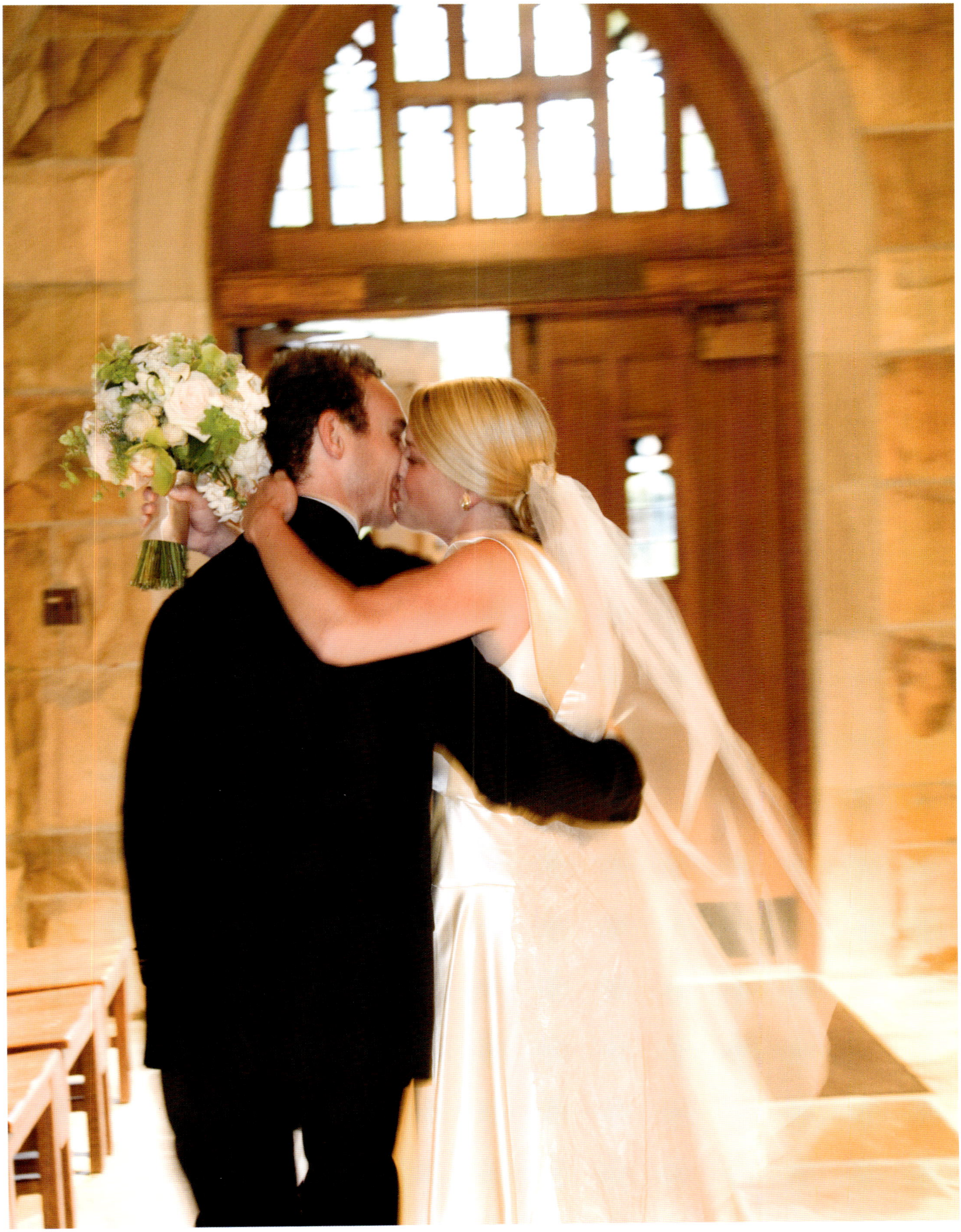

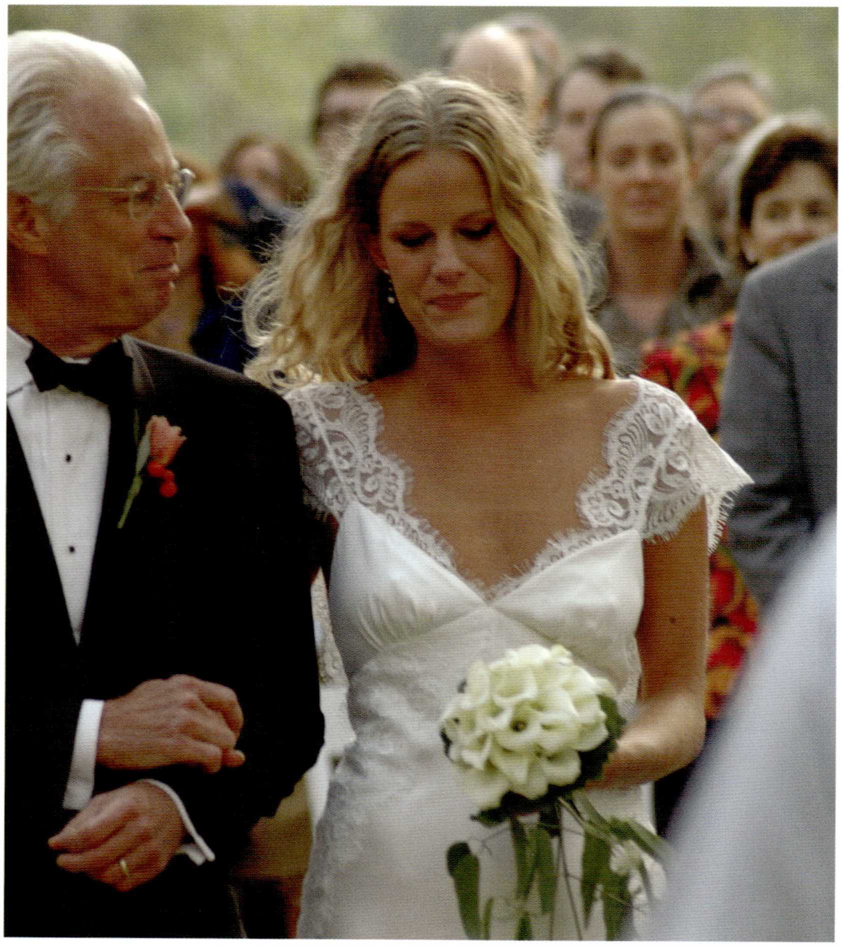

ELIZABETH & NED

green acres is the place to be

When I saw the barn—the site of the reception—for the first time my inner voice told me I was doomed. But then I remembered what works every time—family, friendships, and a team effort. Elizabeth's Daddy is ingenious, and he would get it to where it needed to be. To start, we had not enough electricity or water pressure, no restrooms, and the wedding was going to be in a grove by a pond that needed to be leveled and cleaned up. The barn was really like an attic, and we needed space for caterers and the valet. But we did it, and the result was magical.

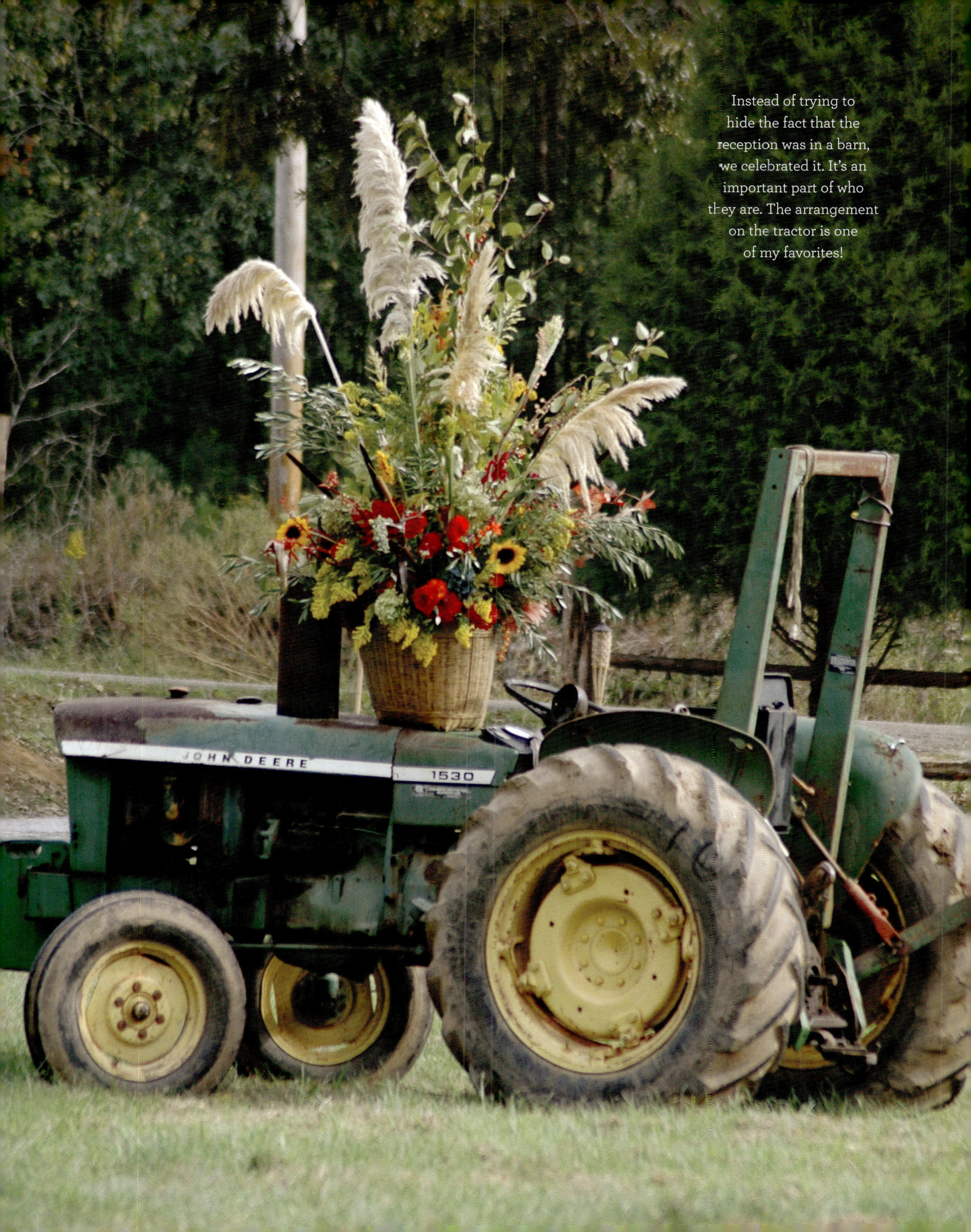

Instead of trying to hide the fact that the reception was in a barn, we celebrated it. It's an important part of who they are. The arrangement on the tractor is one of my favorites!

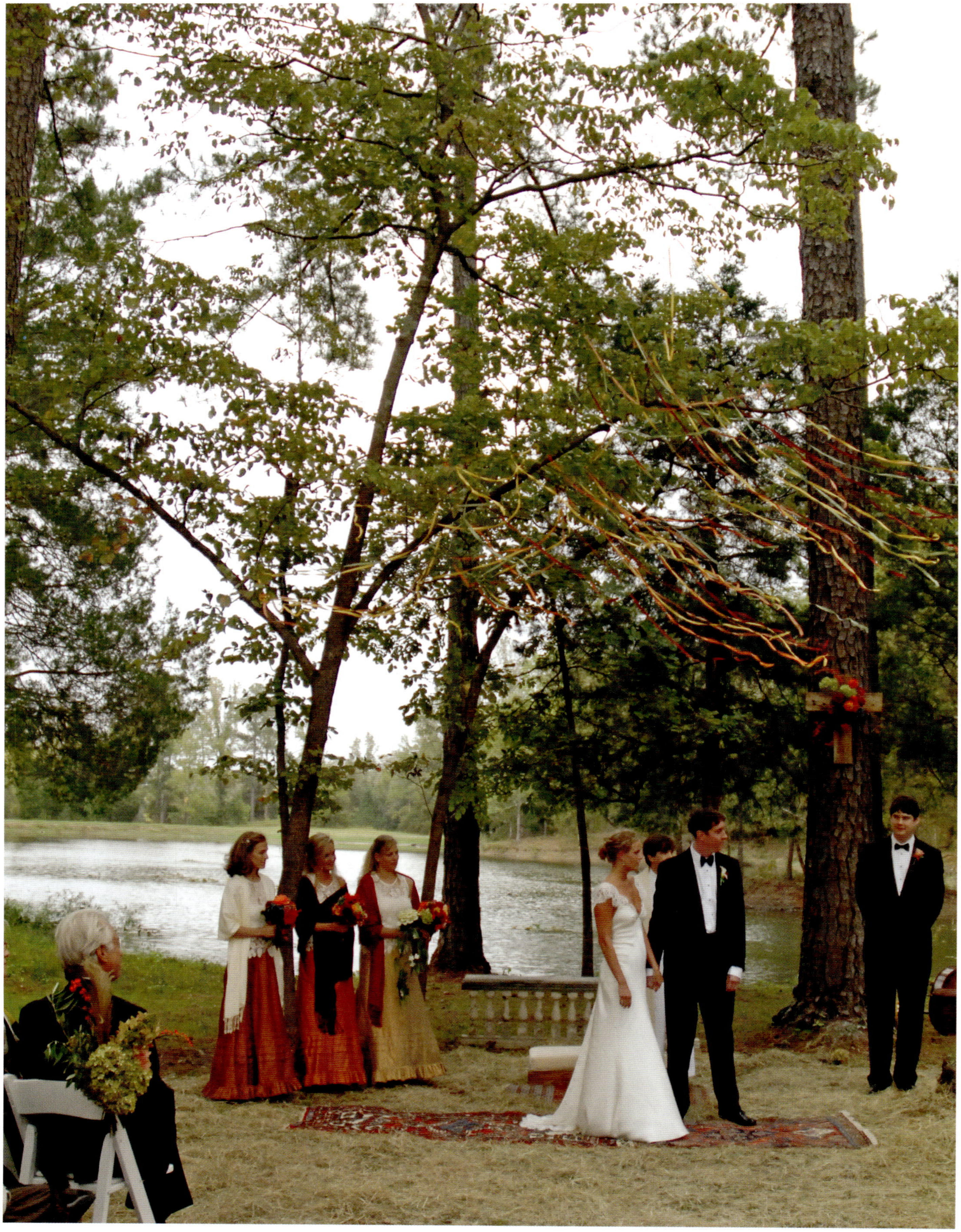

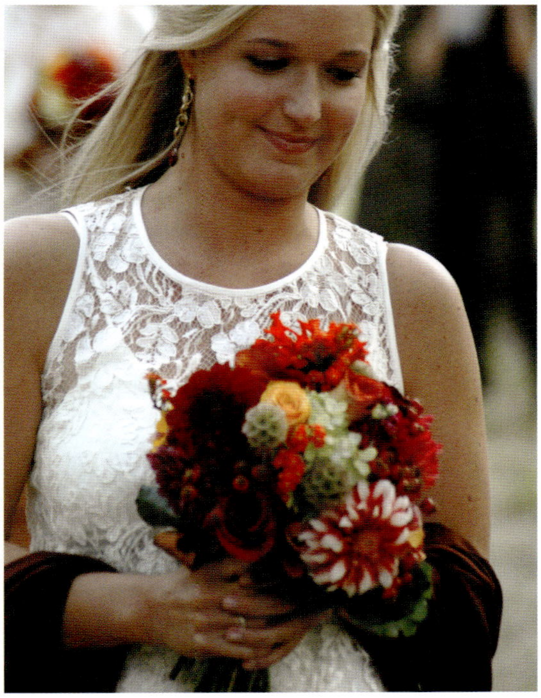

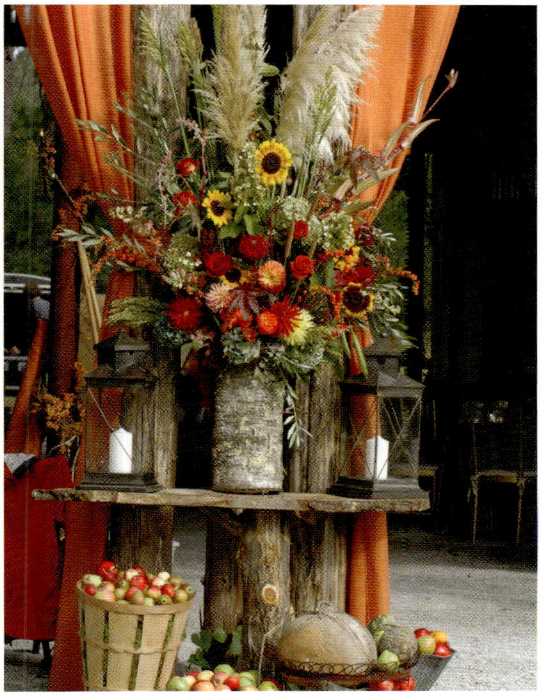

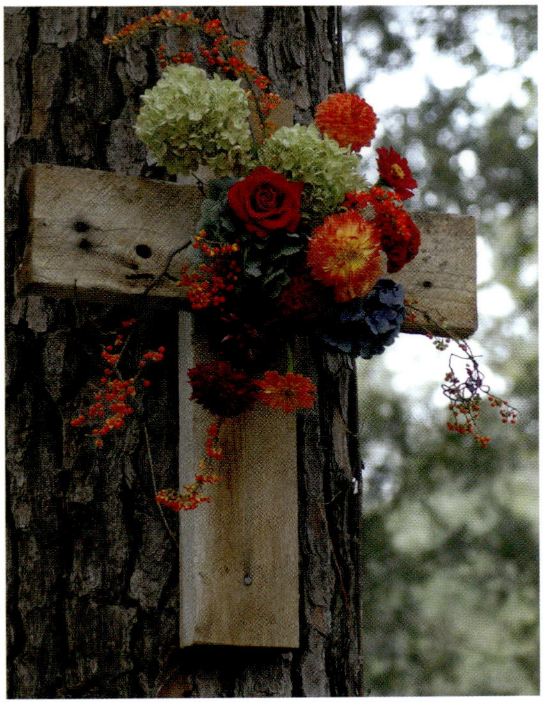

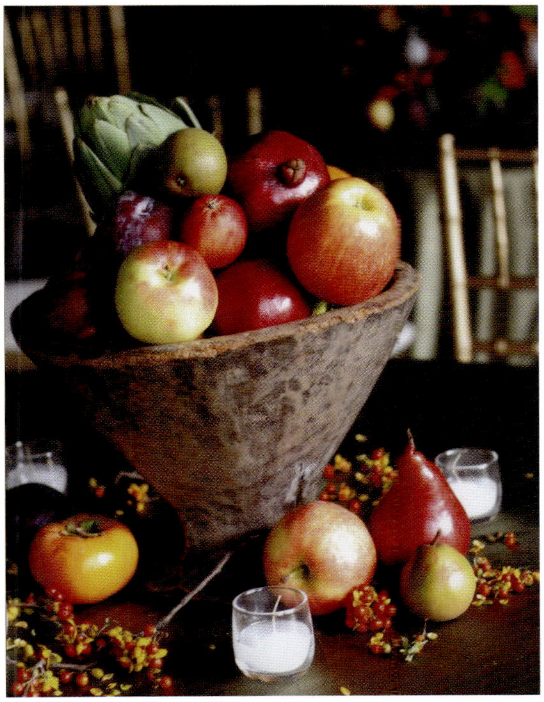

'NO' IS NOT AN ANSWER I'LL ACCEPT. SO WHEN THE SUNFLOWERS I PLANTED DIDN'T MAKE IT, WE FOUND A GROWER WHO HAD MORE.

In addition, Elizabeth's dad hauled in gigantic wisteria vines to climb up the support poles along the front of the barn to soften the space. We also decided on pumpkin/rust colored linen draperies to hang across the entry. We hung ribbon from the trees in the grove to decorate the wedding. The whole effect was relaxed and sophisticated and evoked stained glass.

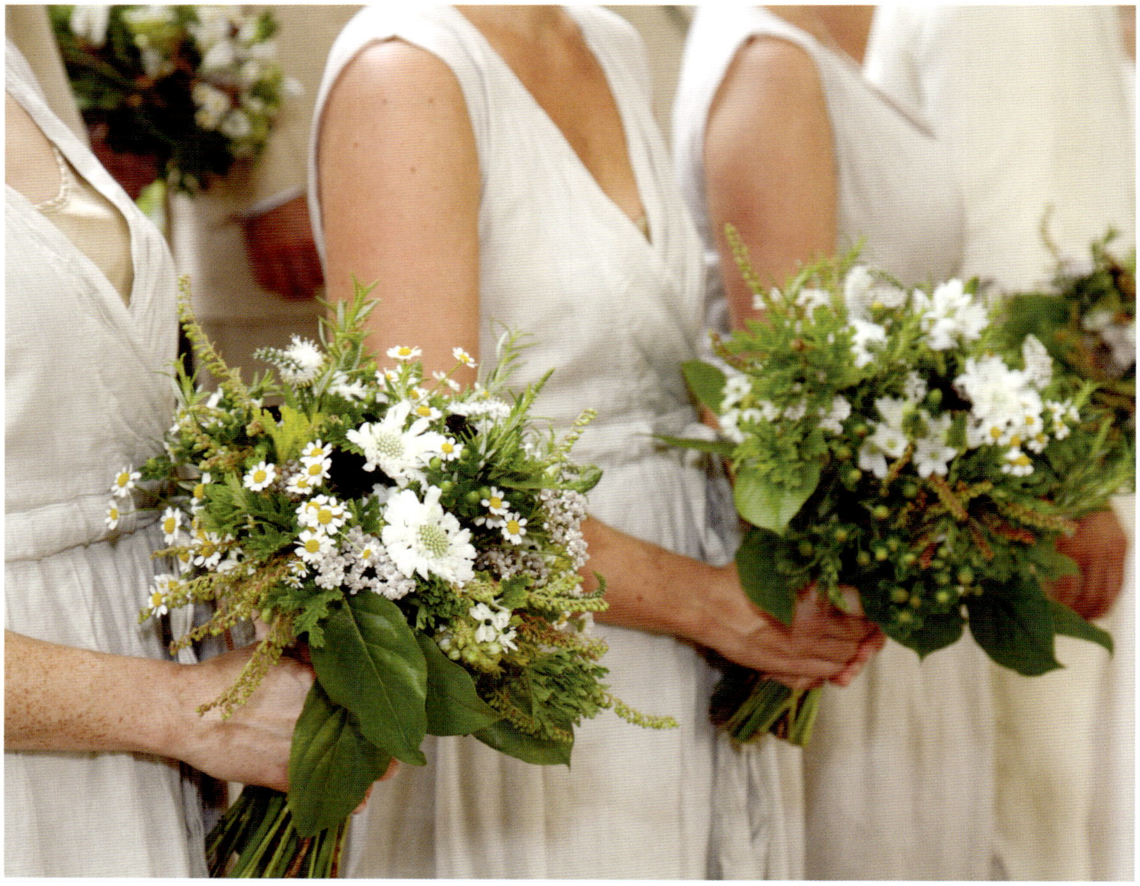

CARTER & ROBERT

an outdoor wedding

Carter really wanted an outdoor wedding and reception, but scheduling constraints worked so the wedding had to be in August. And if you know Alabama, you know that August here is unbearable. But we worked it out. They were married under an open air tent with ceiling fans above. Guests then boarded buses to be transported to the reception site—a lawn that overlooks the city of Birmingham. It was a magical evening, amazingly cool despite the time of year, and everyone had a great time.

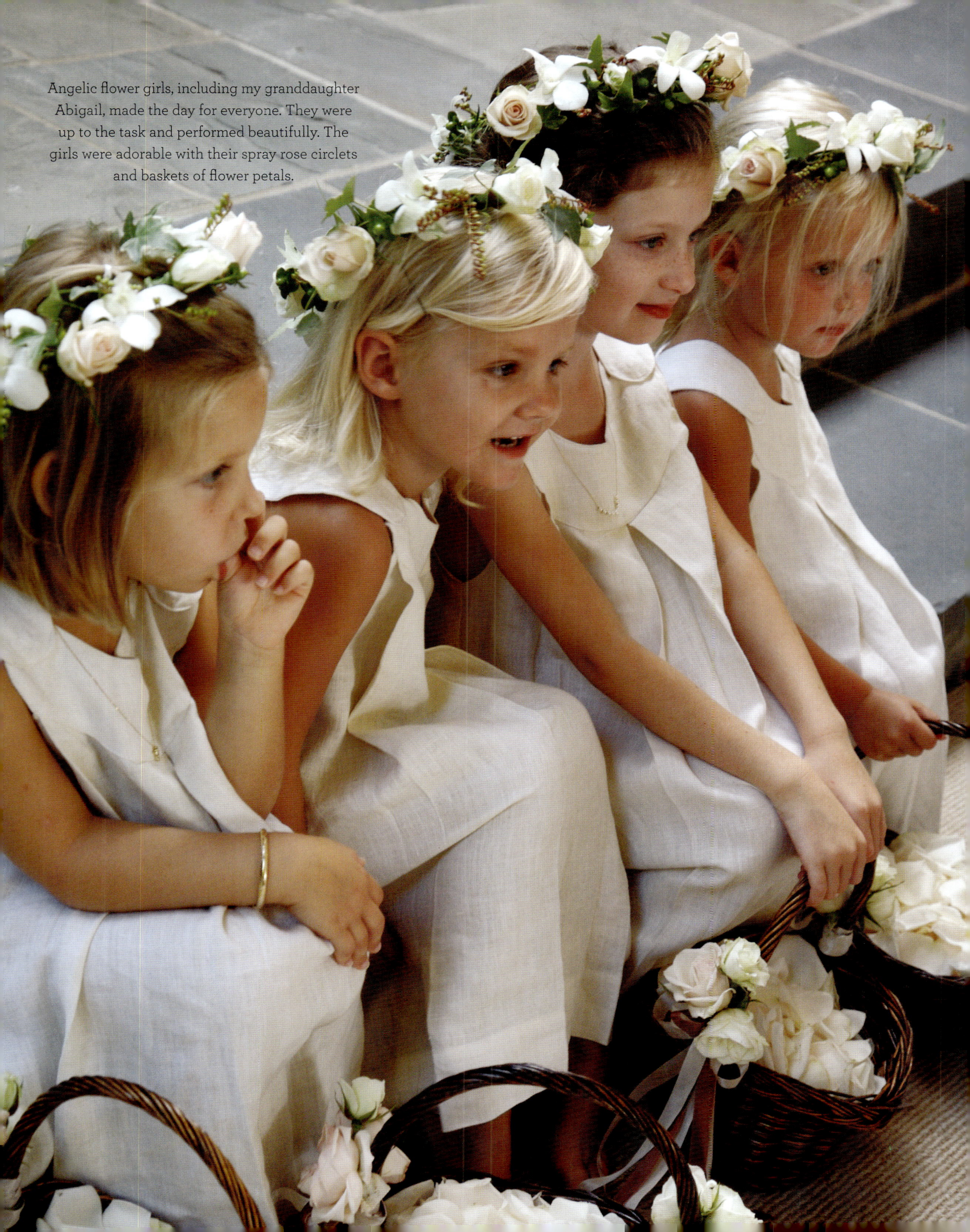

Angelic flower girls, including my granddaughter Abigail, made the day for everyone. They were up to the task and performed beautifully. The girls were adorable with their spray rose circlets and baskets of flower petals.

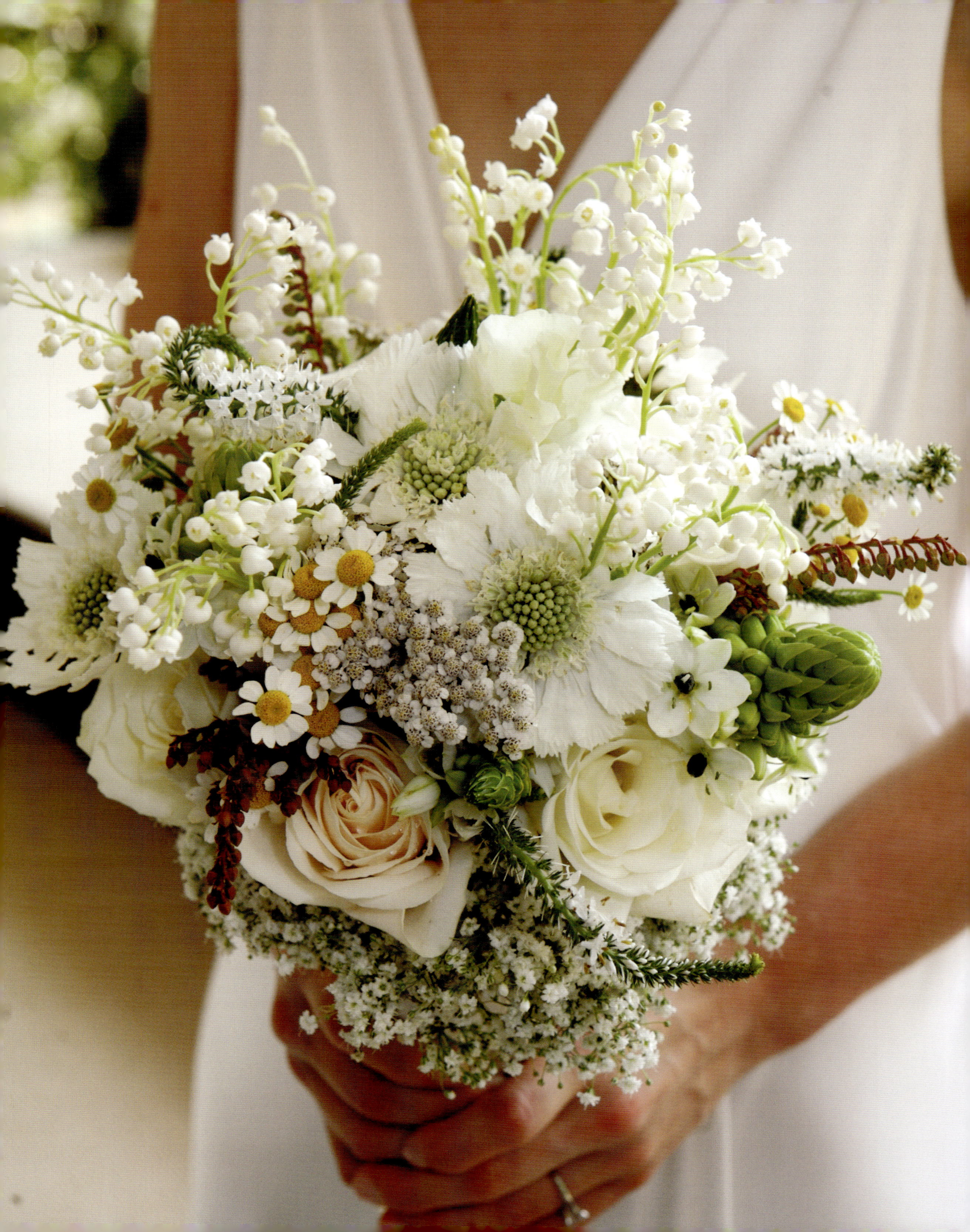

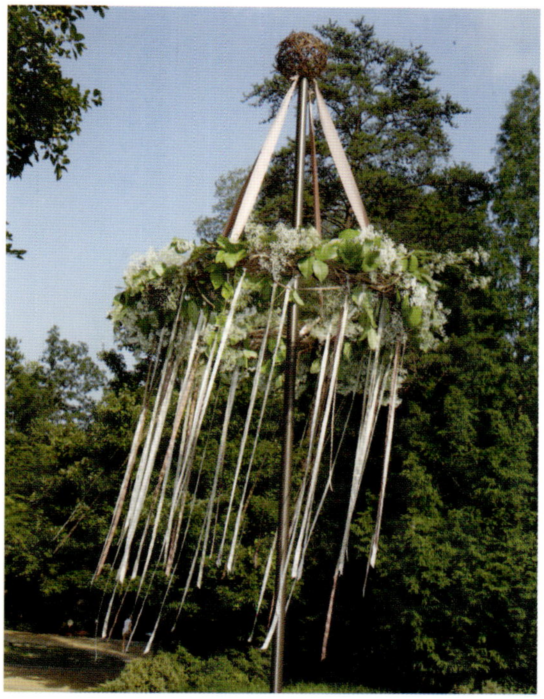
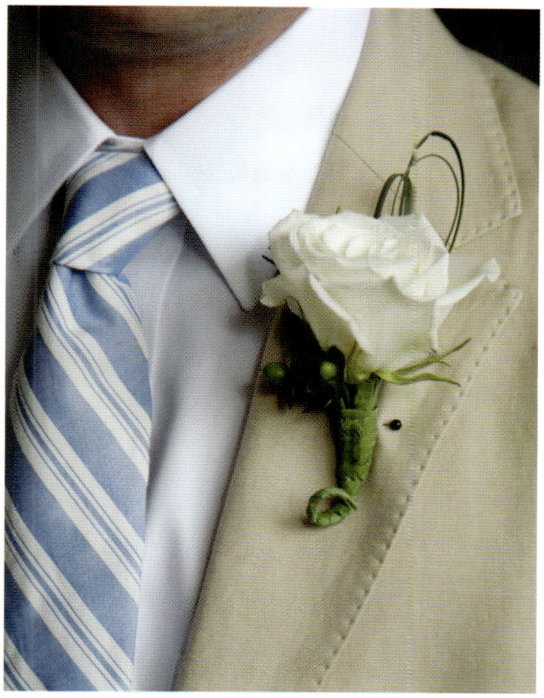
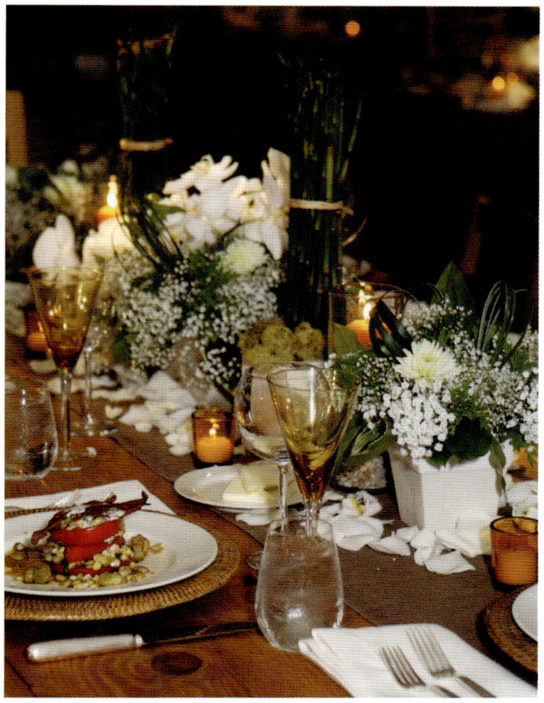
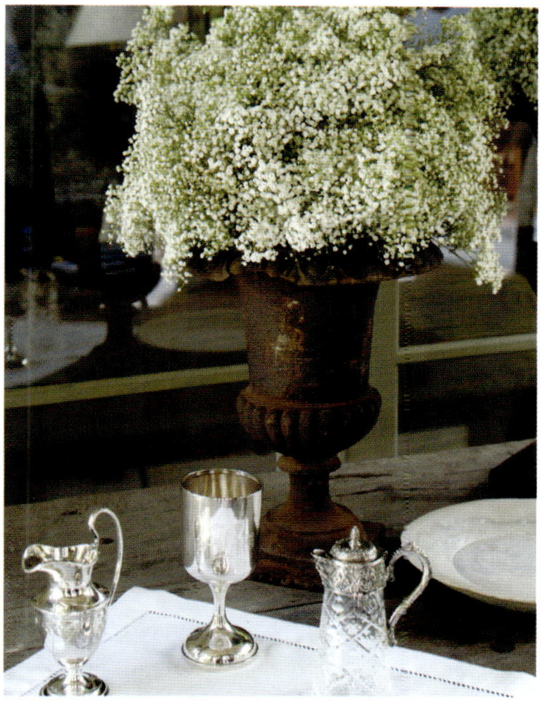

IT'S FUN TO REMINISCE ABOUT CARTER'S WEDDING, ESPECIALLY SINCE THEY HAVE NOW WELCOMED A NEW BABY TO THEIR FAMILY.

Our maypole greeted guests. Bouquets and arrangements filled with herbs, sprays of orchids, baby's breath, and roses kept everyone feeling fresh and cool on a hot summer evening. The caterer was Chris Hastings, a famous Birmingham chef known for his use of locally grown and harvested produce.

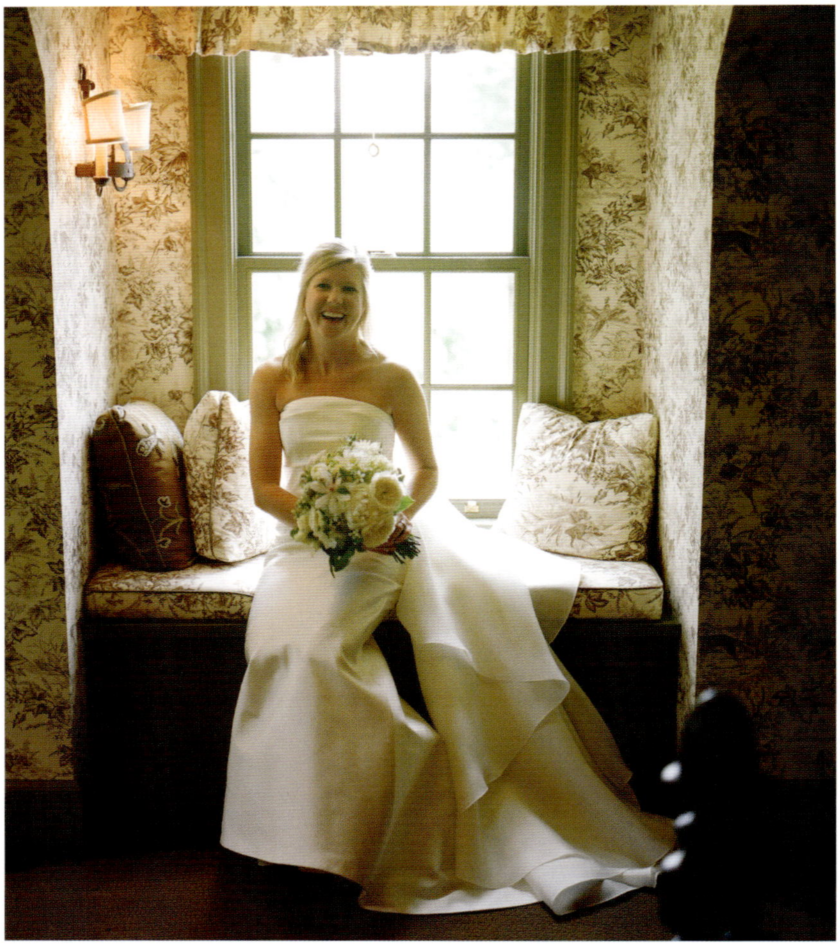

LIBBY & WHIT

mountaintop wedding

Libby's idea of a wedding in the mountains came from a long time love of this particular place on earth. She had spent many childhood summers hiking and canoeing and camping here. She and her two sisters attended Camp Merrie-Woode just down the road, and amazingly enough I did too. I understood her mindset. There were many many hurdles involved in a destination/at-home wedding. But to get Libby married under the open sky with a view of Whiteside Mountain in the distance made for the backdrop of the century.

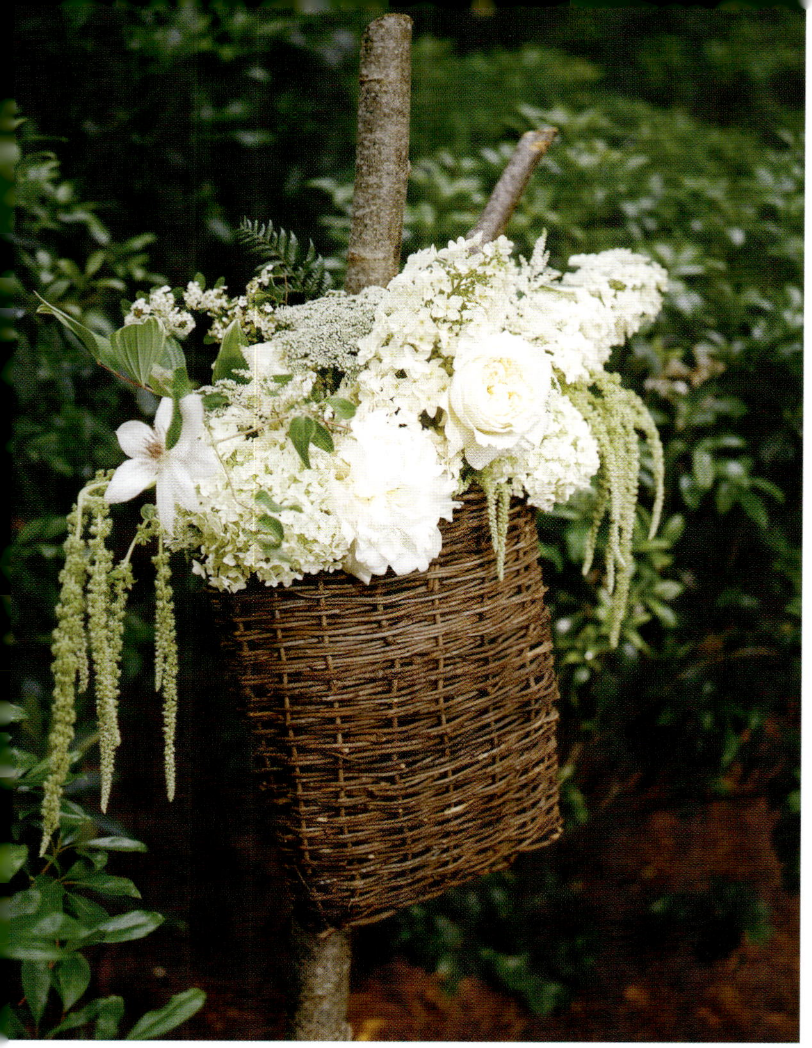

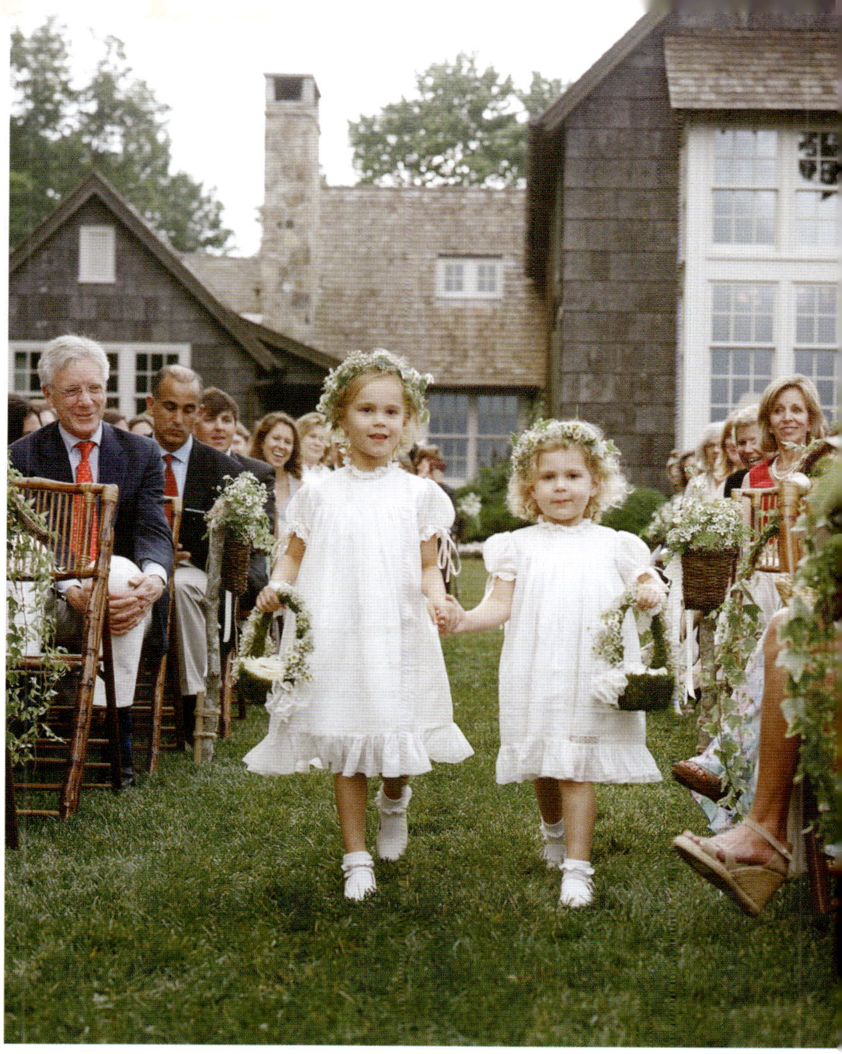

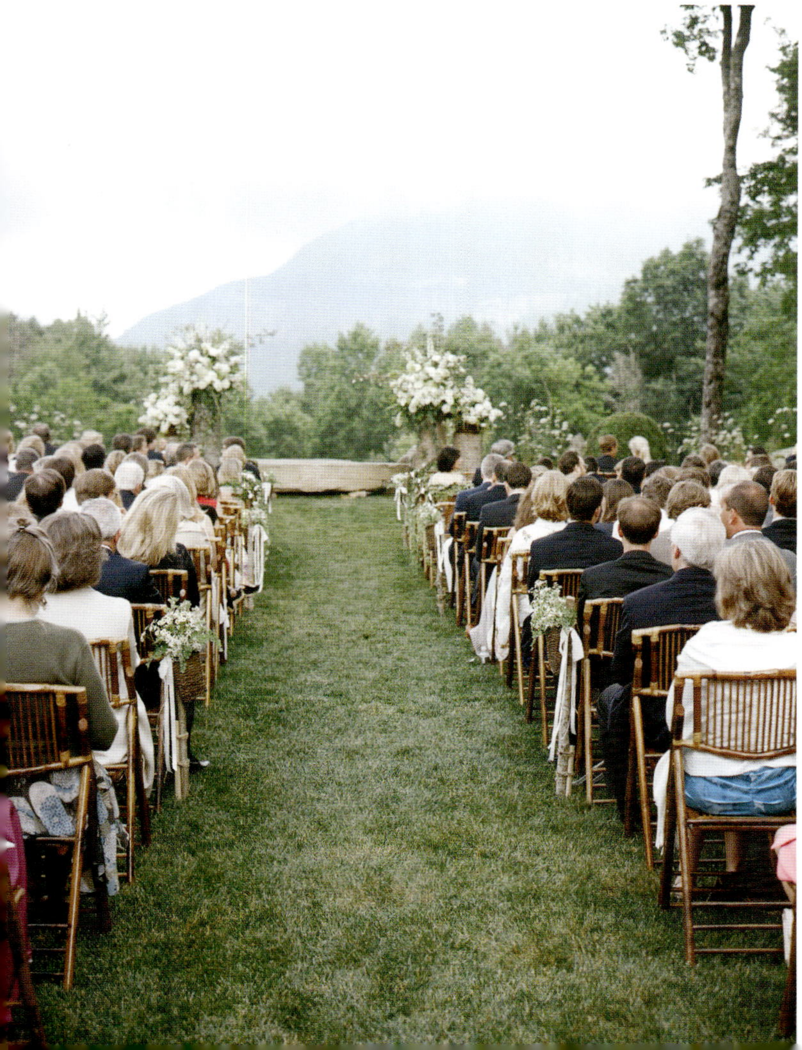

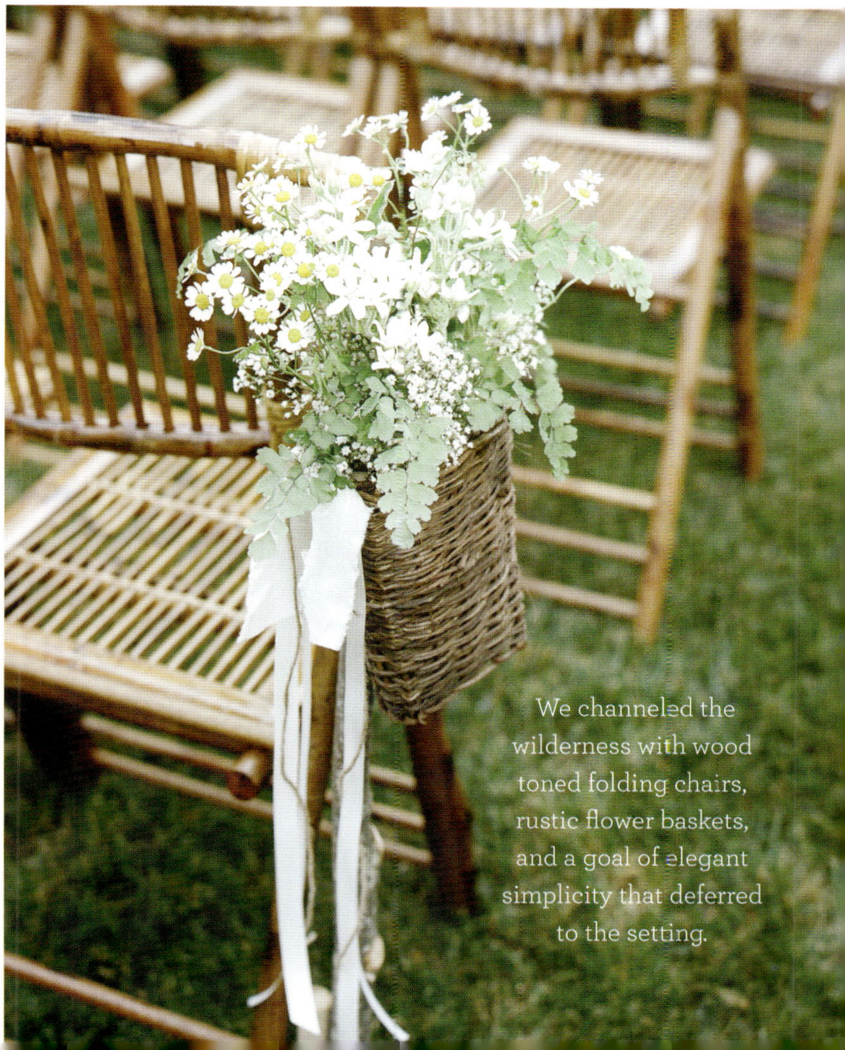

We channeled the wilderness with wood toned folding chairs, rustic flower baskets, and a goal of elegant simplicity that deferred to the setting.

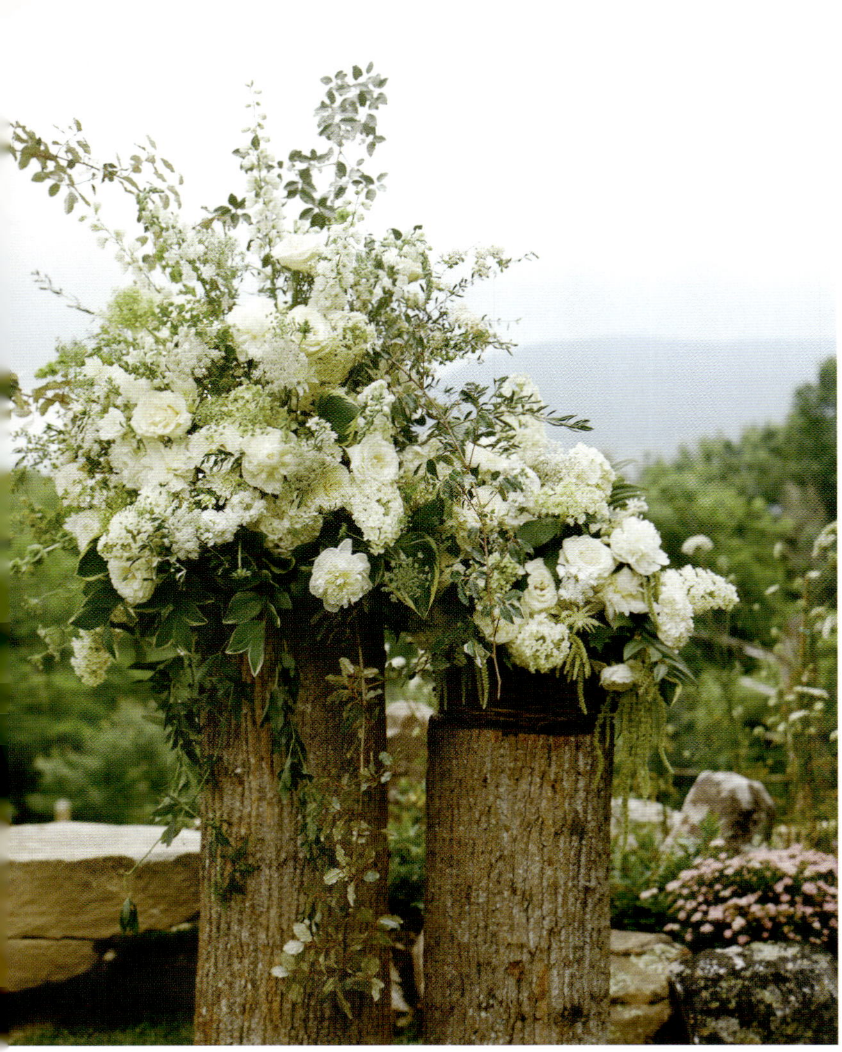
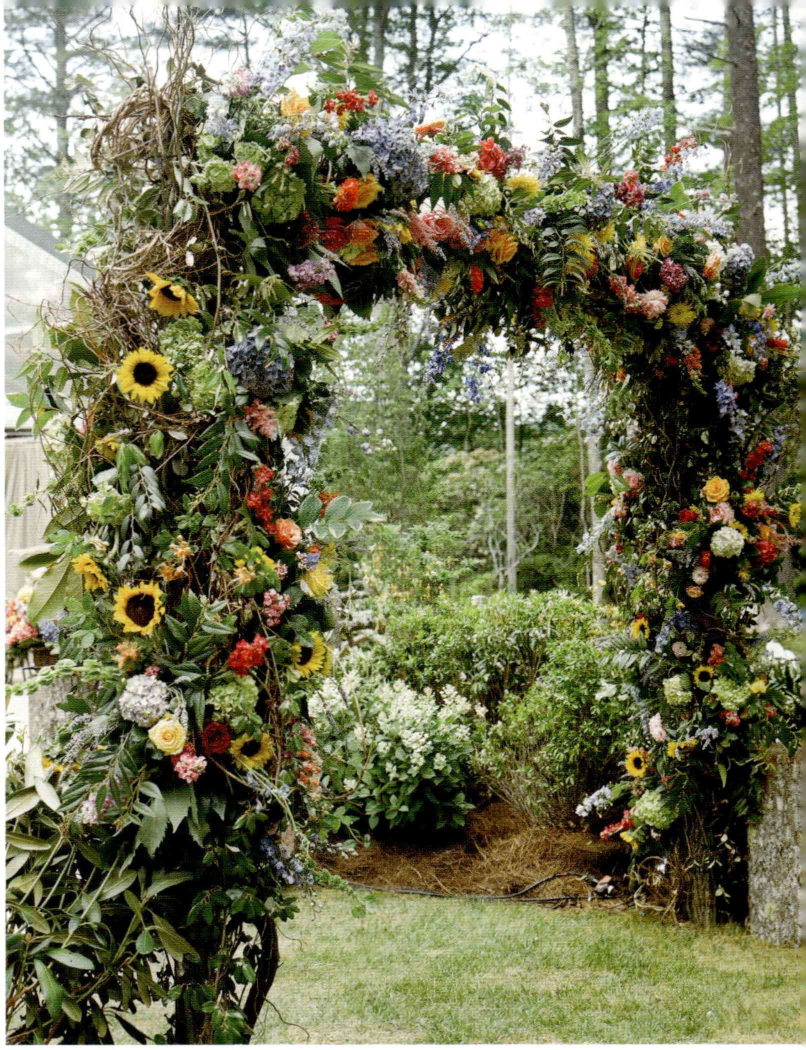
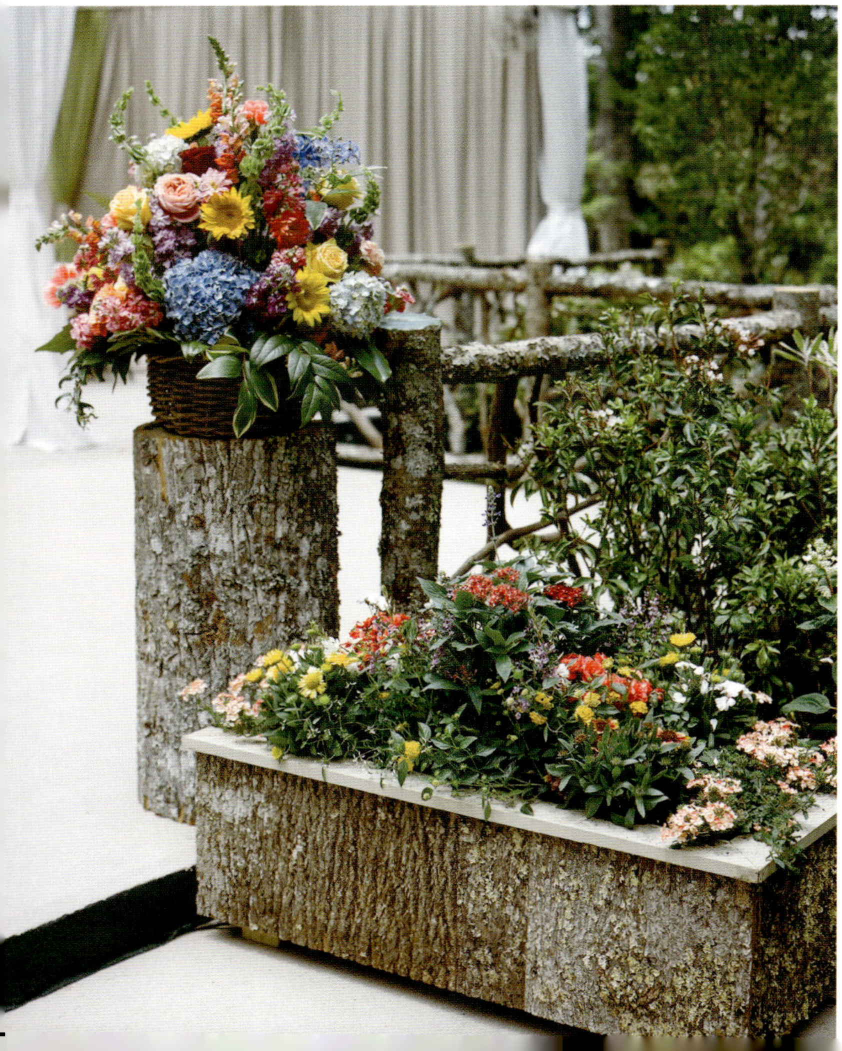
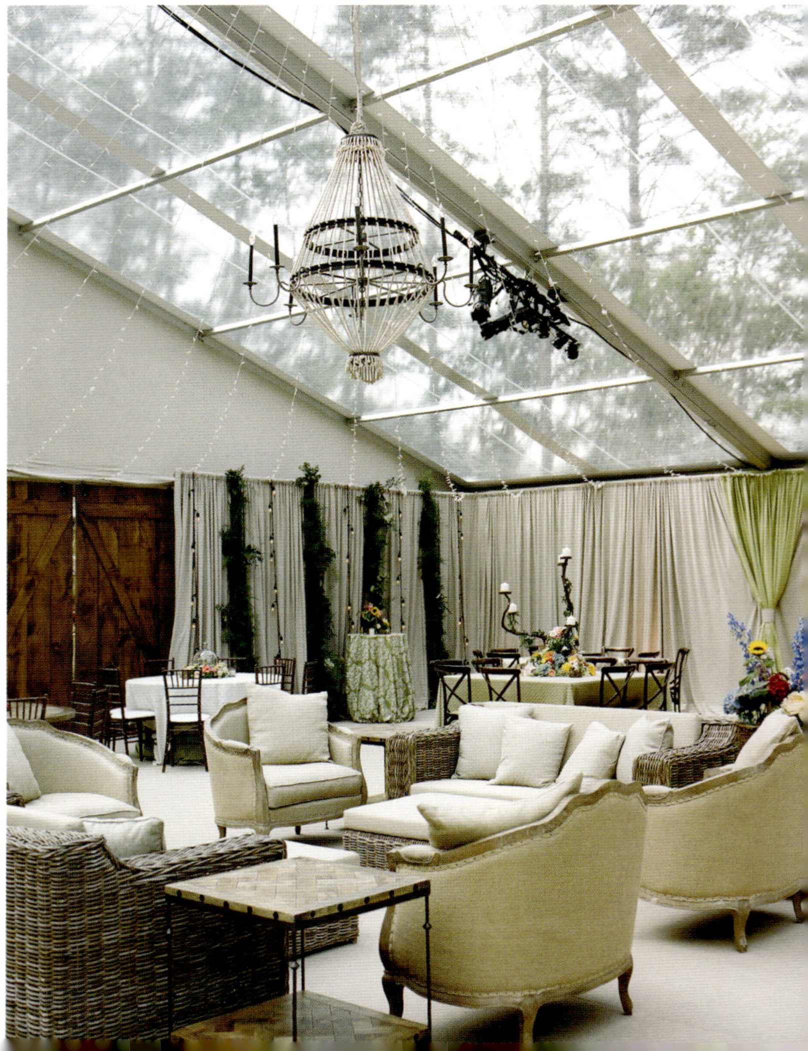

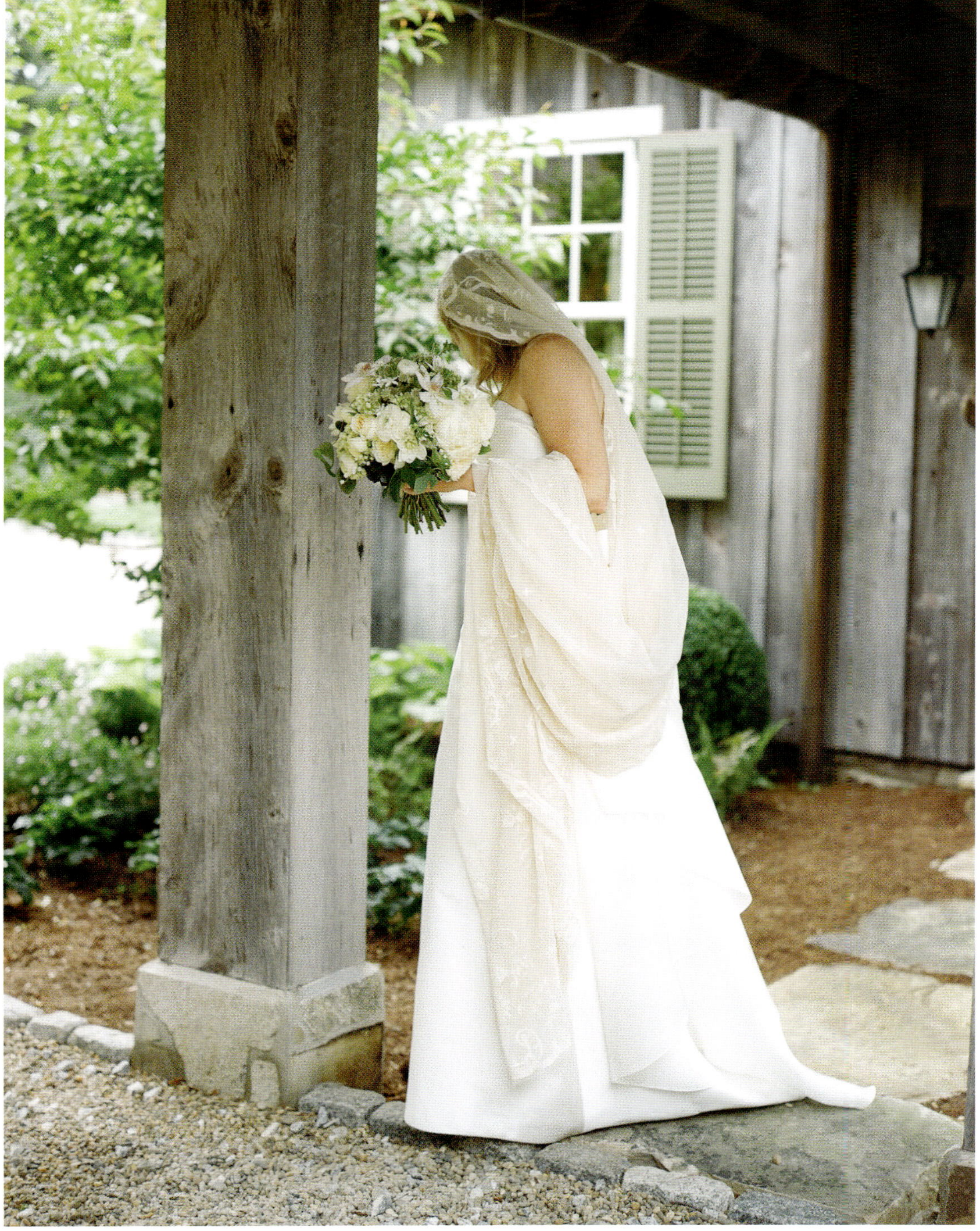

WHEN WE SAW THE FIELD WHERE THE RECEPTION TOOK PLACE, I SAW MY "FIELD OF DREAMS." IT WAS ALMOST COMPLETELY LEVEL!

The whole idea was to balance the rustic setting with the lushness of the garden. We used hollowed out log containers, gathered hydrangeas and shrubs, and then got more chic at the reception. There we created rooms within the tent, divided by oversize barn doors and built and hung garden chandeliers above and around the sunken dance floor.

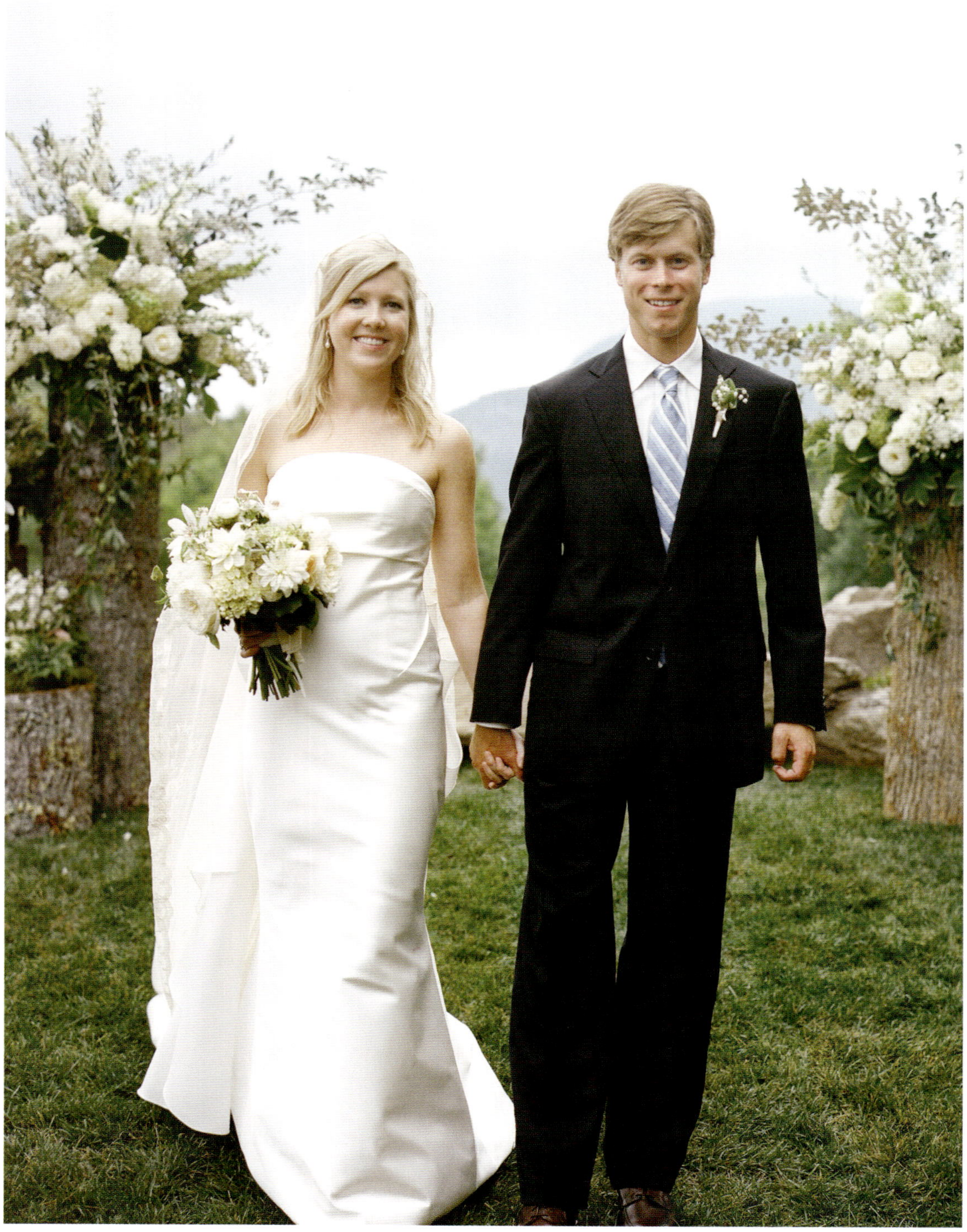

I'M ONLY FIVE-FEET-TALL, BUT I JUMPED HURDLES IN HIGH SCHOOL, WHICH IS WHY I KNEW I COULD PULL THIS OFF.

We covered a portion of the tables with chartreuse ikat and left some tables bare to coordinate with the furniture in the seating area. Two of my favorite ideas are that every table had a different centerpiece and the hanging flowers flanking the sunken dance floor.

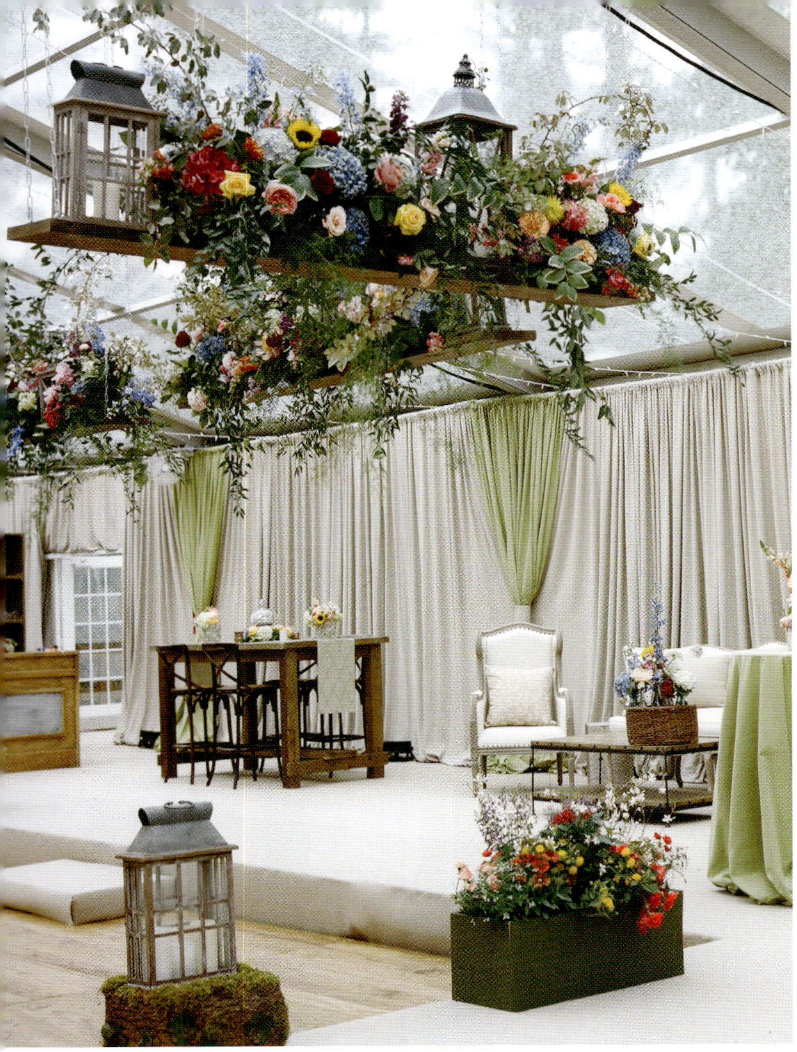
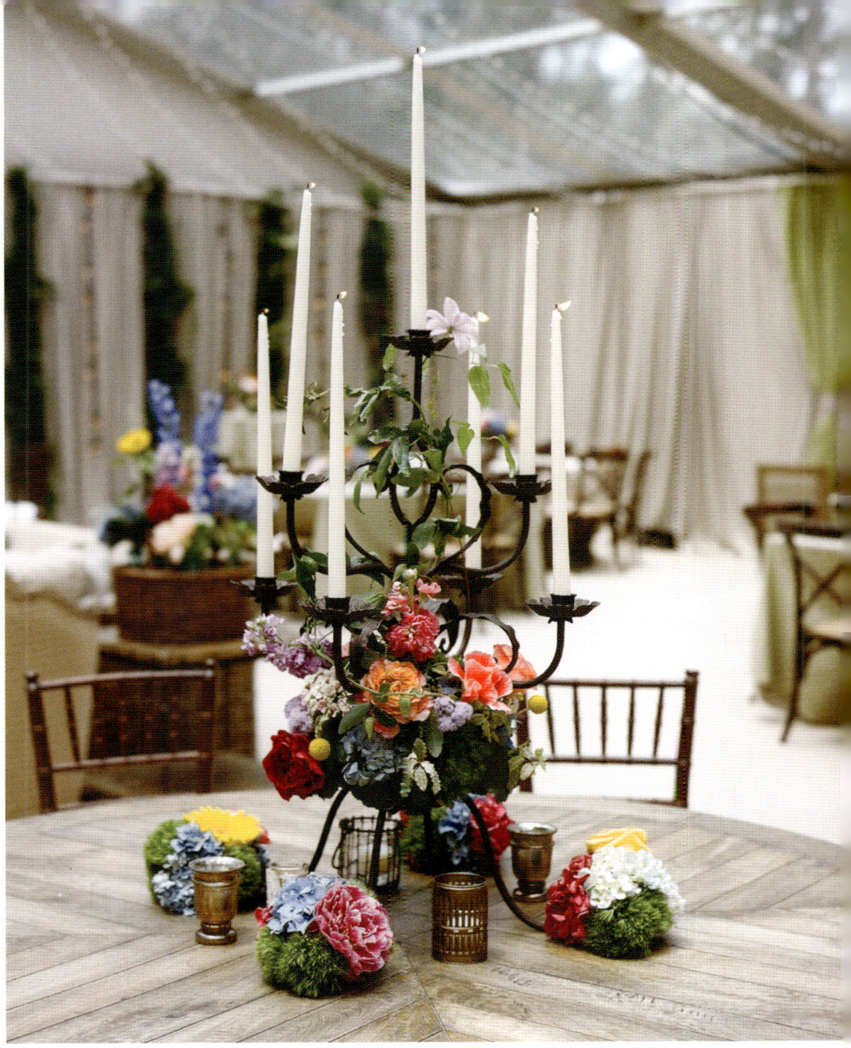
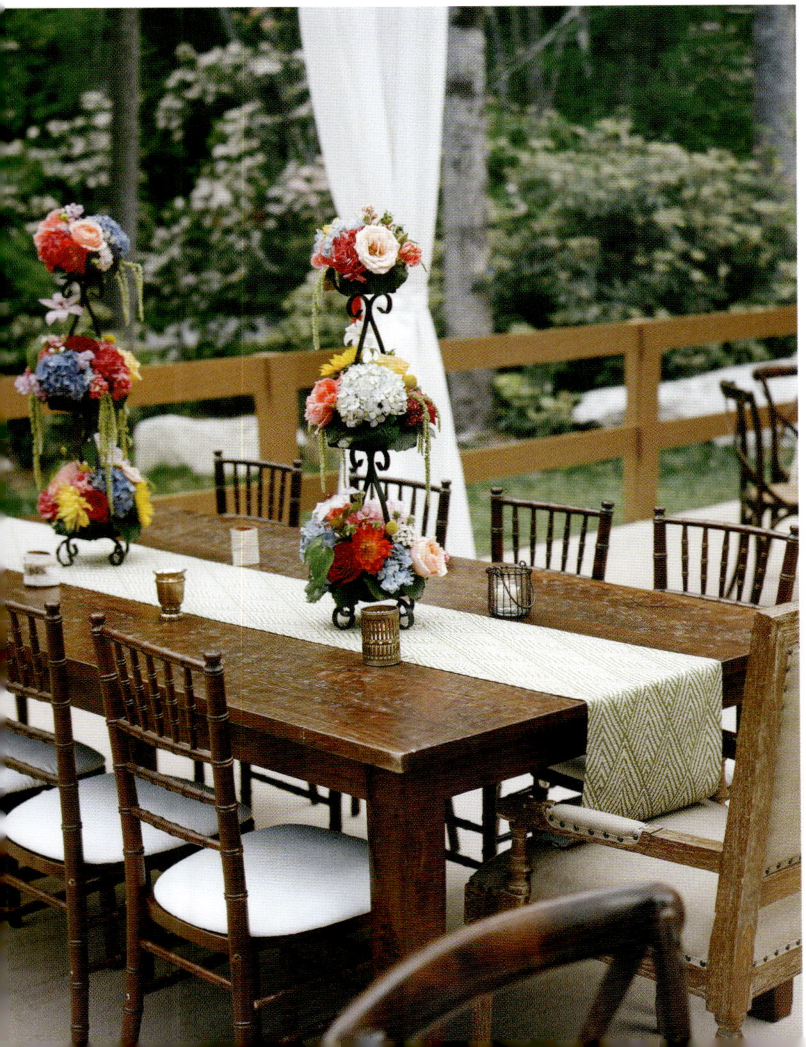
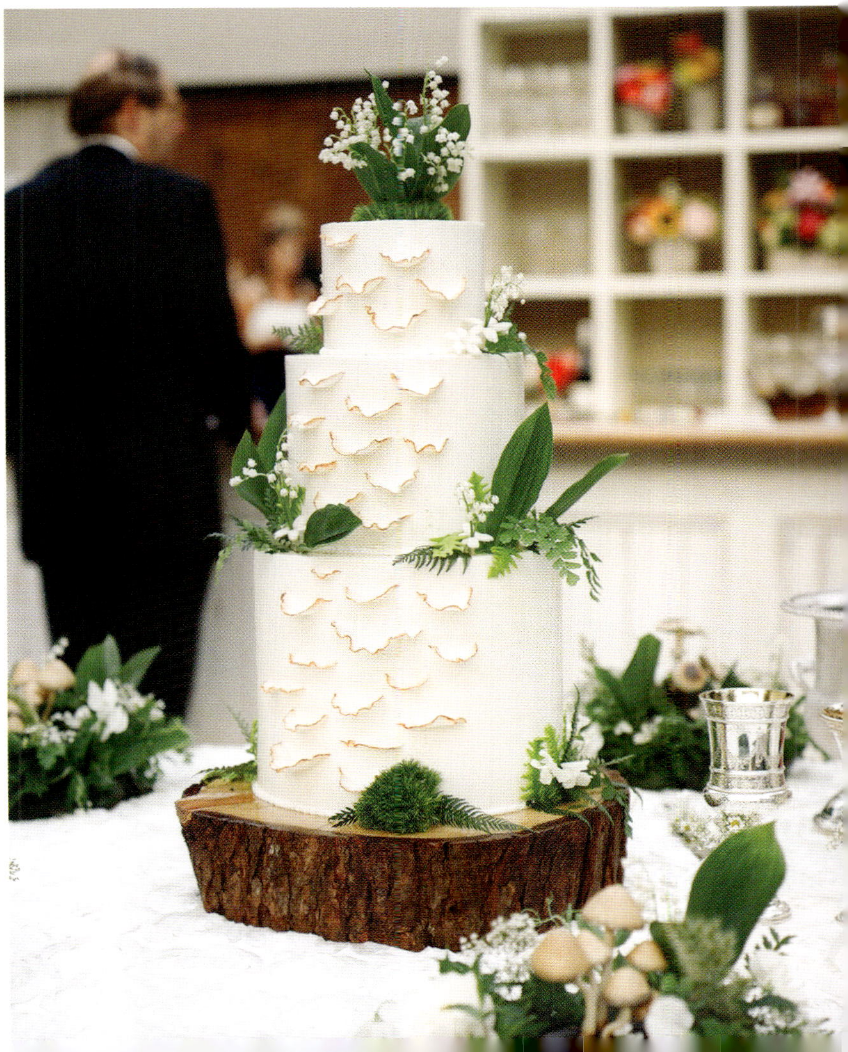

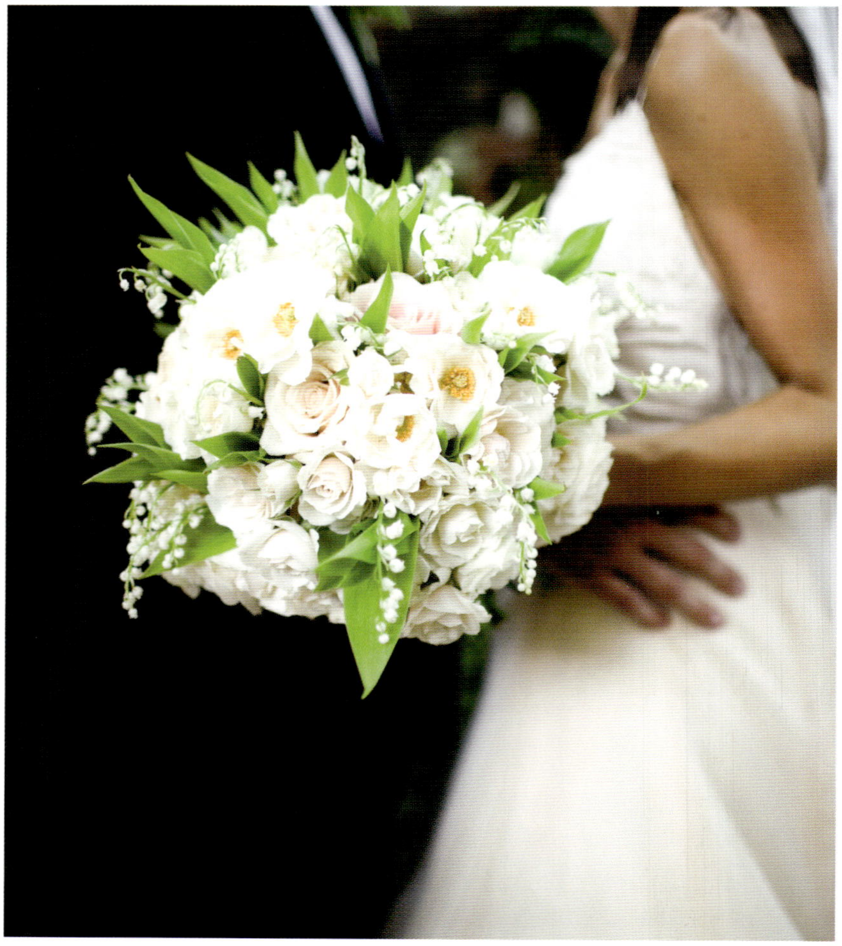

GINGER & WILL

give it up for tradition

I was an attendant in Ginger's mama and daddy's wedding years ago. Ginger wanted to pay homage to them and to their wedding that was held in her grandmother's formal garden at her gorgeous Colonial-style home. We recreated the summer garden feel in the big ballroom of the Birmingham Country Club with trellis and topiaries and loads of pink roses and oversized floral wreaths.

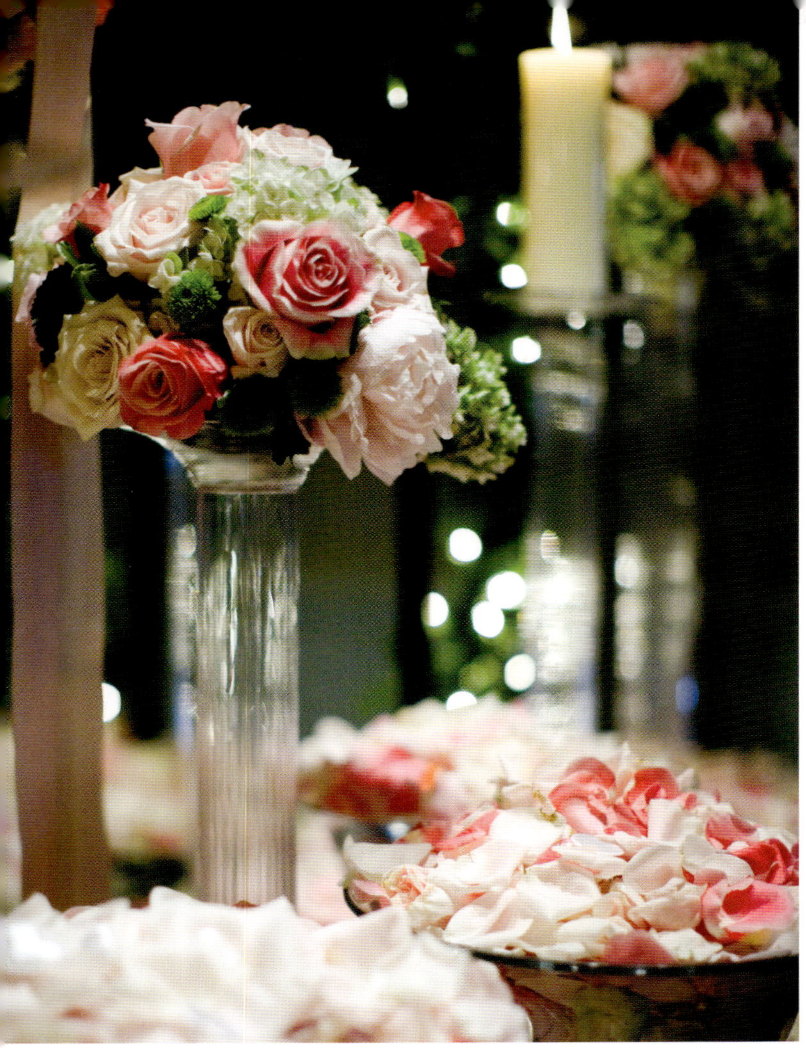

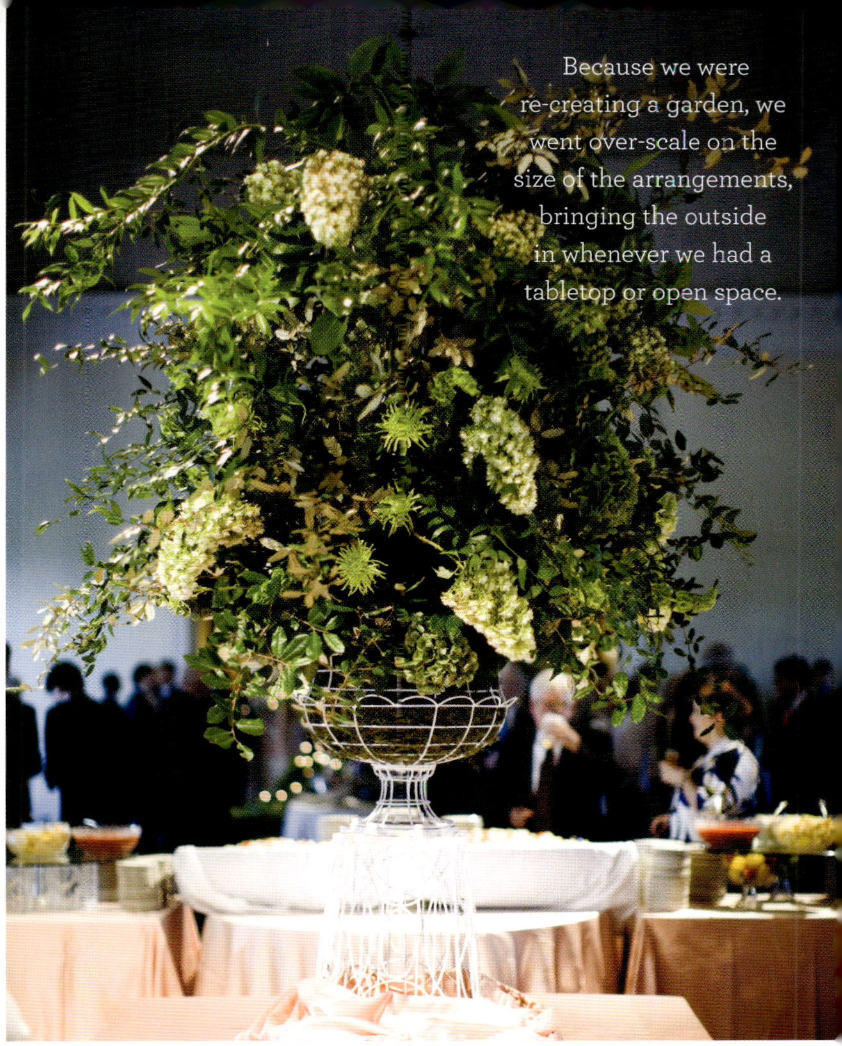

Because we were re-creating a garden, we went over-scale on the size of the arrangements, bringing the outside in whenever we had a tabletop or open space.

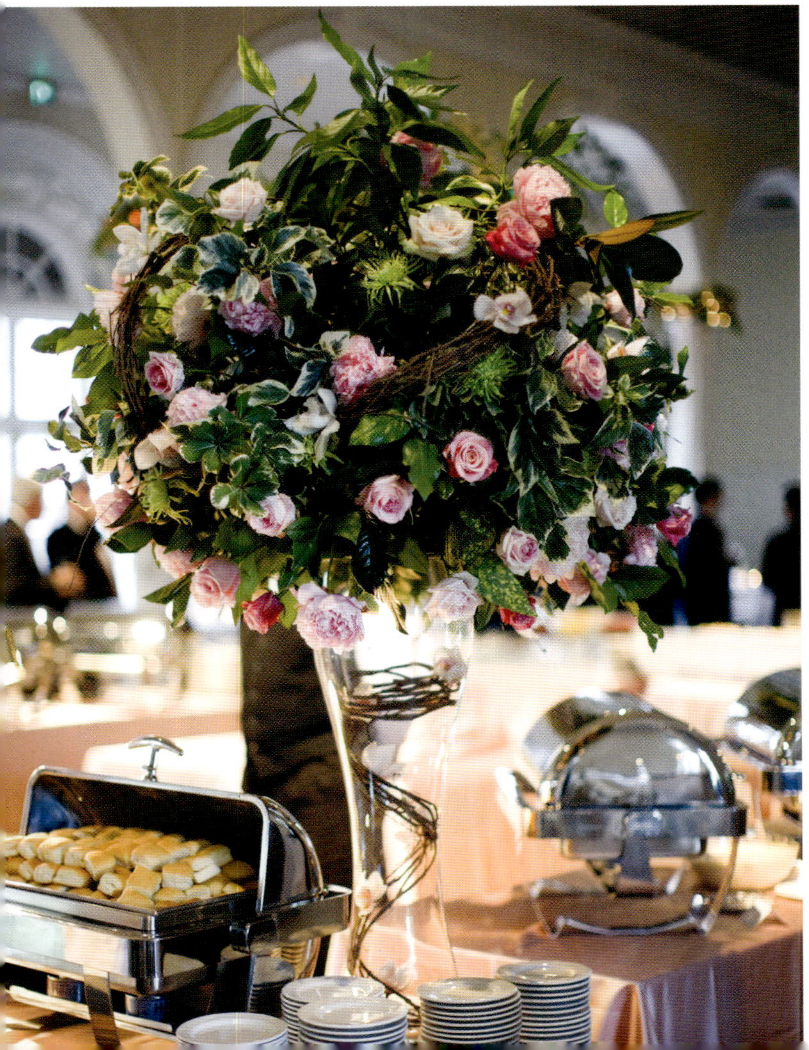

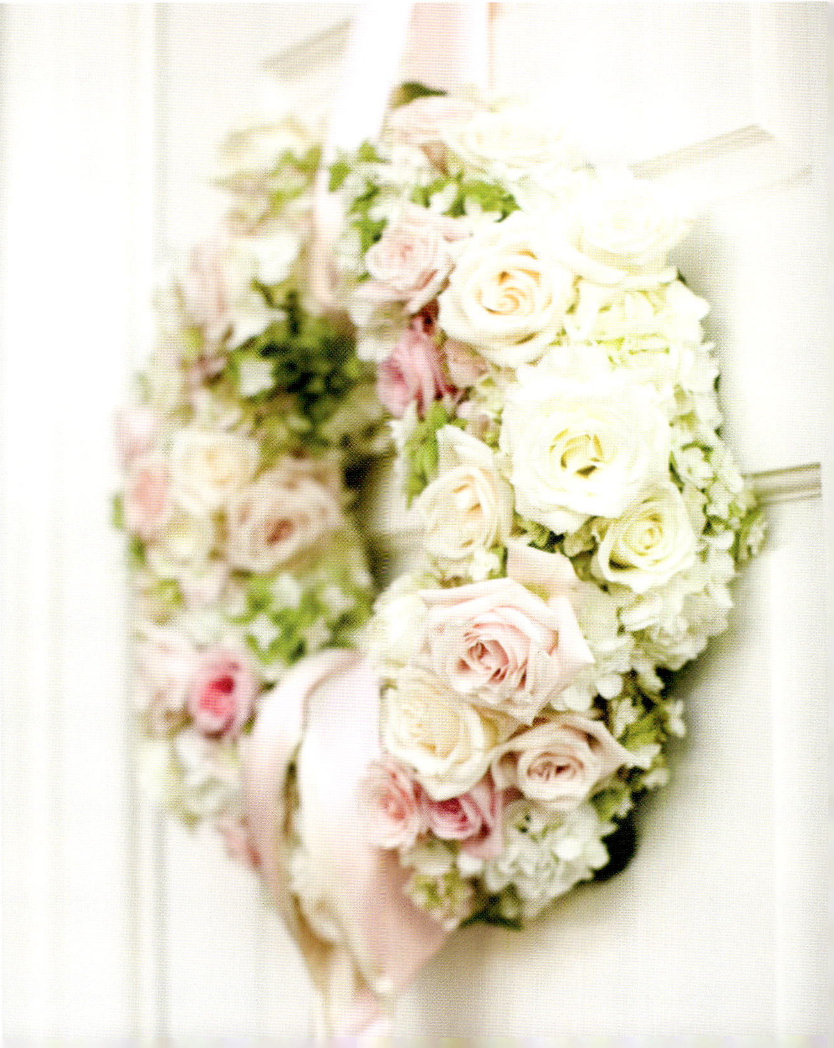

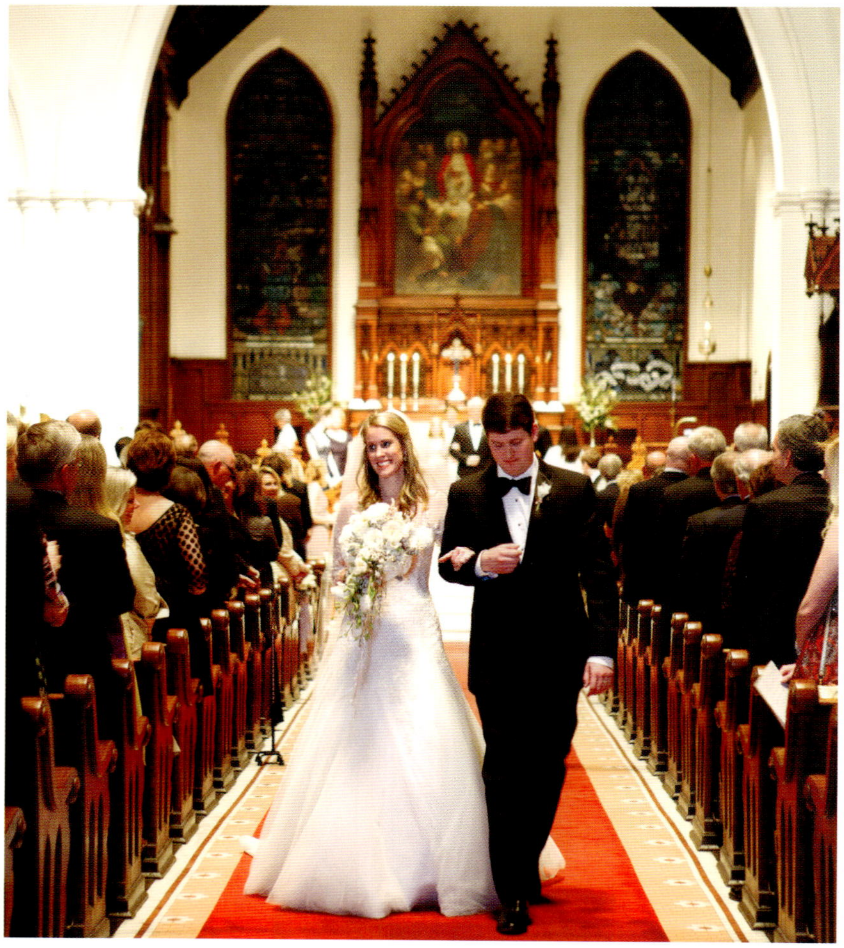

ABBY & JOSEPH

a fine romance

Abby has been a friend of mine for years. She worked at *flower* magazine and is one of the sharpest young women I have the pleasure of knowing. So when she asked me to work on her wedding, I wanted to do her and her passion justice. The wedding was at one of Birmingham's most traditional cathedrals, and the reception was at the newest, hippest music venue in the city. My challenge was to soften the reception venue, to keep the fun and festoon the setting so that it made sense for Abby.

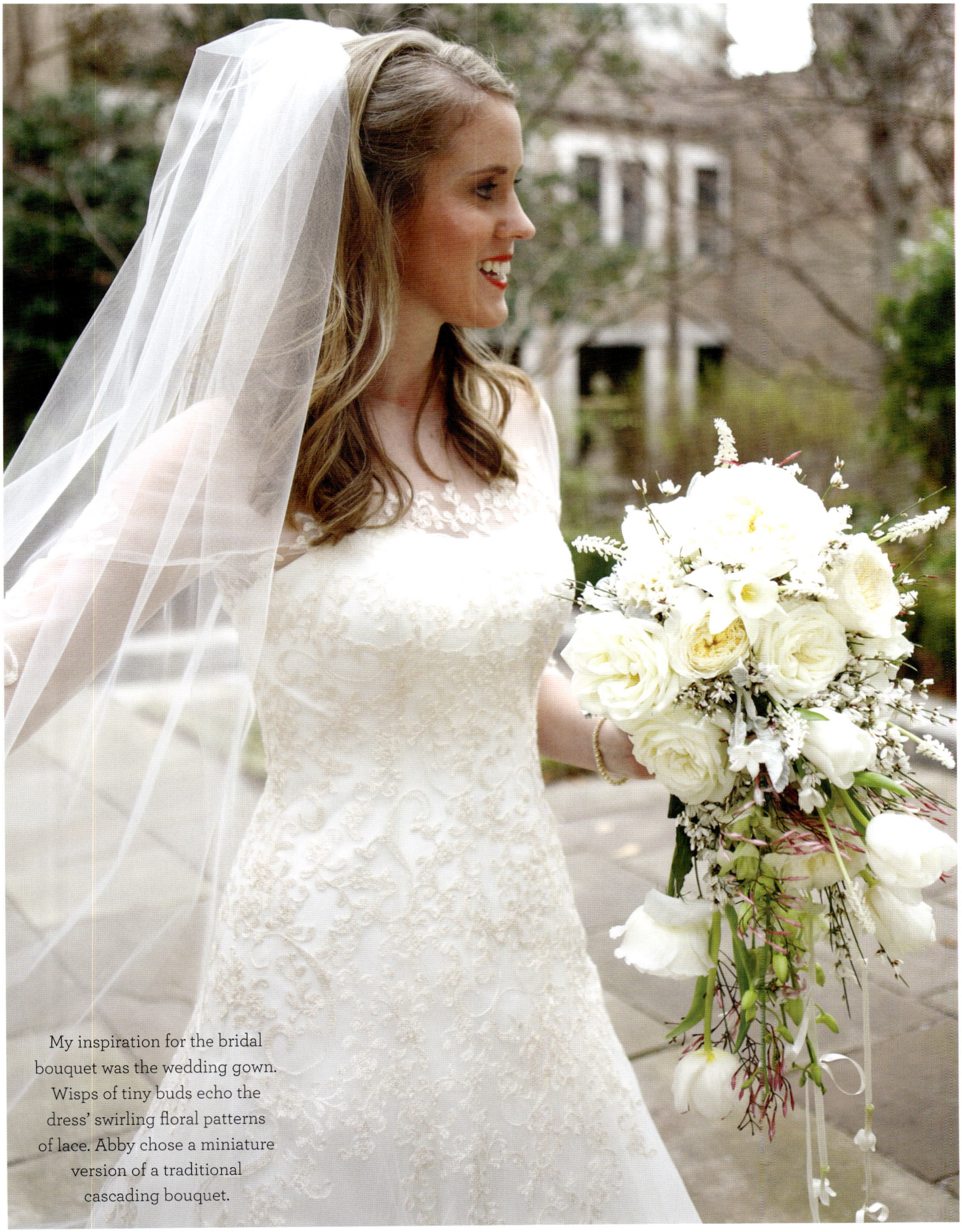

My inspiration for the bridal bouquet was the wedding gown. Wisps of tiny buds echo the dress' swirling floral patterns of lace. Abby chose a miniature version of a traditional cascading bouquet.

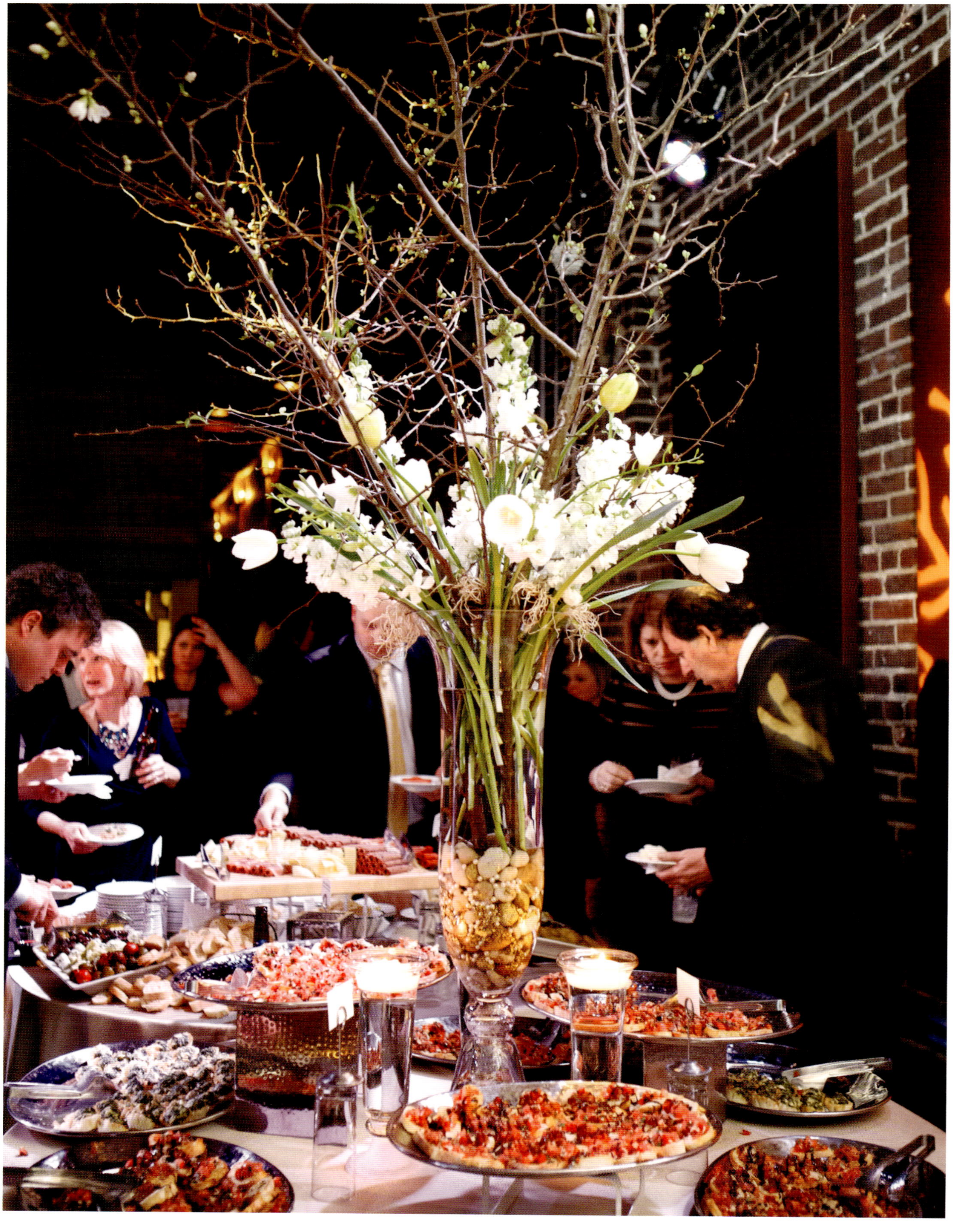

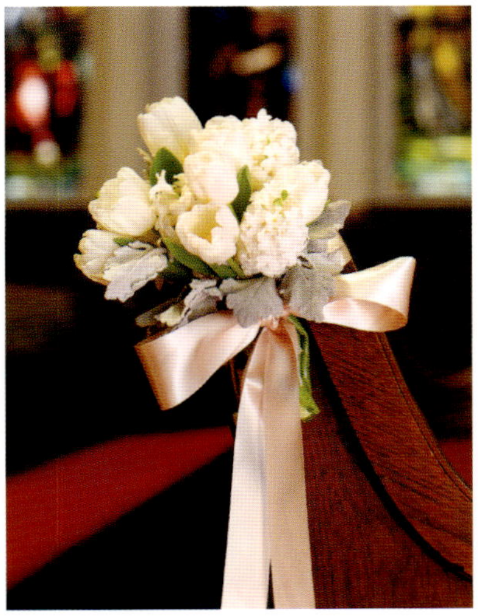
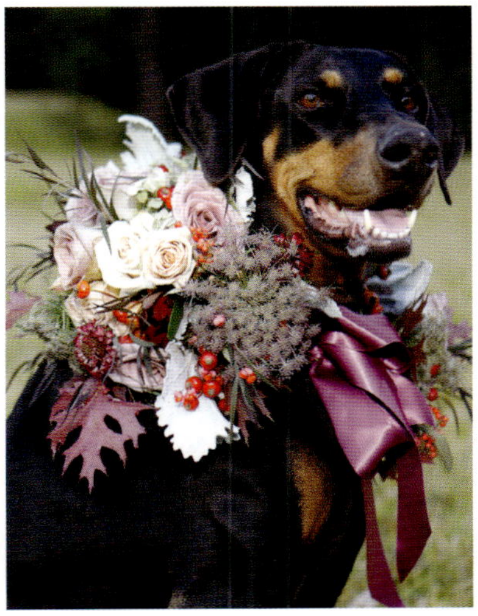
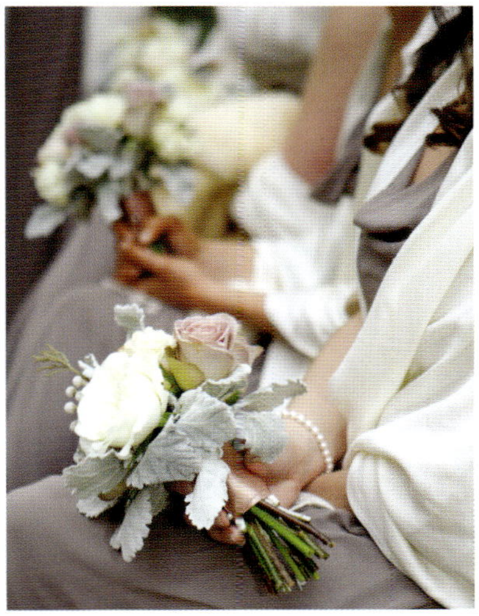
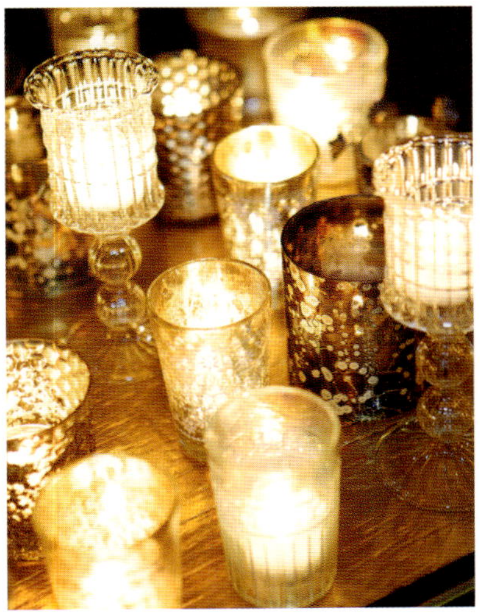
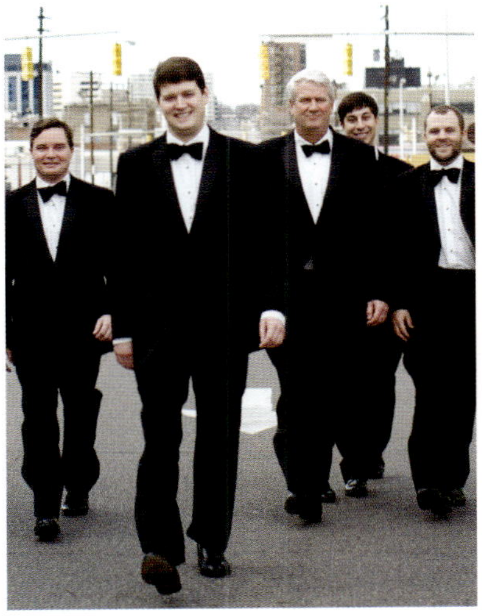
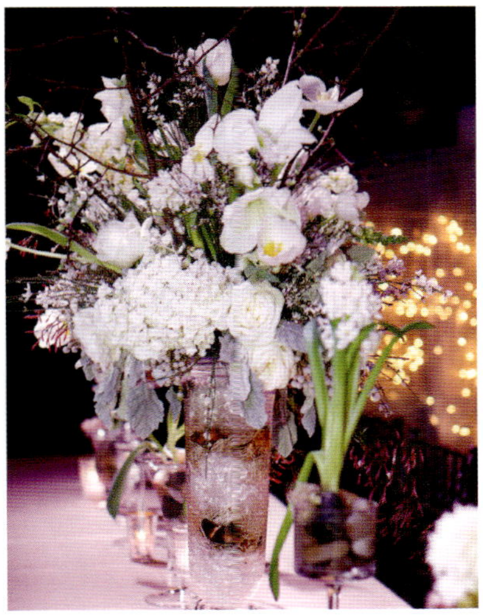
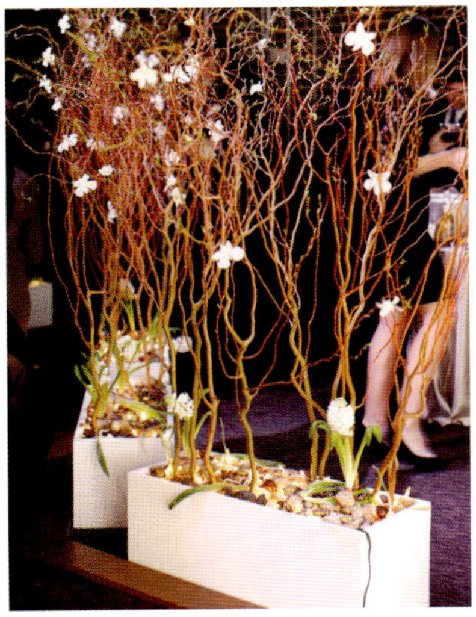
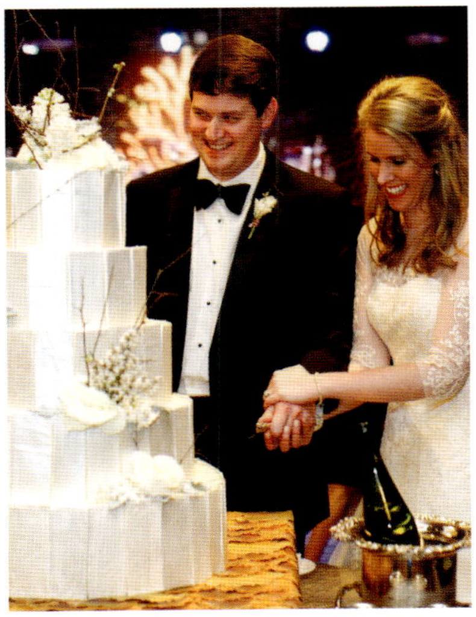
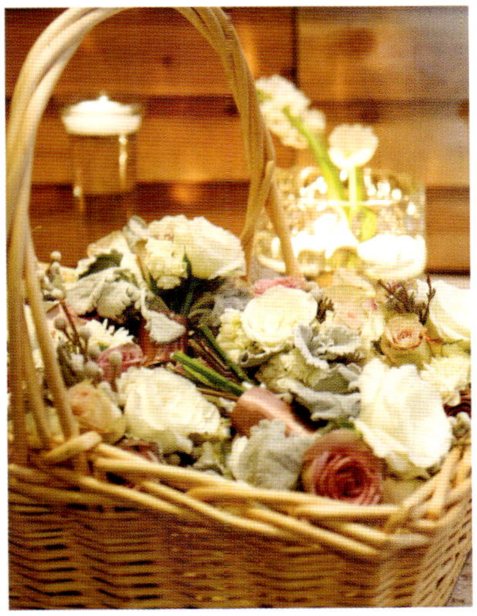

I created special areas for hors d'oeuvres, which were on a raised small stage. I used wooden planter boxes that we painted white. These held concrete blocks, and we used the blocks to support willow twigs to stand upright across the edge of this raised area. We then filled the boxes with white rocks and loosely wove strings of lights at the feet of the branches to create a glow. We attached white dendrobium orchid blooms to the twigs. The effect was of magical blooming spring trees.

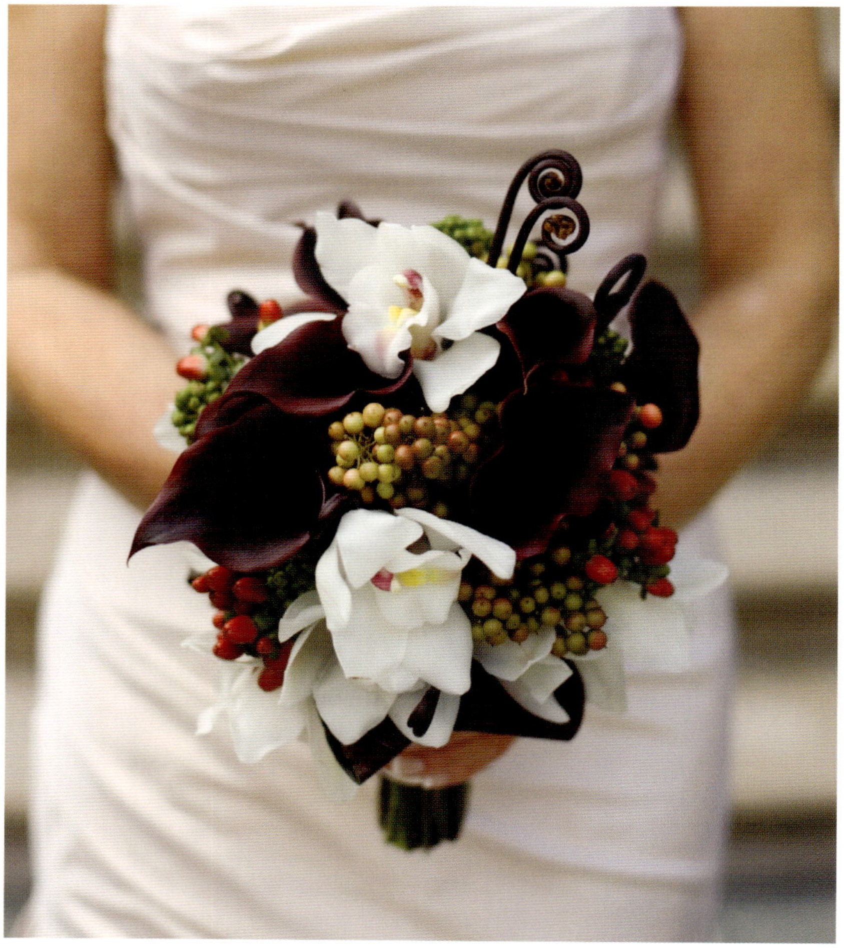

KAYE & MARK

some enchanted evening

I have worked with Kaye for years, and it was thrilling to be so involved in planning their intimate at home family wedding, followed by an extraordinary dinner under a tent in their backyard. We mixed orchids and calla lilies with fern fronds, berries, and green lotus pods to create an elegant autumnal feeling. The cake—a croquembouche—was a delicious departure from Southern tradition.

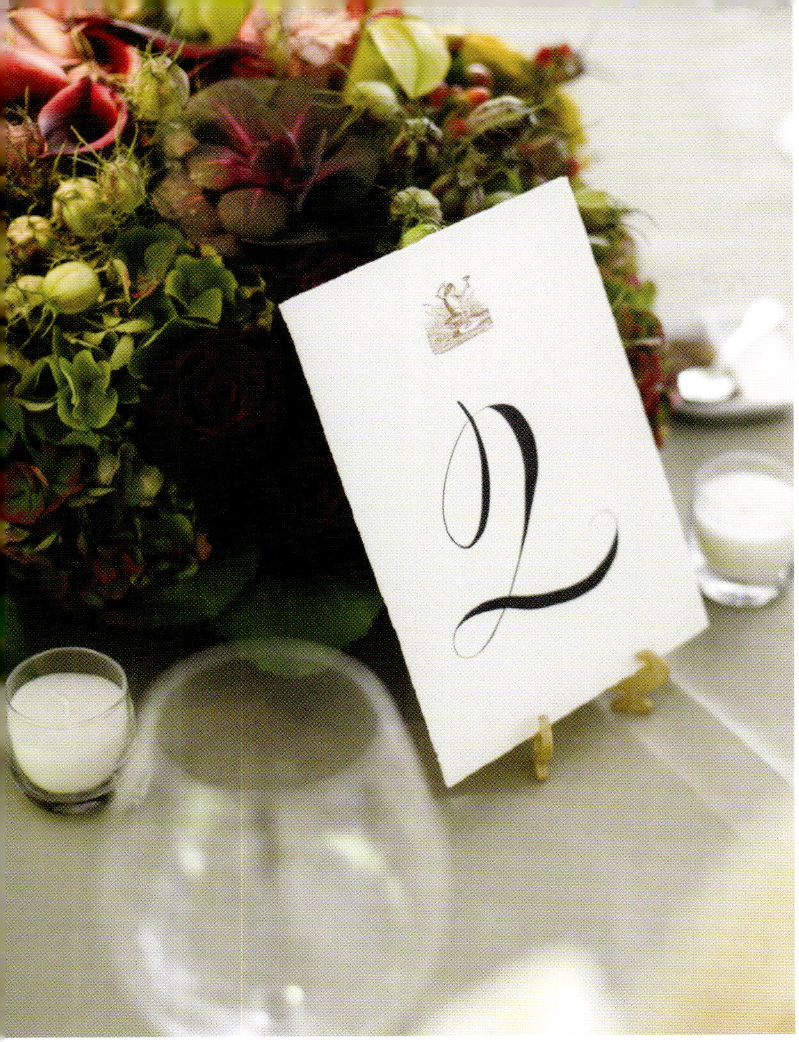
2

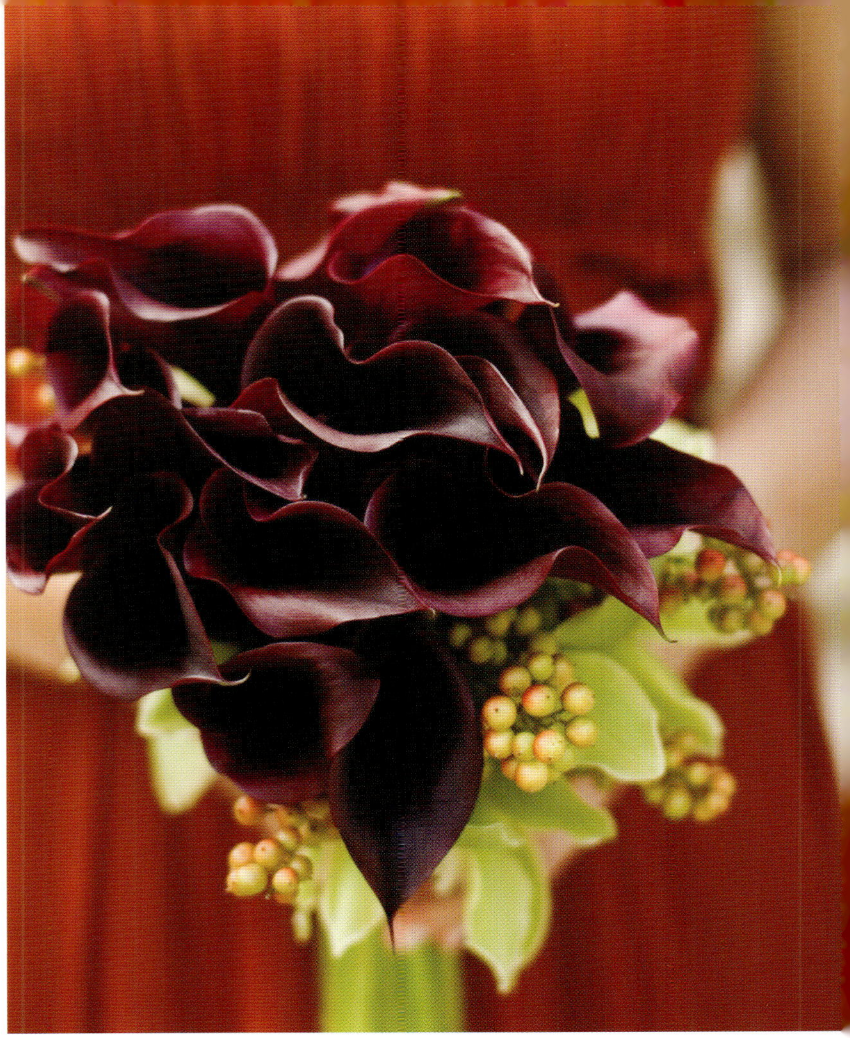

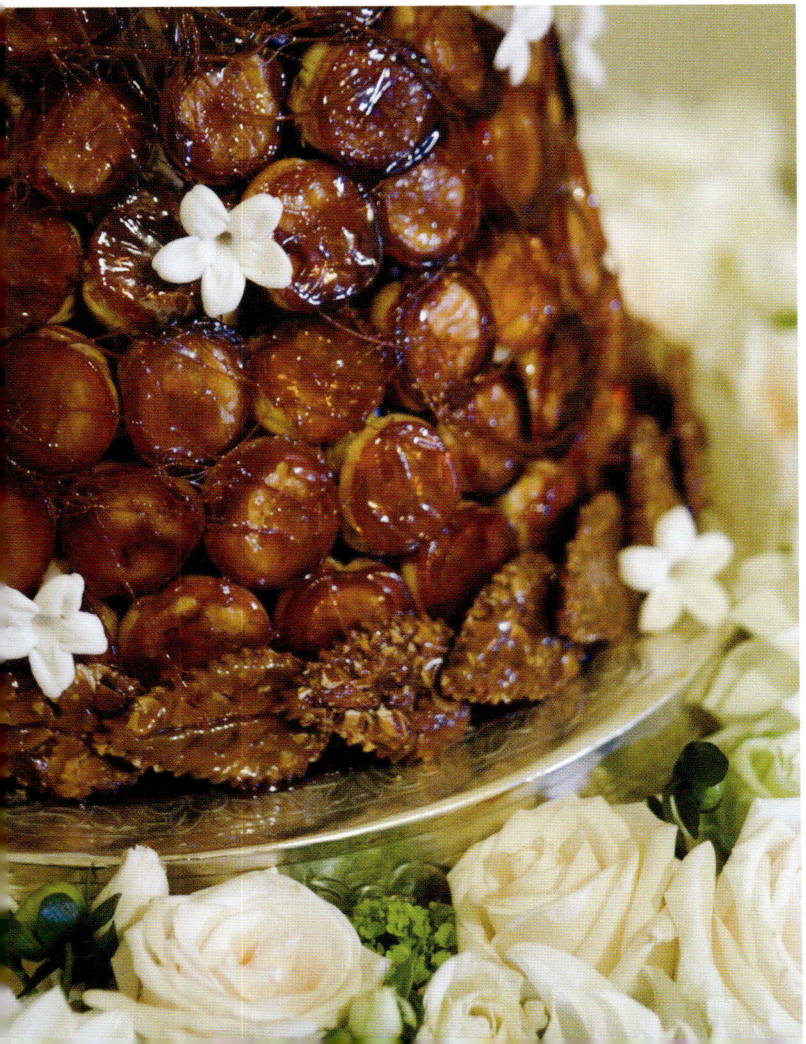

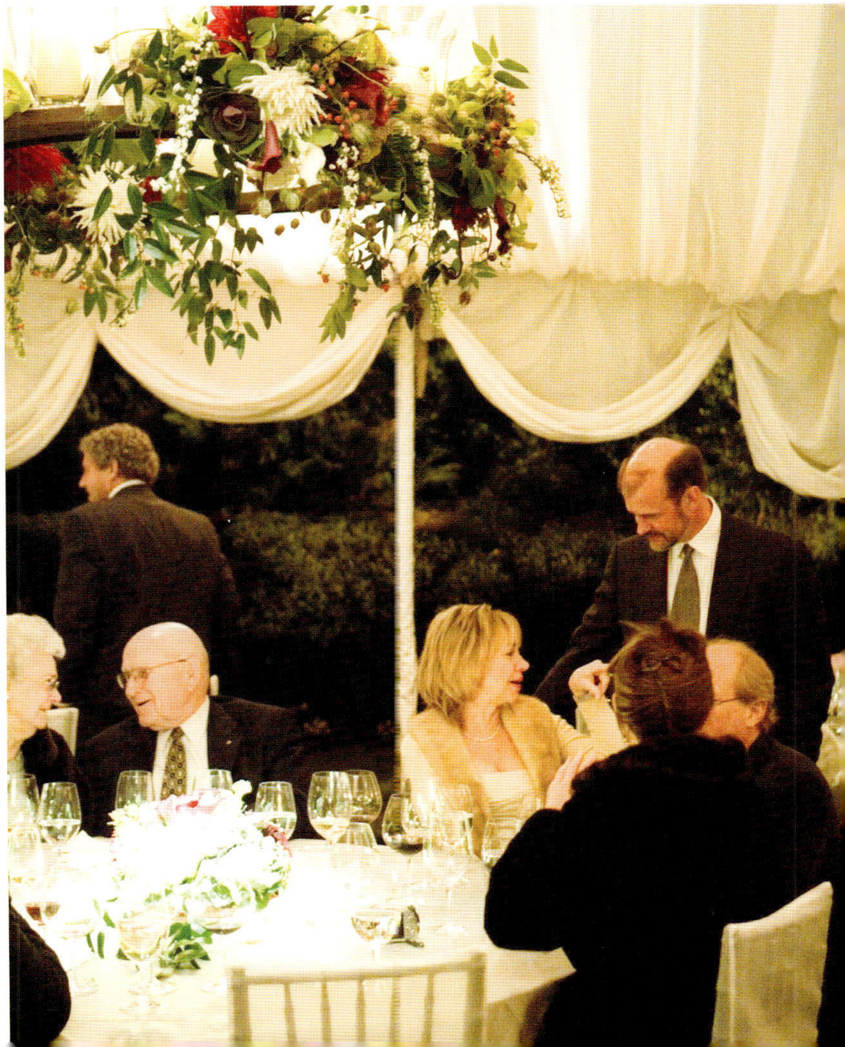

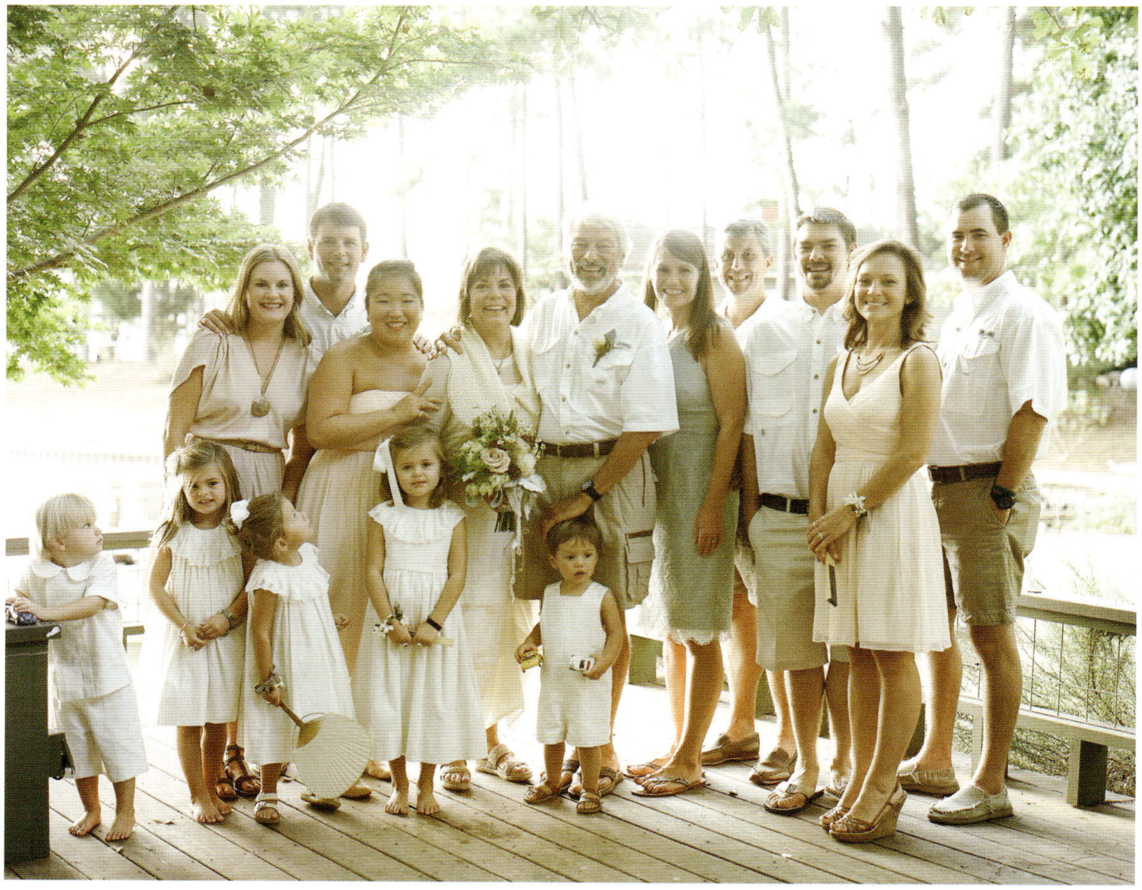

KIT & MAC

cue the music... at last...

Kit and I have a very deep bond as well as being next door neighbors. She and Mac were celebrating the 20th anniversary of their first date at the best, best spot in town. They came home and got comfy to watch some tv before Mac left for the evening. I got a call. Kit asked me to meet her out back, and she sounded serious. I was worried. She came over in her Granny robe and slippers and showed me her engagement ring in the light of my landscaping lamp. The hooting and hollering were heard all over the neighborhood.

one rose in a forest

by Charles McNair

I came to Sybil's attention in a most roundabout way. Years ago, I befriended in Mallet Hall, the men's honors dorm at the University of Alabama, a brilliant pre-law student named Bill Sylvester. We had good adventures together, road trips (Bill drove tirelessly) and wins on the volleyball court (Bill played formidably). He went on to law school; I went wandering into the wild world to search for success as a writer.

With our paths parted, I didn't learn for many years that Bill had been bewitched by his charming Sybil, and that this pair of good people had built a life together in Birmingham. By the time we reconnected, Bill had made a great success of himself as a lawyer. Sybil made a name in her own right with Wildflower Designs, her event planning and floral design business.

By chance, in April of 2015, I ran into Sybil in a restaurant in Atlanta. As she excitedly explained her concept for a book on the use of flowers in creative design, she couldn't have known that flowers, wild and domesticated alike, have forever been a part of my life.

The day I was born on a cold January morning, nurses placed a bowl of camellia blossoms by the delivery bed.

My grandparents ran Rose Hill Nursery in Dothan, Alabama, my hometown. My brother, Clay, majored in horticulture and operated a nursery. I now live in Bogota, where I'm in love with a beautiful Colombian ophthalmologist ... named Adela Rosa. I buy fresh flowers for our apartment once a week.

Sybil's wonderfully creative book presents a paradox. She has civilized the wildflower, turned the bloom by the side of a stream ... mainstream. It strikes me that Sybilization could well be a term we all now use to describe art made with fresh wildflowers.

One thing's for sure. The pleasure that Sybil's ideas and invention will bring a reader make this book worthy of any home or library. These pages inspire, delight, and awaken unexpected beauty.

They also stir old memories.

I hope you won't mind if I share one of mine.

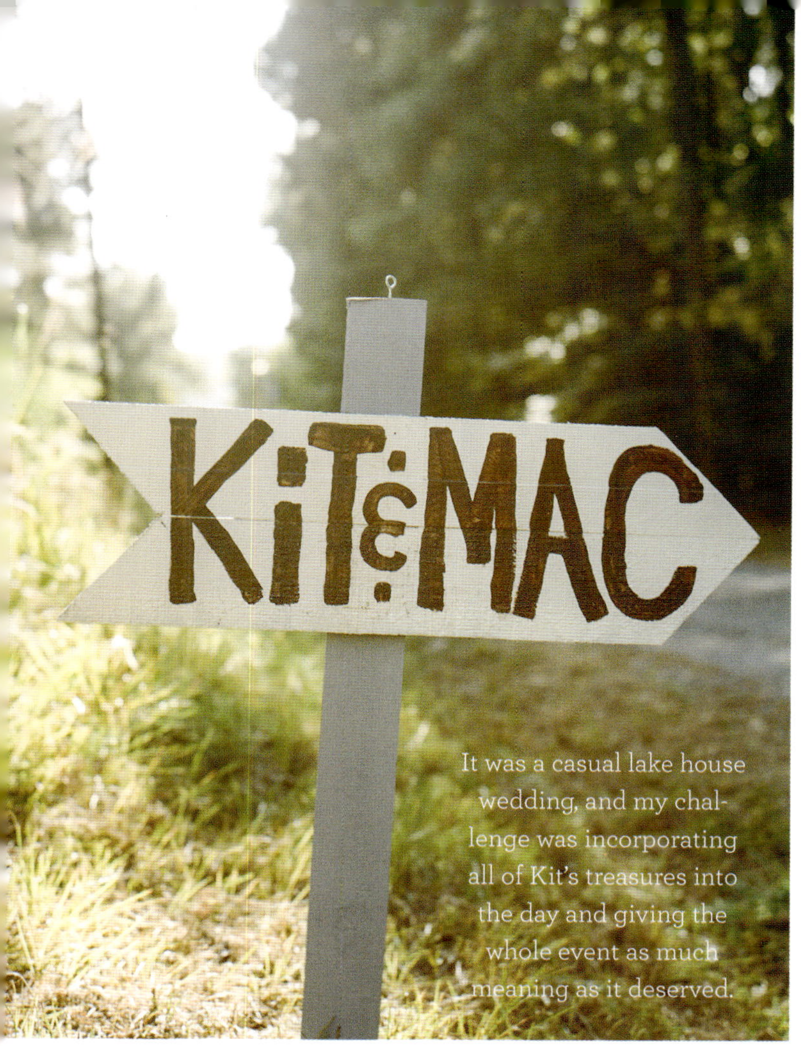

It was a casual lake house wedding, and my challenge was incorporating all of Kit's treasures into the day and giving the whole event as much meaning as it deserved.

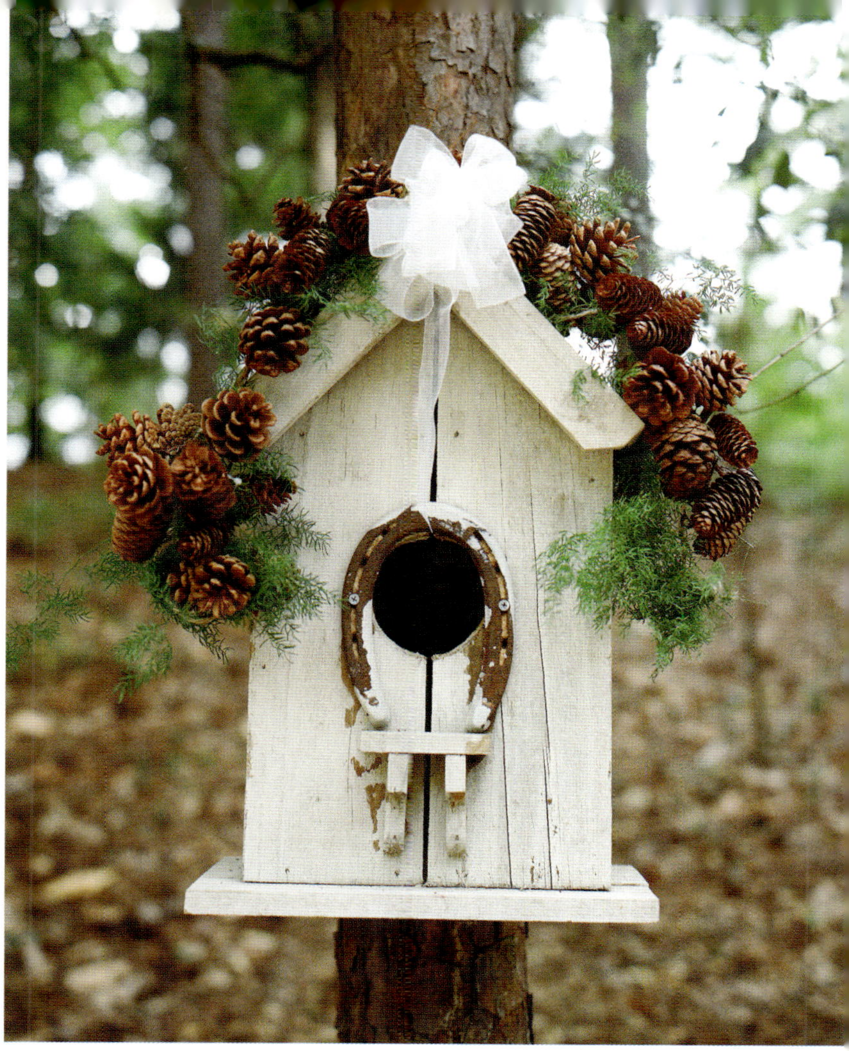

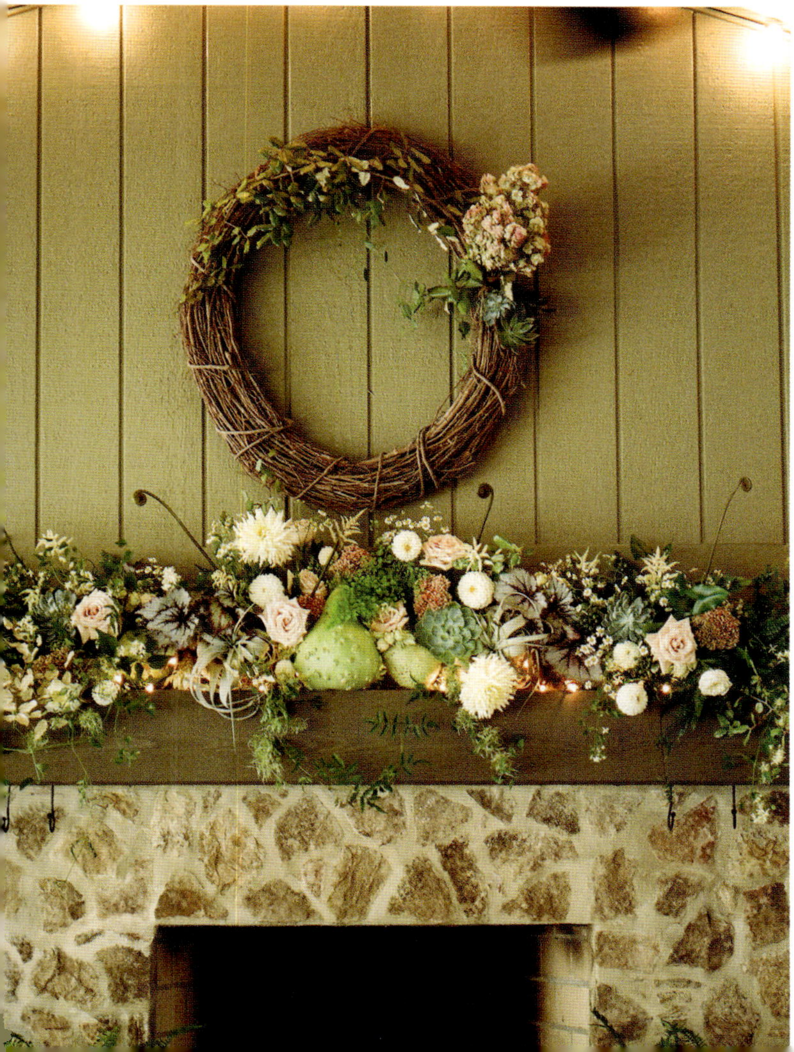

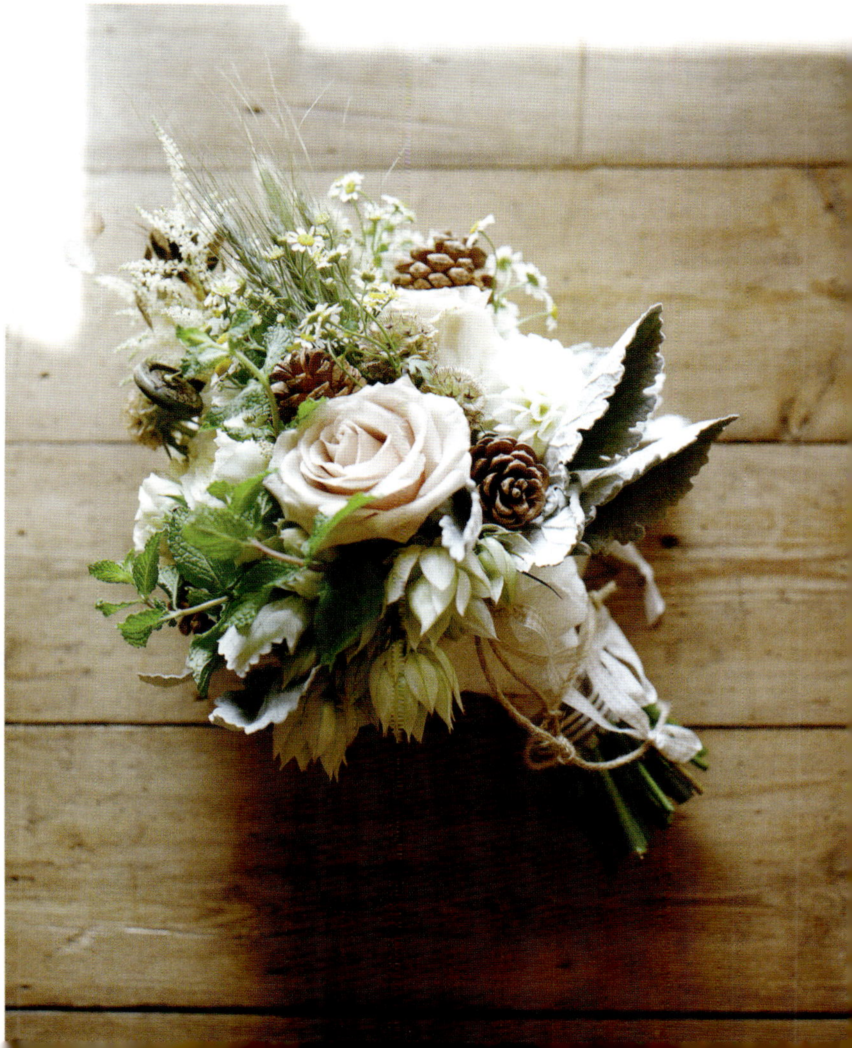

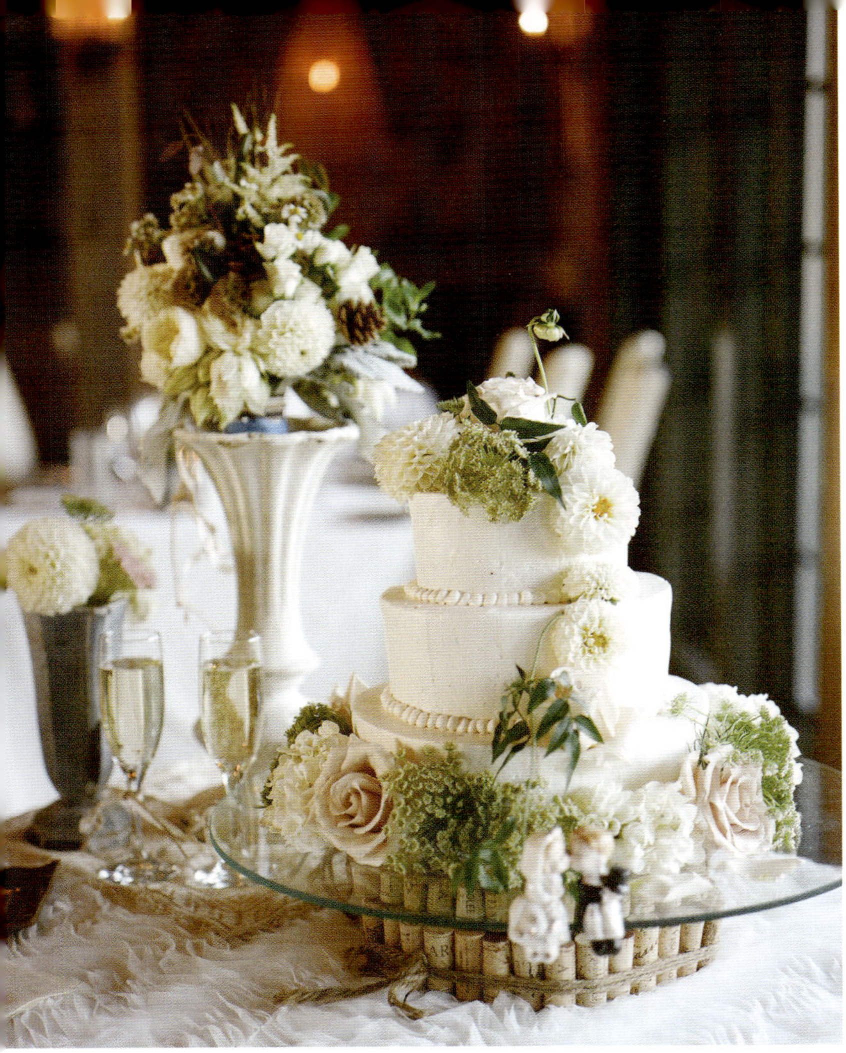

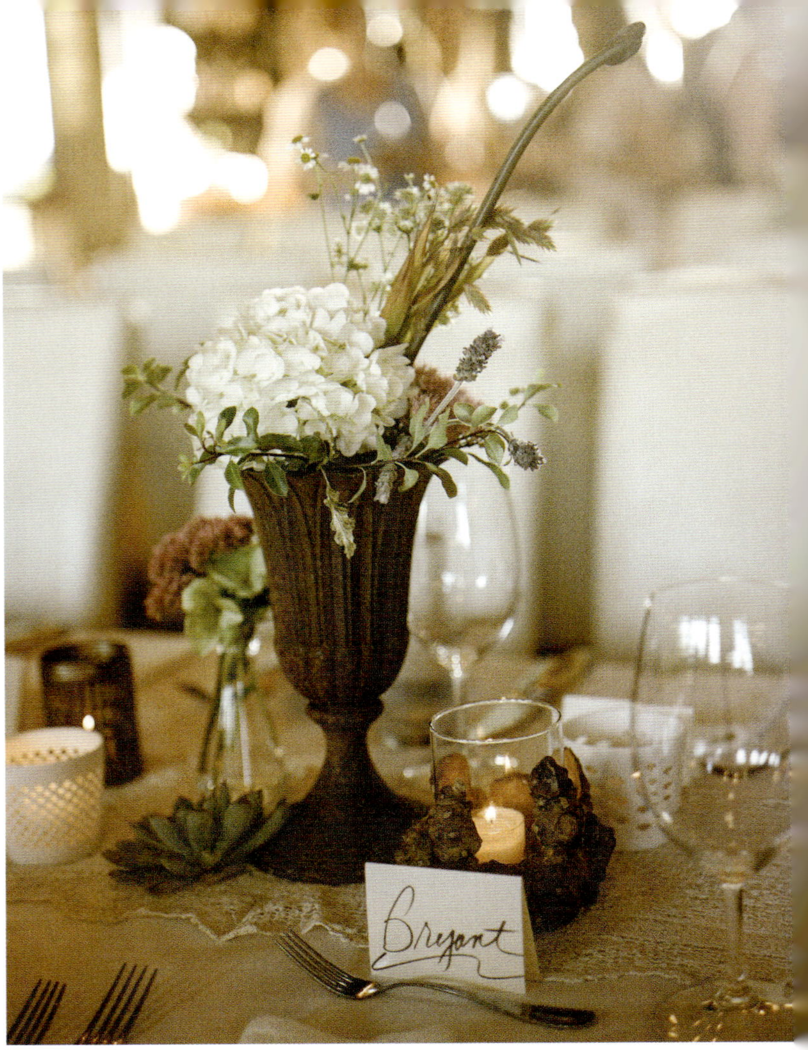
Bryant

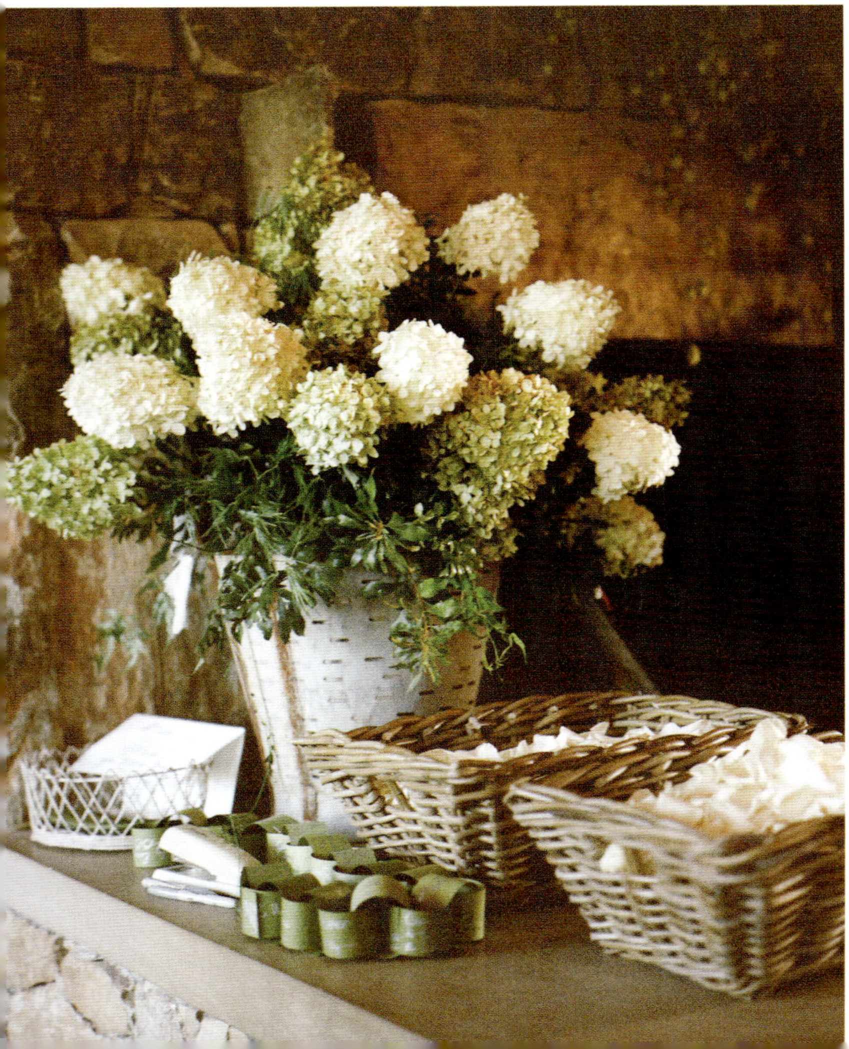

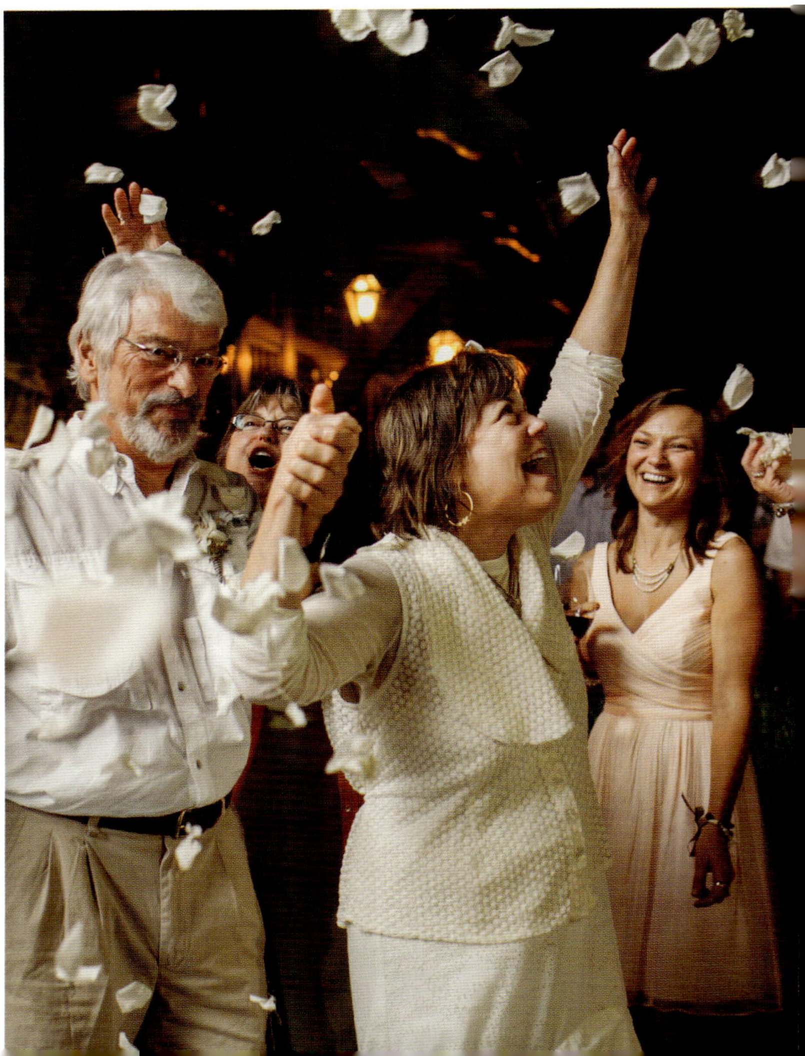

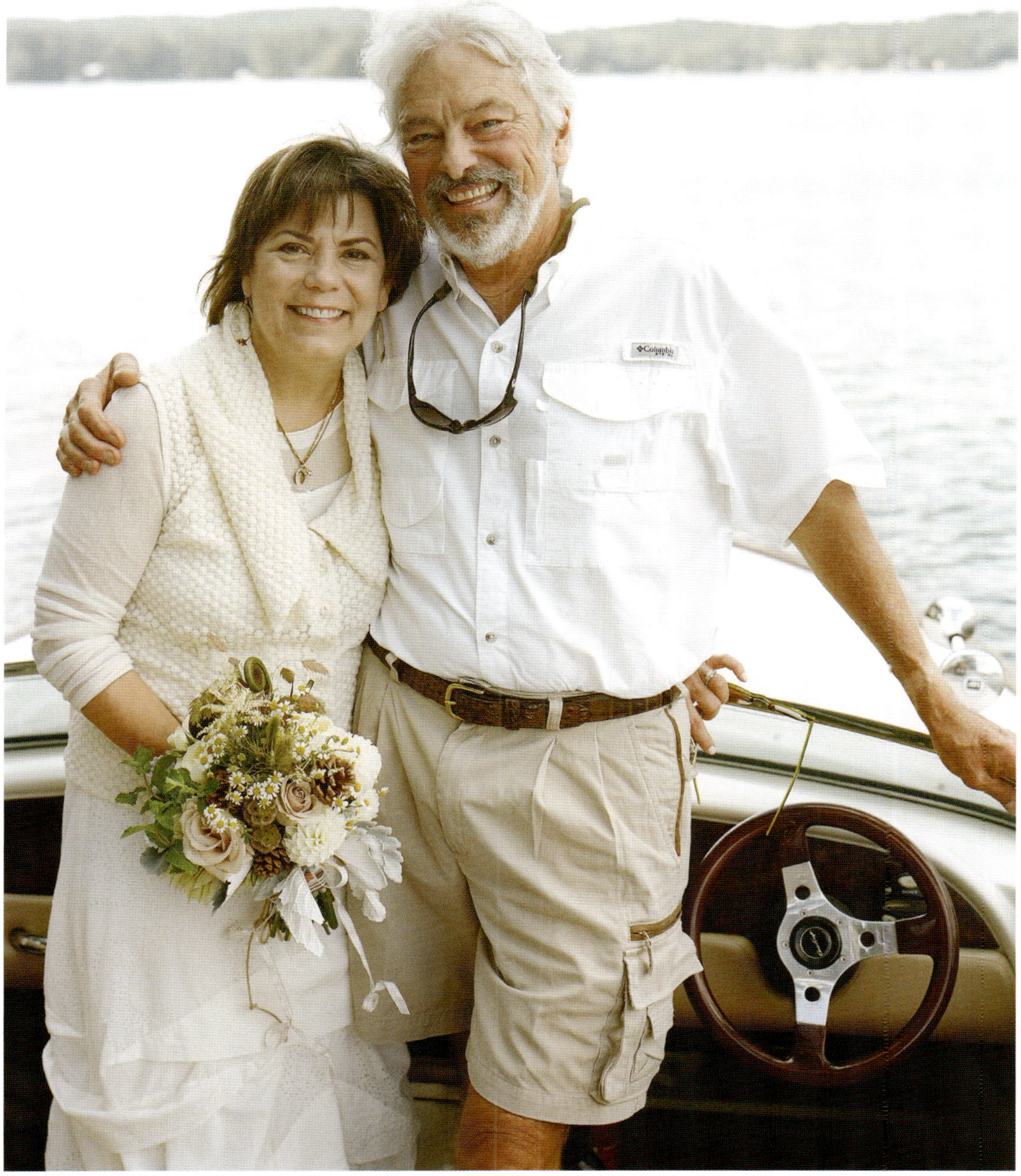

I LOVE THEIR SPIRIT, AND THE WHOLE WEDDING VIBE. IT WAS JUST RIGHT. NOT FANCY BUT A REFLECTION OF THEIR APPROACH TO LIFE, WHICH IS FUN AND FUNNY AND SO FULL OF KINDNESS AND GENEROSITY.

The sweet family wedding, with all the grown children and grandchildren, who were the attendants and participants, left not a dry eye in the house. It was so special to be surrounded by close family and dear friends and celebrate a long-awaited union. It left us all with a true and complete and satisfying feeling that all is right in the world.

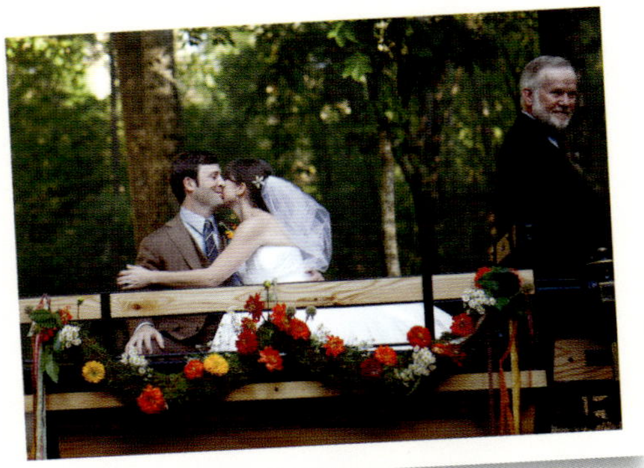

THE GETAWAY

the final touch

Just like dressing the entryway to the reception as a way of welcoming friends and family, I believe strongly in decorating the bride and groom's getaway vehicle. My goal is to celebrate their union, to put a "The End" symbol on the event. But it also transports the couple to their new life together. And what better method than a flower-decked carriage or jeep, boat or vintage automobile?

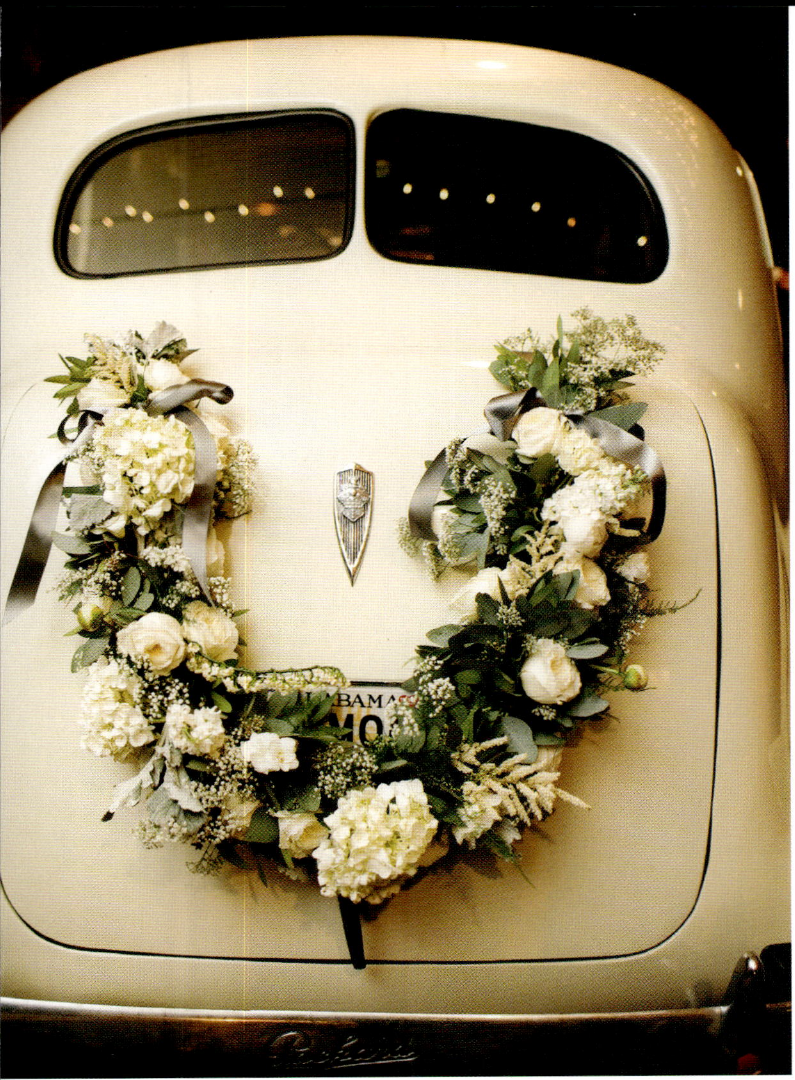

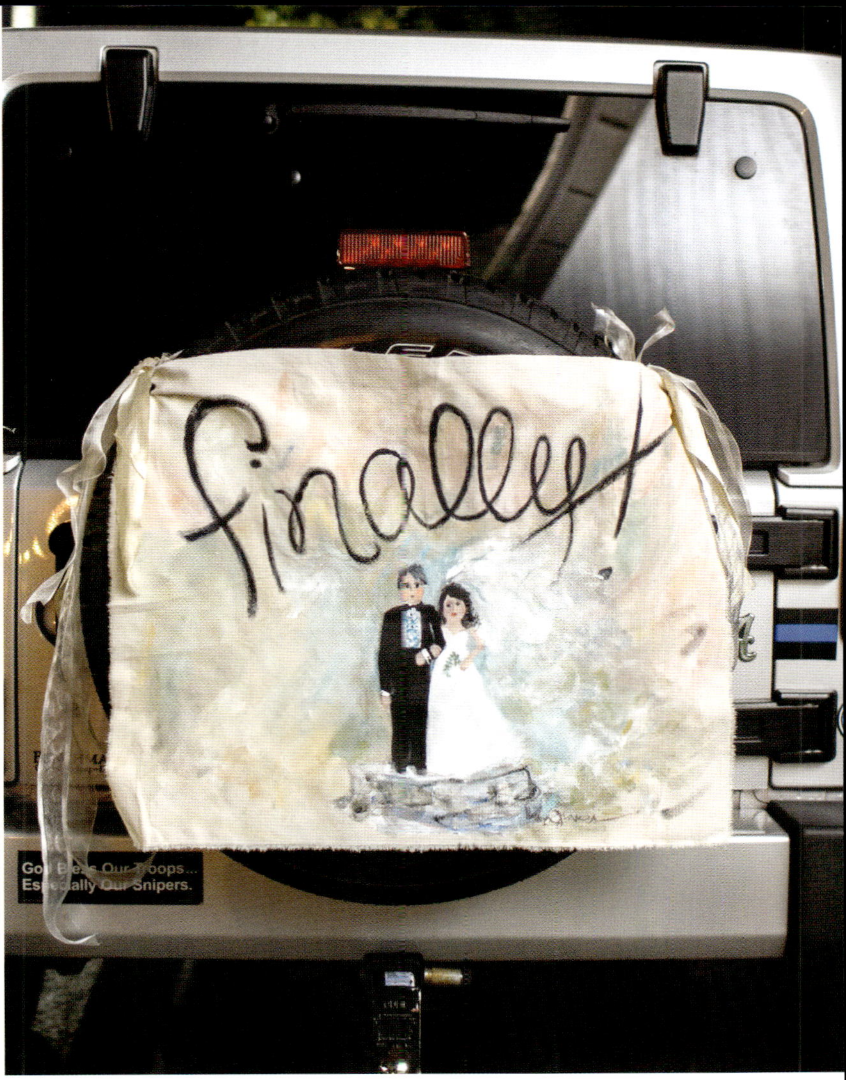
finally!

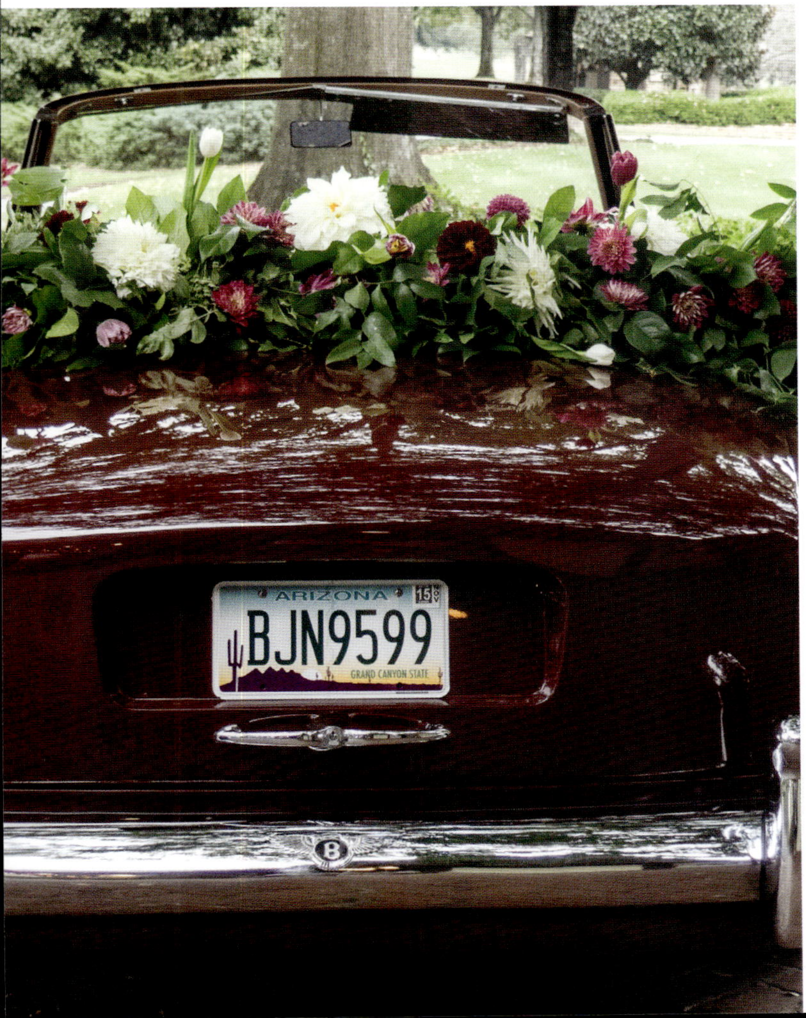
ARIZONA
BJN9599
GRAND CANYON STATE

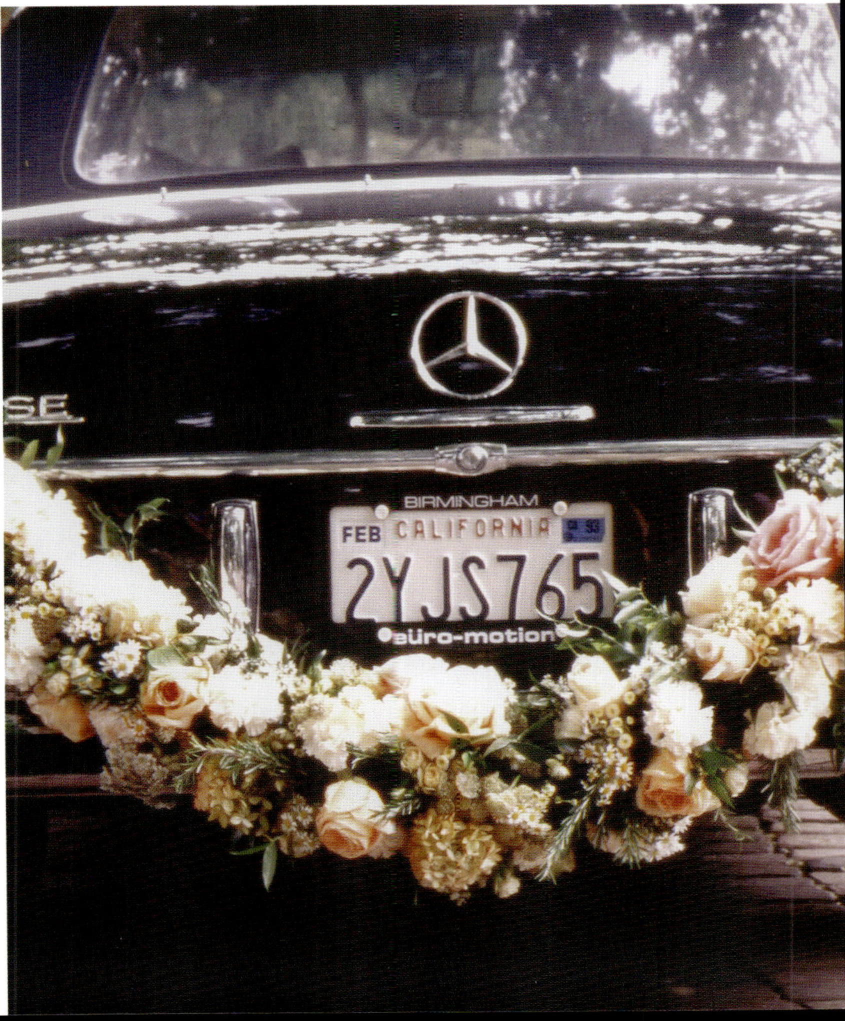
BIRMINGHAM
FEB CALIFORNIA
2YJS765
euro-motion

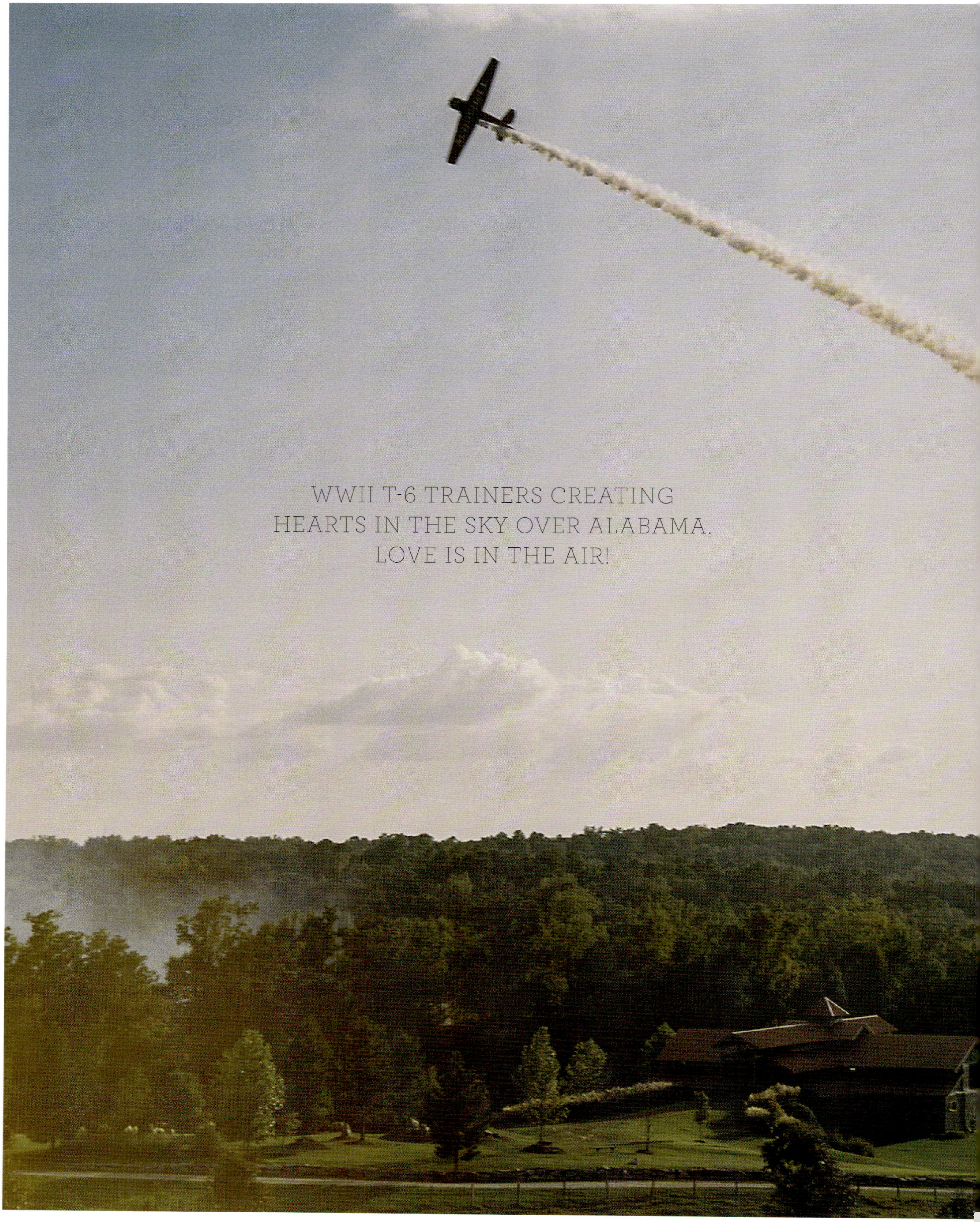

WWII T-6 TRAINERS CREATING
HEARTS IN THE SKY OVER ALABAMA.
LOVE IS IN THE AIR!

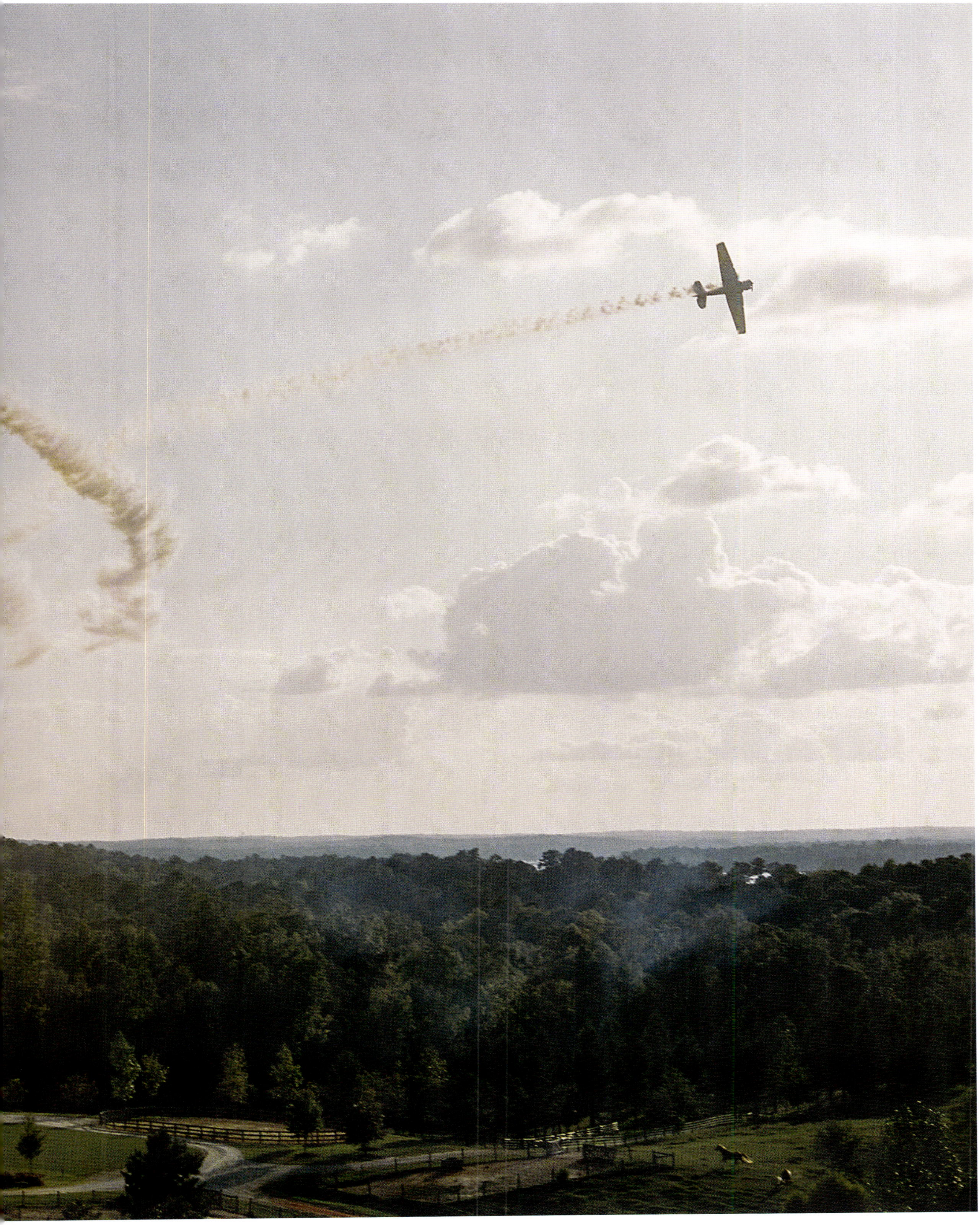

how-to

I have a specific goal when I am on stage demonstrating floral designs or when I am teaching a flower class. I want to encourage my audience to feel empowered to actually attempt flower arranging. Many people feel self critical, shy or intimidated by flowers, and I want to lift the fear and help you dive right in. I was determined to include some instructional information in my book so you can see what goes on behind the scenes and make some magic of your own.

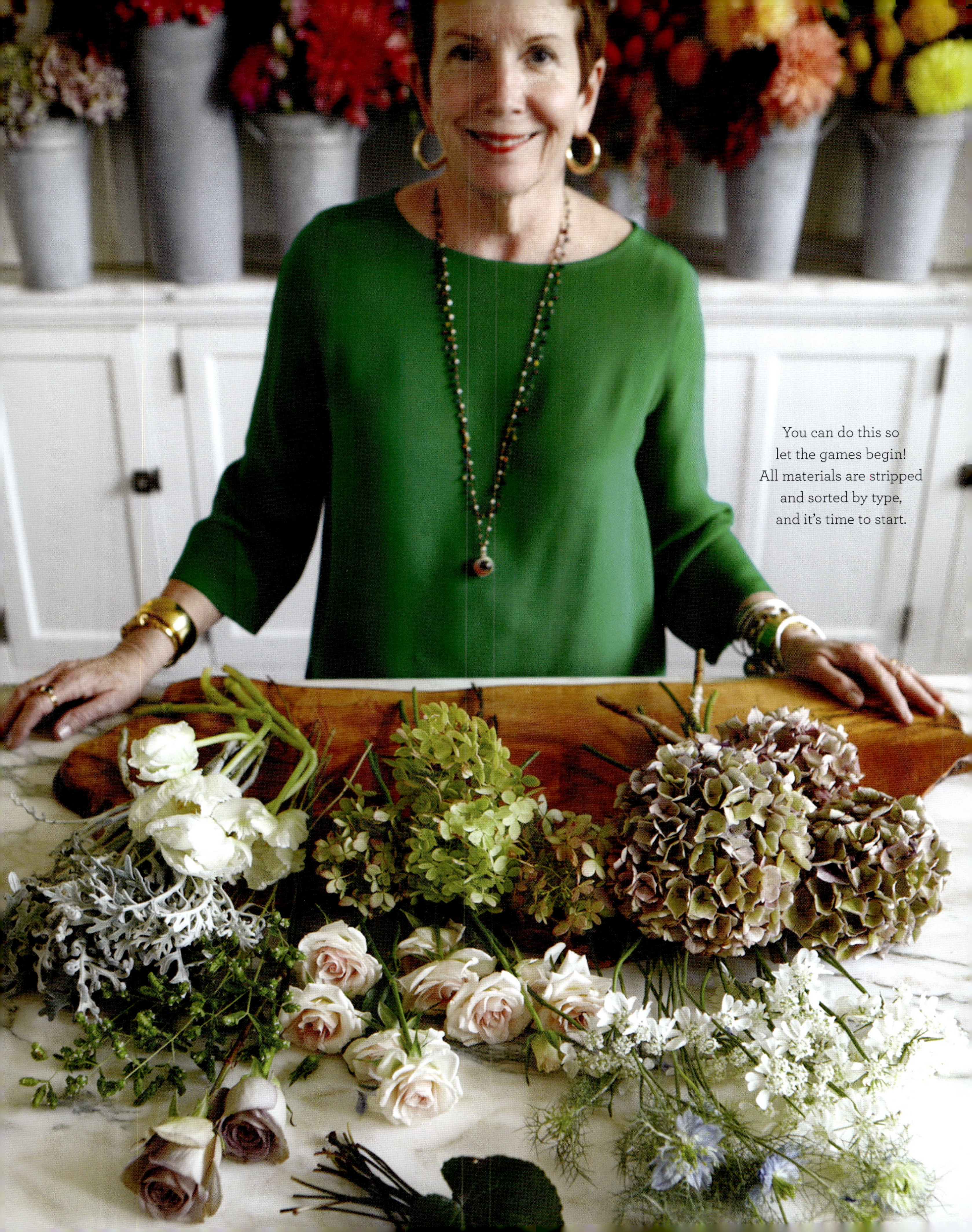

You can do this so let the games begin! All materials are stripped and sorted by type, and it's time to start.

FIRST RULE

prep the flowers

I may forsake traditional habits of flower arranging at every turn, but I do follow a tried-and-true routine when I am prepping arrangements—so that the blossoms look as good as possible and last long.

Clean the base of your container and dry it thoroughly. We use Windex for glass containers. If you are using a clear glass vase, and it is cloudy, fill the vase with water and drop an Efferdent tablet inside. The glass almost always comes clean.

Buy or cut your flowers from the garden. If cutting flowers from your garden, cut early in the day or late in the afternoon. NEVER in the HEAT of the day.

Strip the stems. All of these steps are vital, and this one will stave off the murky stinky water that arrangements get when submerged leaves and stems start to rot. We strip all stems of thorns and leaves, occasionally leaving a small tuft of leaves at the top. Here's are a few methods:

- Snap the greenery off with your fingers.
- Clip greenery with clippers. Some floral designers will only use a knife.
- Strip leaves with a metal clamp.
- There's even a machine to do it, kind of like a sawmill.
- Heavy rubber gloves make stripping and snapping easy and painless.
- An old-fashioned soap dish liner with knobs lets you strip everything and preserve the outside membrane of the stem, which is very important.

My take: I strip everything with my hands to protect the flowers as much as possible and preserve the delicate stems so they don't rot. But that is my personal preference. I work with people who have all sorts of different methods to prep the flowers.

Trim the stems at an angle to allow them more surface from which to drink. And drop the stem in water. We use a three-second rule. Three seconds from being trimmed to getting water. The water should reach halfway up the stem.

Find a cool spot to let the flowers drink for a bit. Ideally overnight; at least 30 minutes if they're going in a vase. Three hours if they'll be in oasis. Treat flowers and greenery from your garden the same, but keep in mind that greenery is delicate.

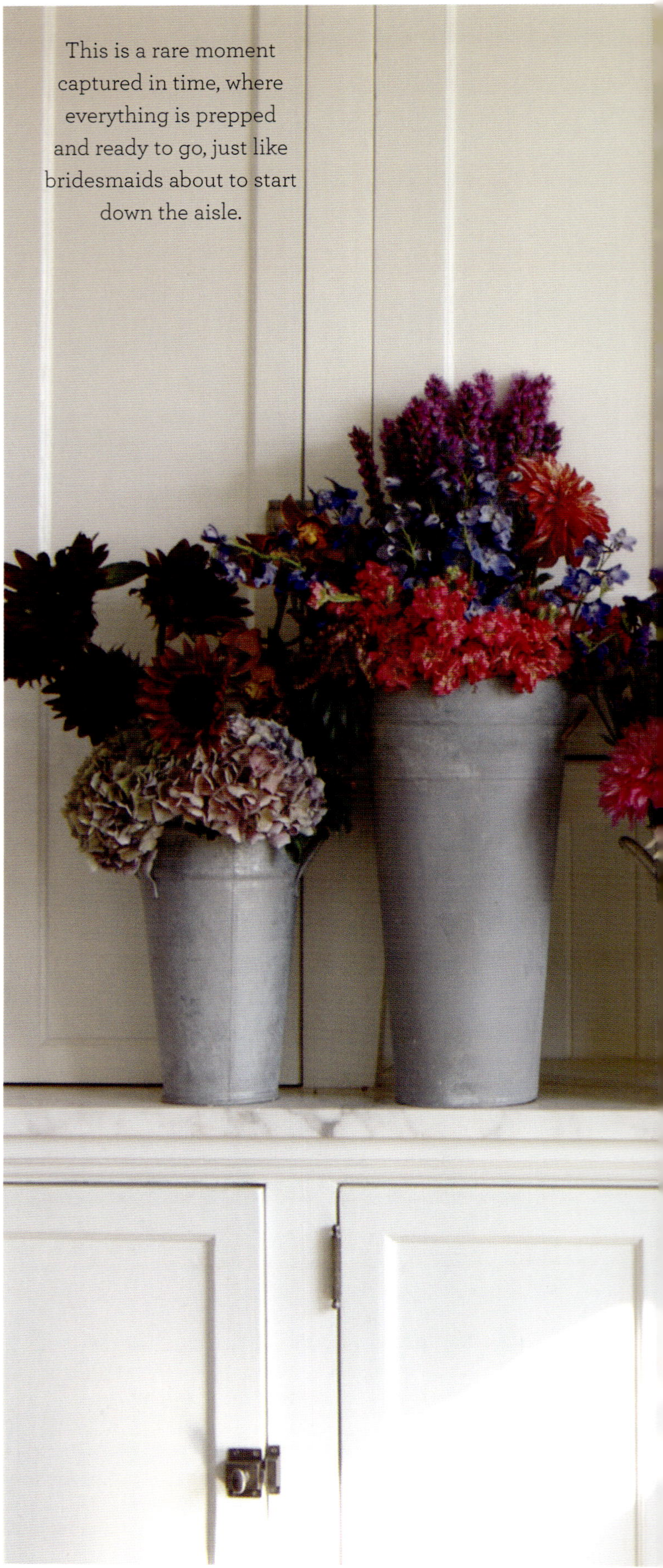

This is a rare moment captured in time, where everything is prepped and ready to go, just like bridesmaids about to start down the aisle.

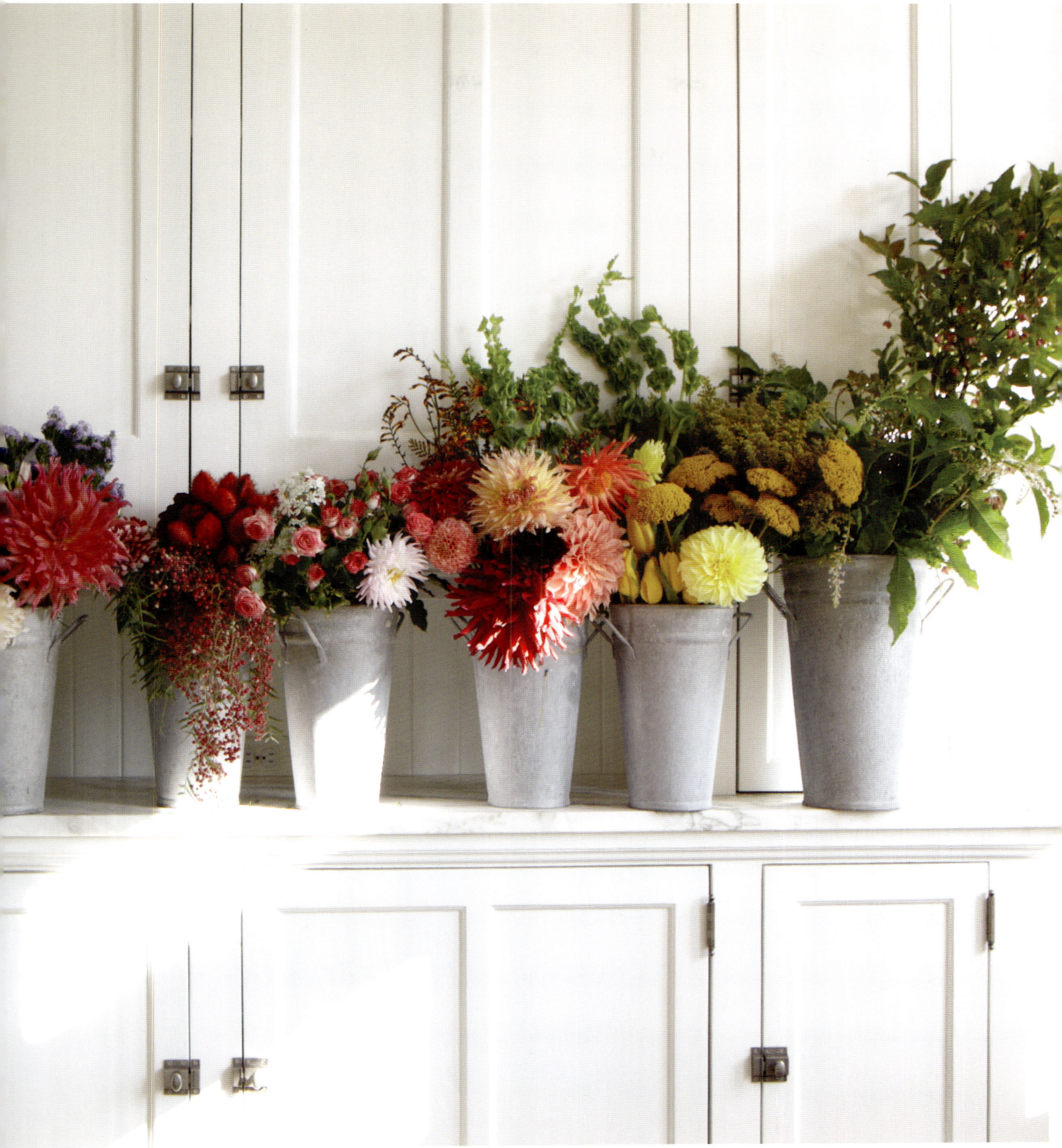

HAND-TIED BOUQUET

a stem-by-stem guide

Preparing your flowers for this project takes longer than actually making the finished bouquet, but proper preparation, which includes stripping all flower stems, thorns, etc., is the key to success.

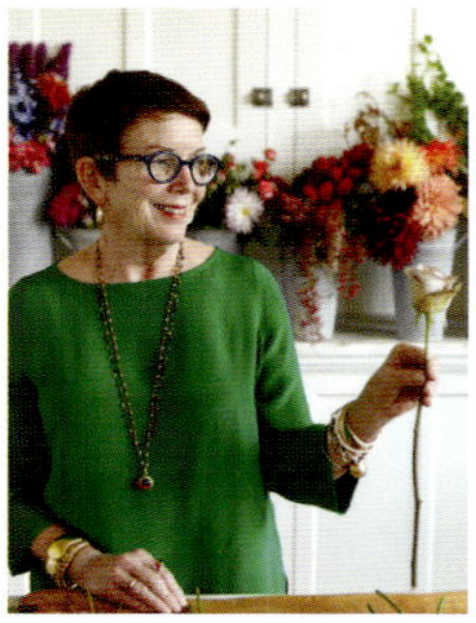

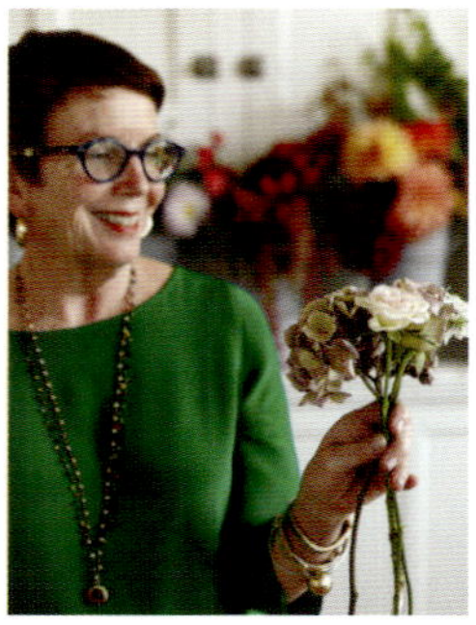

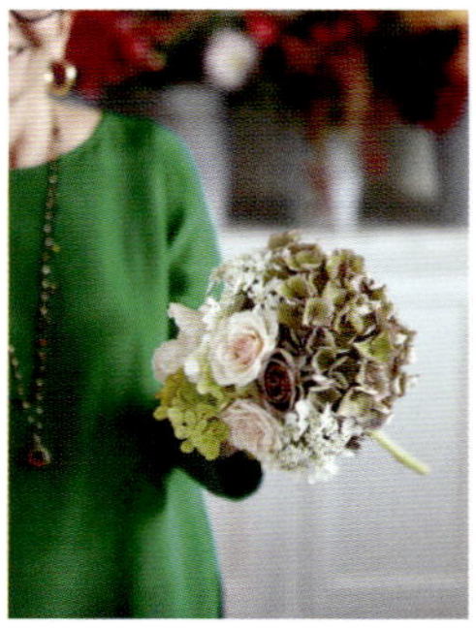

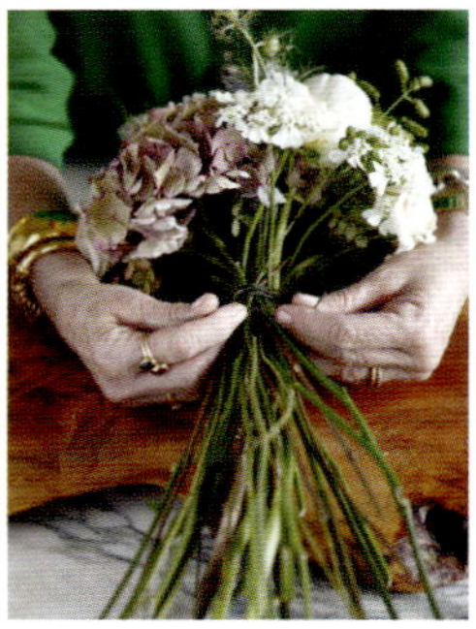

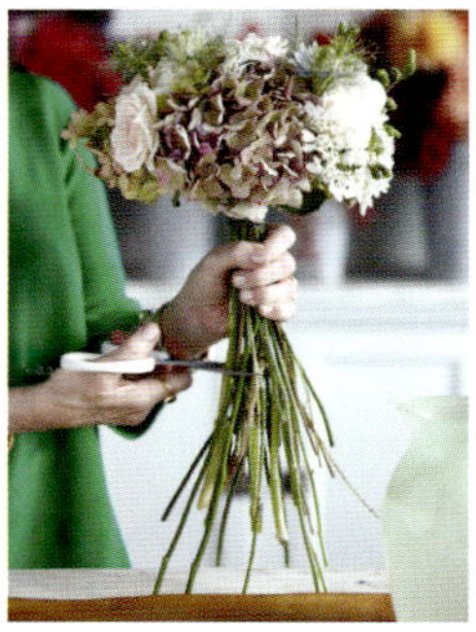

step 1

Choose your strongest flower wtih a straight stem. It's your starter. Hold it gently, approximately two inches down the stem, below the head, between your thumb and forefinger. Think of this flower as the center spoke of a bicycle wheel.

step 2

Add two additional flowers, diagonally, across the center stem (with heads to the left of the first blossom ... stems to the right). Just tuck stems in between your fingers to keep in place. Turn this entire grouping around so that the newly added flowers are to the right of the center flower.

step 3

Continue adding flowers, blossoms to the left; stems crossing the center stem and extending to the right. Turn the bouqet clockwise and continue to add flowers or greenery with the same technique—head of flower to the left, stems crossing to the right.

step 4

When complete, tie your bouquet off in a tight double knot using binding wire (paper coated wire product) or sticky floral tape.

step 5

Re-cut all stems evenly and place the entire bouquet in water.

the flowers

Antique Hydrangeas, Pee Gee Hydrangeas, White and Green stripe Parrot Tulips, Dusty Miller, Amnesia Rose, Nigella, Orlaya, Candy Bianca Rose, Oregano, Galax

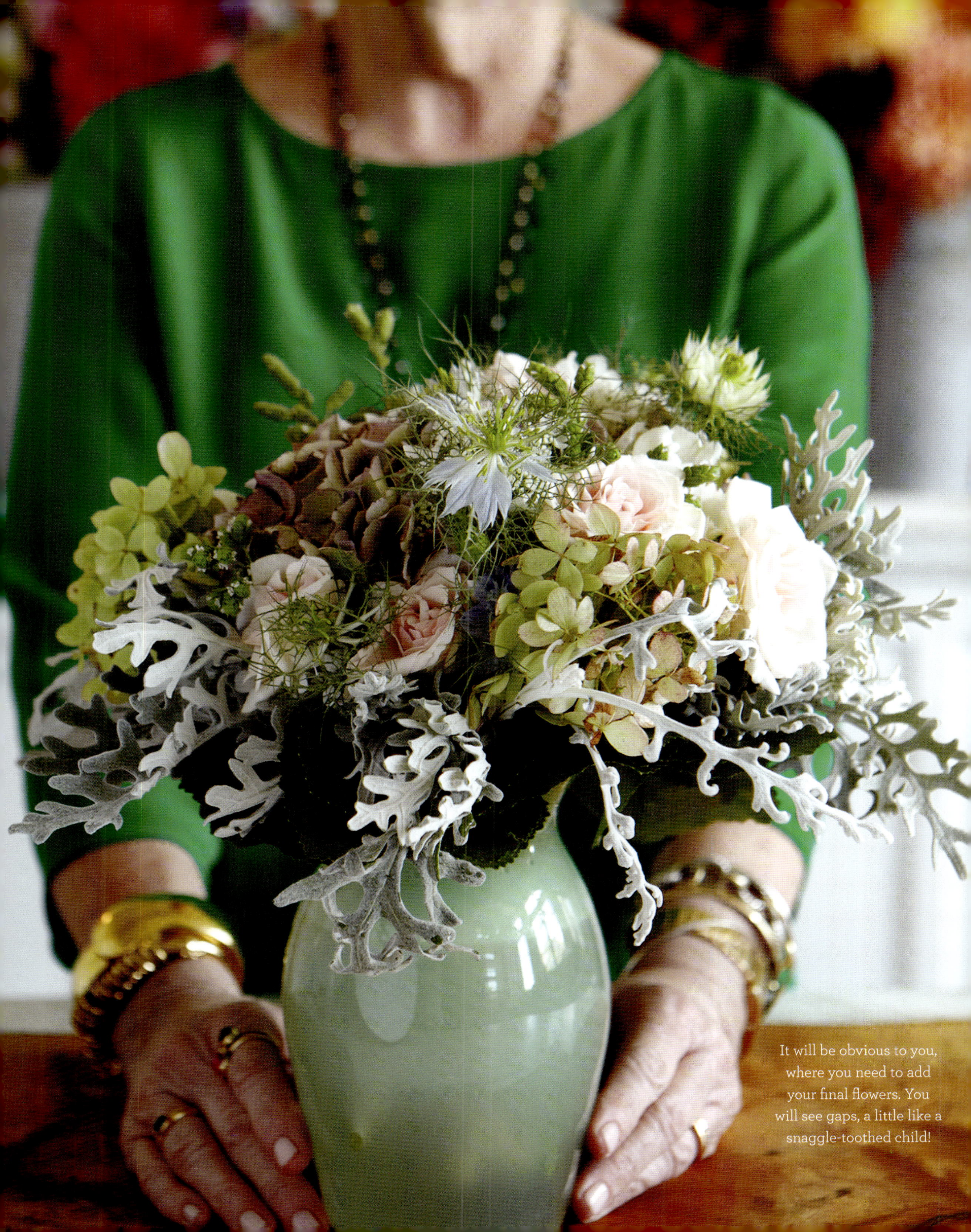

It will be obvious to you, where you need to add your final flowers. You will see gaps, a little like a snaggle-toothed child!

LADY ON A PIANO

classically loose and lovely

What goes around comes around, and flower frogs and pin holders are back in fashion. Back in the day, my mama disapproved of my using oasis, so I worked hard to come up with alternatives, this being one of them.

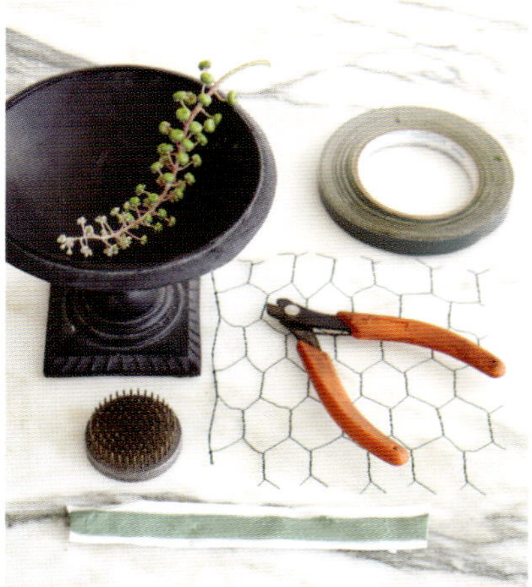

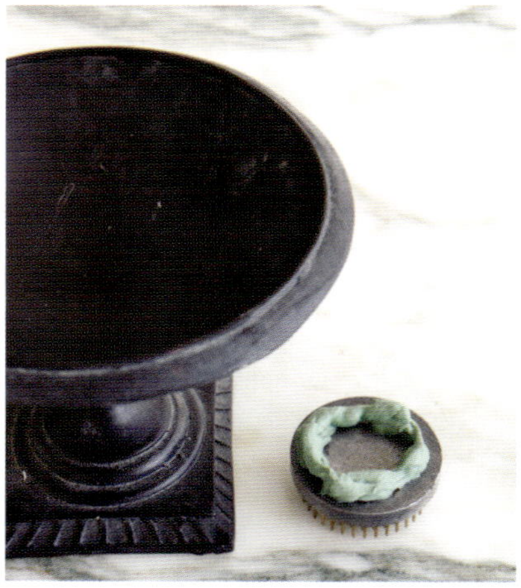

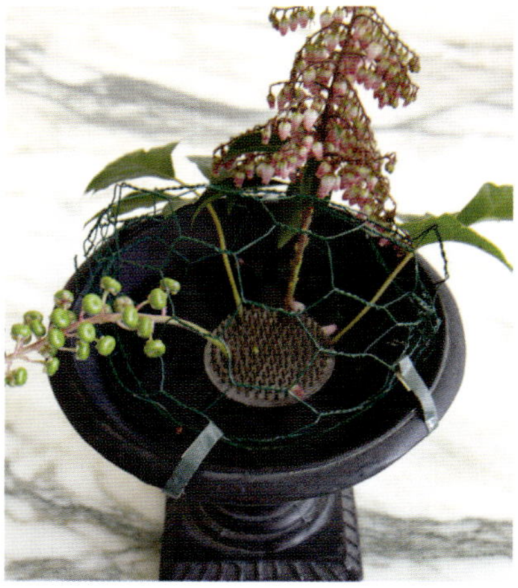

step 1

An important step is to be sure the inside of your container is totally dry.

step 2

Use a two- to three-inch length of Cling floral adhesive. Play with it, warming it up in your hands. When it is more pliable, stretch it out like a piece of ribbon and coil it onto the bottom of your pin holder.

step 3

Use a towel to protect your hands from the pin spikes. Press it firmly into place in the middle of the bowl of your container. Keep pressing and holding for a good minute to secure the Cling. Next place a dome-shaped piece of chicken wire into the lip of the container and tape this down to the outside of the vase to secure the wire. BE SURE TO ADD WATER.

the flowers

Dahlias, Neapolitan Queen Anne's Lace, Pokeweed Berries, Oregano, Antique Hydrangea, Pierus, Beauty Berry, Oak Leaf Ivy, Chilean Fern

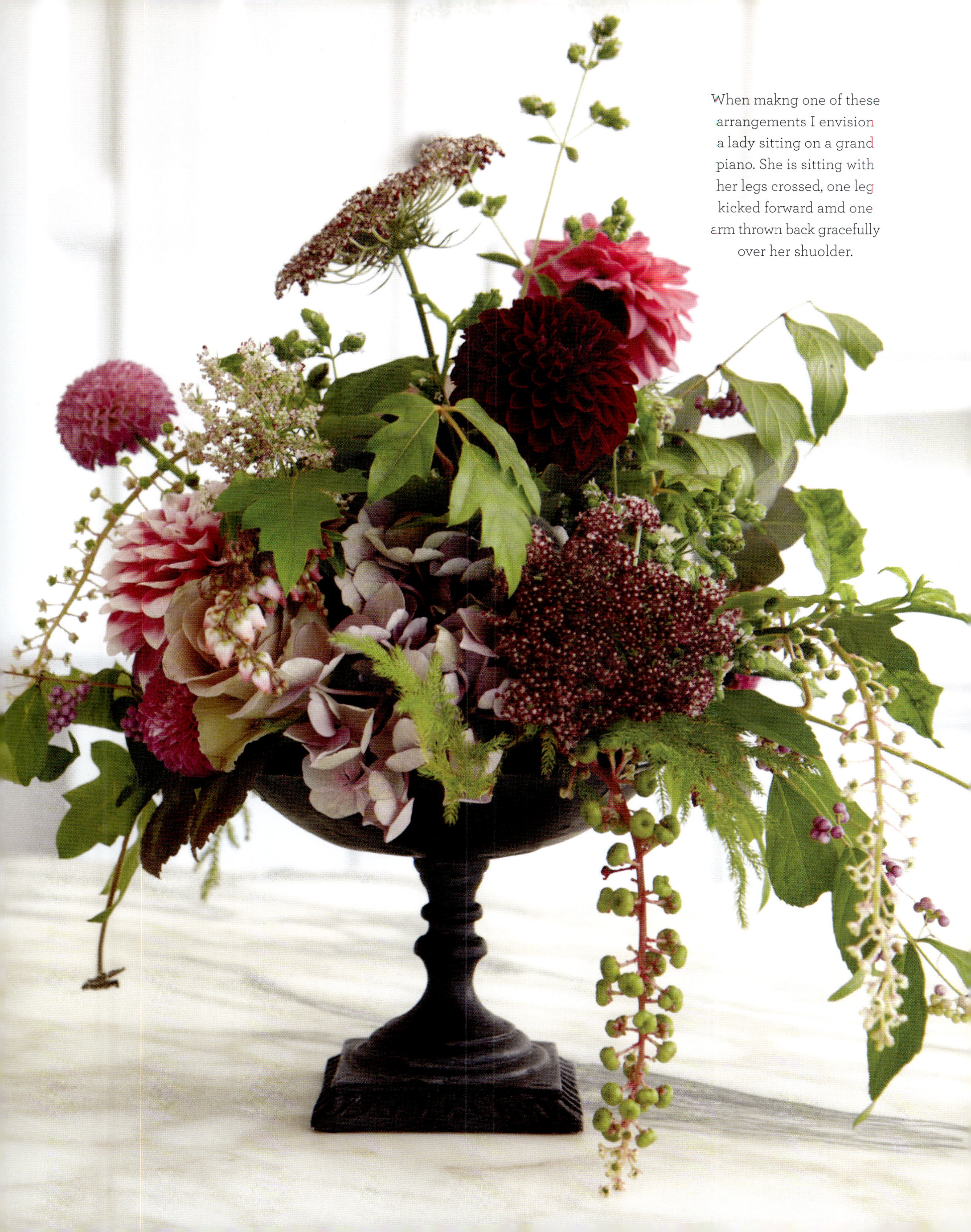

When makng one of these arrangements I envision a lady sitting on a grand piano. She is sitting with her legs crossed, one leg kicked forward amd one arm thrown back gracefully over her shuolder.

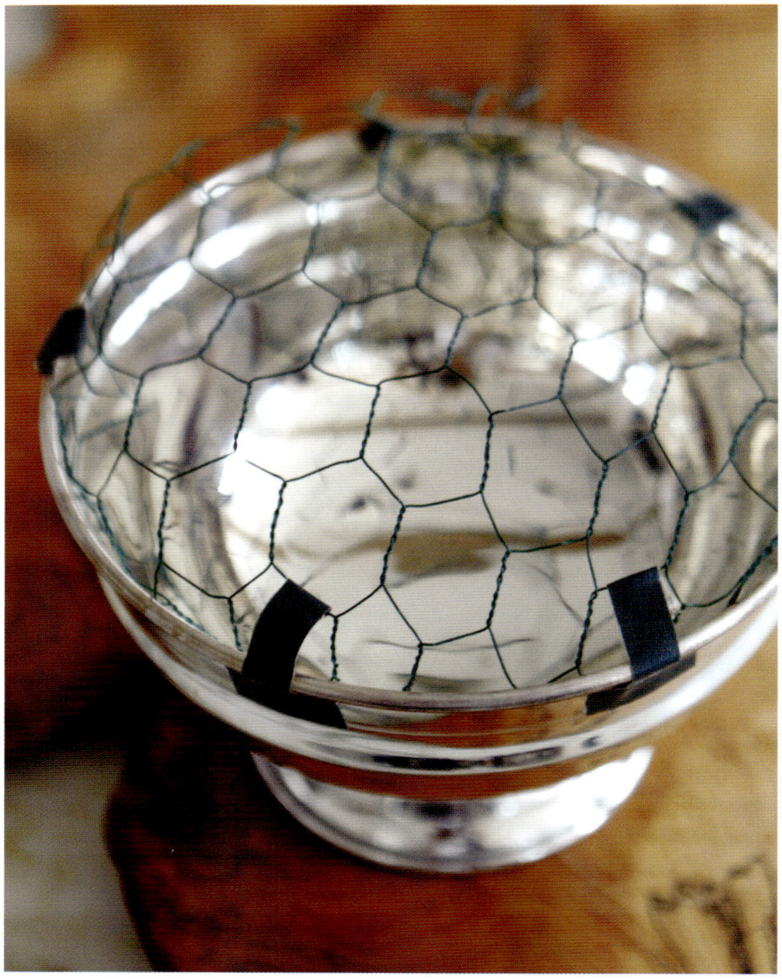

STOP THE FLOP

chicken wire and taped grids

Always working to please my mama, I came up with more and more techniques to avoid using oasis. And honestly the flowers last longer when the stems are allowed to drink straight from fresh water. This technique works exceptionally well for large-mouthed vases. Using wire clippers, cut a piece of chicken wire a little bit larger than the mouth of your vase and tape it in place. Essentially tape to tape makes it affix better. For a taped grid (opposite), I lay strips across the mouth in one direction, securing over the lip of the container. Cross with additional strips going in the oppsite direction to create a grid over the mouth. Secure with one long piece of tape all the way around the mouth, taping down each individual piece of tape to keep them from popping loose.

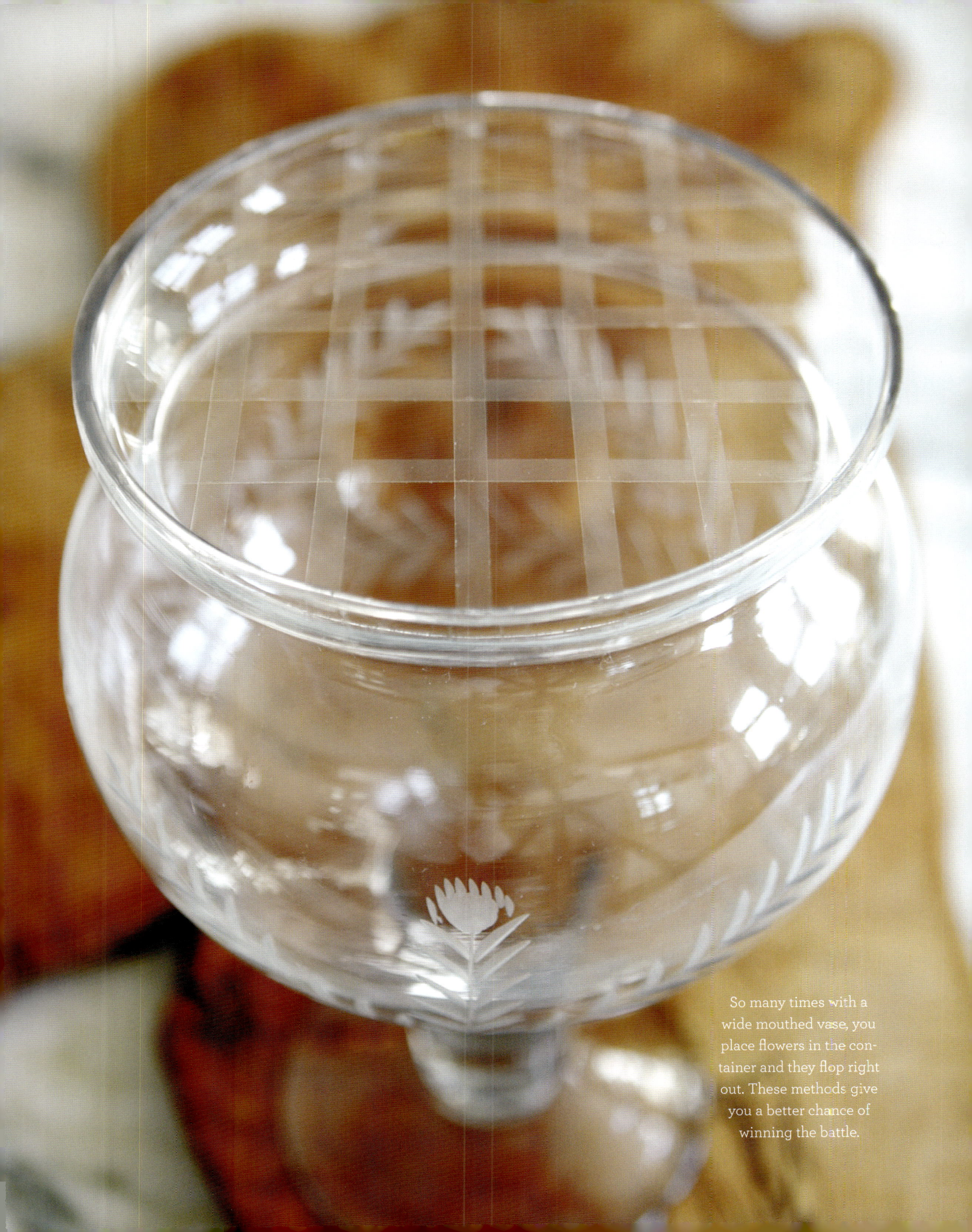

So many times with a wide mouthed vase, you place flowers in the container and they flop right out. These methods give you a better chance of winning the battle.

FRUIT & FLOWERS

adding texture and form

I love the seasonality that produce lends to a bouquet, but there is a method to the beauty. They're usually heavier than flowers, and you have to create a stem. I use wooden floral picks or bamboo kabob skewers as stand-ins for stems.

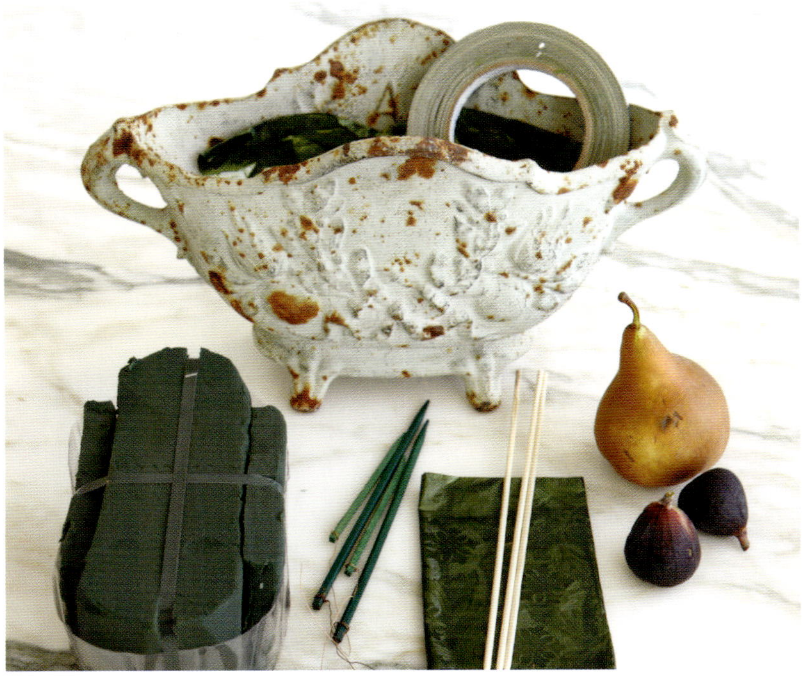

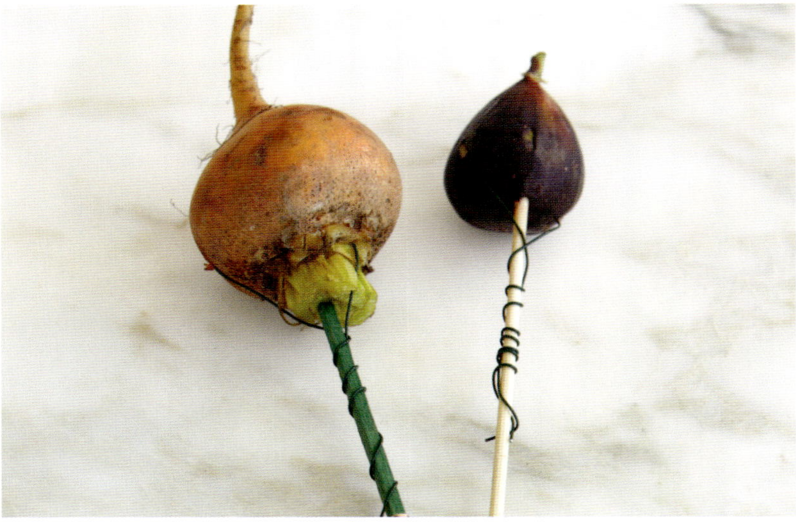

step 1

I lined the contaner with green floral foil. I found a cheap plastic vessel that fit inside. I cut oasis to fit the vessel. I like the oasis to stand 1 1/2 inches above the lip of the container. I make an X over the top with floral tape that reaches to the lip of the container to hold it in place.

step 2

Decide which side of the fruit or vegetable you want to highlight and spear the opposite side with your skewer. Many times I will speare the base of the produce with a length of wire, twisting it down the skewer to ensure stability.

step 3

Push the skewer into the oasis to secure. Be careful: your skewer must be long enough for stability. But if it's too long it will break through the the entire fruit.

step 4

Weave your flowers and greenery in among your produce.

the flowers

Dahlias, Oak Leaf Ivy, English Ivy, Nandina, Woodland Oats, Montbretia

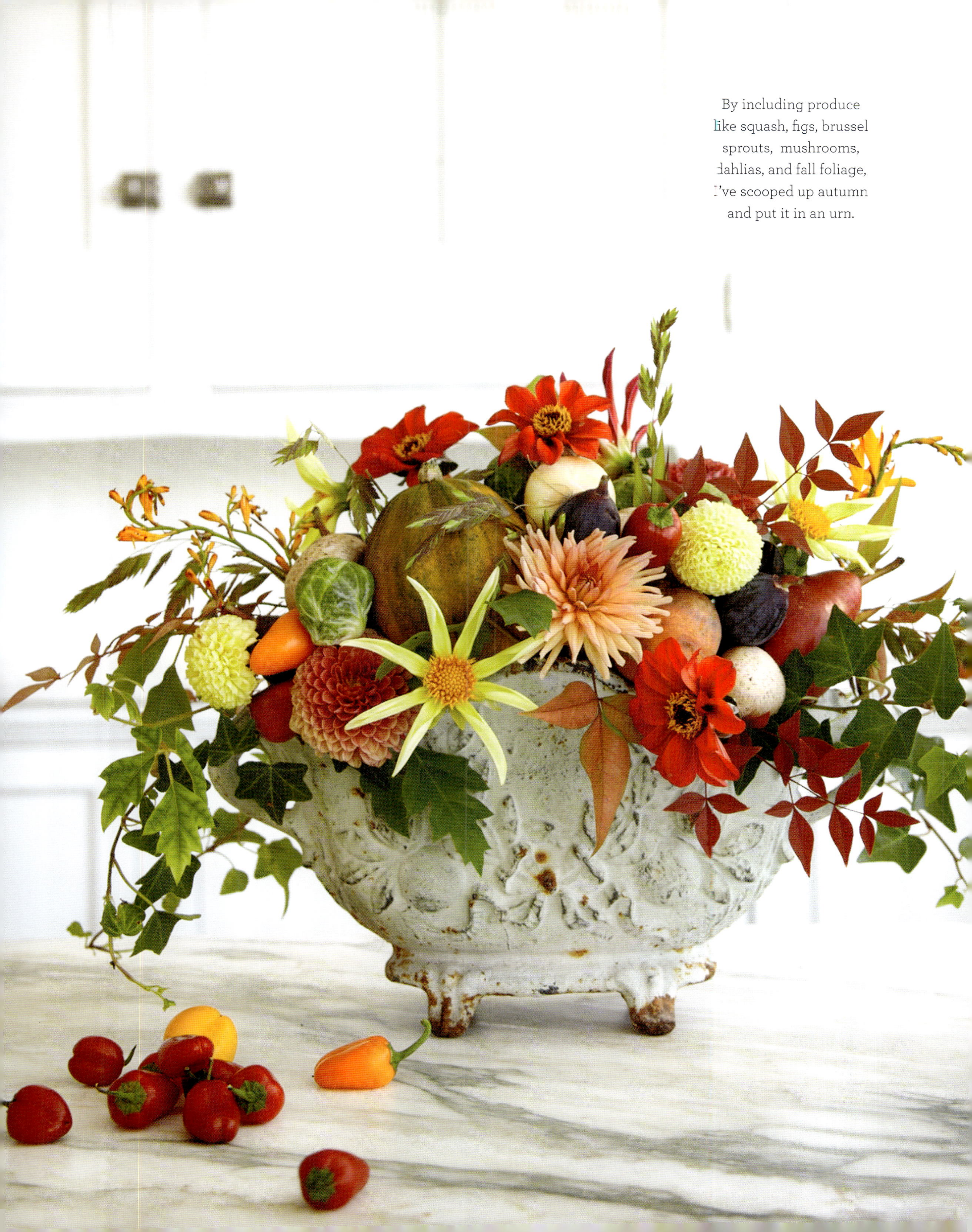

By including produce like squash, figs, brussel sprouts, mushrooms, dahlias, and fall foliage, I've scooped up autumn and put it in an urn.

EXPOSING THE ROOTS

getting that just dug-up look

Often to create even more interest in an arrangement, we choose forced bulbs or plants (orchids, hyacinths, daffodils, amaryllis, etc.) that have hardy roots and become a part of the overall composition.

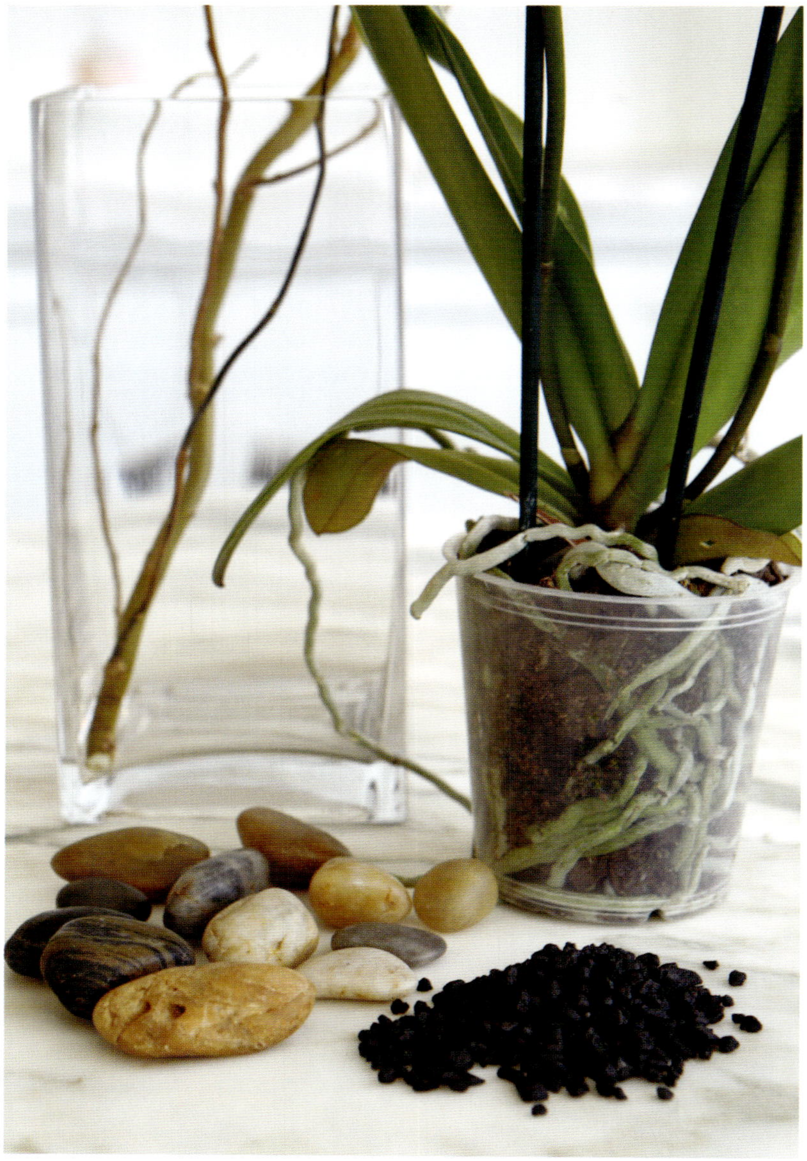

step 1

Remove plants from their dirt. Gently wash dirt away—this takes patience and a gentle touch.

step 2

Place river stones or even gravel, if you choose, in the base of a container or vase to add height and another earthy dimension.

step 3

Place your plant or bulbs inside your container, layering it with additional rocks and gravel. Here I used natural twigs in place of the nursery stake to support the orchid stems and tied them into place with natural raffia.

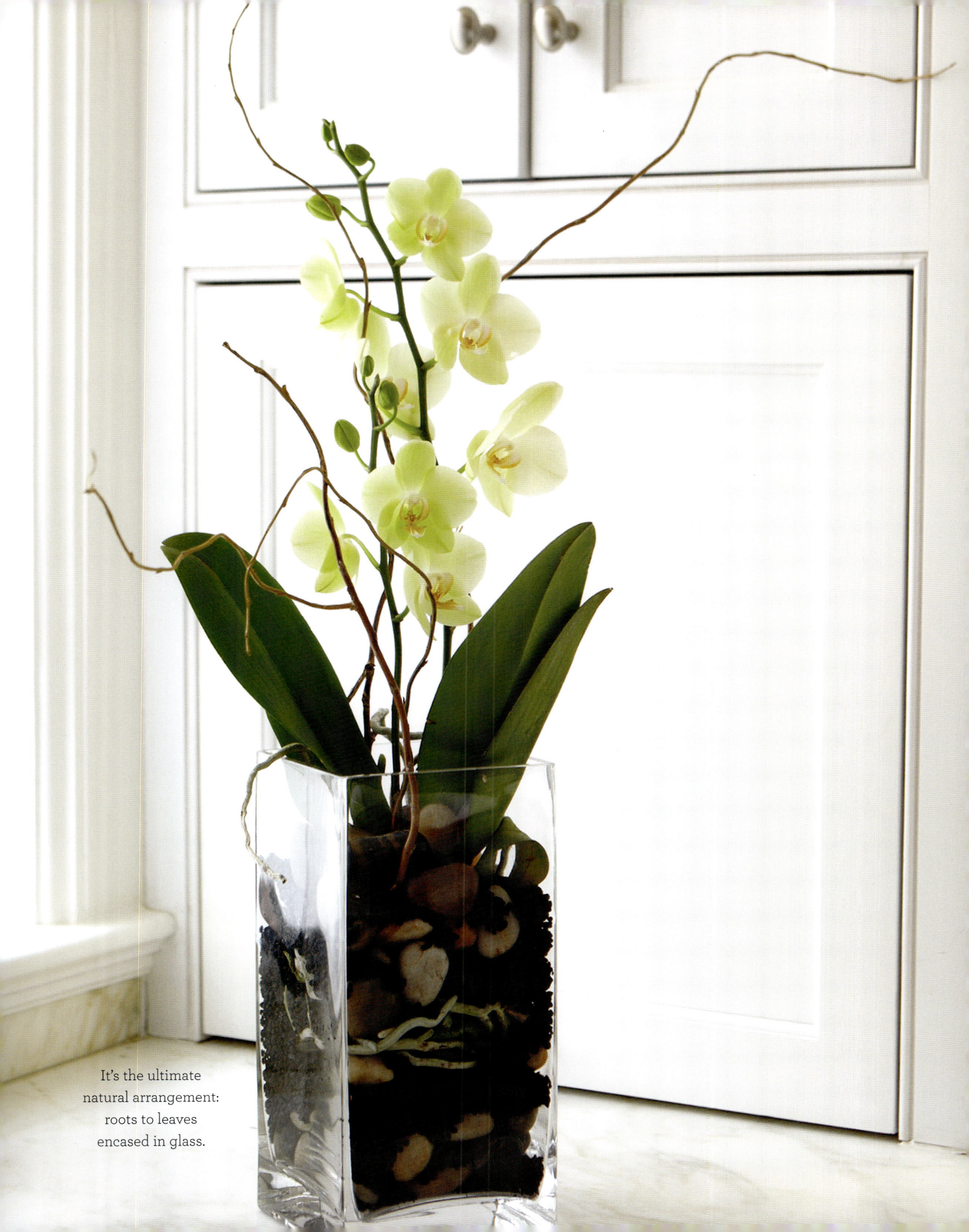

It's the ultimate natural arrangement: roots to leaves encased in glass.

LONG LIVE THE TOPIARY

topiaries are historic in garden and floral design

They are so French and clipped and controlled. It just makes the beholder happy to look upon them. I made many in my "dried flower" era, perfecting the methods of getting a lifelike looking trunk.

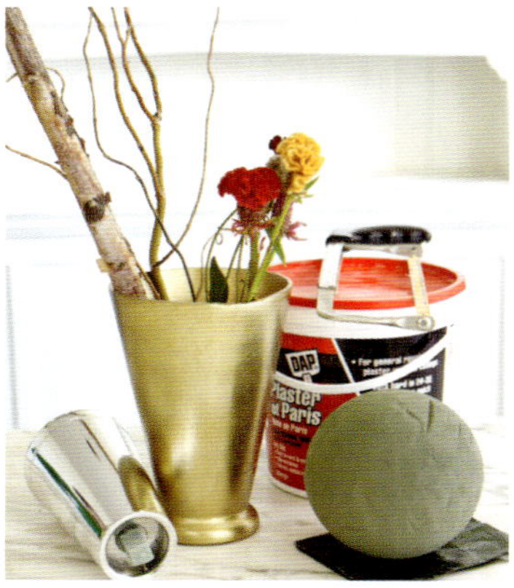

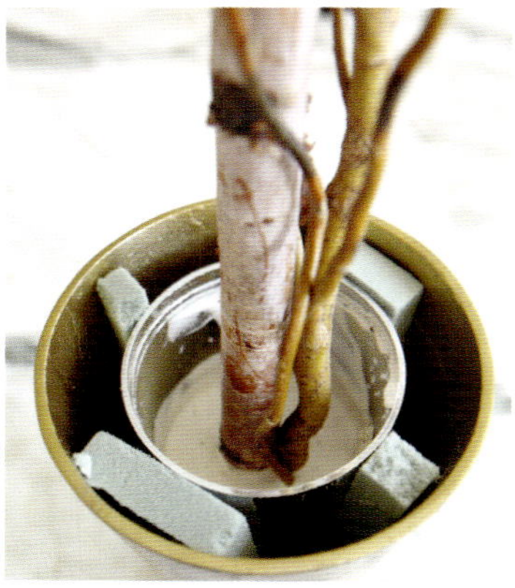

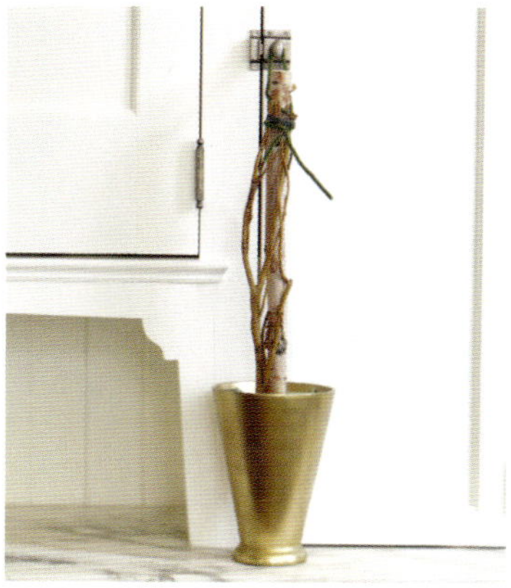

1 Gather your supplies and line the vessel with floral foil. Place a plastic container inside and fill it 2/3 full with Plaster of Paris.

2 Working quickly, tape together the "stems" of curly willow at the base and the top and put the base in the Plaster of Paris. Hold or tie them securely to keep them straight until the Plaster of Paris begins to set.

3 Meanwhile, soak a 3 to 6 inch sphere of floral foam/oasis until it is saturated. After plaster is hardened, spear the foam sphere onto the end of the branches.

4 Add pieces of wet/ soaked oasis on top of the Plaster of Paris and at the base of the stems.

5 Cut flower heads and buds and insert them into the sphere until it is covered on all sides.

6 Finish by covering the base of the arrangement with greenery and flowers.

the flowers

Sedum, Cocks Comb, Nigella Pods, Hearts a Burstin, Blushing Bride Protea, Snowberry, Woodland Oats, Oak Leaf Ivy, Yarrow, Autumn Clematis

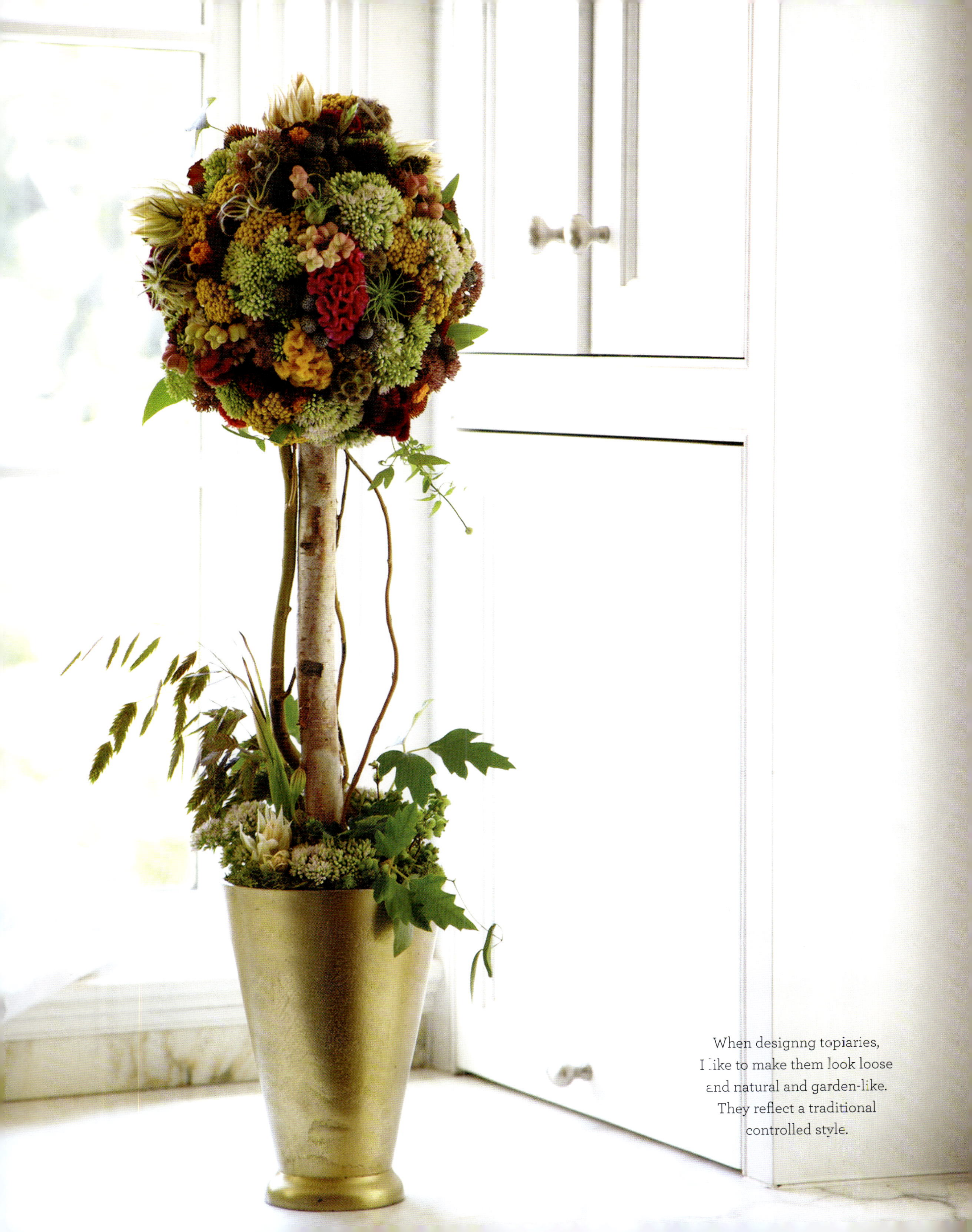

When designng topiaries, I like to make them look loose and natural and garden-like. They reflect a traditional controlled style.

REMEMBERING CONSTANCE SPRY

from birmingham's best gardens

One day, while working in the garden, it became clear to me that as I cut each flower, branch, and vine, I was designing the completed arrangement in my mind, a peaceful and meditative task for me.

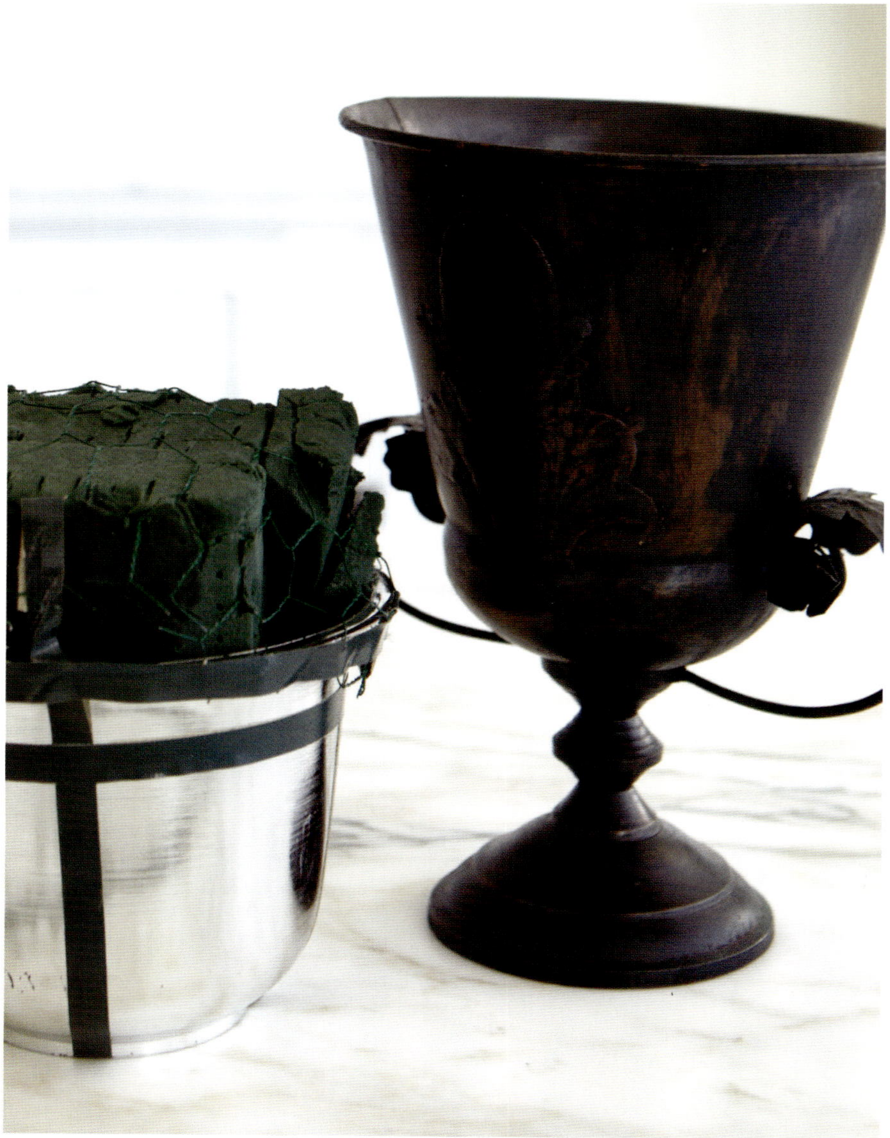

step 1

When the occasion arises to use floral foam, I use the Oasis brand "Instant Deluxe." I start to soak the oasis as soon as I've selected my container. Do not push the oasis down in the water. Lay it on top of the water and let the oasis drink at its own pace.

step 2

Line the urn with floral foil. Cut the oasis to fit the liner, leaving the oasis to stand approimately two inches above the lip of the container. I laid chicken wire over the oasis and taped it taut in place. Imagine a swimming cap with a strap under the chin. The floral tape is the strap that holds the oasis in place. Don't forget to add water to the container.

step 3

When creating a greenery arrangement, I prefer to add the bolder branches first to establish my lines. Then I fill in with smaller materials.

the flowers

Abelia, Leucothoe, Pee Gee Hydrangea, Eleagnus, Hearts a Burstin', Dogwood, Barberry, Amsonia, Rosemary, Japanese Maple, Chinaberry

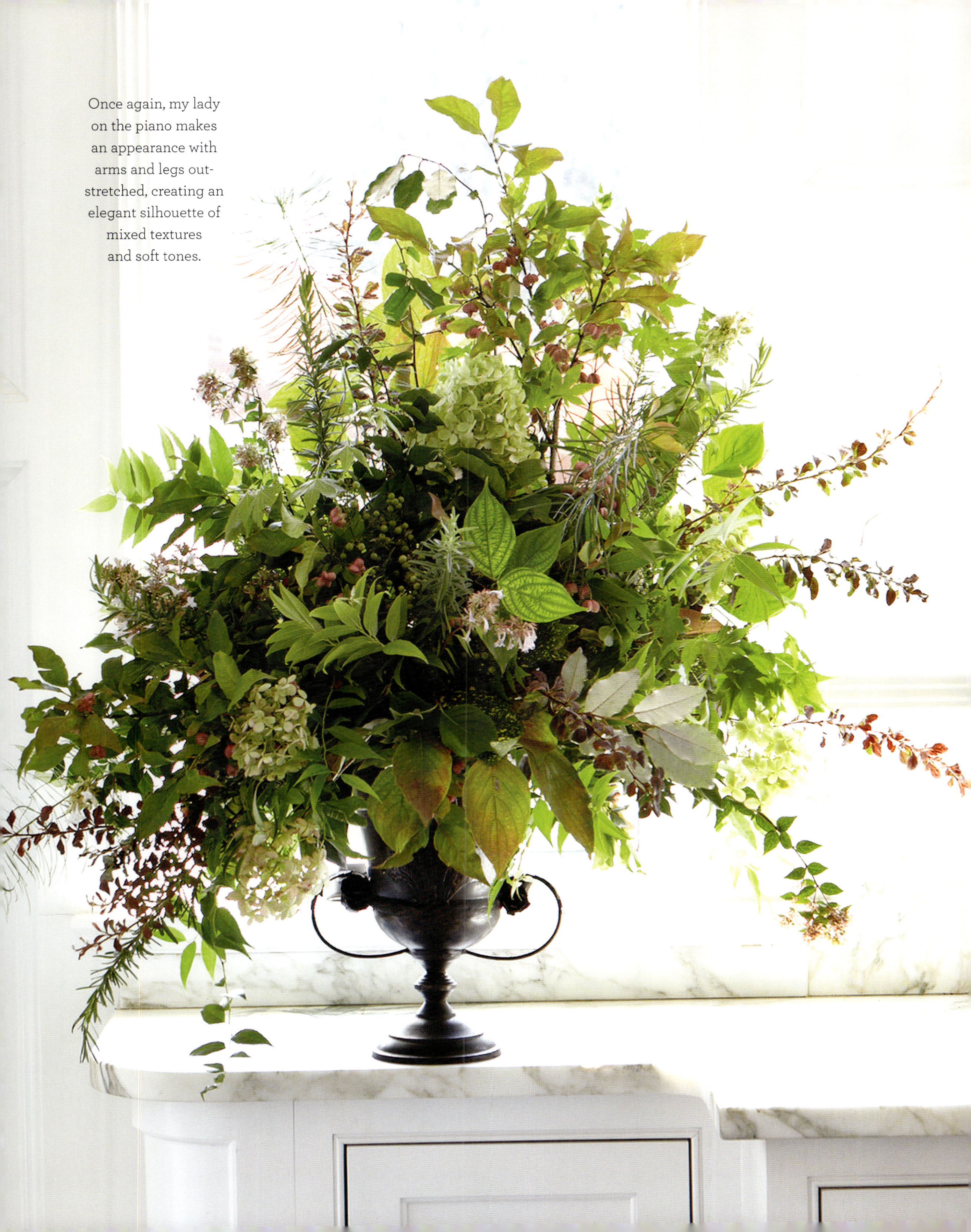

Once again, my lady on the piano makes an appearance with arms and legs outstretched, creating an elegant silhouette of mixed textures and soft tones.

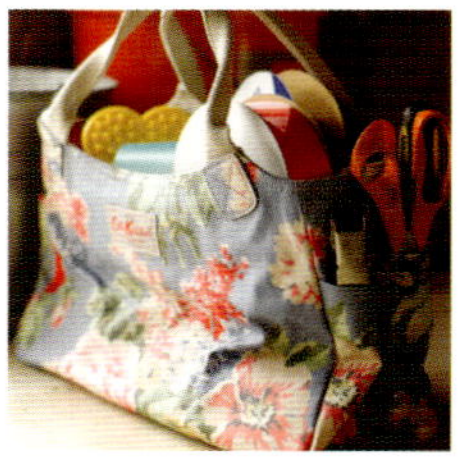

THE TOOLS
of the trade

Below is the list of the items I require in every toolbox.

1 Floral foil: my preference is green on green
2 Glass cleaner.
3 Oasis Floracage and Igloo Holder
4 Goo Gone to remove sticky label residue from glass or other containers
5 Mister or spray bottle
6 Clear plastic liners: "Lomey" dishes
7 Various beautiful ribbons to tie off buquets or to dress up a gift arrangement
8 Binding wire and jute twine that I use to secure the hand-tied bouquet
9 Cling and various floral tapes
10 Florist scissors
11 Floral knife
12 Ribbon scissors
13 Wire clippers
14 Pruning sheers
15 Floral wire
16 Pipe cleaners or chenilles
17 Wired floral picks
18 Spool wire
19 Bamboo skewer
20 Staple gun
21 Candle pick
22 Pearl-headed pins
23 Moss pins
24 Boutonniere pins
25 Water tubes and water pick
26 Chicken wire
27 Metal stem stripper and rubber stem stripper
28 Round floral pin and a square floral pin box

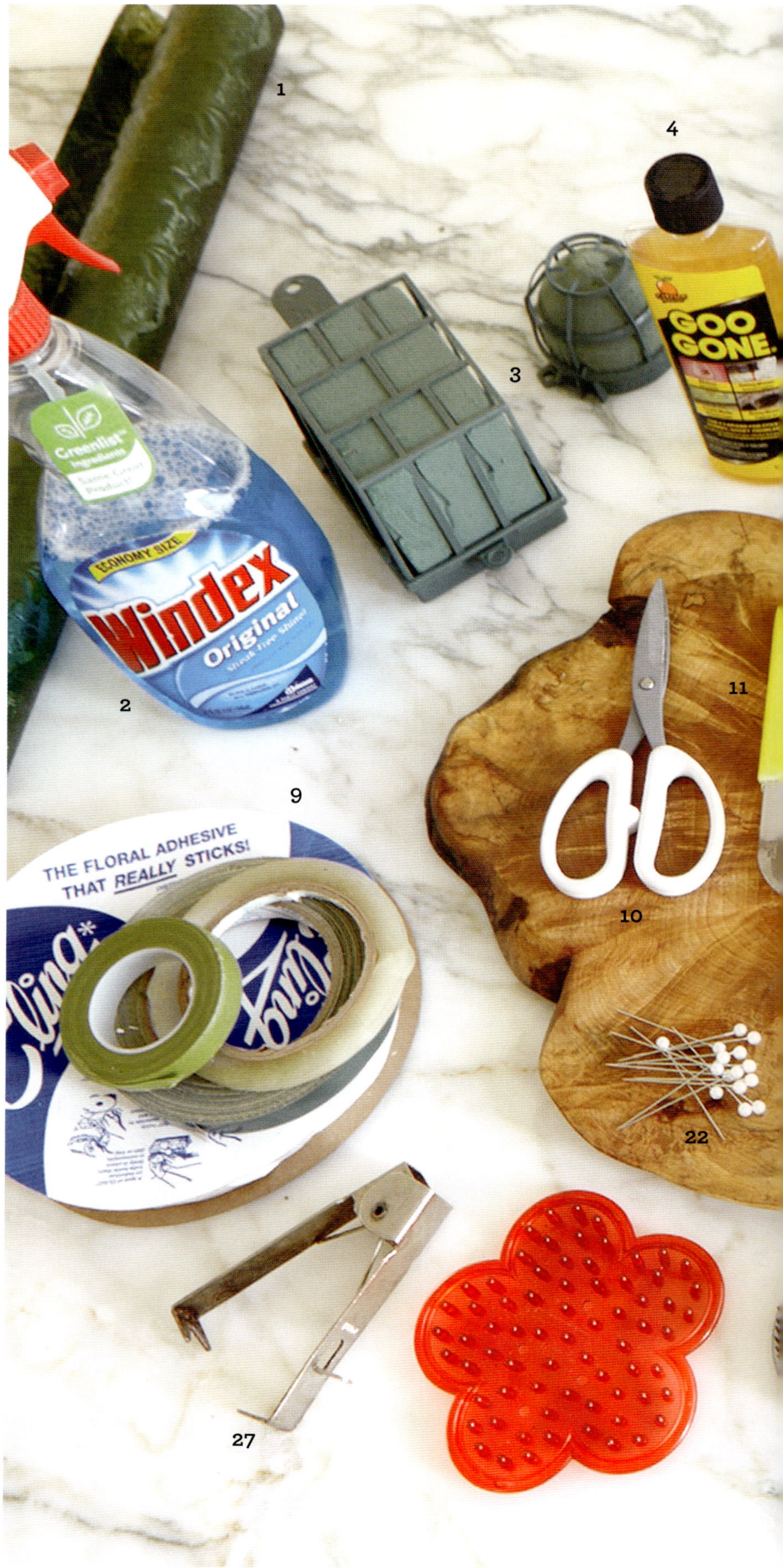

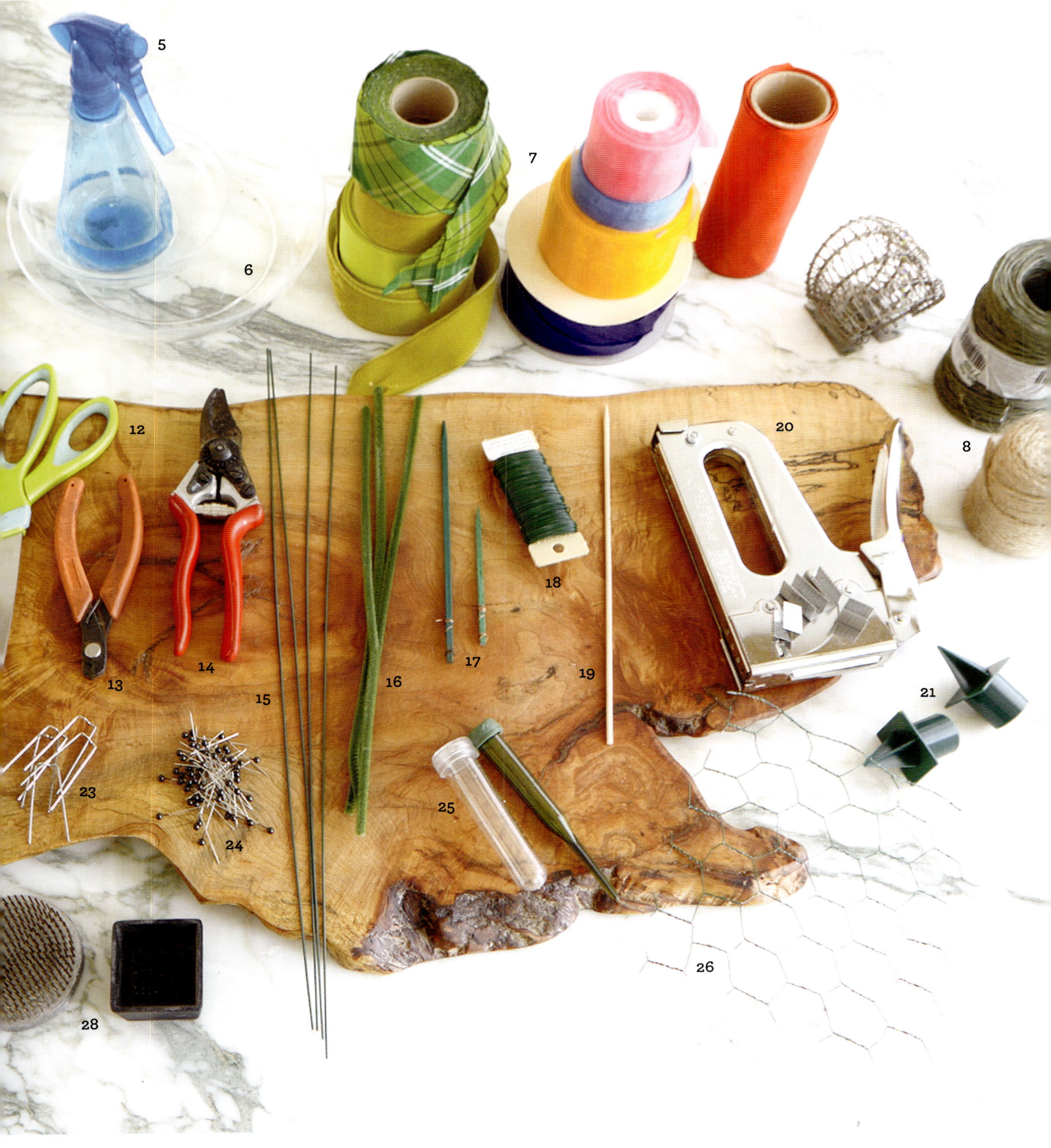
5
6
7
8
12
13
14
15
16
17
18
19
20
21
23
24
25
26
28

GREENERY GARLAND

a garland deconstructed

This technique can be used to make any type of garland—extremely simple to extraordinarily complicated. The final product is up to your imagination.

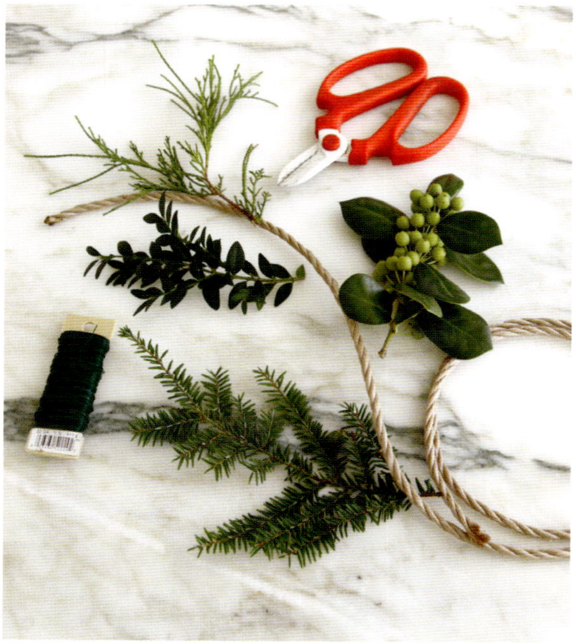

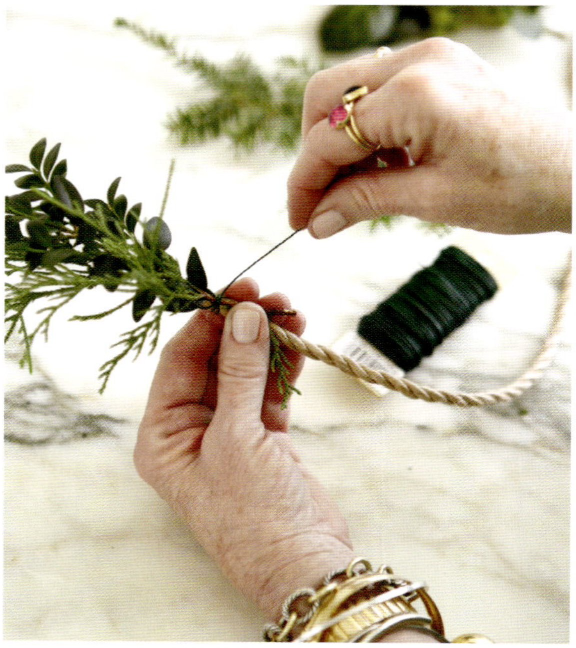

step 1

Cut a piece of string (for a lightweight small scale garland) or a small diameter rope (for a heavy mixed material garland) to the desired length.

step 2

Place the string on the floor and divide greenery beside the string, all stems pointed in one direction. Then move the greenery to cover the string, overlapping so that the stems are hidden (like scales on a fish).

step 3

Using spool wire, securely bind the greenery to the string, going over and over and down the string, pulling tightly to secure the stems to the string.

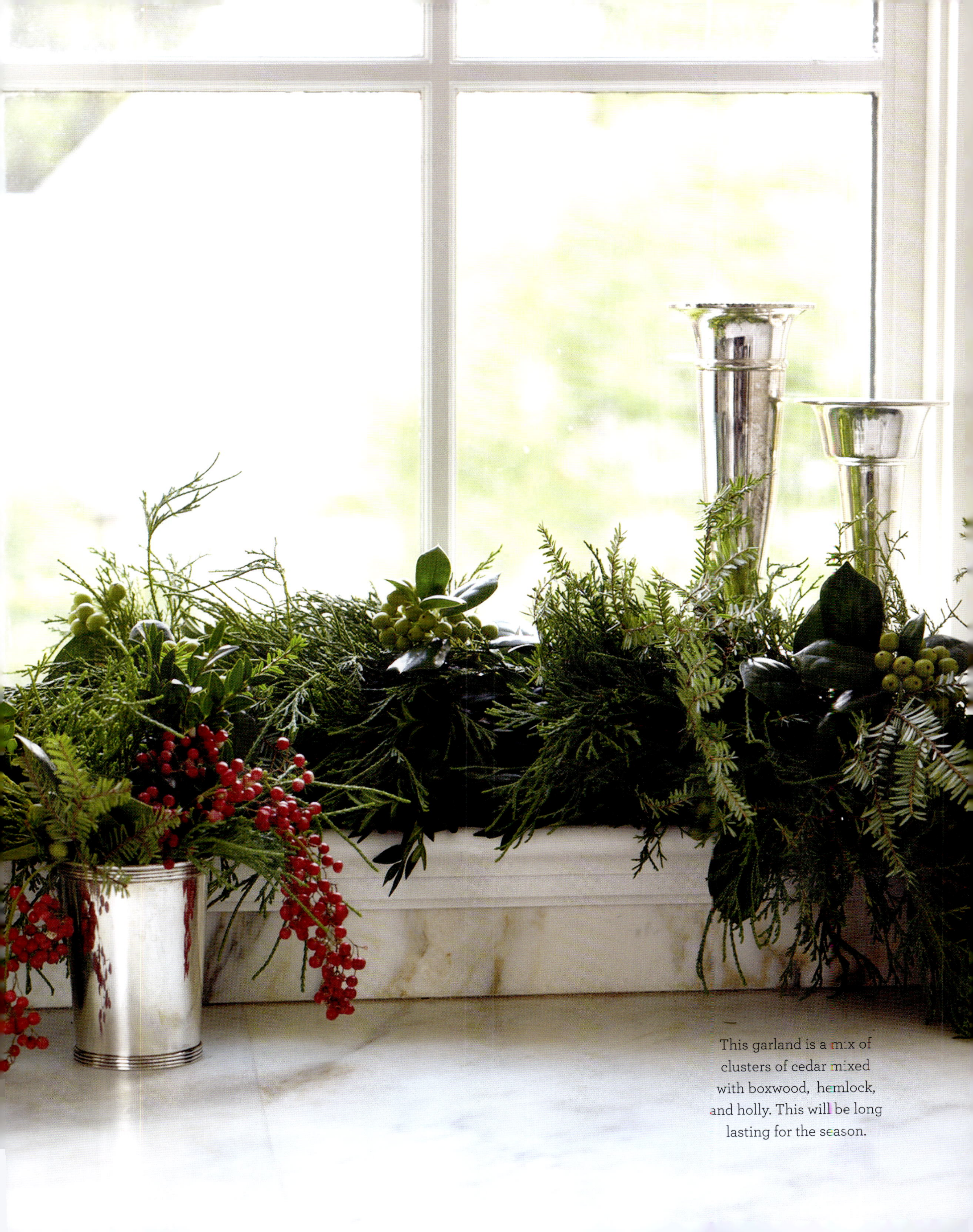

This garland is a mix of clusters of cedar mixed with boxwood, hemlock, and holly. This will be long lasting for the season.

A FLOWER CIRCLET

not just for the flower girl

I use the same technique to make a circlet as I do when I make a garland.

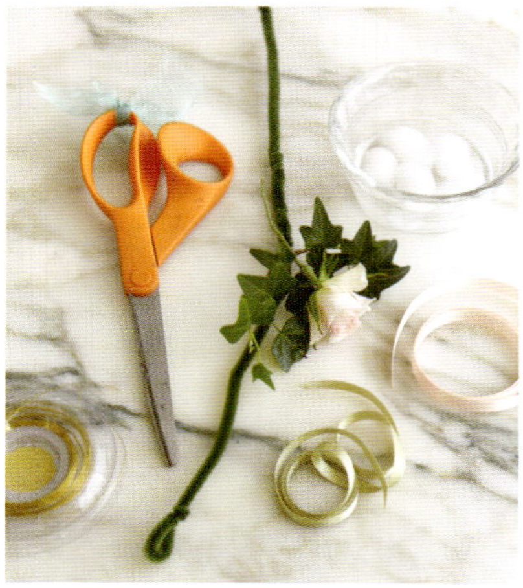

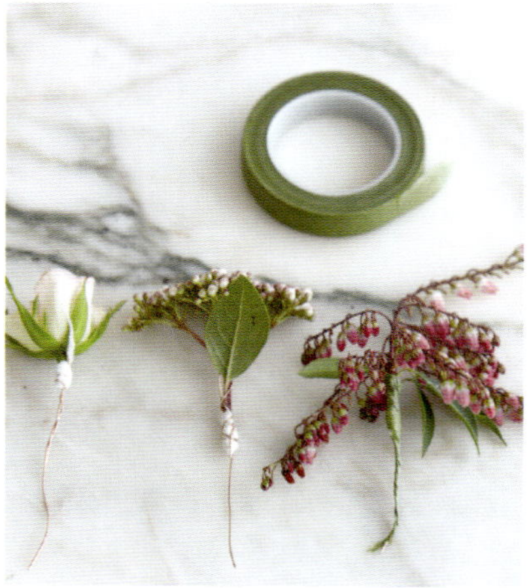

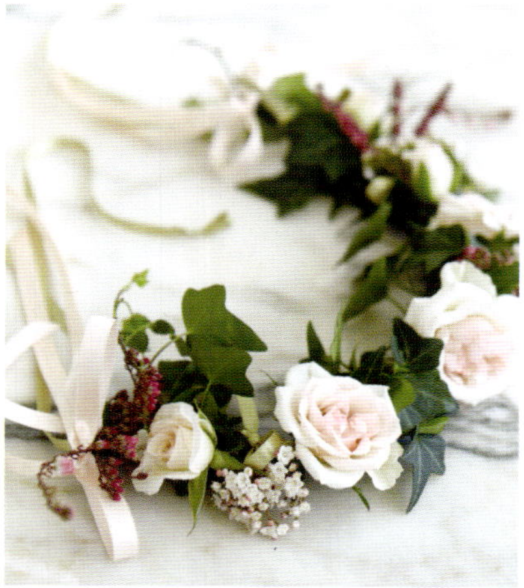

step 1

Begin by binding pipe cleaners together and cutting to the required length. I create a loop at both ends of the pipe cleaner for ribbons.

step 2

Working with soft greenery or herbs, cover the pipe cleaner using the same techniqe for making a garland.

step 3

If adding f.lowers, they must be hand wired and wrapped with floral tape prior to inserting them in the greenery. When complete, tie pretty ribbon to the end of the pipe cleaner loops. The flower circlet is complete.

the flowers

English Ivy, Pierus , Viburnum, Majolica Spray Rose

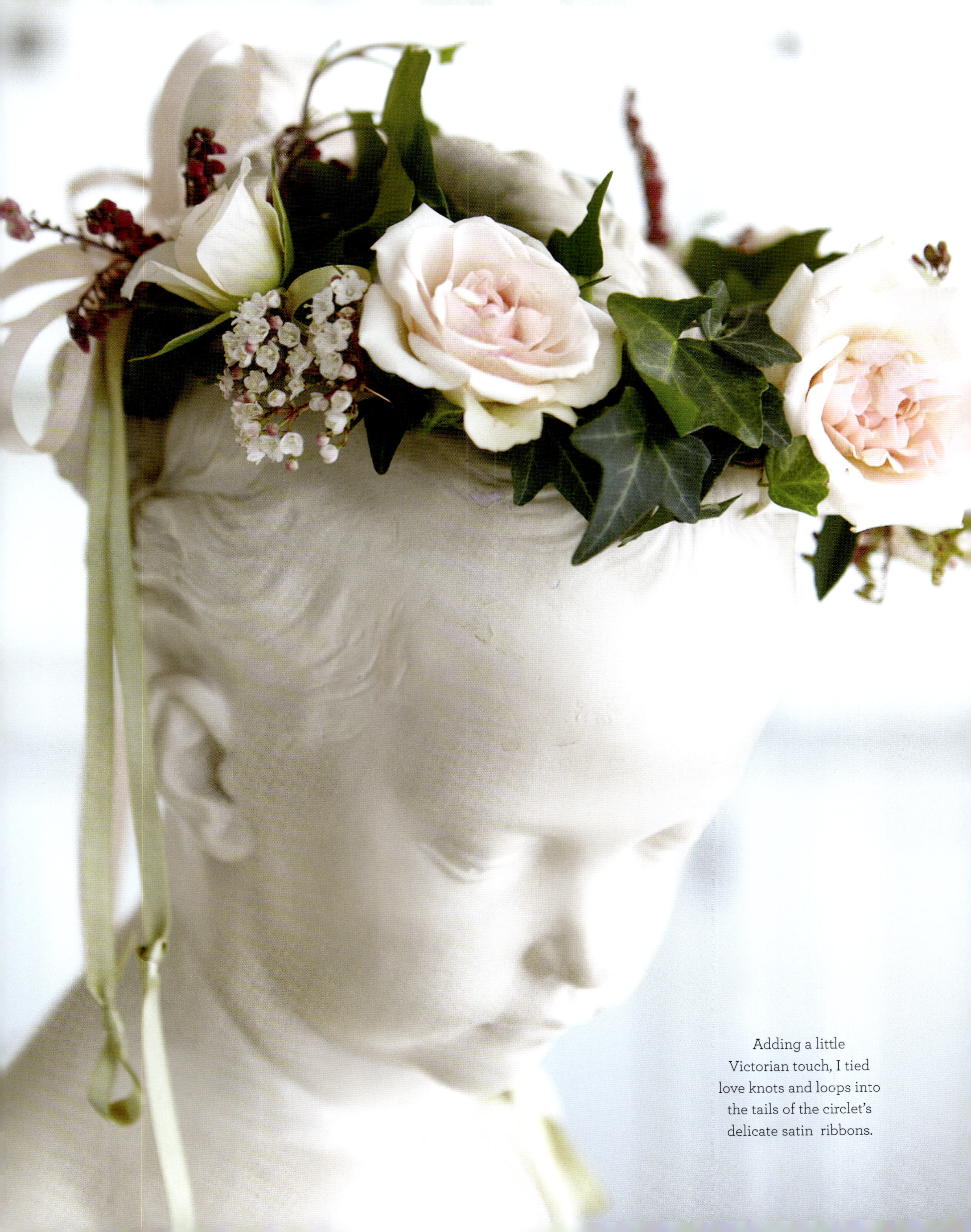

Adding a little Victorian touch, I tied love knots and loops into the tails of the circlet's delicate satin ribbons.

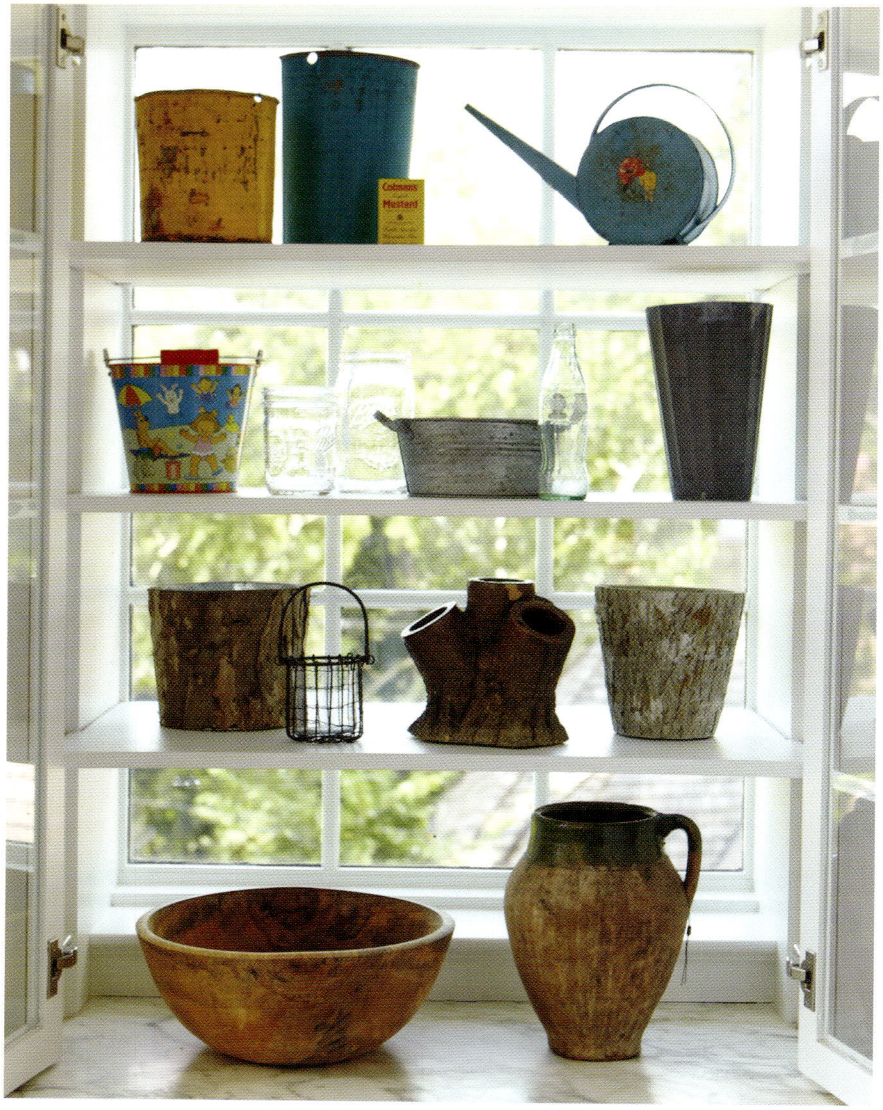

THE CONTAINERS

my ever-expanding collection

I'm passionate about my containers—When I opened the shop, I said that I would never create an arrangement in or sell a container that I wouldn't want to own myself. My mother and grandmother had plastic and pressed glass floral vases jammed into cabinets. I said, "No way!" I shopped garage sales, flea markets, and gift markets for unique things at a good price point that could be used again.

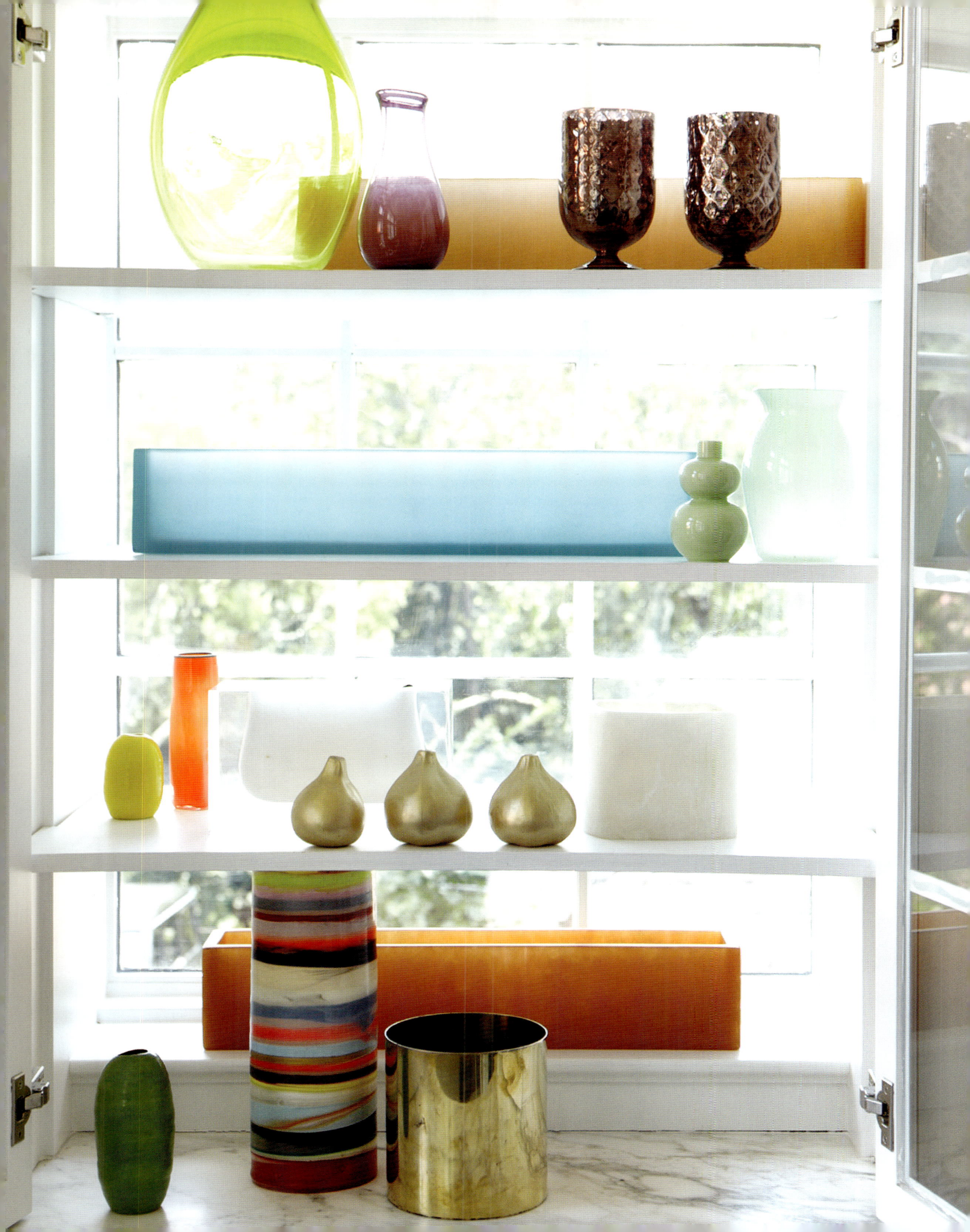

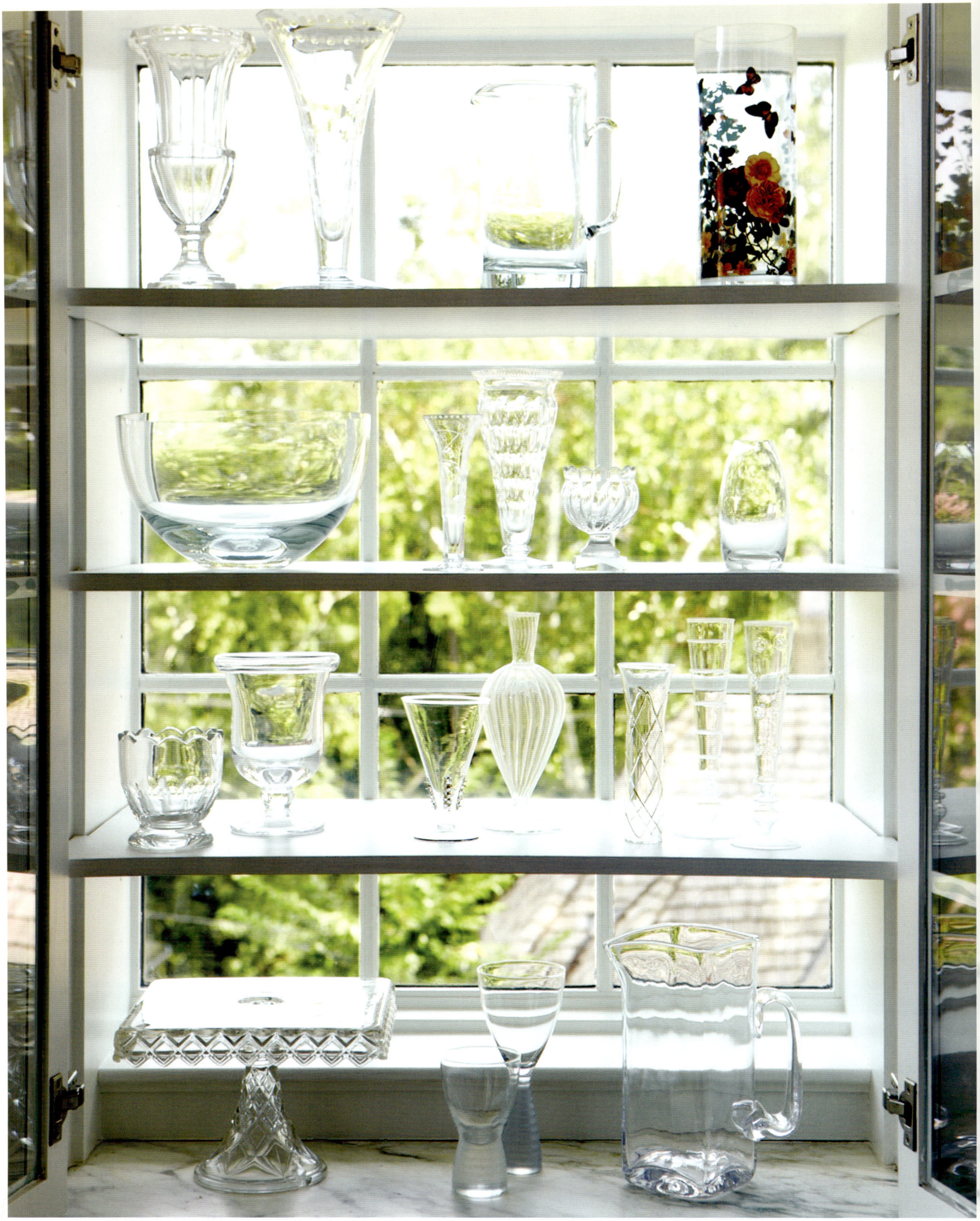

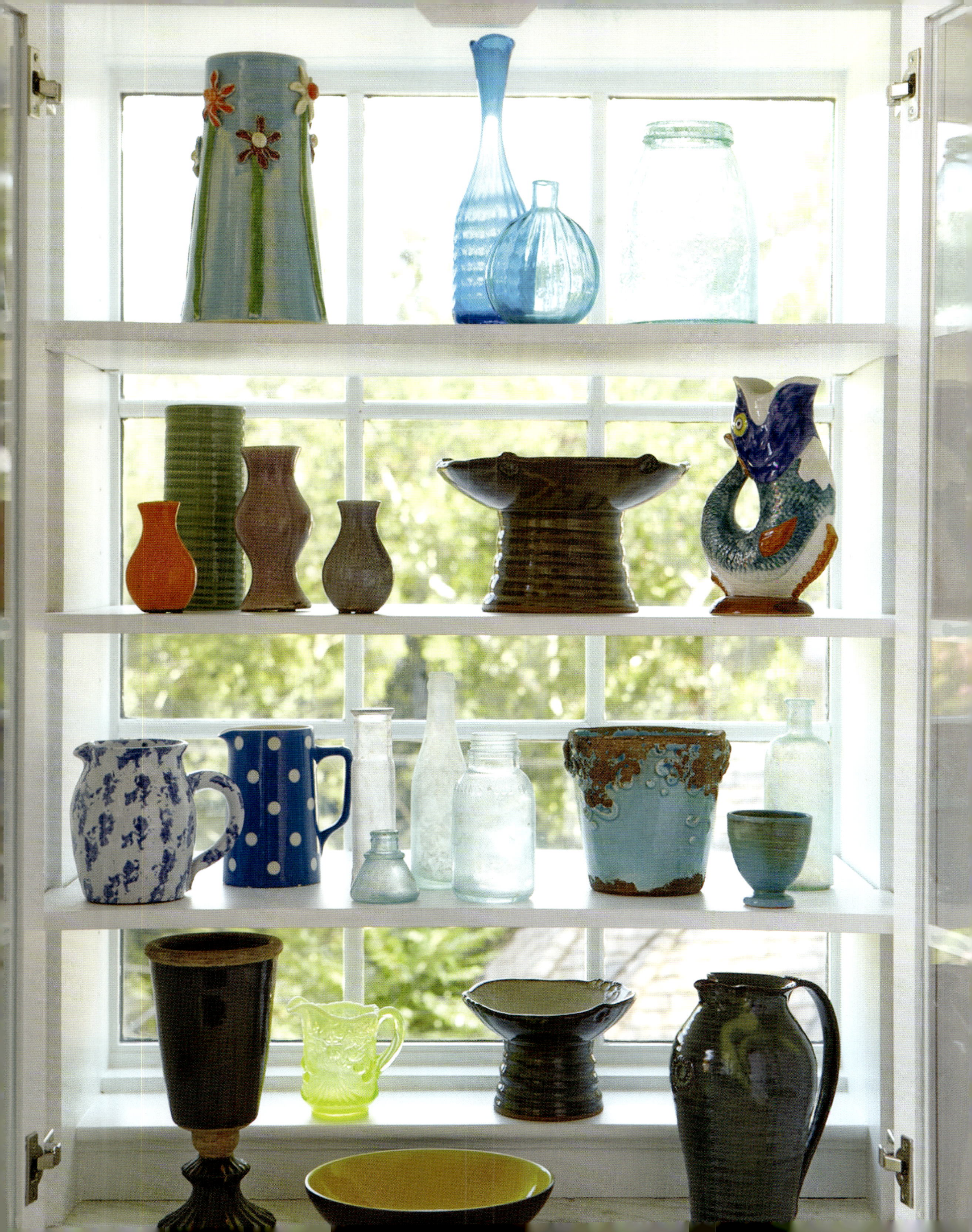

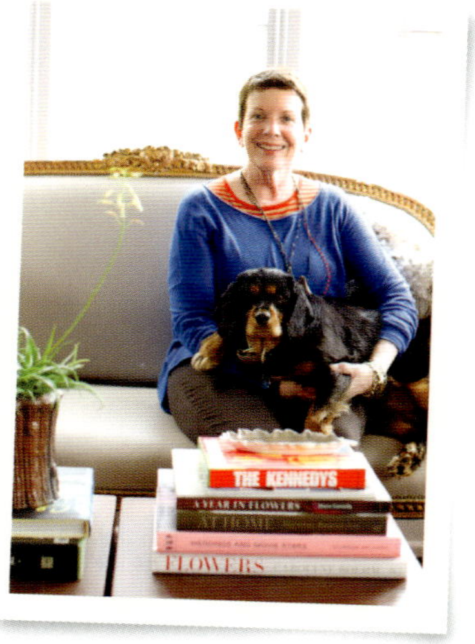

This is just the tip of the iceberg from my vast collection of containers. What you see here—crystal and glass, modern and traditional, rustic and primitive—shows my ability to create different moods and feelings for events and occasions through the choice of container.

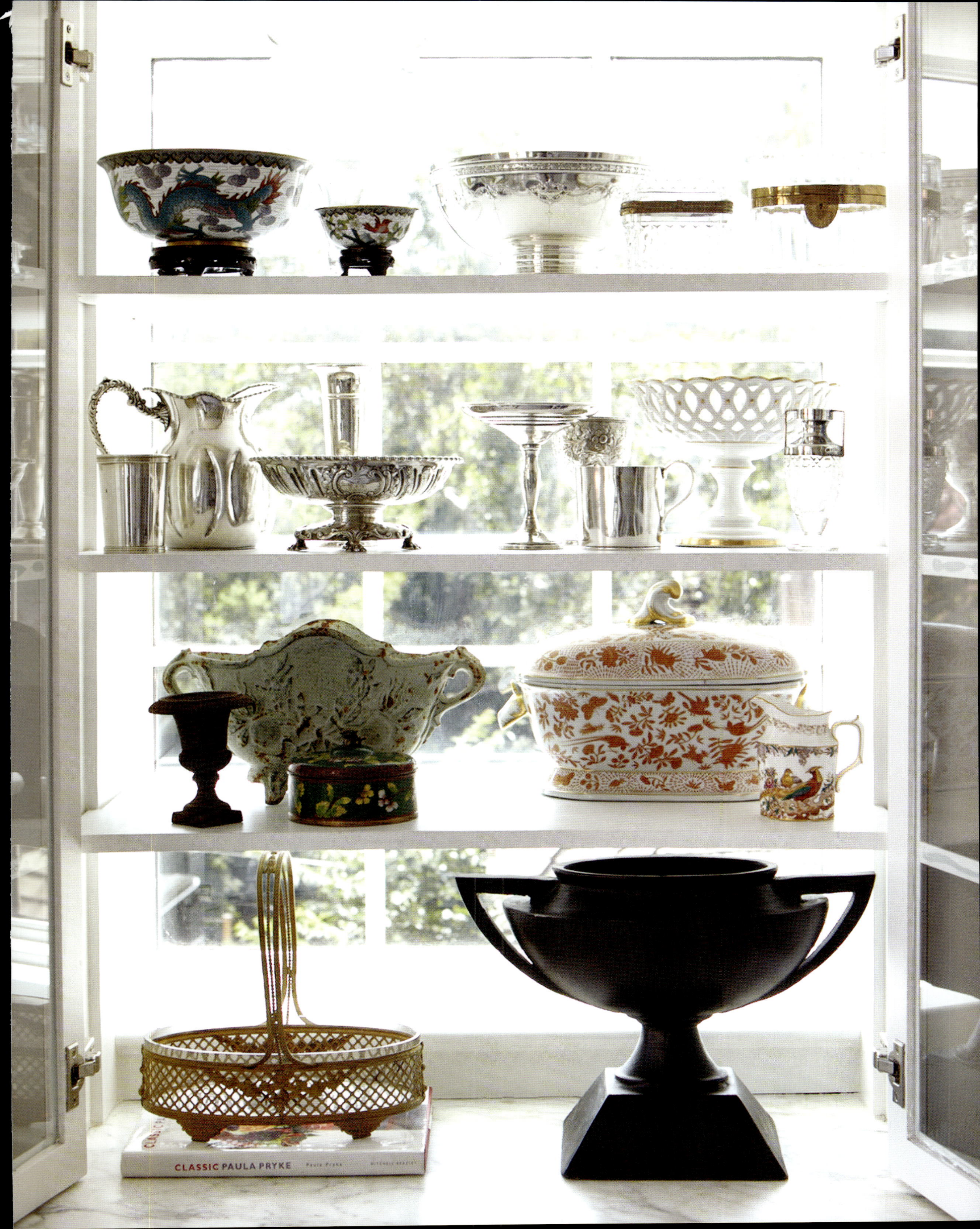
CLASSIC PAULA PRYKE

the flowers

The more time I spend working with flowers, teaching flower school and doing floral demonstrations, the more I realize how important it is to give all the specifics. On the following pages you will see a sampling of what I made, how I accomplished it and the flowers I used, and you can then do whatever you want to make the arrangements your own, using these creations to inspire your own fresh ideas.

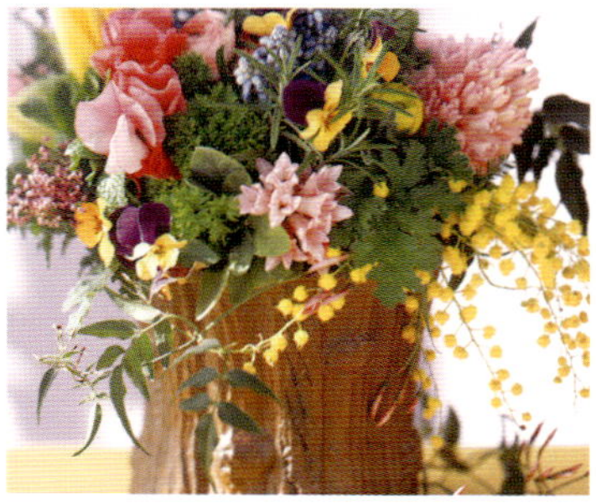

page 17

Parsley, Sage, Rosemary
Scented Geranium, Mimosa
Sweet Peas, Johnny-Jump Ups
Muscari, Hyacinth
Tulips, Ranunculus, Jasmine
Viburnum

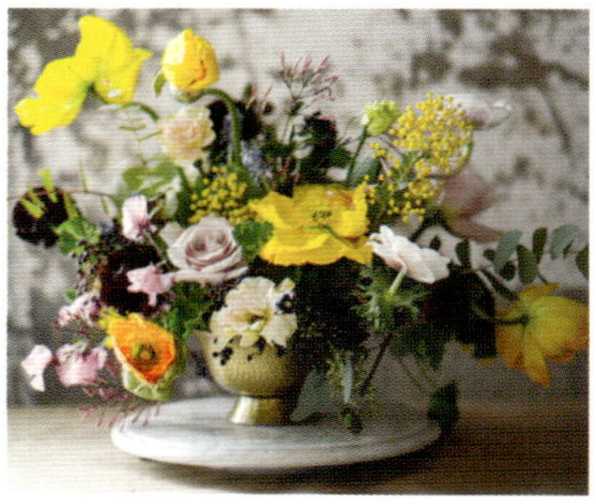

page 18

Lisianthus, Poppies
Anemones, Blackberries
Mimosa, Ranunculus
Sweet Peas, Jasmine
Eucalyptus, Tinus Viburnum
Muscari
Scented Geranium

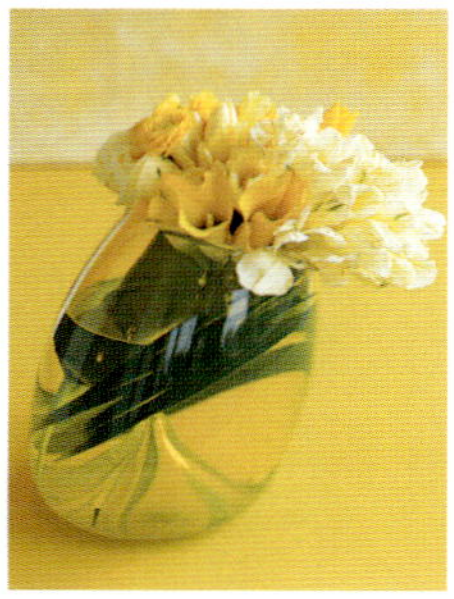

page 19

Calla Lilies
Ranunculus
Tulips
Parrot Tulips
Lily Grass

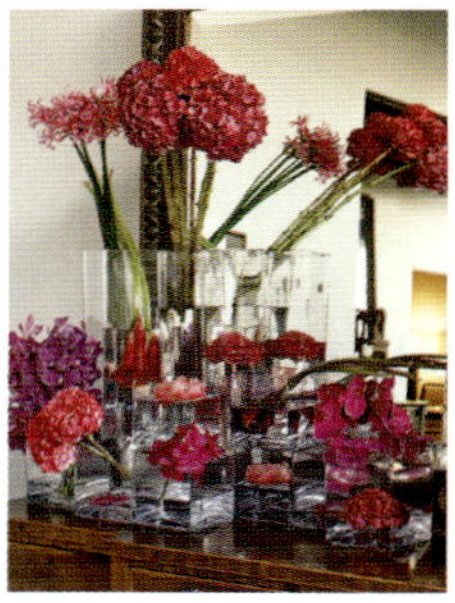

page 20

Pink Nerines
Calla Lilies
Hydrangeas
Vanda Orchids
Phalaenopsis Orchids
Coral Peonies

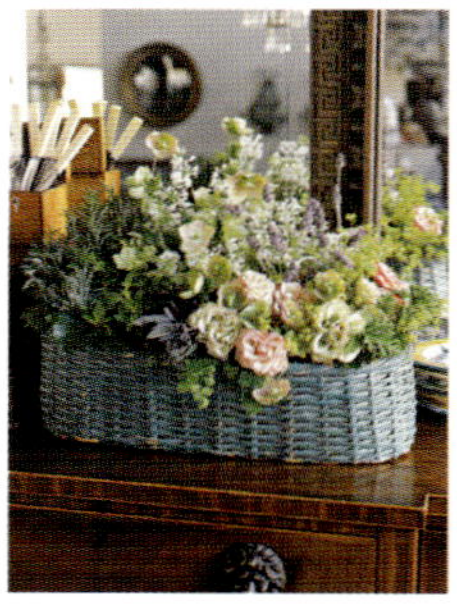

page 21

Lenten Rose
Rosemary
Lavender, Lilac
Lady's Mantle
Scented Geranium
Sage, Mint
Maidenhair Fern
Illusion Roses

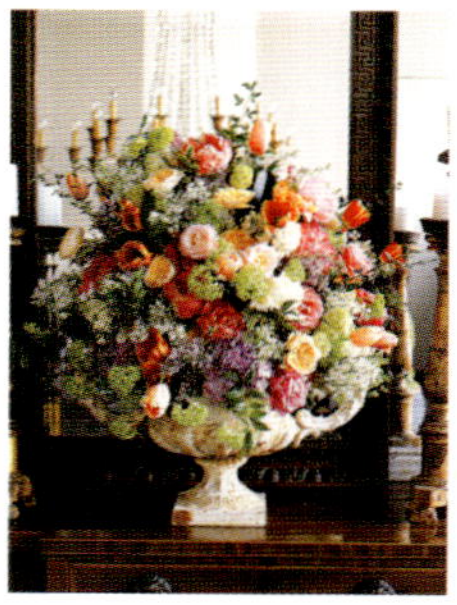

page 22

Garden Greenery
French Hydrangeas
Coral Peonies
Garden Roses
Phlox
French Tulips
Lilacs
Viburnum Clusters
Orange Tulips

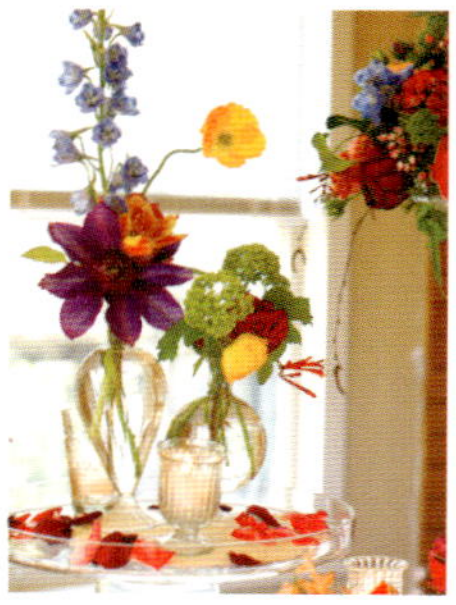

page 24

Delphinium
Poppies
Clematis
Bi-Color Tulip
Viburnum
Hyacinth
Phlox

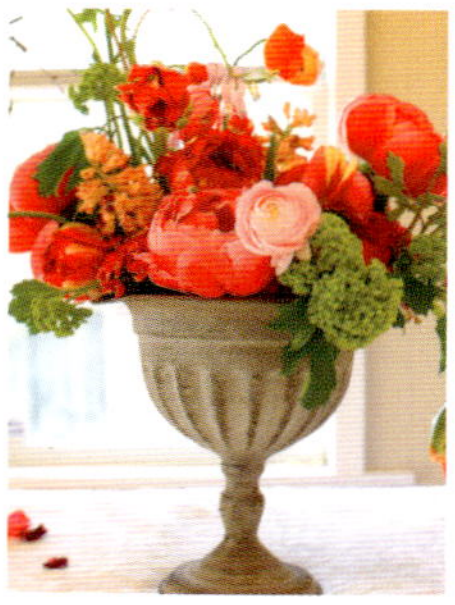

page 25

Double Tulips
Viburnum
Bi-Color Tulips
Coral Charm Peony
Hyacinth
Ranunculus
Poppies
Bleeding Hearts

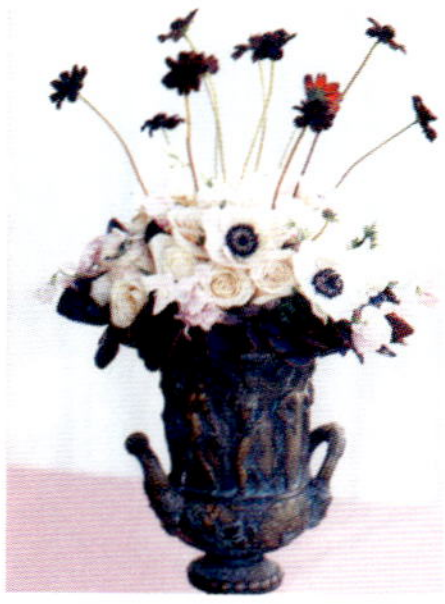

page 26

Smoke Tree Foliage
Blush Sweet Peas
Blush Anemones
Sahara Roses
Chocolate Cosmos

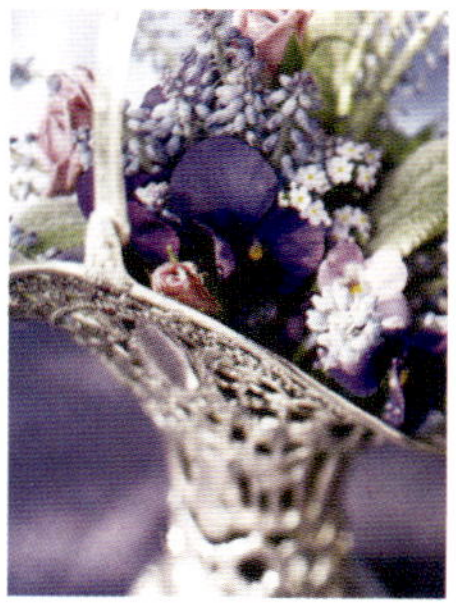

page 27

Forget-me-Nots
Lambs Ear
Little Silver Spray Rose
Violas
Pansies
Muscari

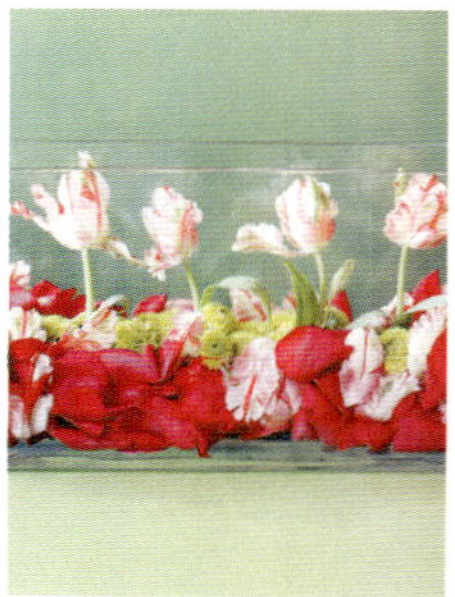

page 28

Peppermint Stripe
French Parrot Tulips
Kermit Mums
Milano Rose Petals

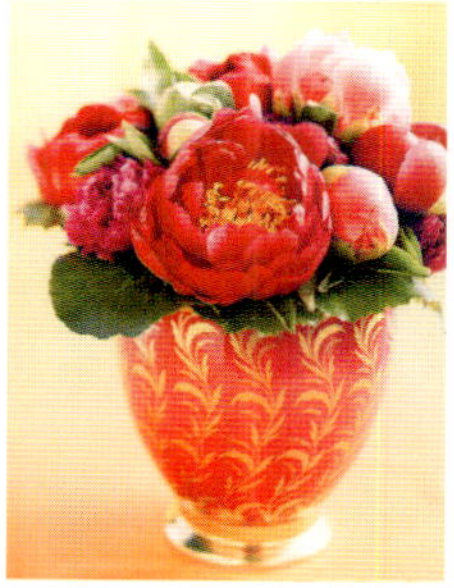

page 29

Coral Charm Peonies
Galax Leaves

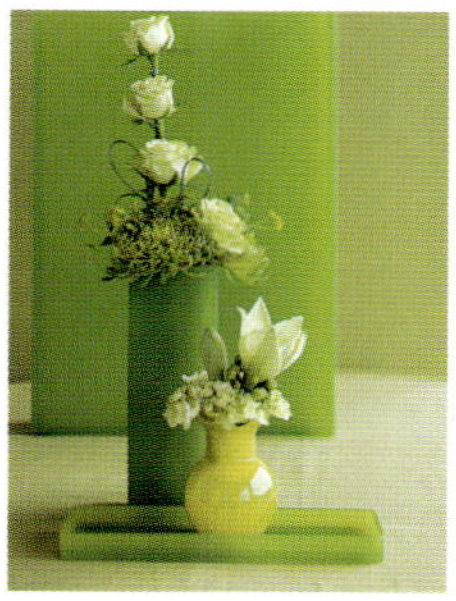

page 30

(left)
Jade Roses
Lily grass
'Shamrock' Fuji mums
Amaryllis 'Lima'
Lady's Mantle
Hydrangea
Hypericum Berries

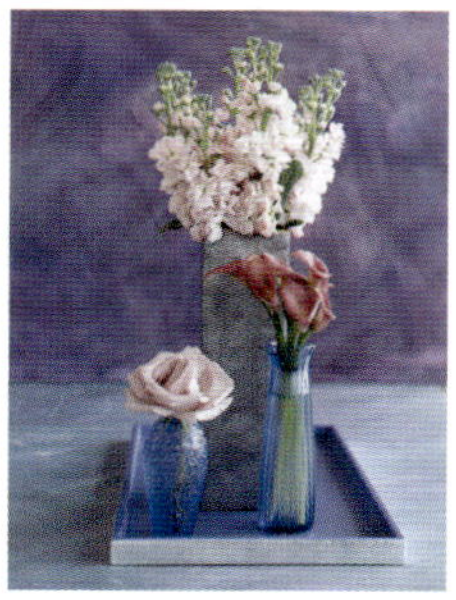

page 30

(right)
Lavendar Stock
'Night Cap' Calla Lillies
Sterling Silver Rose

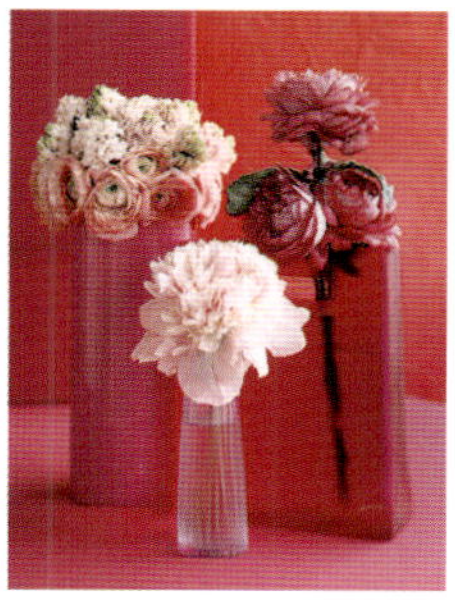

page 31

(left)
Catherine Fontaine
Peony
Yves Piaget Garden
Roses
Pale Pink Hyacinth
Ranunculus

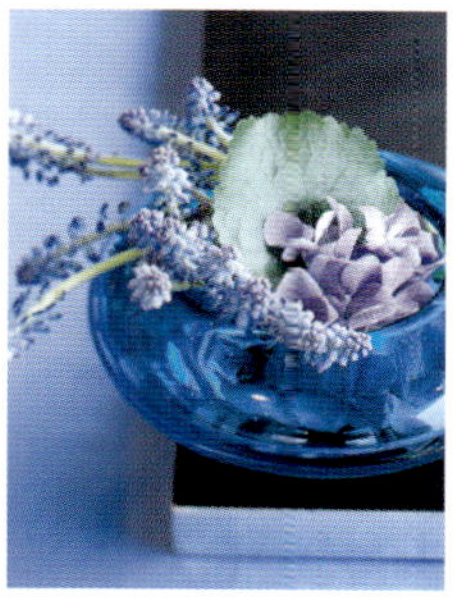

page 31

(right)
Blue Muscari or Grape
Hyacinth
Purple Hydrangea
Galax Leaf

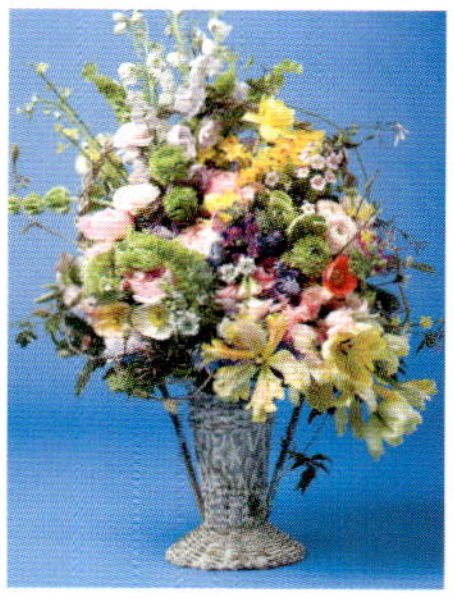

page 32, 33

Candytuft, Hybrid Delphinium
Bells of Ireland
Double Green Ranunculus
Pink Peonies, Daffodils
Soleil d'Or Narcissus
Euphorbia, Sweet Peas, Muscari,
Lavender, Viburnum
Lenten Roses, Poppies,
Jasmine, Tulip Magnolia Pods
Parrot Tulips, Primula

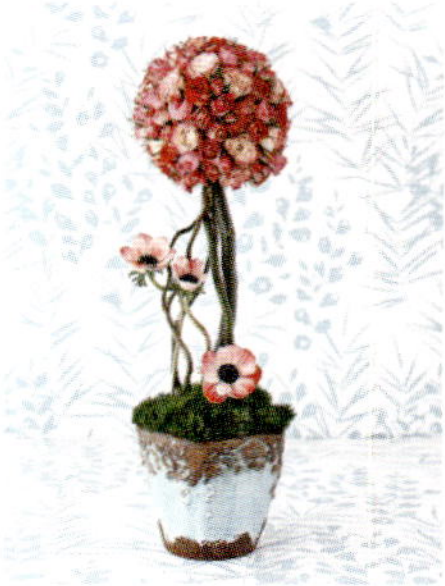

page 34

Light Pink Anemones
Pink Spray Roses
(Electra, Gem Pearl,
Gem Star)
Chilean Moss
Curly Willow

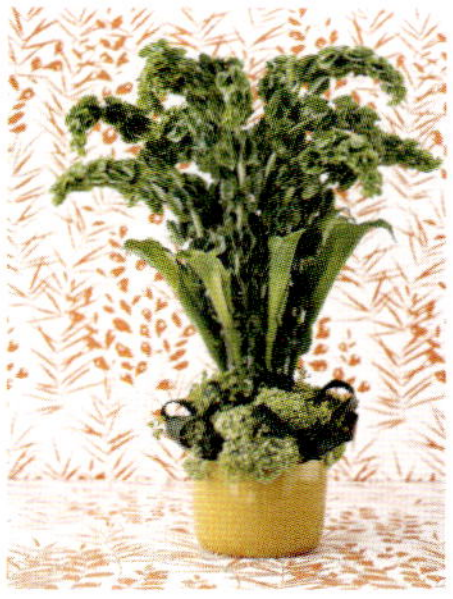

page 35

(left)
Bells of Ireland
Green Goddess Calla
Lillies
Viburnum
Ladies Mantle
Aspidistra Leaves

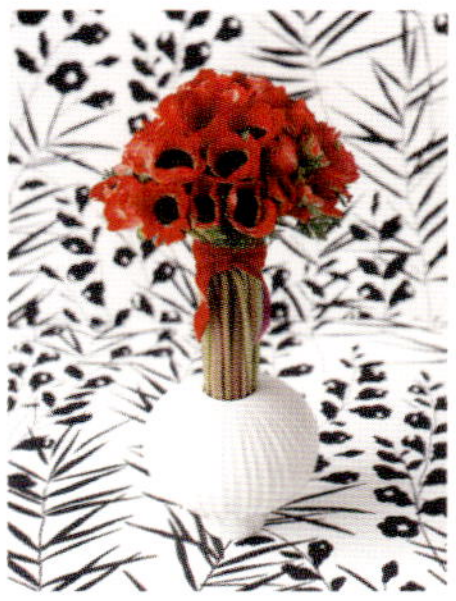

page 35

(right)
Red Anemones

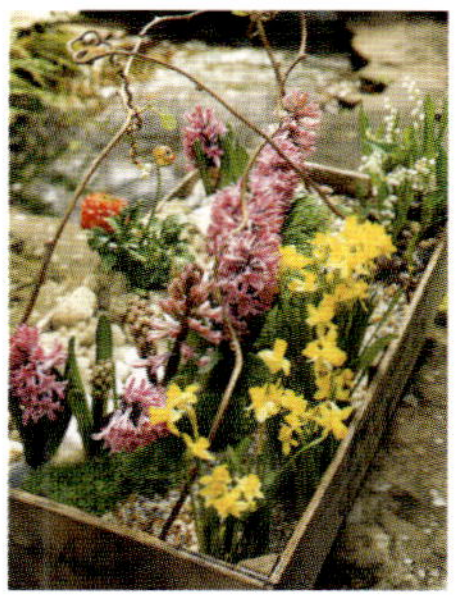

page 37

(top left)
Kiwi Branches
Daffodils
Ranunculus
Hyacinth
Lily of the Valley
Baby Tears

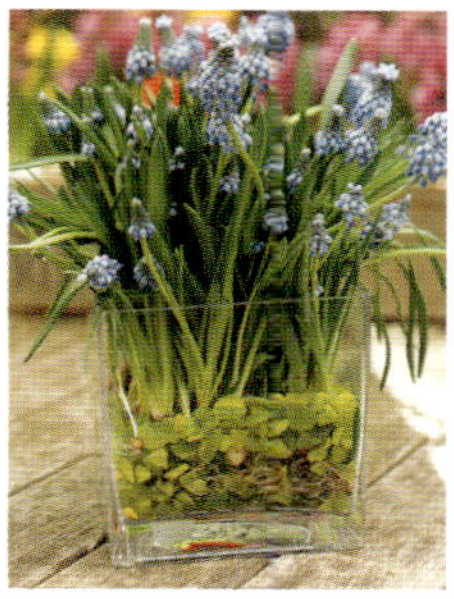

page 37

(top right)
Green sea glass
Muscari Bulbs

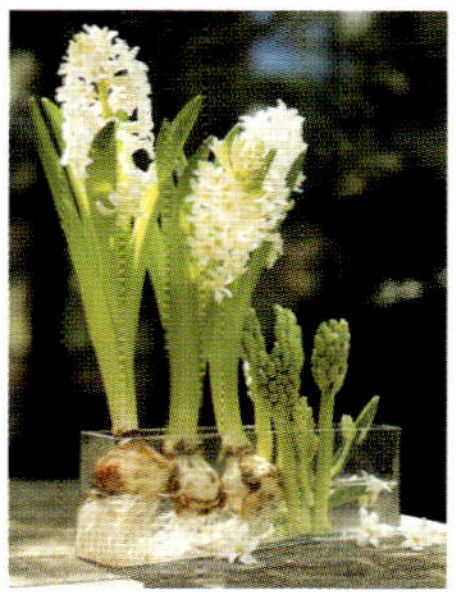

page 37

(bottom left)
Hyacinth Bulbs
Immature Cut Hyacinth
Stems
Hyacinths

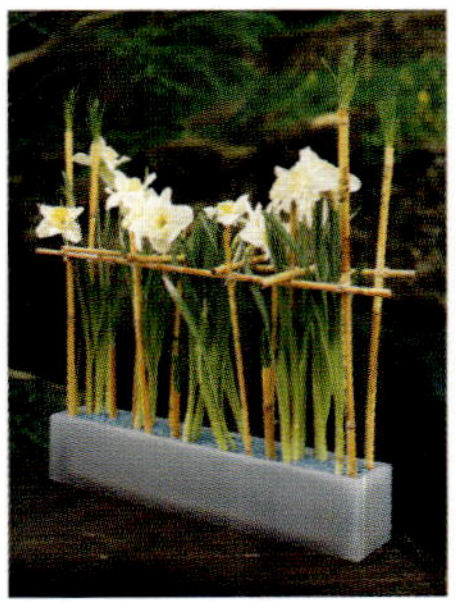

page 37

(bottom right)
Aquarium Gravel
Bamboo Poles
Raffia
Daffodils
Wheat Grass Tassels

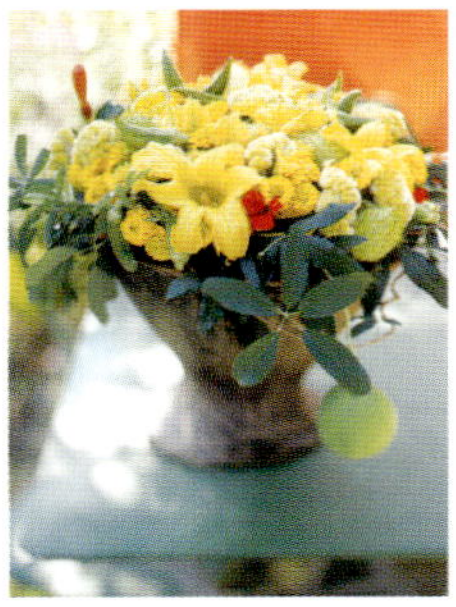

page 39

Squash Blossoms
Miniature Okra
Passion Vine & Fruit
Trumpet Vine
Zinnias
Nasturtiums
Cockscomb
Asclepias Pods

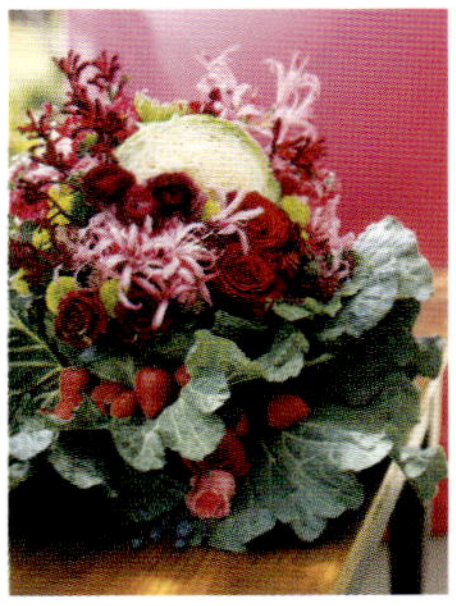

page 40

Cabbage
Strawberries
Burgundy Ranunculus
Black Magic Roses
Hocus Pocus Roses
Kermit Mums
Soft-Pink Nerines
Hot Pink Stock
Shamrock Fuji Mum
Burgundy Kangaroo Paws
Blackberries on the Vine

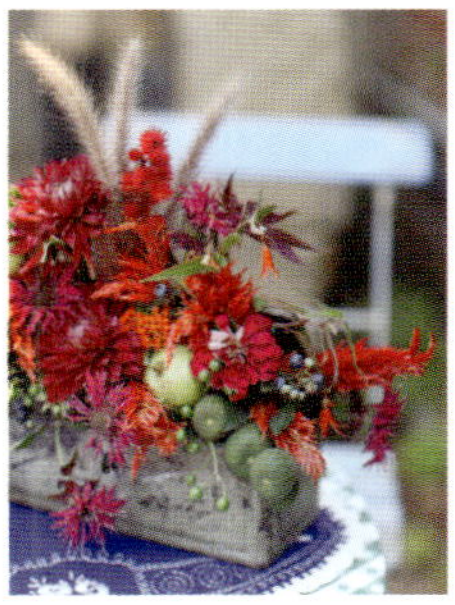

page 41

Dahlias
Feather Celosia
Chinaberry
Angel Wing Begonia
Monarda
Castor Beans
Zinnias
Grasses
Blueberries
Figs
Green Apples

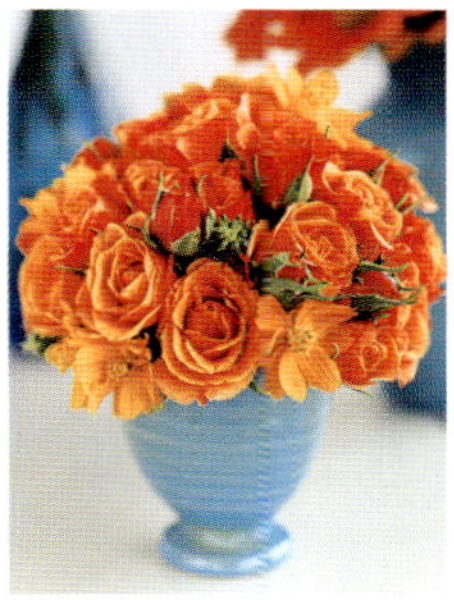

page 42

Ignace Spray Roses
Coreopsis

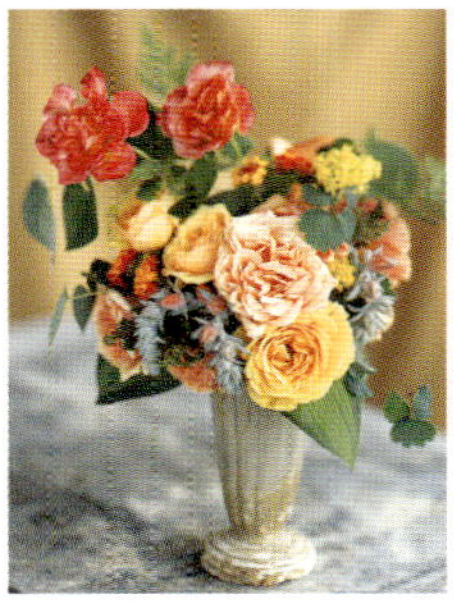

page 43

Lantana
Arborvitae Ferns
Hosta Leaves
Succulent blooms - echevaria
Garden Roses

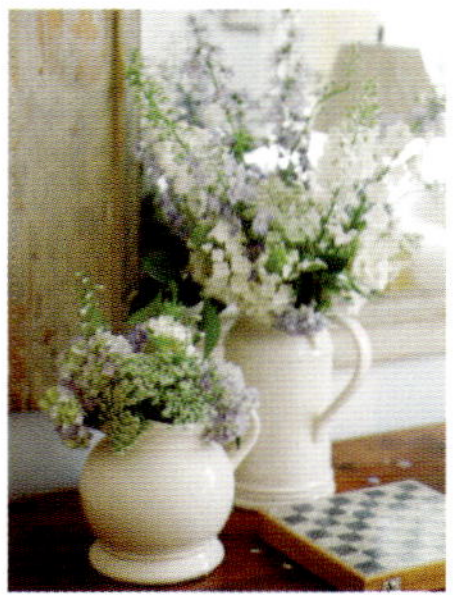

page 44

Hybrid Delphiniums
Snowflake Hydrangeas
French Hydrangeas
Queen Anne's Lace
Camellia

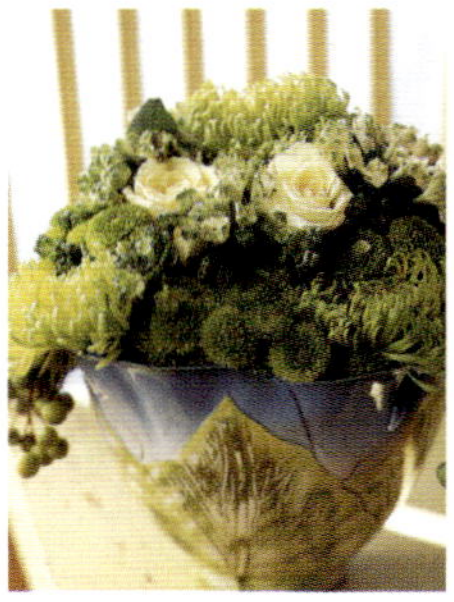

page 45

Chinaberry Clusters
Shamrock Fuji Mums
Kermit Mums
Green Bouvardia
Green Tea Roses

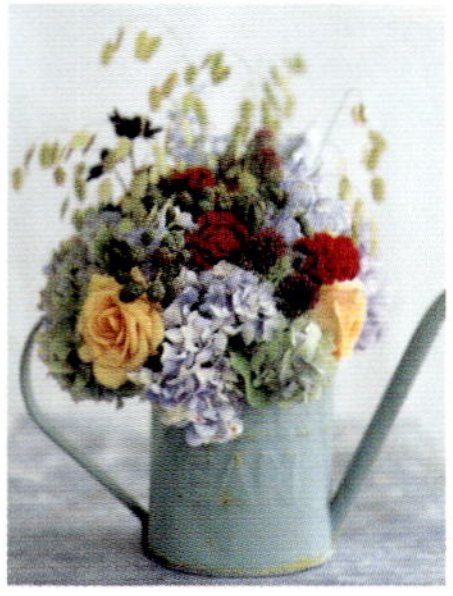

page 46

Nikko Hydrangeas
Bullet Allium
Celosia- Coxcomb
Chocolate Cosmos
Sea Oats
Blackberry Branches
High and Lucky Roses
Delphiniums
Nigella Pods

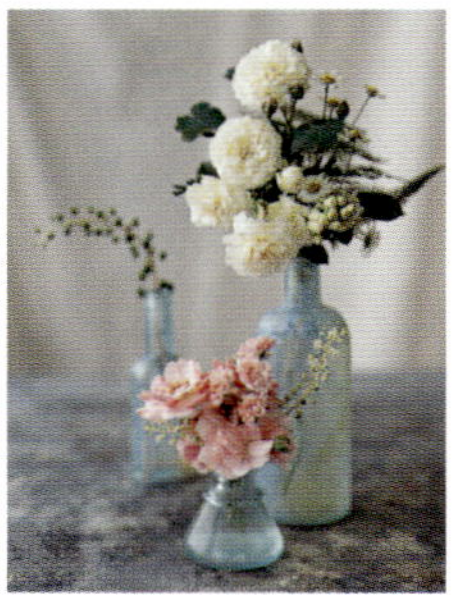

page 47

Climbing Garden
PurityRoses
Chamomile—Daisy
Variety
Tuberose
Maidenhair Fern
Pokeweed Berry Clusters

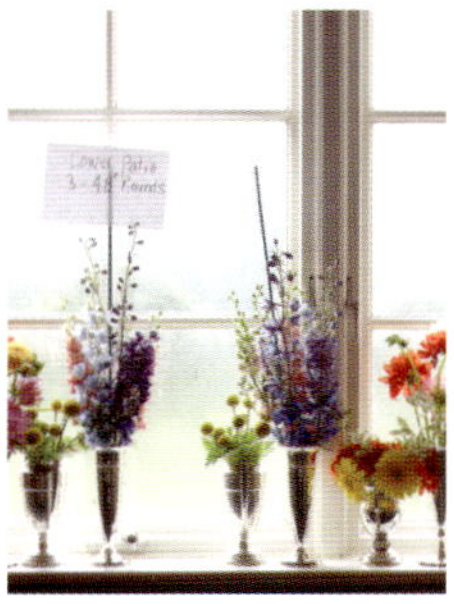

pages 48, 49

Delphinium
Dahlia
Stock
Larkspur
Gerbera Daisy
Billy Balls
Scented Geranium
Hosta

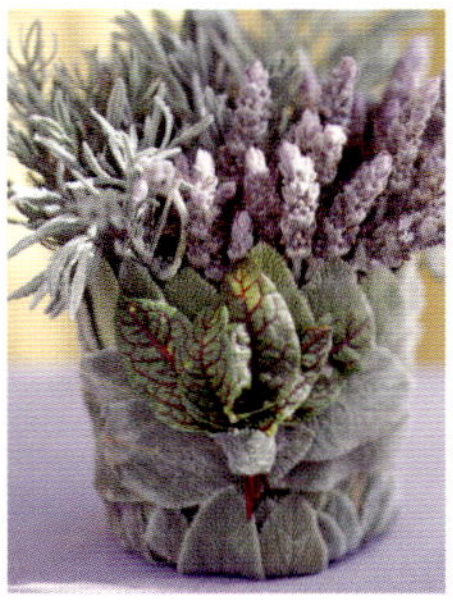

page 50

Lavender Blooms
Lavender Foliage
Lamb's Ear
Sorrel Leaves

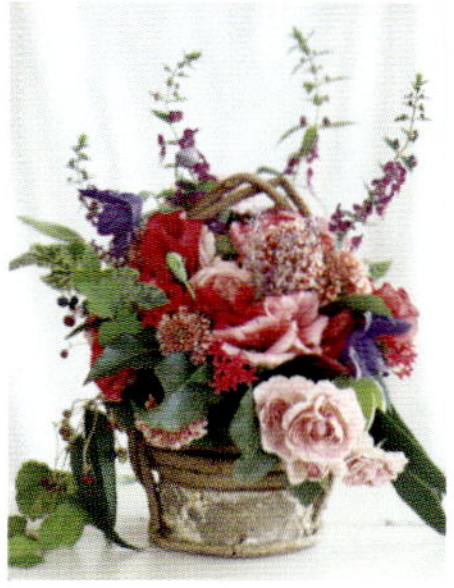

page 51

Porcelain Vine
Evergreen Clematis
Garden Roses
Lisianthus
Balloon Flower
Pentas
Lenten Rose Foliage
Pink Scabiosa
Angelina
Hosta Leaves

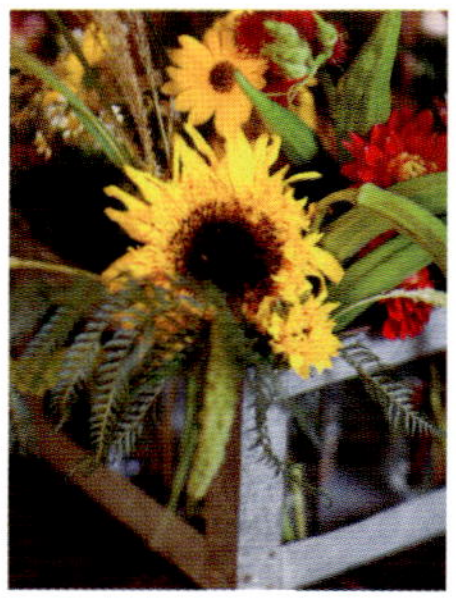

pages 52-53

Sunflowers
Zinnias
Dahlias
Coreopsis
Castor Beans
Okras
Chamomile
Millet
Eschinops
Seed Heads

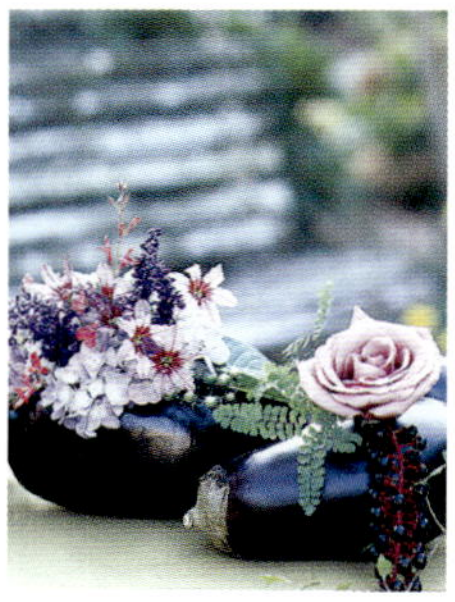

page 54

Muscari
Hydrangeas
Maidenhair Fern
Pokeweed Berries
Baby Green Cherry Tomatoes
Garden Spray Roses
Gomphrena Sterling Silver
Rose, Angelina, Ivy
Dark Ranunculus
Leucocorine

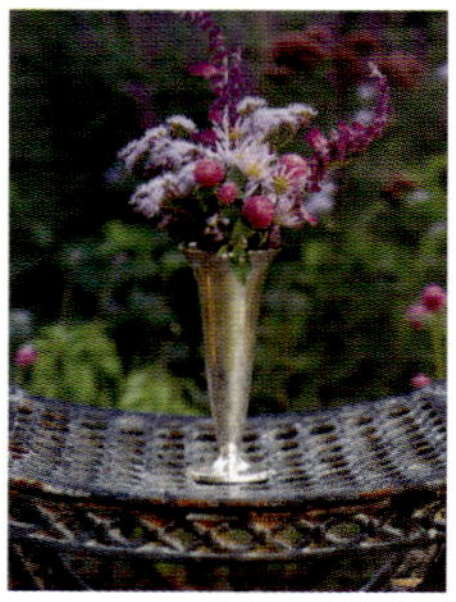

page 55

Mexican Sage
Ageratum
Gomphrena
Asters

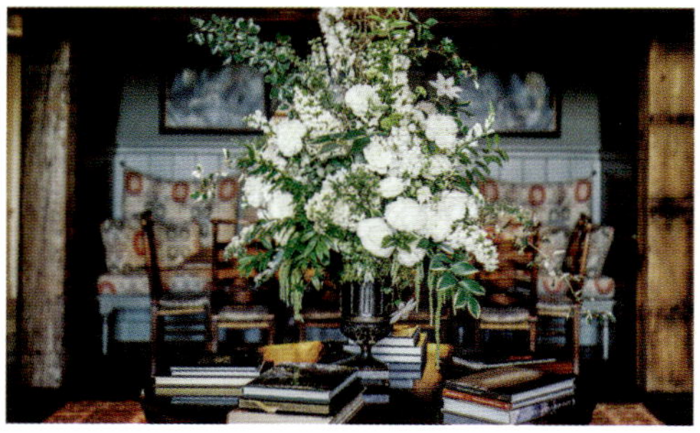

page 56

Assorted Garden Greenery, Solomon's Seal,
Leucothoe, Elaeagnus, Harry Lauder's Walking
Stick, Hybrid Delphinium, Snowflake Hydrangeas,
Peonies, Clematis, Spirea, Snapdragons
Hanging Amaranthus, French Hydrangeas
Polo Roses, Garden Roses

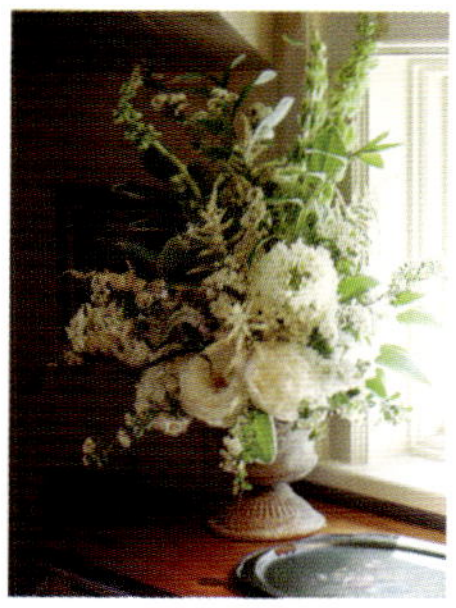

page 57

Snowflake Hydrangeas
Astilbe
Veronica
Bells of Ireland
Solomon's Seal
Hosta, Viburnum
Peony, Garden Roses
Stock

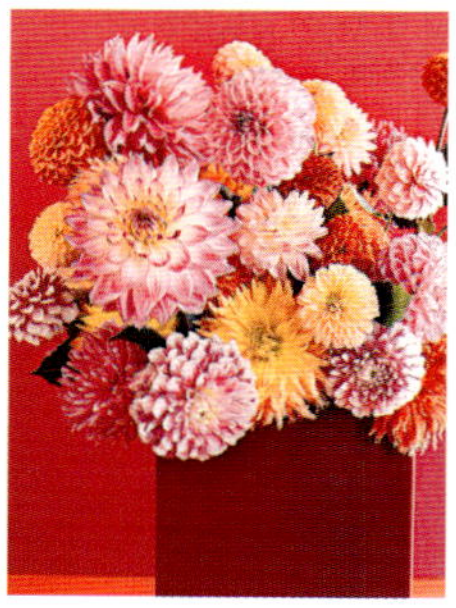

page 58

Dahlias

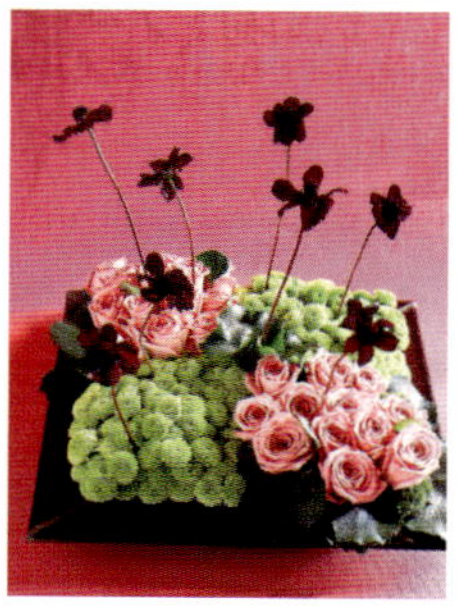

page 59

(left)
Kermit Mums
Pink Roses
Galax Leaves
Chocolate Cosmos

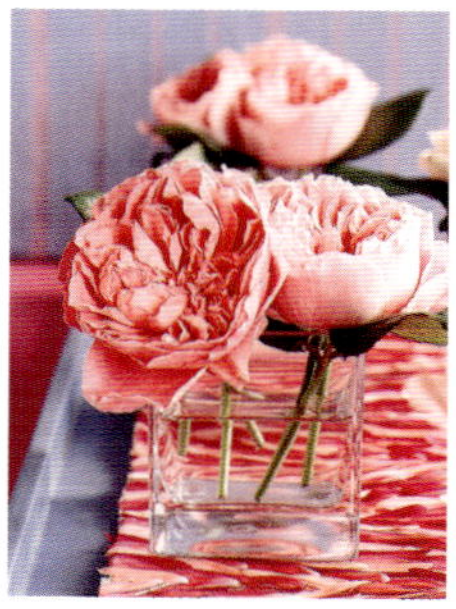

page 59

(right)
Gerbera Daisies
Olivia and Portia David
Austin Roses

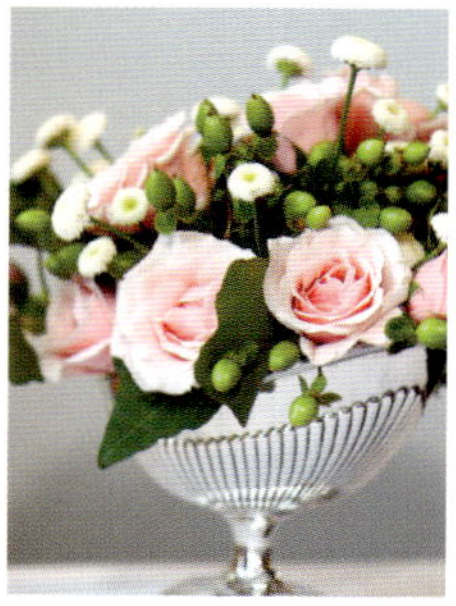

page 61

(top left)
Majolica Spray Roses
Button Chamomile
Hypericum Berry
Ivy

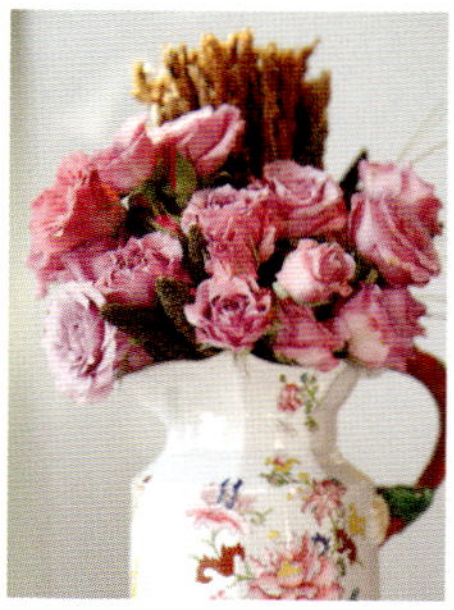

page 61

(top right)
Mixed Tones of Garden
Spray Roses
Grasses

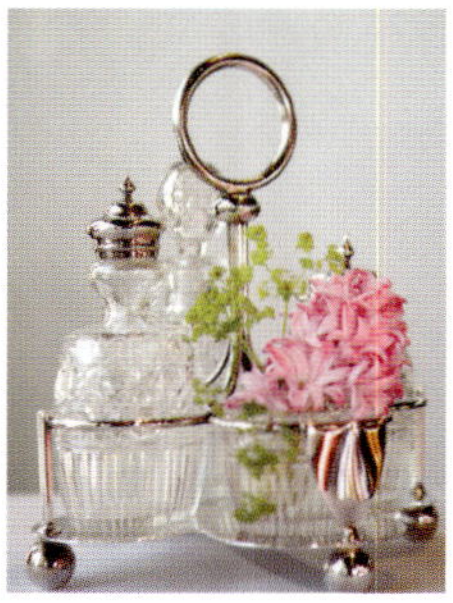

page 61

(bottom left)
Lady's Mantle
Hyacinth

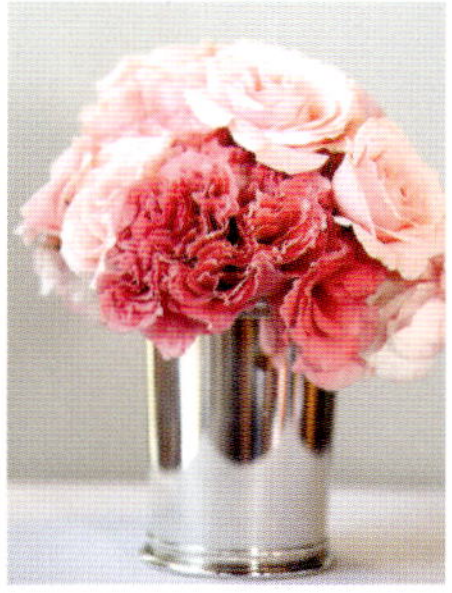

page 61

(bottom right)
Majolica Spray Roses
Pink French Hydrangeas

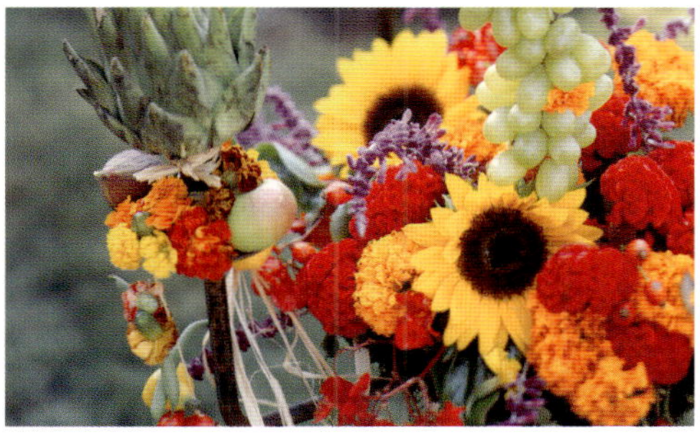

page 63

Rose Hips, Nasturtiums, Sunflowers
Mexican Sage, Marigolds, Coxcomb, Begonia,
Figs,Lady Apples, Artichokes, Grapes
Pittypan Squash, Zucchini Squash
Peppers, Haricots Verts

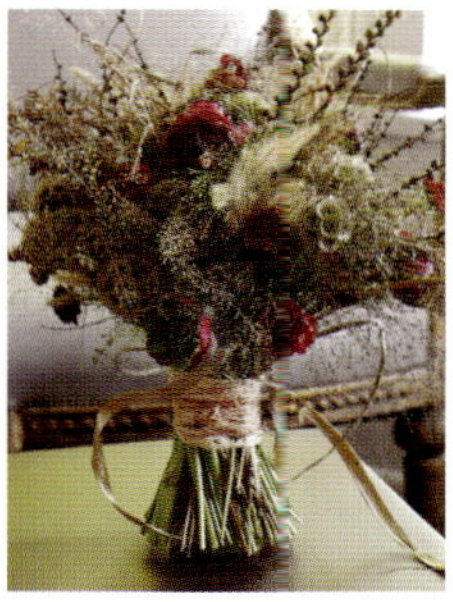

page 65

Dried Roadside Grasses
Scabiosa Pods
Ranunculus
Montbretia Pods
Cottage Scabiosa
Explosion Grass

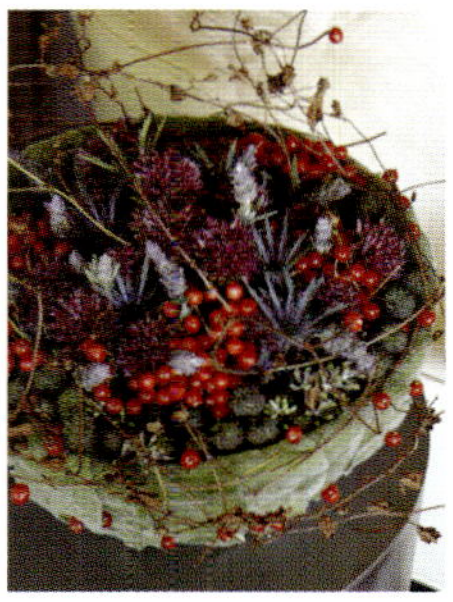

page 66

Lamb's Ears
Echinops
Viburnum Berry
Lavender
Castor Beans
Bullet Allium
Dried Morning Glory
Vine

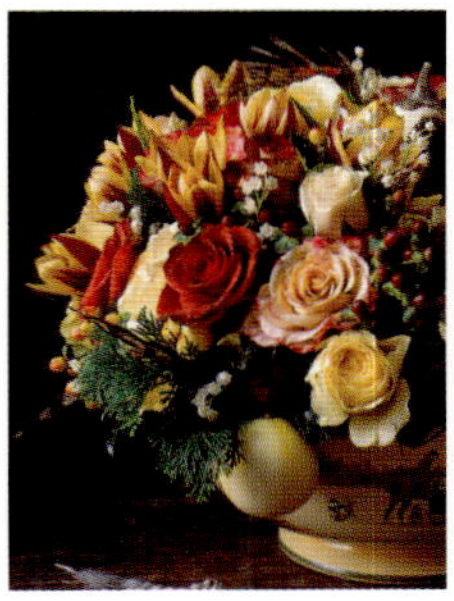

page 67

Evergreen Foliage-Hinoki
Cedar, White Eggplants
Skimmia, Rudbedkia
Pheasant Feathers
Hypericum Berries
Lily of Valley
Gardel and Campanella
Garden Roses
Leonidis Roses
Exotic Curiosa
Vendella
Bi-Color Pointed Tulips

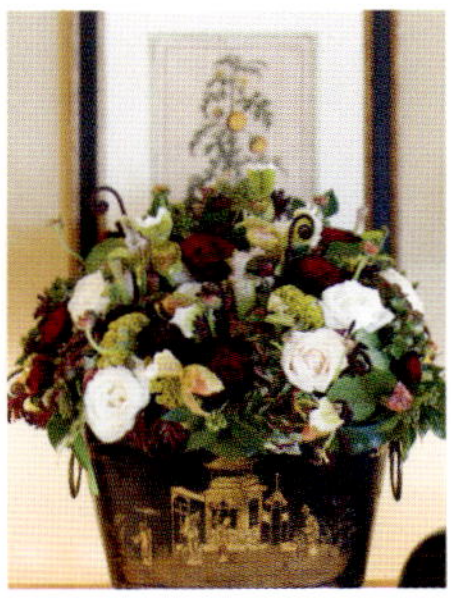

page 68

Lady Slipper Orchids
Fern Fronds, Seracina
Poppy Pods, Tree Ivy
Dark Ranunculus
Cockscomb
Burgundy Kanagaroo Paw
Antique Hydrangeas
Sahara Roses
Vendella Roses
Black Beauty Roses
Galax Leaves

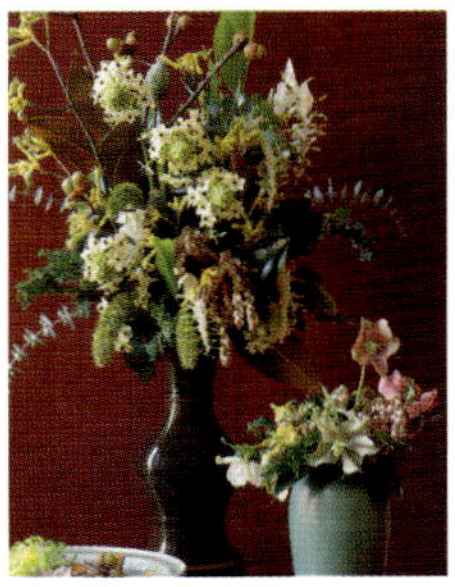

page 69

Ginger Lily, Pierus,
Acorns, Poppy Pods,
Millet, Eucalyptus
Arabicum, Yellow
Kangaroo Paw
Cedar, Little Gem
Magnolia,
Lenten Rose, Cedar
Pierus, Yellow
Kangaroo Paw
Shamrock Fuji Mum,
Magnolia Leaf

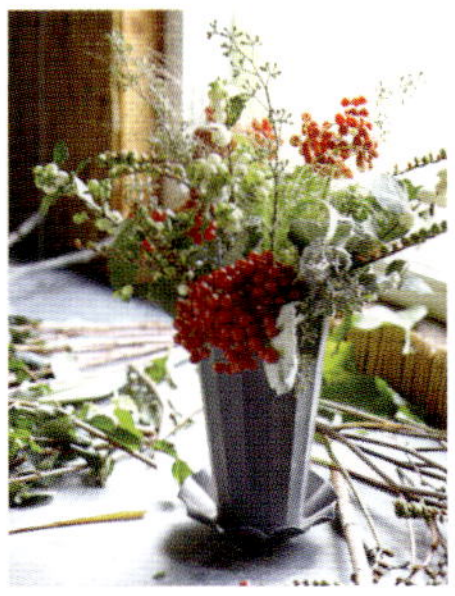

page 71

Dusty Miller
Seeded Eucalyptus
Snowberry
Montbretia Pods
Viburnum Berries
Explosion Grass

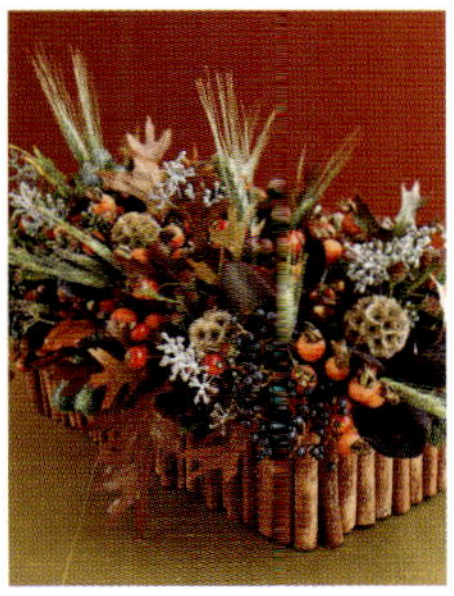

page 72

Seeded Eucalyptus
Scabiosa Pods
Tinus Viburnum Berries
Smoke Tree &
Oak Leaves
Wheat, Rose Hips
Leucadendron Pods
Pine Needles
Cinnamon Sticks
Aspidistra Leaves
Castor Beans

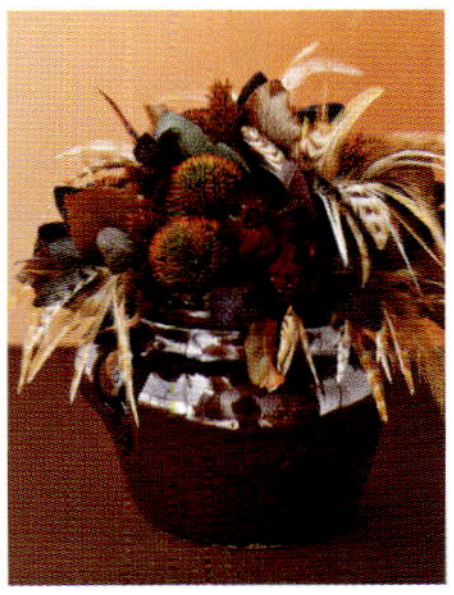

page 73

Smoke Tree Foliage
Echinacea Pods
Preserved Beech Foliage
Phalaris
Chocolate Cosmos
Feather Clusters

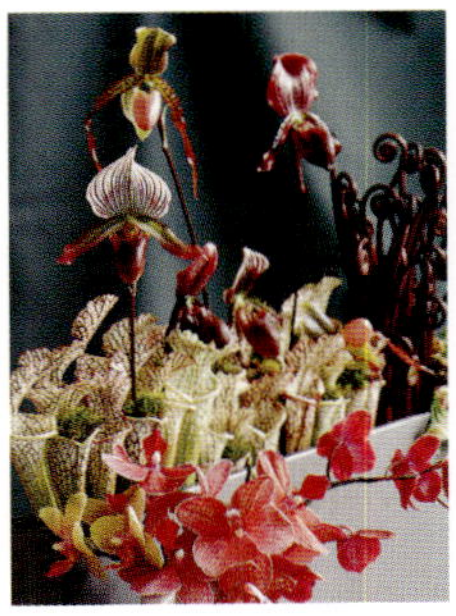

page 74

(left)
Allium Sicilum Hanging
Sarracenia
Lady's Slipper Orchids
Fern Fronds
Phalaenopsis Orchids

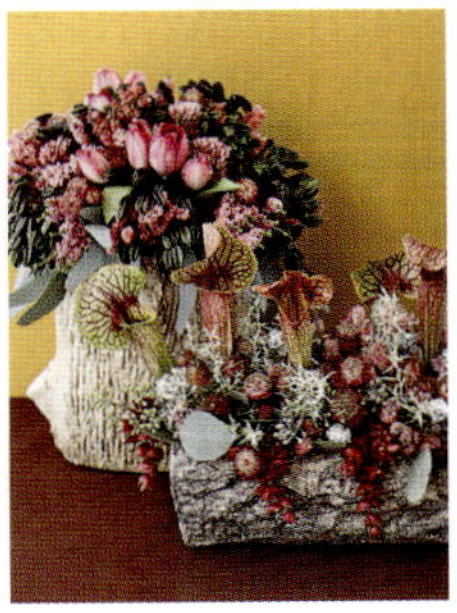

page 74

(right)
Sedum Blooms
Lily Seedpods
Seeded Eucalyptus
Eucalyptus Foliage
Kochia
Lavender Tulips
Allium
'Rubia' Astrantia
Sarracenia, Red Shuttle

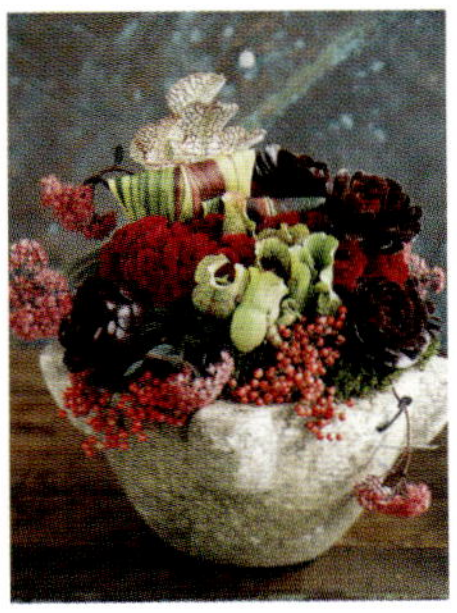

page 75

(left)
Black Echeveria Heads
Pepper Berry
Sedum Blooms
Sarracenia
Cockscomb
Variegated Ti Leaf

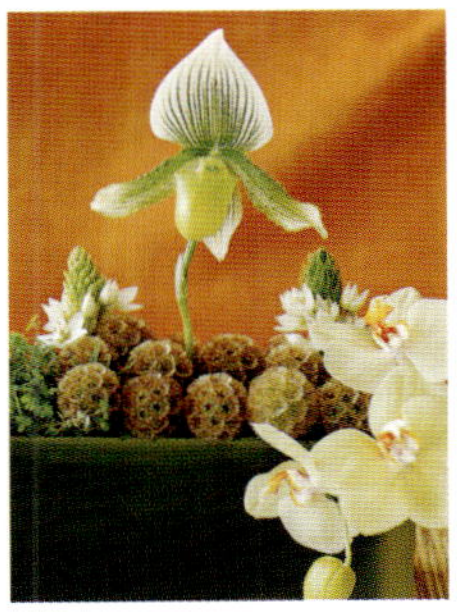

page 75

(right)
Baby Tears
Stars of Bethlehem
Scabiosa Pods
Maudie 'Lady Slipper'
Orchids
Green Phalaenopsis

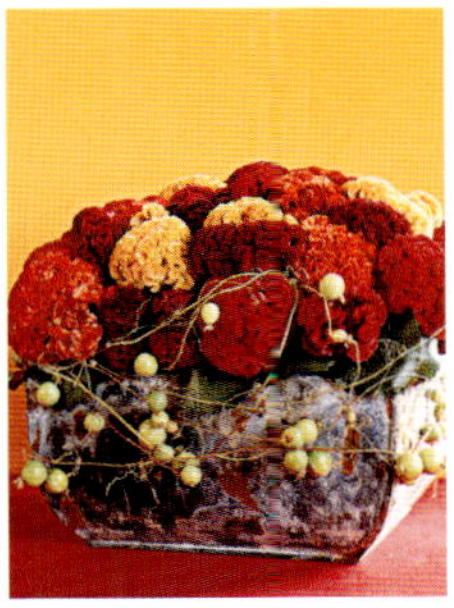

pages 76

Cockscomb Heads
Sour Gherkin Vine
Galax Leaves

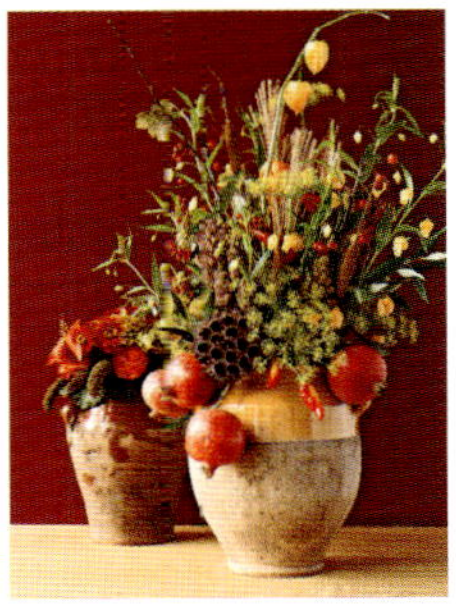

page 77

Sorghum, Dill, Cattails
Pyracantha Berries
Dried Lotus Pods
Pomegranates
Peppers, Grasses
Sandersonia, Crabapples
Japanese Lanterns
Millet, Zinnias
Calla Lilies, Roses

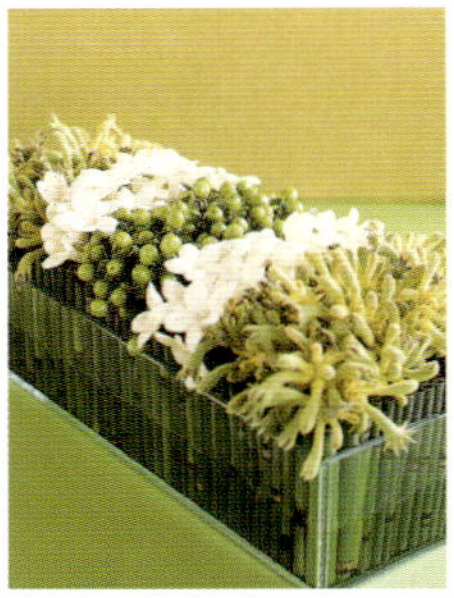

page 78

Horsetail Reeds
Stephanotis
Green Kangaroo Paw
Green 'Ivy Flair' Hypericum Berries

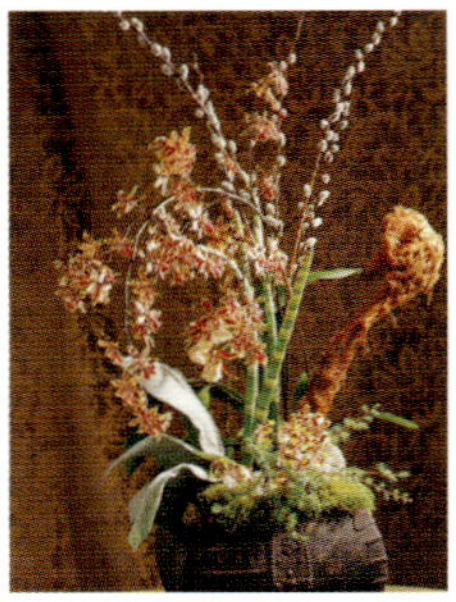

page 79

Giant Fern Frond
Pussy Willow
Giant Equisetum
Mosses
Deodar Cedar

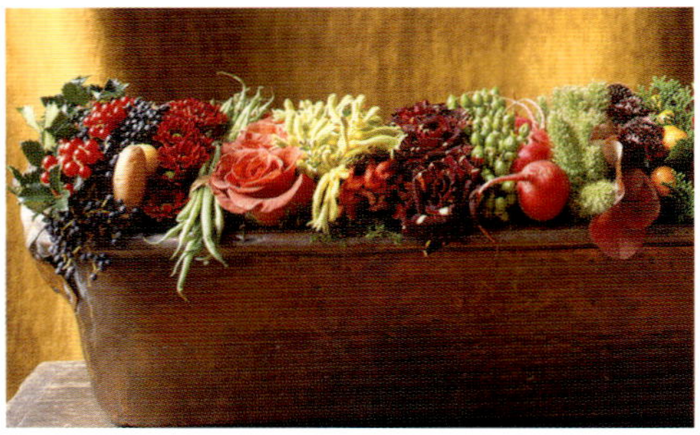

page 80

Mums , Green Beans
Terra-Cotta & Black Beauty Roses
Hocus Pocus Roses
Swiss Chard Stems , Scabiosa
Kangaroo Paws
Bunny Tail Grass, Rose Hips
Echinacea, Seed Heads
Hypericum Berries, Radishes
Kumquats, Red Roses
Broccolini, Kermit Mums, Tulips
Seeded Eucalyptus

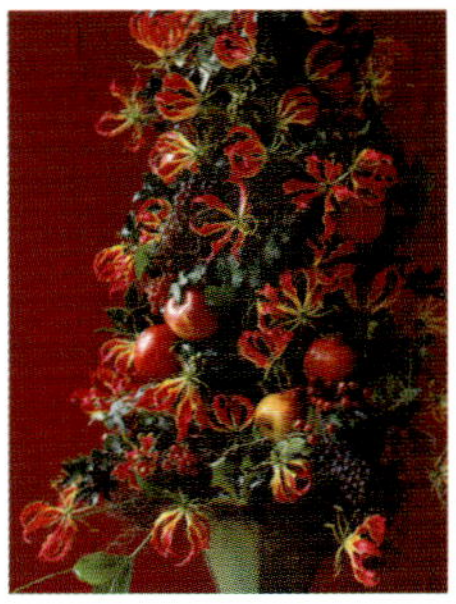

page 81

Pears
Pomegranates
Apples
Champagne Grapes
Ivy
Berried Ivy
Viburnum Berries
Gloriosa Lilies

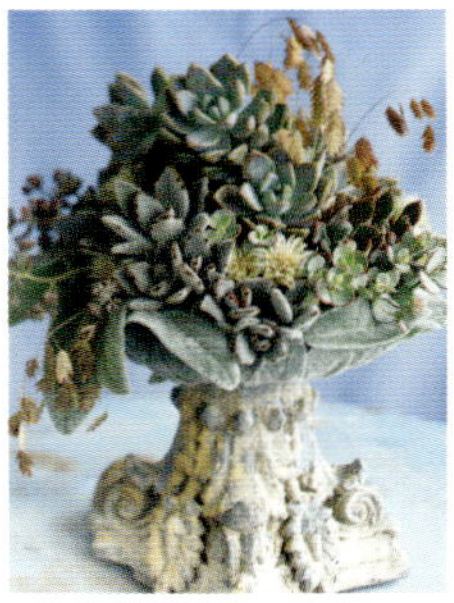

page 82

Lamb's Ear
Succulents
Sea oats
New Zealand Protea
Foliage

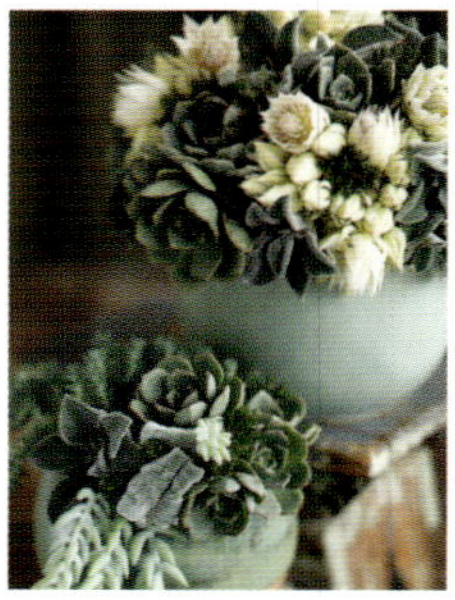

page 83

White Blushing Bride
Protea
Chilean Moss
Various Echeverias

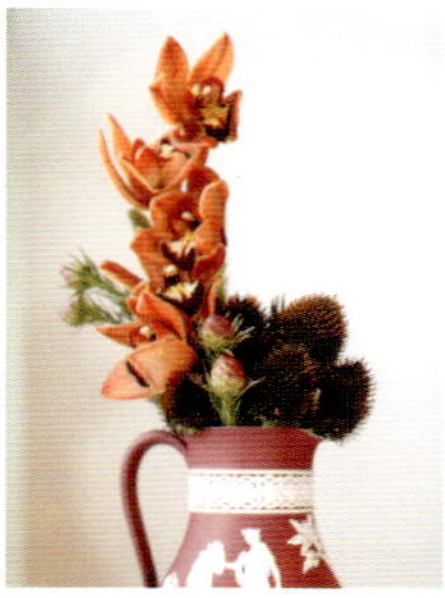

page 84

Echinacea Seed Heads
Leucadendron Pods
Mini Chocolate Cymbidium Orchids

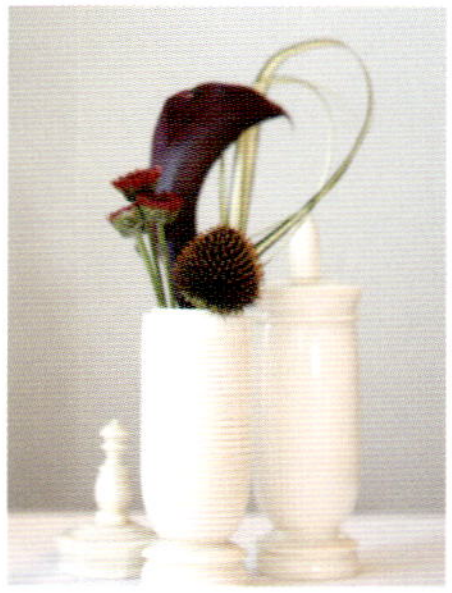

page 85

Dark Calla Lily
Echinacea Seed Head
Chocolate Mums
Zebra Grasses

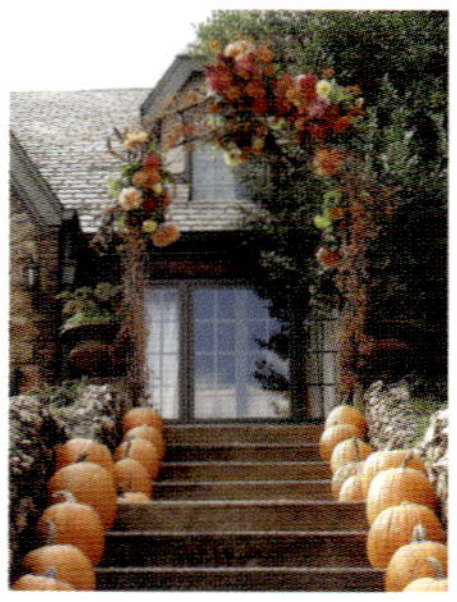

page 86

Bittersweet, Dahlias
Coral Charm Peonies
Terra-Cotta Roses
Black Magic Roses
Mango Calla Lillies
Black Millet
Red Kangaroo Paw
Amaranthus, Zinnias
Pumpkins

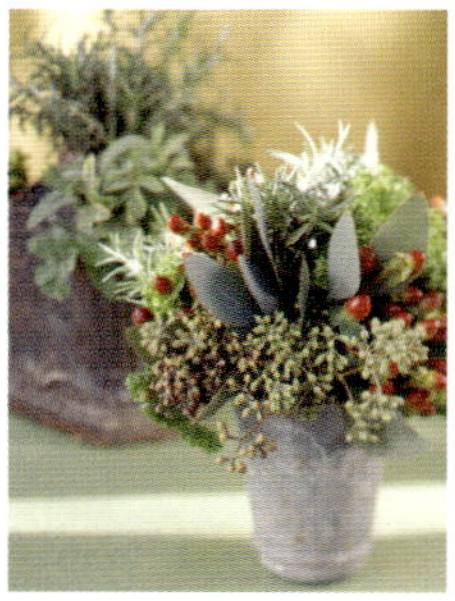

page 87

Seeded Eucalyptus
Eucalyptus Leaves
Hypericum Berries
Parsley
Rosemary

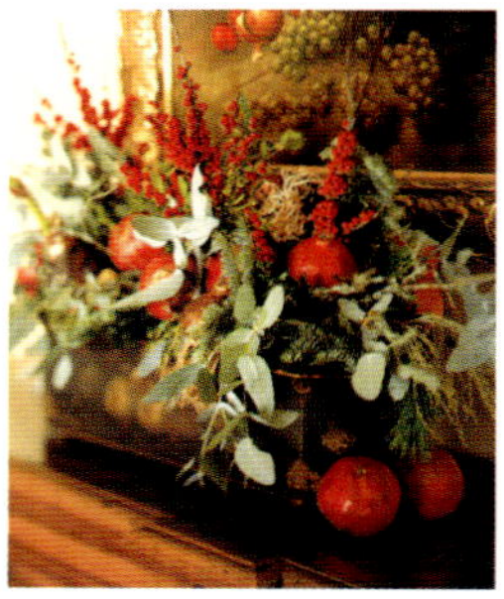

page 89

Seasonal Greens
Pomegranates
Ilex Berries
Lichen-Covered Twigs
Eucalyptus
Acacia
Young Amaryllis Sprouts
(with their bulbs and
roots exposed)

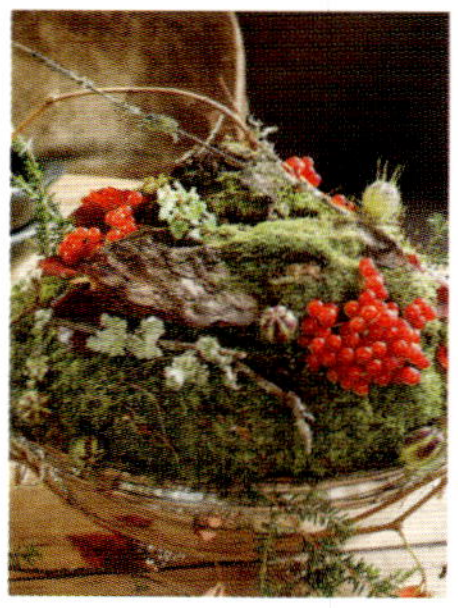

page 90

Moss-Encrusted Bark
Lichen-Covered Branches
Nigella Seed Pods
Viburnum Berries
Deodar Sprigs
Virginia Creeper Vine

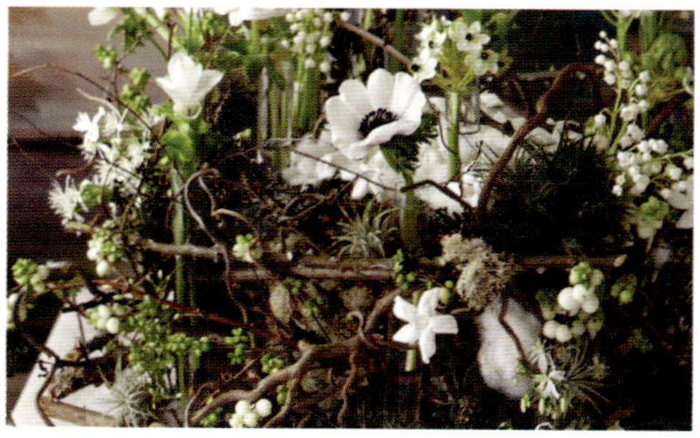

page 91

Wood Branches, Rose Stems
Harry Lauder's Walking Stick
Mosses, Cotton Boles
Autumn Clematis, Snowberry
Anemones, Ranunculus, Stephanotis
Lily of the Valley, Tillandsia
Arabicum, Curcuma

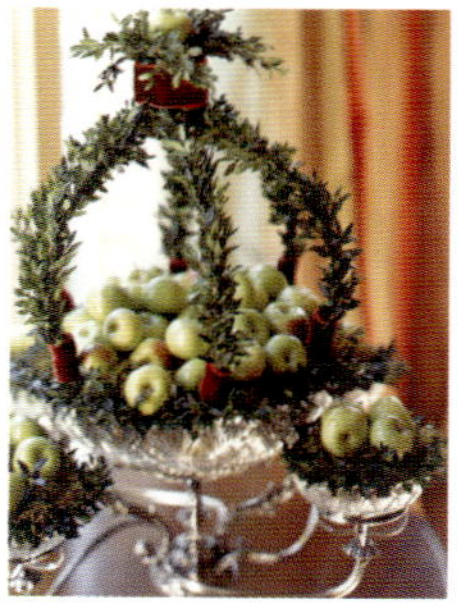

page 92

Boxwood
Lady Apples
Moss

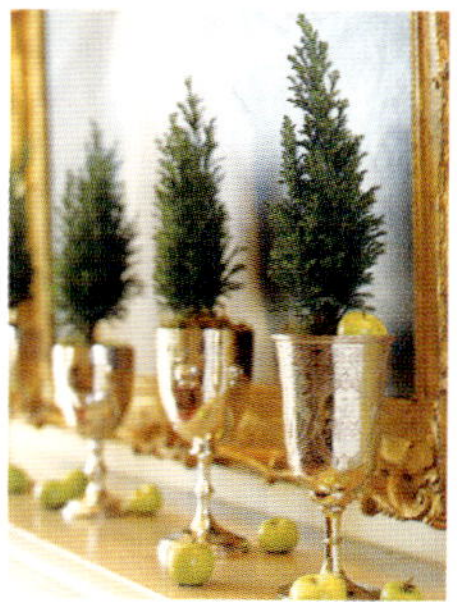

page 93

(left)
Miniature Cedar Trees
Lady Apples

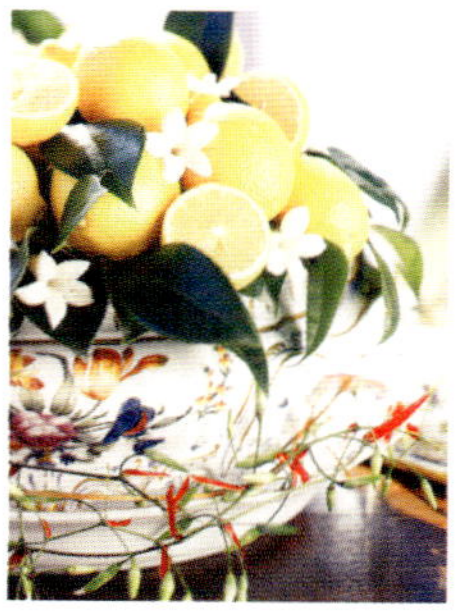

page 93

(right)
Lemons
Camellia Foliage
Stephanotis
Firecracker Vine

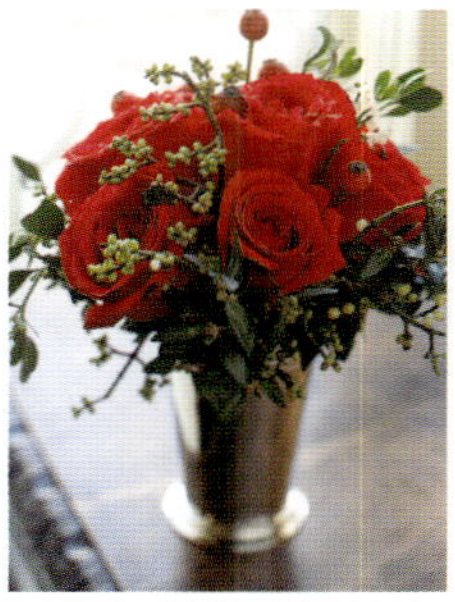

page 94

Charlotte Roses
Boxwood
Mistletoe
Rose Hips

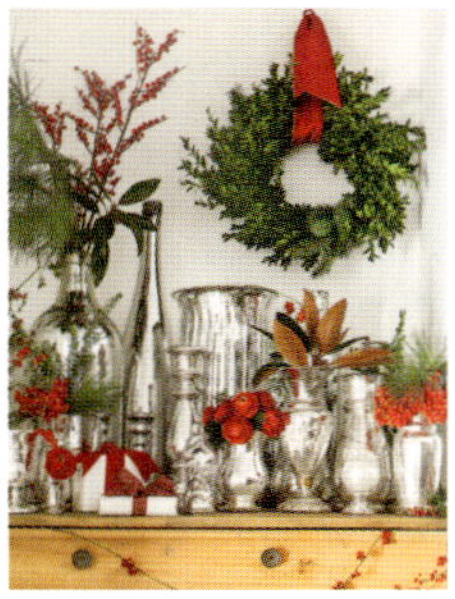

page 95

Pine
Magnolia
Red Viburnum Berries
Ranunculus
Ilex Berry
Carolina Snailseed Vine
Boxwood
Fir

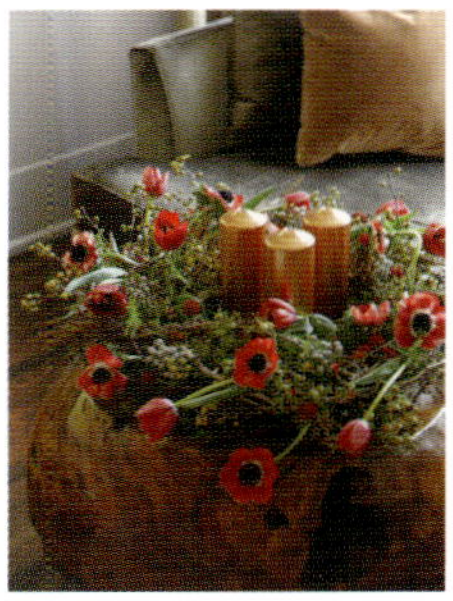

page 97

Eucalytus Berries
Silver Brunia
Pierus
Chilean Fern
Tulips
Anemones
Echinacea Seed Pods
Rose Hips
Bittersweet

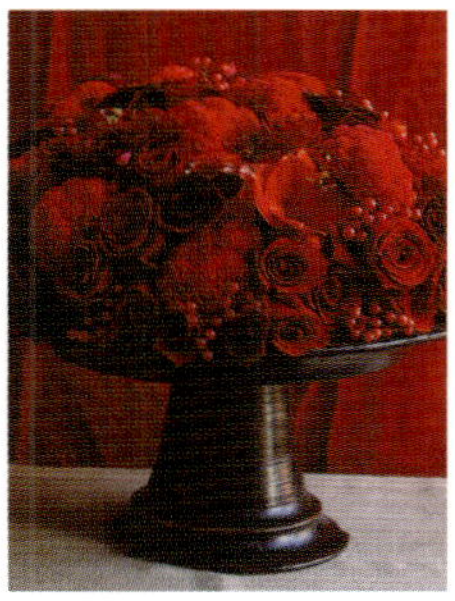

page 98

Red Lion Amaryllis
Coxcomb
Black Magic Roses
Currants

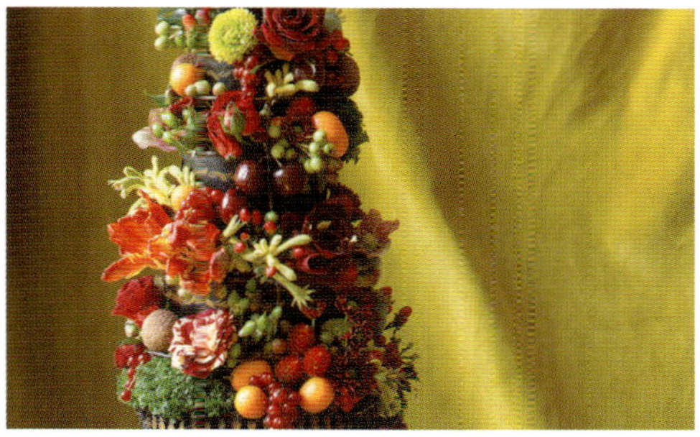

page 99

Irish Moss, Red Lion Amaryllis
Lychee Nuts, Kumquats
Red Currants, Gomphrena, Cherries
Santini Chrysanthemum
Chartreuse Kangaroo Paw, Crabapples
Jade Flair and Dual Flair Hypericum Berries,
Rococo Tulips, Fire King Spray Rose
Hellebores, Black Beauty Roses
Holly, Tree Ivy

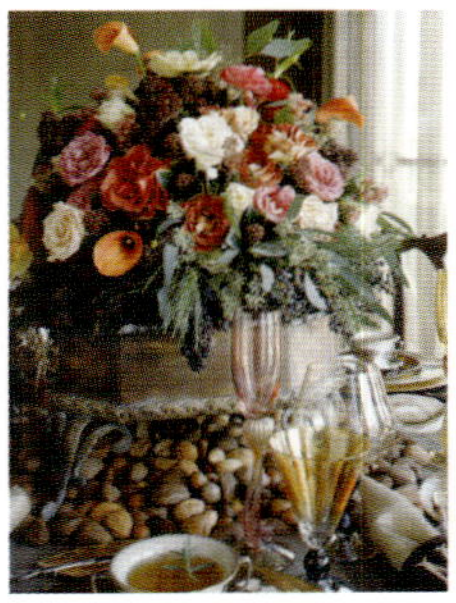

page 100

Seeded Eucalyptus
Pine
Fir
Privet Berries
Skimmia
Mini Calla Lilies
Leonidas, Sahara, Camel, Patience, Terra-Cotta Roses
Ranunculus

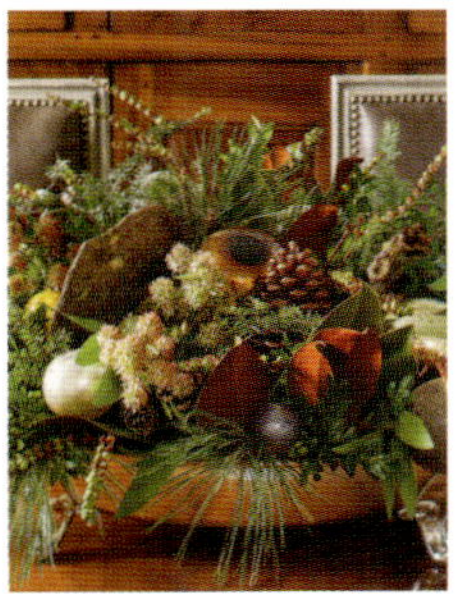

page 101

Little Gem Magnolia
Pine
Abelia Seed Heads
Pine Cones
Dried Shelf Mushrooms
Montbretia Pods
Fir
Boxwood
Camellia
Bay Leaves

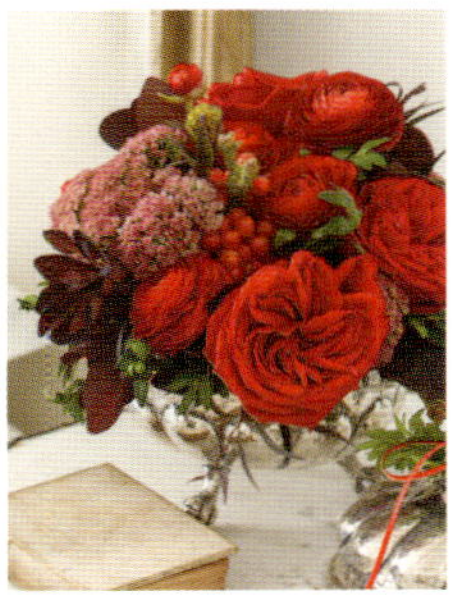

page 102

Sedum
Smoke Bush
Ranunculus
Leucadendron Pods
Viburnum Berries
Boxwood
Piano Rose

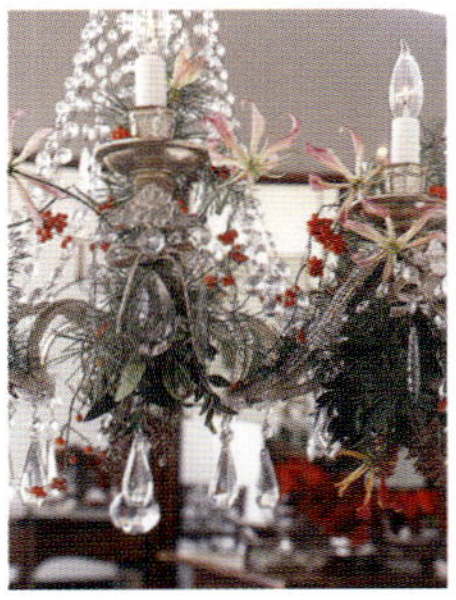

page 103

(left)
Boxwood
Fir
Skimmia
Gloriosa Lily
Red Berry Vine

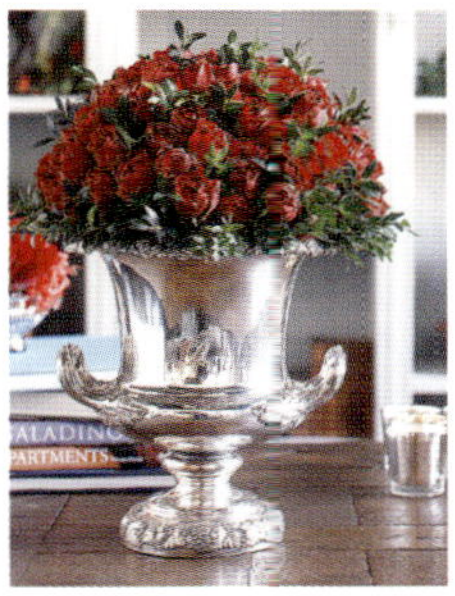

page 103

(right)
Boxwood
Tamango Spray Rose

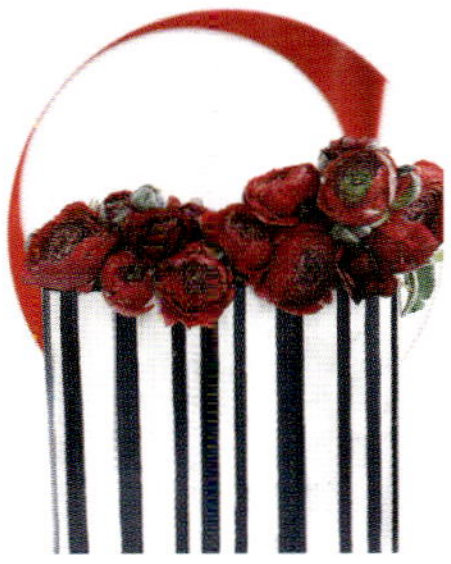

page 104

(left)
Ranunculus

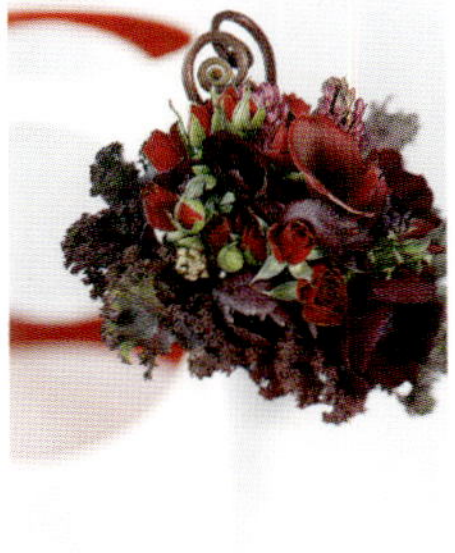

page 104

(right)
Kale
Calla Lilies
Tamango Spray Rose
Fiddlehead Fern Fronds
Hyacinth

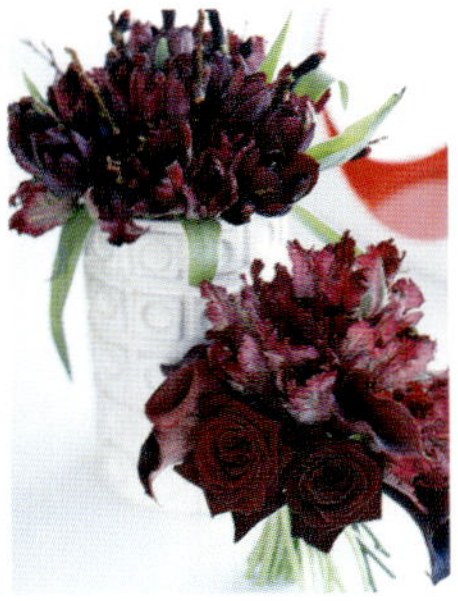

page 105

(left)
Tulips
Pussy Willow Twigs
Dark Calla Lilies
Black Baccaro Roses

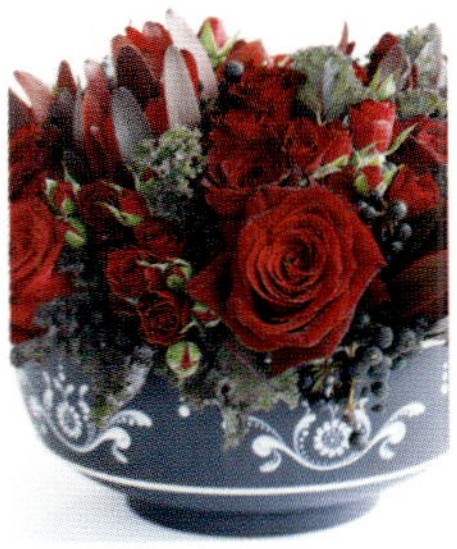

page 105

(right)
Black Baccaro Roses
Garden Roses
Tamango Spray Roses
Safari Sunset Protea
Kale
Viburnum Berries

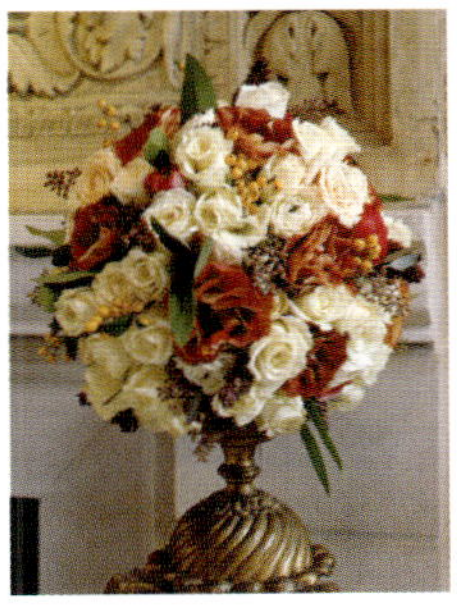

page 106

Terra-Cotta Rose
Vendela Rose
Yellow Ilex Berries
Seeded Eucalyptus
Bay Leaf
Oregano
Celestial and Carla Romantica Spray Rose

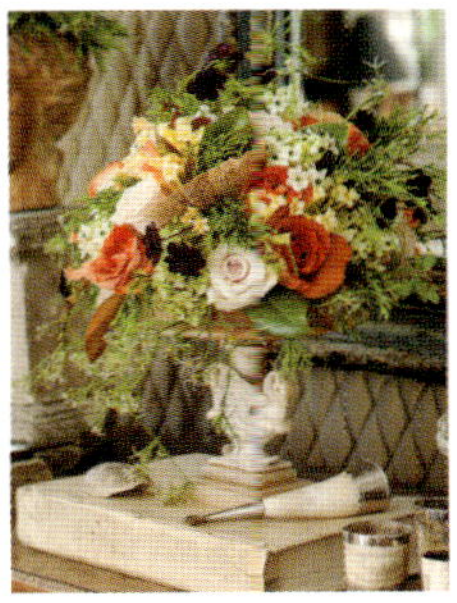

page 107

Sahara Rose
Terra-Cotta Rose
Peegee Hydrangea
Little Gem Magnolia
Cedar, Arabicum
Montbretia Pods
Old Man's Beard
Cyrtanthus
Chocolate Cosmos

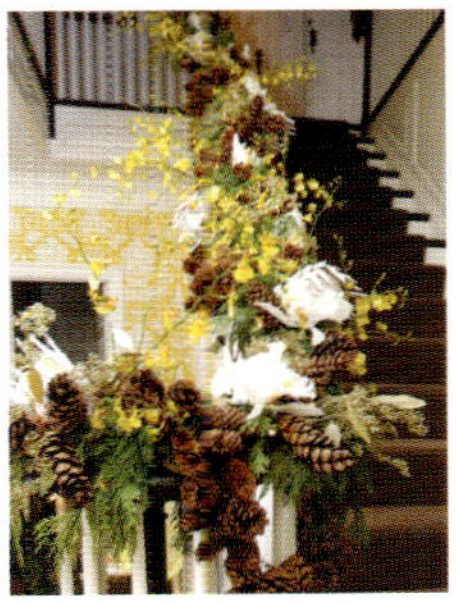

pages 108–109

Heavy Deluxe Garland
Pine Garland
Seeded Eucalyptus
Spray-Painted King Protea
Yellow Oncidium Orchids
Cattleya Orchids

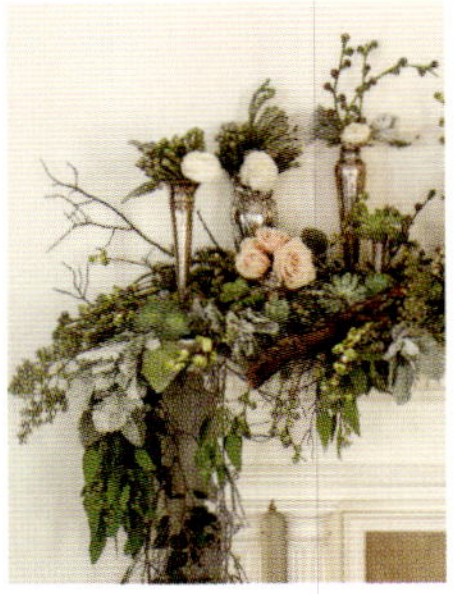

page 110

Eucalyptus Pods
Eucalyptus
Dusty Miller
Snowberry
Lichen Branches
Brunia
Succulents
Ranunculus
Arabicum
Sahara Rose

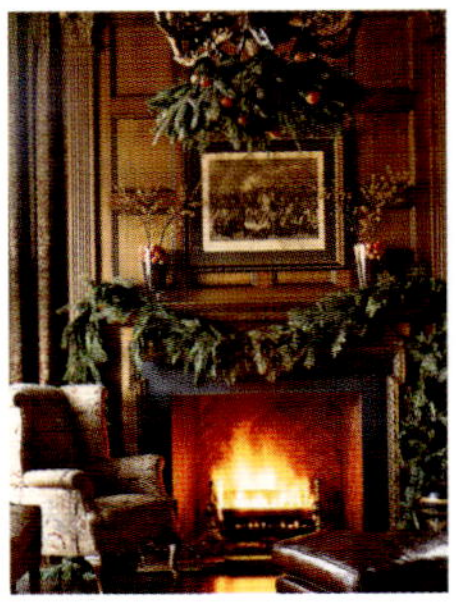

page 110

Miniature Pine Cones
Crabapples
Yellow Ilex Berries
Deluxe Mixed Garland

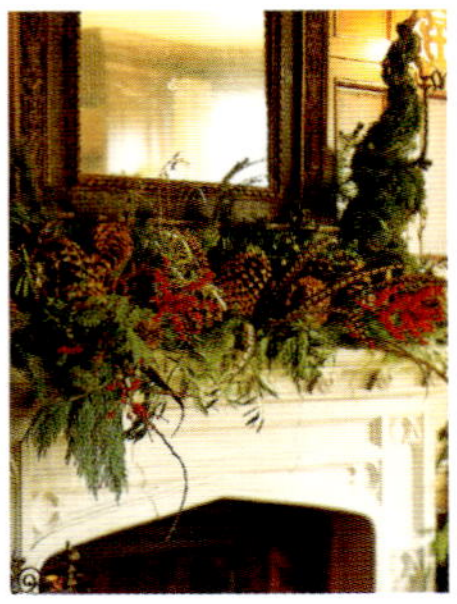

page 110

Cedar
Fir
Olive
Ilex Berries
Pheasant Feathers
Pine Cones
Preserved Juniper
Topiaries
Boxwood
Mistletoe

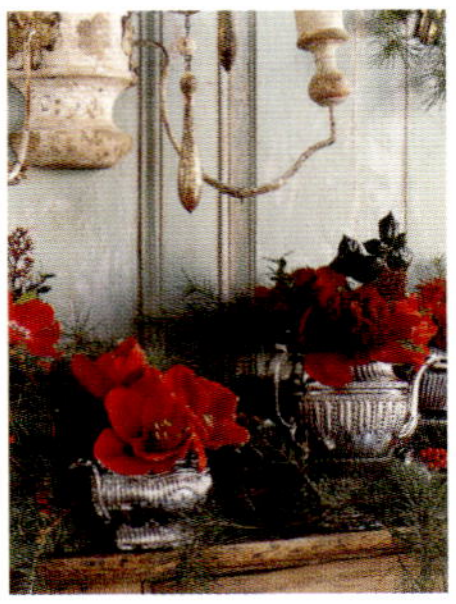

page 110

Red Lion Amaryllis
Inspector Laverne Peony
Ranunculus
Anemones
Holly
Skimmia
Carolina Snailseed Vine
Deodar Cedar
Red Nerines

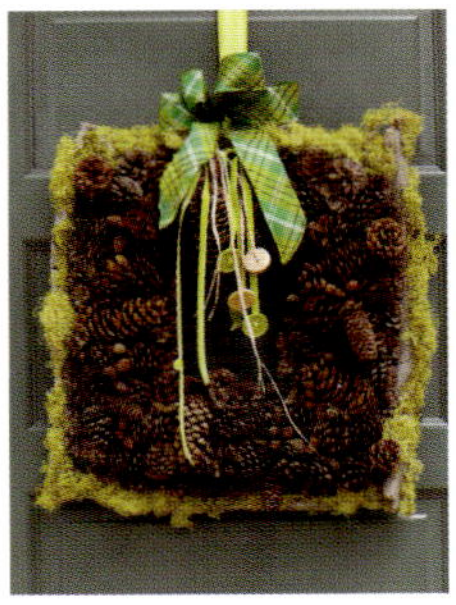

page 112

Lichen twigs
Pine Cones
Ribbon
Buttons

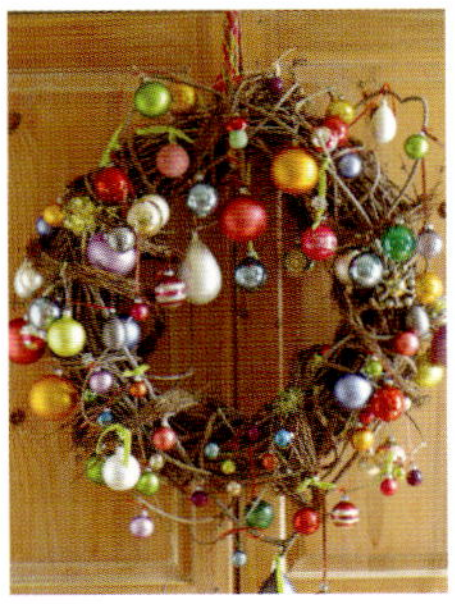

page 112

Modern, vintage
ornaments
Vine wreath form

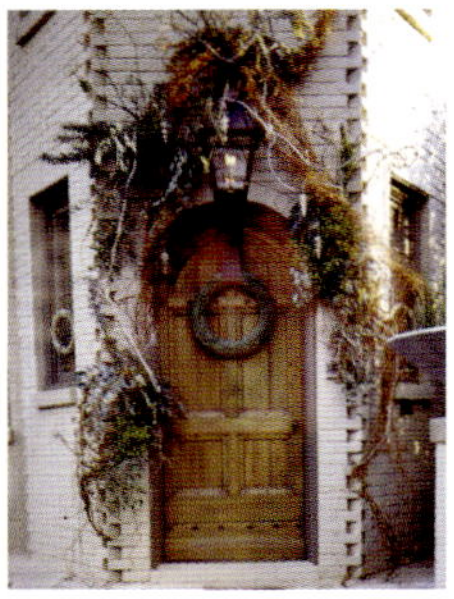

page 112

Lamb's Ear Wreath
Honeysuckle Vine
Eucalyptus Branches
Lichen Branches
Rosemary
Metallic Ribbon
Mistletoe Clusters

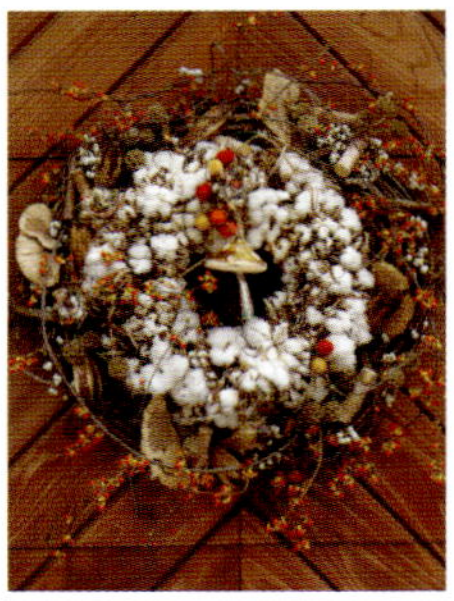

page 112

Vine Wreath Form
Cotton Boles
Scabiosa Pods
Bittersweet
Dried Shelf Mushrooms
Birch Logs, Tallow Berry
Felt Acorns
Mushroom Ornament

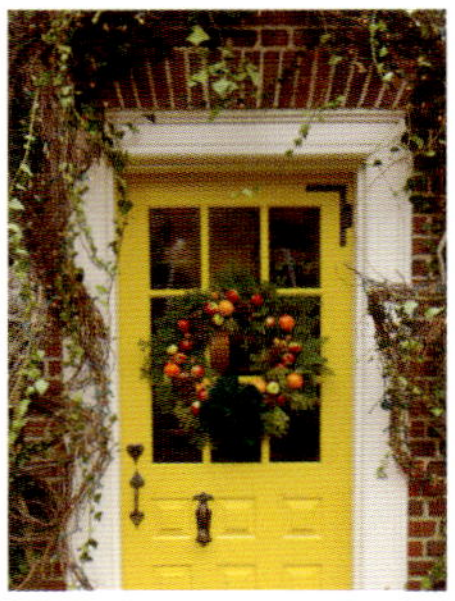

page 112

Pinecones
Tangerines
Kumquats
Lady Apples

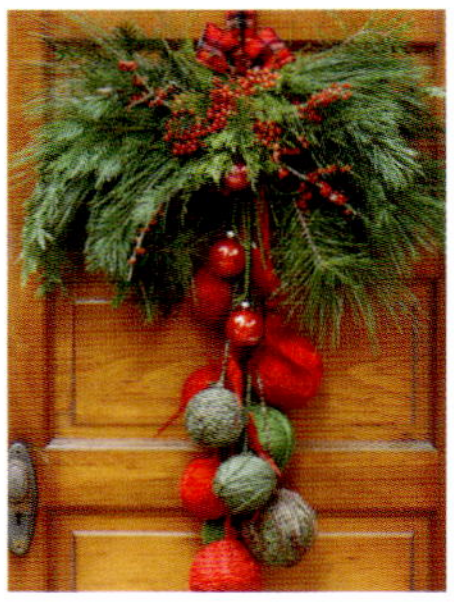

page 112

Cedar
Fir
Pine
Ilex Berry
Plaid Ribbon
Yarn covered ornament
cluster

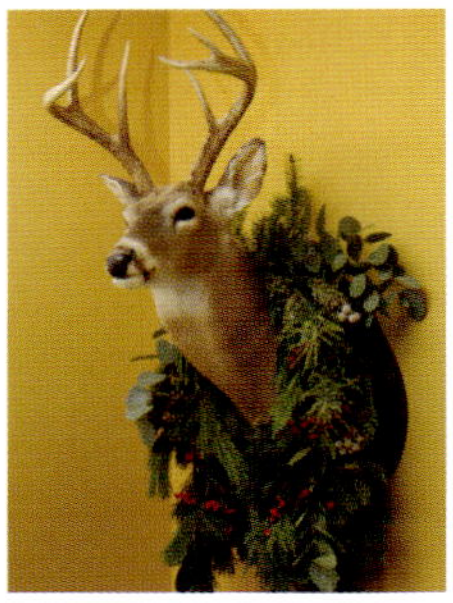

page 112

Handmade Garland
Pine
Cedar
Silver Dollars
Eucalyptus
Acacia
Brunia
Rose Hips

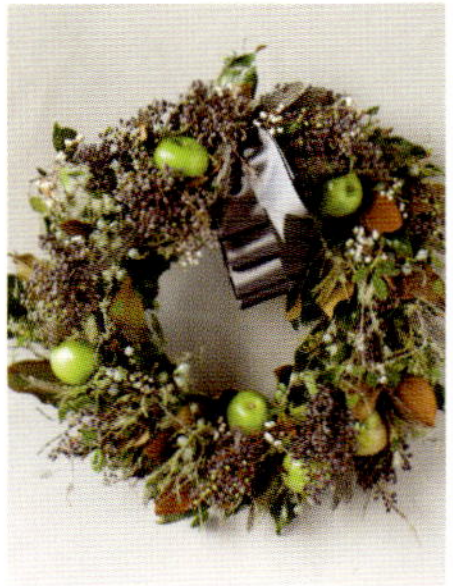

page 112

Little Gem Magnolia
Lichen Twig
Privet Berries
Seeded Eucalyptus
Green Apples
Acacia
Feathers
Tallow Berries

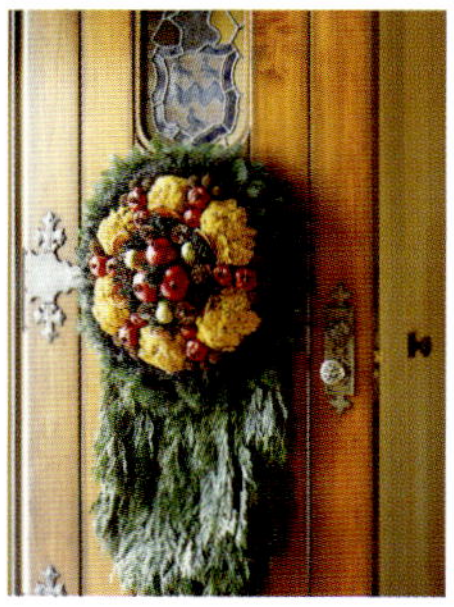

page 112

Dried Yarrow
Dried Pomegranates
Dried Orange Slices
Pine Cones
Preserved Boxwood
Cedar

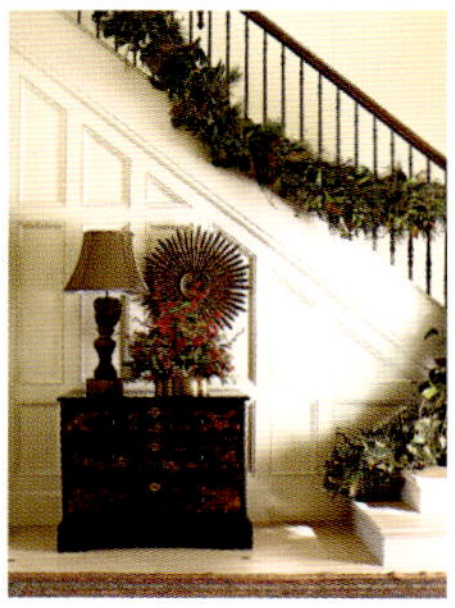

page 114

Handmade California
Garland
Lichen Twigs
Mixed Greenery
Long Leaf Pine
Seeded Eucalyptus
Magnola

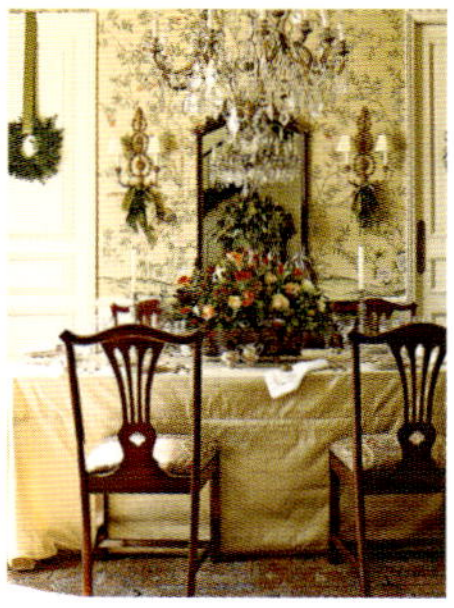

page 115

Ranunculus
Calla Lilies
Roses
Mistletoe
Olive
Protea Pods
Safari Sunset

ACKNOWLEDGMENTS

thank you...

The road to getting *fresh* to fruition has been a very, very long trip, starting when I volunteered to be a member of the planning committee for Art in Bloom in 1998 at the Birmingham Museum of Art. As fate would have it, I was asked to "take care of" Paula Pryke, a London florist who was our keynote speaker and teacher for two flower workshops. "Take care of" meant procuring all of her flowers and supplies needed for her floral demonstration and two workshops and making sure she was set and ready for everything as well as squiring her to a series of special events and parties that were all held in her honor. It was an exhilarating week and the beginning of our long-time friendship and many fun times together and collaborations! We truly connected and bonded. Paula has written and published 17 beautiful books on floral design, and she has always encouraged me to write my own book.

I recall purchasing the book *How to Publish a Book, For Dummies* in 1999 and Jon Davis, my right hand at my shop, and I began the process. We wrote and re-wrote and gathered materials for a portfolio and brainstormed concepts. Many of my employees helped along the way with this endeavor, always encouraging me and helping me collect photos and film, as well as writing and rewriting. Fonda Shaia brought all her styling creativity to the team from the very beginning. Mimi Brown was a real trooper and helped me stay after it even though we were constantly so busy at our real job! Mimi and Jon—we must share a toast soon! Concurrently, I was being encouraged by Karen Carroll, Editor in Chief and Francie MacDougall, Executive Editor with *Southern Accents* magazine to pursue a book deal, as well. Thank you, Karen, your belief in me has always kept me going. And for introducing me to your fabulous, creative staff members Rebecca Hawkins and Amanda Fowler, who always were there to support me. Francie and I began a series of meetings to strategize our approach and those meetings are happening on a daily basis, still to this day, literally, some ten years later! They introduced me to Jill Simpson, a freelance writer who took up my project truly as her mission. Through all of this help I was able to put together what I thought was an acceptable book proposal.

My good friend and soul mate, Margot Shaw, began *flower* magazine in 2006. The cover of her preview issue featured her daughter's wedding that I had done for them at their family farm. It was such an honor, and Margot has continued to support me and is always there when things need to be hashed over with her best, sound advice. I love being a contributing editor to her beautiful magazine, and I thank you, Margot! As part of Paula's encouragement, she introduced me to a wonderful man, Jamie Becker, Creative Director and Visual Manager for Marshall Field & Company. Through Jamie, I met in 2005 with Marta Hallett in New York. Jamie, we must celebrate this book together soon!!! Marta had started Glitterati in 2002, and she met with me as a friend of Jamie's to see my prepared book proposal and give me her best advice. Through Marta's support and enthusiasm about my project I was filled with hope. She arranged for me to meet Karen Gantz Zahler, a literary agent in New York, and we were off to the races in 2007.

Things were slow—loads of likes but no "takers" and then there was that call on January 28, 2008 (my husband's and my 19th wedding anniversary) when Karen called to say we had our deal! What a day!!! I will never forget that feeling. If my memory serves me correctly it was about this point that Jill needed to step away and my enthusiastic friend, Beatty Coleman, stepped in to help me edit.

Then slowly, the book industry started to change. And then more rapidly. Within 18 months, my book still wasn't published, and they decided to "Drop the Deal". Again, another day I won't be forgetting (this one, though, I really try hard to forget)! It's difficult to not have the wind taken out of you when something like this happens, but I pushed to keep my business productive and not give up on my dream.

Francie and I began the process of re-vamping the proposal and updating it once again, probably in 2010. We would meet sporadically and make changes or try new approaches. Finally, in January 2014, I vowed that I would focus on the book to have a proposal in hand and take myself to New York again (before the end of 2014). Late Fall that year, I did it and went to New York. Thank you, Francie! I was back at the beginning, nine years later, meeting with Marta for her to look at my work, seeking her guidance, once again having a lovely lunch in New York and enjoying catching up.

Let's jump forward to January 30, 2015—the day I heard back from Marta that SHE wanted to publish my book!!! NOW, THAT IS THE DAY TO REMEMBER!!! So thank you to Marta Hallett and Kiara Cobb and all your wonderful staff at Glitterati Incorporated. You believe in me—it is an amazing feeling!

My Birmingham team of supporters has been amazing. Thank you would never say it all …leading the helm is Francie MacDougall, my Editor, rudder and true, true friend along with Karen Downs, our photo guru extraordinaire as well as masterful photography genius. Karen, you are one cool cookie! To get to today there have been a series of Art Directors: Jennifer Madara, who is the incredibly talented artist who created this beautiful book design. I'm missing you, girl! Ellen Padgett, who saved a floundering ship with such grace and enthusiasm, as well as amazing talent. Last but never least, my two sweet friends—you know who you are—you are both masters at organization, detail, and creativity, and the breath of fresh air … You are something else!!! To Jennie Shannon, for your computer savvy. I would be deep in the weeds trying to accomplish what you have done for us.

There are photos from 22 photographers in my book and without their beautiful images of my fleeting creations I wouldn't be writing this today! Thank you to each and every one of you, for your talent and ability to capture my designs in such flattering light and for your support and friendship throughout this process—each of you has been my Hero this year. Thank you to Charles McNair for your beautiful words and willingness to be a part of my dream. Your contribution to my book is so lovely and sweet and will certainly capture the heart of each of my "garden club ladies" who understand the spirit of those competitions. Billy and I look forward to seeing you very soon.

To Megan LaRussa, now Chenoweth, you rock!! Particularly when I need to get fabulous and confident for a photo shoot!!

To Scott Shepherd and his sweet family who put up with all of my intrusions, along with everyone at Cut Flower Wholesale in Atlanta. Scott you are an invaluable member to my Team! Thank you for all your hard work, friendship, and dogged determination and beautiful fleurs!

And to, Jeff Serafini, I miss our fun days of collaboration.

To 20 years worth of employees and Wildflower Gang members. Here's to each of you!! I could never have done this on my own. I am not worthy!!!!

To all my lovely brides and fabulous clients, thank you for allowing me to part of their life celebrations and for saying, "I Do!" Wildflower Style—haven't we had fun!

A special thanks to all the "garden club ladies" for your support and encouragement.

And to, Paula Pryke—you are the wind beneath my sails. I truly value our friendship.

Lastly, To my family and friends who have put up with my madness and still love me in spite of it all. It just shows…if you stick to it, dreams do come true.

I have really tried to follow this path and acknowledge everyone, if I have left you off—I am the one at fault. Thank you for what you have done to get this book published!

PHOTOGRAPHERS

an amazing thank you

COVER: Becky Luigart-Stayner

Elizabeth Adams: 15, 157-9, 229 (bottom right)
Jean Allsopp: 112 (top left, top center, middle right, middle left), 194, 197 (bottom left)
Arden Photography: 55, 60-1, 84-85, 119, 124-5, 136-141,168-173, 202-9, 218-221
Kim Box: 52-53, 164-167, 228
Clark Brewer: 180-185
Monica Buck: 20-2, 34-5, 58-9, 72-3, 74 (right), 75 (left), 76-8, 103, 110 (bottom right)
Robbie Caponetto: 122
Mary Margaret Chambliss: 198-201
Stephen DeVries: 186-189
Karen J. Downs: 229 (bottom left)
Bob Farley/f8Photo: 142-145
Dana Gallagher: 67, 69, 80-1, 98-9
Irene Thames Gardner: 190, 191 (top right, bottom left)
Mick Hales: 100, 102
Beth Hontzas: 11, 24-5, 41, 62, 108-9, 112 (bottom left, middle center), 128-131, 260, 272
A. Bryan Johnson: 6, 32-3, 44, 56-7, 160-163, 192-3, 196, 197 (top left, top right, bottom right), 210-215, 216-217, 224-7, 229 (top left, right), 230-1, back cover
Helen Norman: 90, 95, 101-2, 107, 110 (top left)
Howard L. Puckett: 146
Becky Luigart-Stayner: 12-3, 17, 23, 26, 27-9, 39-40, 45, 48-50, 54, 63, 65-6, 70-1, 87, 89, 91, 92-4, 96-7, 110 (bottom left), 112 (bottom right), 120-1, 148-155, 176-9, 232-259, 261
Ann Stratton: 108 (top right), 114-117, 126-7, 132-135
Laura Walker: 18
Jason Wallis: 68, 86, 174-5, 222-3
Charles E. Walton IV: 19, 30-1, 37, 42-3, 46-7, 51, 74 (left), 75 (right), 79, 82-3, 104-5, 112 (top right)

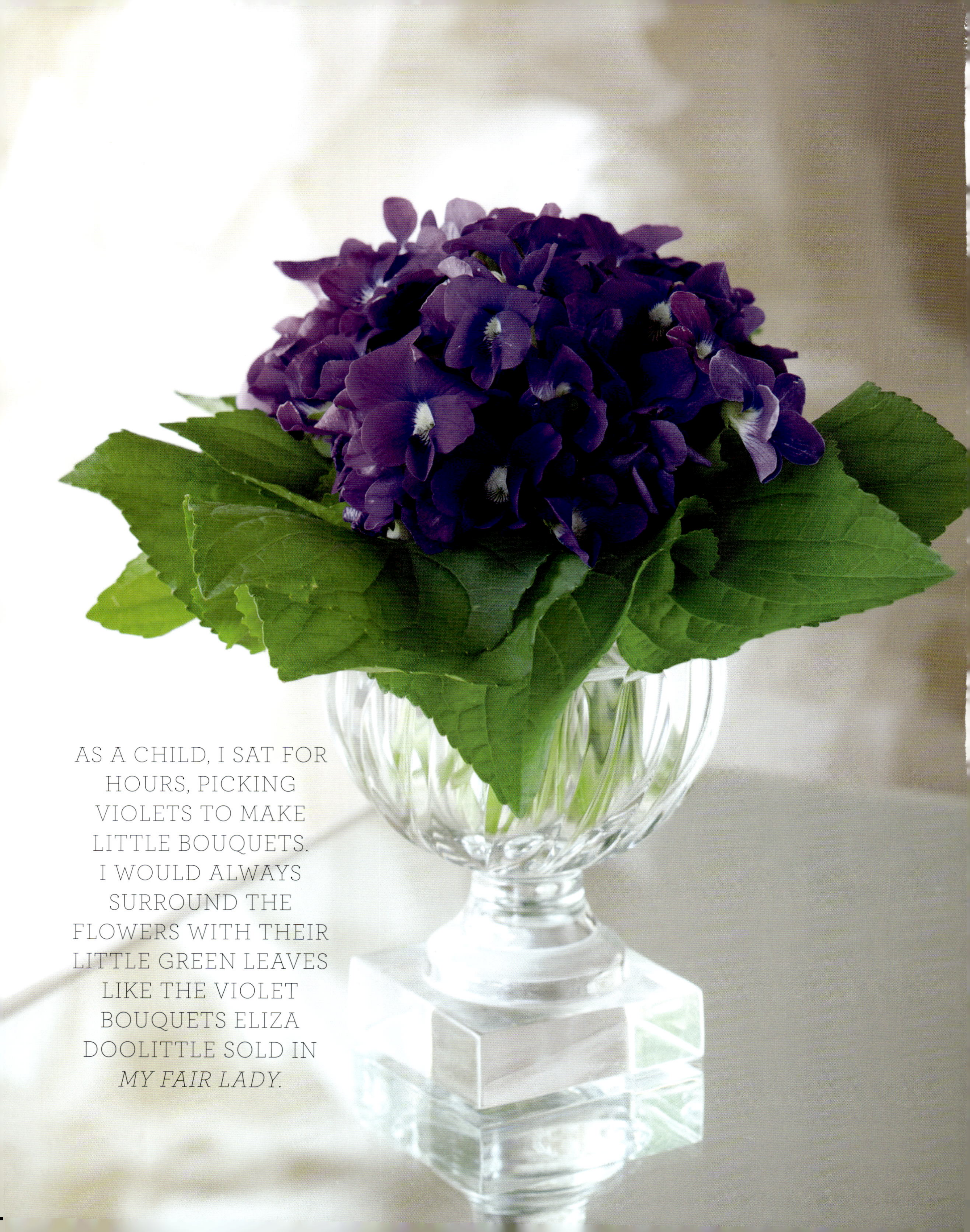

AS A CHILD, I SAT FOR HOURS, PICKING VIOLETS TO MAKE LITTLE BOUQUETS. I WOULD ALWAYS SURROUND THE FLOWERS WITH THEIR LITTLE GREEN LEAVES LIKE THE VIOLET BOUQUETS ELIZA DOOLITTLE SOLD IN *MY FAIR LADY.*